The
Call to the Believers in the Clear Qur'ān

[Nidā' al-Mu'minīn fi 'l-Qur'ān al-Mubīn]

The Call to the Believers in the Clear Qur'ān

[Nidā' al-Mu'minīn fi 'l-Qur'ān al-Mubīn]

SHAIKH AḤMAD FATḤU'LLĀH JĀMĪ

TRANSLATED FROM THE ARABIC BY MUHTAR HOLLAND

AL-BAZ PUBLISHING, INC.
FT. LAUDERDALE, FLORIDA

Dome and Minaret of the Prophet's Mosque, Medina, Saudi Arabia

Cover photography for paperback edition: Peter Sanders

Peter Sanders is an internationally known photographer. Born in London, he established himself in the 1960's photographing most of the pop musicians of that era, such as Jimi Hendrix, Bob Dylan, Eric Clapton, The Rolling Stones, The Doors and many more. In 1971 he was granted the unique opportunity to photograph the Hajj in Saudi Arabia. These images appeared in the Sunday Times magazine, The Observer, Paris Match and other major journals of that time in recognition of their rareness. His empathy with the people he meets has opened doors to him and he has often been granted permission to take pictures of people never photographed before. It has been said of his work '...he captures the spiritual beauty of creation itself.'

Cover Design: Dryden Design, Houston, Texas
Pivot Design, Inc., Fort Lauderdale, Florida

Body text set in Ghazali and Jilani fonts by Al-Baz Publishing, Inc.

Printed on acid-free paper

Library of Congress
Catalog Card Number: 99-62847

First Edition April 2000

ISBN: 1-882216-19-9 Paperback
ISBN: 1-882216-20-2 Hardcover

Published for Al-Durra Publishing by:

Al-Baz Publishing, Inc.
P.O. Box 348, Fort Lauderdale,
FL 33302-0348, U.S.A.
(954) 567-4072 Fax: (954) 563-1311
E-mail: albaz@bellsouth.net

Printed and bound in the United States of America by McNaughton & Gunn.

Table of Contents

Biography of the Author of "The Call to the Believers in the Clear Qur᾿ān"

In the Name of Allāh, the All-Merciful, the All-Compassionate.
Bismi'llāhi 'r-Raḥmāni 'r-Raḥīm.

Praise be to Allāh, the Lord of All the Worlds, and the most perfect salutation to our master Muḥammad, his family and all his Companions.

The following is a brief account of certain aspects of the life of our Shaikh, my master and my spiritual support:

Shaikh Aḥmad Fatḥu'llāh Jāmī

—the Shaikh of the Shādhilī Order [*Ṭarīqa*], the native of Mush [in Eastern Turkey], the Khālidī by descent, the Shāfiʿī by school of Islāmic Law [*madhhab*], the resident of Marash.

May Allāh protect him and look after him well. May Allāh (Exalted is He) grant him long life, and may He enable the Muslims to derive great benefit from him. *Āmīn.*

1. His family background (may Allāh the Exalted keep him safe!):

He was born into a family of noble descent, with a reputation for pious devotion, righteousness and learning, as well as for courage and readiness to help those in distress. His grandfather, Shaikh ʿAbdullāh Jāmī (may Allāh the Exalted bestow His mercy upon him), was one of the outstanding religious scholars of his time. The same can be said of his ancestor, Shaikh Ismāʿīl (may Allāh bestow His mercy upon him), through whom he is related to Shaikh Mullā Jāmī (may Allāh the Exalted bestow His mercy upon them all).

As for our Shaikh's father, Fatḥu'llāh Jāmī (may Allāh the Exalted bestow His mercy upon him), he was prevented from acquiring religious knowledge, because of the conditions prevailing during the First World War, since he took part in many of the military campaigns against the Russian armed forces. He was renowned for his bravery and his bold initiative. In one of the battles, almost all of the soldiers in his company took flight in face of the Russian offensive, so that he and one other man were the only ones left on the battlefield. The other man did not stay long, however. He also turned in retreat, saying to Fatḥu'llāh Jāmī (may Allāh bestow His mercy upon him): "By Allāh, never in my life have I beaten a retreat from a battlefield, leaving any member of my army behind me to fight the enemy; never until now! You have surpassed me in the contest of patient endurance!"

Once he was left there entirely alone, Fatḥu'llāh Jāmī (may Allāh the Exalted bestow His mercy upon him) did recognize the wisdom of retreating, in order to join a troop of the Muslims, so he withdrew. Somewhere along his route, he came upon a Muslim woman, who was trying to find help, to avoid falling prey to the Russians. As he looked around (may Allāh the Exalted bestow His mercy upon him), he noticed that the area was almost empty of its inhabitants. They were fleeing from the Russian army, which was fanning out in every direction. Caravans of refugees were passing by that woman, but no one among them would help her, because their own plight was so desperate. He therefore halted beside her (may Allāh bestow His mercy upon him) and felt obliged to assist her, so he carried her behind him on his horse, until he delivered her to the Muslims, safe and sound.

This explains why, in a period when so many wars were being waged, he was unable (may Allāh the Exalted bestow His mercy upon him) to pursue his study of noble religious knowledge, as his father, Shaikh ʿAbdullāh (may Allāh the Exalted bestow His mercy upon him), had done. Nevertheless, he was eager to see his own son—meaning our excellent Shaikh (may Allāh keep him safe)—become a seeker of knowledge, and that he should follow the path of the religious scholars. He therefore introduced him to someone who could teach him the noble knowledge, that teacher being Shaikh Ḥaqq Shūnās (may Allāh the Exalted bestow His mercy upon him). This arrangement proved to be impossible, however, since he [Fatḥu'llāh Jāmī] (may Allāh bestow His mercy upon him) passed away, leaving several orphans. Our Shaikh (may Allāh keep him safe) was the eldest of these, although he was then barely eight years old. This meant that his acquisition of knowledge (may Allāh the Exalted keep him safe) was inevitably delayed, due to the conditions of orphanhood and the upbringing of his brother, Muḥammad, and his sisters.

2. His quest for knowledge (may Allāh the Exalted keep him safe):

When he had reached the age of twenty, he embarked on the acquisition of Islāmic legal knowledge [*ʿilm sharʿī*], with a serious commitment that never wavered. At the same time, he began to travel, and to make progress in the struggle with the lower self, by following the spiritual path [*ṭarīqa*] of the Naqshbandī Order. Before very long, however, he suffered a grave misfortune. During the very first stage of his travels and studies, Allāh (Exalted is He) concluded the life of his full brother, Muḥammad. He bore this loss with patience, displayed the steadfastness of the unshakable mountains in dealing with trial and tribulation, and entrusted his affair to Allāh (Exalted is He).

He continued his travels, his spiritual journey, and his effort in the pursuit of knowledge. As he moved from village to village, from town to town, and from one country to another, his single purpose was to discover the most suitable setting for spiritual progress and development, and the devout and righteous teacher from whom to acquire knowledge. Allāh (Exalted is He) granted him that favour, for all of his teachers belonged to the community of genuine Ṣūfism [*taṣawwuf*].

He received instruction in Islāmic jurisprudence [*fiqh*] and the Arabic language from Shaikh ʿAbd al-Hādī al-ʿUmarī al-Būṭī (may Allāh bestow His mercy upon him), who was a qualified teacher in the Naqshbandī Order. He also pursued these studies at the hand of Shaikh ʿAbd ar-Raḥmān al-ʿUmarī al-Būṭī (may Allāh bestow His mercy upon him), from whom he learned many other subjects besides. Another teacher, from whom he likewise acquired knoweldge of many subjects, was Shaikh Muḥammad Ẓāhir al-Malāz Kurdī, he being the teacher of his teacher, Shaikh ʿAbd ar-Raḥmān al-ʿUmarī (may Allāh the Exalted bestow His mercy upon them both).

While he was in the state of seeking knowledge (may Allāh the Exalted keep him safe), he made many wise remarks in the company of his teachers. On one occasion, for instance, he was together with one of them in a big open space, in the springtime, when the earth was in full bloom. He gazed at those clean plants, trembling in the breeze, and he said to his teacher: "O my master, the heart of the human being is clean and sound, just like this place, so if he preserves it from all other objects of worship, and none but Allāh (Exalted is He) enters into it, it will remain sound and clean. On the other hand, if it is entered by other objects of worship, by this world and the devil, they will make a mess of it, defile it and pollute it. The heart will then turn dark, after being in a state of pure whiteness, just as would happen here, if herds of animals were to enter this field, make a mess of the plants, and trample them down." His teacher was delighted and amazed at him for making such a valuable observation.

On another occasion, he was together with one of his teachers among trees of various kinds. He gazed at them with his lordly glances, and reflected on their conditions and their shapes, then he said to his teacher: "O my master, I am looking at this tree, from which the branches it does not need have been trimmed. I notice how straight and tall it has grown. I am also looking at those trees that have not been trimmed, and I notice that they are short, twisted, and close to the ground. That is just how it is with the believer [*muʾmin*]. When his attachments to this world are cut off, and he becomes attached to Allāh (Exalted is He), he goes straight toward the highest height, since he is able to develop properly." His teacher was delighted to hear this wise observation.

He once told one of his teachers: "I seem to feel a sense of embarrassment, whenever I say: 'Glory be to Allāh [*Subḥāna 'llāh*],' since the meaning of that is: 'I exempt Allāh (Exalted is He) from every deficient attribute.' Is there any deficiency in Him? Far be that from Him! Exalted and Sanctified is He!"

This was typical of him, of course. He was known for his prolonged silence, for he seldom spoke at all, except when really necessary. He was also renowned (may Allāh keep him safe) for eating very little and fasting frequently, and for his love of secluded retreats [*khalawāt*]. Most of his retreats used to last for an entire month. All of his spiritual brethren were familiar with his reputation for prolonged silence, and one of the seekers of knowledge, who came from Mesopotamia, was no exception. This brother once said to me, when he had noticed his many pearls of wise advice (may Allāh keep him safe): "Glory be to Allāh! Can this be the one who never used to speak, except to say very little indeed, and who was so well known for his seclusion? How can he be uttering all these pieces of wisdom and sound advice?" Then he quoted the words of the Prophet (Allāh bless him and give him peace), in the noble tradition [*ḥadīth*]:

> When you notice that the believer is silent, you should draw close to him, for he will communicate wisdom.

The following incident occurred during the time when he was receiving instruction in various subjects from his teacher, Shaikh ʿAbd ar-Raḥmān al-ʿUmarī al-Būṭī (may Allāh bestow His mercy upon him): In the blessed month of Ramaḍān, on the night of the Festival [*ʿĪd*], he left the mosque by himself, after the evening prayer [*ṣalāt al-ʿishāʾ*]. He went to the local graveyard, which was situated in a high, mountainous area, covered by enormous trees. There in the graveyard was the shrine of Shaikh ʿAbdullāh ash-Shāwarī (may Allāh bestow His mercy upon him), one of the ancestors of his teacher, Shaikh ʿAbd ar-Raḥmān. The graveyard was fear-inspiring, due to the intense darkness, its high elevation and its remoteness from the village. The shrine itself was also fear-inspiring, so that people would not enter it in the daytime, let alone at night. When he reached the shrine, he stood there and said to himself: "I shall not enter this shrine, until I see something." As he said later (may Allāh the Exalted keep him safe), he did see some amazing phenomena, so he went inside the shrine. The Shaikh's tomb was encased in a wooden frame, so he sat down on the left side of the tomb, and spent the night of the Festival there, until the call was given for the dawn prayer [*fajr*]. He then returned to the mosque, where he performed the dawn prayer.

Throughout the period when he kept moving from one place to another in pursuit of knowledge (may Allāh the Exalted keep him safe), he was always reliant upon Allāh (Exalted is He) and in Him he put all his trust. He never asked, not even once, about the means of livelihood in the place he was heading towards, he and his family. The only questions he always asked, as far as we knew, were about the teacher, his moral character, his truthfulness, and his method of spiritual development.

In this regard, he used to say (may Allāh the Exalted keep him safe): "I have taken my lessons from those who are truly devout, and my training has been based on their rules of conduct, until they awarded me their scholarly diplomas. This is all due to the gracious favour of Allāh (Exalted is He). I have lived with the righteous, and I have adopted the path of the truthful."

After all that, Allāh (Exalted is He) endowed him with abundance of knowledge, and he became a Shāfiʿī by school of law [*madhhab*]. Although he is extremely well versed in Ḥanafī jurisprudence [*fiqh*], his expertise in Shāfiʿī jurisprudence is in no way lacking. He read the book known as the Commentary [*Ḥāshiya*] of Ibn ʿĀbidīn more than seven times, for the purposes of study and teaching, and his extensive knowledge of it earned him a distinguished reputation. The circuits of legal consultation in Turkey began to send him many of their difficult cases for resolution. Alongside all this, he paid constant attention to the Spiritual Path.

Through his love of the noble Sacred Law [*Sharʿ*], he attained to high degrees, for he was keenly devoted to the Sacred Law of Allāh (Exalted is He). Everything else became insignificant in his sight, by comparison with the Sacred Law, so that he once said: "As long as we live, we shall never deviate, if Allāh (Exalted is He) so wills, from the Sacred Law of Allāh (Exalted is He). Even if I had thousands of spirits, I would sacrifice them all, one spirit after another, as ransom for this Sacred Law. We must not deviate from the Sacred Law on account of our own selves, so how can we deviate from it on account of other people?"

3. His progress on the road of the people [of the Spiritual Path]:

As we have previously mentioned, he embarked on his travels and the spiritual journey (may Allāh the Exalted keep him safe) at the time when he began the quest for noble religious knowledge. He was initiated into the Naqshbandī Order [*Ṭarīqa*] by our master Shaikh Ibrāhīm Ḥaqqī (may Allāh the Exalted bestow His mercy upon him), and he adhered to it for a lengthy period of his life. He tells us (may Allāh the Exalted keep him safe): "I received my training at the hand of Shaikh Ibrāhīm Ḥaqqī (may Allāh the Exalted bestow His mercy upon him), and I stayed with him until the very last moment of his life. Then, with my own hands, I performed his funeral ablution and wrapped him in his burial shroud (may Allāh the Exalted bestow His mercy upon him)." After his Shaikh's death, he set out in search of a spiritual guide [*murshid*] to direct him. His search for a new guide extended from Mesopotamia [*al-Jazīra*] to the borders of Istanbul, and he spent seventeen years in this condition.

Throughout these years, he engaged in the struggle with his lower self, in accordance with the method of Imām al-Ghazālī (may Allāh the Exalted bestow His mercy upon him), and he frequently practised secluded retreats [*khalawāt*]. He eventually became acquainted with his Shaikh in the Shādhilī Order, my master Shaikh ʿAbd al-Qādir ʿĪsā al-Ḥalabī (may Allāh bestow His mercy upon him), and obtained a copy of the Shaikh's book, entitled *Ḥaqāʾiq ʿani 't-Taṣawwuf* [True Facts about Ṣūfism]. He took his time, however, and was not in a hurry to make the pledge of allegiance [*mubāyaʿa*]. "Where this religion of mine is concerned," he said, "I must not act hastily." He waited for one whole year (may Allāh the Exalted keep him safe), while reading the book of the True Facts [*Ḥaqāʾiq*] and praying for right guidance. Then Allāh (Exalted is He) made him aware of the real value of this blessed Shādhilī path, so he wrote to our master, Shaikh ʿAbd al-Qādir ʿĪsā, requesting permission to come and visit him. He included in his message the assertion that, if he should leave this world before meeting the Shaikh, he would bear witness to Allāh (Exalted is He) that he was one of the people of this path. Our master Shaikh ʿAbd al-Qādir did grant him permission to come and visit him, and he entered the Order [*Ṭarīqa*]. The Shaikh put him into a retreat [*khalwa*] for a period of ten days, then he authorized him to practise the general litany [*wird*]. After several years, he gave him permission to conduct both the general and the special litany. He is now the Successor [*Khalīfa*] of the Shaikh (may Allāh bestow His mercy upon him).

He has many things to say about this [and other subjects], so we have made the following selection:

• He says (may Allāh the Exalted keep him safe): "During those years after the death of my first Shaikh, while I was searching for the guide,

I was always in contact with my master, Shaikh ʿAbd al-Qādir al-Jīlānī (may Allāh the Exalted bestow His mercy upon him), through his spiritual influence [*rūḥāniyya*], and I used to see the wonders that he made visible. The object of my quest, however, was neither a mystical disclosure [*kashf*] nor a charismatic marvel [*karāma*]. My quest was for something other than this, until Allāh (Exalted is He) graciously connected me with our master, Shaikh ʿAbd al-Qādir ʿĪsā (may Allāh bestow His mercy upon him)."

• He says, on another subject: "When I first began to practise remembrance [*dhikr*], I never refrained from seeking support from Allāh's Messenger (Allāh bless him and give him peace), as well as from my master al-Jīlānī, my master Ibn Mashīsh, and my master Ibn al-Ḥasan ash-Shādhilī (may Allāh bestow His mercy upon them), until I experienced the opening [*fatḥ*] that I eventually experienced."

• In similar vein, he says: "The method of Imām al-Ghazālī (may Allāh the Exalted bestow His mercy upon him) is my technique of spiritual progress [*sulūk*], while the Path of Imām ash-Shādhilī (may Allāh the Exalted bestow His mercy upon him) suits my personal disposition [*mashrab*]. I therefore apply the former in the case of spiritual exercises [*riyāḍāt*], and the latter in the case of remembrance [*dhikr*]."

• He says (may Allāh the Exalted keep him safe): "People today are in a valley, and the spiritual path is in another valley. Where are the people of the path, when it comes to the practice of secluded retreats? By Allāh, never until now have I had enough of retreats, and it is impossible for me to give them up!"

• He says (may Allāh the Exalted keep him safe), concerning his own view of the goal of the spiritual path: "What I see as the goal of the spiritual path is servitude [*ʿubūdiyya*] to Allāh (Almighty and Glorious is He), and that I may follow in the footsteps of our master Abraham [*Ibrāhīm*] (blessing and peace be upon him), the dearest of all creatures until after our master, the Messenger of Allāh (Allāh bless him and give him peace). It is that I may follow in the footsteps of our master, the Messenger of Allāh (Allāh bless him and give him peace), in the worshipful servitude he refers to when he says:

> "If I were to choose a bosom friend [*khalīl*], I would surely choose Abū Bakr as a bosom friend, but he is my [spiritual] brother and my companion, and Allāh has chosen your Companion [Muḥammad] as a bosom friend.

"For me, the goal of the spiritual path is that I may travel like this, but we cannot do without service, and we must hope that Allāh (Exalted is He) will grant us help and support."

•He says (may Allāh the Exalted keep him safe), concerning the exemplary guide [*qudwa*]: "If someone does not follow the example set by his righteous predecessors, he cannot be relied upon. If someone has no respect for the Shaikhs, maintained both while they are alive and afterwards, that person cannot be relied upon. How can he qualify as an exemplary guide, if he is not a follower of his righteous predecessors? We follow the example set by our righteous predecessors in the practice of religion [*dīn*], and we do not think to ourselves: "This is our own way to proceed." As for myself, I follow the example of my master, Badīʿ az-Zamān an-Nūrsī (may Allāh the Exalted bestow His mercy upon him). I follow the example of Imām al-Ghazālī (may Allāh bestow His mercy upon him). I likewise follow my first Shaikh (may Allāh bestow His mercy upon him), my master Ibrāhīm Ḥaqqī, and my Shaikh ʿAbd al-Qādir ʿĪsā (may Allāh the Exalted bestow His mercy upon him). I actually met these last two Shaikhs (may Allāh bestow His mercy upon them both), and I derived great benefit from them. I saw each one of them in a very favourable light, but I have found that people who love them are few indeed."

•One of his pupils once asked him: "O my master, how did you achieve what you have achieved?" To this he replied (may Allāh the Exalted keep him safe): "By means of three things: truthfulness [*ṣidq*], sincere devotion [*ikhlāṣ*], and extinction of the 'I' [*maḥw al-ana*]. For the self that instigates evil [*an-nafs al-ammāra bi-'s-sūʾ*], these are among the hardest things to bear."

4. His service to his Shaikhs (may Allāh the Exalted keep him safe):

We shall mention one example of the service he rendered to his first teacher, Shaikh ʿAbd al-Hādī (may Allāh the Exalted bestow His mercy upon him):

A member of his teacher's family once fell sick, and the invalid asked for ice-water to drink. There was no electricity available at that time, and there were no refrigerators. When he heard (may Allāh the Exalted keep him safe) that the invalid was asking for ice-water, the summer temperature was in the range of forty degrees centigrade [over one hundred degrees Fahrenheit]. The only snow in those parts was up on the peak of a mountain, and it would take a whole day to get there. He therefore went to and from that mountain on foot (may Allāh the Exalted keep him safe), taking a day to walk there and a day to walk back, in order to carry the snow in flasks slung over his back. He endured all the hardships involved, until he had collected and delivered the very last remnant of snow.

As for the service he rendered to our master Shaikh ʿAbd al-Qādir ʿĪsa (may Allāh the Exalted bestow His mercy upon him), especially during his illness, he spoke about it freely. The Shaikh's brethren from Aleppo, who used to pay bedside visits to Shaikh ʿAbd al-Qādir (may Allāh bestow His mercy upon him), are particularly well informed on this score, so we shall leave the reporting of it to them.

5. His patience and endurance in coping with misfortunes:

Allāh (Exalted is He) has graciously endowed him with endurance of misfortunes and adversities, and with considerable patience in coping with them. I shall describe some scenes that will serve to illustrate his patience:

1. In the course of his migrations, his travels and his spiritual journey, he transplanted his family on more than ten occasions. He did not move from one place to another without leaving at least one of his small children beneath the layers of the ground, since no fewer than eleven children died in the course of those travels. He always performed their funeral ablution with his own hands. He was patient, willing to sacrifice, resigned to committing his affair to Allāh (Exalted is He), and he gave thanks to Allāh (Exalted is He) for all his conditions and circumstances, content with whatever Allāh (Exalted is He) had chosen for him. Indeed, he would often say (may Allāh the Exalted keep him safe): "Praise be to Allāh, in any case! [*al-ḥamdu li'llāhi ʿalā kulli ḥāl*], for I do not know if these young children will survive. Perhaps I shall not be able to complete the quest for knowledge, the travels and the spiritual journey."

2. He suffered the loss of his eldest son, Sayyid Muḥammad Ṣabīḥ (may Allāh bestow His mercy upon him), and of his daughter Ṭayyiba

(may Allāh bestow His mercy upon her), who was married but had no children, as well as being personally afflicted with numerous fractures in his body. These were the tragic results of a traffic accident, in which a car of his (may Allāh keep him safe), driven by his son Muḥammad Ṣabīḥ, was reduced to a total wreck. Prior to this accident, his eldest daughter was bereaved of her husband, who left her with three small children.

During the period immediately following the accident, he used to perform the ritual prayers while lying on his back. Then his health improved, so he took to praying in a sitting position for a certain length of time, without being able to perform the prostration [*sujūd*]. This state of affairs was agonizing for him, and he kept asking himself questions: How long would it be, he wondered, before he could make the prostration again? When would he be able to set his forehead on the ground, prostrating himself before his Patron (Glory be to Him and Exalted is He)? His most frequent supplication was that Allāh (Exalted is He) might enable him to make prostration on his forehead, until relief came at last from Allāh (Exalted is He).

"By Allāh," says he (may Allāh the Exalted keep him safe), "I cannot calculate the extent of my relief, my joy and my gratitude to Allāh, at the moment when I performed the act of prostration on the ground, for the sake of Allāh (Exalted is He), for the first time after the accident!" He also performed a special prostration of gratitude [*sujūd shukr*] to Allāh, because Allāh had honoured him with the prostration.

3. He was stripped of all his worldly goods, on more than four occasions, while he was engaged in the pursuit of knowledge, for, in his sight, the quest for knowledge took precedence over wealth. He abandoned his real-estate properties during his travels, so some of his relatives seized the opportunity and took possession of the estates, taking advantage of his absence and his preoccupation with the pursuit of knowledge. After his return from his journeys, he tried to reclaim his properties, but they rejected his claim. He did not enter into litigation with them, however, on account of the kinship between them. Instead, he entrusted his business and theirs to Allāh (Exalted is He), feeling sure that Allāh (Exalted is He) had compensated him with something far better than that.

6. His merciful compassion and his tender kindness towards the creatures of Allāh, especially the orphans:

How could he fail to exhibit this excellence of character, when the Prophet (Allāh bless him and give him peace) tells us:

> As for the compassionate, the All-Merciful treats them with merciful compassion. Have mercy on those who inhabit the earth, so that those in heaven will treat you mercifully.[1]

How could he fail to take good care of the orphans, when Allāh's Messenger (Allāh bless him and give him peace) tells us:

> "I and the guardian of the orphan are in the Garden [of Paradise] like this...," pointing with his index finger and his middle finger, and leaving hardly any space between the two.[2]

He used to take care of his fellow orphans when he himself had just become an orphan, after the death of his father (may Allāh bestow His mercy upon him), and he continued to care for them later on. The children of his eldest daughter eventually gathered under his wing, when her husband died and left her with three infants. These were soon joined by the four children of his son Muḥammad Ṣabīḥ (may Allāh bestow His mercy upon him). He thus added the children of his son to the children of his daughter, and all of these to his own children, and he became a custodian of them all. May Allāh reward him well!

As for his compassionate treatment of people, everyone who ever met him has acknowledged the extent of his merciful compassion for his fellow creatures in general, and for the sinners in particular. He would often say: "The spiritual path is centred on two things: The first is compliance with the commandment of Allāh (Exalted is He). The second is tender kindness towards the creatures of Allāh, without any element of flattery."

He used to shed many tears, feeling very sad, whenever he noticed that someone was painfully afflicted in his religion or his physical body.

As for his tender kindness towards people, and his courage, it once happened while he was at home (may Allāh the Exalted keep him safe), that a gang of men burst in upon a neighbour of his. Because of some quarrel between them, they intended to humiliate him and give him a

1 Reported by at-Tirmidhī.

2 Related by al-Bukhārī.

beating. The Shaikh (may Allāh keep him safe) rushed out to confront them, as soon as he noticed that his neighbour was all alone, with no family or relatives to defend him. He tried to persuade them to leave, but they refused to display anything but harshness, cruelty and arrogance toward his neighbour, on whom they wished to inflict a beating in his own home. The Shaikh (may Allāh keep him safe) went quickly to his house next door, came back with a big stick, and told them what he had in mind: "I had hoped to persuade you to depart with decency, leaving this poor fellow unharmed, but you offered nothing but harshness. By Allāh, if any one of you strikes him, I will surely break this stick on your heads!" He bellowed at them all, so they ran away in a pack, having failed to achieve the purpose that had brought them to his neighbour.

Yes indeed, he has always been eager to draw near to Allāh (Exalted is He) by all the paths. He has entered the presence of Allāh (Exalted is He) by the doorway of the penitents. He has entered His presence by the doorway of truthfulness. He has entered His presence by the doorway of sincere devotion. He has entered His presence by the doorway of knowledge and practice. He has entered His presence by the doorway of the custodianship of orphans. He has entered His presence by the doorway of tender kindness towards the creatures of Allāh. He has entered His presence by the doorway of service to the believers and love of what is best for them. He has entered His presence by the doorway of patience. He has entered His presence by the doorway of migration in the pursuit of knowledge and experience. He has entered His presence by the doorway of migration in the service of the spiritual path. He migrated at one point from his home town to Aleppo, where he stayed for quite some time, and where he acquired abundant means to make life comfortable, such as a house and a family, as well as other benefits. Then he migrated again, this time in every sense of the term migration [*hijra*].

All doorways to the inheritance of Allāh's Messenger (Allāh bless him and give him peace) have thus become accessible to him. Praise be to Allāh! May Allāh (Exalted is He) reward him on our behalf, and on behalf of all the true believers, with the most excellent reward. Everything we have mentioned about him, or that others may have to tell, is no more than a tiny fraction of the story concerning his first appearance and his travels in pursuit of knowledge and experience. He deserves to be regarded by the Islāmic Community [*Umma*] as an exemplary guide, a pillar of support and an illuminating beacon, on account of his worshipful servitude to Allāh (Exalted is He). It also befits the Community to accept his pearls of wise counsel, as they emerge from the ocean of his Qur'ānic traits of character and his luminous comportment. Let us therefore place our hand in his hand, until we reach the shore of safety with the permission of Allāh (Exalted is He), so that we may be together with him in truthfulness [*ṣidq*] and sincere devotion [*ikhlāṣ*], both in private and in public.

All that we have recounted, by Allāh, is merely a drop from the ocean of his blessed emanations [*fuyūḍāt*]. We have drawn attention, as many others have done, to the fact that he is entitled to the station of inheritance from Allāh's Messenger (Allāh bless him and give him peace). It is not possible, however, for the juvenile to fully understand the adult, so how can the student at the first stage understand his teacher perfectly? How can that student fully understand his teacher, the scope of his knowledge, his characteristics and his spiritual states? Nevertheless, we have no option but to travel on, step by step, in compliant and submissive recognition of the inheritor of Allāh's Messenger (Allāh bless him and give him peace).

One of the means to success, which Allāh (Exalted is He) bestowed upon him, was a righteous wife. She lived with him throughout those lengthy periods of time, far away from her family, close relatives and kinsfolk. She moved with him from place to place, steadfastly enduring the absence from home, the poverty and all the severe hardships. Witness to this is borne by everyone with firsthand knowledge of their situation and their high-minded family. No one ever heard her speak, or even give the slightest hint, of being worried or bored or discontented. Nor did she seek the luxuries of this world, for herself or for her children, and all this was true of her to the very end.

May Allāh (Exalted is He) reward her, on our behalf, with the best of all rewards! Yes indeed, for she was with him throughout the process of development, in character-building, in the acquisition of knowledge and in spiritual culture [*taṣawwuf*], deriving benefit from his state of being and what he had to say. May Allāh (Exalted is He) preserve them all!

We beg Allāh (Exalted is He) to assist us, through His enabling grace, to act in harmony with our Shaikh, and to follow him obediently. We also beseech Allāh (Exalted is He) to accept our fellowship with him as evidence in our favour, not against us. Of whatever He wills, He is surely Capable! May Allāh bless our master Muḥammad, his family and his Companions, and may He grant them peace. Praise be to Allāh, the Lord of All the Worlds.

Abū Manṣūr ʿAbd al-Bāqī Ḥasan

In the Name of Allāh, the All-Merciful, the All-Compassionate.

Author's Introduction

Praise be to Allāh, the Lord of All the Worlds! Blessing and peace be upon the Best of His creatures, and upon his family and all his Companions!

Glory be to You, O Allāh! We have no knowledge except that which You have taught us. You are indeed the All-Knowing, the All-Wise.

I praise Him for the constant flow of His gracious favour, with oft-repeated praise, for He has illumined the hearts of His devoted servants with the light of His clear Book. He has made the Qur'ān a remedy for what the breasts contain, and a guidance and a mercy for the true believers. In Him I put my trust, consigning my business to Him and seeking His protection. I testify that there is no god but Allāh, Alone without partner, with a testimony that leaves the heart of the testifier tranquil and enlightened.

I also testify that our master Muḥammad is His servant and His Messenger, whom He has endowed, from His grace, with glory and dignity and honour. Blessing and peace be upon the Seal of the Prophets, the most noble of the Messengers, our master, Muḥammad the Trustworthy (Allāh bless him and give him peace), by means of whom He has opened hearts that were hard, and has brought people out of the darkness into the light. I also invoke blessing and peace upon the good and pure members of his family, upon his Companions, those righteous guides, and upon all who follow them in active goodness, until the Day of Judgement.

Zaid ibn Arqam (may Allāh be well pleased with him) is reported as having said: "Allāh's Messenger (Allāh bless him and give him peace) stood up to address us one day, at a watering place called Khammā',[3]

[3] Khammā': the valley containing water.

between Mecca and Medina. He gave praise to Allāh and extolled Him. He pronounced an exhortation and a reminder, then he went on to say:

> "O you people, I am only a mortal human being. The Messenger of my Lord will soon come to me, so I shall respond. I am leaving you with two heavy loads: One of them is the Book of Allāh, the contents of which are guidance and light, so take the Book of Allāh and hold it with a firm grip.

"He stressed the importance of the Book of Allāh, and aroused our interest in it, then he said:

> "And the people of my household. I urge you to remember Allāh, where the people of my household are concerned. I urge you to remember Allāh, where the people of my household are concerned. I urge you to remember Allāh, where the people of my household are concerned."[4]

According to Abū Huraira (may Allāh be well pleased with him), the Prophet (Allāh bless him and give him peace) once said:

> I have left you with two things, and so long as you hold fast to them both, you will never go astray. [They are] the Book of Allāh and the Sunna of His Prophet (Allāh bless him and give him peace).[5]

The greatest of all the sciences, and the noblest of them all, is the science of Qur'ānic exegesis [*tafsīr*]. Since the Qur'ān comprises all kinds of knowledge, and since it addresses all classes of society in every age, no universally appropriate commentary on it can be produced from the understanding of a single individual. It is necessary for the commentator to be free from fanatical attachment to his particular method and school of thought. His own understanding is peculiar to himself, and it is not for him to ask others to adopt it, unless it is accepted by the majority [of the religious scholars]. Research should likewise be conducted objectively.

It is therefore essential to have meticulous scholars, who inspire general confidence and the trust of the majority, and who are conscientiously committed to the welfare of the Muḥammadan Community. They will thus be in a position to clarify the enigma of consensus [*ijmā'*], which can serve as a basis for legal rules and statutes, but only if it is truly credible, and properly established by sound exercise of judgement. They will not agree on what is false, for they are the trustees of the Community.

4 This tradition is reported by Muslim.

5 This tradition is reported by Imām Mālik.

As reported by Ibn ʿAbbās (may Allāh be well pleased with him and his father), Allāh's Messenger (Allāh bless him and give him peace) once said:

> If someone speaks about the Qurʾān without knowledge, let him occupy his seat in the Fire of Hell.[6]

Abū Bakr aṣ-Ṣiddīq [the Champion of Truth] (may Allāh be well pleased with him) was asked about Allāh's saying (Exalted is He):

> And fruits and grasses.
> *wa fākihatan wa abbā.* (80:31)

He replied: "What heaven would shade me, and what earth would carry me, if I spoke about Allāh's Book without knowledge?"

That is why I have not written anything without first reading what the traditional commentators [*mufassirūn*] have written, in the principal books of commentary. I have combined this with scrupulous research, to the extent of my capacity and ability, in order to establish the authenticity of the sayings quoted, and to select the most acceptable of them. I have limited my own rôle to quotation and selection, except that I have added a few relevant comments of my own at the end of each of the Calls, for the benefit of the believers.

I give thanks to the Master (Glorious and Exalted is He) for making this work easy for me. Whenever I read the Qurʾān, the sound of the Call from my Lord would penetrate my heart, with His saying (Exalted is He):

> O you who truly believe!
> *yā ayyuha 'lladhīna āmanū.*

—in which I would find the special quality of the address to the believer, filled with providential care. I would also find His address to the ennobled Prophet (Allāh bless him and give him peace):

> O Prophet!
> *yā ayyuha 'n-Nabiyyu.*

—as in His saying (Exalted is He):

> O Prophet, We have sent you as a witness
> *yā ayyuha 'n-Nabiyyu innā arsalnā-ka shāhidan*
> and a bringer of good tidings and a warner.
> *wa mubashshiran wa nadhīrā.* (33:45)

[6] Reported by at-Tirmidhī and Aḥmad.

—and I would find His address to the people at large, in His saying (Exalted is He):

> O humankind, We have created you male and female,
> *yā ayyuha 'n-nāsu innā khalaqnā-kum min dhakarin wa unthā*
> and have made you nations and tribes
> *wa ja'alnā-kum shu'ūban wa qabā'ila*
> so that you may know one another.
> *li-ta'ārafū.*
> Surely the noblest among you in the sight of Allāh
> *inna akrama-kum 'inda 'llāhi*
> is the one of you who is most truly devout.
> *atqā-kum.* (49:13)

I would pause at each verse containing a Call, and contemplate what Allāh meant this Call to signify for me. It occurred to my heart that I should collect them and write them down, but I did not decide to act on that feeling, until I was moved to do so by Allāh's enabling grace. That came about through a conversation between me and my Shaikh, Shaikh 'Abd al-Qādir 'Īsā (may Allāh bestow His mercy upon him). We discussed the subject of the Call in the Qur'ān, and the commandment or prohibition it conveyed, in the course of one of his visits to us in Mar'ash. Then, some time later, I went to visit him in 'Ammān, Jordan, and he said (may Allāh the Exalted bestow His mercy upon him): "You must write, compile, and translate into Turkish, for the benefit of the believers!"

After I came home from that journey, I wrote these Calls with the help of Allāh (Exalted is He). The religious scholars of Mar'ash kept asking me what title I would give to the collection, so I replied: "I have been instructed to write the Calls, to compile them and translate them, but not to give them a title."

During his last visit to us (may Allāh bestow His mercy upon him), some twenty-five days before his demise, I told him about that, so he said (may Allāh bestow His mercy upon him): "Entitle it: 'The Call to the Believers, and how it conveys commandment, prohibition and information.'" I suggested to him: "Let us name it: 'The Call to the Believers in the Clear Qur'ān,'" and, praise be to Allāh, he agreed.

Allāh has graciously enabled me to compile these Calls, of which there are eighty-nine in the noble Qur'ān. I have arranged them in the order in which they occur in the noble Sūras, beginning with the Sūra of the Cow [*al-Baqara*], and concluding with the Sūra of the Forbidding [*at-Taḥrīm*].[7]

I have worked for the sole purpose of obtaining His good pleasure, hoping that He will accept my work as dedicated purely to His noble countenance, and that He will preserve it as a treasure for me on the Day of Judgement. I beseech Allāh to let the believers derive benefit from it, and that those who read it may offer a righteous supplication on my behalf, which will be to my advantage on the Day of Return. May Allāh bless our master Muḥammad, his family and his Companions, and may He grant them peace in abundance.

Written by the poor beggar in need of his Lord,
Aḥmad Fatḥu'llāh Jāmī

8th Rajab A.H. 1417
19th November 1996 C.E.

[7] If the reader finds any passage or meaning difficult to understand, please refer to the sources mentioned in the footnotes supplied with each Call.

Translator's Introduction

Qur'ānic commentary is an indispensable source for the understanding of Islām. Muslims believe the Qur'ān to be the Book of Allāh, the One Almighty God, revealed to His Messenger Muḥammad (blessing and peace be upon him). Even if they know the text of the Qur'ān by heart, and can recite it from beginning to end, they must also understand its meaning, if they are to put its message into active practice. As for non-Muslim students of Islām, their curriculum will be woefully inadequate, if it does not include the traditional interpretation or exegesis [*tafsīr*] of the Qur'ān.

The author of the present work, Shaikh Aḥmad Fatḥu'llāh Jāmī, has performed a tremendously valuable service, by assembling a vast array of excerpts from traditional Islāmic commentaries, and by adding his own insightful and enlightening observations. Most importantly, he has drawn his quotations from a wide range of sources, providing everything from linguistic and grammatical details, historical background, differences of opinion concerning matters of religious doctrine and jurisprudence [*fiqh*], to profoundly wise advice for those who follow the Spiritual Path.

At first glance, it may seem that the Shaikh has dealt, however extensively, with no more than eighty-nine verses [*āyāt*] from the entire Qur'ān. As the reader will soon notice, however, the verse containing the Call to the Believers is frequently accompanied by several others, preceding and/or following the Call. Within each chapter, numerous other verses are also quoted and discussed, so that several hundred Qur'ānic verses are treated in the course of the whole work. The primary emphasis, of course, is on those verses that contain the address: "O you who truly believe [*yā ayyuha 'lladhīna āmanū*]," for reasons explained in the Author's Introduction (pp. xxv-xxix above).

In that introduction, the Shaikh mentions that he once told some religious scholars in Turkey: "I have been instructed to write the Calls, to compile them and translate them...." This may suggest that he considered translating them into his native Turkish, but the published work, on which my English translation is based, was written in Arabic.

The Qur'ān itself was revealed in the Arabic language:

> We have revealed it as a Qur'ān in Arabic.
> *innā anzalnā-hu Qur'ānan 'arabiyyan.* (12:2)

This fact may seem too well-known to need mention, but I wish to underline it here, in order to clarify certain features of the translation, and to explain some of the challenges faced by the translator:

• Since commentaries are based on the Arabic text, that text is supplied throughout, in romanized transliteration.[8] Even if the reader has little or no knowledge of the Arabic language, reference to the transliteration will often prove helpful.

• The Arabic script makes no distinction between lower and upper case. Capital letters are occasionally supplied in the transliteration, mostly for proper names. In the English translation, on the other hand, capitals are frequently used, especially to distinguish adjectives and pronouns that refer to Allāh (Almighty and Glorious is He). This convention is generally conducive to clarity, especially where the relevance of pronouns is concerned. It should always be remembered, however, that even the most "exact" translation is inevitably a form of interpretation. Consider the following passage from the 53rd Call:

> You cannot harm Him at all.
> *wa lā taḍurrū-hu shai'ā.* (9:39)

—the pronoun refers to Allāh (Exalted is He), so the meaning is: "You cannot harm Allāh at all, because He is Independent of all the worlds...." According to some, the pronoun refers to Allāh's Messenger (Allāh bless him and give him peace), so the meaning is: "You cannot harm Muḥammad (Allāh bless him and give him peace) at all, for Allāh is his Helper against his enemies...."

If we accept the second interpretation, our translation should be: "You cannot harm him (small 'h') at all." To allow for both, we could

[8] There is no universally established system of transliteration, but the one adopted here is widely used in academic literature, with occasional minor variations.

resort to: "You cannot harm Him [Allāh] (or him [the Messenger]) at all." This may be a rather exceptional case, but it does serve to illustrate the importance of the transliteration, and the need to regard the English rendering as an interpretation, not as a definitive text.

As for the challenges facing the translator, the best example is provided by the very first Call to the Believers (pp. 1-5 below):

> O you who truly believe,
> *yā ayyuha 'lladhīna āmanū*
> do not say: "Take care of us,"
> *lā taqūlū rā'i-nā*
> but say: "Look after us," and listen.
> *wa qūlu 'nẓur-nā wa 'sma'ū.* (2:104)

Fortunately, the significance of this prohibition and commandment is explained, at length and in detail, in the commentary supplied by the author. Otherwise, the translation would need to be something like: "O you who truly believe, do not use the expression *rā'i-nā* [meaning 'take care of us,' or 'guard us,' or 'watch over us,' etc., in Arabic], because that is a term of abuse in another language, used by certain unbelievers. You must rather say: *unẓur-nā* [meaning 'look after us' in Arabic]." I trust that my handling of the translation, at this point, will not cause the reader to refrain from using the English expression: "Take care of us," when that has no sinister meaning in any other language, to the best of my knowledge!

May Allāh (Exalted is He) bestow His blessed grace in abundance on Shaikh Aḥmad Fatḥu'llāh Jāmī, on the generous sponsors of this translated edition of his admirable work, and on all those who heed the Call to the Believers in the Clear Qur'ān.

Muhtar Holland

The
Call to the Believers in the Clear Qur'ān

[Nidā' al-Mu'minin fi 'l-Qur'ān al-Mubīn]

The First Call

In the Name of Allāh, the All-Merciful, the All-Compassionate.
Bismi'llāhi 'r-Raḥmāni 'r-Raḥīm.

O you who truly believe,
yā ayyuha 'lladhīna āmanū
do not say: "Take care of us,"
lā taqūlū rā'i-nā
but say: "Look after us," and listen.
wa qūlu 'nẓur-nā wa 'sma'ū.
And for the unbelievers [there will be]
a painful torment.
wa li'l-kāfirīna 'adhābun alīm. (2:104)

'Abdu'llāh ibn Mas'ūd is one of several righteous early believers [*salaf*] (may Allāh be well pleased with them all) who said: "When you hear Allāh say:

> O you who truly believe!
> *yā ayyuha 'lladhīna āmanū.*

"—you must listen carefully to His words, for they are about something good that He is commanding, or something bad that He is forbidding."[1]

Allāh has addressed the believers with His words:

> O you who truly believe!
> *yā ayyuha 'lladhīna āmanū.*

—in eighty-nine places in the Qur'ān. This is the first instance, in this Sūra, where He addresses the believers with the direct summons, indicating that it is explicitly aimed at them. By using the name "believers" to summon those addressed, He is reminding them that faith or true belief [*īmān*] requires its owner to respond to the commandments and prohibitions of Allāh with excellent obedience and full compliance.[2]

The name "believer [*mu'min*]" is the most noble of all names and descriptions. Since He has addressed us in this world with the most noble of all names and descriptions, we may hope that, of His gracious favour, He will treat us in the Hereafter with the best kinds of treatment.[3]

It should be understood that, when Allāh (Exalted is He) exposed the shameful actions of the Jews, prior to the mission of our master Muḥammad (blessing and peace be upon him), He thereby intended to expose their shameful actions at the time of the mission of our master Muḥammad (blessing and peace be upon him). He intended to expose their strenuous efforts to vilify him and discredit his religion. This is the first example from this category.[4]

The point is that Allāh (Exalted is He) has forbidden the believers to imitate the unbelievers in word and deed. Allāh's Messenger (Allāh bless him and give him peace) has told us:

> If someone imitates a group of people, he is one of them.

This saying has been reported by Imām Aḥmad and Abū Dāwūd, on the authority of 'Umar's son (may Allāh be well pleased with them both). It implicitly indicates the stern prohibition, the menace and the threat, directed against imitating the unbelievers in their actions, their words, their style of clothing, their festivals [*a'yād*], their forms of worship [*'ibādāt*], and other affairs of theirs, which have not been made lawful for us, and which we must not adopt.[5]

The believers used to say to Allāh's Messenger (Allāh bless him and give him peace), when he presented them with some item of knowledge: "Take care of us [*rā'i-nā*], O Messenger of Allāh"—in other words, 'watch over us [*rāqib-nā*]'—"and wait for us to understand it and commit it to memory!" The Jews had a word, in either Hebrew or Syriac, which they used as a term of abuse, and that word was pronounced "*rā'inā*." So, when they heard the believers saying "*rā'i-nā*," they seized the opportunity to use it when they addressed the Messenger (Allāh bless him and give him peace), intending it to convey that abusive sense. That is why the believers were forbidden to use it, because its meaning in the language of the Jews was "O stupid fool!" [Instead of "*rā'i-nā*,"] they were commanded to use the synonymous expression "*unẓur-nā* [look after us]."[6]

As stated by Abū Naʿīm in "Proofs [*Dalāʾil*] from Ibn ʿAbbās (may Allāh be well pleased with him and his father)," the occasion of the revelation of the Qurʾānic verse [*āya*] was as follows:

The Jews used to say that to the Messenger (Allāh bless him and give him peace) in secret, for it is a term of foul abuse in their language. Then, when they heard his Companions (blessing and peace be upon him) saying it, they took to uttering it in public, laughing among themselves as they did so. That is why Allāh (Exalted is He) revealed this Qurʾānic verse [*āya*].

It is related that Saʿd ibn ʿUbāda (may Allāh be well pleased with him) once heard that from them, so he said: "O enemies of Allāh, may Allāh's curse be upon you! By the One who holds my soul in His hand, if I ever hear a man among you saying that to Allāh's Messenger (Allāh bless him and give him peace), I will surely cut off his head!" To this they replied: "But you say it yourselves, do you not?" The verse [*āya*] was therefore revealed.[7]

Allāh (Exalted is He) has said:

> O you who truly believe, do not say: "Take care of us"
> *yā ayyuha 'lladhīna āmanū lā taqūlū rāʿi-nā* (2:104)

In other words: "Watch over us, and grant us some delay, until we are able to grasp what you have presented to us."

> but say: "Look after us," and listen.
> *wa qūlu 'nẓur-nā wa 'smaʿū.* (2:104)

In other words: "Say: 'Wait for us, await us in expectation,' and obey the commandments of Allāh, and do not be like the Jews, when they say: 'We hear and we disobey.'"

> And for the unbelievers [there will be] a painful torment.
> *wa li'l-kāfirīna ʿadhābun alīm.* (2:104)

In other words: "For the Jews who slandered and abused the Messenger (Allāh bless him and give him peace) there will be a terribly painful torment."[8]

The verse [*āya*] implicitly commends the implementation of precautionary measures [*sadd adh-dharāʾiʿ*].[9] This principle is established by the Book and the Sunna. The term *dharīʿa*[10] is applied to something that is not forbidden in itself, though committing it is dangerous, since it is likely to result in transgression, as in the instance to which the noble verse [*āya*] refers. A precautionary measure was called for, in that case, because the Jews were using that expression, which was a term of abuse in their own language. Since Allāh knew what they were doing, He placed an absolute ban on the use of that expression, because it was an indirect cause [*dharīʿa*] of verbal abuse. He has obstructed access to things of dubious legality [*shubuhāt*], because of the danger of transgression into things that are strictly unlawful [*muḥarramāt*], and that amounts to the precautionary measure of "stopping the means."

Allāh's Messenger (Allāh bless him and give him peace) has told us:

> Before the servant [of the Lord] can attain to being one of the truly devout [*muttaqīn*], he must abandon that which is harmless, as a precaution against that which is harmful.[11]

These are my own comments:

This call is addressed to you by Allāh (Exalted is He). You are known to be a believer, praise be to Allāh, so hear what your Lord has promised you in exchange for your belief, in the way of success, salvation, and the mighty triumph, in His words:

> Alif, Lām, Mīm.
> *Alif–Lām–Mīm.*
>
> This is the Book, no doubt about it; a guidance for the righteous,
> *dhālika 'l-Kitābu lā raiba fī-h: hudan li'l-muttaqīn.*
> who believe in the Unseen, and perform the prayer,
> *alladhīna yu'minūna bi'l-ghaibi wa yuqīmūna 'ṣ-ṣalāta*
> and spend out of what We have provided for them;
> *wa mimmā razaqnā-hum yunfiqūn.*
> who believe in what has been sent down to you,
> *wa 'lladhīna yu'minūna bi-mā unzila ilai-ka*
> and what has been sent down before you,
> *wa mā unzila min qabli-k.*
> and are certain of the Hereafter
> *wa bi'l-ākhirati hum yūqinūn.*
> These follow guidance from their Lord,
> *ulā'ika ʿalā hudan min Rabbi-him*
> and it is they who will prosper.
> *wa ulā'ika humu 'l-mufliḥūn.* (2:1–5)

There is no discrepancy in His promise (Glory be to Him and Exalted is He). He has summoned you in the Qur'ān to true faith, and He has assigned success and right guidance to your faith.

O truly believing brother, it is therefore essential for you to act in accordance with your faith. You must not follow the footsteps of the Devil, nor let yourself be ridden by passionate desire. You must follow the exemplary custom of the Chosen One [*Sunnat al-Muṣṭafā*] (peace be upon him), so that you become one of the triumphant.

O Allāh, complete our shortcomings, and accept our prayer. You are the Lord of Bountiful Grace and Mercy. *Āmīn*. Peace be upon the Messengers, and praise be to Allāh, the Lord of All the Worlds. There is no might nor any power, except with Allāh, the All-High, the Almighty. May Allāh bless our master Muḥammad, his family and his Companions, and may He grant them peace.

The Second Call

In the Name of Allāh, the All-Merciful, the All-Compassionate.
Bismi'llāhi 'r-Raḥmāni 'r-Raḥīm.

O you who truly believe,
seek help through patience and prayer;
yā ayyuha 'lladhīna āmanu 'staʿīnū bi'ṣ-ṣabri wa 'ṣ-ṣalāh.
surely Allāh is together
with those who are patient.
inna 'llāha maʿa 'ṣ-ṣābirīn. (2:153)

Allāh (Blessed and Exalted is He) has summoned His believing servants with the word of faith, in order to arouse their aspirations toward compliance with the Divine commandments. This is the second call issued in this noble Sūra.

He has said (Exalted is He):

> Seek help through patience and prayer.
> *istaʿīnū bi'ṣ-ṣabri wa 'ṣ-ṣalāh.*

In other words: "Seek help, in dealing with your affairs of this world and the Hereafter, through patience and prayer. Through patience you will acquire every virtue, and through prayer you will be restrained from every vice.[12]

This verse is an incentive from Allāh (Exalted is His remembrance), urging obedience to Him and endurance of physical and material discomforts, for He has said:

> O you who truly believe, seek help through patience and prayer.
> *yā ayyuha 'lladhīna āmanu 'staʿīnū bi'ṣ-ṣabri wa 'ṣ-ṣalāh.*

—meaning: "in order to practise obedience to Me, to perform My obligatory observances [*farāʾiḍ*], and to submit to My commandment, so that you do what I order you to do, at the time when it is incumbent upon you, and refrain from it after I have directed you to refrain from it. In this you must persevere, even if you suffer discomfort in the process, from the false accusations hurled at you by your enemies among the unbelievers, or from physical hardship, or from shortage of material goods. You must persevere in this, and in the struggle and combat with your enemies in My cause, with the help of patience and prayer."[13]

Patience is the means of control. Allāh (Exalted is He) has commanded patience in the practice of obedience, and in abstinence from disobedience. If someone patiently abstains from sinful acts of disobedience, he is thereby patient in worshipful obedience. Patience in the endurance of pain, and in the performance of acts of worshipful obedience, is essential to the struggle with the lower self [*jihād li'n-nafs*], to taming its lustful desires, and to checking its arrogant assumption of superiority. Patience is one of the moral virtues of the Prophets and the righteous.[14]

Patience means compelling the lower self to bear with things that are unpleasant, for the sake of Allāh (Exalted is He), and making it accustomed to enduring hardships and refraining from agitation. If someone succeeds in subjecting his lower self and his heart to this humiliation, it will be easy for him to perform the required acts of worshipful obedience.

As for seeking help through prayer [*ṣalāt*], the point is that prayer must be performed with an attitude of humility and submissiveness toward the One who is worshipped, and with sincere devotion to Him. The worshipper must concentrate his interest and his inner feeling on the prayer, and on the Qur'ānic recitation included therein, so that he contemplates both the promise and the threat, both the attraction and the intimidation. That is why Allāh (Exalted is He) has told us:

> The ritual prayer helps to prevent indecency
> *inna 'ṣ-ṣalāta tanhā ʿani 'l-faḥshā'i*
> and reprehensible behaviour.
> *wa 'l-munkar.* (29:45)

That is why we see that the people of goodness are of one accord, when faced with disasters, in taking refuge in prayer. It is related that the Prophet (blessing and peace be upon him), whenever he experienced a serious problem, would always take refuge in prayer,[15] for it is the essential requirement for the perfection of closeness to Him.[16]

It is related that ʿAbdu'llāh ibn ʿAbbās (may Allāh be well pleased with him and with his father) was told of the death of his brother—or, by some accounts, of a daughter of his—while he was on a journey. He exclaimed:

> To Allāh we belong, and to Him we are returning.
> *innā li'llāhi wa innā ilai-hi rājiʿūn.* (2:156)

Then he said: "If there is any private part exposed, may Allāh cover it. If there is any provision needed, may Allāh supply it sufficiently. If any recompense is due, may Allāh convey it." He then stepped aside from the road, and performed the ritual prayer. Then he went over to his riding animal, while reciting the words of Allāh (Exalted is He):

> Seek help through patience and prayer.
> *istaʿīnū bi'ṣ-ṣabri wa 'ṣ-ṣalāh.*[17]

It is easy to explain why He has mentioned patience and prayer specifically, since patience is the hardest of all internal practices in its impact on the physical body, while the ritual prayer is the hardest of all external practices. This is because the ritual prayer is a combination of acts of worshipful obedience of various kinds, including basic essentials [*arkān*], customary elements [*sunan*] and refinements [*ādāb*], as well as the state of present awareness, submissive humility, focus of attention, calm composure, and other ingredients, far from easy to remember without the enabling grace of Allāh (Exalted is He).[18]

Patience is of several types:

1. Patience in abstaining from things that are unlawful and from sins.
2. Patience in the performance of acts of worshipful obedience and charitable deeds. The second is greater in terms of spiritual reward, because it is positively intentional.
3. Patience in the endurance of misfortunes and disasters, for that is also a necessary duty, like seeking forgiveness for faults and failings, repentance, and turning in contrition to Allāh.

It was Zain al-ʿĀbidīn ibn al-Ḥusain (may Allāh be well pleased with him and with his father) who said: "When Allāh gathers the first and the last, a herald will proclaim: 'Where are the patient ones, that they may enter the Garden of Paradise before the Reckoning?' A prominent group of people will thereupon arise, and the angels will welcome them, saying [to each one]: 'Where are you going, O son of Adam?' They will reply: 'To the Garden of Paradise,' so the angels will say: 'Before the Reckoning?' The answer will be 'Yes,' so they will ask: 'Who are you?' 'We are the patient ones,' they will reply, so the next question will be: 'And what was the nature of your patience?' They will say: 'We were patient in obedience to Allāh, and we were patient in abstaining from disobedience to Allāh, until Allāh brought our earthly lives to an end.' The angels will then say: 'Enter the Garden, for excellent is the recompense of those who do good work!'"

This is confirmed by His words (Exalted is He):

> Surely those who are patient will be paid their wages in full
> *innamā yuwaffa 'ṣ-ṣābirūna ajra-hum*
> without reckoning.
> *bi-ghairi ḥisāb.* (39:10)[19]

That is to say: "Because of the patience you practised for My sake, in bearing the discomfort involved, and the hardship imposed upon you, and in enduring the trouble and the burden of it all, as well as because of your taking refuge in ritual prayer for My sake, in the midst of the horrors afflicting you. Through patient endurance of adversities, you will obtain My good pleasure, and, through ritual prayer performed for My sake, you will experience the satisfaction of your wishes in My presence, and the fulfillment of your needs in My sight."[20]

Then He has told us:

> Surely Allāh is together with those who are patient.
> *inna 'llāha maʿa 'ṣ-ṣābirīn.* (2:153)

That is to say, Allāh is together with those who are patient in that He provides them with help and assistance, protection and support.[21] It seems that He (Exalted is He) has guaranteed them that, if they seek help by obeying Him through patience and ritual prayer, He will grant them extra enabling grace, direction and kind favours:

> Allāh increases in right guidance those who are rightly guided.
> *wa yazīdu 'llāhu 'lladhīna 'htadaw hudā.* (19:76)[22]

He is saying, in effect: "I am together with those who are patient in carrying out My obligatory requirements [*farāʾiḍ*] and in refraining from acts of disobedience toward Me. I shall assist them, take good care of them and nourish them, until they succeed in obtaining what they seek."[23]

His words can be understood to mean: "Surely Allāh is together with those who are patient—in terms of providing help," because togetherness or 'being with' [*maʿiyya*] is of two types:

1. Togetherness in a general sense, relating to the knowledge and power [of Allāh]. This is of general application with respect to everyone.
2. Togetherness in a specific sense, meaning togetherness involving [divine] help and assistance. This is specifically relevant to those who are truly devout [*muttaqīn*], to those who practise active goodness [*muḥsinīn*], and to those who are patient [*ṣābirīn*]. This is why Allāh (Exalted is He) has told us:

> Surely Allāh is together with those who are truly devout,
> *inna 'llāha maʿa 'lladhīna 'ttaqaw*
> and those who are active in goodness.
> *wa 'lladhīna hum muḥsinūn*. (16:128)

When He says: "Surely Allāh is together with those who are patient," you must understand that He is together with those who perform the ritual prayer, *a priori*.[24] He does not explicitly state: "with those who perform the ritual prayer," for the simple reason that, if He (Exalted is He) is with those who are patient, He must necessarily be with those who perform the ritual prayer, since patience is intrinsic to the ritual prayer.[25]

This explains why, after saying:

> And give glad tidings to those who are patient.
> *wa bashshiri 'ṣ-ṣābirīn*. (2:155)

—Allāh (Exalted is He) goes on to say:

> As for those, blessings from their Lord are upon them.
> *ulāʾika ʿalai-him ṣalawātun min Rabbi-him*. (2:157)

It is said that those who are patient deserve the ultimate treasure and the height of dignity, inasmuch as they have acquired the togetherness [*maʿiyya*] of Allāh, for He has said (Exalted is He):

> Surely Allāh is together with those who are patient.
> *inna 'llāha maʿa 'ṣ-ṣābirīn*. (2:153)[26]

The following are my own observations:

This call is addressed to you by Allāh (Exalted is He). You are known to be a believer, praise be to Allāh, so hear and remember Allāh's promise in His noble Book, which the noble Messenger has conveyed to you. Allāh (Glory be to Him and Exalted is He) has said:

> Successful indeed are the true believers,
> *qad aflaḥa 'l-mu'minūn:*
> who are humble in their prayers.
> *alladhīna hum fī ṣalāti-him khāshi'ūn.* (23:1,2)

In another of the verses [*āyāt*] of the Qur'ān, He has said (Glory be to Him and Exalted is He), concerning the splendid qualities [of the true believers]:

> Those are the inheritors, who will inherit Paradise,
> *ulā'ika humu 'l-wārithūn: alladhīna yarithūna 'l-Firdaws:*
> wherein they will abide forever.
> *hum fī-hā khālidūn.* (23:10,11)

It would be absurd for you to deny yourself the attribute of true belief [*īmān*], for you are definitely a true believer [*nu'min*], and you are therefore included among those to whom this divine summons is addressed. It is essential for you to strive with earnest endeavour, in order to obtain this enormous profit, and to ensure that you do not let it go to waste, by following the lower self and the temptation of the devil, and through greedy desire for this inferior world. May Allāh guide you to the straight path. *Āmīn.*

You must therefore seek help in your worldly affairs, through the practice of ritual prayer [*ṣalāt*], and likewise in matters pertaining to your life hereafter. As reported by Imām Muslim, it was Rabī'a ibn Ka'b al-Aslamī (may Allāh be well pleased with him) who said:

"I used to spend the night at the home of Allāh's Messenger (Allāh bless him and give him peace), so I attended to his ritual ablution [*wuḍū'*] and other needs, and he said to me: 'Ask [me for something].' To this I replied: 'O Messenger of Allāh, I ask you for your companionship in the Garden of Paradise.' He said: 'Or something else, perhaps?' I said: 'That is it,' so Allāh's Messenger (Allāh bless him and give him peace) told me: 'In that case, you must train your lower self through the frequent practice of prostration [*sujūd*].'"

O Allāh, grant us the ability to accomplish that. *Āmīn*. Peace be upon the Messengers, and praise be to Allāh, the Lord of All the Worlds. There is no might nor any power, except with Allāh, the All-High, the Almighty. May Allāh bless our master Muḥammad, his family and his Companions, and may He grant them peace.

The Third Call

In the Name of Allāh, the All-Merciful, the All-Compassionate.
Bismi'llāhi 'r-Raḥmāni 'r-Raḥīm.

O you who truly believe!
yā ayyuha 'lladhīna āmanū
Eat of the good things with which
We have provided you,
kulū min ṭayyibāti mā razaqnā-kum
and give thanks to Allah,
if you truly worship Him alone.
wa 'shkurū li'llāhi in kuntum iyyā-hu ta'budūn. (2:172)

From the beginning of the Sūra up to this point, Allāh (Glory be to Him and Exalted is He) has spoken of the proofs of Divine Oneness [*Tawḥīd*] and Prophethood [*Nubuwwa*], and He has provided a detailed refutation of the Jews and the Christians. From this point on, He embarks on the exposition of the rules of law [*aḥkām*].[27] He says (Glorious and Exalted is He):

O you who truly believe!
yā ayyuha 'lladhīna āmanū

—for it was the usual practice of Allāh, in His Book, to summon the inhabitants of Mecca with the call: "O you people! [*yā ayyuha 'n-nās*]," and to summon the inhabitants of Medina with: "O you who truly believe! [*yā ayyuha 'llādhīna āmanū*]."[28]

I mention this because the Meccan verses [*āyāt*] are concerned with religious belief [*i'tiqād*], and are therefore addressed to the general population, as in the verse:

O mankind, eat of that which is lawful and wholesome in the earth,
yā ayyu-ha 'n-nāsu kulū mimmā fi 'l-arḍi ḥalālan ṭayyibā:
and do not follow the footsteps of the devil.
wa lā tattabi'ū khuṭuwāti 'sh-shaiṭān:

He is indeed an open enemy for you.
inna-hu la-kum ʿaduwwun mubīn. (2:168)

—whereas the Medinan verses are concerned with Islāmic legislation [*tashrīʿ*], and are therefore addressed to the specific audience [of the believers], as in the verse:

O you who truly believe!
yā ayyuha 'lladhīna āmanū
Eat of the good things with which We have provided you,
kulū min ṭayyibāti mā razaqnā-kum
and give thanks to Allah, if you truly worship Him alone.
wa 'shkurū li'llāhi in kuntum iyyā-hu taʿbudūn. (2:172)

The purpose of singling them out in this fashion, after the earlier generalization, is to honour them with such an address, and to prepare the way for inviting gratitude.[29] When He says "Eat!" the word is addressed to the true believers, because they are the ones who benefit by the Lordly instructions. The meaning implied is: "Eat, O true believers, of the foods you enjoy, and of the lawful sustenance that is pleasing to your taste, which Allāh has provided for you."[30]

You should know that eating may be:

1. Strictly necessary [*wājib*]. That is when it is required in order to prevent the individual concerned from suffering harm.
2. Highly recommended [*mandūb*]. That is because the guest feels obliged to refrain from eating, if he has to do so alone, though he feels comfortable about it if he is happily entertained.
3. Simply permissible [*mubāḥ*]. That is when none of these factors is involved.

The basic assumption is that no special factors need to be considered, and that eating can undoubtedly be classed as simply permissible. This being the case, His saying "Eat!" in this context implies neither strict obligation nor strong recommendation, but rather simple permission.[31]

Then Allāh (Exalted is He) goes on to say:

of the good things with which We have provided you.
min ṭayyibāti mā razaqnā-kum

The expression: "Eat of the good things with which We have provided you" signifies: "Let your meals consist of the kind of sustenance that is lawful [*ḥalāl*], the kind that We have permitted to you. Since I have declared them lawful to you, it is good for you to consume foodstuffs and drinks that you used to consider unlawful, even though I had not forbidden them to you."[32]

The commandment to eat of the good things raises two important points:

1. Their eating is motivated by the commandment [of the Lord], not by natural instinct, so they are distinguished from the animals, and they emerge from the veil of darkness through the light of the Sacred Law.

2. They will be granted spiritual reward for complying with the commandment to eat.[33]

The consumption of lawful food is the means to acceptance of supplication [*du'ā'*] and worship [*'ibāda*], just as the consumption of unlawful food prevents the acceptance of supplication and worship. This has been stated in the noble tradition [*ḥadīth*] handed down from Abū Huraira (may Allāh be well pleased with him), who said: "Allāh's Messenger (Allāh bless him and give him peace) once said:

> "O you people, Allāh is Good, and He only accepts what is good. Allāh has issued to the believers the same command that He gave to the Messengers, for He said:
>
> O you Messengers, eat of the good things,
> *yā ayyuha 'r-Rusulu kulū mina 'ṭ-ṭayyibāti*
> and do right. I am indeed Aware of what you do.
> *wa ''mālū ṣāliḥā : innī bi-mā ta'malūna 'Alīm.* (23:51)
>
> "He also said:
>
> O you who truly believe!
> *yā ayyuha 'lladhīna āmanū*
> Eat of the good things with which We have provided you.
> *kulū min ṭayyibāti mā razaqnā-kum* (2:172)

"Then he mentioned the man who undertakes a very long journey, describing him as follows: 'Unkempt, covered in dust, he stretches his hands toward the sky, [crying]: "O my Lord! O my Lord!" His source of food is unlawful, his source of drink is unlawful, his clothing is unlawful, and he sustains himself unlawfully, so how can he expect a response to his appeal?'"

(This tradition has been reported by Aḥmad [ibn Ḥanbal], Muslim and at-Tirmidhī.)[34]

Then He said:

> and give thanks to Allah, if you truly worship Him alone.
> *wa 'shkurū li'llāhi in kuntum iyyā-hu taʿbudūn.* (2:172)

—in other words: "Give thanks to Allāh for His gracious favours, which are too many to be counted, even if you tried to count them. Give thanks to Him through worship, and by worshipping no one apart from Him."[35]

Thankfulness requires the servant to direct all his outer and inner parts toward that which has been created for his benefit. This is not a matter of simple permission, but rather of strict necessity, since there can be no doubt that it is necessary for the intelligent person to be convinced, in his heart, that the One who brought him into being, and blessed him with countless magnificent blessings, is entitled to the utmost reverence, and that he should express that with his tongue and with all his limbs and organs.[36]

The Qurʾānic verse also contains an implicit instruction, namely: "You must be firmly convinced that blessings come to you from Allāh, and that gratitude for them is therefore strictly necessary, while its negation amounts to a form of unbelief [*kufr*]." Or the meaning may be: "You must be aware of Allāh at every moment, acknowledging that every blessing is from Allāh." According to this interpretation, gratitude is highly recommended, because this is the spiritual station of the privileged few,[37] and the real significance of thankfulness is that you do not breathe in anything but the good pleasure of the Lord of Truth, as long as you still have the strength to consume that food.[38]

As for His words:

> if you truly worship Him alone.
> *in kuntum iyyā-hu taʿbudūn.* (2:172)

—it is as if He were saying: "Give thanks to Him, because you single Him out for worship, and your doing so indicates that you wish that worship to be perfect, as befits His Grandeur. It can only be perfected by giving thanks, because the expression of gratitude is one of the most splendid acts of worship, and it has therefore been made to constitute one half of faith.[39] If you are truly aware of Allāh and His blessings, you must therefore thank Him for them."[40]

According to a traditional report that has reached us from Abu 'd-Dardā', Allāh (Exalted is He) says:

> I and humankind and the jinn are in a terrible story:
> *Ana wa 'l-insu wa 'l-jinnu fī naba'in 'aẓīm:*
> I create, yet others are worshipped instead of Me!
> *akhluqu wa yu'badu ghairī:*
> I provide sustenance, yet thanks are given to others instead of Me![41]
> *arzuqu wa yushkaru ghairī.*

You may say that worship is identical with thankfulness, because giving thanks is an action that expresses the glorification of the Benefactor [*al-Mun'im*] on account of His being Beneficent. It can also be said that worship without thanks is possible, since Allāh is worshipped because He is entitled to be worshipped, not because he is a Benefactor to the grateful recipient.[42]

I must say, however, that Allāh (Almighty and Glorious is He) has granted the servant a tremendous blessing, by enabling him to acknowledge his debt. The absence of thankfulness is therefore inconceivable, because gratitude for the blessing is intrinsic to the acknowledgement thereof. I have called this the station of worshipful servitude ['*ubūdiyya*], because worship ['*ibāda*] is for the common folk, while worshipful servitude ['*ubūdiyya*] is for the élite, and full servanthood ['*ubūda*] is for the élite of the élite [*khawāṣṣ al-khawāṣṣ*].

These are my personal observations:

Wisdom calls for eating to be repeated on a regular basis, because of the regular repetition of acts of religious obedience. If someone eats at frequent intervals, that person will surely devote his energy to worship on a frequent basis, so that he comes to be clearly distinguishable from the animals. Just as a meal is nourishment for the physical body, acts of worship are likewise nourishment for the spirit. Eating without performing acts of obedience may strengthen the body, but it does not fortify the spirit. Eating may thus be a misfortune for the believer, on the one hand, and an act of obedience on the other. If it gives him the energy to disobey Allāh, it is a misfortune where he is concerned. If it gives him the energy to obey Allāh, it counts as an act of worshipful obedience.

If the believer eats because of the commandment, he will take a sufficient amount of food, neither more nor less than that, after making sure that it is lawful [*ḥalāl*]. He must abstain from taking that which belongs to other people, for Imām al-Qushairī (may Allāh be well pleased with him) once said: "Lawful food is that to which no one else has a claim, and good food is that for which no other creature has a desire. If the servant [of the Lord] can find a meal that matches both descriptions, it is both lawful and good."

It is essential for the human being to understand that what belongs to him is bound reach him, and that what belongs to someone else will never reach him. It is therefore essential for intelligent believers to realize that they are being addressed with Divine instructions, and that they must adhere to the Qur'ānic rules and the Prophetic example, so that they may included among the truly devout. Allāh (Exalted is He) has said:

> And know that Allāh is with the truly devout.
> *wa 'ʿlamū anna 'llāha maʿa 'l-muttaqīn.* (2:194)

He has also said (Exalted is He):

> Allāh accepts only from those who are truly devout.
> *inna-mā yataqabbalu 'llāhu mina 'l-muttaqīn.* (5:27)

He has also said (Exalted is He):

> Allāh loves those who are truly devout.
> *inna 'llāha yuḥibbu 'l-muttaqīn.* (9:4))

The matter relates entirely, therefore, to true devotion [*taqwā*]. A righteous man once said to one of our Shaikhs: "Give me a piece of good advice!" To this the Shaikh replied: "Let me offer you this advice, which the Lord of All the Worlds has given to those of earlier and later times. He said (Exalted is He):

> And We advised those who received the Book before you,
> *wa la-qad waṣṣaina 'lladhīna ūtu 'l-Kitāba min qabli-kum*
> and you as well, to practise true devotion to Allāh.
> *wa iyyā-kum ani 'ttaqu 'llāh:* (4:131)"

We beg Allāh to grant us true devotion and righteous work. *Āmīn.* Peace be upon the Messengers, and praise be to Allāh, the Lord of All the Worlds. There is no might nor any power, except with Allāh, the All-High, the Almighty. May Allāh bless our master Muḥammad, his family and his Companions, and may He grant them peace.

The Fourth Call

In the Name of Allāh, the All-Merciful, the All-Compassionate.
Bismi'llāhi 'r-Raḥmāni 'r-Raḥīm.

O you who truly believe,
yā ayyuha 'lladhīna āmanū
retaliation is prescribed for you
in the matter of the murdered;
kutiba ʿalai-kumu 'l-qiṣāṣu fi 'l-qatlā:
the freeman for the freeman,
and the slave for the slave,
al-ḥurru bi'l-ḥurri wa 'l-ʿabdu bi'l-ʿabdi
and the female for the female.
wa 'l-unthā bi'l-unthā:
As for him who receives some exemption
from his brother,
fa-man ʿufiya la-hu min akhī-hi shaiʾun
let there be prosecution according to fair usage
fa-'ttibāʿun bi'l-maʿrūfi
and payment to him in kindness.
wa adāʾun ilai-hi bi'l-iḥsān:
That is an alleviation and a mercy from your Lord.
dhālika takhfīfun min Rabbi-kum wa raḥma:
He who transgresses after that,
fa-mani 'ʿtadā baʿda dhālika
for him there will be a painful torment.
fa-la-hu ʿadhābun alīm.

And there is life for you in retaliation,
wa la-kum fi 'l-qiṣāṣi ḥayātun
O men of understanding,
yā uli 'l-albābi
for then you may practise true devotion.
laʿalla-kum tattaqūn. (2:178,179)

Before embarking on the commentary, we need to discuss the occasion of this revelation, by drawing attention to the following three points:

1. The purpose of the revelation was to abolish the legal rules [*aḥkām*] that had become established prior to the mission of our master Muḥammad (Allāh bless him and give him peace). This was necessary because the Jews were insisting that killing alone was obligatory, while the Christians were prescribing pardon alone. As for the Arabs, they were sometimes prescribing killing, and sometimes prescribing the payment of blood money [*diya*]. In the application of either of these rules, however, they were clearly guilty of wrongful excess. In the case of killing, the problem was as follows: When a murder involved two tribes, one of them more noble than the other, the nobles used to say: "In retaliation for one of our slaves, we must kill one of their freemen; for one of our women, one of their men; and for one of our men, two men of theirs." They would also count their wounds as twice the wounds of their opponents, or sometimes even more than that. It is related that somebody once murdered one of the nobles, whereupon the close relatives of the murderer assembled in the presence of the victim's father, and said: "What do you want?" He replied: "One of three things." When they asked him what they were, he told them: "Either you bring my son back to life, or you fill my house with the stars of the sky, or you herd the whole of your tribe here to me, so that I can kill the lot of them. Even then, I shall not see myself as having received sufficient compensation." As for the wrong committed in the case of blood money, it lay in the fact that they sometimes set the nobleman's blood money at several times the value of the common man's. When Allāh sent our master Muḥammad (Allāh bless him and give him peace), He demanded the implementation of justice, and prescribed equality among His servants with respect to the law of retaliation [*qiṣāṣ*], so He revealed this Qurʾānic verse.

2. It was revealed in connection with the incident involving the murder of Ḥamza (may Allāh be well pleased with him).

3. According to as-Suddī, [the tribes of] Quraiẓa and an-Naḍīr, in spite of their devout commitment to the Scripture, were following the path of the Arabs in transgression.[43] Allāh (Exalted is He) therefore said:

O you who truly believe,
yā ayyuha 'lladhīna āmanū
retaliation is prescribed for you in the matter of the murdered.
kutiba ʿalai-kumu 'l-qiṣāṣu fi 'l-qatlā.

In other words: "It is made obligatory for you to exact retaliation for the murdered victim from his murderer, on the basis of equality, without injustice or hostility."

The freeman for the freeman, and the slave for the slave,
al-ḥurru bi'l-ḥurri wa 'l-ʿabdu bi'l-ʿabdi
and the female for the female.
wa 'l-unthā bi'l-unthā.

In other words: "You must exact retaliation from the actual perpetrator, and from no other. If a freeman murders a freeman, you must kill the former for the latter. If a slave murders a slave, you must kill the former for the latter. Similarly in the case of a female, if she murders a female, the rule of like-for-like must be applied. Do not transgress by killing someone other than the actual perpetrator, for, if the life of anyone else is taken, it will not count as retaliation, but rather as wrongfulness and transgression."[44]

The legal experts are unanimously agreed on the following, where the murderer is concerned:

1. If he does not repent, and persists in refraining from repentance, retaliation is legally decreed in his case, as a punishment from Allāh (Exalted is He).

2. If he is repentant, they agree that retaliation cannot be classed as a divine punishment, because all the evidence points to the fact that repentance is accepted. Allāh (Exalted is He) has said:

And He it is who accepts repentance from His servants,
wa Huwa 'lladhī yaqbalu 't-tawbata ʿan ʿibādi-hi
and pardons evil deeds.
wa yaʿfū ʿani 's-sayyiʾāti. (42:25)

Since repentance is accepted, the penitent can no longer be deserving of divine chastisement, because the Prophet (Allāh bless him and give him peace) has told us:

Repentance eradicates the gap [*at-tawbatu tamḥu 'l-jawba*].

In the version related by Abū Nu'aim, the wording is:

> Repentance washes the jar [*kūba*], and good deeds drive bad deeds away.

It is thus established that, while retaliation is legally decreed in the case of the penitent, it cannot be classed as a divine punishment. On this point, however, there has been some disagreement, since our colleagues have said: "Allāh does whatever He wills, and there is no opposition to Him in anything."[45]

> As for him who receives some exemption from his brother....
> *fa-man 'ufiya la-hu min akhī-hi shai'un....*

That is to say: "As for him who is granted some exemption from [paying with his life for] the blood of his murdered brother, in that the victim's guardian refrains from exacting revenge and forgoes retaliation, being satisfied to accept the payment of blood money [*diya*]...."[46]

Exemption is the opposite of punishment. It may be said: "You have exempted so-and-so," when you have pardoned him and declined to punish him. In the words of the Prophetic tradition [*ḥadīth*] reported by Ibn Māja:

> I have exempted you from the alms-due [*ṣadaqa*] assessed on horses and slaves.[47]

It was az-Zajjāj who said, in commenting on the expression:

> As for him who receives some exemption....
> *fa-man 'ufiya la-hu ....*

"That is to say: 'As for him whose life is spared, in exchange for the blood money,'[48] while

> from his brother....
> *min akhī-hi shai'un....*

—means: 'from [full payment for] the blood of his brother.'"

It has been said that the brother referred to is the guardian of the murdered victim, and that, when Allāh mentioned him in terms of brotherhood, He did so in order to awaken sympathy between the two parties, through recognition of their affinity and the brotherhood of Islām.[49]

> Let there be prosecution according to fair usage
> *fa-'ttibā'un bi'l-ma'rūfi*
> and payment to him in kindness.
> *wa adā'un ilai-hi bi'l-iḥsān:*

That is to say: "The person granting exemption must then prosecute the murderer in accordance with fair usage, by claiming the blood money [*diya*] from him without cruelty or violent pressure. The murderer, for his part, must pay the blood money to the person granting exemption, the guardian of the victim, without delay and without subtraction."[50] Furthermore, the expression:

> Let there be prosecution according to fair usage
> *fa-'ttibā'un bi'l-ma'rūfi*

—means: "Let the guardian prosecute the murderer in accordance with fair usage, so that he does not take more than his due, and does not treat him harshly."

The Qur'ānic verse also makes it clear, by implication, that the murderer does not become an unbeliever [*kāfir*], and that the transgressor is still a believer [*mu'min*]. In this connection, the following points should be noted:

1. Allāh (Exalted is He) has addressed him, after the murder, in the context of belief [*īmān*], and He has called him a believer [by including him] in His statement:

> O you who truly believe, retaliation is prescribed for you.
> *yā ayyuha 'lladhīna āmanū kutiba 'alai-kumu 'l-qiṣāṣu.*

He has thereby called him a believer, since he is subject to the retaliation prescribed, and he became subject to it only after the murder was committed by him. When murder is committed with deliberate intent and hostile motivation, it is classed as one of the major sins [*kabā'ir*], by general consensus, so this goes to prove that the perpetrator of a major sin is still a believer.

2. Allāh (Exalted is He) has confirmed the existence of brotherhood between the murderer and the blood-guardian, in His words:

> As for him who receives some exemption from his brother....
> *fa-man 'ufiya la-hu min akhī-hi shai'un....*

By brotherhood, He meant the brotherhood of belief [*ukhuwwat al-īmān*], for, if belief no longer applied to the murderer, brotherhood could not be affirmed of him.

3. Allāh (Exalted is He) has urged the granting of exemption to the murderer, and exemption is appropriate only in the case of the believer, not in that of the unbeliever.[51]

Let us now consider His statement (Exalted is He):

> That is an alleviation and a mercy from your Lord.
> *dhālika takhfīfun min Rabbi-kum wa raḥma.*

This is a way of saying: "As for what I have prescribed for you, regarding the sparing of life and the payment and acceptance of blood money, this is an alleviation bestowed upon you by your Lord, and a mercy from Him to you. The payment of blood money is an alleviation for the murderer, and its acceptance is a benefit for the guardians of the victim." Where the penalty for murder is concerned, Islām strikes a balance between justice and mercy. It gives the guardians of the victim the right to retaliation, if they demand it, and that is an act of justice. If they waive their right to inflict retaliation on the murderer, it prescribes the acceptance of blood money instead, and that is an act of mercy.[52]

This sentence from the Qur᾽ānic verse may be viewed from different perspectives:

1. Allāh's statement: "That [*dhālika*]..." may be taken to mean: "The rule prescribing retaliation and blood money is an alleviation for you [Muslims], because the granting of exemption and the acceptance of blood money were both forbidden to the people of the Torah, and retaliation was prescribed for them absolutely. On the other hand, both retaliation and blood money were forbidden to the people of the Gospel, and exemption was strictly prescribed for them. The members of this [Islāmic] Community have been allowed to choose between retaliation, blood money and [total] pardon, as a way of increasing their options and making things easier for them." This is what Ibn ʿAbbās (may Allāh be well pleased with him and his father) had to say on the subject.

2. Allāh's statement: "That [*dhālika*]..." may be seen as referring to His statement:

> Let there be prosecution according to fair usage
> *fa-'ttibāʿun bi'l-maʿrūfi*
> and payment to him in kindness.[53]
> *wa adā᾽un ilai-hi bi'l-iḥsān:*

As for His next statement (Exalted is He):

> He who transgresses after that,
> *fa-mani 'ʿtadā baʿda dhālika*
> for him there will be a painful torment.
> *fa-la-hu ʿadhābun alīm.*

—this means: "If anyone transgresses against the murderer, after acceptance of the blood money, that person will suffer a painful torment in the Hereafter."[54] In the words of the Prophetic tradition [*ḥadīth*] traced to Samura, and reported by Abū Dāwūd:[55]

> I shall not grant exemption to anyone who kills [in retaliation] after accepting the blood money.

When Allāh (Glory be to Him and Exalted is He) prescribes retaliation, in the first of the two Qur'ānic verses cited above, this prompts a question, since retaliation involves the infliction of agonizing pain. The question is: "How can it be in keeping with the perfection of His mercy, to cause the feeble servant to suffer agony?" In order to dispel this question, He goes on to explain the wisdom of prescribing retaliation,[56] for He says (Exalted is He):

> And there is life for you in retaliation, O men of understanding,
> *wa la-kum fi 'l-qiṣāṣi ḥayātun yā uli 'l-albābi*
> for then you may practise true devotion.
> *laʿalla-kum tattaqūn.* (2:179)

In other words: "For you, O men of understanding, in the kind of retaliation that I have prescribed, there is life—and so much life! This is because, if someone knows that he will be killed for the murder of a living soul, he will be deterred and restrained from committing murder. He will thereby preserve both his own life and the life of the person he intended to kill. The shedding of blood is thus prevented, and human life is preserved."[57]

Let us now consider the meaning of "life":

1. It may be the life of this world. This is the obvious meaning, because, in the prescription of retaliation and the knowledge of it, there is something which makes the potential murderer terrified of committing murder. It is therefore the means of keeping two souls alive in this generation. [In earlier generations] they used to kill someone other than the actual murderer, and sometimes many in retaliation for one. This provoked conflict among them, and often led to the outbreak of

intertribal warfare. When retaliation is confined to the actual murderer, all the other folk are safe and sound, so this becomes a means of preserving their lives.

2. As for the life of the Hereafter, it is also relevant here, for the following reason: When retaliation is exacted from the murderer in this world, he will not be subject in the Hereafter to chastisement on the victim's account.

When Allāh (Exalted is He) says:

> O men of understanding!
> *yā uli 'l-albābi.*

—the meaning is: "O you who have minds that are free from the contamination of passionate desire." When He singles them out at this point, although the summons was previously addressed to the believers in general, He does so because they are the ones best qualified to contemplate the wisdom of retaliation. They can appreciate its contribution to the survival of spirits and the preservation of living beings. These words also indicate, it has been said, that the rule applies specifically to adults, to the exclusion of minors.[58]

As for His words:

> For then you may practise true devotion.
> *la'alla-kum tattaqūn.*

—they signify: "For then you may act with restraint, and beware of things that are unlawful and sinful in the sight of Allāh."[59] These interpretations should also be noted:

1. According to al-Ḥasan and al-Aṣamm, the meaning is: "For then you may beware of committing murder, specifically, for fear of retaliation."

2. The reference is to true devotion [*taqwā*] in all its aspects, and the Qur'ānic verse does not specify one aspect in particular. It better, therefore, to understand it in the most comprehensive sense. It is well known that, when Allāh (Exalted is He) prescribed painfully difficult matters for His servants, retaliation being one of these, His only purpose was to make them beware of the Fire [of Hell], by avoiding sinful acts of disobedience and taking precautions against them. Since this is the fundamental intention, it is necessary to construe His words accord-

ingly.[60] *Taqwā* [true devotion] is a term that embraces both the performance of acts of obedience and the abandonment of things that are reprehensible.

Sins must be considered in three distinct categories:

1. Those that fall between the servant and Allāh (Exalted is He), through the commission of acts that are prohibited by Him, such as fornication or adultery [*zinā*] and sodomy [*liwāṭa*]. Backbiting [*ghība*] and slander [*buhtān*] also belong in this category, but only when the person maligned is unaware of the calumny against him. If it comes to his notice and he exonerates the culprit, and if the sinner repents, we may hope that Allāh will forgive him.

Likewise in the case where a man is guilty of sexual misconduct with a married woman, and the husband does not exonerate that man, Allāh will not forgive the offender, because his quarrel is with the human being concerned. If he repents, however, and if the husband exonerates him, Allāh will forgive him. For the husband to exonerate the offender, it is sufficient for him to say, without mentioning the sexual misconduct: "I have every right to prosecute you, but I have exculpated you from that, and from all litigation between me and you." This represents a concession by the known to the unknown, and it is permissible as a gracious favour to this [Islāmic] Community [*Umma*], because the earlier religious communities were not granted forgiveness unless the sin was mentioned.

2. Those that fall between the sinner and the deeds required by Allāh (in other words, the divine duties), through neglect of the commanded obligations. These sins are committed by someone who fails to perform the ritual prayer [*ṣalāt*], the fast [*ṣawm*], the pilgrimage [*ḥajj*], and payment of the alms-due [*zakāt*]. Repentance is not sufficient, so long as he does not make up the ritual prayer and other duties he has neglected, because repentance has a precondition: namely, that he must fulfil whatever he has failed to perform. If he does not act accordingly, it will be as if he had not repented.

3. Those that fall between the servants of Allāh. Such are the sins committed when someone misappropriates the possessions of his fellow servants, or strikes them, or vilifies them, or kills them. Repentance is

not sufficient, unless the offender's legal adversary is prepared to acquit him, or he dedicates himself to righteous works, so that Allāh enables them to be reconciled on the Day of Resurrection. If the servant repents, when he owes debts to his fellow servants, it is incumbent upon him to restore those dues to their owners. If he is unable to deliver them, yet Allāh wishes to grant him forgiveness, He will say to his adversary on the Day of Resurrection: "Lift up your head!" When he looks up, he will notice lofty palaces, so he will say: "O my Lord, whose are these?" Allāh (Exalted is He) will reply: "You are capable of acquiring them, for their price is your exoneration of your brother." He will then say: "I have exonerated him," so Allāh (Exalted is He) will say: "Take your brother by the hand, and go, both of you, to the Garden of Paradise."

The intelligent person must kill his passionate nature, through the practice of stringent spiritual exercises, and he must revive his heart, by always living the good life. O Allāh, enable us to heal these sick hearts! *Āmīn*.[61]

The right to retaliation is a legal right, though exoneration is better. If someone is inclined to exercise his right, it is therefore placed at his disposal. If someone is willingly to forfeit his right, on the other hand, he is a charitable benefactor. The former is competent for service [*ʿibāda*], and even for servitude [*ʿubūdiyya*], while the latter is qualified for chivalry [*futuwwa*] and, more than that, for liberty [*ḥurriyya*].[62]

These are my own observations:

The physical body [*jirm*] of the human being is small, but his sinfulness [*jurm*] is great. Punishment is based on the size of the offence, not on the size of the physical body. That is why, small though his body may be, if a person refuses to obey the Law of Allāh (Almighty and Glorious is He), he is fit for nothing but the Fire of Hell. The only refuge is with Allāh (Exalted is He). The Qurʾān directs so many warning threats at this human being, yet he is immersed in his state of heedlessness, and will not return to His right guidance:

> O human being! What has deceived you
> *yā ayyuha 'l-insānu mā gharra-ka*
> concerning your Lord, the All-Generous?
> *bi-Rabbi-ka 'l-Karīm*. (82:6)

If a human being warned you of what would happen if you did something, and he was capable of putting his warning into effect, would you disregard him? Surely not! How, then, after Allāh has issued His warning and His threat, can you transgress the limits set by Allāh (Almighty and Glorious is He)? This does not befit an intelligent human being, for he can see that the gracious blessings of Allāh (Almighty and Glorious is He) are constantly bestowed upon him.

It behoves us to feel a sense of shame before Allāh (Almighty and Glorious is He), the One who has prepared the Garden of Paradise for those who obey, and the Fire of Hell for those who disobey. You must beware of wrongdoing, for wrongdoing [*ẓulm*] is what forms the darknesses [*ẓulumāt*] of the Day of Resurrection. The wrongdoer [*ẓālim*] loses his stake in the Hereafter, just as he loses his stake in this world. If someone wrongs other people, when he has good things to his credit, his victims will take them from him. As for the person who wrongs himself, by committing violations of the Sacred Law, he loses his benefit in both this world and the Hereafter. He will therefore gnaw at the fingers of remorse on the Day of Resurrection, but alas, remorse will not avail him. Allāh (Exalted is He) has said:

> And on the day when the evildoer will gnaw at his own hands,
> *wa yawma yaʿaḍḍu 'ẓ-ẓālimu ʿalā yadai-hi*
> he will say: "Ah, if only I had chosen
> *yaqūlu yā-laita-ni 'ttakhadhtu*
> a way together with the Messenger [of Allāh]!
> *maʿa 'r-Rasūli sabīlā.*
>
> Alas for me! Ah, would that I had never taken such a one for friend!
> *yā-wailatā laita-nī lam attakhidh fulānan khalīlā.*
>
> He led me astray from the Reminder after it had reached me."
> *la-qad aḍalla-nī ʿani 'dh-dhikri baʿda idh jāʾa-nī:*
> Satan was always man's deserter in the hour of need.
> *wa kāna 'sh-shaiṭānu li'l-insāni khadhūlā.* (25:27–29)

This means, O genuine believer, that you must choose the way of Allāh's Messenger (Allāh bless him and give him peace), for then you will be happy in the Two Abodes [in this world and the Hereafter], and you will be included among the people of justice. You will otherwise be a tyrant, because every way apart from the way of Allāh's Messenger (Allāh bless him and give him peace) consists of tyranny and hostility.

We beg Allāh to include us among those who hold fast to the guidance of His Messenger (Allāh bless him and give him peace), and we beg Him to endow us with a genuine repentance, for He is indeed Capable of whatever He wills, and He is Competent to grant such requests. Peace be upon the Messengers, and praise be to Allāh, the Lord of All the Worlds. There is no might nor any power, except with Allāh, the All-High, the Almighty. May Allāh bless our master Muḥammad, his family and his Companions, and may He grant them peace.

The Fifth Call

In the Name of Allāh, the All-Merciful, the All-Compassionate.
Bismi'llāhi 'r-Raḥmāni 'r-Raḥīm.

O you who truly believe!
Fasting is prescribed for you,
yā ayyuha 'lladhīna āmanū kutiba
ʿalai-kumu 'ṣ-ṣiyāmu
even as it was prescribed for those before you,
ka-mā kutiba ʿala 'lladhīna min qabli-kum
in order that you may practise true devotion.
laʿalla-kum tattaqūn:

[You must fast] a certain number of days.
ayyāman maʿdūdat:
And whoever of you is sick, or on a journey,
fa-man kāna min-kum marīḍan aw ʿalā safarin
[let him fast the same] number of other days;
fa-ʿiddatun min ayyāmin ukhar:
and for those who are capable of it
there is a ransom:
wa ʿala 'lladhīna yuṭīqūna-hu fidyatun
the feeding of a man in need.
ṭaʿāmu miskīn:
But if someone acts well of his own accord,
fa-man taṭawwaʿa khairan
it is better for him;
fa-huwa khairun la-h:
and that you should fast is better for you,
wa an taṣūmū khairun la-kum
if you did but know.
in kuntum taʿlamūn. (2:183,184)

When Allāh (Exalted is He) says:

> O you who truly believe! Fasting is prescribed for you,
> *yā ayyuha 'lladhīna āmanū kutiba ʿalai-kumu 'ṣ-ṣiyāmu*
> even as it was prescribed for those before you.
> *ka-mā kutiba ʿala 'lladhīna min qabli-kum*

—it is clear from the first words of His call, addressed to the true believers, that He is speaking (Glorious and Exalted is He) as a friend speaks to a friend. It was Jaʿfar aṣ-Ṣādiq who said: "There is a sweetness in the call, by which toil and trouble are eliminated from the act of worship." As he points out, the lover would make haste to obey the command of his Beloved, even if He commanded him to throw himself into the fire.[63] By summoning them with reference to their true belief [*īmān*], He arouses within them the feelings of worshipful obedience, and kindles within them the firebrand of faith.

> Fasting is prescribed for you
> *kutiba ʿalai-kumu 'ṣ-ṣiyāmu*

—that is to say: "Fasting is required of you, as a religious duty, in the month of Ramaḍān."

> even as it was prescribed for those before you
> *ka-mā kutiba ʿala 'lladhīna min qabli-kum*

—in other words: "even as it was required, as a religious duty, of the communities before you."[64]

This means that this form of worship has been an obligation prescribed for all the Prophets and communities, from the time of Adam until your own era. Allāh has not exempted any community from its strict observance; He has not imposed it upon you alone. This point is worth emphasizing, because fasting is a difficult act of worship, and, when something difficult is universally required, it is much easier to bear.[65]

In the Sacred Law, fasting [*ṣawm*] is defined as: abstinence from all things that break the fast [*mufṭirāt*], combined with the intention [*niyya*] to keep it, from the rising of the dawn [*fajr*] until the setting of the sun. In non-technical language, the Arabic word *ṣawm* is synonymous with *imsāk* [abstaining].

Fasting is brought to perfection through the avoidance of things that are prohibited, and the absence of transgression into things that are unlawful, in keeping with the saying of the Prophet (Allāh bless him and give him peace):

> If someone fails to desist from uttering falsehood, and from acting upon it, Allāh will attach no importance to the fact that he is desisting from his food and his drink.[66]

As for His saying (Exalted is He):

> in order that you may practise true devotion.
> *la'alla-kum tattaqūn:*

—this means: "in order that you may be included among those who are truly devoted to Allāh, being careful to avoid all things that He has declared unlawful."[67] The word *la'alla* [in order that] has several possible connotations:

1. Allāh (Glory be to Him) has used this expression to explain that fasting is conducive to true devotion [*taqwā*], since it entails the disappointment of lustful appetite and the cessation of passionate desire. It thus prevents wantonness, arrogant behaviour and the commission of immoral deeds, and belittles the pleasures and the leadership of this world. That is because fasting breaks the appetite of the stomach and the sexual organ, which are the only two stimulants of ordinary human endeavour. If someone makes a frequent practice of fasting, these two will become unimportant to him, and he will find their burden light. This will serve to prevent him from committing unlawful and immoral deeds. It will also make him lose interest in the business of leadership in this world.

There we have all the factors conducive to true devotion, so the meaning of the Qur'ānic verse must be: "I have made fasting a religious duty for you, so that you may be included among the truly devout, among those whom I have commended in My Book, and whom I have informed that this Book is a guidance for them." Since He has specified fasting in this particular sense, it is clearly appropriate for Allāh (Exalted is He) to say, when declaring it obligatory:

> in order that you may practise true devotion.
> *la'alla-kum tattaqūn:*

—because, if something can prevent the lower self [*nafs*] from committing acts of sinful disobedience, it should undoubtedly be an obligatory duty.

2. The meaning may also be: "Fasting is necessary for you, in order to reinforce your hope of achieving true devotion."

3. "In order that you may practise true devotion, through your fasting and your abandonment of lustful appetites." The greater the desire for something, the harder it is to abstain from that object, and the desire for food and sexual indulgence is far more intense than the desire for other things. Since devotion to Allāh becomes easier for you, through your abstinence from food and sexual indulgence, abstinence from other things must be easier and lighter still, as a means of achieving devotion to Allāh.

4. "In order that you may be arrayed, by reason of this act of worship, in the company of the truly devout, because fasting is their emblem. Allāh knows best!"[68]

As for those who fast, they practise various kinds of fasting:

1. The fast of the ordinary believers [*ʿawāmm al-muʾminīn*]. Their fasting amounts to abstinence during the daytime, with the declared intention of avoiding the well-known causes of fastbreaking, which constitute the major part of what the natural instincts desire.

2. The fast of the élite [*khawāṣṣ*], this being abstinence from all forbidden things.

3. The fast of the élite of the élite [*khawāṣṣ al-khawāṣṣ*], this being abstinence from everything apart from Allāh (Exalted is He).

Fasting breaks the lustful appetite, which is the source of acts of sinful disobedience. As the Prophet (blessing and peace be upon him him) once said:

> O young men, if any of you is capable of all that marriage demands [*al-bāʾa*], he should marry, for that is the best safeguard of modesty and chastity. If someone is incapable of that, let him practise fasting, since fasting will be a [form of] castration [*wijāʾ*] for him.[69]

The Arabic term *al-bāʾa* signifies the ability to consummate a marriage sexually, and to provide the home required for married life. As for the term *wijāʾ*, it signifies a kind of gelding [*ikhṣāʾ*], that is to say, the severance of sexual appetite.[70]

When Allāh (Exalted is He) says:

> a certain number of days.
> *ayyāman maʿdūdat:*

—the meaning is: "The days of fasting are only a few. You are not obliged to fast every day of the year, as an alleviation and a mercy for you."

> And whoever of you is sick, or on a journey,
> *fa-man kāna min-kum marīḍan aw ʿalā safarin*
> [let him fast the same] number of other days.
> *fa-ʿiddatun min ayyāmin ukhar:*

In other words: "If someone is suffering from an illness, or is travelling, he should break his fast. It will then be incumbent upon him to make up for this, by devoting a corresponding number of other days to fasting [after the month of Ramaḍān]."

> And for those who are capable of it there is a ransom:
> *wa ʿala 'lladhīna yuṭīqūna-hu fidyatun*
> the feeding of a man in need.
> *ṭaʿāmu miskīn:*

That is to say: "As for those who are capable of fasting, despite the difficulty caused by senility or weakness, but who nevertheless break the fast, they must pay a ransom, amounting to the food required by a needy person, for every day concerned."

> But if someone acts well of his own accord,
> *fa-man taṭawwaʿa khairan*
> it is better for him;
> *fa-huwa khairun la-h:*

In other words, if someone pays more than the amount specified above, by way of ransom:

> it is better for him.
> *fa-huwa khairun la-h:*

Then Allāh (Exalted is He) goes on to say:

> And that you should fast is better for you,
> *wa an taṣūmū khairun la-kum*
> if you did but know.
> *in kuntum taʿlamūn.*

—which means: "Keeping the fast is better for you than breaking it and paying the ransom, if you did but know what the fast contains, in the way of spiritual reward and excellent merit."[71]

As for His expression:

> if you did but know.
> *in kuntum taʿlamūn.*

—this may be interpreted in several ways:

1. "Fasting is incumbent upon you, so you must acknowledge the truth of Our statement:

> And that you should fast is better for you."
> *wa an taṣūmū khairun la-kum*

2. The last part of this Qur'ānic revelation is directly linked to the first, and the implicit meaning is:

> Fasting is prescribed for you—
> *kutiba ʿalai-kumu 'ṣ-ṣiyāmu*—
> and that you should fast is better for you.
> *wa an taṣūmū khairun la-kum*

In other words: "If you reflect, you will recognize the spiritual contents of fasting, which are conducive to true devotion [*taqwā*], as well as the other points We have mentioned in the central part of this Qur'ānic revelation."

3. When someone truly knows Allāh, the fear of Allāh is bound to reside in his heart, in accordance with His words (Exalted is He):

> Among His servants, only those who have knowledge fear Allāh.
> *inna-mā yakhsha 'llāha min ʿibādi-hi 'l-ʿulamā'*. (35:28)

He refers to knowledge [when He says: "if you did but know"], and the implicit reference is to the sense of fear. When someone feels that sense of fear, he is sure to practise caution, and caution is inherent in the act of fasting. It has been said, in effect: "If you did but know Allāh, so well that you came to fear Him, fasting would be better for you."

Allāh (Exalted is He) has also explained the time when fasting is prescribed, for He has said:

> The month of Ramaḍān, in which
> *shahru Ramaḍāna 'lladhī*
> the Qur'ān was sent down, as a guidance for mankind,
> *unzila fī-hi 'l-Qur'ānu hudan li'n-nāsi*
> and clear proofs of the guidance, and the Criterion.
> *wa bayyinātin mina 'l-hudā wa 'l-Furqān.*
>
> So every one of you who is present [at home] during the month
> *fa-man shahida min-kumu 'sh-shahra*
> should spend it in fasting; and if any one of you is sick,
> *fa-l-yaṣum-h : wa man kāna marīḍan*
> or on a journey, then a number of other days.
> *aw ʿalā safarin fa-ʿiddatun min ayyāmin ukhar:*

Allāh desires ease for you, He does not desire hardship for you;
yurīdu 'llāhu bi-kumu 'l-yusra wa lā yurīdu bi-kumu 'l-ʿusr:
and that you should fulfil the number,
wa l-tukmilu 'l-ʿiddata
and magnify Allāh for having guided you;
wa li-tukabbiru 'llāha ʿalā mā hadā-kum
and perhaps you will be thankful.
wa laʿalla-kum tashkurūn. (2:185)

When He says (Exalted is He):

The month of Ramaḍān, in which
shahru Ramaḍāna 'lladhī
the Qurʾān was sent down, as a guidance for mankind,
unzila fī-hi 'l-Qurʾānu hudan li'n-nāsi
and clear proofs of the guidance, and the Criterion.
wa bayyinātin mina 'l-hudā wa 'l-Furqān.

—He is clearly referring to the time when fasting is prescribed.

The Arabic word *shahr* [month] is derived from *shuhra,* which means the visible appearance of something. The new moon [*hilāl*] was called a *shahr* because of its visibility [*shuhra*] and its clarity, and the term *shahr* thus came to signify "a month," as the name of the period inaugurated by the new moon.

As for *Ramaḍān,* it has been reported, on the authority of al-Khalīl, that the word is derived from *ramḍāʾ*, which is a rain that falls before the autumn season, clearing the dust from the face of the earth. In similar fashion, the month of Ramaḍān washes the members of this Islāmic Community [*Umma*], clearing their sins away and making their hearts pure.[72]

In the Qurʾānic revelation, the meaning is: "As for the 'certain number of days [*ayyāman maʿdūdāt*],' which I have prescribed for you, O true believers, they constitute the month of Ramaḍān, the month during which the revelation of the Qurʾān began. The Qurʾān is rightly described as 'a guidance for human beings,' because of all that it contains in the way of instructive direction, inimitable wonder [*iʿjāz*], and clear signs that distinguish between the true and the false."

So every one of you who is present during the month
fa-man shahida min-kumu 'sh-shahra
should spend it in fasting;
fa-l-yaṣum-h.

That is to say: "Every one of you who is at home during the month should spend it in fasting."

> and if any one of you is sick, or on a journey,
> *wa man kāna marīḍan aw ʿalā safarin*
> then a number of other days.
> *fa-ʿiddatun min ayyāmin ukhar*

In other words: "If someone is sick, or travelling, let him break the fast. He will then be required to fast on other days." Allāh has repeated this particular injunction here, in case its abrogation might be assumed, through misinterpretation of the general nature of the reference to being present during the month.

> Allāh desires ease for you, He does not desire hardship for you.
> *yurīdu 'llāhu bi-kumu 'l-yusra wa lā yurīdu bi-kumu 'l-ʿusr.*

That is to say: "By granting this concession, Allāh intends to make things easier for you, not to cause difficulty."

> And that you should fulfil the number,
> *wa l-tukmilu 'l-ʿiddata*

In other words: "And that you should complete the number of days in the month, by making up for those on which you have broken the fast."

> and magnify Allāh for having guided you.
> *wa li-tukabbiru 'llāha ʿalā mā hadā-kum*

That is to say: "You should also praise Allāh for the signposts of the religion, by which He has guided and directed you towards Him."[73] It means, furthermore: "You should magnify Allāh, at the conclusion of the fast, for having guided you to this act of worshipful obedience." This signifies that the glorification of Allāh is an expression of gratitude, a way of thanking Him for enabling you to perform this act of worshipful obedience. You must understand that, if it is to be complete, this magnification must be expressed not only in words, but also through genuine conviction and active practice.

As for its verbal expression, this calls for the affirmation of His exalted attributes and His most beautiful Names [*Asmāʾi-hi 'l-ḥusnā*]. It calls for the declaration of His absolute freedom from everything that does not apply to Him, such as an equal partner, a female consort, a son, and any resemblance to creatures. Before any such expression can be genuine, there must first be genuine conviction in the heart.

As for active practice, this means the worshipful performance of religious duties, such as the ritual prayer [*ṣalāt*], fasting [*ṣiyām*] and pilgrimage [*ḥajj*]. Since this raises many detailed questions, on which expert opinion may differ, I advise the reader to consult the relevant works of Islāmic jurisprudence [*fiqh*].

Let us now consider His words (Exalted is He):

> And perhaps you will be thankful.
> *wa la'alla-kum tashkurūn.*

Allāh (Exalted is He) has commanded the magnification [of His Glory]. For this command to be obeyed completely, the servant must truly recognize the Majesty of Allāh, His Grandeur, His Might and His Sublimity, and the fact that He is far too Great to be reached by the minds of the intelligent, the descriptions of those who attempt to describe, and the remembrance of those who remember. The servant must also realize that, regardless of His Majesty, His Might, and His Independence from all created entities, not to mention this miserable wretch, Allāh (Glory be to Him) has granted him the special favour of this momentous guidance. That must surely be taken as an invitation to the servant, calling him to dedicate himself to thanking Him, and to extolling Him with constant diligence, to the fullest extent of his capacity and his ability. This explains why He said:

> And perhaps you will be thankful.[74]
> *wa la'alla-kum tashkurūn.*

Concerning the special cases, it should be noted that fasting while on a journey is more meritorious, except when the traveller is afraid for his life, or when he has companions who are sharing the provisions with him, and they choose to break the fast.[75] Another exception is the traveller who has reason to believe that, if he travels throughout the day, he will not be able to break the fast [when evening comes].[76]

In the words of Allāh (Exalted is He):

> O you who truly believe! Fasting is prescribed for you.
> *yā ayyuha 'lladhīna āmanū kutiba 'alai-kumu 'ṣ-ṣiyāmu*

—it is implicitly stated that fasting applies, not only to the outer being [*ẓāhir*], but equally to the inner being [*bāṭin*]. From the inner perspective, the statement indicates that, in the fasting of the heart, the spirit and the innermost being [*sirr*] of those who truly believe, there is evidence of the lights of presence in the company of Allāh.

•The fasting of the heart refers to its fasting from the sources of intellectual speculations [*ma'qūlāt*].

•The fasting of the spirit is abstinence from paying attention to spiritual concerns [*rūḥāniyyāt*].

•The fasting of the innermost being means its preservation from witnessing anything other than Allāh. If someone merely abstains from those [external] things that break the fast, his fasting ends with the advent of the night. If someone abstains from all others [apart from Allāh], his fasting ends with the vision of the Truth [*Ḥaqq*].

When He says (Exalted is He):

> Fasting is prescribed for you.
> *kutiba 'alai-kumu 'ṣ-ṣiyāmu*

—His injunction applies to every member of the outer body, and to every attribute of the inner being.

•The fasting of the tongue is from lying, obscenity and backbiting.

•The fasting of the eye is from looking at things in a state of heedlessness and suspicion.

•The fasting of the ear is from listening to unlawful utterances and frivolities.

•The fasting of the rest [of the bodily parts] can be inferred from these examples.

•The fasting of the instinctive self [*nafs*] is from desire, greed and lustful appetites.

•The fasting of the heart [*qalb*] is from the love of this world and its trifling ornaments.

•The fasting of the spirit [*rūḥ*] is from the bliss of the Hereafter and its delights.

•The fasting of the innermost being [*sirr*] is from noticing and affirming the existence of anything other than Allāh.

When He goes on to say (Exalted is He):

> even as it was prescribed for those before you.
> *ka-mā kutiba 'ala 'lladhīna min qabli-kum*

—we are implicitly being told: "Prior to their combination, the various components of the human being, some physical and some spiritual, were in a state of fasting from all sources of input. Then, when the spirit was attached to the heart, the components of the human form became desirous of the luxuries of life, both animal and spiritual, with the energy supplied by the spirit. As for the spirit, it drew strength from the feelings of the heart, and began to enjoy both spiritual and animal sources of nourishment. That is why fasting has been prescribed for human beings, now that they have been assembled in combination, just as it was prescribed for 'those before you,' meaning those separate elements."[77]

As for the other rules applicable to fasting, they are expounded in detail in the books of Islāmic jurisprudence [*fiqh*], which should therefore be consulted.

Fasting is of two kinds: There is the outer fast, which is kept by abstaining from all things that break it [*mufṭirāt*], and which must be undertaken with declared intention [*niyya*]. Then there is the inner fast, which is kept by preserving the heart from evil influences, then by preserving the spirit from deficiencies, and then by preserving the innermost being from distractions.

It is also said, concerning the fasting of the worshipful, that its perfection is contingent on preserving the tongue from backbiting [*ghība*], and preventing the eye from gazing with suspicion [*rība*]. In the words of the traditional report [*khabar*]:

> When someone fasts, let his hearing and his sight keep the fast!

Whenever you fast, you must make sure that the fast is kept by your hearing, your sight, your tongue and your hand. Such is the meaning of the Prophetic tradition [*ḥadīth*]:

> If someone fails to desist from uttering falsehood, and from acting upon it, Allāh will attach no importance to the fact that he is desisting from his food and his drink.[78]

These are my own remarks:

Your days in the life of these world are numbered, and everything that is numbered must come to and end. You must therefore seize the opportunity your life provides, by making a good approach to Allāh, through your obedient following of the Prophet (Allāh bless him and give him peace). You must observe how he kept the fast (Allāh bless him and give him peace), and try to follow him in that regard, so that you may enter the station of active goodness [*iḥsān*]. At the same time, your worship of your Lord must be practised between the stations of vigilant awareness [*murāqaba*] and direct perception [*mushāhada*]. When someone enters this station, he will not disobey his Patron. If his foot should ever slip, he will not persist in disobedience. Far from it! He will correct his mistake at once, and seek forgiveness. This is someone who will not fall from the providential care of Allāh (Almighty and Glorious is He).

We beg Allāh (Almighty and Glorious is He) to steer us on the course of those who are sure to reach their destination, through the blessed grace of the Chief of the Messengers, our master Muḥammad (Allāh bless him and give him peace). *Āmīn*. Peace be upon the Messengers, and praise be to Allāh, the Lord of All the Worlds. There is no might nor any power, except with Allāh, the All-High, the Almighty. May Allāh bless our master Muḥammad, his family and his Companions, and may He grant them peace.

The Sixth Call

In the Name of Allāh, the All-Merciful, the All-Compassionate.
Bismi'llāhi 'r-Raḥmāni 'r-Raḥīm.

O you who truly believe,
yā ayyuha 'lladhīna
come into [the religion of] peace, altogether.
āmanu 'dkhulū fi 's-silmi kāffa:
And do not follow the devil's footsteps.
wa lā tattabiʿū khuṭuwāti 'sh-shaiṭān:
He is indeed an obvious enemy to you.
inna-hu la-kum ʿaduwwun mubīn.

And if you slide back
fa-in zalaltum
after the clear proofs have come to you,
min baʿdi mā jāʾat-kumu 'l-bayyinātu
then know that Allāh is Almighty, All-Wise.
fa-'ʿlamū anna 'llāha ʿAzīzun Ḥakīm. (2:208,209)

This you must know: When Allāh (Exalted is He) described the hypocrite [*munāfiq*] as striving to cause mischief in the land, and to destroy the crops and the cattle, He commanded the Muslims to behave in a manner completely opposite to that. He commanded harmony in Islām, and compliance with its sacred laws [*sharāʾiʿ*], for He said:

> O you who truly believe, come into [the religion of] peace, altogether.[79]
> *yā ayyuha 'lladhīna āmanu 'dkhulū fi 's-silmi kāffa.*

In other words: "Come into Islām in its entirety, in obedience to all its rules and sacred laws. You must not accept one rule and disregard another. You must not accept the ritual prayer [*ṣalāt*], for instance, while refusing to pay the alms-due [*zakāt*]. You must not refuse to dress in a modest fashion, and overstep the limits…, for Islām is a single whole, which cannot be divided into separate parts."[80]

As for the Arabic term *silm* that occurs in the Qur'ānic verse, its meaning is: "peace [*ṣulḥ*], and the forsaking of warfare and conflict." The words:

> O you who truly believe, come into [the religion of] peace, altogether.
> *yā ayyuha 'lladhīna āmanu 'dkhulū fi 's-silmi kāffa.*

—can therefore be understood to mean: "You must be harmonious, united in support of the religion and in the endurance of misfortune for its sake. You must not follow the footsteps of the devil, by letting him carry you off in pursuit of this world, and into conflict with other people." This seems to echo the words of Allāh (Exalted is He):

> And do not dispute one with another,
> *wa lā tanāza'ū fa-tafshalū*
> in case you falter and your spiritual energy departs.
> *wa tadhhaba rīḥu-kum.* (8:46)

He has also said (Exalted is He):

> O you who truly believe, endure with patience.
> *yā ayyuha 'lladhīna āmanu 'ṣbirū.* (3:200)

> And hold fast, all of you together, to the lifeline of Allāh,
> *wa ''taṣimū bi-ḥabli 'llāhi jamī'an*
> and do not separate.
> *wa lā tafarraqū.* (3:103)

The Prophet (Allāh bless him and give him peace) has told us:

> The true believer is pleased for his brother to have what he is pleased to have for himself.

In addition to these interpretations, which have been mentioned by the majority of the commentators, I have some other points to offer:

1. In His words (Exalted is He):

> O you who truly believe!
> *yā ayyuha 'lladhīna āmanū*

—there is an implicit reference to intimate knowledge [*ma'rifa*] and confirmation by the heart.

2. In His words (Exalted is He):

> Come into [the religion of] peace, altogether.
> *udkhulū fi 's-silmi kāffa.*

—there is an implicit reference to the abandonment of sins and acts of disobedience. That is because disobedience means opposition to Allāh and to His Messenger, so its abandonment is appropriately called "peace [*silm*]." The intended meaning may otherwise be:

• "Become submissive to Allāh by performing acts of obedience, and refraining from things that are forbidden." That is because, according to our doctrine [*madhhab*], belief can coexist with the commission of acts of disobedience. This is the obvious interpretation.

• The term "peace [*silm*]" may be intended to signify that the servant [of the Lord] should be content, and that his heart should not be disturbed. This is compatible with the Prophetic tradition [*ḥadīth*]:

> Contentment with destiny's decree [*ar-riḍā bi'l-qaḍā'*] is Allāh's most splendid gateway.

• The forsaking of vengeance may be the meaning intended, as in His words:

> And when they pass by idle talk, they pass by with dignity.
> *wa idhā marrū bi'l-laghwi marrū kirāmā.* (25:72)

> Keep to forgiveness, and enjoin kindness,
> *khudhi 'l-'afwa wa ''mur bi'l-'urfi*
> and turn away from the ignorant.
> *wa a'riḍ 'ani 'l-jāhilīn.* (7:199)

Such are the points discussed in the various interpretations of this Qur'ānic verse.[81]

As for the occasion of the revelation of this verse [*āya*], according to more than one report from Ibn 'Abbās (may Allāh be well pleased with him and his father), it was revealed in connection with 'Abdu'llāh ibn Salām and his companions. Their situation was as follows: When they came to believe in the Prophet (Allāh bless him and give him peace) and in his laws, they also believed in the laws of our master Moses (peace be upon him), so they attached great importance to the Sabbath. Even after they had accepted Islām, they detested the meat and milk of the camel. When the Muslims reproached them on that account, they said: "We are adamant on these matters." They said to the Prophet (Allāh bless him and give him peace): "The Torah is the Book of Allāh, so let us act in accordance with it." Allāh thereupon revealed this verse of the Qur'ān, addressing it to the believers among the People of the Scripture.

There are some who maintain, however, that it is addressed to the sincere Muslims, since the term *silm* signifies "the nation of Islām," while *kāffa* refers to its state of unity. The meaning of the revelation is therefore: "Enter, O you Muslims who believe in our master Muḥammad (Allāh bless him and give him peace), into the nation of true belief [*sha'b al-īmān*] in its entirety, and do not invalidate any of its rules."[82]

Let us now consider His words (Exalted is He):

> And do not follow the devil's footsteps.
> *wa lā tattabi'ū khuṭuwāti 'sh-shaiṭān:*
> He is indeed an obvious enemy to you.
> *inna-hu la-kum 'aduwwun mubīn.*

This is a way of saying: "Do not follow the paths of the devil and his temptation, for he is an enemy to you, and his enmity is clearly apparent."[83]

As for the fact that he tries to cause us harm, that is simply the fact of the matter, except that Allāh (Exalted is He) can prevent him from succeeding. It is certainly his intention to cause us harm, but that does not necessarily mean that he is capable of achieving his object.

As for the fact that he makes flagrant use of insinuation [*waswasa*], it is well known that the embellishment of sinful acts of disobedience, the stimulation of lustful appetites, and all such influences, result in the fall of the human being into futility. The victim is thereby deprived of spiritual reward, so that is one of the most serious features of enmity.[84]

The meaning is that the devil's enmity is plain and apparent, to anyone whose insight is illuminated by Allāh, and whom He wishes well. He has said (Exalted is He):

> As for the righteous, when a visitation from the devil disturbs them,
> *inna 'lladhīna 'ttaqaw idhā massa-hum ṭā'ifun mina 'sh-shaiṭāni*
> they have only to remember [Me], and then they see clearly.
> *tadhakkarū fa-idhā-hum mubṣirūn.* (7:201)[85]

Let us now consider His words (Exalted is He):

> And if you slide back, after the clear proofs have come to you....
> *fa-in zalaltum min ba'di mā jā'at-kumu 'l-bayyinātu....*

That is to say: "If you deviate from entry into Islām, after brilliant arguments and decisive proofs have been presented, to establish that it is the Truth...."[86] Or, in other words: "If you deviate from the path that you have been commanded to follow...."

According to this interpretation, both major and minor sins are significant in this context, since the cause of deviation may be relatively trivial, just as it may be very considerable. That is why Allāh (Exalted is He) has warned against all those sins, to deter the believers from leaving the right path. The believer must therefore beware of committing any offence, whether it be small or great. Where any of the major sins is concerned, the need to be on guard against it is unquestionable. If it is not known whether a particular sin is a major one, it is uncertain whether punishment is incurred by its commission. That being the case, it must also be guarded against, as a necessary precaution.[87]

His expression (Exalted is He):

> after the clear proofs have come to you.
> *min ba'di mā jā'at-kumu 'l-bayyinātu*

—is a comprehensive reference to all kinds evidence, both intellectual and traditional.

As for intellectual proofs, they relate to matters that must be established before the validity of the Prophethood of our master Muḥammad (Allāh bless him and give him peace) can be confirmed. Consider, for example, the knowledge of the emergence of the universe, and its need for a Creator, who is Cognizant of all knowable facts, Capable of all possibilities, Independent of all needs. Another example is the knowledge of the difference between the true miracle [*mu'jiza*] and illusory magic [*siḥr*]. Then there is the knowledge that the miraculous provides evidence of the truth. All of these constitute intellectual proofs.

As for traditional proofs, they are the evidence provided by the Qur'ān, and the evidence provided by the Sunna.

All of these are included among the "clear proofs [*bayyināt*]" referred to in the Qur'ānic verse. Nevertheless, a person charged with religious duty will not cease to make excuses, even when all these clear proofs have been presented.[88]

> And if you slide back....
> *fa-in zalaltum....*

That is to say: "If you turn away from the path of rectitude...." The term *zalal* [slip; slide] originally applied to the foot, then it came to be used with reference to beliefs, opinions, and other subjects.

The Qur'ānic verse contains evidence that, in the case of someone who knowingly commits a sin, the penalty is greater than that incurred by someone who commits it in ignorance. If the summons of Islām has not reached an individual, his failure to observe the sacred laws does not make him an unbeliever [*kāfir*]. As related by Naqqāsh, when Ka'b al-Aḥbār accepted Islām, he used to study the Qur'ān. The person who was teaching him recited to him: "Then know that Allāh is Forgiving, Merciful [*fa-'lamū anna 'llāha Ghafūrun Raḥīm*]." On hearing this, Ka'b exclaimed: "That does not sound right to me!" A man passed by the pair of them, so Ka'b said to him: "How would you recite this verse?" The man replied:

> Then know that Allāh is Almighty, All-Wise.
> *fa-'lamū anna 'llāha 'Azīzun Ḥakīm.* (2:209)

"That is exactly how it ought to be," said Ka'b.[89]

The significance of this verse is as follows: "Know that Allāh is All-Prevailing [*Ghālib*]. It is not impossible for Him to exact retribution from anyone who disobeys Him. He is All-Wise in His creation and His handicraft."[90] It is an established fact that He (Glory be to Him and Exalted is He) is Capable of all possibilities, so He is Almighty in the absolute sense. The verse may therefore be interpreted: "Then know that Allāh is All-Powerful over you. No obstacle can keep Him from you, so He will not fail to obtain from you whatever He wishes." This is the ultimate form of threat, since it inspires more types of fear than a threat in which the punishment is mentioned.

He is rightly called "All-Wise [*Ḥakīm*]," because wisdom entails the ability to distinguish between the benefactor and the evildoer. Just as it is proper for the All-Wise to deliver torment to the evildoer, it is likewise proper for Him to deliver reward to the benefactor. Indeed, the latter is more appropriate to wisdom, and closer to mercy.[91]

This message is also conveyed by the Qur'ānic verse: "The true believer is obliged to make peace with everyone else, but not with his own lower self [*nafs*], for it functions only in opposition to his Master. If someone makes peace with his lower self, he will slacken in his spiritual strivings. That can cause any aspirant to come to a halt, and it induces laxity in any seeker. If someone has a reputation for treachery, he cannot be relied upon when trust is essential."[92]

These are my own observations:

Allāh (Glorious and Exalted is He) has commanded us to enter into Islām, in total acceptance of all its rules, whether they be of minor or major importance. The first of them is belief [*īmān*] in its six pillars [*arkān*]. The pillars of Islām include the testimony of faith [*shahāda*], the ritual prayer [*ṣalāt*], the alms-due [*zakāt*], the fast [*ṣawm*] and the pilgrimage [*ḥajj*]. Yet even with all of these, though without belief, the believer is not a true believer. Nor can the Muslim be characterized by Islām, unless he has built the pillars of Islām on the foundation of belief.

Furthermore, in another verse of the Qur'ān, Allāh has given us this command:

> Forsake the outer aspect of sin, and the inner aspect of it as well.
> *wa dharū ẓāhira 'l-ithmi wa bāṭina-h.* (6:120)

It is therefore incumbent upon us, as Muslims, to adhere to the moral standards that Allāh has enjoined upon His servants in the Noble Qur'ān. Those are the moral standards of Allāh's Messenger (Allāh bless him and give him peace). As long as we live, we must adhere to the moral standards of the Qur'ān. When the lady 'Ā'isha (may Allāh be well pleased with her) was asked about the character of her husband (Allāh bless him and give him peace), she replied: "The Qur'ān is his character." At the head of all virtuous qualities stand true devotion [*taqwā*] and truthfulness [*ṣidq*], because Allāh (Exalted is He) instructed His Messenger to convey to the believers:

> O you who truly believe, you must practise true devotion to Allāh,
> *yā ayyuha 'lladhīna āmanu 'ttaqu 'llāha*
> and be with the truthful.
> *wa kūnū ma'a 'ṣ-ṣādiqīn.* (9:119)

Truthfulness is the perfection of sincerity [*ikhlāṣ*], and sincerity is the fruit of righteous intention. Allāh (Glory be to Him and Exalted is He) has linked His approval to truthfulness, for He has said, in another verse of the Qur'ān:

> This is a day in which their truthfulness will benefit the truthful.
> *hādhā yawmu yanfa'u 'ṣ-ṣādiqīna ṣidqu-hum.* (5:119)

The Garden of Paradise is not the only benefit in store for them, since He also said:

> Allāh is well pleased with them, and they are well pleased with Him.
> *abadā: raḍiya 'llāhu ʿan-hum wa raḍū ʿan-h.* (5:119)

So long as togetherness with the truthful is our first priority, we are bound to be included among the truthful. If we are incapable of truthfulness, due to the weakness of our human nature, we must be together with the truthful, in order to acquire truthfulness from them.

We beg Allāh (Glorious and Exalted is He) to endow us with truthfulness, true devotion and good moral values, from His grace and His mercy. The truthful have never been, and will never be, entirely absent from the Community of our master Muḥammad (Allāh bless him and give him peace) in any place or at any time, until the advent of the Final Hour. We must not be so deceived by instinctive misgivings, and by satanic inclinations, as to say: "They do not exist in this day and age." Remember the saying of Allāh's Messenger (Allāh bless him and give him peace):

> In my Community, there will always be a group of people who uphold the truth. Those who oppose them will not harm them.[93]

—for this is evidence to prove that the truthful will never become extinct.

We beg Allāh to gather us in their company at the Resurrection. *Āmīn*. Peace be upon the Messengers, and praise be to Allāh, the Lord of All the Worlds. There is no might nor any power, except with Allāh, the All-High, the Almighty. May Allāh bless our master Muḥammad, his family and his Companions, and may He grant them peace.

The Seventh Call

In the Name of Allāh, the All-Merciful, the All-Compassionate.
Bismi'llāhi 'r-Raḥmāni 'r-Raḥīm.

O you who truly believe,
yā ayyuha 'lladhīna āmanū
spend from what We have provided for you,
anfiqū mimmā razaqnā-kum
before a day comes when there will be no trading,
min qabli an ya'tiya yawmun lā bai'un fī-hi
nor friendship, nor intercession.
wa lā khullatun wa lā shafā'a:
The unbelievers, they are the wrongdoers.
wa 'l-kāfirūna humu 'ẓ-ẓālimūn. (2:254)

Allāh (Exalted is He) has said:

> O you who truly believe,
> *yā ayyuha 'lladhīna āmanū*
> spend from what We have provided for you.
> *anfiqū mimmā razaqnā-kum*

In other words: "Spend, for the sake of Allāh's cause, from the wealth of Allāh, which He has bestowed upon you. You must pay the alms-due [*zakāt*], and spend in support of goodness, charity, and righteous endeavours."[94]

Concerning His expression (Exalted is He):

> from what We have provided for you.
> *mimmā razaqnā-kum*

—Ibn Juraij and Sa'īd ibn Jubair maintained: "This Qur'ānic verse refers both to the obligatory alms-due [*zakāt*] and to voluntary spending [*taṭawwu'*]." Ibn 'Aṭiyya said: "This may be correct, although the preceding verses are concerned with the subject of fighting, and how Allāh urges the believers to challenge the unbelievers. It is more probable, therefore, that this summons refers only to spending for the sake of Allāh's cause. This is emphasized by His saying, at the end of the verse:

> The unbelievers, they are the wrongdoesrs.
> *wa 'l-kāfirūna humu 'ẓ-ẓālimūn.*

"In other words: 'You must confront them [*kāfiḥū-hum*]* in battle, in personal combat and by spending your wealth.'" (*That is to say: "You must meet them face-to-face." When people confront [*kāfaḥa*] their enemies, this is said to mean: "They approach them in battle with their faces exposed, without using shields or other means of protection.")

According to this interpretation, the expenditure of wealth is sometimes strictly required, and sometimes merely recommended, depending on whether or not the holy war [*jihād*] has been explicitly declared.

Allāh (Exalted is He) has commanded His servants to spend from what He has provided for them and graciously bestowed upon them. He has also warned them against withholding, until a day comes when there can be no buying and selling, and no acquisition of livelihood. As He has said (Exalted is He):

> And he says: "My Lord, if only You would reprieve me
> *fa-yaqūla Rabbi law lā akhkharta-nī*
> for a little while, then I would donate to charity."
> *ilā ajalin qarībin fa-aṣṣadaqa.* (63:10)[95]

The message seems to be: "You had better obtain the benefits of the Hereafter while you are still in this world, for, once you have departed from this world, you will not be able to obtain or acquire them in the Hereafter."

[The heretics known as] the Mu'tazila have argued that [divine] provision cannot be other than lawful [*ḥalāl*], since He has said:

> Spend from what We have provided for you.
> *anfiqū mimmā razaqnā-kum*

We say: "Allāh (Exalted is He) has commanded expenditure from everything that constitutes provision, by general consensus. As for that which is unlawful [*ḥarām*], its expenditure is not permissible. This leads to the definite conclusion that [divine] provision cannot be unlawful." The Companions said: "While the Qur'ānic verse apparently conveys the order to spend everything that constitutes provision, we apply this commandment specifically to the expenditure of everything that constitutes lawful provision."[96]

As for His words (Exalted is He):

> before a day comes when there will be no trading,
> *min qabli an ya'tiya yawmun lā bai'un fī-hi*
> nor friendship, nor intercession.
> *wa lā khullatun wa lā shafā'a:*

—the meaning is: "Before the coming of that dreadful day, when you will not be able to ransom yourselves with any wealth you may offer, as if in making trade. When that day comes, you will not find any friend to keep the torment from you, nor any intercessor to intercede on your behalf, in order to rid you of your evil deeds, unless permission is granted by Allāh, the Lord of All the Worlds."[97]

"There will be no trading [*lā bai'un*]" signifies: "You must forward something for yourselves, from the wealth you have in your possession, before the day comes when there will be no commerce and no business contract, so that something of value can be earned.

"Nor any friendship [*wa lā khullatun*]" signifies: "Nor any loving affection."

For the sake of comparison, consider what Allāh (Exalted is He) has said in these other Qur'ānic verses:

> Friends on that Day will be foes to one another,
> *al-akhillā'u yawma'idhin ba'ḍu-hum*
> except those who were truly devout.
> *li-ba'ḍin 'aduwwun illa 'l-muttaqīn.* (43:67)

> And all their aims will collapse with them.
> *wa taqaṭṭa'at bi-himu 'l-asbāb.* (2:166)

> Then on the Day of Resurrection you will deny each other
> *thumma Yawma 'l-Qiyāmati yakfuru ba'ḍu-kum bi-ba'ḍin*
> and curse each other.
> *wa yal'anu ba'ḍu-kum ba'ḍā.* (29:25)

> Now we [unbelievers] have no intercessors,
> *fa-mā la-nā min shāfi'īn*
> nor any loving friend.
> *wa lā ṣadīqin ḥamīm.* (26:100,101)

Wrongdoers have no helpers,
wa mā li'z-zālimīna min anṣār. (2:270)
nor any intercession.
wa lā shafā'a. (2:254)

You must know that the absence of friendship and intercession, on the Day of Resurrection, will be due to several causes:

1. Everyone will be preoccupied with himself:

Every man that day will have business to suffice him.
li-kulli 'mri'in min-hum yawma'idhin sha'nun yughnī-h. (80:37)

2. Everyone will be utterly overwhelmed by extremely intense fear:

On the day when you behold it,
yawma tarawna-hā
every nursing mother will forget her nursling
tadhhalu kullu murḍi'atin 'ammā arḍa'at.
and every pregnant one will be delivered of her burden,
wa taḍa'u kullu dhāti ḥamlin ḥamla-hā
and you will see mankind as drunken,
wa tara 'n-nāsa sukārā
yet they will not be drunken,
wa mā hum bi-sukārā
but the doom of Allāh will be strong.
wa lākinna 'adhāba 'llāhi shadīd. (22:2)

3. Since the torment is inflicted because of unbelief and depravity, the sufferer will come to hate these two vices. Then, when he has come hate them, he will also come to hate anyone who is characterized by them.[98]

The Arabic term *khulla* denotes friendship in the sense of genuine loving affection. It is derived from the *takhallul* [intermingling] of the innermost beings [*asrār*] that occurs between friends. Allāh (Exalted is He) has informed us that there will be no such friendship in the Hereafter, and no intercession, except with His permission. The real experience of it is a mercy from Him, with which He honours anyone whom He allows to practise intercession.[99]

The summons:

O you who truly believe,
yā ayyuha 'lladhīna āmanū
spend from what We have provided for you.
anfiqū mimmā razaqnā-kum

—implies: "[Spend] in obedience to Me, since those who do not believe in Me are spending in disobedience to Me. You must do so now, before there comes a day when there will be no trading. The people of unbelief will then have to settle for what they neglected in their worldly business. There will be no friendship for them on that day, no friend to protect them from Me. They will have no intercessor to intercede with Me on their behalf, no one whose intercession could save them from My punishment."[100]

When Allāh (Exalted is He) says: "Nor intercession [*wa lā shafāʿa*]," the implication is: "for anyone, unless the All-Merciful first grants permission to whomever He wishes and approves." He is thereby indicating that no one will have the power to obtain some advantage for himself, by any manner of means. If a person owes a debt, for instance, he will not be able to pay it by making a sale, nor by getting help from his friends, nor by finding someone to intercede on his behalf, in order to seek a reduction. All of these options will have ceased to exist, and the only source of help will be Allāh.[101]

> The unbelievers, they are the wrongdoesrs.
> *wa 'l-kāfirūna humu 'ẓ-ẓālimūn.*

That is to say: "Among those who appear before Allāh on that day, no one who has been wronged will be counted as an unbeliever. The disbeliever in Allāh is the wicked wrongdoer, who deserves to suffer punishment."

ʿAṭāʾ ibn Dīnār is reported as having said: "Praise be to Him who said:

> The unbelievers, they are the wrongdoesrs.
> *wa 'l-kāfirūna humu 'ẓ-ẓālimūn.*

—"and did not say: 'The wrongdoers, they are the unbelievers [*wa 'ẓ-ẓālimūna humu 'l-kāfirūna*].'" What he meant was that, if the revelation had come in this form, every wrongdoer would be judged guilty of unbelief, so no one would be innocent of it, except those kept immune by Allāh.

NOTE: The term *kufr* [unbelief] may be understood in either the literal or the figurative sense. The label *kāfir* [unbeliever] may thus be applied to someone who fails to pay the alms-due [*zakāt*], as az-Zamakhsharī suggested when he said: "['The unbelievers, they are the wrongdoers'] means: 'Those who fail to pay the alms-due, they are the wrongdoers [*wa 't-tārikūna li'z-zakāti humu 'z-zālimūna*].'" By choosing this expression, Allāh intended to strike a harsh and threatening note, as in the verse about the Pilgrimage [*Ḥajj*]:

> And Pilgrimage to the House is a duty unto Allāh for mankind,
> *wa li'llāhi ʿala 'n-nāsi Ḥijju 'l-Baiti*
> for him who can find a way thither.
> *mani 'staṭāʿa ilai-hi sabīlā:*
> As for him who disbelieves,
> *wa man kafara*
> Allāh is indeed Independent of all the worlds.
> *fa-inna 'llāha Ghaniyyun ʿani 'l-ʿālamīn.* (3:97)

—where He uses the expression: "As for him who disbelieves [*wa man kafara*] instead of: "As for him who does not perform the Pilgrimage [*wa man lam yaḥujj*]." He has also included failure to pay the alms-due among the attributes of unbelief, in His words:

> Woe to the idolaters, who do not pay the alms-due,
> *wa wailun li'l-mushrikīn : alladhīna lā yu'tūna 'z-zakāta*
> and who are disbelievers in the Hereafter.
> *wa hum bi'l-ākhirati hum kāfirūn.* (41:6,7)[102]

It was ar-Rāghib who said: "Allāh has urged the true believers to spend from what He has provided for them, in the way of spiritual as well as physical benefits. While the obvious reference is to the expenditure of wealth, it may also signify the sacrifice of body and soul in the sacred struggle with the [satanic] enemy and the passions, as well as all other forms of worshipful service. This world is the abode of earning and tribulation, while the Hereafter is the abode of reward and recompense. As He has therefore explained, there is no way for the human being to obtain what is of benefit to him [once he has come to be] in the Hereafter, so he is tested by the mention of these three things, because they are the means of procuring the relevant benefits:

1. Contractual exchange, of which commercial dealing is the most important form.
2. That which is obtained through loving affection, meaning that to which terms like "gifts" and "presents" apply.
3. That which is achieved through the assistance of another person; that is to say, through intercession.'[103]

The message conveyed by the Qurʾānic verse is this: "You must seize the opportunity that makes it possible to send good conduct on ahead, before the fading of energy and the expiration of hope."[104]

These are my own remarks:

Six things provide protection from Allāh's torment and the threat He has issued to the believers, namely:

1. Repentance.
2. Seeking forgiveness.
3. Good deeds that erase the bad ones.
4. Patience in the face of worldly misfortunes.
5. The intercession of the accepted intercessor [he being the Prophet (Allāh bless him and give him peace)].
6. The mercy of the Most Merciful of the merciful.

Since these are effective means of preventing the threat of torment from being implemented, we beseech Allāh (Glorious and Exalted is He) to let us be included among those who repent, who seek forgiveness, and who follow bad deeds with good deeds. We request of Him, through His compassion, that He may enable Allāh's Messenger (Allāh bless him and give him peace) to intercede on our behalf, and that He may bestow His mercy upon us, for He is the Most Merciful of the merciful. *Āmīn.* Peace be upon the Messengers, and praise be to Allāh, the Lord of All the Worlds. There is no might nor any power, except with Allāh, the All-High, the Almighty. May Allāh bless our master Muḥammad, his family and his Companions, and may He grant peace to them all.

The Eighth Call

In the Name of Allāh, the All-Merciful, the All-Compassionate.
Bismi'llāhi 'r-Raḥmāni 'r-Raḥīm.

O you who truly believe,
yā ayyuha 'lladhīna āmanū
do not render your charitable
donations null and void
lā tubṭilū ṣadaqāti-kum
with reproach and insult,
bi'l-manni wa 'l-adhā
like him who spends his wealth
ka-'lladhī yunfiqu māla-hu
only to be seen by other people,
riʾāʾa 'n-nāsi
and does not believe in Allāh
and the Last Day.
wa lā yuʾminu bi'llāhi wa 'l-yawmi 'l-ākhir.

His likeness is as the likeness of a rock
fa-mathalu-hu ka-mathali ṣafwānin
on which there is a layer of soil,
ʿalai-hi turābun
but then a rainstorm smites it,
fa-aṣāba-hu wābilun
leaving it smooth and bare.
fa-taraka-hu ṣaldā:
They have no control of anything
of what they have acquired.
lā yaqdirūna ʿalā shaiʾin mimmā kasabū
And Allāh does not guide the unbelieving folk.
wa 'llāhu lā yahdi 'l-qawma 'l-kāfirīn. (2:264)

O you who truly believe,
yā ayyuha 'lladhīna āmanū
do not render your charitable donations null and void
lā tubṭilū ṣadaqāti-kum
with reproach and insult
bi'l-manni wa 'l-adhā

That is to say: "Do not waste their reward through reproach and injury."[105]

with reproach
bi'l-manni

The term *mann* [reproach; taunting] is applied to the conduct of a person who does someone a favour, then casts that favour in the recipient's face, making him feel that he is entitled to far more evidence of gratitude. In other words: "Do not taunt them with your charitable donations, as when the reproachful donor says: 'I treated you like that as an act of charity, and I have done you so much good!'"

and insult
wa 'l-adhā

This signifies that the donor adopts an attitude of insolence towards the recipient, on account of the favour he has granted him. In other words: "Do not insult him, as when the insolent donor says: 'I gave you so much, but you have shown no gratitude,' or: 'How long will you keep coming and bothering me?' or: 'How much do you want? Have you no sense of shame?'" If he acts like that, he will have no spiritual reward for his charitable donation. He will bear the burden of sin for his taunting of the pauper, as well as the burden of sin for insulting him.

As for what is meant by rendering charitable donations null and void, it signifies the cancellation of their spiritual reward. Once a charitable gift has been made, and has already been delivered, its annulment cannot possibly mean the annulment of the gift itself. It can only mean the cancellation of its spiritual recompense and reward. Since the reward has not yet been obtained, its annulment is right and proper, because of the reproach and insult committed by the donor.[106]

like him who spends his wealth only to be seen by other people,
ka-'lladhī yunfiqu māla-hu riʾāʾa 'n-nāsi

That is to say: "like the ostentatious hypocrite, who renders his expenditure null and void by pretentious display."[107] The reference is to the hypocrite, because the unbeliever is frank about his unbelief, not hypocritical. In other words: "Do not render them null and void in the manner of the hypocrite, meaning someone who:

> spends his wealth only to be seen by other people
> *yunfiqu māla-hu ri'ā'a 'n-nāsi*

—in order to make a good impression on them, and so they will call him noble and generous."[108]

> and does not believe in Allāh and the Last Day.
> *wa lā yu'minu bi'llāhi wa 'l-yawmi 'l-ākhir.*

That is to say: "He does not believe in the Meeting with Allāh, so he neither hopes for any reward nor dreads any punishment."[109] His expenditure is not for the purpose of gaining Allāh's good pleasure, nor the reward of the Hereafter, for he is an ostentatious hypocrite, and the expenditure of the ostentatious hypocrite is designed to attract attention and praise from other people.[110]

Allāh (Exalted is He) has expressed unacceptability and deprivation of reward in terms of rendering null and void. The reference is to the charitable donation that is used as a pretext for reproach and insult, not to any other. It is an article of faith [*ʿaqīda*] that bad deeds do not render good deeds null and void, so reproach and insult linked to one charitable donation do not annul any other.

In the context of this Qur'ānic verse, according to the majority of the religious scholars: "When Allāh knows that the giver of a charitable donation is using it as a pretext for reproach and insult, it will not be accepted." Some say: "Allāh has already put the angel in charge of it, so he will not record it [to the donor's credit]." Ibn Sīrīn once heard a man say to another man: "I have done you a favour, and what have you done to deserve it?" So he told him: "Be quiet, for there is no good in an act of kindness, if it is held against the recipient."

The Prophet (Allāh bless him and give him peace) is reported as having said:

> Beware of using an act of kindness as a pretext for reproach, for it will annul the appreciation and cancel the reward.

Then he recited:

Do not render your charitable donations null and void
lā tubṭilū ṣadaqāti-kum
with reproach and insult.[111]
bi'l-manni wa 'l-adhā.

❧ ☙

His likeness is as the likeness of a rock
fa-mathalu-hu ka-mathali ṣafwānin
on which there is a layer of soil
ʿalai-hi turābun

That is to say: "The likeness of the ostentatious hypocrite, in his expenditure, is as the likeness of the smooth stone covered by a layer of soil, which the observer supposes to be good and fruitful earth."

but then a rainstorm smites it, leaving it smooth and bare.
fa-aṣāba-hu wābilun fa-taraka-hu ṣaldā:

In other words: "When heavy rain falls on it, the soil is washed away, leaving it smooth and bare, without a single speck of dust." This hyprocrite is just like that. On a practical level, he seems to have righteous deeds to his credit, but when the Day of Resurrection dawns, they will vanish and disappear.[112] Reproach and insult will expose the intention in the Hereafter, so the charitable donation will be rendered null and void, just as the rainstorm exposes the naked rock.[113]

They have no control of anything of what they have acquired.
lā yaqdirūna ʿalā shaiʾin mimmā kasabū:

That is to say: "They will discover no reward for it, so nothing beneficial will be derived from it."

And Allāh does not guide the unbelieving folk.
wa 'llāhu lā yahdi 'l-qawma 'l-kāfirīn.

In other words: "He does not guide them to the path of goodness and right direction."[114] That is to say: "They will derive no benefit from what they have done in pretentious display, and they will not find any reward for it, none whatsoever." As He has said (Exalted is He):

And We shall advance upon the work they have done,
wa qadimnā ilā mā ʿamilū min ʿamalin
and make it into scattered particles of dust.
fa-jaʿalnā-hu habāʾan manthūrā. (25:23)

Having declared the invalidity of charitable donation followed by reproach and insult, Allāh (Exalted is He) has explained the nature of the resulting annulment of its reward, by making two comparisons:

1. The likeness of someone who spends his wealth only to be seen by other people, and who is also an unbeliever in Allāh and the Last Day. As for the nullity of the reward for what this unbeliever spends, it is more obvious than the nullity of the reward of the donor who follows his donation with reproach and insult.

2. The rock on which a layer of soil and dust accumulates, but then the rain pours down on it and removes that dust, until comes to be as if there had never been any soil and dust on it at all.

The unbeliever is like the rock, and the soil is like that expenditure. The rainstorm is like the unbelief that cancels the deed of the unbeliever, and like the reproach and insult that cancel the deed of this hypocrite. Just as the rainstorm removes the soil that had coated the rock, reproach and insult are bound to annul the reward for the expenditure after its occurrence. That is explicitly stated in the reference to cancellation and the charge of unbelief.

As for why reproach and insult deprive the charitable donor of his entitlement to the promised reward, the explanation is as follows: For a good deed to result in the promised reward, the doer must perform it in a spirit of worship and obedience, seeking only the reward and good pleasure to be found with Allāh, and acting in accordance with His saying (Exalted is He):

> Whatever good you forward for your own selves,
> *wa mā tuqaddimū li-anfusi-kum min khairin*
> you will surely find it with Allāh,
> *tajidū-hu ʿinda 'llāhi*
> better and greater in recompense.
> *huwa khairan wa aʿẓama ajrā.* (73:20)

—and with His saying (Exalted is He):

> Allāh has bought from the believers
> *inna 'llāha 'shtarā mina 'l-muʾminīna*
> their persons and their goods,
> *anfusa-hum wa amwāla-hum*
> the Garden [of Paradise] being theirs for the price.
> *bi-anna la-humu 'l-janna.* (9:111)

If a person's good deed is motivated solely by the desire for what Allāh has promised to those who are sincerely devout, he is in compliance with the norms of reciprocity between the deed and the reward. He is therefore entitled to the reward, which Allāh (Exalted is He) has promised to anyone whose work is sincerely devoted to Allāh (Exalted is He). Since his transaction is really with Allāh (Exalted is He), there can be no question of his reproaching the pauper to whom he gives a charitable gift, nor of his insulting him, by saying something like: "Take it, and may Allāh grant you blessing in the use of it!" If the donor reproaches him or insults him, he has turned away from the direction of reciprocity with Allāh, and moved in the direction of donating to the pauper without seeking Allāh's countenance. He has thus brought his deed under the heading of invalidity, from the outset. He is therefore deprived of the recompense promised by Allāh to anyone who lends Allāh a fine loan, since his deed did not take the form of lending.

There is also an allusion to the fact that ostentation, reproach and insult are all characteristics of the unbelievers, and that the believers are obliged to avoid them. One of the religious scholars is reported as having said: "The likeness of someone who practises worshipful obedience, but only to put on a show and acquire a good reputation, is as the likeness of a man who goes out to the market, having filled his sack with pebbles, so that people will say: 'How full is this man's sack!' He gains no benefit, apart from the way people talk. If he wished to buy something with it, he would not get anything in exchange.

The Prophet (Allāh bless him and give him peace) once said:

> The polytheism [*shirk*] I fear for you the most, is the lesser form thereof.

"O Messenger of Allāh," they said, "what is the lesser form of polytheism?" He replied:

> Hypocritical ostentation [*riyā'*]. Allāh will say to them, on the Day when He will recompense the servants for their deeds: 'Go to those whom you sought to impress, and see if you can find any reward in their presence.'[115]

The Prophet (Allāh bless him and give him peace) also said:

> When the Day of Resurrection arrives, Allāh (Exalted is He) will reveal Himself to the servants, to judge between them, and every community will fall on its

knees. The first to be summoned will be a man who compiled the Qur'ān, a man who was killed in Allāh's cause, and a man of great wealth. Allāh will say to the reader of the Qur'ān: 'Did I not teach you what I revealed to My Messenger?' The man will reply: 'Yes indeed, O my Lord!' Then He will say: 'So why did you not practise what you were taught?' The man will say: 'I used to recite the Qur'ān in the watches of the night, and at the ends of the day!' Allāh (Exalted is He) will then say: 'You have told a lie!' The angels will also tell him: 'You have told a lie!' Allāh (Exalted is He) will say: 'You only wanted to be spoken of as "So-and-so, the Qur'ān-reciter," and that came to be said....'

The owner of wealth will be brought to the fore, and Allāh (Exalted is He) will say to him: 'Did I not enrich you so abundantly, that I did not leave you in need of anyone?' The man will reply: 'Yes indeed, O my Lord!' Then He will say: 'So what did you do with the wealth I gave you?' The man will say: 'I used to support family ties, and give charitable donations.' Allāh (Exalted is He) will then say: 'You have told a lie!' The angels will also tell him: 'You have told a lie!' Allāh (Exalted is He) will say: 'You only wanted to be spoken of as "So-and-so, the generous one," and that came to be said....'

The man who was killed in Allāh's cause will then be brought forward, and He will say to him: 'In what cause were you killed?' The man will reply: 'O my Lord, I was commanded to wage the sacred struggle [*jihād*] in Your cause, so I fought until I was killed.' Allāh (Exalted is He) will then say: 'You have told a lie!' The angels will also tell him: 'You have told a lie!' Allāh (Exalted is He) will say: You only wanted to be spoken of as "So-and-so, the brave hero," and that came to be said.'

Allāh's Messenger (Allāh bless him and give him peace) then went on to say:

These three will be the first of Allāh's creatures to be fuel for the Fire of Hell on the Day of Resurrection.[116]

As the Qur'ānic verse indicates, when transactions are mixed with ulterior motives, they contain a kind of deviation. If someone deviates from the truth, he has moved towards falsehood. If he moves towards falsehood, he has nullified his rights in the deeds performed, for what is there after the truth, except error? We have been forbidden to render deeds of righteousness null and void, by deviating from the quest for the truth, and by moving towards falsehood, in His saying (Exalted is He):

Do not render your charitable donations null and void.[117]
lā tubṭilū ṣadaqāti-kum

Allāh (Exalted is He) has then coined another simile for the believer who spends his wealth in search of of Allāh's good pleasure, for He has said:

And the likeness of those who spend their wealth
wa mathalu 'lladhīna yunfiqūna amwāla-hum
in search of Allāh's good pleasure,
mubtighā'a marḍāti 'llāhi
and for the commitment of their lower selves,
wa tathbītan min anfusi-him
is as the likeness of a garden on a hill.
ka-mathali jannatin bi-rabwatin
The rainstorm smites it and it brings forth
its fruit twofold.
aṣāba-hā wābilun fa-ātat ukula-hā ḍi'fain:
And if the rainstorm does not smite it,
then the shower.
fa-in lam yuṣib-hā wābilun fa-ṭall:
Allāh is All-Seeing of what you do.
wa 'llāhu bi-mā ta'malūna Baṣīr. (2:265)

As for His saying (Exalted is He):

> And the likeness of those who spend their wealth
> *wa mathalu 'lladhīna yunfiqūna amwāla-hum*
> in search of Allāh's good pleasure....
> *mubtighā'a marḍāti 'llāhi....*

—that is to say: "They spend it in search of His good pleasure, believing in the Meeting with Him, and seeking to realize the reward."[118]

> and for the commitment of their lower selves
> *wa tathbītan min anfusi-him.* (2:265)

In other words: "for the firm commitment of part of their lower selves to faith and worshipful obedience, in order to rid them of the vice of niggardliness and of the love of wealth, attachment to it and reluctance to spend it." The lower self may be naturally disposed to the love of wealth and dislike of physical acts of worshipful obedience, but it develops the habits to which you make it accustomed. As the author of *al-Burda* [The Cloak] expressed it in poetry:

> The lower self is like an infant; if you neglect him,
> he will grow up loving to be suckled,
> but if you wean him, he will be weaned from the breast.
> *wa 'n-nafsu ka-'ṭ-ṭifli in tuhmil-hu shabba 'āla*
> *ḥubbi 'r-raḍā'i wa in tafṭim-hu yanfaṭimi.*

Whenever you neglect the lower self, it becomes accustomed to laziness, idleness and stinginess. Its attachment to wealth prevents it from spending on acts of worshipful obedience and the requirements of faith. On the other hand, if you impose obligations upon it, and train it to bear the hardships of acts of worshipful service, both physical and material, it will come to obey you, and it will be purified of its natural habits.[119]

> as the likeness of a garden on a hill.
> *ka-mathali jannatin bi-rabwatin*

That is to say: "as the likeness of an orchard abounding in trees, in an elevated site on the earth." The term *rabwa* is applied to a hill because of the beauty of its trees and the purity of their fruit.[120] According to al-Farrā᾽: "If the orchard contains date palms, it is an earthly garden. If it contains grapevines, it is a Garden of Paradise [*Firdaws*]."

> The rainstorm smites it and it brings forth its fruit twofold.
> *aṣāba-hā wābilun fa-ātat ukula-hā ḍiʿfain:*

In other words: "It yields its fruit in two varieties." According to some: "It produces as much fruit in one year as others produce in two years." Some say: "It bears fruit twice in the same year."[121] In other words: "Heavy rain smites it, so it produces its fruits ready to be gathered, twice as many as those produced by any other garden on the earth."

> And if the rainstorm does not smite it, then the shower.
> *fa-in lam yuṣib-hā wābilun fa-ṭall:*

That is to say: "If heavy rain does not descend upon it, light rain is sufficient for it," or: "The dew is sufficient for it, on account of its excellent quality, the nobility of its soil and the fineness of its air, so it will be highly productive in any event."[122]

Allāh (Exalted is He) has coined this simile for the work of the sincere believer, in his expenditure and his other good deeds. It is as if Allāh (Exalted is He) is saying: "Just as this garden is fertile and fruitful in every situation, and never lags behind, whether the rain be little or much, Allāh will likewise double the value of the offering made by the sincere believer, in his charitable donation and his expenditure, so long as he does not follow it with reproach and insult, whether his expenditure be little or much."[123]

> Allāh is All-Seeing of what you do.
> *wa 'llāhu bi-mā ta'malūna Baṣīr.*

In other words: "Nothing is hidden from Him among the deeds of His servants.[124] He sees your deeds, however much or little you do, and He knows your intentions in performing them, whether they amount to hypocritical ostentation or sincere devotion."[125]

Having mentioned the likeness of the spender who is reproachful and insulting, Allāh (Exalted is He) has also mentioned the spender who is not like that. In this verse, He has explained (Exalted is He) that the purpose of these spenders is twofold: the quest for Allāh's good pleasure (Exalted is He), and the firm commitment of the lower self. The latter bears several interpretations:

1. It means that they train their lower selves to observe this act of worshipful obedience, and to refrain from anything that corrupts it. That includes refraining from following it with reproach and insult. This is the view of al-Qāḍī.

2. Mujāhid supports his opinion by citing the words:

> and for the commitment of their lower selves
> *wa tathbītan min anfusi-him*

—which he takes to mean: "establishing, in the presence of the believers, that they are true to the faith and sincerely devoted to it."

3. The lower self has no steadfastness in the station of servitude, unless it is brought under control by earnest striving. Its ardent desire is for two things: the present life and material wealth.

If the lower self is obliged to practise the expenditure of wealth, it becomes subdued in certain respects. If it is also obliged to make spiritual efforts, it becomes subdued in other respects, so a degree of commitment is bound to result. This is explains the insertion of the preposition *min* [of; from], which indicates division into parts. The meaning of:

> and for the commitment of their lower selves
> *wa tathbītan min anfusi-him*

—is that, if someone spends his wealth for the sake of Allāh's countenance, he has committed part of his lower self. If someone spends his wealth and his spirit together, he has then committed the whole of it. Such is the import of His saying (Exalted is He):

> And strive for Allāh's cause
> *wa tujāhidūna fī sabīli 'llāhi*
> with your wealth and your own selves.
> *bi-amwāli-kum wa anfusi-kum.* (61:11)

This interpretation, which is mentioned by the author of *al-Kashshāf*, is a good explanation and a subtle commentary.

4. This occurred to me at the time of writing this passage: Steadiness of the heart is experienced only through the remembrance of Allāh, as He has said (Exalted is He):

> It is truly in the remembrance of Allāh
> *a-lā bi-dhikri 'llāhi*
> that hearts feel comfortably at rest.
> *taṭma'innu 'l-qulūb.* (13:28)

Even if someone spends his wealth in support of Allāh's cause, he will not automatically obtain tranquillity of heart thereby, unless his expenditure is purely for the purpose of servitude. This explains why ʿAlī (may Allāh be well pleased with him), when speaking of his expenditure, is reported to have uttered the words:

> "We feed you only for Allāh's countenance.
> *inna-mā nuṭʿimu-kum li-Wajhi 'llāhi*
> We desire no recompense from you, nor thankfulness."
> *lā nurīdu min-kum jazā'an wa lā shukūrā.* (76:9)

Allāh has also described the expenditure of Abū Bakr (may Allāh be well pleased with him), for He has said (Exalted is He):

> And he confers no favour on anyone for recompense,
> *wa mā li-ʿaḥadin ʿinda-hu min niʿmatin tujzā*
> but seeking only the countenance of his Lord the Most High;
> *illa 'btighā'a wajhi Rabbi-hi 'l-Aʿlā*
> and he will surely be satisfied.
> *wa la-sawfa yarḍā.* (92:19–21)

When the servant's expenditure is for the sake of servitude to the Lord of Truth, not for any personal motive or selfish purpose, only then will his heart find peace. His lower self will then become stable, and there will be no conflict between his lower self and his heart.

To this I would add: The point is that, in the view of those who learn from Allāh, and who understand the enmity of the lower self towards its owner, there is a collision and a battle between the lower self and the heart. That is why He said about this expenditure, first of all, that it is for the sake of Allāh's good pleasure, then followed that with His saying:

> and for the commitment of their lower selves
> *wa tathbītan min anfusi-him*

5. It is well established in the intellectual sciences, that the repetition of actions is a cause of the development of traits of character. (Let me add: This is a definite fact, according to those who are close associates of the people of Allāh, meaning those who focus on Reality.) If you recognize this, we can go on to say: If someone is diligent in expenditure, time after time, in search of Allāh's good pleasure, he will obtain two things from that diligence:

- The acquisition of this spiritual content.
- This searching and seeking will become an established characteristic in the self. As a result, even if the heart gave vent to an action by way of heedlessness, the heart would immediately return to the presence of Holiness. That is because worshipful service has become like the habit and natural disposition of the spirit. The servant's fulfilment of obedience to Allāh, in search of Allāh's good pleasure, will result in this established characteristic, which is referred to in the Qur᾿ān as the commitment of the lower self. Such is the import of His saying (Exalted is He):

> Allāh confirms those who believe.
> *yuthabbitu 'llāhu 'lladhīna āmanū.* (14:27)

With the acquisition of this commitment, the spirit comes to consist, in this universe, of the nature of the spiritual angels and of the holy essences. The servant thus comes to be, as one of the masters of Reality put it: "Absent, present, on the move, at home."

6. According to az-Zajjāj: "What is meant by commitment is that, when they spend their wealth, they are firmly convinced that Allāh (Exalted is He) will not let their work go to waste, and that He will not disappoint their hope, because it is connected with reward and punishment and the Resurrection, contrary to what the hypocrite believes."

7. According to al-Ḥasan, Mujāhid and ʿAṭāʾ: "The meaning is that the spender becomes committed to giving charitable donations, so He includes him among the people of righteousness and virtue." It was al-Ḥasan who said: "If a man is serious about a charitable donation, it must be a firm commitment. If it is for the sake of Allāh, he should give it, but if his motive is mixed, he should withhold it."[126]

Would any of you like to have a garden
a-yawaddu aḥadu-kum an takūna la-hu jannatun
of palm trees and vines,
with rivers flowing underneath it,
min nakhīlin wa aʿnābin tajrī min taḥti-ha 'l-anhāru
with all kinds of fruit for him therein;
la-hu fī-hā min kulli 'th-thamarāti
and old age has stricken him,
and he has feeble offspring;
wa aṣāba-hu 'l-kibaru wa la-hu dhurriyyatun ḍuʿafāʾu
and a fiery whirlwind strikes it
and it is consumed by fire?
fa-aṣāba-hā iʿṣārun fī-hi nārun fa-'ḥtaraqat:
Thus Allāh makes the signs plain to you,
ka-dhālika yubayyinu 'llāhu la-kumu 'l-āyāti
so that you may reflect.
laʿalla-kum tatafakkarūn. (2:266)

Would any of you like to have a garden
a-yawaddu aḥadu-kum an takūna la-hu jannatun
of palm trees and vines
min nakhīlin wa aʿnābin

That is to say: "Would any of you love to have a garden of riches, containing various kinds of palm trees and vines in great abundance?"

with rivers flowing underneath it
tajrī min taḥti-ha 'l-anhāru

In other words: "with rivers flowing beneath its trees."

with all kinds of fruit for him therein
la-hu fī-hā min kulli 'th-thamarāti

In other words: "where all fruits grow for him, of every lovely sort."

and old age has stricken him, and he has feeble offspring
wa aṣāba-hu 'l-kibaru wa la-hu dhurriyyatun ḍuʿafāʾu

That is to say: "Senility has afflicted him, so he is too weak to earn a livelihood, and he has small children, who are incapable of earning."

> and a fiery whirlwind strikes it and it is consumed by fire
> *fa-aṣāba-hā iʿṣārun fī-hi nārun fa-'ḥtaraqat:*

In other words: "A violent hurricane has struck that garden, together with a fire, so the fruits and the trees have all been burned, though the person is greatly in need of them."[127]

> and it is consumed by fire
> *fa-'ḥtaraqat:*

—so all its bounties have departed, and its foundation has been destroyed. The man is left bewildered, finding no means to restore the garden. He lacks the strength to plant the like of it, and he can expect no help from his offspring, since they are weak and unable to assist him. As you can see, this is a portrayal of the state of someone who does good deeds, but mixes them with something that annuls them, such as hypocritical display and injurious behaviour, resulting in sorrow and remorse. When the Day of Resurrection dawns, his need for those good deeds will be urgent and intense, but he will find them cancelled. Allāh has likened such people to someone who roams, with his innermost being, in the realm of Sovereignty [*Malakūt*], and advances in his contemplation to the gardens of Dominion [*Jabarūt*], but then turns on his heels and retreats to the realm of perfidy, concentrates on that which is other than the truth, and reduces all his effort to scattered particles of dust.[128]

> Thus Allāh makes the signs plain to you,
> *ka-dhālika yubayyinu 'llāhu la-kumu 'l-āyāti*
> so that you may reflect.
> *laʿalla-kum tatafakkarūn.*

That is to say: "By the like of this clear illustration, in this perfectly splendid allegory, Allāh makes plain to you His signs in His wise Book, so that you may reflect and consider the admonitions and exhortations contained therein."[129]

Sincerity is therefore essential to good deeds, for the fruits depend upon the root. Muʿādh ibn Jabal (may Allāh be well pleased with him) is reported as having said, when he was sent on a mission to Yemen:

"O Messenger of Allāh, give me some good advice!" He told him:

> Be sincere in your religion, for then just a little work will suffice you.[130]

According to al-Bukhārī, in his commentary on this Qur'ānic verse, 'Umar ibn al-Khaṭṭāb (may Allāh be well pleased with him) said one day, to the Companions of the Prophet (Allāh bless him and give him peace): "Concerning whom do you suppose this verse was revealed:

> Would any of you like to have a garden
> *a-yawaddu aḥadu-kum an takūna la-hu jannatun*
> of palm trees and vines?"
> *min nakhīlin wa a'nābin*

They replied: "Allāh knows best," so 'Umar (may Allāh be well pleased with him) became angry and he said: "Say: 'We know,' or, 'We do not know'!" Ibn 'Abbās (may Allāh be well pleased with him and his father) then said: "I have some idea about it, O Commander of the Believers." 'Umar said: "O son of my brother, speak up, and do not underestimate yourself," so Ibn 'Abbās (may Allāh be well pleased with him and his father) said: "I have coined a simile, using a pattern of conduct." 'Umar (may Allāh be well pleased with him) asked: "What pattern of conduct?" Ibn 'Abbās replied: "A rich man acts in obedience to Allāh, then Allāh sends the devil to him, so he commits sinful acts of disobedience, until he has drowned all his good deeds."

This traditional report contains sufficient in the way of commentary on this Qur'ānic verse. It explains the allegory in terms of the conduct of someone who acts well at first, but then reverses his course, thereby exchanging the good deeds for bad deeds. Let us take refuge from that with Allāh![131]

In these Qur'ānic verses, Allāh (Exalted is He) has made frequent allegorical references to the sincere believer and the hypocrite, comparing the former to someone who spends in support of Allāh's cause, and the latter to someone who spends his wealth in futility. The former will obtain nobility and progeny, while the latter will receive nothing in the present but rejection, and nothing in the future but loss. The effort of the former will always be appreciated, while the latter will suffer ruin and exposure to a blazing inferno. The deeds of the former will flourish, their wealth will increase, their spiritual states will be exalted in the sight of Allāh, and communion will be their final destination. The deeds of the latter will be nullified, their spiritual states will be damaged, their hopes will come to a bad end, and their evil outcome will be multiplied against them. The former, it is said, are like someone who plants a crop, so it takes root, its stems grow, its branches rise high, and its benefit is abundant. As for the latter, they are like someone whose business makes a loss, whose merchadise is stolen, whose skill is wasted (because of his arrogant pride), and whose troubles multiply in every shape and form, and at every moment. Are the two equivalent in likeness? Is there any similarity between them?[132]

These are my own comments:

You must sever the roots of the stem of hypocritical display, and cut them out entirely. Its roots consist of three things:

1. The love of this world and attachment to its lustful appetites, both outwardly and inwardly.
2. Short-term pleasure, and preferring it over the Hereafter.
3. Taking notice of one's fellow creatures, and being influenced by their praise or their blame.

If created beings were to bow in prostration before a mere creature, and offer him their praise, there would be no escape from death, not for those who bowed in prostration, nor for the one who received their tribute. Since the return is towards Allāh (Almighty and Glorious is He), it is essential for us to heed the admonition of Allāh (Almighty and Glorious is He), and to reflect upon it.

O Allāh, grant us the ability to accomplish all that. *Āmīn*. Peace be upon the Messengers, and praise be to Allāh, the Lord of All the Worlds. There is no might nor any power, except with Allāh, the All-High, the Almighty. May Allāh bless our master Muḥammad, his family and his Companions, and may He grant them peace.

The Ninth Call

In the Name of Allāh, the All-Merciful, the All-Compassionate.
Bismi'llāhi 'r-Raḥmāni 'r-Raḥīm.

O you who truly believe,
yā ayyuha 'lladhīna āmanū
spend from the good things you have earned,
anfiqū min ṭayyibāti mā kasabtum
and from that which We produce
for you from the earth,
wa mimmā akhrajnā la-kum mina 'l-arḍ:
and do not seek the bad, to spend therefrom,
wa lā tayammamu 'l-khabītha min-hu tunfiqūna
when you would not take it for yourselves,
except with disdain;
wa lastum bi-ākhidhī-hi illā an tughmiḍū fī-h:
and know that Allāh is Self-Sufficient,
Praiseworthy.
wa 'ʿlamū anna 'llāha Ghaniyyun Ḥamīd.

The devil promises you poverty,
ash-shaiṭānu yaʿidu-kumu 'l-faqra
and instructs you to behave with gross indecency.
wa yaʾmuru-kum bi'l-faḥshāʾ:
But Allāh promises you forgiveness from Him
and gracious favour.
wa 'llāhu yaʿdu-kum maghfiratan min-hu wa faḍlā:
Allāh is All-Embracing, All-Knowing.
wa 'llāhu Wāsiʿun ʿAlīm.

He gives wisdom to whomever He will,
yuʾti 'l-ḥikmata man yashāʾ:
and he to whom wisdom is given,
wa man yuʾta 'l-ḥikmata
he has truly received abundant good.
wa man yuʾta 'l-ḥikmata fa-qad ūtiya khairan kathīrā:
But none remember except people
of understanding.
wa mā yadhdhakkaru illā ulu 'l-albāb. (2:267–69)

Praise be to Allāh, who has commanded the believers to spend [on worthy causes], so that their lower selves may grow in purity, free from the rubbish of bad character. Praise be to Him who has guided the insightful to sacrifice their material wealth and their spirits, so that the gates of triumphant opportunities may be opened up for them.[133]

O you who truly believe,
yā ayyuha 'lladhīna āmanū
spend from the good things you have earned
anfiqū min ṭayyibāti mā kasabtum

That is to say: "Spend from that which is lawful and good in the wealth you have earned." In other words: "from that which is fine, not that which is vile."

and from that which We produce for you from the earth
wa mimmā akhrajnā la-kum mina 'l-arḍ:

That is to say: "and from the good things that We have produced for you, such as grains and fruits."

and do not seek the bad, to spend therefrom
wa lā tayammamu 'l-khabītha min-hu tunfiqūna

In other words: "and do not look for what is vile and despicable, in order to make charitable donations from it."[134] According to one of the worthy scholars, when he interpreted *ṭayyib* [good] in the sense of *jayyid* [fine, excellent], rather than *ḥalāl* [lawful], he did so for the simple reason that lawfulness can be inferred from the commandment, since spending from what is unlawful [*ḥarām*] would never be commanded. The meaning may also be expressed as: "Spend from what is pleasing among your earnings."[135]

when you would not take it for yourselves, except with disdain
wa lastum bi-ākhidhī-hi illā an tughmiḍū fī-h:

That is to say: "You would not accept it, or receive it as a gift, without belittling it and treating it with disdain, so how can you use it to pay what is due to Allāh, when He has said (Exalted is He):

You will never attain to piety
lan tanālū 'l-birra
until you spend from that which you love.
ḥattā tunfiqū mim-mā tuḥibbūn. (3:92)?[136]

The scholars have disagreed about the meaning of *infāq* [spending; expenditure] in this context. According to ʿAlī ibn Abī Ṭālib (may Allāh be well pleased with him), ʿUbaidat as-Salmānī and Ibn Sīrīn: "It is the obligatory alms-due [*zakāt*]. In the payment thereof, people have been forbidden to spend from what is vile, instead of what is fine." Ibn ʿAṭiyya said: "According to al-Barrāʾ ibn ʿĀzib, al-Ḥasan and Qatāda, it is obvious that the Qurʾānic verse applies to voluntary expenditure on good causes. When making voluntary contributions to charity, people have been urged to choose only what is fine. The verse covers both aspects [the compulsory and the voluntary]."

As reported by al-Barrāʾ, a man once dangled [as an offering] a bunch of shrivelled dates. (Dates sometimes dry before ripening, and so become bad.) Allāh's Messenger (Allāh bless him and give him peace) noticed it, so he said: "What rotten stuff you have dangled!" The Qurʾānic verse was thereupon revealed.

In the version recorded by an-Nasāʾī, the wording is as follows: "ʿAwf ibn Mālik is reported as having said: 'Allāh's Messenger (Allāh bless him and give him peace) once went out with a staff in his hand. A man dangled a bunch of shrivelled dates, so he struck out at that bunch, and he said:

> "'If he wished, the owner of this charitable offering could donate something better than this. The owner of this charitable offering will eat shrivelled dates on the Day of Resurrection!'""

On the basis of this saying, the injunction is a strong recommendation, rather than a strict commandment.[137]

It was Sahl ibn ʿAbdi'llāh who said: "Ibn al-Mubārak was asked about the case of a man who wishes to earn, and who intends by his earning to support family ties, to engage in the sacred struggle, and to do good works, but who gets into trouble in his endeavour to earn for these purposes. He replied: 'If he has livelihood sufficient to keep himself independent of other people, it is better to refrain from this [problematic extra effort]. That is because, if he seeks what is lawful, and spends on what is lawful, he will be questioned about it, and about his earning, and about his expenditure. To refrain from that is pious abstinence [*zuhd*], for pious abstinence consists in refraining from what is lawful."

It was Ibn Khuwaiz Mindād who said: "On the strength of this Qur'ānic verse, it is permissible for the father to consume the earnings of his son. That is because the Prophet (Allāh bless him and give him peace) once said:

> Your sons are part of your good earnings, so consume some of the wealth of your sons, and feel free to enjoy it![138]

> and know that Allāh is Self-Sufficient, Praiseworthy.
> *wa 'ʿlamū anna 'llāha Ghaniyyun Ḥamīd.*

In other words: "Allāh (Glory be to Him) is Independent of your charitable expenditures, and He is Praiseworthy, for He bestows the most excellent reward upon the beneficent."[139] Allāh (Glory be to Him and Exalted is He) has hereby drawn attention to the quality of the One who is Self-Sufficient. That is to say: "Allāh has no need of your charitable offerings. If someone wishes to draw near [to Him], and to seek a spiritual reward, let him do that to the best of his ability and capacity, for he is investing in his own future." The meaning of *Ḥamīd* [Praiseworthy] is "Worthy of praise in every situation."[140]

You should know, O human beings, that Allāh (Almighty and Glorious is He) is Independent of your charitable donations, and of everything else. He has commanded you to make those donations, and imposed them as duties on your wealth, simply as a mercy from Him to you, in order to enrich your dependants, to strengthen the weak among you, and to make your reward for them abundant in the Hereafter, not because He has any need of His own to receive them from you.

> Praiseworthy.
> *Ḥamīd.*

That is to say: "[He is] Worthy of praise from His creatures, for all the blessings that He has bestowed upon them, and for all the gracious favour that He has made available to them."[141]

> The devil promises you poverty,
> *ash-shaiṭānu yaʿidu-kumu 'l-faqra*
> and instructs you to behave with gross indecency.
> *wa ya'muru-kum bi'l-faḥshā':*

In other words: "The devil makes you afraid of poverty, if you make charitable donations, and he incites you to stinginess and the withholding of the alms-due [*zakāt*]."

> But Allāh promises you
> *wa 'llāhu ya'du-kum*
> forgiveness from Him and gracious favour.
> *maghfiratan min-hu wa faḍlā:*

That is to say: "In exchange for your expenditure in support of His cause, Allāh (Glory be to Him) promises you forgiveness of sins, and more in addition to the principal invested."

> Allāh is All-Embracing, All-Knowing.
> *wa 'llāhu Wāsi'un 'Alīm.*

In other words: "He is All-Embracing in gracious favour and generous giving, All-Knowing of those who deserve commendation."[142]

According to Ibn 'Abbās (may Allāh be well pleased with him and his father): "In this Qur'ānic verse, there are two [promises] from Allāh, and two from the devil." As related by at-Tirmidhī, on the authority of 'Abdu'llāh ibn Mas'ūd, Allāh's Messenger (Allāh bless him and give him peace) once said:

> The devil has a suggestion for the human being, and the angel has a suggestion. As for the suggestion of the devil, it is the promise of evil and the denial of the truth. As for the suggestion of the angel, it is the promise of goodness and the acceptance of the truth. If someone experiences the latter, he should know that it is from Allāh, so let him praise Allāh. If someone experiences the former, let him take refuge with Allāh from the devil.

Then he recited the words of Allāh (Exalted is He):

> The devil promises you poverty,
> *ash-shaiṭānu ya'idu-kumu 'l-faqra*
> and instructs you to behave with gross indecency.
> *wa ya'muru-kum bi'l-faḥshā':*

(According to at-Tirmidhī, this is an authentic Prophetic tradition [*ḥadīth*].)

> But Allāh promises you
> *wa 'llāhu ya'du-kum*
> forgiveness from Him and gracious favour.
> *maghfiratan min-hu wa faḍlā:*

Forgiveness means pardon for His servants in this world and the Hereafter, while gracious favour means sustenance and bliss in the Hereafter. Allāh (Exalted is He) has promised both. As noted by an-Naqqāsh: "Some people take this verse to mean that poverty is more meritorious than wealth, because it is only by making the servant afraid of poverty, that the devil keeps him far away from goodness."[143]

You should notice that Allāh (Exalted is He), after urging the human being to spend the very best of what he possesses, has gone on to warn him against the whispering of the devil, for He has said:

> The devil promises you poverty
> *ash-shaiṭānu ya'idu-kumu 'l-faqra*

In other words: "If you spend the very best, you will become a pauper." You must pay no attention to what he says, however, because the All-Merciful:

> promises you forgiveness from Him and gracious favour.
> *ya'du-kum maghfiratan min-hu wa faḍlā:*

The scholars hold differing opinions concerning the devil [*shaiṭān*]. Some say he is Iblīs, while others maintain that the other devils [*shayāṭīn*] are referred to here. According to some, [*shaiṭān* is a collective term for] the devils of humankind and the jinn. It is also said to mean the lower self that is always instigating evil [*an-nafs al-ammāra bi's-sū'*].

As for the real meaning of *waswasa* [the whispering of the devil], Allāh (Exalted is He) has drawn attention, in this Qur'ānic verse, to the following subtle point: The devil starts by making the servant afraid of poverty, then, using this frightening prospect, he goes on to instruct him to behave with gross indecency, and incites him to the stinginess that is typical of the lower self. That is because stinginess is a blameworthy characteristic in everyone's sight, so the devil cannot make it seem attractive, without first instilling the fear of poverty. As for the interpretation of:

> with gross indecency.
> *bi'l-faḥshā':*

—it means that the devil says: "Do not spend the finest of your property in obedience to Allāh, in case you become a pauper." Then, if the man obeys the devil in that, the devil grows bolder, and prevents him from spending altogether, so that he gives neither the good nor the bad. He prevents him from meeting his strict obligations, so he does not pay the alms-due [*zakāt*], does not support his family, and does not return the deposit held in trust. Once this stage is reached, the impact of sins no longer affects his heart, and he ceases to be concerned about their commission. The gap now widens, and he becomes audacious in committing every kind of sin. That constitutes *faḥshā'* [gross indecency].

In other words: "The devil incites you to stinginess, with the incitement instilled by a commander in someone under his command."

Every creature has two sides and a middle. On the perfect side, he spends everything he owns in support of Allāh's cause, both the excellent and the inferior. On the side that is defective and indecent, he spends nothing in support of Allāh's cause, neither the excellent nor the inferior. As for the middle, that is where he hoards the excellent and spends the inferior. If the devil wishes to transfer him from the virtuous side to the indecent side, he can only succeed by moving him into the middle. If a person disobeys the devil in this area, his interest in him will cease, but if he obeys him here, the devil will be keen to move him from the middle to the indecent side. The middle is referred to in His saying (Exalted is He):

> The devil promises you poverty,
> *ash-shaiṭānu ya'idu-kumu 'l-faqra*

—and the indecent side in His saying:

> and instructs you to behave with gross indecency.
> *wa ya'muru-kum bi'l-faḥshā'*:

Then, having mentioned the stages of the devil's whispering, Allāh (Glory be to Him and Exalted is He) has followed them by mentioning the inspirations of the All-Merciful, for He has said:

> But Allāh promises you
> *wa 'llāhu ya'du-kum*
> forgiveness from Him and gracious favour.
> *maghfiratan min-hu wa faḍlā*:

Forgiveness alludes to the benefits of the Hereafter, while gracious favour is an allusion to progeny in this world. It is related that the Prophet (Allāh bless him and give him peace) once said:

> The angel cries every night: 'O Allāh, grant offspring to every generous spender, and loss [*talaf*] to every greedy withholder.'[144]

To this I would add: The angels seek forgiveness for those on the earth. They plead on their behalf, and they do not plead against them. In this instance, they plead for them to experience loss [*talaf*] in the sense of expenditure, not the destruction [*itlāf*] of property.

The Qur'ānic verse contains this subtle point: The devil promises you poverty in your future worldly life, while the All-Merciful promises you forgiveness in your future Otherworldly life, and the promise of the All-Merciful is more worthy of acceptance.[145]

> He gives wisdom to whomever He will,
> *yu'ti 'l-ḥikmata man yashā':*
> and he to whom wisdom is given,
> *wa man yu'ta 'l-ḥikmata*
> he has truly received abundant good.
> *wa man yu'ta 'l-ḥikmata fa-qad ūtiya khairan kathīrā:*

That is to say: "He gives useful knowledge, conducive to righteous conduct, to whomever He will among His servants." In the words of a traditional saying, related by Ibn Mardawaih on the authority of Ibn Mas'ūd, but without a complete chain of transmission:

> The summit of wisdom is the fear of Allāh.

> and he to whom wisdom is given,
> *wa man yu'ta 'l-ḥikmata*
> he has truly received abundant good.
> *wa man yu'ta 'l-ḥikmata fa-qad ūtiya khairan kathīrā:*

In other words: "If someone is granted wisdom, he has been granted abundant good, because the outcome for its owner is everlasting felicity."[146]

As you should also know, having mentioned in the preceding verse that the devil promises poverty and commands gross indecency, and that the All-Merciful promises forgiveness and gracious favour, Allāh (Glory be to Him and Exalted is He) has now explained why the promise of the All-Merciful is preferable to the promise of the devil. The reason is that the promise of the All-Merciful is preferred by wisdom and intelligence, whereas the promise of the devil is preferred by lustful desire and the lower self, since these two demand the acquisition of present pleasure, and compliance with the rules of imagination and fantasy. Beyond any doubt, the rule of wisdom and intelligence is the honest rule, which is free from deviation and disorder, whereas the rule of the senses, lustful desire and the lower self will only plunge the human being into trial and tribulation. The rule of wisdom and intelligence is therefore more worthy of acceptance. The Qur'ānic verse raises several questions:

1. The meaning [of wisdom] may be either knowledge or correct conduct. Muqātil is reported as having said: "There are four interpretations of the term *ḥikma* [wisdom], as it is used in the Qur'ān:

a. The admonitions and exhortations [*mawā'iẓ*] of the Qur'ān:

> And what He has revealed to you of the Book and of wisdom,
> *wa mā anzala 'alai-kum mina 'l-Kitābi wa 'l-ḥikmati*
> by which He exhorts you.
> *ya'iẓu-kum bi-h.* (2:231)

> Allāh has revealed to you the Book and wisdom.
> *wa anzala 'llāhu 'alai-ka 'l-Kitāba wa 'l-ḥikmata.* (4:113)

b. Wisdom in the sense of understanding and knowledge:

> And We gave him wisdom when a child.
> *wa ātainā-hu 'l-ḥukma ṣabiyyā.* (19:12)

> And We did indeed give Luqmān wisdom.
> *wa la-qad ātainā Luqmāna 'l-ḥikmata.* (31:12)

c. Prophethood [*Nubuwwa*], as in His saying:

> Those are they to whom We gave the Book and wise judgment.
> *ulā'ika 'lladhīna ātainā-humu 'l-Kitāba wa 'l-ḥukma.* (6:89)

> And We gave him wisdom and decisive speech.
> *wa ātainā-hu 'l-ḥikmata wa faṣla 'l-khiṭāb.* (38:20)

d. The Qur'ān, because of the marvellous secrets it contains:

> Summon to the way of your Lord with wisdom.
> *ud'u ilā sabīli Rabbi-ka bi'l-ḥikmati.* (16:125)

In actual fact, these are all aspects of knowledge. You must therefore pay careful attention, O miserable wretch, for Allāh (Exalted is He) has bestowed but little in the way knowledge. He has said (Exalted is He):

> And of knowledge you have been given only a little.
> *wa mā ūtītum mina 'l-'ilmi illā qalīlā.* (17:85)

2. As for wisdom in the sense of correct conduct, it is said to mean modelling one's character and behaviour on the standards set by Allāh, to the extent of human ability. This is based on the saying of the Prophet (Allāh bless him and give him peace):

> You must model your character and conduct on the standards set by Allāh (Exalted is He).

You should know that wisdom [*ḥikma*] cannot bear any meaning apart from these two. That is because the perfection of the human being resides in two things: He must acknowledge the Truth for its own sake, and goodness for the sake of putting it into practice,[147] for Abraham (peace be upon him) is reported as having said:

> My Lord, grant me wise judgment.
> *Rabbi hab lī ḥukman* (26:83)

That is abstract wisdom, while:

> and join me with the righteous.
> *wa alḥiq-nī bi'ṣ-ṣāliḥīn.* (26:83)

—refers to practical wisdom.

> But none remember except people of understanding.
> *wa mā yadhdhakkaru illā ulu 'l-albāb.*

That is to say: "None take lessons from the parables of the Qur'ān and its nuggets of wisdom, except those endowed with luminous faculties of understanding, free from passionate desire.[148] (In other words: "free from the murky lower self.")

The meaning is that, when the human being sees the nuggets of wisdom and the insights received in his heart, then ponders and reflects, and realizes that they could only have been obtained through the giving of Allāh and His facilitation, he is then included among the people of understanding. That is because he did not stop at the secondary causes, but progressed beyond them to their primary causes. This progress, from the secondary to the primary cause, is the remembrance that is experienced only by the people of understanding. As for someone who attributes these spiritual states to his own self, and believes that he is the direct cause of their receipt and their obtainment, he is obviously one of those who are incapable of progressing from the secondary to the primary causes.[149]

As reported by Sa'īd ibn Jubair, the Muslims used to make charitable donations to the poor among the protected non-Muslims [*ahl adh-dhimma*]. Then, when there came to be many impoverished Muslims, Allāh's Messenger (Allāh bless him and give him peace) said:

> Do not give charitable donations except to the people of your religion.

The Qur'ānic verse:

> Their guidance is not your duty,
> *laisa 'alai-ka hudā-hum*
> but Allāh guides whom He will.
> *wa lākinna 'llāha yahdī man yashā':*
> And whatever good thing you spend,
> *wa mā tunfiqū min khairin*
> it is for yourselves, when you do not spend
> *fa-li-anfusi-kum wa mā tunfiqūna*
> except in search of Allāh's countenance.
> *illa 'btighā'a Wajhi 'llāh.* (2:272)

—was thereupon revealed, permitting the giving of charitable gifts to those who do not belong to the religion of Islām.[150] Allāh's Messenger (Allāh bless him and give him peace) also said:

> Envy is appropriate in two cases only: (1) the case of a man to whom Allāh gives wealth, and he uses it to avert his destruction, for the sake of the Truth, and (2) the case of a man to whom Allāh grants wisdom, and he puts it into practice and teaches it.[151]

According to 'Abdu'llāh ibn Mas'ūd (may Allāh be well pleased with him), Allāh's Messenger (Allāh bless him and give him peace) once said:

> Allāh has allotted your characters among you, as He has allotted your provisions among you. Allāh gives this world to those whom He loves, and also to those He does not love, but He does not give the religion to any but those He loves. If He gives the religion to someone, He must love him. By the One who holds my soul in His hand, a servant does not surrender [to his Lord] until his heart and his tongue surrender, nor does he believe until his neighbour feels safe from his afflictions.

They said: "What are his afflictions [*bawā'iq*], O Prophet of Allāh?" He replied:

> His deception and his wrongdoing. If a servant acquires wealth by unlawful means, then spends from it [on a good cause], he will never receive any blessing. If he donates it to charity, it will never be accepted of him. If he leaves it behind him as a legacy, it will only add to his torment in the Fire of Hell. Allāh does not erase the bad with the bad, but He does erase the bad with the good. That which is evil does not erase that which is evil.[152]

To this I would add: The intelligent person is obliged to be diligent in observing the practices of remembrance [*adhkār*], both at night and during the day, and to give charitable donations to the poor and the indigent, with purity of intention and conviction, at all times.

It was al-Ghazālī who said: "If wealth is lacking, the state of the servant must be contentment. If wealth is available to him, he must practise altruism, generosity, and abstinence from stinginess. The Prophet (Allāh bless him and give him peace) once said:

> Generosity is one of the trees of the Garden of Paradise. Its branches droop to the earth, so, if anyone grasps one of its branches, that branch will lead him to the Garden. Greed is a tree in the Fire of Hell, so, if anyone is greedy, he will grasp one of its branches, and he will not let go of that branch until it takes him into the Fire.[153]

These are my own remarks:

There is none more truthful than Allāh (Exalted is He), and He is the One who says (Magnificent is His Glory):

> Surely Satan is an enemy to you,
> *inna 'sh-shaiṭāna la-kum ʿaduwwun*
> so treat him as an enemy.
> *fa-'ttakhidhū-hu ʿaduwwā.* (35:6)

Your Lord (Blessed and Exalted is He) has informed you that Satan is an enemy to you, and He has commanded you to treat him with hostility, to oppose him in his contravention, and to turn a deaf ear to his whispering. Allāh (Exalted is He) has said:

> He promises them and stirs up desires in them,
> *yaʿidu-hum wa yumannī-him:*
> and Satan promises them only to beguile.
> *wa mā yaʿidu-humu 'sh-shaiṭānu illā ghurūrā.* (4:120)

You must be on your guard against him, so, when he attacks you, seek refuge with Allāh (Exalted is He), for He sees you and He sees him. You must be sincerely devoted to Allāh (Almighty and Glorious is He), for then He may select you and include you among the truly virtuous. If you become one of them, you will be a beloved servant in the sight of Allāh. He is the One who says (Blessed and Exalted is He):

> My servants, over them you have no power,
> *inna ʿibādī laisa la-ka ʿalai-him sulṭān* :
> and your Lord suffices as Guardian.
> *wa kafā bi-Rabbi-ka Wakīlā.* (17:65)

Satan, therefore, will surely not beguile you. As Allāh (Exalted is He) has told us, quoting the words of Iblīs:

> "I shall beguile them every one,
> *la-ughwiyanna-hum ajma'īn*.
> except Your truly virtuous servants among them."
> *illā 'ibāda-ka min-humu 'l-mukhlaṣīn*. (38:82,83)

—for they are beyond the devil's reach.

O Allāh, include us among Your truly virtuous servants, for the sake of the Chief of the Messengers, our master Muḥammad (Allāh bless him and give him peace), through Your mercy, O Most Merciful of the merciful. Peace be upon the Messengers, and praise be to Allāh, the Lord of All the Worlds. There is no might nor any power, except with Allāh, the All-High, the Almighty. May Allāh bless our master Muḥammad, his family and his Companions, and may He grant them peace.

The Tenth Call

In the Name of Allāh, the All-Merciful, the All-Compassionate.
Bismi'llāhi 'r-Raḥmāni 'r-Raḥīm.

Those who consume usury cannot rise up,
alladhīna ya'kulūna 'r-ribā lā yaqūmūna
except as he arises whom the devil
has prostrated by touch.
illā ka-mā yaqūmu 'lladhī
yatakhabbaṭu 'sh-shaiṭānu mina 'l-mass:
That is because they say:
"Trade is just like usury,"
dhālika bi-anna-hum qālū inna-ma 'l-bai'u
mithlu 'r-ribā:
though Allāh has permitted trading
and forbidden usury.
wa aḥalla 'llāhu 'l-bai'a wa ḥarrama 'r-ribā:
When an admonition comes to someone
fa-man jā'a-hu maw'iẓatun
from his Lord, and he refrains,
min Rabbi-hi fa-'ntahā
he may keep that which is past,
fa-la-hu mā salaf:
and his affair is with Allāh.
wa amru-hu ila 'llāh:
As for those who relapse,
wa man 'āda
such are the rightful owners of the Fire,
fa-ulā'ika aṣḥābu 'n-nār:
wherein they will dwell eternally.
hum fī-hā khālidūn.

Allāh blights usury
yamḥaqu 'llāhu 'r-ribā
and He makes charitable donations fruitful.
wa yurbi 'ṣ-ṣadaqāt:

Allāh does not love the unrighteous
and the guilty.
wa 'llāhu lā yuḥibbu kulla kaffārin athīm.

Those who truly believe and do righteous deeds,
inna 'lladhīna āmanū wa 'amilu 'ṣ-ṣāliḥāti
and perform the prayer and pay the alms-due,
wa aqāmu 'ṣ-ṣalāta wa ātawu 'z-zakāta
their reward is with their Lord,
la-hum ajru-hum 'inda Rabbi-him:
and no fear shall come upon them,
wa lā khawfun 'alai-him
nor shall they grieve.
wa lā hum yaḥzanūn.

O you who truly believe,
practise dutiful devotion to Allāh,
yā ayyuha 'lladhīna āmanu 'ttaqu 'llāha
and give up what remains from usury,
wa dharū mā baqiya mina 'r-ribā
if you are true believers.
in kuntum mu'minīn.

And if you do not, then be warned of war
fa-in lam taf'alū fa-''dhanū
from Allāh and His Messenger.
bi-ḥarbin mina 'llāhi wa Rasūli-h:
And if you repent, then you have your principal.
wa in tubtum fa-la-kum ru'ūsu amwāli-kum:
Do not wrong, and you shall not be wronged.
lā taẓlimūna wa lā tuẓlamūn.

And if he is in straitened circumstances,
wa in kāna dhū 'usratin
then postponement until ease;
fa-naẓiratun ilā maisara:
and that you remit the debt as charity
wa an taṣaddaqū
would be better for you, if you did but know.
khairun la-kum in kuntum ta'lamūn.

And be on your guard against a day
wa 'ttaqū yawman
in which you shall be brought back to Allāh.
turja'ūna fī-hi ila 'llāh:

Then every soul shall be paid in full
for what it has earned,
thumma tuwaffā kullu nafsin mā kasabat
and they shall not be wronged.
wa hum lā yuẓlamūn. (2:275–81)

To understand His saying (Exalted is He):

Those who devour usury cannot rise up
alladhīna ya'kulūna 'r-ribā lā yaqūmūna
except as he arises whom the devil has prostrated by touch.
illā ka-mā yaqūmu 'lladhī yatakhabbaṭu 'sh-shaiṭānu mina 'l-mass:

—you should know that the relationship between usury [*ribā*] and charitable donation [*ṣadaqa*] amounts to total contrast. That is because charitable donation [*ṣadaqa*] refers to the reduction of wealth, in accordance with Allāh's commandment to that effect. Usury [*ribā*], on the other hand, is a term for the effort to obtain an increase in wealth, in spite of Allāh's prohibition thereof. The two are therefore complete opposites, and this explains why He has said (Exalted is He)

Allāh blights usury and He makes charitable donations fruitful.
yamḥaqu 'llāhu 'r-ribā wa yurbi 'ṣ-ṣadaqāt:

Since this kind of relationship exists between these two subjects, it is hardly surprising that He has mentioned the subject of charitable donations immediately after the subject of usury.[154]

Those who consume usury
alladhīna ya'kulūna 'r-ribā

That is to say: "Those who deal in usury, and suck people's blood." This expression of His (Exalted is He) alludes to the benefit derived from usury, because consumption normally applies to the intake of things that are beneficial. That is equally relevant to the giver and the recipient, for, as Jābir said: "Allāh's Messenger (Allāh bless him and give him peace) cursed the consumer of usury, and its provider, and clerk who records it, and its two witnesses. 'They are all on an equal footing,' said he."[155]

cannot rise up except as he arises
lā yaqūmūna illā ka-mā yaqūmu 'lladhī
whom the devil has prostrated by touch.
yatakhabbaṭu 'sh-shaiṭānu mina 'l-mass:

They will not arise from their graves on the Day of Resurrection, except as the crazy epileptic arises from his fit of insanity, stumbling and falling, and unable to walk straight. They will arise in a state of mental disorder, like crazy epileptics. That is their distinctive feature, by which they will be recognized at the Place of Standing [at the Resurrection], to their shame and disgrace. According to Sa'īd ibn Jubair: "That will be the mark of the consumer of usury, on the Day of Resurrection."

> That is because they say: "Trade is just like usury."
> *dhālika bi-anna-hum qālū inna-ma 'l-bai'u mithlu 'r-ribā:*

That staggering and stumbling is due to their treating as lawful that which Allāh has made unlawful, and to their saying: "Trade is just like usury, so why should it be unlawful?"[156] They have grouped usury and trade in a single category, because both are conducive to profit, thereby attributing the lawfulness of one to the other. They say: "It is permissible to sell one dirham [silver coin] for two dirhams, just as it is permissible to sell an article worth one dirham for two dirhams." What they are really saying is that usury is the same as normal trade.

Concerning the people of the Time of Ignorance, it is related that, when the money of one of them fell due to his creditor, and he demanded it of him, the creditor would say to the debtor: "Take some extra time to repay me, and I will increase the amount of money you owe me." They would act accordingly, and they would say: "It is all the same to us, whether the increase is added at the beginning of a sale, to make a profit, or at the due date, in exchange for deferred repayment [of a loan]."[157] Allāh has declared them false, by His saying:

> Allāh has permitted trading and forbidden usury.
> *wa aḥalla 'llāhu 'l-bai'a wa ḥarrama 'r-ribā:*

That is to say: "Allāh has permitted trading because it involves the mutual exchange of benefits, and He has forbidden usury because it entails serious detriment to the individual and to society, since it involves an extra charge that is exacted from the effort of the debtor and his flesh."

> When an admonition comes to someone
> *fa-man jā'a-hu maw'iẓatun*
> from his Lord, and he refrains,
> *min Rabbi-hi fa-'ntahā*
> he may keep that which is past
> *fa-la-hu mā salaf:*

In other words: "When Allāh's prohibition of usury reaches him, and he refrains from acting in accordance with it, he may keep what belongs to the past, before the prohibition."

> and his affair is with Allāh.
> *wa amru-hu ila 'llāh.*

That is to say: "His affair is entrusted to Allāh. If He wishes, He will pardon him, and if He wishes, He will punish him."

> As for those who relapse,
> *wa man 'āda*
> such are the rightful owners of the Fire,
> *fa-ulā'ika aṣḥābu 'n-nār:*
> wherein they will dwell eternally.
> *hum fī-hā khālidūn.*

In other words: "If someone relapses into dealing in usury, and regards it as lawful after Allāh has forbidden it, he is one of those who will dwell eternally in the Fire of Hell."[158]

As related by al-Baghawī, in a report transmitted by ath-Tha'labī on the authority of Abū Sa'īd al-Khudrī (may Allāh be well pleased with him), Allāh's Messenger (Allāh bless him and give him peace) once said, concerning the story of the Heavenly Journey [*Isrā'*]:

> Gabriel took me to a numerous group of men. Every man has a belly like a huge house [*bait ḍakhm*], and they are arranged in layers [*munaḍḍadīn*] in the path [*sābila*] of the people of Pharaoh. The people of Pharaoh are being exposed to the Fire, in the morning and the evening time, so they move like insatiably hungry camels [*ibil manhūma*], crashing against the rocks and the trees, neither hearing nor understanding.
>
> When the owners of those bellies notice them, they stand up and bump them with their bellies, so they fall to the ground. Then one of them stand up, so he bumps him with his belly, and he falls down again. They will not be able to desist, until the people of Pharaoh overcome them, by repelling them from in front and from the rear. That is their torment in the interval [*barzakh*] between this world and the Hereafter. The people of Pharaoh say: "O Allāh, let the Hour never come," but He has said:
>
> Cause the people of Pharaoh to enter the most terrible torment.
> *adkhilū āla Fir'awna ashadda 'l-'adhāb.* (40:46)
>
> I said: 'O Gabriel, who are these?' He said: 'These are the ones who consume usury. They do not arise except as those arise whom the devil has prostrated by touch.

As for his saying: "a belly like a huge house [*bait ḍakhm*]," the term *ḍakhm* means *ʿaẓīm* [enormous]; *kabīr* [big]; *ghalīẓ* [gross; crude]. The term *munaḍḍadīn* means "placed one on top of another." The term *sābila* means *ṭarīq* [path]. As for the expression: "like insatiably hungry camels [*ibil manhūma*]," the corresponding noun *naham* signifies a voracious appetite for food, resulting from hunger.[159]

> **Allāh blights usury and He makes charitable donations fruitful.**
> *yamḥaqu 'llāhu 'r-ribā wa yurbi 'ṣ-ṣadaqāt:*
> **Allāh does not love the unrighteous and the guilty.**
> *wa 'llāhu lā yuḥibbu kulla kaffārin athīm.*

Allāh blights usury and He makes charitable donations fruitful.
yamḥaqu 'llāhu 'r-ribā wa yurbi 'ṣ-ṣadaqāt:

That is to say: "He takes away its fruitfulness and eradicates its goodness, even though it appears to represent an increase."[160] In other words: "He makes it worthless, ruins it, and takes away its blessedness." According to Ibn ʿAbbās (may Allāh be well pleased with him and his father): "Allāh will accept from him [the usurer] no charitable offering [*ṣadaqa*], no pilgrimage [*ḥajj*], no sacred struggle [*jihād*], and no act of piety [*ṣila*]."[161]

and He makes charitable donations fruitful.
wa yurbi 'ṣ-ṣadaqāt:

In other words: "He multiplies charitable donations, and makes them grow, even if they seem insignificant."[162] That is to say: "He increases the wealth of someone who makes charitable donations from it, and blesses him for doing so." In the words of the Prophetic tradition:

> Almsgiving from wealth is never worthless.[163]

As reported by Abū Huraira (may Allāh be well pleased with him), Allāh's Messenger (Allāh bless him and give him peace) once said:

> Whenever someone gives his charitable donation from something good—and Allāh accepts only that which is good—the All-Merciful receives it with His right hand. Even if it is no more than a date, it will grow in the palm of the All-Merciful, until it is bigger than a mountain, just as one of you causes his foals or his young camels to grow.[164]

To this I would add: That is to say: "His spiritual reward will be great in the sight of Allāh. His reward will be in Allāh's providential care."

Allāh does not love the unrighteous and the guilty.
wa 'llāhu lā yuḥibbu kulla kaffārin athīm.

In other words: "He does not love anyone who is ungrateful at heart, sinful in word and deed." The Qur'ānic verse contains a severe rebuke in the matter of usury, and a declaration that it is one of the practices of the unbelievers,[165] because love from Allāh is confined to those who repent.[166]

Those who truly believe and do righteous deeds,
inna 'lladhīna āmanū wa 'amilu 'ṣ-ṣāliḥāti
and perform the prayer and pay the alms-due
wa aqāmu 'ṣ-ṣalāta wa ātawu 'z-zakāta

Allāh has spoken in terms of praise for the believers who obey His commandment, concerning the performance of the ritual prayer and the payment of the alms-due. In other words: "Those who believe in Allāh, and do the righteous deeds that include the performance of the ritual prayer and the payment of the alms-due...."

their reward is with their Lord,
la-hum ajru-hum 'inda Rabbi-him:
and no fear shall come upon them, nor shall they grieve.
wa lā khawfun 'alai-him wa lā hum yaḥzanūn.

That is to say: "They shall have their perfect reward in the Garden of Paradise. They shall not be afraid on the Day of the Greatest Terror, nor shall they grieve for what they have missed in this world."

Let me say at this point: Since the preceding verses are closely connected with those to come, I have inscribed them at the outset, because they contain severe warning for those who practise usury, and commendation and praise for those who abstain from it, in obedient compliance with the commandment of Allāh (Glorious and Exalted is He). He speaks (Exalted is He) as One commanding His believing servants to practise dutiful devotion, while forbidding them to do things that will bring them close to His displeasure, and keep them far removed from His good pleasure.

O you who truly believe, practise dutiful devotion to Allāh,
yā ayyuha 'lladhīna āmanu 'ttaqu 'llāha
and give up what remains from usury,
wa dharū mā baqiya mina 'r-ribā
if you are true believers.
in kuntum mu'minīn.

That is to say: "Be afraid of offending your Lord, be vigilantly aware of Him in all that you do, and abandon whatever claim you have on people in the form of usury, if you are really and truly believers in Allāh."[167]

As for the context in which this Qur'ānic verse came down, it is said to have been revealed in connection with the tribe of Thaqīf. They had made an agreement with the Prophet (Allāh bless him and give him peace) on the following terms: As for usurious interest owed to them by other people, it would be theirs to collect, while that which they owed to other people would be remitted. When the due dates arrived, they sent emissaries to Mecca for the settlement of accounts. The debts were owed to the Banū 'Abda, they being the clansmen of 'Amr ibn 'Umair, of the tribe of Thaqīf. They were owed by the Banu 'l-Mughīra, the Makhzūmī tribesmen, but the Banu 'l-Mughīra said: "We shall not give anything, for usury has been abolished." They presented their case to 'Attāb ibn Usaid, so he informed Allāh's Messenger (Allāh bless him and give him peace) about it in a written message. This Qur'ānic verse was then revealed, so Allāh's Messenger (Allāh bless him and give him peace) sent a letter about it to 'Attāb. He told Thaqīf about it, so they withdrew their claim.

This is an abridged account of the occasion for the verse, gathered from the reports of Ibn Isḥāq, Ibn Juraij, as-Suddī and others. The meaning is: "Place a defensive shield between you and the torment of Allāh, by forsaking what remains due to you from usury, and by desisting from its practice."[168]

When Allāh (Exalted is He) declared, in the preceding verse, that if someone refrains from usury he may keep what is past, it might have been assumed that there was no difference between the debt already collected and the amount still owed, so He went on to say:

> and give up what remains from usury
> *wa dharū mā baqiya mina 'r-ribā*

—thereby explaining that, if people still owe a usurious debt, and it has not been collected, the increase is unlawful, and the creditors may recover their principals only. Allāh (Exalted is He) has strongly emphasized that point, for the following reason: In case someone waits a long time for the due date to arrive, then the moment comes, and he assumes that he can collect the interest on the loan, it is necessary to deter him most emphatically. Allāh (Exalted is He) has therefore said:

> Practise dutiful devotion to Allāh,
> *yā ayyuha 'lladhīna āmanu 'ttaqu 'llāha*
> and give up what remains from usury
> *wa dharū mā baqiya mina 'r-ribā*

That is to say: "If you have already collected something, He will pardon you for it. If you have not collected it, however, or you have not collected part of it, you are forbidden to collect what you have not yet collected, in whole or in part."

> if you are true believers.
> *in kuntum mu'minīn.*

According to al-Qāḍī: "The condition 'if you are true believers' is like an indication that belief cannot be perfected, so long as the human being persists in a major sin. Before he can become a believer in the absolute sense, he must refrain from all of the major sins." The response to this is as follows: While the many indications mentioned in the commentary on His saying:

> Those who believe in the Unseen....
> *alladhīna yu'minūna bi'l-ghaibi....* (2:3)

—do point to the fact that practice [*'amal*] is not included in the definition of belief [*īmān*], this Qur'ānic verse covers both the perfection of belief and its legal obligations. It must therefore be interpreted to mean: "If you are people who act in accordance with the legal obligations of belief."[169]

It has also been said [that the verse was relevant] because it referred to the initial stage of their entry into Islām.[170] They used to deal in usury during the Time of Ignorance, so, when they accepted Islām, they were commanded to take only their principals."[171]

> And if you do not, then be warned of war
> *fa-in lam taf'alū fa-''dhanū*
> from Allāh and His Messenger.
> *bi-ḥarbin mina 'llāhi wa Rasūli-h:*

In other words: "If you do not refrain from dealing in usury, you can be sure that Allāh and His Messenger will be at war with you."

The Prophet (Allāh bless him and give him peace) is reported as having said:

> Usury has seventy-three categories, the least significant of which is like a man having sexual intercourse with his own mother.[172]
>
> A single dirham [silver coin] of usury, consumed by a man who knows what he is doing, is more serious than thirty-six acts of adultery or fornication.[173]

As reported by Muslim: "Allāh's Messenger (Allāh bless him and give him peace) cursed both the consumer of usury and its provider." According to Ibn ʿAbbās (may Allāh be well pleased with him and his father): "On the Day of Resurrection, the consumer of usury will be told: 'Take hold of your weapon for war!'"[174]

Allāh's war is His Fire of Hell, and the war of His Messenger (Allāh bless him and give him peace) is the war of the sword. The scholars have differed over the meaning of this warfare. According to some: "It signifies the extreme nature of the threat and the warning, rather than war itself." Others say: "No, it does mean war itself. That is because, if someone persists in the consumption of usury, and does so with deliberate knowledge, the ruler will arrest him and subject him to the judgment of Allāh, by inflicting punishment and imprisonment until his repentance becomes manifest.[175]

Suppose someone says: "How could He command warfare with the Muslims?" We shall reply: This expression is applied to those who disobey Allāh, not in a general sense. Consider its use in the traditional report [*khabar*]:

> If someone scorns me as a guardian, he has engaged me in warfare.[176]

As reported by Jābir, the Prophet (Allāh bless him and give him peace) also said:

> If someone does not refrain from the practice of sharecropping [*mukhābara*],* let him be warned of war from Allāh and His Messenger.[177]

*The term *mukhābara* refers to the practice whereby the landowner gives the peasant farmer some land to cultivate, on condition that he will receive a share of the produce from it, such as a third or a quarter. According to the Prophetic tradition, sharecropping [*mukhābara*] has been forbidden.

Many of the commentators and jurists maintain that His saying (Exalted is He):

The only reward of those
inna-mā jazā'u 'lladhīna
who make war on Allāh and His Messenger....
yuḥāribūna 'llāha wa Rasūla-hu.... (5:33)

—is an allusion to highway robbery committed by the Muslims, so it is established that this kind of warning threat, extended to include the Muslims, does indeed occur in the Book of Allāh and in the Sunna of His Messsenger (Allāh bless him and give him peace).[178]

And if you repent, then you have your principal.
wa in tubtum fa-la-kum ru'ūsu amwāli-kum:
Do not wrong, and you shall not be wronged.
lā taẓlimūna wa lā tuẓlamūn.

That is to say: "If you turn away from usury and abandon it, you shall have your principal, meaning the amount you handed over [as a loan], with neither increase nor reduction."[179]

In his sermon during the Farewell Pilgrimage [*Ḥajjat al-Wadā'*], Allāh's Messenger (Allāh bless him and give him peace) said:

All usury in the Time of Ignorance has been cancelled from you—all of it. You are still entitled to your principals. Do not wrong, and you shall not be wronged. The first usury to be cancelled was the usury of al-'Abbās ibn 'Abd al-Muṭṭalib. All of it will be cancelled.[180]

To this I would add: It becomes a case of usury when the lender hands over the principal sum, and later collects the increase. After that, if he spends his usurious profit, his expenditure will consist of something unlawfully acquired. This is not permissible, for Allāh (Exalted is He) has said:

Spend from the good things you have earned.
anfiqū min ṭayyibāti mā kasabtum. (2:267)

Since it is unlawful to spend from that which is unlawfully acquired, one must be afraid for its owner, if he hopes for the reward.

The reader should refer to the books of jurisprudence [*fiqh*], for the rules are elaborately detailed.

According to our own scholars, if someone has unlawful wealth in his possession, the procedure of repentance is as follows: If his wealth consists of usurious profit, he must return it to the person from whom he exacted it, seeking him out if he is not present. If he despairs of finding him, he must give that amount as a charitable donation on his behalf. If he has acquired his wealth by wrongdoing, he must act it that same manner, in relation to the person he wronged.

If the matter is complicated for him, and he does not know how much of what he has in his possession is unlawful, and how much is lawful, he must conduct a thorough investigation. He must determine the exact amount that he is obliged to return, from the total in his possession, so there can be no doubt that what remains is genuinely his own. From that which he has excluded from his possession, he must then return what is due to those he is aware of having wronged or treated usuriously. If he despairs of finding a victim, he must give the relevant amount as a charitable donation on his victim's behalf.

If the misdeeds for which he is responsible are overwhelming, and he recognizes that he owes more than he will ever be capable of repaying, his repentance must be expressed by disposing of everything in his possession, either to the poor and the needy, or else for some purpose conducive to the welfare of the Muslims at large. He must continue like this, until he has nothing left in his possession, except a very small amount, sufficient to clothe himself properly for the ritual prayer [*ṣalāt*]. He needs enough cloth to cover his private parts, from his navel to his knees, and enough food to sustain him for the day at hand.[181]

To this I would add: The point is to ensure that he does not return to Allāh while he is still in charge of unlawful wealth, for which he will be tormented.

> And if he is in straitened circumstances,
> *wa in kāna dhū ʿusratin*
> then postponement until ease.
> *fa-naẓiratun ilā maisara:*

That is to say: "If the debtor is in straitened circumstances, you are obliged to grant him respite until the time of ease. You must not act like the people of the Time of Ignorance, one of whom would say to his debtor: 'Either you make the repayment that is now due, or else you will be charged usurious interest.'"[182]

Allāh's Messenger (Allāh bless him and give him peace) once said:

> Whenever a debt owed by a Muslim man falls due, and he [his creditor] grants him postponement, he will be credited with a charitable donation for each day [of respite he has granted].

As reported by Abū Umāma Asʿad ibn Zarāra, Allāh's Messenger (Allāh bless him and give him peace) also said:

> If someone cherishes the hope that Allāh will shade him, on the Day when there will be no shade but His, let him grant ease to someone in difficult straits, or cancel his debt altogether.

In the version reported by Muslim, the wording is:

> If someone cherishes the hope that Allāh will deliver him from grief, on the Day of Resurrection, let him grant relief to someone in difficult straits, or cancel his debt altogether.

Concerning Abū Qatāda al-Ḥārith ibn Rabʿī al-Anṣārī, Aḥmad said: "A man owed Abū Qatāda a debt, and he kept approaching the debtor, seeking repayment, so the man used to hide from him. When he came one day, a young boy emerged, so he asked him if he knew the man's whereabouts, 'Yes,' said the boy, 'he is in the house, eating.' He called to him, saying: 'O so-and-so, come outside! I have been informed that you are here.' The man came out to him, so he said: 'What is keeping you away from me?' The man replied: 'I am in difficult straits, and I have nothing in my possession.' Abū Qatāda said: 'Allāh! Are you really in difficult straits?' 'Yes,' said the man, so Abū Qatāda burst into tears, then he said: 'I have heard Allāh's Messenger (Allāh bless him and give him peace) say:

> If someone grants relief to his debtor, or cancels his debt altogether, he will be in the shade of the Heavenly Throne on the Day of Resurrection.'"[183]

As reported by Ḥudhaifa (may Allāh be well pleased with him), Allāh's Messenger (Allāh bless him and give him peace) once said:

> Allāh will bring one of His servants before Him on the Day of Resurrection, and He will say: 'What have you done for My sake in the lower world?' The servant will say: 'O my Lord, I have not done an atom's weight for Your sake in the lower world, seekng to please You by it.' He will say this three times, then he will add: 'O my Lord, You used to grant me surplus wealth, and I was a man who traded with people. Permissiveness was part of my character, so I used to make things easy for the affluent, and I would grant respite to anyone in straightened circumstances.' Allāh (Almighty and Glorious is He) will then say: 'I am the Most Worthy of those who grant ease. Enter the Garden of Paradise!'[184]

and that you remit the debt as charity
wa an taṣaddaqū
would be better for you, if you did but know.
khairun la-kum in kuntum taʿlamūn.

That is to say: "If you remit what the debtor owes you, that is more noble and more meritorious, if you did but know what it entails, in the way of handsome repute and enormous reward." Allāh (Exalted is He) has then warned His servants to beware of that frightful Day, on which nothing will be of any use to them, apart from righteous conduct, for He has said:

> And be on your guard against a day
> *wa 'ttaqū yawman*
> in which you shall be brought back to Allāh.
> *turja'ūna fī-hi ila 'llāh:*
> Then every soul shall be paid in full for what it has earned,
> *thumma tuwaffā kullu nafsin mā kasabat*
> and they shall not be wronged.
> *wa hum lā yuẓlamūn.*

In other words: "Beware of a day when you will be returned to your Lord. Then every soul will settle its account in full, and you will not be wronged." These noble verses have concluded with this comprehensive and cautionary verse, which was the last of the Qur'ān to be revealed. Its revelation marked the end of the inspiration [*waḥy*], and it contains a reminder for the servants [of the Lord] of that fiercely scorching day.

According to Ibn Kathīr: "This verse is the last of the glorious Qur'ān to be revealed. The Prophet (Allāh bless him and give him peace) lived for nine nights after its revelation, then he moved on to the Companion Most High [*ar-Rafīq al-A'lā*]."[185]

While the Prophet (Allāh bless him and give him peace) was standing at 'Arafa, down came the verse:

> Today I have perfected your religion for you,
> *al-yawma akmaltu la-kum dīna-kum*
> and I have completed My blessing upon you,
> *wa atmamtu 'alai-kum ni'matī.* (5:3)

Then came the revelation:

> And be on your guard against a day
> *wa 'ttaqū yawman*
> in which you shall be brought back to Allāh.
> *turja'ūna fī-hi ila 'llāh.*

—and Gabriel said: "Set it at the head of one hundred and eighty verses of the [Sūra of the] Cow [*al-Baqara*]."

According to al-Qāḍī: "The day referred to is a particular time, which cannot be guarded against by preventing its occurrence. One can only guard against the violence and the terrors that will happen in the course of it, and guarding against those terrors is possible only in the domain of this world, through the avoidance of sinful acts of disobedience." His saying (Exalted is He):

> And be on your guard against a day
> *wa 'ttaqū yawman*

—thus comes to include the imposition of all types of legal obligation.

> in which you shall be brought back to Allāh.
> *turjaʿūna fī-hi ila 'llāh.*

The return to Allāh is not meant to be understood in terms of physical location and direction, for that is inconceivable in relation to Allāh (Exalted is He). Nor does it mean returning to His knowledge and His safekeeping, for He is with them wherever they may be. In every Qur'ānic reference to returning to Allāh, there are two meanings to consider:

1. Human beings experience three conditions, in the following sequence:

a. Their state of being in their mothers' wombs. During this stage, they have no control over what is to their benefit or to their detriment. No one exercises any control over them, except Allāh (Glory be to Him and Exalted is He).

b. Their state of being after having emerged from their mothers' wombs. At this stage, those initially responsible for their proper development are the parents. Then, in due course, they influence one another in the external domain.

c. After death. At this stage, no one really controls them outwardly, except Allāh (Exalted is He). It is as if, after departing from this world, the human being returns to the state he was in before entering this world. This is what is meant by returning to Allāh.

2. The second meaning is that they will be brought back to what Allāh has prepared for them, be it reward or punishment.

Both interpretations are quite consistent with the wording of the text.[186] This verse has been placed between the Verse of Debt [Ā*yat* *ad-Dain*] and the Verse of Usury [*Āyat ar-Ribā*], in order to reinforce the prohibition of usury.[187]

These are my own observations:

You must sense the terror of standing in the presence of Allāh (Almighty and Glorious is He) on the Day of Resurrection. You will be on the bridge of Hell, so you will look to your right, and you will see nothing but that which you have forwarded. Then you will look to your left, and you will see only that which you have forwarded. Then you will look straight ahead, and you will see nothing but the Fire. You will be in the presence of the Sovereign Omnipotent, the One who knows the secret and what is more deeply hidden still, so what will you say to your Lord (Almighty and Glorious is He) on the Day of Resurrection, if He asks you: "My servant, how did you dare to consume unlawful wealth, in the form of usurious profit and in other ways?"?

You must feel a sense of shame before Allāh (Almighty and Glorious is He), because the scope of what is lawful [*ḥalāl*] is sufficient for your needs, O true believer. You must not forget that He has not granted you anything except for a wise reason, and that He has not withheld anything from you except for a wise reason. The measure of noble generosity is not material wealth. He has said (Exalted is He):

> As for man, whenever his Lord tries him,
> *fa-amma 'l-insānu idhā ma 'btalā-hu Rabbu-hu*
> and honours him, and blesses him, then he says:
> *fa-akrama-hu wa na'ama-h:*
> "My Lord has honoured me."
> *fa-yaqūlu Rabbī akrama-n.*
> But when He tries him by stinting his provision,
> *wa ammā idhā ma 'btalā-hu fa-qadara 'alai-hi rizqa-h:*
> then he says: "My Lord has despised me."
> *fa-yaqūlu Rabbī ahāna-n.* (89:15,16)

No indeed, the standard by which it is measured is true devotion [*taqwā*]. He has said (Exalted is He):

> Surely the noblest among you in the sight of Allāh
> *inna akrama-kum 'inda 'llāhi*
> is the one of you who is most truly devout.
> *atqā-kum.* (49:13)

—and true devotion includes the abandonment of usury [*ribā*], and refraining from taking people's goods by misappropriation and by wielding the sword of shame.

We beg Allāh to bless us with contentment, and to deliver us from this world in safety from its unwholesomeness. He is indeed Capable of all things. Peace be upon the Messengers, and praise be to Allāh, the Lord of All the Worlds. There is no might nor any power, except with Allāh, the All-High, the Almighty. May Allāh bless our master Muḥammad, his family and his Companions, and may He grant them peace.

The Eleventh Call

In the Name of Allāh, the All-Merciful, the All-Compassionate.
Bismi'llāhi 'r-Raḥmāni 'r-Raḥīm.

O you who truly believe,
yā ayyuha 'lladhīna āmanū
when you contract a debt for a fixed term,
record it in writing.
idhā tadāyantum bi-dainin ilā ajalin
musamman fa-'ktubū-h:
Let a scribe record it in writing
between you in equity.
wa l'-yaktub baina-kum kātibun bi'l-ʿadl:
No scribe should refuse to write
as Allāh has taught him,
wa lā yaʾba kātibun an yaktuba ka-mā ʿallama-hu 'llāhu
so let him write, and let him
who incurs the debt dictate,
fa-l'-yaktub: wa l'-yumlili 'lladhī ʿalai-hi 'l-ḥaqqu
and let him practise true devotion
to Allāh, his Lord,
wa l'-yattaqi 'llāha Rabba-hu
and diminish nothing thereof.
wa lā yabkhas min-hu shaiʾā:
But if he who owes the debt
is of low understanding
fa-in kāna 'lladhī ʿalai-hi 'l-ḥaqqu safīhan
or weak, or unable himself to dictate,
aw ḍaʿīfan aw lā yastaṭīʿu an yumilla huwa
then let the guardian of his interests
dictate in equity.
fa-l'-yumlil waliyyu-hu bi'l-ʿadl:
And call to witness, from among your men,
two witnesses.
wa 'stashhidū shahīdaini min rijāli-kum:

And if two men are not there,
then a man and two women,
fa-in lam yakūna rajulaini fa-rajulun wa 'mra'atāni
of such as you approve as witnesses,
mim-man tarḍawna mina 'sh-shuhadā'i
so that, if one errs, one of them
will remind the other.
an taḍilla iḥdā-humā fa-tudhakkira iḥdā-huma 'l-ukhrā:
And the witnesses must not refuse
when they are summoned.
wa lā ya'ba 'sh-shuhadā'u idhā mā du'ū
Do not be averse to writing it down,
wa lā tas'amū an taktubū-hu
whether it be small or great,
with the term thereof.
ṣaghīran aw kabīran ilā ajali-h:
That is more equitable in the sight of Allāh,
dhālikum aqsaṭu 'inda 'llāhi
and more sure for testimony,
wa aqwamu li'sh-shahādati
and the best way of avoiding doubt between you,
wa adnā allā tartābū
except only in the case when it
is actual merchandise
illā an takūna tijāratan ḥāḍiratan
which you transfer among yourselves
from hand to hand.
tudīrūna-hā baina-kum
In that case it is no sin for you
if you do not write it down.
fa-laisa 'alai-kum junāḥun allā taktubū-hā:
And have witnesses when you sell to one another,
wa ashhidū idhā tabāya'tum:
and let no harm be done to scribe or witness.
wa lā yuḍārra kātibun wa lā shahīd:
If you do, it is a sin in you.
wa in taf'alū fa-inna-hu fusūqun bi-kum:
Practise true devotion to Allāh,
wa 'ttaqu 'llāh:
and Allāh will teach you.
wa yu'allimu-kumu 'llāh:
Allāh is Aware of all things.
wa 'llāhu bi-kulli shai'in 'Alīm.

If you are on a journey and cannot find a scribe,
wa in kuntum ʿalā safarin wa lam tajidū kātiban
then a pledge in hand.
fa-rihānun maqbūḍa:
And if one of you trusts another,
fa-in amina baʿḍu-kum baʿḍan
let him who is trusted fulfil his trust,
fa-l'-yu'addi 'lladhi ''tumina amānata-hu
and let him practise true devotion
to Allāh, his Lord.
wa l'-yattaqi 'llāha Rabba-h:
Do not hide testimony.
wa lā taktumu 'sh-shahāda:
If someone hides it, his heart is surely sinful.
wa man yaktum-hā fa-inna-hu āthimun qalbu-h:
Allāh is Aware of what you do.
wa 'llāhu bi-mā taʿmalūna ʿAlīm. (2:282,283)

Allāh (Exalted is He) has already mentioned usury [*ribā*], and explained why it is so foul and disgusting, because it is an increase extracted from the veins and flesh of the debtor, and a vile form of earning, detested and forbidden by Islām. He followed that with mention of the fine loan without interest, and He has now set forth the rules applicable to debt, commerce and pawning, all of them honourable ways of causing wealth to grow and increase, because they are good for the individual and society. The verse of debt [*āyat ad-dain*] is the longest verse in the Qur'ān, without exception, which indicates Islām's concern for sound economic systems.

O you who truly believe,
yā ayyuha 'lladhīna āmanū
when you contract a debt for a fixed term,
idhā tadāyantum bi-dainin ilā ajalin musamman
record it in writing.
fa-'ktubū-h:

That is to say: "When your dealings involve a fixed-term debt, record it in writing." This is a directive from Allāh (Exalted is He) to His servants, requiring them to record their fixed-term dealings in writing, since that is the best way to keep track of the amount and the date of the transaction.[188] In other words: "When one of you contracts a debt with another, and deals with him on the basis of deferred payment, either as a creditor or as a debtor." The point of adding the noun *dain* [debt] is to dispel any idea that the verb *tadāyantum* could refer to indebtedness in the metaphorical sense, as in the saying: "As you repay, so you will be repaid [*ka-mā tadīnu tudān*]." The instruction is complex, in that it refers to the present and the future, and that it is an incentive to writing.

> when you contract a debt for a fixed term
> *idhā tadāyantum bi-dainin ilā ajalin musamman*

—of days and months, or a year, or any specification that favours knowledge and dispels ignorance:

> record it in writing.
> *fa-'ktubū-h:*

That is to say: "[record] the debt with its term, because that is more reliable and provides better protection against dispute." The majority opinion is that it is a strongly recommended practice.[189]

> Let a scribe record it in writing between you in equity.
> *wa l'-yaktub baina-kum kātibun bi'l-ʿadl:*

In other words: "Let an equitable scribe record it for you, meaning a trustworthy person who will not treat either side unfairly."[190] His expression (Exalted is He):

> between you
> *baina-kum*

—is intended to indicate that the scribe must place himself between the two parties to the contract, that he must record what each of them has to say, and that he must not consider it sufficient to note what only one of them says. The person who acts as the scribe must record with equal fairness, without leaning in favour of either party, and neither adding nor subtracting. It is also a commandment to the two parties, instructing them to choose a scribe who is well-versed in legal and religious knowledge, and whose recording can be relied upon as consistent with the Sacred Law.[191] [They must choose such a person] because he is true to the religion, since he knows that his right is confined to the act of recording, and he must neither ask for anything more, nor present any demand before the expiration of the term.

To this I would add (and this is a rule of jurisprudence [*fiqh*]): If the debtor sees fit to repay what he owes, before the expiration of the term, the creditor is obliged to reduce his debt by the amount corresponding to the remainder of the term, if he added to the price of what he sold him on terms of deferred payment. If the debtor is aware of that added cost, however, he is not allowed to refuse payment, nor to deduct from the amount of the debt he owes. This is the advantage of recording the contract in writing, so Allāh (Exalted is He) has commanded it.

The scholars have disagreed about this recording in writing. Some maintain that it is strictly necessary, that being the doctrine of ʿAṭāʾ, Ibn Juraij and an-Nakhaʿī, and the preferred opinion of Muḥammad ibn Jarīr aṭ-Ṭabarī. Others maintain that the imperative should be construed as an admonition and a strong recommendation, so there is no serious harm in failure to comply. This is the opinion of the majority of the religious scholars. It has also been said that recording in writing, summoning witnesses, and pledging pawns [*rahn*], were all obligatory at first, but then their compulsory character was abrogated by His saying (Exalted is He):

> And if one of you entrusts to another,
> *fa-in amina baʿḍu-kum baʿḍan*
> let him who is trusted fulfil his trust,
> *fa-l'-yuʾaddi 'lladhi ''tumina amānata-hu*

Such is the opinion of al-Ḥasan, ash-Shaʿbī and al-Ḥakam ibn ʿUyaina.[192]

> No scribe should refuse to write as Allāh has taught him
> *wa lā yaʾba kātibun an yaktuba ka-mā ʿallama-hu 'llāhu*

That is to say: "None should refuse to write with fairness, as Allāh has taught him."[193] The scholars have disagreed about the obligation of the scribe to record, and of the witness to bear witness. Some maintain the strict necessity of both, because the obvious meaning of the sentence is that it forbids refusal to write, and imposes it as a duty on every scribe. If a qualified person is asked to record a contract, or to bear witness to it, he is therefore obliged to act accordingly.

Others assign the obligation to the category of *farḍ al-kifāya* [collective duty, incumbent on the Islāmic community as a whole, though not on every individual Muslim]. According to this opinion, which is held by ash-Shaʿbī, if only one person is available, it is incumbent upon him to perform the task. Some consider it a matter of positive advice and recommendation. That is because, when Allāh (Exalted is He) taught him how to write, He honoured him with that skill, so it is commendable for him to act as a scribe, to meet the need of his Muslim brother, and also to give thanks for that blessing bestowed on him by Allāh. It is also said that recording and bearing witness used to be incumbent on the scribe and the witness, but then Allāh abrogated both duties by His saying (Exalted is He):

> and let no harm be done to scribe or witness.
> *wa lā yuḍārra kātibun wa lā shahīd:*

❧ ❧

> as Allāh has taught him
> *ka-mā ʿallama-hu 'llāhu*

In other words: "as Allāh has ordained for him and commanded him to do."[194]

> so let him write, and let him who incurs the debt dictate
> *fa-l'-yaktub: wa l'-yumlili 'lladhī ʿalai-hi 'l-ḥaqqu*

That is to say: "let the debtor dictate to the scribe, and tell him what to write." This should be done by the one who incurs the debt, because the debt is the object of testimony.[195]

The scribe must write without adding or subtracting anything. He must record what will be useful as evidence, if the need arises. He must not favour the interest of one of the two parties, rather than the other, and each of the two must be sure that his right will not be annulled. What he records must conform to the standard generally agreed upon by the religious scholars, and he must be wary of formulations that are subject to dispute. To meet these criteria, the scribe must be well-versed in jurisprudence, language, and the doctrines of the religious scholars.

In other words: "The person who incurs the debt must make a verbal statement, acknowledging and describing the debt he is incurring. He must mention its amount, its nature, its term, and so on." The terms *imlāl* and *imlā'* are classical Arabic synonyms [both meaning "dictation"].[196]

> and let him practise true devotion to Allāh, his Lord,
> *wa l'-yattaqi 'llāha Rabba-hu*
> and diminish nothing thereof.
> *wa lā yabkhas min-hu shai'ā:*

That is to say: "Let him be afraid of offending Allāh, the Lord of All the Worlds, and let him diminish nothing of what is rightfully due."[197] This applies to the person making the dictation, not to the scribe, as some say, in view of His saying (Exalted is He):

and diminish nothing thereof.
wa lā yabkhas min-hu shai'ā:

In other words: "[nothing of] the debt which he is dictating to the scribe," for he is the one more likely to withhold something, whereas the scribe is more likely to add than to omit. There is good reason for the twofold imposition on the person making the dictation, combining the commandment to practise true devotion with the prohibition of diminution, because he has strong incentives to do what has been forbidden. The human being is naturally disposed to shielding himself from things that are to his disadvantage, and lightening the burden of his liabilities.[198]

But if he who owes the debt is of low understanding, or weak
fa-in kāna 'lladhī ʿalai-hi 'l-ḥaqqu safīhan aw ḍaʿīfan

That is to say: "If the debtor is an intellectually deficient spendthrift, or if he is a feeble youth or a senile old man...."[199] According to ash-Shāfiʿī: "The *safīh* is the spendthrift who squanders his wealth and his religion."[200]

or unable himself to dictate,
aw lā yastaṭīʿu an yumilla huwa
then let the guardian of his interests dictate in equity.
fa-l'-yumlil waliyyu-hu bi'l-ʿadl:

In other words: "If he cannot dictate by himself, due to stammering, dumbness or poor command of the language, let his guardian or his agent make the dictation, in fairness, without subtraction or addition."[201]

According to Ibn ʿAbbās (may Allāh be well pleased with him and his father): "In this context, the *waliyy* is the creditor. In other words: 'If the debtor is incapable of dictating, the creditor must do it, because he knows best what is due to him.'"[202]

As for the insertion of the particle *aw* [or] between these three expressions—(1) of low understanding, (2) weak, (3) unable himself to dictate—it signifies that these are different cases. Since the meaning is:

"If any one of these three attributes can be ascribed to the debtor, let his guardian dictate with equity," it must be concluded that each of the three cases is different. Once this has been established, the three groups can be disstinguished as follows:

1. The term *safīh* applies to adults who are feeble in understanding and intellectually deficient.
2. The term *ḍaʿīf* applies to the immature youth, the lunatic and the senile old man, they being those who are totally lacking in intellectual capacity.
3. The expression *lā yastaṭīʿu an yumilla* refers to someone who cannot dictate because his tongue is too weak for the purpose, due to dumbness, or because he does not know exactly what is owed to him and what he owes.

None of the above are capable of valid acknowledgement and dictation, so there is no alternative to having someone else act on their behalf.[203]

> And call to witness, from among your men, two witnesses.
> *wa 'stashhidū shahīdaini min rijāli-kum:*

That is to say: "Along with the recording in writing, you must seek two witnesses from among the Muslims, as an extra guarantee of authenticity."[204] As for the expression:

> from among your men
> *min rijāli-kum:*

—there are several interpretations: (1) "from among the members of your own religious community, they being the Muslims." (2) "the free men." (3) "those whom you are accustomed to calling as witnesses, because of their fairness."[205]

> And if two men are not there, then a man and two women,
> *fa-in lam yakūna rajulaini fa-rajulun wa 'mraʾatāni*
> of such as you approve as witnesses
> *mim-man tarḍawna mina 'sh-shuhadāʾi*

That is to say: "If two male witnesses are not available, then a man and two women should be called to witness, from among those whose commitment to religion and fairness can be trusted."[206] The testimony of women together with men is permissible in matters of property, by consensus, but not in cases involving legal penalties [*ḥudūd*] and retaliation, where only men can serve as witnesses.[207] As you should also understand, this Qur'ānic verse indicates that not everyone is qualified to act as a witness.

The jurists have attached the following ten preconditions to the acceptance of testimony:

1. The witness must be a free man.
2. He must be an adult.
3. He must be a Muslim.
4. He must be equitable.
5. He must know and understand what he is testifying to.
6. He must gain no personal advantage from that testimony.
7. He must not be using it to shield himself from some personal disadvantage.
8. He must not have a reputation for making many mistakes.
9. He must not have a reputation for unchivalrous behaviour.
10. There must be no enmity between him and the person he testifies against.[208]

As for His saying (Exalted is He):

> so that, if one errs, one of them will remind the other.
> *an taḍilla iḥdā-humā fa-tudhakkira iḥdā-huma 'l-ukhrā:*

—that is to say: "if one of the two women forgets what the testimony is about, the other will remind her of it." This is the reason for requiring two women, because they are typically less retentive.[209] Forgetfulness is predominant in the nature of women, due to the large proportion of coldness and moisture in their constitutions. It is reasonable to assume, however, that forgetfulness is less likely to affect two women together, than one woman on her own. Two women can therefore be substituted for one man, since even if one of them were to forget, the other would remind her. This is the import of the Qur'ānic verse.[210]

As reported by Muslim in his *Ṣaḥīḥ*, on the authority of Abū Huraira (may Allāh be well pleased with him), the Prophet (blessing and peace be upon him) once said:

> O womenfolk, you must be truthful, and you must seek forgiveness frequently, for I have seen that you account for the majority of the inhabitants of the Fire of Hell.

A woman among them, who happened to be extremely intelligent, thereupon spoke up and said: "What is wrong with us, then, O Messenger of Allāh, that we should be the majority of the inhabitants of the Fire of Hell?" To this he replied:

> You do a lot of cursing, and you accuse your mate of infidelity. I have not seen any group, apart from you, in which those deficient in intelligence and religion outnumber the discerning.

"O Messenger of Allāh," she asked, "what do you mean by deficiency in intelligence and religion?" He said:

> As for the deficiency of her intelligence, the testimony of two women is equivalent to the testimony of one man, so this is the deficiency of her intelligence. She spends the nights without performing the ritual prayer, and breaks her fast during Ramaḍān, so this is deficiency in religion.[211]

> And the witnesses must not refuse when they are summoned.
> *wa lā ya'ba 'sh-shuhadā'u idhā mā du'ū*

That is to say: "The witnesses must not refuse to perform the act of witnessing, nor to testify, if that is asked of him."[212] From this it can also be inferred that bearing witness is a collective duty [*farḍ kifāya*], and such is the doctrine of the majority.

In His saying (Exalted is He):

> And the witnesses must not refuse when they are summoned.
> *wa lā ya'ba 'sh-shuhadā'u idhā mā du'ū*

—the summons applies to performing the act of witnessing. As for "the witnesses [*ash-shuhadā'*]," the term *shāhid* [sing. of *shuhadā'*] actually applies to someone who bears witness. If he is summoned to perform the act of witnessing, he is obliged to respond, but only if his personal duty requires him to do so, otherwise it is a collective responsibility [*farḍ kifāya*]. Allāh knows best, of course. According to Mujāhid: "If you are summoned to act as a witness, you are free to choose. If you have acted as a witness, and you are summoned [to testify], you must respond."

According to an established report in the *Ṣaḥīḥ* of Muslim and the *Sunan*, transmitted by Mālik ibn 'Abdu'llāh on the authority of Zaid ibn Khālid, Allāh's Messenger (Allāh bless him and give him peace) once said:

> Shall I tell you who is the best of witnesses? He who provides his testimony before he is asked for it.[213]

As indicated in this Qur'ānic verse, the witness is he who presents himself to the judge. This is a basic principle of the Sacred Law. It has been followed in practice in every age, and understood by every community.[214] Where the witness is concerned, you should be aware of these two cases:

1. He is individually responsible [as the only qualified person available], so he is strictly obliged to perform the act of witnessing.
2. There are many potential witnesses, so that obligation becomes a collective duty [*farḍ kifāya*].[215]

> Do not be averse to writing it down,
> *wa lā tas'amū an taktubū-hu*
> whether it be small or great, with the term thereof.
> *ṣaghīran aw kabīran ilā ajali-h:*

In other words: "Do not be too impatient to record the debt in writing, whether it be small or great, little or much, with the time when repayment falls due."

> That is more equitable in the sight of Allāh,
> *dhālikum aqsaṭu 'inda 'llāhi*
> and more sure for testimony,
> *wa aqwamu li'sh-shahādati*
> and the best way of avoiding doubt between you
> *wa adnā allā tartābū*

That is to say: "To record the debt in writing, as We have commanded you, is more equitable in His judgement (Exalted is He), more reliable when it comes to testimony, so that you do not forget, and more likely to keep you from harbouring doubts about the amount of the debt and its term."[216] You should know that recording in writing is:

> more equitable in the sight of Allāh
> *aqsaṭu 'inda 'llāhi*

—for the simple reason that, if the debt is written down, it is closer to certainty and truthfulness, and farther from ignorance and falsehood, and therefore more equitable in the sight of Allāh. He has also said (Exalted is He):

> Proclaim their real parentage.
> *udʿū-hum li-ābāʾi-him*
> That will be more equitable in the sight of Allāh.
> *huwa aqsaṭu ʿinda 'llāh.* (33:5)

In other words: "That will be closer to reality than if you assign them to others, instead of to their own parents."

> and more sure for testimony
> *wa aqwamu li'sh-shahādati*

—because the written record is the means of safekeeping and recollection, so it is closer to the right path. The difference between the first advantage and the second is that (1) the first has to do with obtaining Allāh's good pleasure, while (2) the second has to do with obtaining the benefit of this world. The first is mentioned before the second, to draw attention to the fact that the religion must be given priority over this world. As for the third advantage:

> and the best way of avoiding doubt between you
> *wa adnā allā tartābū*

—that is to say: "It is more likely to remove doubt and suspicion from the hearts of the debtor and the creditor." As for the difference between the first two and this third, it is that the first two concern the procurement of benefit—the procurement of religious benefit in the first case, and the procurement of worldly benefit in the second—while the third is about keeping oneself and the other party out of harm's way.

As for the element of self-protection, one is spared from wondering about the nature of the business, and from asking oneself: "What I just said, was it true or false?" As for the protection accorded to the other party, the point is that he might otherwise accuse one of lying and shortcoming, and so incur the punishment for backbiting and slander. How fine are these advantages, how compatible with equity, and how excellent is their arrangement![217]

> except only in the case when it is actual merchandise
> *illā an takūna tijāratan ḥāḍiratan*
> which you transfer among yourselves from hand to hand.
> *tudīrūna-hā baina-kum*

In other words: "unless it is an immediate hand-to-hand sale, and the price is received there and then."

> In that case it is no sin for you if you do not write it down.
> *fa-laisa ʿalai-kum junāḥun allā taktubū-hā:*

That is to say: "There is no harm in failing to record it in writing, in that case, since the need for precaution does not exist."

> And have witnesses when you sell to one another
> *wa ashhidū idhā tabāyaʿtum:*

In other words: "Have witnesses to your rightful due, in every case, whether the sale is complete or on terms of deferred payment, because that is the best way to avoid dispute and disagreement."[218] According to most of the commentators: "The point is that, while they are relieved of the obligation to have hand-to-hand trading recorded in writing, they have not been relieved of the obligation to have it witnessed, because witnessing without recording is less troublesome, and because, if the need arises, there is no risk of forgetfulness. As you should also know, the purpose of this commandment is undoubtedly to provide guidance towards the path of caution."[219] The commandments contained in the noble Qurʾānic verse are meant to be understood in the sense of strong recommendation, according to the majority.[220]

> and let no harm be done to scribe or witness.
> *wa lā yuḍārra kātibun wa lā shahīd:*

That is to say: "The creditor must not harm the scribe and the witnesses."[221] The verb *yuḍārra* may be grammatically active or passive. If it is understood to be a contraction of *yuḍārira*, and therefore active [meaning "cause harm," not "be harmed"], it signifies that the scribe and the witnesses are forbidden to refuse to respond, and to make any distortion or alteration in the record and the testimony. [If it is understood to be a contraction of *yuḍārara*, and therefore passive], it signifies that harm must not be done to them. It is harmful to them, for instance, if they are pressed to deal hastily with something important, or bothered with things that are none of their business, or if the scribe is not given a fee, and the witness is not compensated for his travel expenses.[222]

With regard to the practice of doing business without calling witnesses, an excellent report has been provided by ad-Dāraquṭnī, who attributes the following account to Ṭāriq ibn ʿAbdi'llāh al-Muḥāribī:

"We travelled in a caravan from ar-Rabdha* and south of ar-Rabdha, until we made camp near Medina. We had a female passenger [*ẓaʿīna*] of ours with us. While we were sitting there, along came a man wearing two white shirts. He saluted us with the greeting of peace, and we returned his salutation. We also had a red camel with us, so the man said: 'Will you sell me this camel of yours?' We said yes, so he asked us: 'For how much?' We said: 'For such-and-such a quantity of dates.' He did not bargain with us for a lower price, and he said: 'I have accepted it.' Then he led the camel away by its head, until he entered Medina and disappeared from our sight. We started blaming one another, saying: 'You gave your camel to someone you do not know!' Our female passenger said: 'You must not blame one another, for I have seen the face of a man who will not betray you. I have seen the face of a man whose face is more like the moon on the night when it is full.' Then, when the evening came, a man approached us and said: 'Peace be upon you! I come to you as the messenger of Allāh's Messenger (Allāh bless him and give him peace), and he has commanded you to eat enough of this to satisfy your hunger, and to measure out as much as you consider your full payment.' We thereupon ate until we were satisfied, and measured out until we had collected our payment in full."

As reported by az-Zuhrī, ʿAmmāra ibn Khuzaima was told by his paternal uncle, who was one of the Companions of the Prophet (Allāh bless him and give him peace), that the Prophet (Allāh bless him and give him peace) once purchased a horse from an Arab nomad. The Arab started saying: "Fetch a witness who will testify that I have sold it to you!" Khuzaima ibn Thābit said: "I bear witness that you have sold it to him," so the Prophet (Allāh bless him and give him peace) approached Khuzaima and said: "To what do you bear witness?" He replied: "To your truthfulness, O Messenger of Allāh." Allāh's Messenger (Allāh bless him and give him peace) thereupon equated the testimony of Khuzaima with the testimony of two men.[223]

*The village of ar-Rabdha, one of the villages of Medina, is situated three miles from Dhāt ʿAraq on the Ḥijāz road. It is the site of the tomb of Abū Dharr al-Ghifārī (may Allāh be well pleased with him).

If you do, it is a sin in you.
wa in taf'alū fa-inna-hu fusūqun bi-kum:

In other words: "If you do what you have been forbidden to do, you have sinned by your departure from obedience to Allāh."

Practise true devotion to Allāh,
wa 'ttaqu 'llāh:
and Allāh will teach you.
wa yu'allimu-kumu 'llāh:

That is to say: "Be afraid of offending Allāh, and be vigilantly aware of Him, for then He will endow you with useful knowledge, which is the key to the felicity of the two abodes [this world and the Hereafter]."[224] This means that He will teach you what you need for guidance and precaution in the sphere of this world, just as He will teach you right guidance in the sphere of religion.[225]

Allāh is Aware of all things.
wa 'llāhu bi-kulli shai'in 'Alīm.

In other words: "He is Aware of those things that are beneficial, and of the consequences, for nothing whatsoever is hidden from Him."[226]

The word "Allāh" is repeated three times in the sentences:

Practise true devotion to Allāh,
wa 'ttaqu 'llāh:
and Allāh will teach you.
wa yu'allimu-kumu 'llāh:
Allāh is Aware of all things.
wa 'llāhu bi-kulli shai'in 'Alīm.

—in order to stress their importance. The first is an exhortation to practise true devotion. The second is a promise of His gracious favour. The third is a magnification of His significance.[227]

If you are on a journey and cannot find a scribe,
wa in kuntum 'alā safarin wa lam tajidū kātiban
then a pledge in hand.
fa-rihānun maqbūḍa:

That is to say: "If you are travelling, and you contract a debt for a fixed term, but you cannot find anyone to a act as a scribe for you, the alternative to recording in writing is a pledge in hand, accepted by the creditor in security for his due."[228]

In this Qur'ānic verse, Allāh (Exalted is He) has distinguished three types of sales:

1. Sale with recording and witnessing.
2. Sale with a pledge in hand.
3. Sale on the basis of trust.

Having commanded recording in writing and the calling of witnesses, in the preceding verse, Allāh (Exalted is He) has acknowledged that it may be impossible on a journey, either because no scribe can be found, or because, though a scribe is available, the necessary instruments are not. Allāh (Exalted is He) has also mentioned another kind of security, that being the receipt of a pledge. This is a more effective precaution than recording in writing and the calling of witnesses.

The jurists today are generally agreed that the pledge is required in every case, both on a journey and at home, whether the scribe is available or not. Mujāhid used to maintain that the pledge is not permissible except on a journey, on the basis of the obvious meaning of the Qur'ānic verse, but his doctrine is not practised today. The verse does make specific mention of the journey, but only because that is the most common situation [in which scribes and witnesses are likely to be unavailable]. Compare His saying (Exalted is He):

> It is no sin for you to curtail the ritual prayer,
> *fa-laisa ʿalai-kum junāḥun an taqṣurū mina 'ṣ-ṣalāti*
> if you fear that those who disbelieve may attack you.
> *in khiftum an yaftina-kumu 'lladhīna kafarū.* (4:101)

—which does not mean that fear is a precondition for the permissibility of curtailment.[229] Besides, the Prophet (blessing and peace be upon him) once pawned his shirt in Medina, when he purchased twenty measures of barley from a Jew. He did so not only to feed his family, but to establish pledging as more reliable than recording in writing, which is likely to be impossible on a journey. In the view of the majority, with the exception of Mālik, pledging is always acceptable.[230]

> And if one of you trusts another,
> *fa-in amina baʿḍu-kum baʿḍan*
> let him who is trusted fulfil his trust,
> *fa-l'-yu'addi 'lladhi ''tumina āmanata-hu*
> and let him practise true devotion to Allāh, his Lord.
> *wa l'-yattaqi 'llāha Rabba-h:*

That is to say: "If the creditor trusts the debtor, to the extent that he does not require the pledge, the person who is trusted must deliver the debt he owes. He must practise true devotion to Allāh, his Lord, by scrupulously observing the duties of trust."[231] The debt is called a trust, because the creditor is assured by his confidence in the debtor. Since he feels safe from the debtor's denial, he does not employ a scribe, does not call witnesses, and does not take a pledge. Nevertheless, Allāh (Exalted is He) has explicitly urged the debtor to justify his creditor's good opinion of him, and to honour his trust by paying him his due. Then He has emphasized that by saying:

> and let him practise true devotion to Allāh, his Lord.
> *wa l'-yattaqi 'llāha Rabba-h:*

In other words: "The debtor must practise that devotion by paying the full amount due when the term expires, without procrastination or denial. He must deal with his creditor in the very best way, just as his creditor thought the very best of him."[232]

Allāh has then returned to the subject of witnessing, for He has said (Exalted is He):

> Do not hide testimony.
> *wa lā taktumu 'sh-shahāda:*
> If someone hides it, his heart is surely sinful.
> *wa man yaktum-hā fa-inna-hu āthimun qalbu-h:*

In other words: "When you are summoned to testify, you must not hide the testimony, for its concealment is a great sin, which renders the heart sinful and its owner immoral." The heart is mentioned specifically, because it is the ruler of the limbs and organs. If the heart is sound, the whole body is sound, but if it is corrupt, the whole body is corrupt. [In the words of the Prophetic tradition]:

> Allāh does not examine your physical forms and your possessions, but He does examine your hearts.[233]

The concealment of testimony means denying knowledge of that which has been witnessed. This is reminiscent of His saying (Exalted is He):

> Or do you say that Abraham and Ishmael
> *am taqūlūna inna Ibrāhīma wa Ismāʿīla*
> and Isaac and Jacob,
> *wa Isḥāqa wa Yaʿqūba*

and the tribes, were Jews or Christians?
wa 'l-asbāṭa kānū Hūdan aw Naṣārā:
Say: "Do you know best, or does Allāh?"
qul a-antum a'lamu ami 'llāh:
And who is more unjust than he who hides
wa man aẓlamu mim-man katama
a testimony that he has received from Allāh?
shahādatan 'inda-hu mina 'llāh. (2:140)

—where the reference is likewise to the denial of knowledge.

Sin is attached to the heart because actions are prompted by motives and stimuli, and these originate in the heart. It is related that 'Umar was teaching an Arab nomad to recite:

The tree of az-zaqqūm
inna shajarata 'z-zaqqūmi
is the food of the sinner.
ṭa'āmu 'l-athīm. (44:43,44)

—but he kept mispronouncing this and saying: "the food of the orphan [*ṭa'āmu 'l-yatīm*]," so 'Umar told him to say: "the food of the immoral profligate [*ṭa'āmu 'l-fājir*]." This indicates that sin [*ithm*], in this context, means immorality [*fujūr*].[234]

Allāh is Aware of what you do.
wa 'llāhu bi-mā ta'malūna 'Alīm.

That is to say: "Nothing is hidden from Him, among all the deeds and actions of His servants."

There are two kinds of knowledge, the kind that is acquired [*kasbī*] and that which is received as a gift [*wahbī*]:

1. The first kind is obtained through dedicated effort, persistent application, and memorization.

2. As for the second kind, it comes by way of true devotion to Allāh, and righteous work, as He has said (Exalted is He):

Practise true devotion to Allāh, and Allāh will teach you.
wa 'ttaqu 'llāh: wa yu'allimu-kumu 'llāh:

This kind of knowledge is called *'ilm ladunī* [esoteric knowledge]:

And We had taught him knowledge from Our presence.
wa 'allamnā-hu min ladun-nā 'ilmā. (18:65)

It is the useful knowledge that Allāh gives to whom He will among

His truly devoted servants. Imām ash-Shāfi'ī alluded to it when he said [in poetry]:

I complained to a stalwart about my poor memory,
so he directed me to stop committing sins.
shakawtu ilā wakī'in sū'a ḥifẓī
fa-arshada-nī ilā tarki 'l-ma'āṣī

He told me that knowledge is a light,
and the light of Allāh does not guide a sinner.
wa akhbara-nī bi-anna 'l-'ilma nūrun
wa nūru 'llāhi lā yuhdī li-'āṣī.[235]

According to a report from Abū Huraira (may Allāh be well pleased with him), Allāh's Messenger (Allāh bless him and give him peace) once told him about a man from among the Children of Israel, who asked a fellow Israelite to lend him a thousand dīnārs [gold coins]. The lender said: "Bring me some witnesses, so that I can have them witness the transaction." The borrower said: "Allāh is sufficient as a witness!" The lender said: "Bring me a guarantor," but the borrower said: "Allāh is sufficient as a guarantor!" The lender said: "You have spoken the truth," so he gave him the loan for a fixed term. The borrower then went out to sea, and attended to his need.

Then he looked for a ship to carry him back, so that he could settle his debt on time. Since he could not find a ship, he took a log of wood, hollowed it out, and inserted a thousand dīnārs, along with a note addressed to the creditor. Then he sealed the hole, and took the log to the sea. "O Allāh," he said, "You know that I asked so-and-so to lend me a thousand dīnārs, so he asked me for a guarantor, but I said: 'Allāh is sufficient as a guarantor!' and he was satisfied with that. When he asked me for a witness, I said: 'Allāh is sufficient as a witness!' and he was satisfied with that. I tried hard to find a ship, so that I could deliver the loan he gave me, but I could not find a ship, so I am entrusting it to Your safekeeping!" He thereupon threw it into the sea, then went off to look for a ship to his homeland.

His creditor went out to see if a ship might be arriving with his money, and lo and behold, there was the log with the money stuffed inside it! He took it home as firewood for his family, and when he broke it, he found the money and the note. Then the man who had borrowed from him arrived, and handed him a thousand dīnārs, saying: "By Allāh, I never stopped trying to find a ship, so that I could bring you your money, but I could not find a ship before the one I have just arrived on." The creditor said: "Did you send me anything?" He replied: "Did I not tell you that I could not find a ship before the one I have just arrived on?" The creditor said: "Well, Allāh has already delivered what you sent in the log of wood, on your behalf, so take your thousand and go on your way, as one who is rightly guided!"[236]

Allāh (Glory be to Him) has commanded His creatures to practise truthfulness, and He has taught them how to conduct their mutual transactions, by taking precautions and calling witnesses, so that they do not wrong one another. That is due to His compassion for them (Glory be to Him), and the result of His tender kindness towards them. So that they will not quarrel and resort to litigation, He has commanded them to preserve their rights by recording them in writing and having them witnessed. He has commanded both the act of witnessing and the subsequent giving of testimony.

The prevention of quarrelling and litigation between them, as prescribed here and now, is even more important as a means of preventing the effects thereof in the Hereafter. In the words of the traditional report [*khabar*]:

> You must give to one another freely in your mutual dealings. I have given you freely that which you owe to me, for, whenever the generous person can do so, he forgives.

Where debt is concerned, the prescription of the Sacred Law includes kind treatment of those in need, because needs take their toll. A needy person may be tempted to play tricks, for his painful feelings are hard to bear, and they may prevent him from begging and appealing for help. He is therefore permitted to borrow, so that he can repair his situation in the immediate present, and look forward to Allāh's grace in the future. A great reward has also been promised for lending, and that is a mark of His tender kindness (Exalted is He).[237]

These are my own remarks:

You must make sure that your food, your drink and your clothing are lawful, for, if someone consumes only that which is lawful, the fountains of wisdom will flow from his heart to his tongue. Allāh (Exalted is He) has said:

> Practise true devotion to Allāh,
> *wa 'ttaqu 'llāh:*
> and Allāh will teach you.
> *wa yu'allimu-kumu 'llāh:*

This refers to esoteric knowledge [*'ilm ladunī*], which Allāh (Exalted is He) grants only to those who climb the ladder of true devotion. You must therefore set to work in earnest, and follow the Prophet (Allāh bless him and give him peace) in your words, your deeds and all your situations, in order to succeed in the two abodes [this world and the Hereafter], by Allāh's leave.

You must also be very wary of cheating or being cheated. If you cheat other people, their property will be transferred to you along with its burden of sin, and if you are cheated, the consequence will rest with you. You may say: "This person has cheated me [so he is fair game]!" You may regard this as justification, but it is by no means certain that the other will absolve you, so anxiety will haunt you till the Day of Resurrection, when he may demand that you repay what you consumed from his property. We beg Allāh the Almighty to keep us safe from all that. *Āmīn*.

Peace be upon the Messengers, and praise be to Allāh, the Lord of All the Worlds. There is no might nor any power, except with Allāh, the All-High, the Almighty. May Allāh bless our master Muḥammad, his family and his Companions, and may He grant them peace.

The Twelfth Call

In the Name of Allāh, the All-Merciful, the All-Compassionate.
Bismi'llāhi 'r-Raḥmāni 'r-Raḥīm.

O you who truly believe,
yā ayyuha 'lladhīna āmanū
if you obey a faction of those
who have received the Book,
in tuṭī'ū farīqan mina 'lladhīna ūtu 'l-Kitāba
they will make you unbelievers after your belief.
yaruddū-kum ba'da īmāni-kum kāfirīn.

How can you disbelieve,
wa kaifa takfurūna
when Allāh's signs are recited to you,
wa antum tutlā 'alai-kum āyātu 'llāhi
and His Messenger is in your midst?
wa fī-kum Rasūlu-h:
And when someone holds fast to Allāh,
wa man ya'taṣim bi'llāhi
he is indeed guided to a straight path.
fa-qad hudiya ilā ṣirāṭin mustaqīm. (3:100,101)

O you who truly believe,
yā ayyuha 'lladhīna āmanū
if you obey a faction of those who have received the Book…
in tuṭī'ū farīqan mina 'lladhīna ūtu 'l-Kitāba…

That is to say: "If you obey a party [*ṭā'ifa*] of those who have received the Book":

they will make you unbelievers after your belief.
yaruddū-kum ba'da īmāni-kum kāfirīn.

In other words: "They will cause you to become unbelievers, after Allāh has guided you to faith." The warning is addressed to the tribes of al-Aws and a-Khazraj, since the Jews were intent on stirring up conflict between them. That was the immediate cause of the revelation, although the wording of the verse is general.[238]

As you should also understand, since Allāh (Exalted is He) has warned the faction of the People of the Book to desist from misguiding and leading astray, in the preceding verse:

> Say: "O people of the Book,
> *qul yā ahla 'l-Kitābi*
> why do you bar those who believe from Allāh's way,
> *li-ma taṣuddūna ʿan sabīli 'llāhi man āmana*
> seeking to make it crooked, when you are witnesses?
> *tabghūna-hā ʿiwajan wa antum shuhadāʾ:*
> And Allāh is not unaware of what you do."
> *wa ma 'llāhu bi-ghāfilin ʿammā taʿmalūn.* (3:99)

—He has now warned the believers, in this Qurʾānic verse [3:100], to beware of their misguidance and deception, and He has prevented them from taking notice of what they say.

It is related that Shāsh ibn Qais, the Jew, was extreme in his unbelief, violently aggressive towards the Muslims, and intensely envious. He happened to pass by a group of the Helpers [*Anṣār*], members of al-Aws and al-Khazraj, and he noticed that they were sitting and conversing together. The hostility that had once existed between them, in the Age of Ignorance, had disappeared through the blessed grace of Islām, and that was disturbing to the Jew. He therefore went and sat beside them, and reminded them of the tribal wars that had come between them in the past. He recited to them some of the poems that had been composed about those wars, so the people started quarrelling and exchanging angry words. They cried: "To arms! To arms!"

News of this reached the Prophet (Allāh bless him and give him peace), so he went out to join them, accompanied by some of the Emigrants [*Muhājirīn*] and the Helpers [*Anṣār*] who were with him at the time. He said:

> Will you go back to the conditions of the Age of Ignorance, while I am in your midst, and when Allāh has honoured you with Islām, and has reconciled your hearts?!

The people immediately recognized that as the work of the devil, and a cunning device of that Jew, so they threw down their weapons and warmly embraced one another. Then they moved away in the company of Allāh's Messenger (Allāh bless him and give him peace). Never did a day start off worse, and have a better ending, than that day! It was then that Allāh (Exalted is He) sent down this Qur'ānic verse, so His saying:

> if you obey a faction of those who have received the Book...
> *in tuṭīʿū farīqan mina 'lladhīna ūtu 'l-Kitāba...*

—probably refers to this particular event. It is also quite conceivable that it refers to all their various attempts to mislead. Allāh (Exalted is He) has thus explained that, if the believers are too receptive, and accept whatever they say, that will lead from one stage to another, until they revert to being unbelievers. Unbelief is bound to result in devastation, in the arena of this world and in the sphere of religion. As for its effect in the worldly arena, it causes destruction through enmity, hatred, the incitement of discord, and the promotion of warfare, which leads to the shedding of blood. As for its effect in the sphere of religion, that is too obvious to need mention.[239]

> How can you disbelieve,
> *wa kaifa takfurūna*
> when Allāh's signs are recited to you,
> *wa antum tutlā ʿalai-kum āyātu 'llāhi*
> and His Messenger is in your midst?
> *wa fī-kum Rasūlu-h.*

This is an expression of incomprehension and incredulity, signifying: "How can unbelief gain access to you, in a situation where Allāh's signs have not ceased to descend upon you, and the revelation has not come to a halt, and Allāh's Messenger is alive in your midst?"[240] After having commanded the Messenger (Allāh bless him and give him peace) to address the People of the Book:

> Say: "O people of the Book...."
> *qul yā ahla 'l-Kitābi....* (3:99)

—Allāh has now addressed them Himself (Glorious and Exalted is He), in order to demonstrate the splendour of their worth, and to make them aware that they are the ones who deserve to be addressed by Allāh, and spoken to by Him.[241]

As for the expression *wa kaifa* [How...?], it signifies amazement, and amazement is only appropriate in the case of someone who is not aware of the cause. Since that is utterly inconceivable where Allāh is concerned, the intention must be to convey interdiction and harsh rebuke. The point is that the recitation of Allāh's signs to them, in one situation after another, together with the fact that the Messenger (Allāh bless him and give him peace) is amongst them, to remove all doubt and to confirm every proof, should be enough to prevent them from lapsing into unbelief. From this perpective, it seems most improbable that unbelief could influence those who were in the presence of the Messenger (Allāh bless him and give him peace), so His saying:

> If you obey a faction of those who have received the Book,
> *in tuṭīʿū farīqan mina 'lladhīna ūtu 'l-Kitāba*
> they will make you unbelievers after your belief.
> *yaruddū-kum baʿda īmāni-kum kāfirīn.*

—must be taken as a warning, to the effect that the ultimate objective, as far as those hypocritical Jews are concerned, is to make the Muslims turn away from Islām. He has then instructed the Muslims to recognize the necessity, not merely of paying no attention to what they say, but of referring every doubt they hear from these Jews to the Messenger (Allāh bless him and give him peace), so that he may dispel it and remove the suspicion it conveys.[242]

This Qurʾānic verse is equally relevant to those who have not seen the Prophet (Allāh bless him and give him peace), because they are familiar with his Sunna [exemplary practice], and that is tantamount to seeing him. According to az-Zajjāj: "It is possible that this was addressed exclusively to the Companions of our master Muḥammad (Allāh bless him and give him peace), because Allāh's Messenger (Allāh bless him and give him peace) was amongst them, and they saw him with their own eyes. It is also possible to understand it as an address to the entire Community, because his traditions, his indications, and the Qurʾān he was given, are all amongst us in the place of the Prophet (Allāh bless him and give him peace), even if we have not actually seen him."

It was Qatāda who said: "There are two signposts in this Qurʾānic verse: the Book of Allāh and Allāh's Prophet. As for Allāh's Prophet, he has passed away." (Let me interject: Adherence to his Sunna has survived, so anyone who adheres to his Sunna will be among the triumphantly successful, through the grace of Allāh.) "As for the Book of Allāh, He has caused it to remain in our midst, as a mercy from Him and a gracious favour, containing what He has made lawful and what He has made unlawful, and what constitutes obedience to Him and disobedience to Him."[243]

Zaid ibn Arqam (may Allāh be well pleased with him) is reported as having said: "Allāh's Messenger (Allāh bless him and give him peace) stood amongst us one day, delivering a sermon at a watering place called Khammā', between Mecca and Medina. He praised Allāh and extolled Him, and he counselled the people and reminded them. Then he said:

> Now hear this, O you people: I am merely a human being. The Messenger of my Lord is about to come for me, so I shall respond. I am leaving you with two weighty matters: The first of them is the Book of Allāh, in which there is guidance and light, so take hold of the Book of Allāh, and cling to it.

"Having stressed the importance of the Book, and excited interest in it, he then went on to say:

> And the people of my household. Let me remind you of Allāh, where the people of my household are concerned. Let me remind you of Allāh, where the people of my household are concerned. Let me remind you of Allāh, where the people of my household are concerned.[244]

> And when someone holds fast to Allāh,
> *wa man ya'taṣim bi'llāhi*
> he is indeed guided to a straight path.
> *fa-qad hudiya ilā ṣirāṭin mustaqīm.*

That is to say: "When someone clings to His true religion, which He has explained through His signs, on the tongue of His Messenger, that person is guided to a very direct path, meaning the path that leads to the Gardens of Bliss."[245] The point is that, after mentioning the threat, He has followed it immediately with this promise. The meaning is: "When someone strictly adheres to Allāh's religion...," and it may also be understood as an exhortation, urging them to take refuge with Him, in order to ward off the evils of the unbelievers.

On the strength of His saying (Exalted is He):

> he is indeed guided to a straight path.
> *fa-qad hudiya ilā ṣirāṭin mustaqīm.*

—our colleagues have argued that the action of the servant is a creation of Allāh (Exalted is He). "That," they say, "is because He has made their holding fast a guidance from Allāh. Since He has made that holding fast an action for them, and a guidance from Allāh, what we have said is confirmed."[246]

You should know that the debate is outwardly with the People of the Book, but inwardly with the scholars of evil, who sell the religion for this world, and who do not put their knowledge into practice. Among them are those who disbelieve in what the Qur'ān has prescribed, such as abstinence from this world, pious restraint and true devotion, forbidding the lower self to follow passionate desire, preferring what is enduring over what is transitory, turning away from creatures and turning towards Allāh, and sparing no effort to reach the goal. Allāh is Witnessing what they do, Present with them, Observing their intentions in the actions of good and evil, so that He may recompense them accordingly.

In their greed for this world and their pursuit of passionate desire, they are misleading those believers who follow them, naïvely thinking well of them and supposing that their actions and their states are based on the foundation of the Sacred Law [*Sharīʿa*] and the process of the Spiritual Path [*Ṭarīqa*]. They are diverting them from the way of Allāh and the path of Truth, to which He commanded the Prophets to summon His creatures, for they are seeking to make the path of Truth crooked, by travelling on the path of falsehood. Allāh has therefore alerted the believers, by His saying:

> O you who truly believe!
> *yā ayyuha 'lladhīna āmanū.*

—so that they will not desert the path of right guidance, after faith, by following their course and their desire. He has said (Exalted is He):

> And do not follow the vain desires of a people
> *wa lā tattabiʿū ahwāʾa qawmin*
> who strayed in former times and led many astray,
> *qad ḍallū min qablu wa aḍallū kathīran*
> and wandered from the straightness of the road.
> *wa ḍallū ʿan sawāʾi 's-sabīl.* (5:77)

According to one of the Shaikhs: "The best kind of knowledge is that which is accompanied by fear. That is because fear arises from knowledge only through recognition of the attributes of the Truth. Fear is the mark of the knowledge that is required by Allāh, while the mark of fear is compliance with the commandment."

Allāh's Messenger (Allāh bless him and give him peace) once said:

> There will come a time when people have nothing left of Islām but its name, and nothing of the Qur'ān but its script. Their hearts will be deprived of guidance, and their mosques will be attended only by their physical bodies. The worst of those who are shadowed by the sky, when that day comes, will be the scholars among them. Discord will emerge, and they will be responsible for it.

If someone devotes himself exclusively to Him, through total absorption in Oneness, his path will be Allāh's straight path. If someone is with Allāh, Allāh will be with him, for He is his Guardian and his Helper. May Allāh protect us, and all of you, at every moment, from the guile of the devil and the cunning deceit of the self that is always instigating evil [*an-nafs al-ammāra bi's-sū'*]. *Āmīn*, O Source of help![247]

To this I would add: He has commanded us to view the servants of Allāh with the eye of compassion, and sincere devotion to Allāh and His Messenger (Allāh bless him and give him peace), to the full extent of our capacity. Allāh is the Guide to the straight path. Allāh (Exalted is He) has said:

> No part of the matter is your concern,
> *laisa la-ka mina 'l-amri shai'un.* (3:128)

—and this Qur'ānic verse contains instruction for us, to the effect that we must not censure the Muslims, nor subject them to negative criticism. If someone has not been guided by Allāh, but he holds fast to Allāh, the guidance will come from Him. As for what the Shaikh said (may Allāh bestow His mercy upon him), when he described the scholars of evil as those for whom there is no hope of improvement, after they have acquired knowledge but do not act in accordance with it, and neither befriend nor accept the people of truth and verification, their affair should actually be entrusted to Allāh. Nevertheless, his method (may Allāh bestow His mercy upon him) is that of admonition, and he is one of those who concentrate on real experience.

As a real experience, holding fast means genuine recourse to Him, permanent escape to Him, and directing all appeals for help to Him. When the veil of separation is removed from someone's inner being, he will realize that not a single atom belongs to anyone but Allāh, and that not a glimmer of light comes from any other source. This is someone who holds fast to Him, for protection from the very One who is clung to!

The chieftain of those of former and of later times (Allāh's blessing be upon him, and may He grant him peace) once said:

> I take refuge with You from You!

If someone holds fast to his own self, without being extinct to his personal power and strength in the process, polytheism [*shirk*] is his abode, and he is unaware.[248]

These are my own comments:

Because of our own inadequacy, it is essential for us to seek refuge with Allāh, appealing to Him in submissive humility. It is very hard, for the likes of us, to keep ourselves safe from the temptations of passionate desire, this world, our fellow creatures and the devil, because we seldom adhere to the path of the righteous and the truly devout. We devote too little time to their companionship, and to gathering the precious pearls of their utterance. As a result, we lack the strength of certitude, which we would need in order to protect our hearts against the influence of others [apart from Allāh], because the heart makes a hundred twists and turns in the space of a single instant.

If someone's heart is rightly guided, he is travelling towards the Truth. We must entreat Allāh to endow us with penitence, readiness to seek forgiveness, and steadfastness in faith. We must implore Him to endow us with love for Him and loyal obedience to His noble Prophet, and with characters modelled on the virtues of the Qur'ān. We must beseech Him to endow us with the real experience of holding fast to Him, and not to include us among those who cling to their own lower selves. We must beg Him to make us extinct to our personal power and strength, and to our attachment to our lower selves.

The Qur'ānic verse conveys this implicit admonition to the genuine believers: "If you obey your lower selves, those instigators of evil will divert you from your adherence to the Sacred Law, and turn you in the direction of your self-centred interests. How can you forget that Allāh has told you:

> Surely the self is always inciting to evil,
> *inna 'n-nafsa la-ammāratun bi's-sū'i.* (12:53)

so do not follow passionate desire.
fa-lā tattabiʿu 'l-hawā. (4:135)?"

Let this be an exhortation for you, inviting you to affirm: "We are together with the truthful, from Allāh's Messenger (Allāh bless him and give him peace) to the end of the chain! We shall not deviate from the straight path, trodden by all the heirs of Allāh's Messenger (Allāh bless him and give him peace), from his time (Allāh bless him and give him peace) till this time of ours." Their path is linked to Allāh's Messenger (Allāh bless him and give him peace) by the sound chain of tradition. They do not agree on anything but the Truth, and the likes of those who constitute this chain could not conceivably agree on falsehood, because Allāh (Exalted is He) says:

O you who truly believe,
yā ayyuha 'lladhīna
you must practise true devotion to Allāh,
āmanu 'ttaqu 'llāha
and be together with the truthful.
wa kūnū maʿa 'ṣ-ṣādiqīn. (9:119)

These truthful heirs have come hand in hand. They never agree on falsehood, and their agreement is a proof of veracity, because their agreement is an act of worshipful obedience to the commandment of Allāh:

and be together with the truthful.
wa kūnū maʿa 'ṣ-ṣādiqīn. (9:119)

They do not seek to promote falsehood, by their unanimity and the unanimity of those who follow them, because they serve as a proof, and they are committed to the Truth. I am absolutely convinced that this radiant circle will endure, from Allāh's Messenger (Allāh bless him and give him peace) to the end of this world, without ever being devoid of the truthful. We beseech Allāh to let us be together with them, and to ensure that we are not diverted by the devils of humankind and the jinn, nor by this deceptive world.

This is our certainty and our conviction, obtained from Allāh's Messenger (Allāh bless him and give him peace) and his heirs. Praise be to Allāh, the Lord of All the Worlds. There is no might nor any power, except with Allāh, the All-High, the Almighty. May Allāh bless our master Muḥammad, his family and his Companions, and may He grant them peace.

The Thirteenth Call

In the Name of Allāh, the All-Merciful, the All-Compassionate.
Bismi'llāhi 'r-Raḥmāni 'r-Raḥīm.

O you who truly believe,
observe your duty to Allāh,
yā ayyuha 'lladhīna āmanu 'ttaqu 'llāha
with the devotion that is truly due to Him,
ḥaqqa tuqāti-hi
and do not die except as those
who have surrendered.
wa lā tamūtunna illā wa antum muslimīn.

And hold fast, all of you together,
to the rope of Allāh,
wa 'ʿtaṣimū bi-ḥabli 'llāhi jamīʿan
and do not separate.
And remember Allāh's favour unto you:
wa lā tafarraqū wa 'dhkurū niʿmata 'llāhi ʿalai-kum
how you were enemies
and He reconciled your hearts
idh kuntum aʿdāʾan fa-allafa baina qulūbi-kum
so that you became brothers by His grace.
fa-aṣbaḥtum bi-niʿmati-hi ikhwānā:
And you were on the brink of a pit of fire,
and He did save you from it.
wa kuntum ʿalā shafā ḥufratin mina 'n-nāri
fa-anqadha-kum min-hā.
Thus does Allāh make clear His signs to you,
ka-dhālika yubayyinu 'llāhu la-kum āyāti-hi
so that you may be guided aright.
laʿalla-kum tahtadūn. (3:102,103)

Having warned the believers to beware of the misguidance and deception of the unbelievers, in the preceding Qurʾānic verse,

Allāh (Exalted is He) has commanded the believers, in these verses, to practise all forms of worshipful obedience and good deeds of every kind. He has commanded them:

1. To practise true devotion to Allāh. In His own words:

   Observe your duty to Allāh
   [u] 'ttaqu 'llāha

2. To hold fast to the rope of Allāh. In His own words:

   And hold fast to the rope of Allāh
   wa '`taṣimū bi-ḥabli 'llāhi

3. To remember the gracious favours of Allāh. In His own words:

   And remember Allāh's favour unto you.
   wa 'dhkurū ni`mata 'llāhi `alai-kum

The reason for this arrangement in sequence is as follows: The conduct of a human being is bound to be motivated either by fearful apprehension or by hopeful aspiration, and fearful apprehension takes precedence over hopeful aspiration, because the repulsion of harm takes precedence over the procurement of benefit. Implicit in His saying:

> Observe your duty to Allāh,
> *[u] 'ttaqu 'llāha*
> with the devotion that is truly due to Him.
> *ḥaqqa tuqāti-hi*

—is the fear-inspiring prospect of Allāh's punishment [if this commandment is disobeyed]. He has then made this a reason for strict adherence to Allāh's religion, and for holding fast to the rope of Allāh. Then He has followed it with hopeful aspiration, in His saying:

> And remember Allāh's favour unto you.
> *wa 'dhkurū ni`mata 'llāhi `alai-kum*

It is as if He had said: "The fear of Allāh's punishment makes that necessary, and the abundance of Allāh's gracious favours also makes that necessary." Human conduct has thus been considered from every standpoint, and the conclusion, in each instance, is the necessity of your compliance with Allāh's commandment, and the necessity of your obedience to Allāh's judgment. It is clear, from all that we have mentioned, that the three points listed above have been set forth in the best possible sequence.[249]

Concerning the true devotion referred to in His summons:

> O you who truly believe, observe your duty to Allāh,
> *yā ayyuha 'lladhīna āmanu 'ttaqu 'llāha*
> with the devotion that is truly due to Him.
> *ḥaqqa tuqāti-hi*

—it was Ibn Mas'ūd (may Allāh be well pleased with him) who said: "[It means] that He must be obeyed and not disobeyed, that He must be remembered and not forgotten, and that He must be thanked and not treated with ingratitude."

> with the devotion that is truly due to Him.
> *ḥaqqa tuqāti-hi*

That is to say: "As He deserves to be treated with devotion," which means: "through the avoidance of all forms of disobedience towards Him."[250]

It has also been said that *ḥaqqa tuqāti-hi* means: "with true devotion and all that it entails, that being the utmost exertion in the performance of duty, and in the avoidance of things that are unlawful." This is in keeping with His saying:

> So practise true devotion to Allāh, as far as you are able.
> *fa-'ttaqu 'llāha ma 'staṭa'tum.* (64:16)[251]

In other words: "You must practise true devotion to the fullest extent, so that you omit nothing that is at all possible."[252]

Other interpretations include: (1) "The devotion that is truly due to Him is the performance of what is incumbent on the servant [of the Lord], to the extent of his ability, for His saying:

> So practise true devotion to Allāh, as far as you are able.
> *fa-'ttaqu 'llāha ma 'staṭa'tum.* (64:16)

—is an explanatory comment on the devotion that is truly due to Him."[253] (2) "True devotion means that its practitioner must neither exceed his own capacity, nor fall short thereof."[254]

Sa'īd ibn Jubair is reported as having said: "When this Qur'ānic verse [3:102] was revealed, the people set to work [on their religious practice] with intense zeal. They kept performing prayers, until the tendons of their calves and heels became sore, and ulcers developed on their foreheads. It was then that Allāh sent down, as a relief for the Muslims:

So practise true devotion to Allāh, as far as you are able.
fa-'ttaqu 'llāha ma 'staṭa'tum. (64:16)"

The devotion that is truly due to Him does require, nevertheless, that they must strive for Allāh's sake:

with all the effort He deserves.
ḥaqqa jihādi-h. (22:78)

They must not incur blame for sin, when striving for the sake of Allāh (Exalted is He). They must uphold justice for the sake of Allāh (Glory be to Him), even against themselves, their fathers and the mothers.[255]

According to one of the commentators: "The first part of this verse [3:102] has been abrogated, but the latter part of it:

and do not die except as those who have surrendered.
wa lā tamūtunna illā wa antum muslimīn.

—has not been abrogated." The majority of the experts have maintained, however, that there are no grounds for this talk of abrogation. They have presented the following arguments against it:

1. It is related, on the authority of Mu'ādh, that the Prophet (blessing and peace be upon him) once asked him: "Do you know what is Allāh's right over His servants?" He replied: "Allāh and His Messenger know best!" He then said: "It is that they must worship Him, and that they must not associate anything with Him."[256] It is inconceivable that this might be abrogated.

2. The meaning of His saying:

Observe your duty to Allāh,
[u] 'ttaqu 'llāha
with the devotion that is truly due to Him.
ḥaqqa tuqāti-hi

—is: "[Observe your duty to Him] as He is entitled to be treated with devotion, that is to say, by avoiding all forms of disobedience to Him." The likes of this cannot conceivably by abrogated, because that would provide a licence for certain forms of disobedience.

3. In view of the above, the meaning of this verse and the meaning of His saying (Exalted is He):

So practise true devotion to Allāh, as far as you are able.
fa-'ttaqu 'llāha ma 'staṭa'tum. (64:16)

—must be one and the same, because, if someone practises true devotion to Allāh, as far as he is able, he is doing so with the devotion that is truly due to Him. The import of His saying:

> with the devotion that is truly due to Him.
> *ḥaqqa tuqāti-hi*

—cannot conceivably be: "with devotion that is humanly impossible," because Allāh (Glory be to Him and Exalted is He) has made it known that:

> Allāh does not charge any soul except to the extent of its capacity.
> *lā yukallifu 'llāhu nafsan illā wus'a-hā.* (2:285)

—and [underdeveloped] capacity [*wus'*] is less than [full-fledged] ability [*ṭāqa*]. Similar to this verse is His saying:

> And strive for Allāh's sake with all the effort He deserves.
> *wa jāhidū fi 'llāhi ḥaqqa jihādi-h.* (22:78)[257]

According to the religious scholars, the stages of true devotion are three:

1. Devout abstinence from polytheistic association [*shirk*].
2. Devout abstinence from heretical innovation [*bid'a*].
3. Devout abstinence from non-fundamental acts of disobedience.

Allāh (Exalted is He) has mentioned them all in one Qur'ānic verse, namely:

> To those who believe and do good works
> *laisa 'ala 'lladhīna āmanū wa 'amilu 'ṣ-ṣāliḥāti*
> no sin shall be ascribed for what they may have eaten.
> *junāḥun fī-mā ṭa'imū*
> So practise true devotion, and do good works;
> *idhā ma 'ttaqaw wa āmanū wa 'amilu 'ṣ-ṣāliḥāti*
> and again: practise true devotion, and believe;
> *thumma 'ttaqaw wa āmanū*
> and once again: practise true devotion, and be active in goodness.
> *thumma 'ttaqaw wa aḥsanū:*
> Allāh loves those who are active in goodness.
> *wa 'llāhu yuḥibbu 'l-muḥsinīn.* (5:93)

1. The first form of true devotion is devout abstinence from polytheistic association [*shirk*], and the corresponding form of belief is the affirmation of Oneness [*tawḥīd*].

2. The second form of true devotion is devout abstinence from heretical innovation [*bid῾a*], and the corresponding form of belief is that which is accompanied by affirmation of the doctrines of the Sunna and the Community.

3. The third form of true devotion is devout abstinence from non-fundamental acts of disobedience. There is no [verbal] affirmation at this stage, since its corresponding expression takes the form of active goodness [*iḥsān*], which means worshipful obedience and steadfastness therein. In other words, of the three stages of true devotion, this is the stage of those who are steadfast in worshipful obedience.

The Qur᾽ānic verse refers to all three stages: the stage of true belief, the stage of the Sunna, and the stage of worshipful obedience and steadfastness therein. This is what the religious scholars have said, in explanation of the meaning of true devotion. To this I would add: It contains an allusion to the active goodness [*iḥsān*] of which the Prophet (blessing and peace be upon him) said:

> You must worship Allāh as if you could see Him, for even if you do not see Him, He surely sees you.[258]

In another well-known tradition [*khabar*], the Prophet (Allāh bless him and give him peace) is reported as having said:

> The truly devout are only called truly devout because of their abstinence from that which is harmless, as a precaution against that which is positively harmful.[259]

It was al-Ghazālī (may Allāh bestow His mercy upon him) who said [of true devotion]: "How much reward and recompense Allāh has promised in exchange for it, and how much happiness He has added thereto! From the sum of all of those blessings, let me count twelve items for you:

1. Praise and commendation:

> But if you persevere and practise true devotion,
> *wa in taṣbirū wa tattaqū*
> then that is of the steadfast heart of things.
> *fa-inna dhālika min ῾azmi 'l-umūr*. (3:186)

2. Safekeeping and protection from the enemies:

> But if you persevere and practise true devotion,
> *wa in taṣbirū wa tattaqū*
> their guile will never harm you.
> *lā yaḍurru-kum kaid-hum shai᾽ā*: (3:120)

3. Helpful support and assistance:

> Surely Allāh is with those who are truly devoted [to Him],
> *inna 'llāha ma'a 'lladhīna 'ttaqaw*
> and those who are active in goodness.
> *wa 'lladhīna hum muḥsinūn.* (16:128)

> And know that Allāh
> *wa ''lamū anna 'llāha*
> is with those who are truly devoted [to Him].
> *ma'a 'l-muttaqīn.* (9:36)

4. Deliverance from severe hardships, and the provision of lawful sustenance:

> And whenever someone practises true devotion to Allāh,
> *wa man yattaqi 'llāha*
> He will prepare a way out for him, and He will provide
> *yaj'al la-hu makhrajā: wa yarzuq-hu*
> for him from sources he could never imagine.
> *min ḥaithu lā yaḥtasib.* (65:2,3)

5. Improvement of conduct:

> O you who truly believe, practise true devotion to Allāh,
> *yā ayyuha 'lladhīna āmanu 'ttaqu 'llāha*
> and speak words that get straight to the point.
> *wa qūlū qawlan sadīdā.*
> He will adjust your works for you.
> *yuṣliḥ la-kum a'māla-kum.* (33:70,71)

6. Forgiveness of sins:

> And He will forgive you your sins.
> *wa yaghfir la-kum dhunūba-kum.* (33:71)

7. The love of Allāh:

> Allāh loves those who are truly devoted [to Him].
> *inna 'llāha yuḥibbu 'l-muttaqīn.* (9:4)

8. Acceptance:

> Allāh accepts only from those who are truly devout.
> *inna-mā yataqabbalu 'llāhu mina 'l-muttaqīn.* (5:27)

9. Honour and high esteem:

> Surely the noblest among you in the sight of Allāh
> *inna akrama-kum 'inda 'llāhi*

is the one of you who is most truly devout.
atqā-kum. (49:13)

10. Good tidings at the point of death:

Those who truly believe and practise true devotion,
alladhīna āmanū wa kānū yattaqūn. (10:63)
theirs are good tidings in the life of this world and in the Hereafter.
la-humu 'l-bushrā fi 'l-ḥayāti 'd-dunyā wa fi 'l-ākhira. (10:63,64)

11. Salvation from the Fire of Hell:

Then We shall rescue those who practised true devotion,
thumma nunajji 'lladhīna 'ttaqaw
and leave the evildoers crouching there.
wa nadharu 'ẓ-ẓālimīna fī-hā jithiyyā. (19:72)

While far removed from it will be the truly devout.
wa sa-yujannabu-ha 'l-atqā. (92:17)

12. Everlasting life in the Garden of Paradise:

And for a Garden as wide as are the heavens and the earth,
wa jannatin ʿarḍu-ha 's-samāwātu wa 'l-arḍu
which has been made ready for those who are truly devoted.
uʿiddat li'l-muttaqīn. (3:133)

"This description of all that is good, and of blissful happiness in the Two Abodes [this world and the Hereafter], comes under the heading of true devotion, so do not forget to earn your share of it, O man!"[260]

Let us now consider the words of Allāh (Exalted is He):

and do not die except as those who have surrendered.
wa lā tamūtunna illā wa antum muslimīn.

That is to say: "You must hold fast to the religion of Islām, and cling to it with all your might, so that, when death overtakes you, it will find you in that condition. You will then die in the state of surrender [*islām*]." The purpose is to command adherence to Islām.[261] That is because, provided they are able to remain steadfast in their commitment to Islām, until death comes to them, it will find them in the state of surrender [*islām*]. Death will coincide with surrender, to the extent that surrender has entered their capability. The same meaning is even more explicit in His saying:

Allāh has chosen for you the [true] religion;
inna 'llāha 'ṣṭafā la-kum 'd-dīna

so do not die except as men who have surrendered [to Him].
fa-lā tamūtunna illā wa antum muslimūn. (2:132)[262]

❧ ☙

and do not die except as those who have surrendered.
wa lā tamūtunna illā wa antum muslimīn.

In other words: "[Do not die unless you are] sincerely devoting your whole beings to Allāh (Almighty and Glorious is He), granting no partnership in them to anything whatsoever apart from Him."

According to one of those who specialize in reality: "In a context like this, Islām does not signify the performance of religious deeds, but rather the inner faith, because deeds are hardly feasible in the state of dying. That is why, in the supplication at the funeral prayer [*duʿāʾ ṣalāt al-janāza*], it is customary to utter the entreaty:

"'O Allāh, as for those of us whom You have kept alive, let them live in accordance with Islām. As for those of us whom You have caused to die, let them die in accordance with true faith [*īmān*].'

"Islām is thus mentioned in the first instance, and faith in the second."[263]

As reported on the authority of Ibn ʿAbbās (may Allāh be well pleased with him and his father): "Allāh's Messenger (Allāh bless him and give him peace) recited this Qurʾānic verse:

Observe your duty to Allāh,
āmanu 'ttaqu 'llāha
with the devotion that is truly due to Him.
ḥaqqa tuqāti-hi
and do not die except as those who have surrendered.
wa lā tamūtunna illā wa antum muslimīn.

"Then he said: 'If a single drop of the [bitter juice of the infernal tree called] *zaqqūm* were to fall into the abode of this world, it would spoil the means of sustenance of all the people of this world. Just imagine, then, how must it be for someone whose whole diet consists of it!'"[264]

And hold fast, all of you together, to the rope of Allāh,
wa 'ʿtaṣimū bi-ḥabli 'llāhi jamīʿan
and do not separate.
wa lā tafarraqū

That is to say: "Cling tight to the religion of Allāh, all of you together, and do not separate from it. Do not differ over the religion, as those before you differed, they being the Jews and the Christians."[265] Allāh has commanded them to persist in holding fast to what is like the root of all virtues and acts of worshipful obedience. As you must also be aware, everyone who walks on the delicate path is afraid that his foot might slip. If he clings tight to a rope that is tied, at both ends, to the sides of that path, he can feel secure from fear. There can be no doubt that the Path of Truth is a delicate path, and that the foot of many a creature has slipped off it. If someone holds fast to the guidance of Allāh, and follows His signposts, only then can he feel secure from fear. The "rope" referred to here is symbolic, it seems, of everything that enables one to arrive at the Truth by the path of the religion. There are many interpretations of the "rope," and each of the traditional commentators has mentioned one of them, for instance:

• According to Ibn ʿAbbās (may Allāh bestow His mercy upon him and his father): "In this context, the rope signifies the covenant mentioned in His saying:

> And fulfil your covenant with Me,
> *wa awfū bi-ʿahdī*
> for then I shall fulfil My covenant with you.
> *ūfi bi-ʿahdi-kum.* (2:40)

"He also said:

> Except with a rope from Allāh and a rope from men.
> *illā bi-ḥablin mina'llāhi wa ḥablin mina 'n-nāsi.* (3:112)

"In other words: 'with a covenant.' He called the covenant a 'rope' because it serves to remove the fear from going to any place one wishes. If someone has a rope to grasp, he loses his sense of fear."

• According to some, it means the Qurʾān. As related on the authority of ʿAlī (may Allāh be well pleased with him), the Prophet (Allāh bless him and give him peace) once said: "There may be serious discord in the future." Someone asked: "What will be the way out of it?" He replied:

> The Book of Allāh. It contains information about those before you, and news of those after you, and judgment on what comes between you. It is the stout rope of Allāh.[266]

As related on the authority of Abū Mas'ūd al-Khudrī, the Prophet (Allāh bless him and give him peace) also said:

> I am leaving you with the two heavyweights: the Book of Allāh (Exalted is He), which is a rope extended from the heaven to the earth, and my stock, meaning the people of my household.[267]

• According to others, it means Allāh's religion, or obedience to Allāh, or sincere repentance.

• Yet others maintain that it represents the community [*jamā'a*], because Allāh (Exalted is He) has followed His mention of it with His injunction:

> and do not separate.
> *wa lā tafarraqū.*

All of these interpretations are quite close to one another. For the sake of verification, consider the situation of a man descending into a well, and how he clings to a rope, to prevent himself from falling down into it. In similar fashion, the Book of Allāh, His covenant, His religion, obedience to Him, and agreement with the community of the believers, all provide protection against falling into the pit of Hell. That constitutes a rope belonging to Allāh, and they have been commanded to hold fast thereto.[268]

> and do not separate.
> *wa lā tafarraqū.*

That is to say: "As the Jews and Christians split into separate factions." According to some, however, the meaning is rather: "As you used to separate in the Age of Ignorance, turning your backs on one another, becoming enemies of one another, and killing one another."

It has also been taken to mean: "Do not introduce innovations that may result in sectarian division, causing you to lose the sense of community and harmony that you now enjoy." It conveys not only the prohibition of separation and dissension, but also the commandment of concord and community, because the truth can only be one, and whatever conflicts with it can only be ignorance and error. That being the case, it is necessary to prohibit dissension and sectarianism in the religion. Those disruptive tendencies were the custom of the people of the Age of Ignorance, so the believers have been forbidden to follow them.[269]

It is reported in the *Ṣaḥīḥ* of Muslim, on the authority of Abū Huraira, that Allāh's Messenger (Allāh bless him and give him peace) once said:

> Allāh approves of three things for you, and disapproves of three thing for you. He approves of your worshipping Him, and not associating anything with Him; of your holding fast, all together, to the rope of Allāh, and not separating; and of your being loyal to those whom Allāh appoints to command you. He disapproves of three things for you: tittle-tattle, asking too many questions, and the wasteful use of property.[270]

> And remember Allāh's favour unto you:
> *wa 'dhkurū niʿmata 'llāhi ʿalai-kum*
> how you were enemies and He reconciled your hearts
> *idh kuntum aʿdāʾan fa-allafa baina qulūbi-kum*
> so that you became brothers by His grace.
> *fa-aṣbaḥtum bi-niʿmati-hi ikhwānā:*

That is to say: "Remember His gracious favour unto you, O you Arabs, when you were bitter enemies before Islām, and he reconciled your hearts through Islām, and brought you together in faith." When Allāh brought Islām, and those entered it who entered it, they became loving brothers, closely interconnected in the Essence of Allāh, helpful to one another in the pursuit of righteousness and true devotion.[271]

You must also know that Allāh's favours to His creatures may be either worldly or Otherworldly, and that He (Exalted is He) has mentioned them both in this Qurʾānic verse. As for the worldly favour, it is described in His saying (Exalted is He):

> how you were enemies and He reconciled your hearts
> *idh kuntum aʿdāʾan fa-allafa baina qulūbi-kum*
> so that you became brothers by His grace.
> *fa-aṣbaḥtum bi-niʿmati-hi ikhwānā:*

As for the Otherworldly favour, it is referred to in His saying:

> And you were on the brink of a pit of fire,
> *wa kuntum ʿalā shafā ḥufratin mina 'n-nāri*
> and He did save you from it.
> *fa-anqadha-kum min-hā.*[272]

Concerning His saying:

> how you were enemies and He reconciled your hearts
> *idh kuntum aʿdāʾan fa-allafa baina qulūbi-kum*
> so that you became brothers by His grace.
> *fa-aṣbaḥtum bi-niʿmati-hi ikhwānā.*

—some say that it refers to the Jew, when he sowed discord between the tribes of Aws and Khazraj. Each of them planned to wage war on the other, so the Messenger (Allāh bless him and give him peace) went out to them, and did not stop relating to them on friendly terms, until the discord was peacefully resolved.

The tribes of Aws and Khazraj were descended from full brothers, but enmity developed between the two, and wars dragged on for a hundred and twenty years, until Allāh extinguished that flame with Islām. The Qur'ānic verse is thus an allusion to them and their conditions. Prior to Islām, they were always fighting each other and hating each other, but then, when Allāh honoured them with Islām, they became loving brothers, mutually sympathetic and loyal. They also became brethren for the sake of Allāh. This is reminiscent of a similar verse, in which He has said:

> And He has reconciled their hearts.
> *wa allafa baina qulūbi-him:*
> If you had spent all that is in the earth,
> *law anfaqta mā fi 'l-arḍi jamī'an*
> you could not have reconciled their hearts,
> *mā allafta baina qulūbi-him*
> but Allāh has reconciled them.
> *wa lākinna 'llāha allafa baina-hum.* (8:63)

Whenever someone concentrates his attention on this world, he is sure to be hostile towards most of his fellow creatures. By contrast, if someone keeps his attention focused on the service of Allāh (Exalted is He), he will not be hostile to anyone. The reason is that he views creatures [*khalq*] from the standpoint of the Truth [*Ḥaqq*], so he sees each one as a prisoner in the grasp of the Divine decree and destiny, and he is therefore hostile to none.

This is why it has been said: "In the case of someone who knows by direct experience, when he gives instructions, he does so in a kind and friendly spirit. He acts as a sincere adviser, who does not scold or criticize, for he is endowed with insight into destiny, through access to Allāh's secret."[273]

> And you were on the brink of a pit of fire,
> *wa kuntum 'alā shafā ḥufratin mina 'n-nāri*
> and He did save you from it.
> *fa-anqadha-kum min-hā.*

In other words: "You were on the verge of falling into the Fire of Hell, but Allāh saved you from it by means of Islām."[274] After having explained the worldly favour, Allāh (Exalted is He) has gone on to describe the Otherworldly favour. If they were to die in unbelief, they would fall into the Fire of Hell. The life after which they would fall into the Fire is therefore likened to sitting on the brink of it. This points to the insignificance of that span of life, for, between that life and the death that would result in falling into the pit, there is nothing more than the space between the edge of a thing and that thing itself.[275]

> Thus does Allāh make clear His signs to you,
> *ka-dhālika yubayyinu 'llāhu la-kum āyāti-hi*
> so that you may be guided aright.
> *la'alla-kum tahtadūn.*

That is to say: "By providing you with such a clear explanation, He is making all the signs apparent to you, so that you may be guided by them towards happiness in the two abodes [this world and the Hereafter],"[276] or: "so that you may expect to receive right guidance," or: "so that you may be guided in the right direction, and towards the means of obtaining spiritual reward."[277]

As you must understand, Allāh (Exalted is He) has commanded the believers to practise true devotion, first of all, then, secondly, to hold fast [to His rope], and then, thirdly, to remember His favour. The intelligent person must therefore comply with Allāh's commandment, obey His judgment, hold fast to His rope, and avoid separation in the religion. It was Shu'aib Abū Madyan ash-Shādhilī (may Allāh bestow His mercy upon him) who said: "What a vast difference there is between someone who aspires to the lovely maidens and palaces [of Paradise], and someone who aspires to the lifting of the veils and everlasting presence [with the Lord]."

According to Sahl (may Allāh be well pleased with him): "The servant has nothing but his Master, and his best prospect is to return to his Master. If he is guilty of disobedience, he must say: 'My Lord, pardon me!' Then, when He pardons him, he must say: 'My Lord, relent towards me!' Then, when He relents towards him, he must say: 'My Lord, grant me Your enabling grace, so that I may do good work!' Then, when he sets to work, he must say: My Lord, grant me Your enabling grace, so that I may be sincerely devoted!' Then, when he becomes sincerely devoted, he must say: 'My Lord, accept from me!' The intelligent person must hold fast to this stout rope, and to the exemplary practice of the chief of the Messengers (may Allāh bless him and his family and his Companions, and may He grant them peace)."[278]

These are my own comments:

It befits you that your business should begin with true devotion, and that it should conclude therewith. There is no way to guarantee a good conclusion, except by obediently following the Prophet (Allāh bless him and give him peace) in what he has brought from his Lord (Almighty and Glorious is He).

You must therefore adhere to the Book and the Sunna, struggling with your lower self and your passions, and securing the safety of your heart by frequent remembrance of Allāh (Exalted is He), in a complete and constant state of awareness, and beseeching your Lord to accept this from you. At the same time, you must be firmly convinced that your worshipful service is not worthy of your Lord (Almighty and Glorious is He).

O Allāh, include us among those to whom the finest reward has gone forth from You, through Your mercy, O Most Merciful of the merciful. *Āmīn*. Peace be upon the Messengers, and praise be to Allāh, the Lord of All the Worlds. There is no might nor any power, except with Allāh, the All-High, the Almighty. May Allāh bless our master Muḥammad, his family and his Companions, and may He grant them peace.

The Fourteenth Call

In the Name of Allāh, the All-Merciful, the All-Compassionate.
Bismi'llāhi 'r-Raḥmāni 'r-Raḥīm.

O you who truly believe,
do not take for confidants
yā ayyuha 'lladhīna āmanū lā tattakhidhū biṭānatan
others apart from your own folk.
They would spare no pains to ruin you.
min dūni-kum lā ya'lūna-kum khabalā:
They love what you find distressing.
Hatred is revealed by their mouths,
waddū mā 'anittum qad badati 'l-baghḍā'u min afwāhi-him
but what their breasts conceal is greater.
wa mā tukhfī ṣudūru-hum akbar:
We have made plain for you the signs,
if you will understand.
qad bayyannā la-kumu 'l-āyāti in kuntum ta'qilūn. (3:118)

Allāh (Exalted is He) has warned the believers against taking the hypocrites for confidants, to whom they impart their secrets, for He has said:

> O you who truly believe, do not take for confidants
> *yā ayyuha 'lladhīna āmanū lā tattakhidhū biṭānatan*
> others apart from your own folk.
> *min dūni-kum.*

In other words: "You must not take the hypocrites for friends, loving them, making them privy to your secrets, and treating them as close companions, rather than your fellow believers."[279]

> Do not take for confidants....
> *lā tattakhidhū biṭānatan....*

A man's confidant [*biṭāna*] is someone who enjoys his intimate trust, someone to whom he imparts his secrets, feeling sure that he can count on his discretion. He resembles the article of clothing [also called *biṭāna* in Arabic] that is worn next to the stomach [*baṭn*]. He also resembles the undergarment [*shiʿār*]. As the Prophet (blessing and peace be upon him) once said:

> The Helpers are an undergarment, while the ordinary people are an overgarment [*al-Anṣāru shiʿār wa 'n-nāsu dithār*].

The undergarment is called a *shiʿār* because it is worn next to the skin [*shaʿr*] of the body. The *dithār* is the article of clothing worn over the *shiʿār*.[280]

Concerning the exact identity of those with whom Allāh has forbidden the believers to associate closely, the experts hold several different opinions:

1. They must be the Jews. That is because the Muslims used to consult them in connection with their business affairs. They related to them on intimate terms, on account of their links of fosterage and contractual ties, supposing that, despite their difference in the sphere of religion, they would deal with them honestly in matters of livelihood. Allāh (Exalted is He) therefore forbade them, in this Qurʾānic verse, to maintain such confidential relations.

2. They must be the hypocrites. That is because the believers used to be deceived by the apparent meaning of what the hypocrites told them. They assumed that they were truthful, so they imparted their secrets to them, and made them privy to their hidden conditions. Allāh (Exalted is He) therefore prevented them from continuing along those lines.

3. They are the unbelievers, of every sort and kind. This is unmistakably implicit in His saying (Exalted is He):

> Do not take for confidants others apart from your own folk.
> *yā ayyuha 'lladhīna āmanū lā tattakhidhū biṭānatan min dūni-kum.*

—since He has barred the believers from taking any others for confidants, apart from the believers, and that amounts to a prohibition against all the unbelievers. He has also said (Exalted is He):

> O you who truly believe, do not choose My enemy
> *yā ayyuha 'lladhīna āmanū lā tattadhidhū ʿaduwwī*

and your enemy for friends.
wa ʿaduwwa-kum awliyāʾa. (60:1)

This view is further substantiated by the following traditional report: Someone said to ʿUmar ibn al-Khaṭṭāb (may Allāh be well pleased with him): "Here is a man from the town of al-Ḥīra. He is a Christian, and no one is known to have a stronger memory, nor a finer style of handwriting, than he. Do you consider it proper for us to choose him for a scribe?" ʿUmar refused to allow that, and he said: "You would then be choosing a confidant from among those who are not believers." ʿUmar (may Allāh be well pleased with him) based his judgment on this Qurʾānic verse, taking it as evidence of the prohibition against choosing [non-Muslim] confidants.[281] He also said (may Allāh be well pleased with him): "For assistance with matters for which you are responsible, you must appeal to those who are afraid of offending Allāh (Exalted is He)."[282]

others apart from your own folk
min dūni-kum

That is to say: "others apart from the Muslims," or: "apart from the members of your religious community [*milla*]." As for His expression:

They would spare no pains to ruin you
lā yaʾlūna-kum khabalā:

—the term *khabāl* signifies corruption and damage, so the meaning is: "They would spare no effort to corrupt you,"[283] or: "They would never desist from their endeavour to harm you and corrupt you."[284]

They love what you find distressing.
waddū mā ʿanittum

In other words: "They take pleasure in your hardship, and in whatever serious injury befalls you."[285] The Arabic verb *wadda* is synonymous with *aḥabba* [both meaning "to love"]. The noun *ʿanat* [corresponding to the verbal form *ʿanittum*] means the distress of injury and hardship. Another verb, from the same root, occurs in His saying (Exalted is He):

Had Allāh willed, He could have caused you distress.
wa law shāʾa ʾllāhu la-aʿnata-kum. (2:220)

The implicit meaning [of *waddū mā ʿanittum*] is: "They would love to harm you in your religion." As for the distinction in meaning between

His saying:

> They would spare no pains to ruin you.
> *lā yaʾlūna-kum khabalā:*

—and His expression:

> They love what you find distressing.
> *waddū mā ʿanittum*

—several interpretations have been suggested, namely:

1. "They would spare no effort to corrupt your religion, but even if they are incapable of that, they love to see you thrown into the worst kinds of harm."
2. "They would spare no effort to corrupt your affairs in this world, but even if they are incapable of that, their hearts go on loving whatever causes you distress."
3. "They would spare no effort to corrupt your affairs, but if even they cannot do so, because of some external obstacle, the love of that prospect never leaves their hearts."[286]

> Hatred is revealed by their mouths,
> *qad badati 'l-baghḍāʾu min afwāhi-him*
> but what their breasts conceal is greater.
> *wa mā tukhfī ṣudūru-hum akbar:*

That is to say: "The signs of enmity towards you are on their tongues. They cannot keep their hatred of you confined within their hearts, so they express it through their mouths, although the hatred they feel for you is even greater than what they display."[287] In the traditional commentary on this verse, these two interpretations are noted:

1. Where the hypocrite is concerned, the content of his speech will inevitably provide evidence of his hypocrisy, and his deviation from the path of integrity in love and sincerity in giving advice. He is like those referred to in His saying (Exalted is He):

> And you will surely know them in the twisting of their speech.
> *wa la-taʿrifanna-hum fī laḥni 'l-qawl.* (47:30)

2. It was Qatāda who said: "The hatred felt by the hypocrites and the unbelievers becomes apparent to their friends, through their making

one another aware of it. If we take this as applying to the Jews, the interpretation of His saying:

> Hatred is revealed by their mouths.
> *qad badati 'l-baghḍā'u min afwāhi-him.*

—must be: 'They reveal their disavowal of your Prophet and your Book, and they associate you with ignorance and stupidity.' If someone views another person from the conviction that he is committed to ignorance and stupidity, he cannot possibly love that other person. No indeed, he is bound to hate him. Such is the import of His saying:

> Hatred is revealed by their mouths."[288]
> *qad badati 'l-baghḍā'u min afwāhi-him.*

❧ ❧

> We have made plain for you the signs, if you will understand.
> *qad bayyannā la-kumu 'l-āyāti in kuntum ta'qilūn.*

That is to say: "We have made clear to you the signs that point to the necessity of sincere devotion to the religion, and of friendship for the believers and hostility towards the unbelievers, if you are intelligent people." This condition is appended to serve as a jolt and a stimulant to the feelings, as though He had said: "If you are a believer, do not cause people harm!"

According to Ibn Jarīr, the meaning is: "If you will understand what Allāh intends by His commandment and His prohibition."[289]

As related by al-Bukhārī, on the authority of Abū Sa'īd al-Khudrī, Allāh's Messenger (Allāh bless him and give him peace) once said:

> Allāh never sent any Prophet, nor appointed any Caliph [*Khalīfa*], unless he had two confidants: a confidant who would command him to do what is good, and would urge him to do so, and a confidant who would command him to do what is bad, and would urge him to do so. He who enjoys protection is he whom Allāh protects![290]

As this Qur'ānic verse clearly indicates, the bearer of another man's secrets must be one of his own kind (meaning one of the people of faith), a reliable and trustworthy individual. It may happen that a man imparts his secret to someone he has not tried and tested in every situation, so his secret becomes public knowledge. You must therefore not be deluded by a person's outward appearance, before you become familiar with his conscience.

According to Imām al-Ghazālī (may Allāh bestow His mercy upon him): "You must not depend on the love of someone you have not yet put to the test of real experience. This means that you must keep him company over a period of time, in one particular home or place, so that you can learn from experience how he reacts to being in or out of work, and to being rich or poor. Other alternatives include travelling with him, or dealing with him financially, or falling on hard times and turning to him in need. If you find yourself well content with him in all these situations, you should adopt him as a father to you, if he is your senior, or as a son, if he is your junior, or as a brother, if he is about the same age as yourself."

If you hear that your brothers have indulged in backbiting, or you see them misbehaving, or they do something that affects you badly, you should entrust your situation to Allāh, and not preoccupy yourself with seeking retribution. That would merely add to the damage, and your life would be wasted on that useless preoccupation. To quote one of the eloquent sayings of az-Zamakhsharī: "As a means of checking the stupid fool, there is nothing like shunning him, and when it comes to giving him free rein, there is nothing like arguing with him."

It was Dhu'n-Nūn (may Allāh bestow His mercy upon him) who said: "In keeping company with Allāh, nothing is appropriate except harmonious compliance; with one's fellow creatures, nothing but sincere advice; with one's own lower self, nothing but opposition; and with the devil, nothing but enmity. The servant [of the Lord] must therefore make haste to acquire goodness of character, and to accustom the lower self to patient endurance of things it finds unpleasant, so that he may succeed along with those who are triumphantly successful."[291]

These are my own remarks:

If the believer is one who loves security in his religion and his worldly estate, he must not be friendly with anyone whose conduct is at odds with the Sacred Law, who distracts him from remembrance and acts of worshipful obedience, and who involves him in matters that do not concern him. If a person stays with the people of righteousness, he will become familiar with the source of his own righteousness, because his senses and his inner feeling will develop in response to what he hears and sees.

O Allāh, keep us safe from all forms of disobedience! Allāh's Messenger (Allāh bless him and give him peace) once said:

> If a crime is committed on the earth, and someone is present as a witness, but disapproves of it, he is like someone who is absent from it, and if someone is absent from it, but approves of it, he is like someone who is present when it is committed.[292]

Most of us are not among those who, when they see something wrong and unfair [*munkar*], attempt to correct it. We prefer to remain silent, and so become participants in the offence. We must take refuge with Allāh from this condition, due to our weakness. If a person's faith is strong, he has nothing to fear from anyone but his Master, because He is his Helper. If he utters no protest against that which is wrong and unfair, then at the very least, if he cannot prevent it with his tongue, he must loathe it with his heart, for that is the weakest form of faith.

According to Ibrāhīm al-Khawwāṣ (sanctified be his innermost being): "The medicines of the heart are five:

1. Recitation of the Qur'ān with meticulous attention.
2. Emptiness of the stomach.
3. Keeping vigil through the night.
4. Humble submission to Allāh.
5. Sitting in the company of the righteous.

"You must cultivate these virtues with great diligence, for then you may attain to purification and spiritual development."

O Allāh, grant us the ability to accomplish all that. *Āmīn*. Peace be upon the Messengers, and praise be to Allāh, the Lord of All the Worlds. There is no might nor any power, except with Allāh, the All-High, the Almighty. May Allāh bless our master Muḥammad, his family and his Companions, and may He grant them peace.

The Fifteenth Call

In the Name of Allāh, the All-Merciful, the All-Compassionate.
Bismi'llāhi 'r-Raḥmāni 'r-Raḥīm.

O you who truly believe,
yā ayyuha 'lladhīna āmanū
do not consume usury,
doubling and redoubling.
lā ta'kulu 'r-ribā aḍ'āfan muḍā'afa:
Practise true devotion to Allāh,
so that you may prosper.
wa 'ttaqu 'llāha la'alla-kum tufliḥūn.

And be on your guard against the Fire
prepared for the unbelievers.
wa 'ttaqu 'n-nāra 'llatī u'iddat li'l-kāfirīn.

And obey Allāh and the Messenger,
wa aṭī'u 'llāha wa 'r-Rasūla
for then you may be treated mercifully.
la'alla-kum turḥamūn. (3:130–32)

This is a prohibition from Allāh (Exalted is He) to His servants, for He has said:

> O you who truly believe,
> *yā ayyuha 'lladhīna āmanū*
> do not consume usury, doubling and redoubling.
> *lā ta'kulu 'r-ribā aḍ'āfan muḍā'afa.*

He has forbidden them to practise usury, and He has added a rebuke for the multiplication thereof, which was common practice in the Age of Ignorance. Ibn Kathīr has told us: "In the Age of Ignorance, when payment of a debt fell due, the creditor used to say: 'Either you settle now, or else you will have to pay usurious interest!' If the debtor did not settle there and then, he would be allowed an extra period, and the due amount would be increased. This would be repeated on an annual basis, so that a small initial sum would eventually be multiplied into a very large one." The subject has been discussed in detail in the section devoted to the Tenth Call, which occurs in the Sūra of the Cow [*al-Baqara*].

> Practise true devotion to Allāh
> *wa 'ttaqu 'llāha*

That is to say: "Be devoutly on guard against His torment, by refraining from what He has forbidden."[293] You must know that true devotion to Allāh is strictly required, with regard to this prohibition, and that prosperity depends upon it. If someone consumes usury, and does not practise true devotion, prosperity will elude him. This Qur'ānic verse provides proof that usury is one of the major sins [*kabā'ir*], not one of the minor offences [*ṣaghā'ir*].[294]

> so that you may prosper.
> *la'alla-kum tufliḥūn.*

In other words: "So that you may be included among those who are triumphantly successful."

The Qur'ānic verse contains a general notification, in which the degrees of multiplication mentioned are neither exclusive nor conditional. The point is simply to explain how people were situated in the Age of Ignorance, and to denounce this practice of theirs, as a flagrant injustice and a plain transgression, since they used to charge multiple compound interest.

It was Abū Ḥayyān who said: "They were forbidden to continue that disgusting situation, in which, through the practice of usury [*ribā*], a trivial borrowing would sometimes result in a claim on the debtor's entire estate. Allāh's expression:

> redoubling.
> *muḍā'afa.*

—indicates that they used to repeat the doubling year after year. Usury is unlawful in all its varieties, so its prohibition is not confined to this particular case."

> And be on your guard against the Fire prepared for the unbelievers.
> *wa 'ttaqu 'n-nāra 'llatī u'iddat li'l-kāfirīn.*

That is to say: "Beware of the Fire of Hell, which has been made ready to receive the unbelievers."[295] This Qurʾānic verse invites the question: Does it prove that the Fire has already been created, or not? The answer must be yes, because He uses the word *uʿiddat* [has been prepared], which is a verb in the past tense, so the thing it refers to must have come into existence.[296]

When the Fire is described as having been prepared for the unbelievers, the intention is to stress the importance of taking precautions. The believers have been told to be on their guard against sinful acts of disobedience. They must also realize that, if they fail to practise true devotion, they will be made to enter the Fire prepared for the unbelievers. Once their minds have grasped the enormity of the punishment in store for the unbelievers, their avoidance of sinful acts of disobedience will be more complete. This is reminiscent of how a father may scare his son, by saying: "If you disobey me, I shall make you enter the lions' den!" That does not mean that no others will enter that den, and the same applies here [in the case of the Fire].[297]

> And be on your guard against the Fire prepared for the unbelievers.
> *wa 'ttaqu 'n-nāra 'llatī uʿiddat li'l-kāfirīn.*

—by being on guard against following their example and their way of doing business. Notice is here being given that the Fire has been made ready for the unbelievers, and, incidentally, for those who are guilty of sinful disobedience.

Imām Abū Ḥanīfa (may Allāh be well pleased with him) used to say: "This is the most frightening verse in the whole Qurʾān, since Allāh has threatened the believers with the Fire prepared for the unbelievers, if they do not practise true devotion to Him, with regard to all His various prohibitions."[298]

This is the hottest level [of Hell], where its torment will be multiplied. It is different from the Fire to be entered by the disobedient sinners of the Community of our master Muḥammad (Allāh bless him and give him peace), for it is lower than that.

The Qurʾānic verse also indicates that the consumption of usury [*ribā*] takes place on the edge of the pit of unbelief.[299] (In other words, it is the work of unbelief.)

> And obey Allāh and the Messenger,
> *wa aṭī'u 'llāha wa 'r-Rasūla*
> for then you may be treated mercifully.
> *la'alla-kum turḥamūn.*

That is to say: "Obey Allāh and the Messenger, so that you will be included among the righteous, who obtain the mercy of Allāh."[300] When He mentioned the threat, He followed it with mention of the promise, in keeping with His regular custom in the Splendid Qur'ān. In other words: "You must obey Allāh in everything He has commanded you to do, and in everything He has forbidden you to do. You must also obey the Messenger, who has brought you His commandments and His prohibitions, hoping for His mercy."

> for then you may....
> *la'alla-kum....*

When used in such contexts, the words *la'alla* and *'asā* point to the rarity ['*izza*] of achieving the proposition to which they are prefixed.[301] (The expression '*izza 'sh-shai'* means that something is in short supply, and therefore unlikely to be found.)

It was al-Qāshānī who said: "It is no secret, to the intelligent person, that the threat against usury is expressed with the force of exaggeration, since the term *la'alla* [maybe; perhaps] is prefixed to the success of one who guards against it and avoids it. The point is that, since the possibility of success and the hope of achieving it are dependent on the avoidance of usury, it is necessary to deny them success, if they do not avoid it and guard against it with their faith.

"Then He has threatened them with the Fire that has been prepared for the unbelievers, despite the fact that they are believers. What disaster could be more enormous, than one that imposes the chastisement of the unbelievers on the believers? What could be more severe than issuing a harsh warning, and then extending that harshness by commanding obedience to Allāh and His Messenger, while intimating that the consumer of usury is totally engrossed in sinful disobedience, and that he has no obedience at all?

"Then He has made the hope of the believers dependent on obedience to Allāh and His Messenger, thereby imparting the knowledge that there can be no hope of mercy, with this kind of sinful disobedience.

This compels the believers to despair of His mercy, because of its being withheld from them on account of their disobedience. Notice how He has inserted harshness into the threat, to the point of linking it to the unbelievers in terms of recompense and punishment!"

You must also know that usury incites greed for the interests of this world. That greed is doubled and redoubled, ad infinitum, as the Prophet (blessing and peace be upon him) has said:

> If the son of Adam had two valleys of gold, he would eagerly desire to add a third to the two of them. Nothing but dust will fill the belly of the son of Adam.[302]

Greed is one of the descending levels of the Fires of Hell, and that is why He said:

> And be on your guard against the Fire prepared for the unbelievers.
> *wa 'ttaqu 'n-nāra 'llatī uʿiddat li'l-kāfirīn.*

Greed for this world is blameworthy and forbidden, as is the effort to acquire and accumulate its benefits. Spending freely on good causes, according preferential treatment to others, detachment from this world, and contentment with little of what it has to offer, all these are praiseworthy and have been commanded. This is indicated by His saying (Exalted is He):

> Allāh has blighted usury and made almsgiving fruitful.
> *yamḥaqu 'llāhu 'r-ribā wa yurbi 'ṣ-ṣadaqāt:* (2:276)

As reported by Abū Bakr al-Warrāq, Abū Ḥanīfa (may Allāh bestow His mercy upon him) once said: "There is one sin that most often snatches faith from the servant [of the Lord] at death, and snatches his faith away most quickly, and that is wrong done to His servants. You must therefore be devoutly wary of Allāh, O believers, and do not wrong the servants of Allāh, by taking their possessions from their hands without proper cause, for that is a major offence. May Allāh protect us, and all of you, from bad conditions."[303]

Allāh has forbidden His servants to practise usury, which includes the lending of one item and demanding two in repayment, yet He has asked you to make Him a single loan, which He will repay seven hundred times or more, ad infinitum. This signifies that noble generosity cannot be ascribed to creatures, but is purely an attribute of Allāh (Glory be to Him).[304]

These are my own remarks:

You must be on guard against your own lower self [*nafs*], in case it asks you for that which is unlawful. This is addressed to you, since you come first, because you are a true believer [*muʾmin*] and faith [*īmān*] is your attribute. It is your duty to obey the commandment of Allāh. You must wake up from the slumber of heedlessness. You must give up hoarding, stinginess, and greed for the vanities of this world. Our sustenance is allotted by destiny. The sphere of the lawful is sufficient for us, and departure from it is part of our misconduct. You must therefore feel a genuine sense of shame before Allāh, so that you may reach the station of those who are truly devoted to Allāh, and to whom Allāh has promised the Garden of Paradise:

> Surely those who practise true devotion will be in a station secure.
> *inna 'l-muttaqīna fī maqāmin amīn.* (44:51)

If someone lays claim to love, without obedience, his claim is false and unacceptable.

We beg Allāh to grant us the blessing of worshipful obedience and faithful following. He is indeed Capable of all things. Peace be upon the Messengers, and praise be to Allāh, the Lord of All the Worlds. There is no might nor any power, except with Allāh, the All-High, the Almighty. May Allāh bless our master Muḥammad, his family and his Companions, and may He grant them peace.

The Sixteenth Call

In the Name of Allāh, the All-Merciful, the All-Compassionate.
Bismi'llāhi 'r-Raḥmāni 'r-Raḥīm.

O you who truly believe,
yā ayyuha 'lladhīna āmanū
if you obey those who disbelieve,
in tuṭīʿu 'lladhīna kafarū
they will make you turn back on your heels,
yaruddū-kum ʿalā aʿqābi-kum
and you will turn back as losers.
fa-tanqalibū khāsirīn.

But Allāh is your Protector,
bali 'llāhu Mawlā-kum
and He is the Best of helpers.
wa Huwa Khairu 'n-nāṣirīn.

We shall cast terror into the hearts
of those who disbelieve
sa-nulqī fī qulūbi 'lladhīna kafaru 'r-ruʿba
because they ascribe to Allāh partners,
bi-mā ashrakū bi'llāhi
for which no warrant has been revealed.
mā lam yunazzil bi-hi sulṭānā:
Their habitation is the Fire,
wa maʾwā-humu 'n-nār:
and awful is the abode of the wrongdoers.
wa biʾsa mathwa 'ẓ-ẓālimīn.

Allāh has made good His promise to you,
wa la-qad ṣadaqa-kumu 'llāhu
since you were slaughtering them by His leave,
waʿda-hu idh taḥussūna-hum bi-idhni-h:
until when your courage failed you
and you disagreed
ḥattā idhā fashiltum wa tanāzaʿtum

about the order and you disobeyed,
fī 'l-amri wa ʿaṣaitum
after He had shown you what you long for.
min baʿdi mā arā-kum mā tuḥibbūn:
There are some of you who desire this world,
min-kum man yurīdu 'd-dunyā
and there are some of you
who desire the Hereafter.
wa min-kum man yurīdu 'l-ākhira:
Then He made you flee from them,
thumma ṣarafa-kum ʿan-hum
so that He might try you.
li-yabtaliya-kum
Yet now He has forgiven you.
wa la-qad ʿafā ʿan-kum
Allāh is the Lord of kindness to believers.
wa 'llāhu Dhū faḍlin ʿala 'l-muʾminīn. (3:149–52)

The noble Qurʾānic verses continue to enumerate the mishaps of the Uḥud campaign, and the lessons and admonitions contained therein. They tell of the causes of the rout, the disgraceful rôle of the hypocrites in that campaign, and their conspiracy against the Islāmic cause, by thwarting the decisions of the believers.

The context of the revelation was as follows: When Allāh's Messenger (Allāh bless him and give him peace) returned to Medina, after they had suffered what befell them on the Day of Uḥud, some people among his Companions said: "From where did this disaster strike us, when Allāh had promised us victory?" It was then that Allāh (Exalted is He) sent down:

> Allāh has made good His promise to you…
> *wa la-qad ṣadaqa-kumu 'llāhu…*

—to His saying:

> There are some of you who desire this world.
> *min-kum man yurīdu 'd-dunyā.*

—referring to the marksmen who did what they did on the Day of Uḥud.

> O you who truly believe,
> *yā ayyuha 'lladhīna āmanū*
> if you obey those who disbelieve….
> *in tuṭīʿu 'lladhīna kafarū….*

That is to say: "If you obey the unbelievers and the hypocrites in what they command you to do…."[305] This also sets out to prevent the believers from following the unbelievers, by explaining the harmful consequences thereof, when they have just been urged to follow the example of the helpers of the Prophets (peace be upon them):

> And with how many a Prophet
> *wa ka-ayyin min Nabiyyin*
> have there been a number of devoted men who fought.
> *qātala maʿa-hum ribbiyūna kathīr:*
> They did not quail because of what befell them in Allāh's cause,
> *fa-mā wahanū li-mā aṣāba-hum fī sabīli 'llāhi*
> nor did they weaken, nor were they brought low.
> *wa mā ḍaʿafū wa ma 'stakānū*
> Allāh loves those who are patient.
> *wa 'llāhu yuḥibbu 'ṣ-ṣābirīn.* (3:146)

That is a description of their excellent virtues, and a summons to show profound concern for its implications. When they are addressed in terms of belief, they are reminded of a condition that precludes any such obedience [to the unbelievers], so the admonition is couched in a most perfect expression.[306]

> those who disbelieve
> *[u] 'lladhīna kafarū*

This is said to be an allusion to Abū Sufyān, for he was the elder of the tribe [of Quraish] on that day. According to as-Suddī: "The reference is to Abū Sufyān, for he was the tree of troubles."[307]

There are some who say: "[This refers to] the hypocrites, ʿAbdu'llāh ibn Ubayy and his followers, for they were the ones who sowed doubts in the hearts of the weak, and who said: 'If Muḥammad had been Allāh's Messenger, this disaster would not have occurred. He is only a man like any other, with one day to his advantage and one day to his disadvantage, so come back to your religion, to which you used to belong.'" Others have said: "[It refers to] the Jews, because there was a tribe of Jews in Medina, and they used to sow doubts in the hearts of the Muslims, especially at the time of this disaster."

As for His saying (Exalted is He):

> if you obey those who disbelieve….
> *in tuṭīʿu 'lladhīna kafarū….*

—it cannot apply to obeying them in everything they say. The meaning must be more precise. Some say: "If you obey them in every error they command you to commit...," while others say: "If you obey them in what they commanded you to do on the Day of Uḥud, which means abandoning Islām...." Yet others say: "[If you obey them] in the conference," or, "in refraining from warfare," which is consistent with their saying:

> "If they had been with us,
> *law kānū ʿinda-nā*
> they would not have died or been killed."
> *mā mātū wa mā qutilū.* (3:156)[308]

❧ ❧

> they will make you turn back on your heels,
> *yaruddū-kum ʿalā aʿqābi-kum*
> and you will turn back as losers.
> *fa-tanqalibū khāsirīn.*

That is to say: "They will make you turn back to unbelief, so they will return you to loss, and there is no greater loss than substituting unbelief for belief."[309] As you should know, when the word "loss" is unqualified, it must include the loss of this world and that of the Hereafter.

As for the loss of this world, there is nothing more excruciating in this world, for intelligent people, than submission and abasement to the enemy, and having to show oneself in need of him.

To this I would add: The most hostile of enemies include the lower self and passionate desire, and submission to them results in loss, the loss of this world and of the Hereafter. As Allāh (Exalted is He) has said:

> Have you seen him who makes his desire his god,
> *a-fa-raʿaita mani 'ttakhadha ilāha-hu*
> and Allāh sends him astray purposely?
> *hawā-hu wa aḍalla-hu 'llāhu ʿalā ʿilmin.* (45:23)

As for the loss of the Hereafter, that is deprivation of the everlasting reward, and falling into the eternal punishment.[310]

> But Allāh is your Protector,
> *bali 'llāhu Mawlā-kum*
> and He is the Best of helpers.
> *wa Huwa Khairu 'n-nāṣirīn.*

The word *bal* indicates dismissal [of the notion expressed in the preceding sentence]. In other words: "They are not helpers to you, that you should obey them, but [*bal*] Allāh is your Helper, so obey His commandment."[311] The point is that you obey the unbelievers so that they will help you and assist you to achieve your goals, but this is due to ignorance, because they are actually incapable and confused. The intelligent person seeks help from Allāh (Exalted is He), because He is the One who will help you against the enemy, and defend you against his cunning. He has then explained that He is the Best of helpers. If the offer of help was not intended by His saying:

> your Protector, and He is the Best of helpers.
> *Mawlā-kum wa Huwa Khairu 'n-nāṣirīn.*

—it would not make sense for Him to use this expression here. Allāh (Exalted is He) is the Best of helpers for several reasons:

1. Allāh (Exalted is He) is the One who is Capable of helping you in whatever you wish. He is the All-Knowing, the One from whom your supplication and your entreaty are not concealed. He is the Generous One, who is not niggardly in His munificence. The mutual assistance of His servants is contrary to that, in each of these respects.
2. He will help you in this world and the Hereafter, but this is not true of anyone other than Him.
3. He will help you before you ask, and even before you recognize your need. As He has said:

> Say: "Who guards you in the night or in the day?"
> *qul man yakla'u-kum bi'l-laili wa 'n-nāhāri.* (21:42)

Here again, this is not true of anyone other than Him.[312]

> We shall cast terror into the hearts of those who disbelieve
> *sa-nulqī fī qulūbi 'lladhīna kafaru 'r-ru'ba*

Allāh (Exalted is He) has given the believers the good tidings that terror will be cast into the hearts of their enemies, for He has said:

> We shall cast...
> *sa-nulqī...*

In other words: "We shall throw fear and alarm into their hearts."[313] The clear implication is that Allāh (Exalted is He) is the One who instils terror and security, hope and dread, and other such feelings, in the hearts of His servants. As the Prophet (peace be upon him) once said:

> The hearts of the servants are in Allāh's hand; He transforms them as He will.[314]

It is therefore incumbent on the servant to entreat Allāh in all humility, and beg Him to grant triumph over the unbelieving lower selves, especially the instigating self [*an-nafs al-ammāra*], for, if he follows its passsion and obeys it in its lustful desire, it will reduce him to the lowest of the low in human nature, and he will be turned into a loser.[315]

> because they ascribe to Allāh partners,
> *bi-mā ashrakū bi'llāhi*
> for which no warrant has been revealed.
> *mā lam yunazzil bi-hi sulṭānā:*

That is to say: "because of their attribution of partners to Allāh, and their worship of other gods together with Him, with neither evidence nor proof [of their divinity]."[316] It is clearly implied that what is relevant to the affirmation of Divine Oneness [*tawḥīd*] is the heavenly proof, not futile opinions and desires. That proof is called a revealed warrant, because it strengthens the case against the adversary and holds sway over him.[317]

> Their habitation is the Fire,
> *wa ma'wā-humu 'n-nār:*
> and awful is the abode of the wrongdoers.
> *wa bi'sa mathwa 'ẓ-ẓālimīn.*

In other words: "Their dwelling-place is the Fire, and awful is the residence of the wrongdoers, the Fire of Hell. In this world they are terrified, and in the Hereafter they will be tormented." In the words of the Prophetic tradition [*ḥadīth*]:

> By terror I was helped to cover the distance of a month-long journey.[318]

> Allāh has made good His promise to you
> *wa la-qad ṣadaqa-kumu 'llāhu*
> since you were slaughtering them by His leave
> *wa'da-hu idh taḥussūna-hum bi-idhni-h:*

That is to say: "Allāh has provided you with all the help he promised you against your enemy, since you were killing them at a rapid pace, and mowing them down with your swords, in accordance with Allāh's will and His decree."[319]

As you should also know, this Qur'ānic verse is linked to what precedes it, in several respects, including:

1. When Allāh's Messenger (Allāh bless him and give him peace) and his Companions returned to Medina, after suffering what they had suffered at Uḥud, some of his Companions said: "How did this come to afflict us, when Allāh had promised us victory?" It was then that Allāh (Exalted is He) sent down this verse.

2. According to some, this promise may be contained in His saying:

> We shall cast terror into the hearts of those who disbelieve.
> *sa-nulqī fi qulūbi 'lladhīna kafaru 'r-ruʿba.*

3. Abū Muslim said: "Having promised them, in the preceding verse, that He would cast terror into their hearts, Allāh confirmed that by reminding them that He had indeed fulfilled the promise of victory in the battle of Uḥud. He had promised them support on condition that they do their duty and endure with patience, so, when they met that condition, Allāh (Exalted is He) had undoubtedly discharged the stipulation and given them support, but then, when they ignored the condition, they forfeited the stipulated assistance."

> since you were slaughtering them by His leave
> *waʿda-hu idh taḥussūna-hum bi-idhni-h:*

As we have mentioned in the story of Uḥud, the Prophet (Allāh bless him and give him peace) set Uḥud behind his back, and turned to face Medina. He stationed the archers beside the hill, commanding them to maintain their position there, and not to depart, whether victory favoured the Mulims or went against them. Then, when the polytheists [*mushrikūn*] approached, the archers started shooting their arrows, while the others struck them with their swords, until they were put to flight, with the Muslims following in their tracks and slaughtering them. According to al-Laith: "The term *ḥass* means rapid slaughter, so *taḥussūna-hum* means: 'you were killing them in a great massacre.'"

> by His leave

bi-idhni-h:

In other words: "with His knowledge." The point being made is as follows: "Allāh (Exalted is He) promised you victory, subject to the condition of dutiful devotion and patience in worshipful obedience. So long as you continued to fulfil that condition, He discharged His promise and helped you against your enemies, but then, when you disregarded the condition and your Lord's commandment, needless to say, that assistance ceased."[320]

until when your courage failed you
ḥattā idhā fashiltum
and you disagreed about the order
wa tanāzaʿtum fi 'l-amri

That is to say: "when you became cowardly and weak, and disagreed about the order to hold the position on the hill."

and you disobeyed,
wa ʿaṣaitum
after He had shown you what you long for.
min baʿdi mā arā-kum mā tuḥibbūn:

In other words: "You disobeyed the order of the Messenger (Allāh bless him and give him peace), after victory had been your ally."[321]

Disagreement came about as follows: The Prophet (blessing and peace be upon him) had commanded the archers not to leave their position, under any circumstances, and he had appointed ʿAbdu'llāh ibn Jubair as their captain. Then, when the polytheists appeared on the scene, the archers attacked them with a heavy shower of arrows, until the polytheists were routed. ʿAbdu'llāh then said: "The Messenger (Allāh bless him and give him peace) has instructed us not to leave this place." They rejected him, however, and set off in serach of the booty. ʿAbdu'llāh stayed behind, with a small band of fewer than ten, until the polytheists killed them. This explains the reference to disagreement.

This Qurʾānic verse gives rise to several questions:

1. Why is the failure of courage mentioned before disagreement and disobedience?

Answer: When the people witnessed the rout of the unbelievers, and eagerly desired to seize the booty, they lost their sense of firm commitment, due to their greed for the spoils. Then they fell into disagreement, by arguing: "Should we go off in search of the booty, or should we not?" Then they [disobediently] concentrated their efforts on the search for the booty.

2. Since leaving those positions was an act of disobedience committed by a particular group, why is this punishment referred to in general terms?

Answer: While it is true that this expression is general, it is rendered specific by His saying, immediately afterwards:

> There are some of you who desire this world,
> *min-kum man yurīdu 'd-dunyā*
> and there are some of you who desire the Hereafter.
> *wa min-kum man yurīdu 'l-ākhira:*

3. What is significance of His saying:

> after He had shown you what you long for?
> *min ba'di mā arā-kum mā tuḥibbūn:*

Answer: Its purpose is to stress the enormity of the disobedience. Since they had witnessed how Allāh (Exalted is He) had honoured them by fulfilling the promise, it was their duty to refrain from disobedience. It is hardly surprising, therefore, that when they committed it, Allāh stripped them of that honour and made them taste the evil consequence of their behaviour.[322]

> There are some of you who desire this world
> *min-kum man yurīdu 'd-dunyā*

That is to say: "[There are some of you who desire] the booty, meaning those who deserted the hill."

> and there are some of you who desire the Hereafter.
> *wa min-kum man yurīdu 'l-ākhira:*

In other words: "[There are some of you who desire] Allāh's reward, they being the ten who held fast to their post, together with their captain, 'Abdu'llāh ibn Jubair (may Allāh be well pleased with him), and then became martyrs."

> Then He made you flee from them,
> *thumma ṣarafa-kum 'an-hum*
> so that He might try you.
> *li-yabtaliya-kum*

That is to say: "He made you turn in flight from the unbelievers, in order to test your faith,"[323] or, "in order to inflict tribulation upon you, so that you might repent to Him and seek His forgiveness." According to some, the meaning is: "so that He might try you, though He knows best, in order to distinguish the believer from the hypocrite, and those who wish for this world from those who wish for the Hereafter."[324]

> Yet now He has forgiven you.
> *wa la-qad ʿafā ʿan-kum*

In other words: "He has pardoned you in spite of disobedience." As this implies, the sin would have deserved even more than what befell them, had it not been for Allāh's pardon. This explains why He said:

> Allāh is the Lord of kindness to believers.
> *wa 'llāhu Dhū faḍlin ʿala 'l-muʾminīn.*

That is to say: "He is the Lord of blessed grace for the believers, at all times and in all situations."[325]

The obvious interpretation is that this applies in the wake of any sin committed by them. According to al-Qāḍī: "If that sin is one of the minor sins [*ṣaghāʾir*], it is correct to say that He has described Himself as having pardoned them without repentance. If it is classed as one of the major sins [*kabāʾir*], however, one must understand that their repentance is implied, since the evidence proves that the perpetrator of a major sin, if he does not repent, will not be included among the recipients of pardon and forgiveness."

As you should know, the sin [under consideration here] is undoubtedly a major sin, because they contravened the explicit instruction of Allāh's Messenger (Allāh bless him and give him peace). That contravention became a cause of the Muslims' defeat, and led to the slaughter of a great number of their distinguished figures. Nevertheless, as indicated by the obvious meaning of the Qurʾānic verse, Allāh (Exalted is He) pardoned them without repentance, because there is no mention of repentance. This must therefore serve as evidence that Allāh (Exalted is He) does sometimes pardon those who are guilty of major sins.[326]

According to al-Baiḍāwī (may Allāh bestow His mercy upon him): "His saying (Exalted is He):

> Yet now He has forgiven you.
> *wa la-qad ʿafā ʿan-kum*

—is a bestowal of gracious favour, since He recognized their remorse over their contravention. This must therefore serve as evidence that Allāh (Exalted is He) does sometimes pardon those who are gulity of major sins, contrary to the assertion of the Muʿtazila."[327]

According to the commentary on *al-Jalālain*, concerning His saying (Exalted is He):

> Yet now He has forgiven you.
> *wa la-qad ʿafā ʿan-kum*

—that is to say: "[He has forgiven you] as a bestowal of gracious favour, because of His knowledge of your remorse over your contravention." This is based on a report from Abu 's-Saʿūd. According to aṣ-Ṣāwī, the meaning is: "He has pardoned the believer among you, after his repentance."

To this I would add: They did set out (may Allāh be well pleased with them) to wage the sacred struggle [*jihād*] with a genuine intention, for the sake of Allāh's countenance (Glorious and Exalted is He), and this resulted in what they experienced because of their dedicated striving. Then they disagreed about whether to leave in pursuit of the booty, or to hold their position on the hill. They disobeyed, but Allāh took notice of their intention, because this intention was originally sound. Even though the noble Qurʾānic verse does not refer explicitly to their repentance, Allāh's knowledge of their sound intentions was sufficient, so He pardoned them. At the end of the verse, Allāh bears witness to their belief, in categorical terms, when He says:

> Yet now He has forgiven you.
> *wa la-qad ʿafā ʿan-kum*
> Allāh is the Lord of kindness to believers.
> *wa 'llāhu Dhū faḍlin ʿala 'l-muʾminīn.*

They are believers by virtue of Allāh's testimony to their belief, and—praise be to Allāh!—their Lord (Glorious and Exalted is He) has pardoned them, even though the noble Qurʾānic verse does not refer explicitly to their repentance. Since Allāh does sometimes pardon some of those who are guilty of major sins, without repentance, it is possible that He pardoned these Companions (may Allāh be well pleased with them), through the blessed grace of Allāh's Messenger (Allāh bless him and give him peace), without repentance. The purpose of this review is to examine the opinions of the commentators concerning their repentance, or their lack of repentance.

You should know that patience, certainty, trust in Allāh, detachment from this world and its vanities, and scrupulous avoidance of opposition to the Messenger (Allāh bless him and give him peace), are factors that necessarily contribute to victory and triumph. As for cowardice, disagreement, attachment to this world, and disobedience to the Messenger (Allāh bless him and give him peace), they are bound to result in trial and tribulation, and in distraction from the enemy. If someone wishes for support against the enemies, both external and internal, he must not follow any other path than that prescribed by the Sacred Law. He must be content with trial and tribulation, and not worry about his afterlife. Indeed, he should find the trouble of seeking the truth more delightful than the bliss of this world and the Hereafter, and he must patiently endure the very painful hardships imposed by the religion.[328]

ʿAlī (may Allāh ennoble his countenance) is reported as having said: "I once said to Abū Bakr, the Champion of Truth [*aṣ-Ṣiddīq*] (may Allāh be well pleased with him), the Caliph of Allāh's Messenger (Allāh bless him and give him peace): 'O Caliph of Allāh's Messenger (Allāh bless him and give him peace), how did you obtain this rank, thereby outstripping us by a distance?' He said: 'By these five things:

"'1. I discovered that people are of two kinds, the seeker of this world and the seeker of the Hereafter, so I became the seeker of the Master.

"'2. Since I entered Islām, I have never eaten my fill of the food of this world, because the delight of intimate knowledge of Allāh has distracted me from the pleasures of this world's food.

"'3. Since I entered Islām, I have never quenched my thirst with the drink of this world, because the love of Allāh has distracted me from the drink of this world.

"'4. Whenever two kinds of work presented themselves to me, the work of this world and the work of the Hereafter, I always chose the work of the Hereafter, rather than the work of this world.

"'5. I befriended the Prophet (Allāh bless him and give him peace) and I found his companionship very pleasing.'"

To this I would add: That is why he did not separate himself for one moment from his close companionship. He eventually entered with him into the cave, and suffered the painful hardships that he suffered for his sake (Allāh bless him and give him peace). Despite those hardships, his heart never swerved from its close connection with him, and he absolutely never considered the idea of contradicting him.[329]

The value of every individual is that of the object to which he aspires. If a person's aspiration is this world, his value is mean and paltry, like this world. If a person's aspiration is the Hereafter, his worth is noble. If someone's aspiration is Lordly [*Rabbāniyya*], he is the chieftain of his time.[330]

These are my own comments:

Allāh is the Source of enabling grace! The Qurʾānic verse contains tremendous benefit for those who ponder and reflect.

As the noble verse points out, the embrace of Allāh's knowledge encompasses all things. He fully Aware of the intentions of His servants, and of what their consciences contain, whether it be sincere devotion combined with desire for this world, or devotion that is both sincere and absolute, accompanied by indifference to this world, so that they desire nothing but His countenance (Exalted is He).

It is therefore appropriate for the human being to supervise his heart, and not to encourage his lower self, because he cannot tell the difference between what is beneficial and what is detrimental, though he supposes that he acting for the best. This is the condition of most creatures, except those who are protected by Allāh. They cannot distinguish between the bad and the good, nor between the good and the best. They cannot escape from the attributes of the instigating self [*an-nafs al-ammāra*]— because only "he who knows himself knows his Lord"—until they become privy to the reality of certainty [*ḥaqīqat al-yaqīn*], and enter the station of active goodness, which Allāh's Messenger (Allāh bless him and give him peace) has described for us:

> You must worship Allāh as if you could see Him, for, even if you do not see Him, He surely sees you![331]

They will then become truly acquainted with the attributes of Allāh, including knowledge, power, hearing and sight, recognizing that Allāh is All-Powerful, All-Hearing, All-Seeing, that He sees and hears what our consciences contain, that nothing is hidden from Allāh, and that:

> He knows the treachery of the eyes,
> *ya῾lamu khā᾿inata 'l-a῾yuni*
> and what the breasts conceal.
> *wa mā tukhfi 'ṣ-ṣudūr.* (40:19)

They will thus have reached their destination, as Allāh (Exalted is He) has said:

> And a gulf is set between them and what they desire.
> *wa ḥīla baina-hum wa baina mā yashtahūna.* (34:54)

In other words: "[between them and their desire] to return to this world," or, according to al-Fakhr ar-Rāzī: "to the pleasures of this world and its delight." This world was an obstacle for them, until they came to be together with the truthful, whose company Allāh urged them to keep, by His saying:

> And be together with the truthful.
> *wa kūnū ma῾a 'ṣ-ṣādiqīn.* (9:119)

The purpose of being together with them is to benefit by their spiritual progress, their spiritual states, their wise counsel and their supplication. Religious problems become easy to solve in their company, because they are the authorized inheritors in this domain.

Suppose it be said: "We have other means of knowing what is best, and we do not need the fellowship of the righteously truthful." Our reply will be: "There is no one more excellent, in the sight of Allāh, than the Companions of Allāh's Messenger (Allāh bless him and give him peace), after the Prophets (may Allāh's blessing be upon them all). Just listen to what Ibn Mas῾ūd (may Allāh be well pleased with him) had to say:

"'We were not aware that any of the Companions of the Prophet (Allāh bless him and give him peace) desired this world, until the Day of Uḥud arrived, and down came the noble Qur᾿ānic verse:

> There are some of you who desire this world,
> *min-kum man yurīdu 'd-dunyā*
> and there are some of you who desire the Hereafter.'"
> *wa min-kum man yurīdu 'l-ākhira.*

These are illumined by the lights of the Messenger (Allāh bless him and give him peace) and his Qur'ānic standards of conduct, together with their truthful certainty, and they are like stars by which to be guided. Allāh has said about them:

> And the first to lead the way,
> *wa 's-sābiqūna 'l-awwalūna*
> the Emigrants and the Helpers,
> *mina 'l-Muhājirīna wa 'l-Anṣāri*
> and those who followed them in active goodness,
> *wa 'lladhīna 'ttaba'ū-hum bi-iḥsānin*
> Allāh is well pleased with them
> *raḍiya 'llāhu 'an-hum*
> and they are well pleased with Him,
> *wa raḍū 'an-hu*
> and He has made ready for them
> *wa a'adda la-hum*
> Gardens underneath which rivers flow,
> *jannātin tajrī min taḥti-ha 'l-anhāru*
> wherein they will abide forever.
> *khālidīna fī-hā abadā:*
> That is the mighty triumph.
> *dhālika 'l-fawzu 'l-'aẓīm.* (9:100)

See how Allāh rebuked them for a single act of disobedience, and took them to task for a single act of disobedience. It is therefore incumbent on the believer to be on guard against non-compliance in following the most noble Messenger (Allāh bless him and give him peace) and his Sunna, to the full extent of his capacity and ability. He is obliged to prefer his commandment, and obedience to him, over the passionate desire of his own lower self. Allāh (Exalted is He) has said:

> Whatever the Messenger gives you, accept it,
> *wa mā ātā-kumu 'r-Rasūlu fa-khudhū-hu*
> and from whatever he forbids you, abstain.
> *wa mā nahā-kum 'anhu fa-'ntahū.* (59:7)

He has also said (Exalted is He):

> And let those who conspire to evade his orders beware,
> *fa-l'-yaḥdhari 'lladhīna yukhālifūna 'an amri-hi*
> lest grief or painful torment befall them.
> *an tuṣība-hum fitnatun aw yuṣība-hum 'adhābun alīm.* (24:63)

The believer must not abandon his path and his procedure, so that he may obtain his intercession (Allāh bless him and give him peace), if Allāh so wills.

O Allāh, grant us the ability to accomplish all that. *Āmīn*. Peace be upon the Messengers, and praise be to Allāh, the Lord of All the Worlds. There is no might nor any power, except with Allāh, the All-High, the Almighty. May Allāh bless our master Muḥammad, his family and his Companions, and may He grant them peace.

The Seventeenth Call

In the Name of Allāh, the All-Merciful, the All-Compassionate.
Bismi'llāhi 'r-Raḥmāni 'r-Raḥīm.

O you who truly believe, do not be
like those who disbelieved
yā ayyuha 'lladhīna āmanū lā takūnū
ka-'lladhīna kafarū
and said to their brethren
who travelled in the land
wa qālū li-ikhwāni-him idhā ḍarabū fi 'l-arḍi
or were fighting in the fray:
"If they had been with us
aw kānū ghuzzan law kānū ʿinda-nā
they would not have died or been killed;"
mā mātū wa mā qutilū
so that Allāh would make it
an anguish in their hearts.
li-yajʿala 'llāhu dhālika ḥasratan fī qulūbi-him:
Allāh gives life and causes death,
wa 'llāhu yuḥyī wa yumīt:
and Allāh is All-Seeing of what you do.
wa 'llāhu bi-mā taʿmalūna Baṣīr.

And even if you are slain in Allāh's cause,
or die therein,
wa la-in qutiltum fī sabīli 'llāhi aw muttum
forgiveness from Allāh and mercy
la-maghfiratun mina 'llāhi wa raḥmatun
are surely better than what they accumulate.
khairun mimmā yajmaʿūn.

Even if you die or are killed,
to Allāh you will surely be gathered!
wa la-in muttum aw qutiltum la-ila 'llāhi tuḥsharūn.
(3:156–8)

You should know that the hypocrites used to reproach the believers, during the sacred struggle with the unbelievers, by saying [about their brothers]:

> "If they had been with us,
> *law kānū ʿinda-nā*
> they would not have died or been killed."
> *mā mātū wa mā qutilū:*

Then some of the believers showed signs of lassitude and faint-heartedness in the sacred struggle, until there befell on the Day of Uḥud what befell, and Allāh graciously pardoned them. He therefore implied, in this Qurʾānic verse, that it is forbidden for any of the believers to say the kind of thing that they [the hypocrites] had said. He told them, in effect: "O you who truly believe, you must not say, to someone about to embark on the sacred struggle: 'If you had not gone forth, you would not have died or been killed,' for Allāh, and He alone, is the One who gives life and causes death. If He decrees survival for someone, he will not be killed in the sacred struggle, and if He decrees death for him, he will not survive, even if he does not engage in the fight." This is the import of His saying:

> Allāh gives life and causes death.
> *wa 'llāhu yuḥyī wa yumīt.*

Furthermore, in the case of someone who was killed in the sacred struggle, even if he had not gone forth to the fray, he would still have died, quite inevitably. Since he was bound to die, it was better for him to be slain in the sacred struggle, and thereby merit the mighty reward, than to die to no avail. This is the import of His saying:

> And even if you are slain in Allāh's cause, or die therein,
> *wa la-in qutiltum fi sabīli 'llāhi aw muttum*
> forgiveness from Allāh and mercy
> *la-maghfiratun mina 'llāhi wa raḥmatun*
> are surely better than what they accumulate.
> *khairun mimmā yajmaʿūn.*

As for His saying:

> O you who truly believe, do not be like those who disbelieved.
> *yā ayyuha 'lladhīna āmanū lā takūnū ka-'lladhīna kafarū.*

—the experts have differed over the meaning of his expression:

> like those who disbelieved.
> *ka-'lladhīna kafarū.*

Some of them have said: "This should be taken in the unrestricted sense, to include every unbeliever who says anything of that kind, regardless of whether or not he is a hypocrite."

Others have said: "It is a particular reference to the hypocrites, because these Qur᾿ānic verses, from the first of them to the last, are specifically concerned with the exposition of their states. That is to say, it refers to ʿAbdu'llāh ibn Ubayy and his companions."

On the basis of these two statements, the Qur᾿ānic verse implies that belief is not a matter of verbal affirmation, since if it were so, the hyprocrite would be a believer, and if he were a believer, Allāh would not have called him an unbeliever.[332]

> and said to their brethren who travelled in the land
> *wa qālū li-ikhwāni-him idhā ḍarabū fi 'l-arḍi*
> or were fighting in the fray....
> *aw kānū ghuzzan....*

In other words: "They said to their brethren among the people guilty of hypocrisy, when they went forth on expeditions and military campaigns, or went forth as warriors in the cause of Allāh...."[333]

According to some, "their brethren" means their brethren in hypocrisy and unbelief, while others take it to mean their blood-related brothers, they being Muslims.

The overall meaning is: "When they [their brethren] travelled in the land, and died, or were fighting in the fray, and were killed,[334] they made that a pretext for discouraging people from engaging in the sacred struggle." That was because the love of life is inherent in human nature, and so is the hatred of death and killing."

Another point worth noting: [When He quotes the hypocrites as saying: "if they *had been* with us..."] Allāh (Exalted is He) is couching a future projection in the past tense of the verb. As this indicates, the purpose is not to convey the literal sense of the statement, but rather to stress their seriousness and their earnestness in seeking to implant this doubt.[335]

"If they had been with us they would not have died or been killed."
law kānū ʿinda-nā mā mātū wa mā qutilū:

That is to say: "If only they had stayed with us, and had not ventured forth, they would not have died or been killed." Allāh (Exalted is He) has then gone on to say, in order to refute them:

so that Allāh would make it an anguish in their hearts.
li-yajʿala 'llāhu dhālika ḥasratan fī qulūbi-him:

In other words: "They said what they said, so that their corrupt belief would become a painful anguish in their feelings."[336] This also refers to the Day of Resurrection, because of the ignominy and remorse they will then experience, in contrast to the blissful happiness and gracious favour experienced by the Muslims.[337]

Allāh gives life and causes death.
wa 'llāhu yuḥyī wa yumīt.

This is a refutation of their statement and their conviction. It signifies: "He (Glory be to Him) is the Giver of Life and the Cause of Death, so death cannot be prevented by staying at home."[338] Allāh (Exalted is He) may keep the traveller and the warrior alive, and He may cause the resident and the stay-at-home to die.[339] As for the Muslim who is firmly convinced that death and life do not exist, except by the foreordainment of Allāh(Exalted is He), and by His destiny and His decree, this painful anguish will not invade his heart."[340]

As I see it, nothing else has any influence on life and death. Allāh's knowledge does not alter, His judgment is not overturned, and His decree does not change. He does whatever He wills, and He decides whatever He wishes.

and Allāh is All-Seeing of what you do.
wa 'llāhu bi-mā taʿmalūna Baṣīr.

This is an admonition to the believers, warning them not to imitate the hypocrites. He is Supervising the actions of His servants, so that He may recompense them appropriately, with good for good and bad for bad.

And even if you are slain in Allāh's cause, or die therein...
wa la-in qutiltum fī sabīli 'llāhi aw muttum....

That is to say: "Even if you are martyred in warfare and the sacred struggle, or if death comes to you while you are preparing to fight them...:"

> forgiveness from Allāh and mercy
> *la-maghfiratun mina 'llāhi wa raḥmatun*
> are surely better than what they accumulate.
> *khairun mimmā yajma'ūn.*

In other words: "That is better than surviving in this world, and accumulating its ephemeral vanities,"[341] or: "It is better than enjoying the benefits and pleasures of this world, throughout the full span of your lives." Someone might ask: "How can forgiveness be described as better than what they accumulate, when there is absolutely no good in what they accumulate, to serve as a basis for comparison?" To this our reply would be: "What they accumulate in this world may consist of that which is lawful [*ḥalāl*], and which is therefore counted as good. Besides, this relates to the way they express themselves, and their firm conviction that those properties are good things, so they have been told: "Forgiveness is better than these things, which you think of as good."[342]

> Even if you die or are killed, to Allāh you will surely be gathered!
> *wa la-in muttum aw qutiltum la-ila 'llāhi tuḥsharūn.*

That is to say: "Whether you die in your beds, or are slain on the field of battle, it makes no difference, because your return is to Allāh in either case, so that He may recompense you for your actions. You must therefore give priority to that which brings you close to Allāh, and which earns you His good pleasure, such as the sacred struggle in Allāh's cause, and the practice of obedience to Him."[343] Here we have an admonition, for Allāh has admonished them by saying, in effect: "Do not flee from the fighting, and from what He has commanded you to do. Flee instead from His punishment and the agony of His torment, for your final return is to Him. No one but He has the power to cause you harm or grant you benefit." Allāh knows best (Glory be to Him and Exalted is He).[344]

You should also know that there are several subtle aspects to His saying:

> to Allāh you will surely be gathered!
> *la-ila 'llāhi tuḥsharūn.*

1. The fact that He did not say: "You will be gathered to Allāh," but rather: "To Allāh you will surely be gathered." This conveys a sense of limitation, in that it signifies: "To Allāh all creatures will be gathered, *and to no one other than Him.*" This implies that there will be no judge on that Day [of Resurrection], and no one capable of causing harm or granting benefit, except Him. He has said (Exalted is He):

> To whom belongs the sovereignty this day?
> *li-māni 'l-mulku 'l-yawm.*
> It belongs to Allāh, the One, the Irresistible.
> *li'llāhi 'l-Wāḥidi 'l-Qahhār.* (40:16)

2. The fact that He uses the verb *tuḥsharūn* [you will be gathered] without naming the agent, although the Agent of that gathering is Allāh. Explicit mention is unnecessary here, because He (Exalted is He) is the Almighty, the Great, the One whom intelligent minds have acknowledged as Allāh, the One who initiates and brings back, the One from whom everything originates, and the One who brings everything back to Him. In a context like this, the omission of explicit reference is a more emphatic indication of sublime majesty. Another example occurs in His saying (Exalted is He):

> And it was said: "O earth, swallow your water."
> *wa qīla yā arḍu 'bla'ī mā'a-ki.* (11:44)

3. The fact that He has linked their gathering [at the Resurrection] to that of others. To the intelligent mind, this gives notice that all creatures are forcibly held in the grip of Divine Power, and subject to the implementation of the Divine Will. Regardless of whether they are alive or dead, they cannot escape from the omnipotence of Lordship [*Rubūbiyya*] and the grandeur of Divinity [*Ilāhiyya*].

4. The fact that His expression *tuḥsharūn* [you will be gathered] is a universally inclusive statement. It implies that all creatures will be gathered and stationed on the field of the Day of Resurrection, and made to stand on the carpet of justice. The victim of wrongdoing will be assembled together with the wrongdoer, and the slain together with the slayer. The Lord of Truth (Glory be to Him and Exalted is He) will then judge between His servants with justice, free from the slightest trace of injustice. As He has said:

> And We shall set up the just balances for the Day of Resurrection.
> *wa naḍa'u 'l-mawāzīna 'l-qisṭa li-yawmi 'l-qiyāmati.* (21:47)

If anyone contemplates His saying (Exalted is He):

> To Allāh you will surely be gathered!
> *la-ila 'llāhi tuḥsharūn.*

—and if he enjoys the support of enabling grace, he will understand that these useful lessons, which we have mentioned, are like a mere drop from the oceans of the secrets stored in this Qur'ānic verse.[345]

You should also know that, in the first verse [3:157], Allāh (Glory be to Him and Exalted is He) has encouraged those engaged in the sacred struggle with the prospect of gathering to receive Allāh's forgiveness, while in this verse He has raised the stakes even higher, for He has encouraged them with the prospect of gathering directly to Allāh.

It is related that Mary's son Jesus (may the blessings and peace of Allāh be upon him) once passed by some people whose bodies were emaciated, and whose faces were extremely pale. He also noticed that they bore the marks of worshipful service, so he said to them: "What are you seeking?" They replied: "We dread the torment of Allāh." Jesus then told them: "He is far too Noble and Generous to deny you salvation from His torment!" Then he passed by some other people, and he noticed that they bore those same marks, so he asked them the same question, and they replied: "We are seeking the Garden of Paradise and the mercy [of Allāh]." Jesus then told them: "He is far too Noble and Generous to withhold His mercy from you." Then he passed by a third set of people, and he noticed that they bore the marks of worshipful servitude, to an even greater extent. When he asked them the same question, they replied: "We worship Him because He is our God and we are His servants, not out of any wish or fear." Jesus then told them: "You are the sincerely devoted servants and the genuine worshippers!"

With this in mind, consider how these Qur'ānic verses are arranged in sequence, for He has said, in the first verse [3:157]:

> forgiveness from Allāh
> *la-maghfiratun mina 'llāhi*

This is relevant to someone who worships Him from fear of His punishment. Then He has added:

> and mercy
> *wa raḥmatun*

This is relevant to someone who worships Him in the hope of His reward. Then He has said, at the very end of the verse [3:158]:

> To Allāh you will surely be gathered!
> *la-ila 'llāhi tuḥsharūn.*

This is relevant to someone who worships Allāh, and who does so purely in recognition of Lordship and servitude. This is the highest of all spiritual stations, and the most advanced form of servitude in elevation of degree.[346]

These are my own remarks:

As indicated by the content of this Qur'ānic verse, there is a very great distinction between being gathered to Allāh and being gathered to Allāh's forgiveness. For the perfect believer, it is essential to practise worshipful obedience purely for the love of Allāh, and in recognition of the status of Lordship, because the lower self has no interest in it, and gracious favour comes only from His mercy (Glorious and Exalted He).

Righteous deeds, performed for the sheer love of Allāh, and in recognition of the status of Lordship, are possible only through vigilant awareness, direct witnessing, and knowledge acquired by experience. As for those performed for the sake of reward, they are seldom devoid of selfish interests. If someone worships Allāh in order to give Lordship its due, he will thereby collect the reward and forgiveness, but without any such intention on his part, because the direct vision of Allāh (Exalted is He) is possible only in the Garden of Paradise. That is why the anonymous poet once said:

> It is not my intent to gain bliss from the Gardens,
> though I do wish for them, so that I may see You.

O Allāh, grant us the blessing of Your love and the love of Your most glorious Messenger (Allāh bless him and give him peace). *Āmīn.* Peace be upon the Messengers, and praise be to Allāh, the Lord of All the Worlds. There is no might nor any power, except with Allāh, the All-High, the Almighty. May Allāh bless our master Muḥammad, his family and his Companions, and may He grant them peace.

The Eighteenth Call

In the Name of Allāh, the All-Merciful, the All-Compassionate.
Bismi'llāhi 'r-Raḥmāni 'r-Raḥīm.

O you who truly believe, endure with patience,
yā ayyuha 'lladhīna āmanu 'ṣbirū
and compete in the exercise of patience,
and be ready for the fray,
wa ṣābirū wa rābiṭū:
and practise true devotion to Allāh,
in order that you may succeed.
wa 'ttaqu 'llāha la'alla-kum tufliḥūn. (3:200)

You must know that Allāh (Exalted is He) has mentioned many kinds of knowledge, in this Sūra, relating to both the roots and the branches. As for the roots, they concern everything connected with the affirmation of Oneness, the establishment of justice, and the nature of Prophethood and the Hereafter. As for the branches, they concern everything connected with the assignment of duty and the rules [of the Sacred Law], such as the performance of the pilgrimage [*ḥajj*] and the sacred struggle [*jihād*], to give only two examples. Allāh has concluded this Sūra with this verse, which embraces all forms of good conduct [*ādāb*]. That is because the situations of the individual human being can be subdivided into two categories: those in which he alone is involved, and those which involve not only him, but others too.

As for the first category, patience [*ṣabr*] is essential in all cases. As for the second category, the essential requirement is competition in the exercise of patience [*muṣābara*]. As for patience itself, it refers to several kinds of endurance, namely:

1. Patient endurance of the hardship involved in the effort to explore and investigate the true significance of the affirmation of Oneness, the

implementation of justice, and the nature of Prophethood and the Hereafter, as well as the hardship involved in discovering how to answer the doubts of those who raise objections. (This fifth element is a collective duty [*farḍ kifāya*].[347])

2. Patient endurance of the hardship involved in the fulfilment of strict duties and strongly recommended obligations.

3. Patient endurance of the hardship involved in guarding against the violation of prohibitions.

4. Patient endurance of the adversities and misfortunes of this world, such as sickness, poverty, famine and drought, and terrifying danger.[348]

When Allāh (Exalted is He) says:

> Endure with patience.
> [*u*] *'ṣbirū*

—He is urging patience in the performance of acts of worshipful obedience, and in the suppression of lustful appetites.[349] This is relevant to all the types of endurance listed above, and endless varieties come under each of those headings.

As for His saying (Exalted is He):

> and compete in the exercise of patience.
> *wa ṣābirū.*

—competition in the exercise of patience [*muṣābara*] is an expression used to indicate endurance of the unpleasant things that happen between one person and another. It also covers the endurance of bad behaviour on the part of members of one's household, the neighbours and close relatives. It also signifies refrainng from taking revenge on those who treat you badly, as He has said:

> And turn away from the ignorant.
> *wa aʿriḍ ʿani 'l-jāhilīn.* (7:199)

> And [those who], when they pass by idle talk, pass by with dignity.
> *wa idhā marrū bi'l-laghwi marrū kirāmā.* (25:72)

It also conveys the idea of treating other people preferentially, as Allāh (Exalted is He) has said:

> But they prefer them above themselves,
> *wa yu'thirūna ʿalā anfusi-him*
> even if they must suffer poverty.
> *wa law kāna bi-him khaṣāṣa.* (59:9)

It also indicates the granting of pardon to those who do you wrong, as He has said:

> To pardon is nearer to true devotion.
> *wa an taʿfū aqrabu li 't-taqwā.* (2:237)

It also covers the enjoining of what is right and fair [*al-amr bi'l-maʿrūf*] and the forbidding of what is wrong and unfair [*an-nahy ʿani 'l-munkar*], since excessive tolerance can sometimes have harmful consequences.

This all goes to prove that His saying (Exalted is He):

> Endure with patience.
> [*u*] *'ṣbirū*

—extends to everything that involves no one but the individual concerned, while:

> and compete in the exercise of patience.
> *wa ṣābirū.*

—extends to everything that involves not only him, but others too.

This you must know and understand: While the human being may try to practise patience [*ṣabr*] and competition in patience [*muṣābara*], there may be blameworthy elements in his character, such as carnal desire, irascibility and greed, and these are the adversaries of patient endeavour. Unless a person dedicates the whole of his life to struggling against these vices, and bringing them under strict control, it will not be possible for him to carry patience and competition in patience to a successful conclusion. This is why He has said (Exalted is He):

> and be ready for the fray.
> *wa rābiṭū:*

This struggle is an active duty, and in every action he performs, the human being must have a motive and an aim. In the case of this struggle, his aim and incentive must be true devotion to Allāh, in order to gain prosperity and success. This is why He has said (Exalted is He):

> and practise true devotion to Allāh,
> *wa 'ttaqu 'llāha*
> in order that you may succeed.
> *laʿalla-kum tufliḥūn.*

The precise significance of this is that actions have their source in the faculties [*qiwā*] of the human constitution. Allāh (Exalted is He) has commanded patience and competition in the exercise of patience, and that is an expression calling for the performance of good deeds, and for the careful avoidance of blameworthy actions. That is also what is meant by readiness for the fray [*murābaṭa*]. Then He has mentioned the means by which to repel those faculties that motivate misdeeds and reprehensible actions, the means being true devotion to Allāh. Then he has mentioned the reason why it is necessary to give precedence to true devotion to Allāh over all other faculties and attributes of character, the reason being the prospect of success.

From all that has been said, it is clear that this Qur'ānic verse, which marks the conclusion of this whole Sūra, represents a comprehensive treasury of wisdom and spiritual secrets. It is also clear that, for all its conciseness, it is like the consummation of everything previously mentioned in this Sūra, concerning knowledge of the roots and the branches. Such is my opinion of it.[350]

According to one interpretation:

> and compete in the exercise of patience.
> *wa ṣābirū.*

—means: "Strive to outdo the enemies of Allāh, in patient endurance of the hardships of war, and combat your own worst enemy, through patient endurance in opposition to passionate desire."

Competition in the exercise of patience [*muṣābara*] is a special kind of patience [*ṣabr*]. It is mentioned after the patient endurance that is strictly required, in order to draw attention to the peculiar hardship and difficulty it entails, and to the fact that it is more perfect and more meritorious than other forms of patient endurance. Patience [*ṣabr*] is also said to mean: "restraining the lower self [*nafs*] from everything of which Allāh does not approve." The first stage in the process is *taṣabbur*, which means the effort to exercise that restraint. Then comes *muṣābara*, which means resisting whatever prevents it. Next comes *iṣṭibār* (the constant practice of patience), which demands careful attention and serious commitment. Then comes *ṣabr* [patience itself] which is the culmination of the process, and which is obtained without artificial contrivance.

> and be ready for the fray.
> *wa rābiṭū:*

That is to say: "Station your bodies and your horses at the front lines, prepared for action, and train your lower selves in obedience." When the Prophet (blessing and peace be upon him) once said:

> Shall I tell you what Allāh uses to wipe away sinful errors, and to exalt the degrees [of His servants]?

—they replied: "Yes indeed, O Messenger of Allāh," so he told them:

> Thorough performance of the ritual ablution [*wuḍū'*], to wash away loathsome things, frequent attendance at the mosques, and waiting for the next ritual prayer [*ṣalāt*], after performing one ritual prayer. That is readiness for the fray [*ribāṭ*].[351]

As reported by ʿAbdu'llāh ibn ʿAmr: "The Prophet (Allāh bless him and give him peace) performed the sunset prayer [*maghrib*] one night, so we prayed with him, then some of us stayed on, and some of us went home. Allāh's Messenger (Allāh bless him and give him peace) arrived [in the mosque] before the people [who had gone home] set out for the evening prayer [*ʿishā'*]. When they arrived, they found him raising his finger [in a counting gesture]. He counted up to twenty-nine, pointing towards the sky with his index finger. Then he pulled his gown away from his shoulder, while saying: 'Rejoice at the good news, all you Muslims! This Lord of yours has opened one of the gates of heaven. He is commending you to the angels, saying: "O My angels, look at these servants of Mine. They have fulfilled one religious duty, and they are waiting for another!"'"[352]

> And practise true devotion to Allāh,
> *wa 'ttaqu 'llāha*
> in order that you may succeed.
> *laʿalla-kum tufliḥūn.*

That is to say: "Practise true devotion to Him through detachment from everything apart from Him, so that you may achieve the utmost success." Or it may mean: "You must abstain devoutly from shameful deeds, in order that you may succeed in attaining the three stations of spiritual progress:

1. Patient endurance [*ṣabr*] of the discomforts and inconveniences involved in acts of worshipful obedience.
2. Competition in the exercise of patience [*muṣābara*] with the lower self [*nafs*], through the disruption of customary patterns of behaviour.

3. Readiness [*murābaṭa*] of the innermost being [*sirr*] for battle on the side of the Truth, in preparation for the onslaughts to come."

These three stations correspond to the Sacred Law [*Sharī'a*], the Spiritual Path [*Ṭarīqa*], and the experience of Reality [*Ḥaqīqa*].[353]

O Allāh, grant us the ability to put this sound advice into practice, and graciously enable us to do what You love and that which pleases You!

These are my personal comments:

It is essential for you to adopt the qualities that Allāh has ascribed to His servants in the Noble Qur'ān. Six qualities are attributed to the successful believers, for He has said (Exalted is He):

> Successful indeed are the true believers,
> *qad aflaḥa 'l-mu'minūn:* (23:1)

1st quality:

> who are humble in their prayers,
> *alladhīna hum fī ṣalāti-him khāshi'ūn:* (23:2)

2nd quality:

> and who turn away from idle conversation,
> *wa 'lladhīna hum 'ani 'l-laghwi mu'riḍūn:* (23:3)

3rd quality:

> and who are active in paying the alms-due,
> *wa 'lladhīna hum li'z-zakāti fā'ilūn:* (23:4)

4th quality:

> and who guard their private parts,
> *wa 'lladhīna hum li-furūji-him ḥāfiẓūn:*
>
> except from their wives or what their right hands possess,
> *illā 'alā azwāji-him aw mā malakat aimānu-hum*
> for then they are not blameworthy;
> *fa-inna-hum ghairu malūmīn:*
>
> but whoever seeks after more than that,
> *fa-mani 'btaghā warā'a dhālika*
> such are the transgressors;
> *fa-ulā'ika humu 'l-'ādūn:* (23:5–7)

5th quality:

> and those who are shepherds of their pledge and their covenant,
> *wa 'lladhīna hum li-amānāti-him wa 'ahdi-him rā'ūn:* (23:8)

6th quality:

> and who faithfully observe their prayers.
> *wa 'lladhīna hum ʿalā ṣalawāti-him yuḥāfiẓūn*. (23:9)

Allāh's Messenger (Allāh bless him and give him peace) has mentioned the excellent merit of cultivating these attributes, which are described in the first ten verses[354] of the Sūra entitled "The Believers [*al-Muʾminūn*]."

Imām Aḥmad [ibn Ḥanbal] reported that ʿUmar ibn al-Khaṭṭāb (may Allāh be well pleased with him) once said: "Whenever the inspiration [*waḥy*] came down to Allāh's Messenger (Allāh bless him and give him peace), a droning sound could be heard beside his face, like the droning of bees. We stayed with him for an hour, one day, so he turned to face the *Qibla*, raised his hands, and said:

> O Allāh, grant us increase, and do not make us suffer diminution. Honour us, and do not belittle us. Grant us gifts, and do not deprive us. Prefer us, and do not prefer others over us. Make us well pleased, and be well pleased with us.

"Then he said:

> Ten verses [of the Qurʾān] have been revealed to me. If anyone acts upon them, he will enter the Garden of Paradise.

"Then he recited:

> Successful indeed are the true believers...
> *qad aflaḥa 'l-muʾminūn*...

—until he completed the ten."[355]

O Allāh, grant us the ability to accomplish all that. *Āmīn*. Peace be upon the Messengers, and praise be to Allāh, the Lord of All the Worlds. There is no might nor any power, except with Allāh, the All-High, the Almighty. May Allāh bless our master Muḥammad, his family and his Companions, and may He grant them peace.

The Nineteenth Call

In the Name of Allāh, the All-Merciful, the All-Compassionate.
Bismi'llāhi 'r-Raḥmāni 'r-Raḥīm.

O you who truly believe, it is not lawful for you
yā ayyuha 'lladhīna āmanū lā yaḥillu
to inherit the women by force,
la-kum an tarithu 'n-nisā'a karhā:
and do not constrain them,
so that you may take away
wa lā ta'ḍulū-hunna li-tadhhabū
a part of what you have given them,
bi-ba'ḍi mā ātaitumū-hunna
unless they are guilty of a flagrant abomination.
illā an ya'tīna bi-fāḥishatin mubayyina:

But consort with them in all fairness,
wa 'āshirū-hunna bi'l-ma'rūf.
for if you hate them, it may happen
that you hate a thing
fa-in karihtumū-hunna fa-'asā an takrahū shai'an
in which Allāh has placed much good.
wa yaj'ala 'llāhu fī-hi khairan kathīrā. (4:19)

O you who truly believe, it is not lawful for you
yā ayyuha 'lladhīna āmanū lā yaḥillu
to inherit the women by force,
la-kum an tarithu 'n-nisā'a karhā:

That is to say: "It is not lawful for you to treat the women like chattels, which are transferred by inheritance from one person to another, nor for you to inherit them under duress, after the death of their husbands."[356]

It was Ibn 'Abbās (may Allāh be well pleased with him and his father) who said: "In the Age of Ignorance [*Jāhiliyya*], when a man died, his guardians were entitled to deal with his wife as they saw fit. If they so wished, one of them would marry her. If they so wished, they would marry her to someone outside their own number, and take her dower [*ṣadāq*] as payment. If they so wished, they could even prevent her from remarrying."[357]

The people of the Age of Ignorance used to hurt the women with many kinds of abusive treatment, and they subjected them to various types of oppression. In this Qur'ānic verse, therefore, Allāh (Exalted is He) forbade them to go on treating the women in that manner.[358]

> and do not constrain them, so that you may take away
> *wa lā taʿḍulū-hunna li-tadhhabū*
> a part of what you have given them.
> *bi-baʿḍi mā ātaitumū-hunna*

In other words: "It is not lawful for you to prevent them from remarrying, or to place restrictions on them,* so that you may take away a part of what you have given them, meaning the dower."[359]

When He says (Exalted is He):

> and do not constrain them
> *wa lā taʿḍulū-hunna*

—to whom are these words addressed? There are several possibilities:

1. Among the people of that time, a man who had taken a strong dislike to his wife, and wished to be separated from her, would treat her badly and impose restrictions upon her, so that she would ransom herself from him for the price of her dower [*mahr*]. This interpretation is preferred by most of the traditional commentators. It is as if Allāh (Exalted is He) had said: "It is not lawful for you to marry them under compulsion, and it is likewise unlawful for you to subject them, after having married them, to constraint and confinement, so that you may take away a part of what you have given them."

2. The person addressed is the inheritor, who is told that he must not prevent the widow, as did the people of the Age of Ignorance, from

*The two negative expressions [It is **not** lawful for you to...; and do **not**...] are virtually synonymous, according to this interpretation, since *wa lā* [and (do) not...] is taken to mean *aw* [or (to...)], and since constraint [*ʿaḍl*] is the same as prevention [*manʿ*].

remarriage to whomever she wishes and chooses. The significance of His saying (Exalted is He):

> so that you may take away a part of what you have given them.
> *li-tadhhabū bi-baʿḍi mā ātaitumū-hunna*

—is that they used to keep the widow in confinement, with the aim of getting her to hand over her share of the dead man's inheritance.

3. Notice is being served on the guardians [of the deceased], who are being forbidden to constrain the widow.
4. Notice is being served on the husbands, because, in the Age of Ignorance, they used to divorce their wives, then constrain them from remarriage and impose restrictions on them, with the aim of getting something from them.
5. This is a general prohibition, applicable to all such cases.[360]

He then goes on to say (Exalted is He):

> unless they are guilty of a flagrant abomination.
> *illā an yaʾtīna bi-fāḥishatin mubayyina.*

In other words: "except in the case where they have committed the abomination of adultery [*zinā*]." It was Ibn ʿAbbās (may Allāh be well pleased with him and his father) who said: "Flagrant abomination means recalcitrance and disobedience."

When He says (Exalted is He):

> But consort with them in all fairness.
> *wa ʿāshirū-hunna bi'l-maʿrūf.*

—the meaning is: "Associate with them in all the ways that Allāh has commanded you to behave, such as speaking pleasantly and treating them positively well."[361] Fairness [*maʿrūf*] is behaviour that is not incompatible with the Sacred Law and chivalry. In the present context, it signifies equity in domestic accommodation and expenditure, decency in speech, and things of that nature.[362]

> For if you hate them, it may happen that you hate a thing
> *fa-in karihtumū-hunna fa-ʿasā an takrahū shaiʾan*
> in which Allāh has placed much good.
> *wa yajʿala 'llāhu fī-hi khairan kathīrā.*

That is to say: "If you come to detest their companionship, you must be patient with them, and persevere in treating them well, for it may happen that Allāh will provide you with the comfort of a righteous son. In something that is strongly disliked, there may prove to be much that is good. As we are told in the Prophetic tradition [*ḥadīth*]:

> A believing man must not hate a believing woman. If he dislikes some aspect of her character, he should find another aspect pleasing.[363]

The lower self [*nafs*] is likely to hate what is most righteous in respect of the religion, most praiseworthy in its ultimate consequence, and closest to goodness, while it loves the very opposite. Your attention must therefore be focused on that which contains goodness and righteousness, instead of on what your lower selves desire.

You must know that consorting with your wives in all fairness, and being patient with them, can only be appropriate in matters that do not conflict with the good pleasure of Allāh (Exalted is He). Otherwise, withdrawal on the grounds of jealousy is strictly required, because honourable jealousy [*ghaira*] is one of the characteristics of Allāh, and one of the characteristics of the Prophets [*Anbiyā'*] and the saints [*awliyā'*]. Allāh's Messenger (Allāh bless him and give him peace) once said:

> You find the jealousy of Sa'd amazing. By Allāh, I am more jealous than he is, and Allāh is More Jealous than I am. One of the most splendid expressions of Allāh's jealousy is the interdiction of abominations, both those that are committed outwardly and those that are committed inwardly.*[364]

Jealousy is expressed by refusing to allow men to enter the wife's presence, and by forbidding her to go out to the marketplaces, except to use the public steam bath [*ḥammām*].

According to Imām Qāḍī Khān (one of those with a preference for the Ḥanafī school of Islāmic jurisprudence): "Access to the public steam bath [*ḥammām*] is legally permissible for both men and women, contrary to what some have maintained."

It is related that Allāh's Messenger (Allāh bless him and give him peace) entered the public steam bath, and spread a depilatory agent [*nūra*] over his skin. (The term *nūra* is applied to a lime paste, which

*He was referring to certain actions of the outer being [*ẓāhir*], which are too obvious to need mention, and to certain states of the inner being [*bāṭin*], especially reliance on anything other than Allāh.

is used in the steam bath for the removal of unwanted hair.) Khālid ibn al-Walīd is known to have entered the public steam bath of Ḥimṣ [Emessa in Syria].

This is only permissible, however, provided there is no one in the bath with his private parts exposed. People in our own time do not refrain from exposing their private anatomy, whether they belong to the highest or the lowest classes of society, so the truly devout must avoid going into the public steam bath without a really good excuse.

The overall conclusion is that, provided the wife is free from serious defects, and deserves to be considered chaste, the husband is obliged to consort with her in all fairness, and to be patient with her bad temper and suchlike, in contrast to the situation where this does not apply to her.

You must also know that dealing with women is much harder than dealing with men, because women are more delicate in religious commitment, weaker in intellectual capacity, and more inflexible in temperament. There is much to be gained, therefore, in the improvement of character, from consorting with them in the best way possible, and being patient with them. The Prophet (blessing and peace be upon him) used to cultivate good relations with his own pure wives.[365] Traditional reports [*aḥādīth*] on this subject are many, so the reader is advised to consult the commentary [*tafsīr*] of Ibn Kathīr.

These are my own remarks:

You must indeed consort with them in all fairness. Just as you love this wife, your mate in this fleeting world, for her beauty, or her wealth, or her affection, or for the satisfaction of carnal desires, it is essential for you to love her religion, so that Allāh will keep her safe from the torment [of the Hereafter]. She will then be your mate in the Garden of Paradise. If you fail in this respect, you are failing to discharge the trusteeship that you undertook to provide for her. Allāh (Exalted is He) has told us:

> And He ordained between you love and mercy.
> *wa ja'ala baina-kum mawaddatan wa raḥma.* (30:21)

He has also said (Exalted is He):

> O you who truly believe, guard yourselves
> *yā ayyuha 'lladhīna āmanū qū anfusa-kum*
> and your families against a Fire.
> *wa ahlī-kum nāran* (66:6)

If a man is patient with the temperaments of women, he is counted as one of those engaged in the sacred struggle. You must not abandon this sacred struggle [*mujāhada*], so that you may be included under His saying:

> As for those who strive in Our cause,
> *wa 'lladhīna jāhadū fī-nā*
> surely We shall guide them to Our paths.
> *la-nahdiyanna-hum subula-nā.* (29:69)

As for legitimate jealousy [*ghaira shar'iyya*], it should not be suppressed with patient endurance. All other traits of character are simply elements of human nature.

May Allāh enable us, and all the Muslims, to apply the rules of the Sacred Law [*Sharī'a*] in practice. *Āmīn.* Peace be upon the Messengers, and praise be to Allāh, the Lord of All the Worlds. There is no might nor any power, except with Allāh, the All-High, the Almighty. May Allāh bless our master Muḥammad, his family and his Companions, and may He grant them peace.

The Twentieth Call

In the Name of Allāh, the All-Merciful, the All-Compassionate.
Bismi'llāhi 'r-Raḥmāni 'r-Raḥīm.

O you who truly believe, do not consume your wealth
yā ayyuha 'lladhīna āmanū lā ta'kulū amwāla-kum
among yourselves in futility,
baina-kum bi'l-bāṭili
except it be a trade by mutual consent,
illā an takūna tijāratan 'an tarāḍin min-kum:
and do not kill your own selves.
wa lā taqtulū anfusa-kum
Surely Allāh is All-Compassionate towards you.
inna 'llāha kāna bi-kum Raḥīmā.

And whoever does that through aggression and injustice,
wa man yaf'al dhālika 'udwānan wa ẓulman
We shall cast him into a Fire,
fa-sawfa nuṣlī-hi nārā:
and that is ever easy for Allāh.
wa kāna dhālika 'ala 'llāhi yasīrā.

If you avoid the major sins
in tajtanibū kabā'ira
that you are forbidden to commit,
mā tunhawna 'an-hu
We shall acquit you of your evil deeds,
nukaffir 'an-kum sayyi'ātikum
and We shall admit you by a gate of honour.
wa nudkhil-kum mudkhalan karīmā. (4:29–31)

Allāh (Exalted is He) has warned against consuming people's wealth to no good purpose, for He has said:

O you who truly believe, do not consume your wealth
yā ayyuha 'lladhīna āmanū lā ta'kulū amwāla-kum
among yourselves in futility.
baina-kum bi'l-bāṭili

That is to say: "O you who believe in Allāh and His Messenger, you must not consume one another's wealth in futility, meaning in any way that is not permitted by the Sacred Law, such as theft, cheating, misappropriation, usury, gambling and the like."[366] As for consuming one's personal wealth in futility, that is done by spending it on sinful acts of disobedience to Allāh. As for consuming the wealth of others, we have already dealt with that.

According to al-Qāḍī: "Allāh has already mentioned the use of wealth for the purpose of marriage, and He has commanded the full payment of marriage dowers and living expenses. He has then gone on to explain the proper disposal of wealth in general, for He has said:

O you who truly believe, do not consume your wealth
yā ayyuha 'lladhīna āmanū lā ta'kulū amwāla-kum
among yourselves in futility.
baina-kum bi'l-bāṭili

"Two points in the verse need further explanation:

1. He has used the particular term *akl* [eating; consumption] because that is the major purpose to which wealth is applied. This is reminiscent of His saying (Exalted is He):

Those who devour the wealth of orphans wrongfully....
inna 'lladhīna ya'kulūna amwāla 'l-yatāmā ẓulman.... (4:10)

2. Futility [*al-bāṭil*] is a term for everything that is not permitted in the Sacred Law, such as usury [*ribā*] and misappropriation [*ghaṣb*]."[367]

except it be a trade by mutual consent
illā an takūna tijāratan 'an tarāḍin min-kum:

That is to say: "Except that which is in keeping with the Sacred Law, like trade that Allāh has made lawful." According to Ibn Kathīr: "The exception is expressed elliptically, and the full meaning is: 'You must not give one another unlawful materials, in the process of acquiring wealth, but you may engage in lawful business transactions, based on mutual consent between the seller and the buyer."[368]

You should know that the consumption of wealth in futility is one of the factors that corrupt a man's religion and his worldly life. It is indeed harmful to his natural self, and can be a cause of his destruction, since the effect of certain actions becomes apparent in this world. As for trade, it must involve lawful means of ownership, such as gifts, inheritance, charitable donations and permissible contracts, so that it will not be contaminated by futility.[369]

> and do not kill your own selves.
> *wa lā taqtulū anfusa-kum*
> Surely Allāh is ever Compassionate towards you.
> *inna 'llāha kāna bi-kum Raḥīmā.*

That is to say: "Do not shed one another's blood," assuming that the reprimand is expressed in terms of self-slaughter for the sake of emphasis. It may be also be interpreted literally, however, in which case it means [that you must not commit] suicide. That reprimand is a token of His merciful compassion (Exalted is He) towards you.[370]

When He used the expression "your own selves," He probably did so on account of the saying of the Prophet (Allāh bless him and give him peace):

> The believers are like one single self [*al-mu'minūna ka-nafsin wāḥida*].[371]

—and because the Arabs say, when one of them is killed: "By the Lord of the Ka'ba, we have been killed!" They say that because, as they see it, the killing of one of them is tantamount to their all being killed.

It has also been said to mean: "Do not commit offences by which you will incur the death penalty, such as murder, apostasy [*ridda*] and adultery [*zinā*], after leading a life of virtue."

> Surely Allāh is All-Compassionate towards you.
> *inna 'llāha kāna bi-kum Raḥīmā.*

He has now explained (Exalted is He) that He is All-Compassionate in dealing with His servants, and that, on account of His merciful compassion, He has forbidden them everything by which they would incur trouble or tribulation. It is said that He (Exalted is He) commanded the Children of Israel to kill themselves, as a means of repentance for them, and as a purification of their sinful errors. Towards you, however, O Community of Muḥammad (Allāh bless him and give him peace), He has been All-Compassionate, inasmuch as He has not imposed those difficult obligations upon you.[372]

> And whoever does that through aggression and injustice,
> *wa man yaf ʿal dhālika ʿudwānan wa ẓulman*
> We shall cast him into a Fire.
> *fa-sawfa nuṣlī-hi nārā:*

That is to say: "If anyone commits what Allāh has forbidden him to do, as a deliberately wrongful aggressor, not inadvertently or by mistake, We shall cause him to enter an enormous Fire, in which he will be consumed."[373]

> through aggression and injustice
> *ʿudwānan wa ẓulman*

In other words: "through going too far in transgressing the limit, and by doing what he has no right to do." According to some, the term *ʿudwān* means aggression against other people, while *ẓulm* means doing wrong to one's own self, because of its liability for [divine] punishment.[374] Injustice [*ẓulm*] is relevant, therefore, when it is a case of deliberate infringement of the obligations imposed by Allāh.[375]

> and that is ever easy for Allāh.
> *wa kāna dhālika ʿala 'llāhi yasīrā.*

That is to say: "It is a simple and easy matter, in which there is no difficulty whatsoever, because nothing is impossible for Allāh (Exalted is He)."[376] The Imām said: "You must know that all possibilities, in relation to the Power of Allāh, are on an equal footing. It cannot therefore be said that certain actions are easier for Him than others." This statement may have been revealed in the style of speech that is customary among us, or it may be intended to add emphasis to the warning threat, by stressing that no one is capable of escaping it, nor of warding it off. Compare his saying:

> and it is easier for Him.
> *wa huwa ahwanu ʿalai-h.* (30:27)

The intelligent person is therefore obliged to avoid falling into situations fraught with danger, and he must go to great lengths in safeguarding all rights. In His admonition, Allāh has established a connection between the preservation of the self and the preservation of wealth, because the latter is the full brother of the former, in that it serves as a means for its subsistence, the attainment of its perfections, and the fulfilment of its excellent qualities.[377]

> If you avoid the major sins
> *in tajtanibū kabā'ira*
> that you are forbidden to commit,
> *mā tunhawna 'an-hu*
> We will acquit you of your evil deeds,
> *nukaffir 'an-kum sayyi'ātikum*

That is to say: "If you refrain, O believers, from the major sins that We have forbidden you to commit, the minor sins will be erased from your records, by Our gracious favour and Our merciful compassion."[378]

The major sin [*kabīra*] is every sin for which the Lawgiver has prescribed a penalty [*ḥadd*], or concerning which He has issued an explicit threat. Anas ibn Mālik (may Allāh be well pleased with him) once said: "You are doing deeds, today, that are less noticeable to your eyes than a hair, though we would have considered them, in the time of Allāh's Messenger (Allāh bless him and give him peace), to be major sins."[379]

According to al-Baiḍāwī: "As defined by the Sacred Law, the unrighteous person [*fāsiq*] is one who departs from the commandment of Allāh by committing major sins. There are three stages to his guilt:

1. Casual stupidity [*taghābī*], which means that he commits them from time to time, while viewing them with repugnance.
2. Total immersion [*inhimāk*], which means that he becomes accustomed to committing them on a regular basis, without giving them a moment's thought.
3. Outright denial of the truth [*juḥūd*], which means that he commits them in the belief that they are entirely right and proper.

"Once he comes in sight of this [third] station, and steps across its lines, he strips the noose of faith from his neck, and dons the attire of unbelief. So long as he remains at the stage of casual stupidity or thoughtless immersion, he cannot be deprived of the name 'believer [*mu'min*],' because he is still characterized by *taṣdīq* [acceptance of the truth], which is synonymous with *īmān* [belief; faith], on the strength of His saying:

> And if two parties of believers fall to fighting....
> *wa in ṭā'ifatāni mina 'l-mu'minīna 'qtatalū....* (49:9)[380]

—although both parties are guilty of hypocrisy in actual practice.

According to Shaikh Zāda (in his marginal commentary on al-Baiḍāwī): "When he says: 'As defined by the Sacred Law, the unrighteous person [*fāsiq*] is one who departs from the commandment of Allāh,' the implied meaning is: 'by abandoning compliance with it.' The term *fāsiq* also applies to someone who departs from His prohibition, if we interpret the prohibition of something as the commandment to abstain from what has been forbidden, or if we understand 'commandment' in the well-known sense implicit in His saying (Glory be to Him and Exalted is He):

> Obey Allāh and the Messenger.
> *aṭī'u 'llāha wa 'r-Rasūl.* (3:32)

"There can be no doubt that obedience refers to obedience with respect to all obligations, whether imposed by commandment or by prohibition. If someone commits any of the major sins, whether or not he does so because of unbelief, he has departed from obedience to Allāh (Exalted is He)."

According to the author of *an-Nihāya* [The Ultimate Goal], in his explanation of the term *kabīr* [major offence]: "It applies to that which is utterly disgusting among the Muslims, and which involves the violation of respect for Allāh (Exalted is He) and the religion. That is a major sin [*kabīra*], otherwise it is a minor sin [*ṣaghīra*]."

According to al-Qāḍī (may Allāh bestow His mercy upon him): "[As mentioned by al-Baiḍāwī] there are three stages in the commission of major sins:

1. Casual stupidity [*taghābī*]. The term is derived from *ghabāwa*, meaning paucity of intelligence.
2. Total immersion [*inhimāk*] in the matter concerned, i.e., intense involvement and stubborn preoccupation with it.
3. Outright denial of the truth [*juḥūd*].

"The noose of faith is mentioned in the Prophetic tradition [*ḥadīth*]:

> "He has stripped the noose of Islām from his neck.[381]

"As for his [al-Baiḍāwī's] citation of the words of Allāh (Exalted is He):

> And if two parties of believers fall to fighting....
> *wa in ṭā'ifatāni mina 'l-mu'minīna 'qtatalū....* (49:9)"

—this is evidence that, even though someone has come in sight of the station of outright denial of the truth [*juḥūd*], he cannot be deprived of the name 'believer.' Civil war [between Muslims] is a major sin, yet Allāh (Glory be to Him and Exalted is He) has applied the term 'believers' to those engaged in fighting one another."[382]

In this context, according to the people of knowledge, major sins are those that amount to the attribution of partners to Allāh [*shirk bi'llāh*]. There is also a clear allusion to concealed polytheism [*shirk khafī*]. That includes taking notice of creatures, delighting in their approval, regarding them with affection, and turning a blind eye to the right of Allāh because of them. It is said that, once the commitment to faith is sound, any subsequent transgression of the limit is remote from the charge of unbelief. It is also said that, since the greatest of major sins is your giving evidence in favour of your own self, if you testify in its rebuttal, you will escape from the prison of trials and tribulations.[383]

Anas ibn Mālik (may Allāh be well pleased with him) is reported as having said: "Allāh's Messenger (Allāh bless him and give him peace) spoke to us about the majors sins, and he said:

> '[The major sins are] the attribution of partners to Allāh, undutiful treatment of one's parents, and the taking of human life [*qatl an-nafs*].'

"He also said: 'I must let you know that the greatest of the major sins is telling lies [*qawl az-zūr*],' or he may have said: 'giving false testimony [*shahādat az-zūr*].'"[384]

According to a report from Abū Huraira (may Allāh be well pleased with him), Allāh's Messenger (Allāh bless him and give him peace) once said:

> You must avoid committing the seven deadly sins [*mūbiqāt*]!

When someone asked: "O Messenger of Allāh, what are they?" he replied:

> Attributing partners to Allāh; witchcraft [*siḥr*]; taking a life that Allāh has declared inviolable, except by legal right; consuming the wealth of the orphan; adultery and fornication [*zinā*]; retreating on the day of the military advance; and falsely accusing the virtuous believing woman of unchastity, when they are merely inattentive.[385]

According to Ibn ʿAbbās: "The major sin is every sin that Allāh has stamped with a fire, or with anger, or with a curse or a torment."

As reported by Saʿīd ibn Jubair, a man once said to Ibn ʿAbbās: "The major sins are seven in number." He replied: "They are closer to seven hundred than to seven, but no sin is major if it is accompanied by a plea for forgiveness, and no sin is minor if it is accompanied by stubborn persistence."[386] Traditional reports on this subject are numerous, so the reader should refer to the sources, if he wishes to know more.

> and We shall admit you by a gate of honour.
> *wa nudkhil-kum mudkhalan karīmā.*

That is to say: "We shall cause you to enter the Garden of Paradise, the abode of honour and bliss, which contains that which no eye has ever seen, of which no ear has ever heard, and which has never occurred to the human heart."[387] You should understand that the avoidance of major sins will result in the pardoning of minor sins. Then, in the absence of both major and minor sins, it will be possible to enter the gate of honour, which is the presence of the Most Noble of the most noble.

> In a sure abode, in the presence of a King All-Powerful.
> *fī maqʿadi ṣidqin ʿinda Malīkin Muqtadir.* (54:55)

O Allāh, provide us with truthfulness! *Āmīn.*

To this I would add: The human being was created as a weakling, as Allāh (Exalted is He) has said:

> For the human being was created weak.
> *wa khuliqa 'l-insānu ḍaʿīfā.* (4:28)

That is to say: "incapable of opposing his passionate desire, unable to control his urges and his energies." As this implies, the human being cannot be patient with Allāh for an instant, on account of his weakness. Such is human nature, the natural constitution with which Allāh created humankind, for He loves them and they love Him, and He deserves praise for this weakness [in His creatures].

You should know that this weakness is a cause of the perfection of the human being, and of his good fortune. It is also a cause of his deficiency and his misfortune. That is because he keeps changing, due to his weakness, from one state to another, and from one condition to another. At one moment, his character is that of an animal, eating, drinking and mating. At another moment, his character is that of an angel, proclaiming the praise of his Lord and sanctifying Him, doing what he is commanded to do, and refraining from what He has forbidden him to do. These shifts and changes are the results of his weakness, and this constitution is peculiar to him. The angel cannot assume the attributes of the animal, and the animal cannot assume the attributes of the angel. Only the human being is endowed with this weakness, to enable his perfection through development based on the standards set by Allāh.[388]

These are my own comments:

Whenever a sin is committed by the servant [of the Lord] in ignorance, and the perpetrator then becomes aware of it, feels remorse, seeks forgiveness and returns to Allāh (Exalted is He), regardless of whether this sin is a major offence or a minor one, he is pardoned for it in the sight of Allāh, on the strength of a Qur᾽ānic text:

> Relenting is only incumbent on Allāh
> *inna-ma 't-tawbatu ʿala 'llāhi*
> towards those who do evil in ignorance,
> *li'lladhīna yaʿmalūna 's-sū᾽a bi-jahālatin*
> and then quickly repent to Allāh.
> *thumma yatūbūna min qarībin*
> These are they towards whom Allāh relents.
> *fa-ulā᾽ika yatūbu 'llāhu ʿalai-him*
> Allāh is All-Knowing, All-Wise.
> *wa kāna 'llāhu ʿAlīman Ḥakīmā.* (4:17)

This Qur᾽ānic verse takes care of the question: "If acts of sinful disobedience are committed in ignorance, since He is the Most Merciful of the merciful, how could He punish the perpetrator, when he has repented, shown contrition and sought forgiveness?"

If a person is blessed with enlightened intelligence, it is incumbent on him to refrain from committing acts of sinful disobedience, whether they be major or minor offences. A seemingly minor offence may be subject to Allāh's wrath, so it will expose you to the anger of Allāh (Magnificent is His Majesty), because this minor sin has been committed with stubborn persistence in your outer being, and with knowledge in your inner being. As we are told in His saying (Exalted is He):

> The relenting is not for those who do evil deeds
> *wa laisati 't-tawbatu li'lladhīna ya'malūna 's-sayyi'āti*
> until, when death attends on one of them,
> *ḥattā idhā ḥaḍara aḥada-humu 'l-mawtu*
> he says: "Now I have repented!"
> *qāla innī tubtu 'l-āna.* (4:18)

Allāh examines your heart, for that is what is significant in His sight (Glorious and Exalted is He).

> He knows the treachery of the eyes,
> *ya'lamu khā'inata 'l-a'yuni*
> and what the breasts conceal.
> *wa mā tukhfi 'ṣ-ṣudūr.* (40:19)

—so He can see that you have not committed those sins in ignorance, but with full knowledge of them and deliberate persistence in them, and postponing repentance has nothing to do with faith and the fear of offending Allāh (Exalted is He).

The human being is heedless by natural inclination, but the demands of his faith include vigilant awareness and remorse for sinful acts of disobedience, since it is possible for a major offence to be treated as minor, if it is accompanied by prompt repentance, and for a minor offence to be treated as major, if it is accompanied by stubborn persistence. The believer must on no account postpone repentance, and he must not persist in committing minor sins. We beg Allāh for safety from every sin that contravenes the good pleasure of Allāh (Exalted is He) and the good pleasure of His Messenger (Allāh bless him and give him peace), either in word or in deed.

O Allāh, grant us the ability to accomplish all that. *Āmīn.* Peace be upon the Messengers, and praise be to Allāh, the Lord of All the Worlds. There is no might nor any power, except with Allāh, the All-High, the Almighty. May Allāh bless our master Muḥammad, his family and his Companions, and may He grant them peace.

The Twenty-first Call

In the Name of Allāh, the All-Merciful, the All-Compassionate.
Bismi'llāhi 'r-Raḥmāni 'r-Raḥīm.

O you who truly believe!
yā ayyuha 'lladhīna āmanū
Do not approach the ritual prayer
lā taqrabu 'ṣ-ṣalāta
when you are intoxicated,
wa antum sukārā
until you know what you are saying,
ḥattā ta'lamū mā taqūlūna
nor when you are in a state of major impurity,
wa lā junuban
except when traversing a road,
illā 'ābirī sabīlin
till you have bathed.
ḥattā taghtasilū.

And if you are ill, or on a journey,
wa in kuntum marḍā aw 'alā safarin
or one of you has come from the toilet,
aw jā'a aḥadun min-kum mina 'l-ghā'iṭi
or you have touched women,
aw lāmastumu 'n-nisā'a
and you have not found water,
fa-lam tajidū mā'an
then head for some fresh topsoil
fa-tayammamū ṣa'īdan ṭayyiban
and rub your faces and your hands.
fa-masaḥū bi-wujūhi-kum wa aidī-kum:
Allāh is indeed All-Pardoning, All-Forgiving.
inna 'llāha kāna 'Afuwwan Ghafūrā. (4:43)

Allāh (Exalted is He) has commanded avoidance of the ritual prayer [*ṣalāt*] in the state of intoxication and major impurity, for He has said:

> O you who truly believe!
> *yā ayyuha 'lladhīna āmanū*
> Do not approach the ritual prayer
> *lā taqrabu 'ṣ-ṣalāta*
> when you are intoxicated,
> *wa antum sukārā*
> until you know what you are saying.
> *ḥattā ta'lamū mā taqūlūna.*

In other words: "You must not perform the ritual prayer in the state of intoxication, because this state is not conducive to submissiveness and humility in intimate converse with Allāh (Glory be to Him and Exalted is He)." This was before the prohibition of strong drink [*khamr*].

As related by at-Tirmidhī,[389] it was 'Alī (may Allāh ennoble his countenance) who said: "'Abd ar-Raḥmān ibn 'Awf had made us a meal, so he invited us to eat and offered us liquor to drink. The liquor had its effect on us, and then the time of the ritual prayer arrived. They appointed me to lead the prayer, so I recited [this garbled version of Q. 109]:

> Say: "O unbelievers, I worship what you worship,
> *qul yā ayyuha 'l-kāfirūn: a'budu mā ta'budūn:*
> and we worship that which you worship."
> *wa naḥnu na'budu mā ta'budūn:*

"Allāh therefore sent down:

> O you who truly believe!
> *yā ayyuha 'lladhīna āmanū*
> Do not approach the ritual prayer
> *lā taqrabu 'ṣ-ṣalāta*
> when you are intoxicated."
> *wa antum sukārā.*

In the wake of this revelation, they refrained from drinking liquor [but only] at the times of the ritual prayer, until Allāh (Exalted is He) sent down:

> Strong drink and games of chance
> *inna-ma 'l-khamru wa 'l-maisiru*
> and idols and divining arrows
> *wa 'l-anṣābu wa 'l-azlāmu*

are only an infamy of Satan's handiwork,
rijsun min ʿamali 'sh-shaiṭāni
so leave it aside, in order that you may succeed.
fa-'jtanibū-hu.laʿalla-kum tufliḥūn.

Satan only seeks to cast among you enmity
inna-mā yurīdu 'sh-shaiṭānu an yūqiʿa
and hatred by means of strong drink
baina-kumu 'l-ʿadāwata wa 'l-baghḍāʾa
and games of chance, and to turn you
fi 'l-khamri wa 'l-maisiri wa yaṣudda-kum
from remembrance of Allāh and from righteousness.
ʿan dhikri 'llāhi wa ʿani 'ṣ-ṣalāh:
Will you then have done?
fa-hal antum muntahūn. (5:90,91)

On hearing this, ʿUmar (may Allāh be well pleased with him) exclaimed: "We have done! We have done!"

Do not approach the ritual prayer
lā taqrabu 'ṣ-ṣalāta

Concerning the term *ṣalāt* in this context, there are two opinions:

1. It means the *masjid* [mosque; place of prayer]. This is the opinion of Ibn Maʿsūd and al-Ḥasan, and it represents the doctrine of ash-Shāfiʿī.
2. In the context of this Qurʾānic verse, the term *ṣalāt* refers to the ritual prayer itself. That is to say: "You must not perform the ritual prayer while you are intoxicated."

As you should understand, difference of expert opinion has a significant bearing on a legal rule [*ḥukm sharʿī*]. On the basis of the first interpretation, the meaning is: "Do not approach the mosque while you are intoxicated, nor when you are in a state of major impurity, unless you are traversing a road. In this case, the exception indicates that it is permissible for someone in a state of major impurity to enter into the mosque. This is the opinion of ash-Shāfiʿī.

If the second opinion is adopted, the meaning is: "You must not approach the ritual prayer while you are intoxicated, nor must you approach it while you are in a state of major impurity, unless you are traversing a road, i.e., unless you are a traveller." This exception indicates that it is permissible, for someone in a state of major impurity [*junub*], to approach the ritual prayer [*ṣalāt*] when water is unavailable (by performing the dry ablution called *tayammum*).

> when you are intoxicated.
> *wa antum sukārā.*

Here again, there are two opinions:

1. The reference is to intoxication caused by strong drink, which is the opposite of mental clarity. This is the opinion of the majority of the Companions [*Ṣaḥāba*] and the Successors [*Tābiʿīn*].
2. The reference is to the intoxication of sleep. There is no doubt that, during sleep, the channels of the spirit become full of coarse vapours, by which those channels are blocked. The seeing and hearing spirit is thus prevented from penetrating to the outside of the body. The Prophet (blessing and peace be upon him) once said:

> If one of you starts dozing off, while performing the ritual prayer, he should lie down and rest, until sleep departs from him. For, if he prays while he is in a doze, he may go away to seek forgiveness, and reproach himself too severely.[390]

You should know that the correct opinion is the first, as indicated by these two considerations:

1. The term *sukr* [intoxication] is properly applied to the intoxication caused by drinking liquor.
2. The traditional commentators are unanimously agreed that this Qurʾānic verse was revealed in connection with the drinking of liquor. According to some of them, this verse was abrogated by the Verse of the Table [*Āyat al-Māʾida*].

In my own opinion, the argument in favour of abrogation can be stated as follows: The scope of the prohibition of approach to the ritual prayer, while in a state of intoxication, is extended to the point where the person concerned knows what he is saying. The rule is thus extended to a certain limit, at which point the rule ceases to apply. This must mean that it is permissible to approach the ritual prayer, though still in a state of intoxication, as soon as the person concerned knows what he is saying. It is well known, however, that when Allāh (Exalted is He) declared strong drink unlawful, in the Verse of the Table [*Āyat al-Māʾida*], He abolished this licence. It is thereby established that the

Verse of the Table [5:90] effectively abrogates some of the provisions of this verse.[391]

nor when you are in a state of major impurity,
wa lā junuban
except when traversing a road
illā ʿābirī sabīlin

That is to say: "And do not approach when you are polluted, meaning when you are not in a state of ritual purity. You must not dismount or enter, unless you are travellers and have not found water. In that case, you must prepare for the ritual prayer by performing the dry ablution [*tayammum*].[392]

The term *junub* is applied to someone who needs to perform the major ablution [*ghusl*]. He is *junub* because he must avoid [*yajtanib*] the ritual prayer, the mosque and recitation of the Qurʾān, until he acquires the necessary state of purity.

except when traversing a road
illā ʿābirī sabīlin

There are two opinions about this: (1) It means journeying to reach the mosque. (2) It refers to long-distance travellers.[393]

And if you are ill, or on a journey,
wa in kuntum marḍā aw ʿalā safarin
or one of you has come from the toilet,
aw jāʾa aḥadun min-kum mina 'l-ghāʾiṭi
or you have touched women,
aw lāmastumu 'n-nisāʾa
and you have not found water....
fa-lam tajidū māʾan....

That is to say: "If you are ill, and water would harm you, or you are travelling, and you have excreted urine or faeces, or been contaminated by some other minor impurity, and you cannot find water...."

or you have touched women
aw lāmastumu 'n-nisāʾa

Ibn ʿAbbās said: "This means sexual intercourse."

and you have not found water
fa-lam tajidū māʾan

In other words: "You have not found the water you need to purify yourselves."

then head for some fresh topsoil
fa-tayammamū ṣaʿīdan ṭayyiban
and rub your faces and your hands.
fa-masaḥū bi-wujūhi-kum wa aidī-kum:

That is to say: "In the absence of water, you must look for pure earth, then use it to purify yourselves, by rubbing your faces and your hands with that earth."[394] The rubbing must be applied to the hands and the lower arms, up to the elbows, according to the consensus [*ijmāʿ*] of the legal scholars.

Note that Allāh (Exalted is He) has mentioned four sets of people here: (1) invalids, (2) travellers, (3) those who have come from the toilet, and (4) those who have touched women.

As for the first two groups, the invalids and the travellers, they may resort to the dry ablution [*tayammum*]. The other two groups are obliged to purify themselves with water, if water is available, and by means of the dry ablution in the absence of water. We shall now discuss each one of these cases in detail:

1. As for the first case, it is referred to in His saying (Exalted is He):

And if you are ill
wa in kuntum marḍā

You should know that three types of illness are relevant in this context:

- The type from which the invalid would die if he used water, such as severe smallpox and massive ulceration.
- The type where the use of water would not result in death, but the invalid would suffer agonizing pains.
- The type where there is no danger of death or serious pain, but the invalid is afraid that some disfigurement or defect could be left on his body.

The Islāmic jurists [*fuqahā*ʾ] consider dry ablution [*tayammum*] permissible in the first two instances, but not in the third.

2. The second case is referred to in His saying (Exalted is He):

or on a journey
aw ʿalā safarin

As the Qurʾānic verse indicates, if the traveller cannot find water, he must perform the dry ablution, whether his journey is long or short.

3. The third case is referred to in His saying (Exalted is He):

> or one of you has come from the toilet
> *aw jā'a aḥadun min-kum mina 'l-ghā'iṭi*

The term *ghā'iṭ* signifies a quiet plot of ground. The plural form is *ghīṭān*. When a man wanted to satisfy a natural need, he would look for a quiet plot of ground, where he could screen himself from people's eyes. Excrement [*ḥadath*] has also come to be called *ghā'iṭ*, through the linguistic process whereby a thing acquires the name of its place.

4. The fourth case is referred to in His saying (Exalted is He):

> or you have touched women
> *aw lāmastumu 'n-nisā'a*

There are two opinions about this:

- It refers to sexual intercourse [*jimā'*]. This is the opinion of Ibn 'Abbās, al-Ḥasan, Mujāhid and Qatāda, as well as that of Abū Ḥanīfa (may Allāh be well pleased with him), based on the fact that touching with the hand does not destroy the state of ritual purity.
- In this context, touching refers to mutual skin contact, whether or not it involves sexual intercourse. This is the opinion of Ibn Mas'ūd, Ibn 'Umar, ash-Sha'bī and an-Nakha'ī, as well as that of ash-Shāfi'ī (may Allāh be well pleased with him).[395]

For each of these two opinions, supporting evidence can be cited from the Qur'ān.

> and you have not found water
> *fa-lam tajidū mā'an*

The conclusion that water is unavailable can only be reached after a search for it has been conducted. As the scholars unanimously agree, if someone does find some water, but he needs it to quench his own thirst, or the thirst of an animal that must be treated with respect, it is permissible for him to perform the dry ablution. In the situation where he finds some water, but not enough for the minor ritual ablution [*wuḍū'*], the question arises as to whether he is obliged to combine the use of that amount of water with the dry ablution [*tayammum*]. According to ash-Shāfi'ī (may Allāh be well pleased with him), that is indeed the required procedure, in accordance with the literal import of the Qur'ānic verse.

then head for some fresh topsoil
fa-tayammamū ṣaʿīdan ṭayyiban

This gives rise to several questions of interpretation, two of which we shall mention here:

1. In ordinary Arabic usage, the term *tayammum* signifies *qaṣd* [setting out with a purpose]. As for *ṣaʿīd*, az-Zajjāj said that it means: "the surface of the earth, whether it be dust or soil or something else."

2. According to Abū Ḥanīfa (may Allāh be well pleased with him): "If we assume that he is in a desert, on which there is no soil, it will be sufficient for the *mutayammim* [person performing the dry ablution] to pat and rub with his hand." According to ash-Shāfiʿī (may Allāh be well pleased with him): "It is essential for some soil to be sticking to his hand."

Fresh topsoil [*aṣ-ṣaʿīd aṭ-ṭayyib*] is earth that contains no manure (if it is salty, it cannot produce plants). There is no doubt that dry ablution with this soil is permissible, by consensus [*ijmāʿ*]. The traveller is therefore obliged to carry fresh topsoil with him, as a precautionary measure, especially since the Prophet (Allāh bless him and give him peace) made a point of describing soil in these terms, for he said:

> The earth has been assigned to me as a mosque [*masjid*], and its soil as a detergent [*ṭahūr*].[396]

Allāh is indeed All-Pardoning, All-Forgiving.
inna 'llāha kāna ʿAfuwwan Ghafūrā.

That is to say: "He grants concessions and makes things easy for His servants, so that they will not lapse into misconduct."[397] It is part of His regular custom (Exalted is He) to pardon those who make mistakes and to forgive the sinners, so He is bound to be One who facilitates, not one who causes difficulty. (I would rather say: We are obliged to be modestly humble, with a true sense of shame.)

The implicit meaning is that the ritual prayer is the heavenly ascension [*miʿrāj*] of the believer, and his opportunity for intimate converse. The worshipper [*muṣallī*] is someone who converses intimately with his Lord. When He tells you, O you who lay claim to true belief:

Do not approach the ritual prayer
lā taqrabu 'ṣ-ṣalāta

when you are intoxicated
wa antum sukārā

—He is saying, in effect: "Do not seek nearness in the ritual prayer, when you are intoxicated by heedless lapses and the pursuit of lustful desires."

Everything that makes the heart neglectful of Allāh (Almighty and Glorious is He) is connected with intoxication. It is therefore necessary to distinguish three types of intoxication:

1. Intoxication caused by strong drink.
2. Intoxication caused by heedlessness, due to the controlling influence of the love of this world.
3. The most serious kind of intoxication, which is your intoxication with your lower self.[398]

These are my own observations:

There are actually four types of intoxication: (1) intoxication due to strong drink; (2) intoxication due to this world; (3) intoxication due to passionate desire; and (4) intoxication due to the love of Allāh (Exalted is He) and His Messenger (Allāh bless him and give him peace). Let us consider each of these in turn:

1. Intoxication due to strong drink. This has been forbidden by Allāh (Exalted is He), in the noble Qur᾽ānic verse:

Strong drink and games of chance
inna-ma 'l-khamru wa 'l-maisiru
and idols and divining arrows
wa 'l-anṣābu wa 'l-azlāmu
are only an infamy of Satan's handiwork,
rijsun min ʿamali 'sh-shaiṭāni
so leave it aside.
fa-'jtanibū-hu. (5:90)

2. Intoxication due to this world. Allāh (Exalted is He) has drawn attention to this in His saying:

So do not let the life of this world delude you,
fa-lā taghurranna-kumu 'l-ḥayātu 'd-dunyā:
and do not let the Deceiver
wa lā yaghurranna-kum
deceive you in regard to Allāh.
bi-'llāhi 'l-Gharūr. (31:33)

—and His saying:

> Whoever desires that which hastens away....
> *man kāna yurīdu 'l-ʿājilata....* (17:18)

3. Intoxication due to passionate desire. This is referred to in His saying (Exalted is He):

> Have you seen him who makes his passionate desire his god?
> *a-fa-raʿaita mani 'ttakhadha ilāha-hu hawā-hu.* (45:23)

4. Intoxication due to the love of Allāh and His Messenger (Allāh bless him and give him peace). This is mentioned in His saying (Exalted is He):

> Those who truly believe
> *wa 'lladhīna āmanū*
> are stauncher in their love for Allāh.
> *ashaddu ḥubban li'llāh:* (2:165)

The love of Allāh makes the heart oblivious of this world and the lower self. It is left with one single concern, and that is the love of Allāh Alone. The love of the Messenger (blessing and peace be upon him) is confirmed by compliance with the immaculate Sunna, because love necessitates obedience, otherwise the lover's claim is false.

You may say: "The pursuit of lawful sustenance, and using it for the purposes commanded by Allāh, make up part of faith" To this I shall reply: "As for the lawful content of this world, even if it is not prohibited, it still has poison in it. Its owner does not know whether or not it is mixed with contamination. Once he recognizes that, he will become aware of its true nature, so he will not preoccupy himself with it, except to the extent of his need. If someone has failed to notice that, he is ignorant, and he will suffer great harm. O Allāh, preserve us!

The heart is single. If it is filled with the love of this world, or passionate desire, nothing else can enter into it, as He has said (Exalted is He):

> Allāh has not assigned to any man
> *jaʿala 'llāhu li-rajulin min*
> two hearts within his body.
> *qalbaini fī jawfi-h:* (33:4)

The heart was created for love alone. Since the heart is single and love is single, there is room for only one Beloved, who has no partner. If someone is totally preoccupied with this world, both inwardly and outwardly, yet claims not merely to love the Hereafter, but to love Allāh, he is lying in making such a claim. Alack and alas!

O Allāh, enable us to obtain Your love. *Āmīn.* Peace be upon the Messengers, and praise be to Allāh, the Lord of All the Worlds. There is no might nor any power, except with Allāh, the All-High, the Almighty. May Allāh bless our master Muḥammad, his family and his Companions, and may He grant them peace.

The Twenty-second Call

In the Name of Allāh, the All-Merciful, the All-Compassionate.
Bismi'llāhi 'r-Raḥmāni 'r-Raḥīm.

O you who truly believe,
obey Allāh and obey the Messenger,
yā ayyuha 'lladhīna āmanū aṭī'u 'llāha
wa aṭī'u 'r-Rasūla
and those of you who are in authority;
wa uli 'l-amri min-kum:
and if you have any dispute about any matter,
fa-in tanāza'tum fī shai'in
refer it to Allāh and the Messenger
fa-ruddū-hu ila 'llāhi wa 'r-Rasūli
if you are believers in Allāh and the Last Day.
in kuntum tu'minūna bi'llāhi wa 'l-yawmi 'l-ākhir:
That is better and more excellent in the end.
dhālika khairun wa aḥsanu ta'wīlā. (4:59)

O you who truly believe,
yā ayyuha 'lladhīna āmanū
obey Allāh and obey the Messenger,
aṭī'u 'llāha wa aṭī'u 'r-Rasūla
and those of you who are in authority.
wa uli 'l-amri min-kum:

That is to say: "Obey Allāh and obey the Messenger, through strict adherence to the Book and the Sunna, and obey the rulers, provided they are Muslims who adhere to Allāh's Sacred Law, since no obedience is due to any creature in disobedience to the Creator. It is implicitly stated in his expression:

of you
min-kum

—that obedience is due to rulers who are Muslims both physically and spiritually, in flesh and in blood, and that it is not enough for them to be Muslims merely in outer form and appearance.[399]

Two points worth noting:

1. His expression (Exalted is He):

> Obey Allāh
> *aṭī'u 'llāha*

—links the word commanding obedience to the word "Allāh." This necessarily means that obedience to Him is incumbent on us for a particular reason: namely, the fact that we are servants to Him, and that He is a Deity [*Ilāh*]. It is thereby established that the duty to obey has its origin in servitude and Lordship, which necessarily means that the duty to obey is permanently incumbent on all responsible persons, till the advent of the Resurrection, and that this principle is ordained in the Sacred Law.

2. He has said:

> Obey Allāh
> *aṭī'u 'llāha*

—thereby singling Himself out for separate mention. Then He has gone on to say:

> and obey the Messenger,
> *wa aṭī'u 'r-Rasūla*
> and those of you who are in authority.
> *wa uli 'l-amri min-kum:*

This is an instruction from Allāh (Glory be to Him) concerning this proper mode of conduct [*adab*]. It tells the believers that they must not mention His Name (Glory be to Him) in direct conjunction with the name of anyone other than Him. Where creatures are concerned, however, that is permissible, as demonstrated by His saying:

> and obey the Messenger,
> *wa aṭī'u 'r-Rasūla*
> and those of you who are in authority.
> *wa uli 'l-amri min-kum:*

[As noted above] this is an instruction concerning this proper mode of conduct.[400]

According to Ibn ʿAbbās (may Allāh be well pleased with him and his father): "Those referred to as:

> and those of you who are in authority.
> *wa uli 'l-amri min-kum:*

—are the experts in Islāmic jurisprudence [*fiqh*] and the religion [*dīn*]."

In the tradition [*ḥadīth*] transmitted on the authority of Abū Huraira (may Allāh be well pleased with him), and which is generally accepted as authentic, Allāh's Messenger (Allāh bless him and give him peace) is reported as having said:

> If someone obeys me, he has obeyed Allāh. If someone disobeys me, he has disobeyed Allāh. If someone obeys my commanding officer [*amīr*], he has obeyed me. If someone disobeys my commanding officer, he has disobeyed me.[401]

These are injunctions requiring obedience to the scholars and the commanding officers, and this is why He said (Exalted is He):

> Obey Allāh
> *aṭīʿu 'llāha*

In other words: "Follow His Book."

> and obey the Messenger
> *wa aṭīʿu 'r-Rasūla*

That is to say: "Adopt his Sunna."

> and those of you who are in authority.
> *wa uli 'l-amri min-kum:*

In other words: "Comply with what they command you to do, in obedience to Allāh, not in disobedience to Allāh, for there can be no obedience to a creature in disobedience to Allāh." As stated in the authentic Prophetic tradition [*ḥadīth*]:

> Obedience is required only in connection with that which is right and proper [*maʿrūf*].[402]

You should understand that, having commanded the custodians and the governors to act justly in their custodianship, Allāh (Exalted is He) has commanded the subjects to obey the governors, for He has said:

> O you who truly believe,
> *yā ayyuha 'lladhīna āmanū*
> obey Allāh and obey the Messenger,
> *aṭīʿu 'llāha wa aṭīʿu 'r-Rasūla*
> and those of you who are in authority.
> *wa uli 'l-amri min-kum:*

This is why ʿAlī ibn Abī Ṭālib (may Allāh be well pleased with him) declared: "The leader [*imām*] has a duty to govern in accordance with what Allāh has revealed, and to discharge the trust. If he does that, the subjects have a duty to hear and to obey."

This Qurʾānic verse is a noble verse, containing most of our knowledge of the basic sources of Islāmic jurisprudence [*fiqh*]. That is because the jurists [*fuqahāʾ*] maintain that the basic sources of the Sacred Law are four in number: the Book, the Sunna, the consensus [*ijmāʿ*] and analogy [*qiyās*]. This verse contains confirmation of these four basic sources, in this order. As for the Book and the Sunna, the allusion to them occurs in His saying:

> Obey Allāh and obey the Messenger.
> *aṭīʿu 'llāha wa aṭīʿu 'r-Rasūla*

Suppose it should be asked: "Is it not true that obedience to the Messenger is obedience to Allāh? What, then, is the meaning of this conjunction?"

Our answer to this would be: "As al-Qāḍī has said: 'The point of that is to clarify the two indications. The Book indicates the commandment of Allāh, then from it we learn the commandment of the Messenger (Allāh bless him and give him peace), quite unmistakably. The Sunna indicates the commandment of the Messenger, then from it we learn the commandment of Allāh, quite unmistakably. It is thus definitely established, on the basis of what we have just stated, that His saying:

> Obey Allāh and obey the Messenger.
> *aṭīʿu 'llāha wa aṭīʿu 'r-Rasūla*

—indicates the strict obligation to follow the Book and the Sunna.'"[403]

As reported by Imām Aḥmad, it was ʿAlī (may Allāh be well pleased with him) who said: "Allāh's Messenger (Allāh bless him and give him peace) once dispatched a military squadron, and he placed in charge of them a man from among the Helpers [*Anṣār*]. Then, when they had set out, he became annoyed with them for some reason, so he said to them: 'Did Allāh's Messenger (Allāh bless him and give him peace) not command you to obey me?' 'Yes indeed,' they replied, so he said: 'In that case, go and collect some firewood for me.' Then he called for a fire, so they kindled the wood. Then he said: 'I adjure you to enter the fire!'

"At that point, a young fellow among them said to them: 'The very reason you fled to Allāh's Messenger (Allāh bless him and give him peace) was to escape the Fire [of Hell], so wait until you meet again with Allāh's Messenger (Allāh bless him and give him peace). Then, if he commands you to enter it, you must enter it.' They promptly returned to Allāh's Messenger (Allāh bless him and give him peace), and told him what had happened, so he said to them:

> "If you had entered it, you would never have re-emerged from it. Obedience is required only in connection with that which is right and proper [*ma'rūf*]."[404]

The gist of it is that Allāh (Almighty and Glorious is He) has enjoined obedience to Him, first of all, and that means compliance with His commandments and avoidance of His prohibitions. Then, in second place, He has enjoined obedience to His Messenger (Allāh bless him and give him peace), in whatever he has commanded and forbidden. Then, in third place, He has enjoined obedience to those in authority. Such is the opinion of the majority [of the scholars], and of Abū Huraira, Ibn 'Abbās and others.

According to Sahl ibn 'Abdi'llāh at-Tustarī: "You must obey the ruler [*sulṭān*] in seven matters: (1) the minting of dirhams and dīnārs [silver and gold coins]; (2) measures and weights; (3) official regulations; (4) the Pilgrimage [*Ḥajj*]; (5) the Friday congregation [*jum'a*]; (6) the two Festivals ['*Īdain*]; (7) the conduct of the sacred struggle [*jihād*]."

Sahl also said: "If the ruler forbids a scholar to act as a legal consultant, he must not be consulted, and if he does give a legal opinion, he is a disobedient sinner, even if he [the ruler] is a tyrannical despot."[405]

> and if you have any dispute about any matter,
> *fa-in tanāza'tum fī shai'in*
> refer it to Allāh and the Messenger
> *fa-ruddū-hu ila 'llāhi wa 'r-Rasūli*

That is to say: "If you disagree over any matter, you must seek a decision on it in the Book of Allāh and the Sunna of His Prophet (Allāh bless him and give him peace)."[406] Since none but the scholars are equipped with the expertise required for making reference to the Book and the Sunna, this proves the validity of the assertion that consulting the scholars is obligatory, and compliance with their formal pronouncement [*fatwā*] is compulsory.

It was Sahl ibn ʿAbdi'llāh (may Allāh bestow His mercy upon him) who said: "It is always good for people to treat the ruler and the scholars with reverence. If they hold these two in high esteem, Allāh will improve their condition in this world and the Hereafter, but if they belittle these two, He will wreak havoc on their worldly and Otherworldly interests."

As for His saying (Exalted is He):

> and if you have any dispute
> *fa-in tanāzaʿtum*

—that is to say: "If you quarrel and disagree, so that it seems as if each person disputes and dismisses the other's argument:

> about any matter
> *fī shaiʾin*

—that concerns your religion."

> refer it to Allāh and the Messenger
> *fa-ruddū-hu ila 'llāhi wa 'r-Rasūli*

In other words: "Refer that decision to the Book of Allāh, or to His Messenger (Allāh bless him and give him peace), by consulting him during his lifetime, or by examining his Sunna after his demise (Allāh bless him and give him peace)." This is the opinion stated by Mujāhid, al-Aʿmash and Qatāda, and it is a sound opinion, as confirmed by ʿUmar ibn al-Khaṭṭāb (may Allāh be well pleased with him), who said: "Reference to the Truth is better than persistence in falsehood."[407]

As Allāh (Exalted is He) has said:

> And in whatever you differ,
> *wa ma 'khtalaftum fī-hi min shaiʾin*
> the verdict therein belongs to Allāh.
> *fa-ḥukmu-hu ila 'llāh.* (42:10)

Whenever a decision is based on the Book and the Sunna, and these two bear witness to its correctness, it must represent the truth, and what is there after the truth, apart from error?[408] This explains why He has said (Exalted is He):

> if you are believers in Allāh and the Last Day.
> *in kuntum tuʾminūna bi'llāhi wa 'l-yawmi 'l-ākhir:*

That is to say: "If you really are believers." Since this conditional expression is not followed by an apodosis, it evidently relates to what precedes it, namely:

> refer it to Allāh and the Messenger.
> *fa-ruddū-hu ila 'llāhi wa 'r-Rasūli*

—and the purpose is to urge adherence to the Book and the Sunna, just as a father may say: "If you are my son, then do not contradict me!"[409] It also implies that if, in a contentious situation, a person fails to appeal to the Book and the Sunna, and does not refer to them in the matter, he cannot be a believer in Allāh and the Last Day.[410]

A literal understanding of His expression:

> if you are believers in Allāh and the Last Day.
> *in kuntum tu'minūna bi'llāhi wa 'l-yawmi 'l-ākhir:*

—requires the conclusion that, if someone does not obey Allāh and the Messenger, he cannot be a believer. This could also signify that the sinner departs from belief, but it is actually construed in the sense of a warning threat. (Because, as previously explained, the believer does not depart from belief through the commission of major sins [*kabā'ir*], so long as that is not accompanied by disavowal of belief.)

> That is better and more excellent in the end.
> *dhālika khairun wa aḥsanu ta'wīlā.*

In other words: "That which He has enjoined upon you, in this Qur'ānic verse, is better for you and more excellent in ultimate outcome." The term *ta'wīl* is applied to the final issue of the thing concerned, to its point of return and its ultimate outcome.[411]

You should know that, in the context of Reality [*Ḥaqīqa*], "those in authority [*uli 'l-amr*]" are the Shaikhs who have reached their spiritual goal, and who are in charge of the training of seekers, for the business [*amr*] of training the seeker has been entrusted [*ūliya*] to his Shaikh. Whenever a truth comes knocking at the door of the seeker's heart, or he receives an inspiration [*ilhām*], or he has an instructive experience concerning deeds or states of being, it is appropriate for the seeker to expose it to the touchstone of his Shaikh's examination. He will thus discover what benefits it contains, as viewed from the Shaikh's perspective. Whether the Shaikh urges him on, or holds him in check, he must comply with his commands and his prohibitions, because the Shaikh is in charge of his business, and "those in authority" do not concur in falsehood.

As for the Shaikh, the authorities in charge of his business are the Book and the Sunna. It is therefore appropriate for him to apply the touchstone of the Book and the Sunna to anything that occurs to him, arriving from the Unseen by the vehicle of truth, in the form of disclosures, visionary experiences, secrets and realities. Whenever these two authorities confirm and validate his receiving, he should accept it, but otherwise not, because the Spiritual Path [*Ṭarīqa*] is defined by the Book and the Sunna, as explained by the consummate Shaikh Najm ad-Dīn al-Kubra in his *Ta'wīlāt* [Interpretations].[412]

These are my own comments:

As indicated by what the Shaikh (may Allāh bestow His mercy upon him) has said, direct perception is an element of the spiritual state of those disciples who take advantage of their opportunities. They are the ones who obtain good fortune in the two abodes [this world and the Hereafter], through vigilant awareness, direct perception and intimate knowledge. May Allāh provide us with that, in honour of the Chieftain of the Messengers (Allāh bless him and give him peace), and through the blessed grace of their supplication and their wise advice.

From this noble Qur'ānic verse:

> Obey Allāh and obey the Messenger,
> *aṭī'u 'llāha wa aṭī'u 'r-Rasūla*
> and those of you who are in authority.
> *wa uli 'l-amri min-kum:*

—it is understood that obedience to Allāh is an absolutely obligatory duty [*farḍ*], so long as the responsible person is alive, and thus until the advent of the Day of Resurrection. Obedience to the Messenger (Allāh bless him and give him peace) is likewise an obligatory duty [*farḍ*], throughout a responsible person's life. The Prophet (Allāh bless him and give him peace) imposed this [during his lifetime] by his noble essence and by inspiration [*waḥy*]. Then, after his conveyance to the Companion Most High [*ar-Rafīq al-A'lā*], his Sunna remained with his Community, and the obligation to follow it likewise remained incumbent on every responsible person [*mukallaf*].

For true knowledge and understanding of this Sunna, it is essential to have religious scholars who give the religion priority over this world. This world cannot play games with them, since they are agreed on the truthfulness that Allāh enjoined upon His servants, by His saying:

> And be together with those who are truthful.
> *wa kūnū maʿa 'ṣ-ṣādiqīn.* (9:119)

These truthful ones will never cease to be among the Community of the Chieftain of the Messengers, until the advent of the Final Hour. Allāh has spoken of them in the Sūra of Repentance [*at-Tawba*]:

> And the first to lead the way, the Emigrés and the Helpers,
> *wa 's-sābiqūna 'l-awwalūna mina 'l-Muhājirīna wa 'l-Anṣāri*
> and those who followed them in active goodness,
> *wa 'lladhīna 'ttabaʿū-hum bi-iḥsānin*
> Allāh is well pleased with them
> *raḍiya 'llāhu ʿan-hum*
> and they are well pleased with Him,
> *wa raḍū ʿan-hu*
> and He has made ready for them for them
> *wa aʿadda la-hum jannātin*
> Gardens underneath which rivers flow,
> *tajrī min taḥti-ha 'l-anhāru*
> wherein they will abide forever.
> *khālidīna fī-hā abadā:*
> That is the mighty triumph.
> *dhālika 'l-fawzu 'l-ʿaẓīm.* (9:100)

As the Qurʾānic verse indicates, those who follow them in their religion, until the Day of Resurrection, will deserve the good pleasure and the reward [of Allāh], provided they follow them in active goodness. The believer must not separate himself from this congregation, and his must not abandon them, because they are the truthful ones. By their truthfulness, they have joined company with those champions of the Truth who preceded them. This is not achieved by mere tittle-tattle, nor by the aspiration of men, but only by the strength of the mercy of the All-Merciful.

O Allāh, to You we declare ourselves detached from our own power, our strength and our actions, and to You we turn for refuge, O Lord of All the Worlds. *Āmīn.* Peace be upon the Messengers, and praise be to Allāh, the Lord of All the Worlds. There is no might nor any power, except with Allāh, the All-High, the Almighty. May Allāh bless our master Muḥammad, his family and his Companions, and may He grant them peace.

The Twenty-third Call

In the Name of Allāh, the All-Merciful, the All-Compassionate.
Bismi'llāhi 'r-Raḥmāni 'r-Raḥīm.

O you who truly believe, take your precautions,
yā ayyuha 'lladhīna āmanū khudhū ḥidhra-kum
then advance in troops, or advance all together.
fa-'nfirū thubātin awi 'nfirū jamīʿā.

Among you there is someone who loiters;
wa inna min-kum la-man yubaṭṭiʾann:
and if disaster overtook you, he would say:
fa-in aṣabat-kum muṣībatun qāla
"Allāh has been gracious to me,
since I was not present with them."
qad anʿama 'llāhu ʿalayya idh lam akun
maʿa-hum shahīdā.

And if a bounty from Allāh befell you,
he would surely cry,
wa la-in aṣāba-hum faḍlun mina 'llāhi la-yaqūlanna
as if there had been no love between you and him:
ka-an lam takun baina-kum wa baina-hu mawaddatun
"If only I had been with them,
yā laita-nī kuntu maʿa-hum
I would have achieved a mighty triumph!"
fa-afūza fawzan ʿaẓīmā. (4:71-3)

Allāh (Exalted is He) has already warned against the hypocrisy of the hypocrites, and ordered obedience to Allāh and obedience to His Messenger (Allāh bless him and give him peace). He has now commanded the greatest of all acts of obedience and deeds of righteousness, that being the sacred struggle in Allāh's cause, for the exaltation of His word and the enlivening of His religion. He has also commanded readiness and preparedness, as a precaution against the surprise attack of the unbelievers. He has then described the condition of those who play truant from the sacred struggle, those hypocrites who frustrate firm resolutions, and He has warned the believers to beware of their wickedness, for He has said (Exalted is He):

> O you who truly believe, take your precautions
> *yā ayyuha 'lladhīna āmanū khudhū ḥidhra-kum.*

That is to say: "O all you believers, be on your guard against your enemy, and be prepared to face him."

> then advance in troops, or advance all together.
> *fa-'nfirū thubātin awi 'nfirū jamīʿā.*

In other words: "Go forth to the sacred struggle in separate companies, one company after another, one detachment after another, or go forth grouped together in a dense military formation." Allāh (Exalted is He) has given you the option between these two approaches to the sacred struggle.[413]

The Qurʾānic verse contains several points requiring clarification:

1. The Arabic terms *al-ḥadhar* and *al-ḥidhr* are synonymous [both meaning "precaution"]. The expression *akhadha ḥidhra-hu* is used when someone becomes alert and takes protective measures against a threatening danger. It is as if he uses the precaution [*ḥidhr*] as an instrument, with which to shield himself and preserve his spirit. The meaning [of the Qurʾānic injunction] is: "You must take precautionary and protective measures against your enemy, and not allow yourselves to come under his control." This is what the author of *al-Kashshāf* has to say on the subject.

According to al-Wāḥidī (may Allāh bestow His mercy upon him), there are two interpretations:

- In this context, *al-ḥidhr* signifies "your weapons," so the meaning [of the injunction] is: "Take your weapons," or more precisely, since the weapons are called precautions: "Take your weapons and be cautiously on guard."
- The expression:

> Take your precautions
> *khudhū ḥidhra-kum.*

—should be understood to mean: "Be cautiously on guard against your enemy," because the command to take such precaution conveys the implicit command to take weapons, since weapons are the means of precaution against the enemy. This interpretation is closely related to the first, but with this difference: According to the first opinion, the command refers explicitly to the taking of weapons, while according to the second, the taking of weapons is merely implied by the tenor of the sentence.

2. Someone may say: "As for that against which Allāh (Exalted is He) has commanded precaution, if its existence must be assumed, precaution is useless, and if its nonexistence must be assumed, there is no need for precaution. In either case, the commandment to take precaution is futile. The Prophet (Allāh bless him and give him peace) is reported as having said:

> Whatever has been foreordained must come to be, so concern is redundant."

It has also been said that taking precaution is of no avail against destiny. If this argument is valid, we must admit that it is pointless to advocate the rules of law [*sharā'i'*], for it may be said: "If a person is one of the people of good fortune, according to Allāh's decree and His destiny, there is no need for faith. If, on the other hand, he is one of the people of misfortune, faith and obedience are useless to him." This amounts to the total nullification of legal responsibility. The correct response must therefore be: "Since everything is predetermined by destiny, the commandment to take precaution must also be included within the scope of destiny." To raise the question: "What is the use of taking precaution?" is to speak in a way that is self-contradictory, because what is the use of this question, designed to discredit precaution, when this precaution is predetermined by destiny?[414]

This call is addressed to the sincere believers of the Community of our master Muḥammad (Allāh bless him and give him peace). It is a commandment instructing them to wage the sacred struggle against the unbelievers, and to go forth in Allāh's cause and in defence of the Sacred Law. It is meant to be understood in the context of the preceding revelations, as part of the following sequence: When He mentioned obedience to Allāh and His Messenger, Allāh commanded the people of obedience to keep His religion alive, and to attach the highest importance to His summons. He also commanded them not to dash against their enemy in a state of ignorance, without first ascertaining their condition and learning how they would react. Since that would be a more positive approach for them, He said:

> Take your precautions.
> *khudhū ḥidhra-kum.*

He thereby taught them how to conduct their military campaigns effectively.

There nothing in the Qur'ānic verse to suggest that taking precaution is of the slightest avail against destiny. We are nevertheless required, as a matter of duty, not to hurl ourselves to destruction. Let us recall the Prophetic tradition [*ḥadīth*]:

> Tie it [the camel], and then have trust.[415]

Since destiny takes its predetermined course, and Allāh does whatever He wishes, the point must be to keep the feelings calm, not to suggest that this can circumvent destiny. Likewise in the case of taking precaution. The proof is that Allāh (Exalted is He) commended the Companions of His Prophet (Allāh bless him and give him peace), in His saying:

> Say: "Nothing befalls us but what Allāh has decreed for us."
> *qul lan yuṣība-nā illā mā kataba 'llāhu la-nā.* (9:51)

—for, if anything could have befallen them apart from what He had decreed for them, this statement would have been meaningless.[416]

3. In His saying:

> then advance in troops, or advance all together.
> *fa-'nfirū thubātin awi 'nfirū jamīʿā.*

—Allāh (Exalted is He) has given them the option, either to fight all together, or to commit only some of them to the fray, by having the leader send one detachment after another into action. This proves that engagement in the sacred struggle is not one of those religious duties that are incumbent on every individual [*furūḍ al-aʿyān*]. The interpretation proposed by al-Baiḍāwī: "[Then advance] combined together, as a single constellation [*kawkaba*]," conveys the sense of a mighty congregation [*jamāʿa*].[417]

Among you there is someone who loiters.
wa inna min-kum la-man yubaṭṭi'ann:

That is to say: "[There is someone who] acts sluggishly and lags behind, to avoid involvement in the sacred struggle." This is a reference to the hypocrites, who were included among the believers because of their expressed determination, and because of their outward show.

and if disaster overtook you
fa-in aṣabat-kum muṣībatun

—in other words: "a slaughter and a defeat,"

he would say: "Allāh has been gracious to me,
qāla qad an'ama 'llāhu 'alayya
since I was not present with them."
idh lam akun ma'a-hum shahīdā.

In other words, that hypocrite would say: "Allāh has treated me with gracious favour, since I did not participate with them in the warfare, for then I would have been among those who were killed."

And if a bounty from Allāh befell you...
wa la-in aṣāba-hum faḍlun mina 'llāhi...

That is to say: "And if there befell you, O believers, a victory, a triumph, and spoils of war...":

he would surely cry, as if there had been no love
la-yaqūlanna ka-an lam takun baina-kum
between you and him: "If only I had been with them,
wa baina-hu mawaddatun yā laita-nī kuntu ma'a-hum
I would have achieved a mighty triumph!"
fa-afūza fawzan 'aẓīmā.

In other words, this hypocrite would surely utter words of remorse and regret, crying, as if there had been no understanding and friendship between you and him: "If only I had been with them in the campaign, I would have obtained a copious share of the booty!" The expression:

as if there had been no...
ka-an lam takun...

—is used to draw attention to the weakness of their faith. This love exists only in the outward appearance of the hypocrite, not in his inner conviction. When he wishes that he had been with the believers, that is not for the sake of the glory of Islām, but simply because of his desire for wealth and the acquisition of worldly vanities. While Allāh (Exalted is He) has blamed the loiterers who hold back from fighting in Allāh's cause, He has encouraged the believers to engage in it, for He has said:

> Let those fight in the way of Allāh who sell
> *fa-l'yuqātil fī sabīli 'llāhi 'lladhīna*
> the life of this world for the Hereafter.
> *yashrūna 'l-ḥayāta 'd-dunyā bi'l-ākhira.* (4:74)[418]

The believer must therefore be in obedience to his Lord, in every aspect of worshipful servitude, for He says, in the first of these Qur'ānic verses:

> O you who truly believe, take your precautions,
> *yā ayyuha 'lladhīna āmanū khudhū ḥidhra-kum*
> then advance in troops, or advance all together.
> *fa-'nfirū thubātin awi 'nfirū jamīʿā.*

It is true that this verse was revealed in connection with warfare, but its wording must be construed in an absolute sense, as referring to the necessity of making haste to acquire all good things, by all possible means, before the opportunity is lost. Allāh's Messenger (Allāh bless him and give him peace) once said:

> Make haste to perform good deeds, before troubles arrive, like the blackout of dark night. A man may be a believer in the early morning, and an unbeliever when evening comes, or he may be a believer in the evening, and an unbeliever the next morning, selling his religion for the merchandise of this world.

It is reported that az-Zubair ibn ʿAdī once said: "Anas ibn Mālik came to us, so we complained to him about the suffering inflicted on us by [the tyrannical governor] al-Ḥajjāj. 'Be patient,' he told us, 'for there will never come a time that is not followed by one that is even worse, until you meet your Lord. I heard this from your Prophet (Allāh bless him and give him peace).'"

As you should also know, the equipment and the weapon for the sacred struggle with the lower self and the devil, meaning the instrument by which to fight them both, is the remembrance of Allāh. That is what the human being must use, to escape from being the prisoner of selfish desire.

Allāh's Messenger (Allāh bless him and give him peace) once said:

> Whenever people remember Allāh, the angels conceal them, mercy covers them, the peace of security descends upon them, and Allāh remembers them among those who are in His presence.[419]

Fleeing towards Allāh is one of the attributes of purposeful seekers, and permanent residence with Allāh is one of the attributes of those who reach their destination. No one can find permanent residence with Allāh, unless he is sincere in fleeing towards Allāh, and fleeing from everything else is the business of everyone who affirms His Oneness.[420]

These are my own observations:

Just as you have been commanded to take your precautions against your external enemy, you have also been commanded to take your precautions against your internal enemy. Your internal enemy is your own lower self and your devil. You must never feel secure from your lower self, no matter what levels of progress you have reached, because it always reverts to its origin, as an instigator of evil [*ammāra bi's-sū'*].

As for your devil, its enmity is clearly described by the text of the Book. You must combat your lower self with scarcity of food, talk and sleep, and be on your guard against it when you satisfy your appetite for lawful food. You must combat your devil with frequent remembrance of Allāh, because it has no influence over those who remember Allāh (Exalted is He) with a heart that is fully aware.

We beseech Allāh (Exalted is He) to help us against our lower selves, our passions and our devils. He is indeed Capable of whatever He wills. Peace be upon the Messengers, and praise be to Allāh, the Lord of All the Worlds. There is no might nor any power, except with Allāh, the All-High, the Almighty. May Allāh bless our master Muḥammad, his family and his Companions, and may He grant them peace.

The Twenty-fourth Call

In the Name of Allāh, the All-Merciful, the All-Compassionate.
Bismi'llāhi 'r-Raḥmāni 'r-Raḥīm.

O you who truly believe,
when you go forth in the way of Allāh,
yā ayyuha 'lladhīna āmanū idhā ḍarabtum fī sabīli 'llāhi
be careful to discriminate,
and do not say to someone who offers you peace:
fa-tabayyanū wa lā taqūlū li-man
alqā ilai-kumu 's-salāma
"You are not a believer," seeking the chance profit
lasta mu'minā: tabtaghūna
of the life of this world.
'araḍa 'l-ḥayāti 'd-dunyā:
With Allāh there are plentiful spoils.
fa-'inda 'llāhi maghānimu kathīra:
You were like that before,
but Allāh has been gracious to you.
ka-dhālika kuntum min qablu fa-manna 'llāhu 'alai-kum
So take care to discriminate.
Allāh is Well-Informed of what you do.
fa-tabayyanū: inna 'llāha kāna bi-mā
ta'malūna Khabīrā. (4:94)

O you who truly believe, when you go forth
yā ayyuha 'lladhīna āmanū idhā ḍarabtum
in the way of Allāh, be careful to discriminate.
fī sabīli 'llāhi fa-tabayyanū

This Qur'ānic verse was revealed in connection with the affair of Mirdās ibn Nahīk, one of the people of Fadak. He had accepted Islām, but no other member of his tribe had done so. The Prophet (peace be upon him) had sent a military detachment to his people, captained by Ghālib ibn Fuḍāla al-Laithī. They fled as soon as the detachment reached them, but Mirdās stayed behind, relying on his Islām for protection. When the Muslims reached Fadak, they proclaimed the Supreme Greatness of Allāh, and Mirdās joined them in proclaiming: "Allāh is Supremely Great [*Allāhu Akbar*]!" He was at the foot of a mountain, together with his sheep and goats, so he went down to meet them, and said: "There is no god but Allāh, and Muḥammad is Allāh's Messenger. Peace be upon you!" Usāma ibn Zaid promptly killed him, and rounded up his sheep and goats.

When they reported this to Allāh's Messenger (Allāh bless him and give him peace), he flew into a rage, and he cried: "You killed him for the purpose of seizing his property, even though he was saying: 'There is no god but Allāh [*lā ilāha illa'llāh*]'!" Usāma responded: "He spoke with his tongue, but not from his heart." (By one account: "He said that only for fear of the sword.") The Prophet (peace be upon him) said: "Why did you not slit his heart open, and look to see whether he was telling the truth or lying?" Then he recited the Qur'ānic verse to Usāma, who said: "O Messenger of Allāh, seek forgiveness on my behalf!" The Messenger replied: "How about doing that by repeating: 'There is no god but Allāh [*lā ilāha illa'llāh*]'?"

Usāma said: "He did not stop repeating it (Allāh bless him and give him peace), until I dearly wished that I had just accepted Islām on that very day. Then he sought forgiveness on my behalf, and commanded the return of the sheep and goats [to the dead man's estate], and the emancipation of a believing slave."[421]

As you should understand, the purpose of this verse is to stress, in no uncertain terms, the unlawfulness of killing believers. For warriors in the sacred struggle, it represents a strict injunction to observe that prohibition with the utmost care, so that they do not shed forbidden blood on some feeble pretext. This heightened emphasis indicates that the preceding verse is also addressed to the believers.[422]

> When you go forth in the way of Allāh, be careful to discriminate
> *yā ayyuha 'lladhīna āmanū idhā ḍarabtum fī sabīli 'llāhi fa-tabayyanū*

That is to say: "When you travel in the course of the sacred struggle [*jihād*], in order to attack the foes, you must proceed at a steady pace, and not be in a hurry to kill, so that you can discriminate clearly between the believer and the unbeliever."

and do not say to someone who offers you peace:
wa lā taqūlū li-man alqā ilai-kumu 's-salāma
"You are not a believer!"
lasta mu'minā.

In other words: "You must not say, to someone who salutes you with the greeting of Islām: 'You are not a believer! You have only said that for fear of being killed,' and then proceed to kill him."[423]

seeking the chance profit of the life of this world.
tabtaghūna ʿaraḍa 'l-ḥayāti 'd-dunyā

That is to say: "While your state is that of people seeking its wealth, which is actually mere rubbish, quick to pass away."[424]

The chance profit of this world is the wealth available therein, whether in cash or in some other form, and whether little or much. As the saying goes: "This world is a pot of luck, from which both the righteous and the shameless eat." Calling it "chance profit" is a way of indicating that it is quick to disappear, and soon to be exhausted.[425]

With Allāh there are plentiful spoils.
fa-ʿinda 'llāhi maghānimu kathīra:

In other words: "In the presence of Allāh there is something far better than that, meaning all that I have promised you in the way of bountiful reward and blissful happiness."[426] That should be enough to keep you from killing someone [who greets you] like that for his property. It also indicates that Allāh's reward is characterized by permanence and everlastingness,[427] as mentioned in His saying (Exalted is He):

And the abiding deeds of righteousness
wa 'l-bāqiyātu 'ṣ-ṣāliḥātu
are better in your Lord's sight for reward,
khairun ʿinda Rabbi-ka thawāban
and better in respect of hope.
wa khairun amalā. (18:46)[428]

You were like that before, but Allāh has been gracious to you.
ka-dhālika kuntum min qablu fa-manna 'llāhu ʿalai-kum
So take care to discriminate.
fa-tabayyanū.

In other words: "You were likewise unbelievers, but He guided you to Islām, and He graciously endowed you with true belief. You must therefore take careful precautions against killing a believer, and compare his condition with your own condition."[429]

> You were like that before
> *ka-dhālika kuntum min qablu*

—in the early stages of your own Islām. The impression you made on people, at that time, was no different from the impression you are now receiving, from the way a newcomer salutes you with the Islāmic greeting, and so on.

> but Allāh has been gracious to you.
> *fa-manna 'llāhu ʿalai-kum.*

—in that He accepted your condition at that stage, using it to protect your life-blood and your property, and that He did not insist on scrutiny of your innermost beings.

> So take care to discriminate.
> *fa-tabayyanū.*

That is to say: "Such being the case, you must seek a clear explanation of this matter. You must compare the person's condition with your own condition, and treat him as Allāh treated you, in your own early stages. In other words, you must accept his condition at face value, without insisting on full correspondence between the outer and the inner."[430] From the fact that the injunction to discriminate is repeated, it is obvious that great emphasis is placed on the warning against wrong behaviour in this matter.[431]

> Allāh is Well-Informed of what you do.
> *inna 'llāha kāna bi-mā taʿmalūna Khabīrā.*

In other words: "Allāh is Well-Informed of what you do, not only in your apparent actions, but also in those that are concealed." He is Well-Informed of the exact nature of those actions, so He will recompense you accordingly. If they are good, the requital will be good, and if they are bad, it will be bad. You must not be impetuous, where killing is concerned, but approach it with circumspection.[432] It was Saʿīd ibn Jubair who said: "This is a warning and a threat."[433]

According to Imām al-Ghazālī (may Allāh the Exalted bestow His mercy upon him): "He who is Well-Informed [*Khabīr*] is One who does not miss the inside stories. Nothing happens in the kingdom of earth and the Kingdom of Heaven, and not an atom moves or keeps still, and not a soul becomes disturbed or tranquil, without there being a report of it in His presence. The term *khabīr* is virtually synonymous with *ʿalīm* [knowledgeable], but when knowledge [*ʿilm*] is linked to the inner secrets, it is properly called *khibra* [expertise; experiential awareness], and he who possesses it is a *khabīr* [expert; one who is fully aware; one who is truly well-informed].

"As for the rôle of the servant [of the Lord] in that, he may become well-informed of what is happening in his own world. His own world consists of his heart, his physical body, and the secret attributes that qualify his heart, such as deception and disloyalty, addiction to the life of this world, concealment of evil behind a show of goodness, and a grudging attitude towards the display of sincere devotion, of which he is personally bankrupt.

"No one really understands the nature of the lower self, unless he is equipped with highly developed expertise [*khibra*]. To fit that description, he must be someone who has thoroughly examined and tested his lower self, become familiar with its guile, its deceit and its treacherous ways, and then declared war on it, briskly countered its hostilities, and taken measures to guard against it. There you have one servant [of the Lord] who truly deserves to be called a well-informed expert [*khabīr*]."[434]

Let us now consider His words (Exalted is He):

> Then He established Himself upon the Throne, the All-Merciful.
> *thumma 'stawā ʿala 'l-ʿarshi 'r-Raḥmānu.*
> Ask someone who is well-informed concerning Him!
> *fa-'sʾal bi-hi khabīrā.* (25:59)

That is to say: "[Ask] someone who has knowledge of His attributes, so that he can make you aware of what has been hidden from you." The identity of that "someone who is well-informed [*khabīr*]" will vary, depending on the identity of the questioner. If the questioner is the Prophet (blessing and peace be upon him), the One who is Well-Informed [*Khabīr*] must be Allāh (Exalted is He). If the questioner is one of his Companions (blessing and peace be upon him), the one who is well-informed [*khabīr*] must be the Prophet (Allāh bless him and give him peace). If the questioner is one of the Successors, the one who is well-informed [*khabīr*] must be one of the Companions (may Allāh be well pleased with them), who received their information from the Prophet (Allāh bless him and give him peace), who received his information from Allāh (Glory be to Him and Exalted is He). That is how the matter proceeds [through a chain of transmission], to the point where the experienced Shaikhs inform the seeker about Allāh. The necessity of intimate knowledge of the affirmation of Oneness [*maʿrifat at-Tawḥīd*] is clearly implied in all this.[435]

As the Qurʾānic verse indicates, the *mujtahid* [person who exercises independent judgment] may make a mistake, as Usāma (may Allāh be well pleased with him) made a mistake. If he does commit a mistake, however, it is regarded as a pardonable error, and not as a punishable offence. While verbal profession is acknowledged as valid, just as the faith of the *muqallid* [unquestioning follower] is considered authentic, it is nevertheless incumbent on the believer to progress from verbal profession to heart-felt profession, and then on to spiritual profession. He will thus obtain specific direction and intimate knowledge, escape from the gloom of ignorance, and be enlightened by the radiance of direct experience, because the human being dies as he lives.[436]

If a Muslim encounters an unbeliever, and the latter has no safe-conduct pass (in other words, he is not protected by a treaty with us), it is permissible for the believer to kill him. This does not apply, however, if he says: "There is no god but Allāh [*lā ilāha illa'llāh*]." In that case, killing him is not allowed, because he has grasped the cord of Islām, which protects his life-blood, his property and his family. If the Muslim kills him after that, he will be killed in retaliation for him.

The abolition of killing, in cases of this kind, was introduced because these incidents occurred in the earliest period of Islām, when the Muslim warriors assumed that if someone spoke like that, he must be acting out of self-defence and fear of the sword, whereas the speech of a person entitled to immunity would be calm and collected. The Prophet (blessing and peace be upon him) therefore let it be known that he was entitled to immunity in any case, however he sounded when he spoke. That is why he said to Usāma: "Why did you not slit his heart open, to find out whether or not he really meant what he said?"[437] (In other words: "To see whether he was a truthful man or a liar.")

That was not a feasible solution, of course, so the only option was to let his tongue state his case. In Islāmic jurisprudence [*fiqh*], where a huge chapter is devoted to this subject, the verdict is that application of the rules of law depends on probable suppositions and external appearances, not on absolute certainty and the examination of consciences.[438]

There is a very useful lesson to be learnt from all this: In your relationships with people, you must base your conduct on how they represent their own conditions. You must not indulge in futile probing into them, for the Custodian of our innermost beings is none but Allāh.[439]

These are my own comments:

This brief survey provides evidence of the tolerance inherent in Islāmic ethics, and the expansiveness of feeling that comes naturally to the Muslims. The basic assumption, in their view, is that all people are good, that we must think well of them all, and that we must accept their outward appearances, while leaving their innermost beings to the Master (Glory be to Him), as a precaution against incurring the condemnation of:

> Some suspicion is a sin.
> *inna ba'ḍa 'ẓ-ẓanni ithmun.* (49:12)

You are commanded to deal with people according to what is apparent, while Allāh (Exalted is He) takes care of their innermost beings. It is within your capacity to know something of what is outwardly apparent, but not to know everything that is visible, so how about the innermost secrets?!

You must therefore entrust the affairs of humankind to Allāh (Exalted is He), the One who knows the secret and what is more deeply hidden still, and think well of your fellow beings, because you are commanded to do so. You are not commanded to think well of yourself, however. Too many people hold a bad opinion of the believers, while thinking well of themselves. "This is the sheer loss [*huwa 'l-khusrānu 'l-mubīn*]" [22:11], so the believer is obliged to refrain from hastily ascribing falsehood to someone who tells the truth with his tongue. He must also refrain from pandering to a liar because of his material wealth, and it is essential for him to be well-informed [*khabīr*].

O Allāh, enable us to be obedient to You, complete our shortcomings, and accept from us. *Āmīn*. Peace be upon the Messengers, and praise be to Allāh, the Lord of All the Worlds. There is no might nor any power, except with Allāh, the All-High, the Almighty. May Allāh bless our master Muḥammad, his family and his Companions, and may He grant them peace.

The Twenty-fifth Call

In the Name of Allāh, the All-Merciful, the All-Compassionate.
Bismi'llāhi 'r-Raḥmāni 'r-Raḥīm

O you who truly believe,
yā ayyuha 'lladhīna āmanū
be staunch upholders of justice,
witnesses for Allāh,
kūnū qawwāmīna bi'l-qisṭi shuhadā'a li'llāhi
even though it be against yourselves
wa law 'alā anfusi-kum
or parents or kindred, whether a rich man
awi 'l-wālidaini wa 'l-aqrabīn: in yakun ghaniyyan
or a poor man, for Allāh is nearer to both.
aw faqīran fa-'llāhu awlā bi-himā

So do not follow passion in case you swerve,
fa-lā tattabi'u 'l-hawā an ta'dilū
and if you twist or turn away,
wa in talwū aw tu'riḍū fa-inna 'llāha
Allāh is ever Aware of what you do.
kāna bi-mā ta'malūna Khabīrā. (4:135)

After having commanded good treatment of wives, and justice in dealing with them, Allāh (Exalted is He) has now commanded the general application of justice in all contexts. He has called for the bearing of witness in the most perfect manner, whether the person testified against be rich or poor, and He has warned against the following of passion. Then [in the verse after this] He has called for belief in all the angels, Books and Messengers.

O you who truly believe,
yā ayyuha 'lladhīna āmanū
be staunch upholders of justice
kūnū qawwāmīna bi'l-qisṭi

That is to say: "O you who believe in Allāh and accept His Book as true, you must be diligent in upholding justice and rectitude." He has used the intensive participle *qawwāmīna* [staunch upholders], to ensure that they will never be guilty of injustice.[440]

The Qur'ānic verse is connected in several respects with those preceding it:

1. It is as if it had been said: "If you are preoccupied with the obtainment of your personal desires, you are for yourself, not for Allāh. On the other hand, if you are preoccupied with the obtainment of the things commanded by Allāh, you are for Allāh, not for yourself, and this station is undoubtedly higher and more noble." This verse is therefore an emphatic confirmation of the obligations previously imposed.

2. Having restrained people from neglecting the reward of this world, and having commanded them to be seekers of the reward of the Hereafter, in His saying (Exalted is He):

> Whoever desires the reward of this world,
> *man kāna yurīdu thawāba 'd-dunyā*
> with Allāh is the reward of this world and the Hereafter.
> *fa-ʿinda 'llāhi thawābu 'd-dunyā wa 'l-ākhira:*
> Allāh is All-Hearing, All-Seeing.
> *wa kāna 'llāhu Samīʿun Baṣīrā.* (4:134)

—Allāh (Exalted is He) has followed it immediately with this verse:

> O you who truly believe,
> *yā ayyuha 'lladhīna āmanū*
> be staunch upholders of justice
> *kūnū qawwāmīna bi'l-qisṭi*

He has explained that, for the human being, the perfection of happiness requires that his speech be for Allāh, that his action be for Allāh, and that his movement and his rest be for Allāh, so that he may come to be one of those who occupy the final ranks of humanity, and the first ranks of the angels. As for the opposite of this case, he will be like the domestic animal, which has no concern beyond the finding of fodder, or like the savage beast, which has no interest beyond causing harm to other animals.

3. Earlier in this Sūra, He has commanded people to practise fairness, as when He said:

> And if you fear that you will not act fairly
> *wa in khiftum allā tuqsiṭū*

in dealing with the orphans....
fi 'l-yatāmā.... (4:3)

He has commanded them to have witnesses present, at the time when the property of orphans is handed over to them. After that, He has commanded them to sacrifice self and wealth in Allāh's cause. He has alluded, in this Sūra, to the story of Ṭuʿma ibn Ubairiq and the conspiracy of his people to defend him by lying, and giving false testimony against the Jews.

In these Qurʾānic verses, Allāh (Exalted is He) has also commanded reconciliation with one's wife. That is known to be a commandment from Allāh to His servants, requiring them to be upholders of justice, witnesses for Allāh against everyone, even against themselves. This verse is therefore like the confirmation of everything that has been mentioned in this Sūra, concerning the various kinds of obligations.[441]

witnesses for Allāh,
shuhadāʾa li'llāhi
even though it be against yourselves
wa law ʿalā anfusi-kum
or parents or kindred
awi 'l-wālidaini wa 'l-aqrabīn:

That is to say: "You must present your testimonies for the sake of Allāh, without bias or partiality, even if that involves testifying against yourselves or against your close relatives. Neither kinship nor self-interest must prevent you from bearing witness in the most perfect manner, for the Lord of Truth is presiding in judgment over every human being."[442] As for bearing witness against oneself, there are two interpretations:

1. The person concerned must acknowledge his own faults, because acknowledgement is like testimony, in that it necessitates the enforcement of the truth.
2. The meaning is: "Even though testifying may have painful consequences for yourselves and your close relatives." That applies to someone who testifies against a tyrannical ruler, or against anyone else whose harmful retribution can be expected.

The commandment to uphold justice precedes the commandment to bear witness, for several reasons:

1. Most people are in the habit of instructing others to do what is right and proper, but when the commandment is directed at themselves, they ignore it. Even if someone is guilty of the most outrageous atrocity, he is disposed to be tolerant of his own offence. On the other hand, even if others behave in the most excellent fashion, he adopts an attitude of negative criticism towards them.

In this Qur'ānic verse, Allāh (Glory be to Him) has therefore drawn attention to the evil of this procedure. He has commanded them (Exalted is He) to uphold justice, first and foremost, then He has commanded them to bear witness against others, in second place. He has thereby served notice that the best procedure is for the individual to put strictness with himself above strictness with other people.

2. The upholding of justice signifies the safeguarding of another from the injury of punishment, when the person concerned is the one who deserves it, despite the natural instinct to give the prevention of harm to oneself priority over the prevention of harm to another.

3. The upholding of justice is an action, while testifying is a verbal utterance, and deeds are stronger than words.

Suppose someone raises the point: "Allāh (Exalted is He) has said:

> Allāh bears witness that there is no god but He,
> *shahida 'llāhu anna-hu lā ilāha illā Huwa*
> and [so do] the angels and the men of learning,
> *wa 'l-malā'ikatu wa ulu 'l-ʿilmi*
> upholding justice.
> *qā'iman bi'l-qisṭ.* (3:18)

—so He has given testimony precedence over the upholding of justice, whereas in this case He has given precedence to the upholding of justice. What is the difference?"

Our answer to this will be: "The testimony of Allāh (Exalted is He) is an expression signifying that He is the Creator of all creatures, while His upholding of justice signifies the care provided by the staunch upholders of justice for the benefit those creatures. In this instance, therefore, it is necessary for the bearing of witness to be given priority over the upholding of justice. As far as His servants are concerned, the upholding of justice signifies that He is a Custodian of justice and an Opponent of injustice. It is well-known that, unless the human being is like that too, his testimony against another will not be accepted.

It is thus established that, in His saying:

> Allāh bears witness....
> *shahida 'llāhu....* (3:18)

—it is necessary for that witnessing to be given precedence over the upholding of justice. In the present case, on the other hand, it is necessary for the bearing of witness to be mentioned after the upholding of justice. If anyone takes careful thought, he will realize that these secrets are unattainable, except through divine assistance. Allāh knows best!"[443]

Allāh (Exalted is He) has then gone on to say:

> whether a rich man
> *in yakun ghaniyyan*
> or a poor man, for Allāh is nearer to both.
> *aw faqīran fa-'llāhu awlā bi-himā*

In other words: "If the person who is testified against is a rich man, you must not pay attention to his wealth, or, if he is a pauper, you must not be dissuaded from testifying against him out of sympathy and compassion. Allāh is nearer to both, and He knows best where their true interest lies. You must therefore observe Allāh's commandment in whatever He has commanded you to do, for He knows the interests of His servants far better than you."[444] If bearing witness against them both were not beneficial to them both, He would not have prescribed it.

In the words of the Prophetic tradition [*ḥadīth*]:

> You must help your brother, whether he be a wrongdoer or a victim.

Someone asked: "O Messenger of Allāh, how can one help him when he is a wrongdoer." To this he replied:

> By steering him away from his wrongdoing, for that is what helping him really means.[445]

To deter the wrongdoer from committing his wrongdoing, is to assist him to obtain the benefit of his religion, and that explains why it is called help. [446]

> So do not follow passion in case you swerve
> *fa-lā tattabiʿu 'l-hawā an taʿdilū*

That is to say: "So do not follow the passion of the lower self, for fear that you may swerve from treating people justly." According to Ibn

Kathīr: "In other words: 'Do not let yourselves be influenced by passion, fanaticism, and the fact that people hate you, so that you abandon justice in dealing with them. You must rather adhere to justice in every situation.'"[447]

The meaning is: "Refrain from following passion, until you deserve to be accorded the attribute of justice." The statement is verified because justice signifies refraining from following passion, and if anyone refrains from either of the two opposites, he automatically acquires the other. The verse may thus be interpreted to mean: "So do not follow passion, to ensure that you act justly," or: "Refrain from following passion, to ensure that you act justly."[448]

> and if you twist or turn away....
> *wa in talwū aw tuʿriḍū....*

In other words: "If your tongues twist and recoil from bearing witness to the truth, or you turn away from upholding it straightforwardly...."[449] It was Mujāhid who said, concerning the expression *talwū* [you twist]: "That is to say: 'You distort the testimony and alter it.' The corresponding noun *layy* signifies distortion and deliberate lying."[450]

As it occurs in the Qur'ānic verse, *talwū* may be interpreted in two senses:

1. It may mean rejecting and recoiling from what people say. The expression *lawā-hu ḥaqqa-hu* [he twisted someone's due] is a way of saying that he deferred it and pushed it aside.
2. It may mean distorting and changing what people say. The expression *lawa 'sh-shai'* [he twisted the thing] is a way of saying that he knotted it together.

In case of the [alternative] reading *talū*, [the corresponding noun] *wilāya* signifies devoting one's attention to something, and becoming fully preoccupied with it, so the meaning is: "If you devote your attention to it, in order to complete it, or you turn away from it."[451]

> Allāh is ever Aware of what you do.
> *kāna bi-mā taʿmalūna Khabīrā.*

He will therefore recompense the accepted doer of good for his beneficence, and the rejected evil-doer for his wickedness. To put it briefly: "If you distort it [the testimony], or turn away from stating it correctly:

> Allāh is ever Aware of what you do.
> *kāna bi-mā ta'malūna Khabīrā.*

This is a dire warning and a threat for the sinners, and a promise of good treatment for the obedient.[452]

The detailed treatment of bearing witness [*shahāda*], and the imperative necessity thereof, has been given in the Eleventh Call [*Nidā'*], in the Sūra of the Cow [*al-Baqara*]. In the opinion of the jurists, the concealment of testimony, in cases involving the *ḥudūd* [legal penalties prescribed by Islāmic law], is more meritorious than its promulgation. This view is based on the saying of the Prophet (Allāh bless him and give him peace), to someone who testified before him in connection with the prescribed penalty:

> If you had kept it hidden in your clothes, it would have been better for you.[453]

—and on his saying (Allāh bless him and give him peace):

> If someone conceals a fault for a Muslim, Allāh will pardon him in this world and the Hereafter.[454]

—as well as on his saying (Allāh bless him and give him peace):

> Whenever a Muslim supports a Muslim, in a place where his honour is being maligned and his dignity is being besmirched, Allāh (Exalted is He) will support him in any situation where he needs His support. If any man leaves a Muslim in the lurch, in a place where his dignity is being maligned, Allāh (Exalted is He) will leave him in the lurch in a place where he needs His support.[455]

—and also on his saying (Allāh bless him and give him peace):

> Ward off the penalties [*ḥudūd*] from the Muslims, as far as you are able.[456]

As stated in the books of jurisprudence [*fiqh*], it is necessary to discharge [the giving of testimony] without waiting to be asked, if the testimony concerns the rights of Allāh (Exalted is He), which are many. (See the *Ḥāshiya* [Margin] of Ibn 'Ābidīn, pt. 5, together with the commentary.) Its concealment is more righteous in cases involving the penalties called *ḥudūd*, on account of the Prophetic saying:

> He who conceals will be concealed [*man satara sutir*].[457]

In short, Allāh (Exalted is He) is commanding His believing servants to be staunch upholders of justice, so they must not swerve from it, neither to right nor to left. They must not be deterred by the blame of any critic, nor must any diversion distract them from it. They must be helpful to one another in it, mutually supportive, cooperative and ready to assist one another.

As for His expression:

> witnesses for Allāh
> *shuhadāʾa li'llāhi*

—and His injunction:

> And keep your testimony upright for Allāh.
> *wa aqīmu 'sh-shahādata li'llāh.* (65:2)

—that is to say: "Discharge it while seeking Allāh's Countenance, for then it will be truly valid and just, free from distortion, alteration and concealment." That is why He has told us:

> even though it be against yourselves
> *wa law ʿalā anfusi-kum*

In other words: "You must bear witness to the truth, even if the consequences are detrimental to you. If you are questioned about the matter, you must tell the truth about it, even if the result is to your disadvantage." For those who obey Him, Allāh will surely provide a relief and a way out of every difficult situation. The Lord of Truth is presiding in judgment over everyone.

Consider the story of ʿAbdu'llāh ibn Rawāḥa: When the Prophet (Allāh bless him and give him peace) dispatched him to the people of Khaibar, to assess the value of their fruit and crops, they tried to gain his sympathy by offering him a bribe, but he said: "By Allāh, I have come from the dearest of creatures to—what can I say? You are more hateful to me than an equal number of monkeys and pigs. Nevertheless, my love of him and my hatred of you will not induce me to treat you unjustly." They exclaimed: "By this the heavens and the earth are set in place!"[458]

A useful note: The term *qisṭ* is synonymous with *ʿadl* [justice; equity; fairness]. Standing by Allāh means acting with justice in the fulfilment of His rights over you yourself, and the fulfilment of His rights over everyone for whom you bear some responsibility. The way to discharge that duty is by enjoining something that is right and proper, or by preventing something that is reprehensible, or by admonishing with sincere advice, or by drawing attention to a rule of law, or by providing guidance to the Truth.[459]

These are my own observations:

Allāh (Exalted is He) revealed the noble Qur'ān to our master, Muḥammad the Chosen [*al-Muṣṭafā*] (on him be the finest blessing and the most perfect salutation), so that he might convey the message to his Community—and to you, O my believing brother, because Allāh is addressing you with this call, which is meant especially for you.

You are included in this, for Allāh's Messenger (on him be the finest blessing and peace) has conveyed these Divine commandments to us all. Our Lord does not seek to profit by our compliance with His commandments, nor does He lose (Glorious and Exalted is He) by our violation of His prohibitions. It is only our welfare that is at stake, since there is benefit, in all the commandments contained in the noble Qur'ān, for our religion and our worldly interests, both collectively and individually. It will be to our detriment if we ignore these commandments.

It is incumbent upon us, O companies of the believers, to adhere to the Muḥammadan Sacred Law, for it came down from the Noble Lord (Glorious and Exalted is He), by means of Gabriel (peace be upon him), to His noble Messenger (Allāh bless him and give him peace). We are answerable for the truth, whether that truth is the Truth of Allāh, or the truth of our own selves, or the truth of the servants [of the Lord]. We are therefore obliged to observe that with great care. We must not let greed and desire for this world induce us to consume people's wealth without entitlement, nor must we be secretive in giving testimony. In all our affairs, both religious and worldly, we must follow the Sunna [the exemplary pattern] of the chief of the Envoys, and we must not follow passionate desire.

We beg Allāh (Exalted is He) to enable us to do what He loves and finds pleasing, and to be truthful in our words and our deeds, in both our outer and our inner dealings, with Allāh and with the servants of Allāh, for the sake of the Chief of the Messengers. *Āmīn*. Peace be upon the Messengers, and praise be to Allāh, the Lord of All the Worlds. There is no might nor any power, except with Allāh, the All-High, the Almighty. May Allāh bless our master Muḥammad, his family and his Companions, and may He grant them peace.

The Twenty-sixth Call

In the Name of Allāh, the All-Merciful, the All-Compassionate.
Bismi'llāhi 'r-Raḥmāni 'r-Raḥīm.

O you who believe, believe in Allāh and His Messenger
yā ayyuha 'lladhīna āmanū āminū bi'llāhi wa Rasūli-hi
and the Book which He has sent down to His Messenger
wa 'l-Kitābi 'lladhī nazzala ʿalā Rasūli-hi
and the Book which He sent down in former times.
wa 'l-Kitābi 'lladhī anzala min qabl:
Whoever disbelieves in Allāh and His angels
wa man yakfur bi'llāhi wa malā'ikati-hi
and His Books and His Messengers and the Last Day,
wa Kutubi-hi wa Rusuli-hi wa 'l-Yawmi 'l-Ākhiri
he has wandered far astray.
fa-qad ḍalla ḍalālan baʿīdā.
(4:136)

Allāh (Exalted is He) is commanding His believing servants to embrace all the basic principles of belief, and its branches, its pillars and its supports. This is not just a matter of acquiring the gist, but rather of perfecting the perfect, confirming it, establishing it and adhering to it constantly. As the believer says in every ritual prayer:

> Guide us in the straight path.
> *ihdina 'ṣ-ṣirāṭa 'l-mustaqīm.* (1:5)

In other words: "Enlighten us in it, increase us in guidance, and set us firmly upon it." He has therefore commanded them to believe in Him and His Messenger, as He has said (Exalted is He):

> O you who believe,
> *yā ayyuha 'lladhīna āmanū*
> believe in Allāh and His Messenger.[460]
> *āminū bi'llāhi wa Rasūli-hi.*

With regard to the connection between this Qurʾānic verse and what was revealed before it, there are two possibilities to consider:

1. It is connected with His saying:

> Be staunch upholders of justice.
> *kūnū qawwāmīna bi'l-qisṭi.* (4:135)

That is because the human being will not be an upholder of justice, unless his footing is firmly rooted in belief in the things mentioned in this Qurʾānic verse.

2. After having expounded the many rules contained within this Sūra, Allāh (Exalted is He) followed them with the verse commanding belief. The traditional commentators have discussed it from several points of view, which may be summed up in two opinions:

• The first opinion is that His saying (Exalted is He):

> O you who believe
> *yā ayyuha 'lladhīna āmanū*

—refers to the Muslims. On the basis of this opinion, the detailed interpretation of the verse gives rise to the following points:

1. The expression:

> O you who believe
> *yā ayyuha 'lladhīna āmanū*

—is intended to convey: "Believe, persist in belief, and be firmly committed to it," and the import of it signifies: "O you who have believed in the past, and who believe in the present, you must also believe in the future." This is similar to His saying [to the Prophet (Allāh bless him and give him peace)]:

> So know that there is no god but Allāh.
> *fa-'ʿlam anna-hu lā ilāha illa 'llāhu.* (47:19)

—even though he was well aware of that.

2. "O you who believe by way of convention [*taqlīd*], you must believe by way of personal verification [*taḥqīq*]."

3. "O you who believe with the knowledge of certainty [*ʿilm al-yaqīn*], you must believe with the eye of certainty [*ʿain al-yaqīn*]."

4. "O you who believe, with the the eye of certainty, in Allāh, His angels, His Books and His Messengers, you must believe, with the truth of certainty [*ḥaqq al-yaqīn*], that the essence of the Might of Allāh is beyond the reach of your minds. You must likewise believe that the conditions of the angels, the secrets of the Books, and the attributes of the Messengers are beyond the logic of our minds."

5. It is related that a group of Jewish rabbis once came to the Prophet (Allāh bless him and give him peace) and said: "O Messenger of Allāh, we believe in you, and in your Book, and in Moses, and in the Torah and in Ezra [*ʿUzair*]. We do not believe in any of the other Books and Messengers." He responded to this by saying (Allāh bless him and give him peace):

> You must rather believe in Allāh, and in His Messengers, and in Muḥammad, and in his Book, the Qurʾān, and in every Book that was before it.

The rabbis said: "We shall not do so!" The Qurʾānic verse was thereupon revealed, and all of them believed.

• The second opinion is that those addressed by His saying:

> [O you who] believe
> [*yā ayyuha 'lladhīna*] *āmanū*

—are not the Muslims. On the basis of this opinion, the detailed interpretation of the verse gives rise to the following points:

1. The summons is addressed to the Jews and the Christians, and the implicit meaning is: "O you who believe in Moses and the Torah, and Jesus and the Gospel, you must believe in Muḥammad and the Qurʾān!"

2. The summons is addressed to the hypocrites, and the implict meaning is: "O you who believe with the tongue, you must believe with the heart!" This interpretation is supported by His saying (Exalted is He):

> Of such as say with their mouths: "We believe,"
> *mina 'lladhīna qālū āmannā bi-afwāhi-him*
> but their hearts do not believe.
> *wa lam tuʾmin qulūbu-hum*. (5:41)

3. The summons is addressed to those who believe at the start of the

day, but disbelieve at the end of it. The implicit meaning is: "O you who believe at the start of the day, you must also believe at the end of it!"

4. The summons is addressed to the idol-worshippers [*mushrikīn*], and the implicit meaning is: "O you who believe in al-Lāt and al-ʿUzzā, you must believe in Allāh."

Most of the scholars have preferred the first opinion, because the term *muʾmin* [believer], without qualification, cannot apply to any but the Muslims.[461]

> and the Book which He has sent down to His Messenger
> *wa 'l-Kitābi 'lladhī nazzala ʿalā Rasūli-hi*

—means the Qurʾān, while:

> and the Book which He sent down in former times.
> *wa 'l-Kitābi 'lladhī anzala min qabl:*

—is a collective expression, referring to all the previous Books. In the case of the Qurʾān, He has used the verb *nazzala*, which indicates that He sent it down in separate instalments, in connection with developing situations, according to the needs of His servants in their worldly and spiritual lives. As for the previous Books, each of them was revealed as a single unit, so He has used the verb *anzala* in His saying (Exalted is He):

> and the Book which He sent down in former times.
> *wa 'l-Kitābi 'lladhī anzala min qabl:*

Then He has gone on to say (Exalted is He):

> Whoever disbelieves in Allāh and His angels
> *wa man yakfur bi'llāhi wa malāʾikati-hi*
> and His Books and His Messengers and the Last Day,
> *wa Kutubi-hi wa Rusuli-hi wa 'l-Yawmi 'l-Ākhiri*
> he has wandered far sstray.
> *fa-qad ḍalla ḍalālan baʿīdā.*

In other words: "He has deviated from the path of right guidance, and has gone as far as could be from the right direction, meaning the straight path."[462]

In this Qur'ānic verse, as you must know, Allāh (Exalted is He) has commanded belief in four things: (1) in Allāh; (2) in His Messenger; (3) in the Book which He has sent down to His Messenger, and (4) the Book which He sent down in former times.

He has also mentioned five categories of disbelief [*kufr*]: (1) disbelief in Allāh; (2) disbelief in His angels; (3) disbelief in His Books; (4) disbelief in His Messengers, and (5) disbelief in the Last Day.

The Qur'ānic verse gives rise to several questions, including the following:

1. Question: Why, in listing the degrees of belief, has He mentioned the Messenger before the Book, and then reversed this order in the degrees of disbelief?

Answer: Because, at the stage of the descent of the knowledge of the Creator to His creatures, the Book came before the Messenger, but then, at the stage of ascent from creatures to the Creator, the Messenger takes precedence over the Book.

2. Question: Why, in listing the degrees of belief, has He mentioned three things: belief in Allāh, in the Messenger and in the Books, whereas, in listing the degrees of disbelief, He has mentioned five things: disbelief in Allāh, in the angels, in the Books, in the Messengers and in the Last Day?

Answer: As for belief in Allāh, in the Messengers and in the Books, when that belief comes about, it inevitably entails belief in the angels and the Last Day. Let us suppose that someone claims to believe in Allāh, in the Messengers and the Books, but then he denies the existence of the angels and rejects the idea of the Last Day, maintaining that the Qur'ānic verses concerning the angels and the Last Day are open to interpretation. If this supposition proves to be a fact, the only possible conclusion is that the denier of the angels and of the Resurrection is a disbeliever in Allāh.[463]

As for the common folk, their degree of belief is referred to in the saying of the Prophet (blessing and peace be upon him):

> You must believe in Allāh, His angels, His books and His Messengers, and in the resurrection after death, the Garden of Paradise, the Fire of Hell, and destiny, both the good of it and the bad of it.[464]

This is second-hand faith [*īmān ghaibī*].

As for the élite, their degree of belief is that of faith based on first-hand experience [*īmān ʿiyānī*]. That is because, when Allāh makes Himself manifest to His servant, through one of His attributes, all parts of that servant's being become humbly submissive to Him. He now believes entirely, from direct experience, after his heart had believed indirectly, while his lower self disbelieved in what his heart believed in. The lower self had been isolated from the fragrance of the perfumes of the Unseen, but then, when the Lord of Truth made Himself manifest to the mountain, He reduced it to dust. The lower self fell prostrate, and then, when it recovered, it said: "I have repented to You, for now I am one of the believers."

As for the élite of the élite, their degree of belief is also that of faith based on first-hand experience [*īmān ʿiyānī*]. In their case, that comes about after the removal of the veils of egoism [*anāniyya*], by the impact of the manifestation of Divine Majesty [*Jalāl*]. As soon as He has made one of them extinct to himself through the attribute of Majesty, He grants him permanent survival through the attribute of Divine Beauty [*Jamāl*]. No *ain* [where] remains for him, and he remains forever in the *ʿain* [eye; essence; source]. Since this is a faith derived from vision of the source [*īmān ʿainī*], it is the real faith [*īmān ḥaqīqī*]. May Allāh grant it to us, and to all of you![465]

The servant attains to this singularity and detachment by means of remembrance [*dhikr*] and the affirmation of Oneness [*tawḥīd*]. In his final advice to ʿAlī (may Allāh be well pleased with him) the Prophet (Allāh bless him and give him peace) told him:

> O ʿAlī, you must safeguard the affirmation of Oneness, for that is my capital. You must be diligent in work, for that is my profession. You must perform the ritual prayer [*ṣalāt*], for that is the comfort of my eye. You must remember the Truth, for that is the succour of my heart. You must put knowledge into active practice. That is my legacy.[466]

The follow meanings are implicit in the Qurʾānic verse:

"O you who believe on the strength of rational proof, you must believe on the strength of clarification, until you come to believe on the strength of disclosure and the experience of direct vision."

"O you who believe by accepting the truth, you must believe by realizing that your salvation depends on His grace, not on your belief."

"O you who believe at the present moment, you must believe by persevering in belief until the final outcome."[467]

These are my own comments:

There are three degrees of faith [*īmān*]:

1. Uncritically conventional faith [*al-īmān at-taqlīdī*].
2. Faith based on rational evidence and proofs [*al-īmān bi'l-istidlāl wa 'l-barāhīn*].
3. Faith based on experience, direct perception, and factors transcending these [*al-īmān adh-dhawqī wa 'sh-shuhūdī wa mā fawqa-humā*].

• As for uncritically conventional faith, it is not acceptable, according to some of the *mujtahidīn* [those who exercise independent judgment], except in the case of a person who is simply a *muqallid* [uncritical follower of convention] by nature. It includes academic faith [*īmān ʿilmī*], where someone takes lessons from a teacher, and does some reading, so that he acquires knowledge of the faith. This is second-hand faith [*īmān ghaibī*].

• As for faith based on rational evidence and proofs, it is the faith of the theologians [*mutakallimīn*], so it is lacking in strength by comparison with the faith of those who are superior to them. That explains the saying: "You must have the faith of old women!" It was ash-Shādhilī (may Allāh bestow His mercy upon him) who said: "We know our Lord directly, without requiring evidence."

• As for faith based on experience, direct perception, and factors transcending these, it develops by stages, until it reaches the level of the faith of the champions of truth [*īmān aṣ-ṣiddīqīn*]. As we are told in the Prophetic tradition [*ḥadīth*]:

> You must worship Allāh as if you could see him, for, even if you do not see him, He surely sees you![468]

That is to say: "Even if you are not among the people of experience and direct perception, and do not behold your Lord (Glorious and Exalted is He) with the eye of your heart, you must at least understand and be fully convinced that He sees you."

In respect of certainty [*yaqīn*], there are three degrees of faith:

1. The knowledge of certainty [*ʿilm al-yaqīn*], as mentioned in His saying (Exalted is He):

> No indeed; if you did but know
> *kallā law taʿlamūna*
> with the knowledge of certainty,
> *ʿilma 'l-yaqīn:*
> you will surely see Hellfire.
> *la-tarawunna 'l-jaḥīm.* (102:5,6)

2. The eye of certainty [*ʿain al-yaqīn*], as mentioned in His saying (Exalted is He):

> Again, you will surely see it with the eye of certainty.
> *thumma la-tarawunna-hā ʿaina 'l-yaqīn.* (102:7)

3. The truth of certainty [*ḥaqq al-yaqīn*], as mentioned in His saying (Exalted is He):

> This is indeed the truth of certainty.
> *inna hādhā la-huwa ḥaqqu 'l-yaqīn.* (56:95)

- As for the faith of the knowledge of certainty, it is possible for it to be invaded by doubts and atheism [*zandaqa*]. This is second-hand faith, the faith of the common people.
- As for the faith of the eye of certainty, it is impossible for it to be invaded by doubts or anything contrary to faith. This is the faith of the élite.
- As for the faith of the truth of certainty, it is the faith of the champions of truth, and above the level of the champions of truth, at the level of Prophethood [*Nubuwwa*].

The human being is veiled by the heedlessness that arises from this world, the lower self, his fellow creatures and the devil. If the veil between the servant and his Creator is removed, the servant will see Reality. If the servant persists in overcoming the obstacles, faith will grow strong, heedlessness will be dispelled, and Reality will shine forth, to become the governor of his heart. That condition will stay with him, until it becomes a spiritual station for him. His heart will then be on intimate terms with his Master, and no impediments will keep him from Allāh (Glorious and Exalted is He).

As you are surely aware, most people are in a state of heedlessness, because they attach importance to themselves, forget their own faults, do not hesitate to oppose Allāh and His Messenger (blessing and peace be upon him), and proceed in accordance with their self-centred desires. Allāh guides aright whomever He will, and if Allāh causes someone to go astray, you will never find a way for him to reach felicity and right guidance.

It is incumbent on us, O believers, to act in accordance with faith, and not to be among those who hear what is said, but do not follow the best of it. To meet the demands of faith, the servant must prefer his life in the Hereafter to his life in this world. He must refrain entirely from disobeying Allāh. He must practise worshipful obedience to the best of his ability, over and above the divinely prescribed obligatory duties, for those he must perform in their entirety.

O Allāh, guide us towards those who will guide us towards You, and acquaint us with those who will acquaint us with You, through Your mercy, O Most Merciful of the merciful. Peace be upon the Messengers, and praise be to Allāh, the Lord of All the Worlds. There is no might nor any power, except with Allāh, the All-High, the Almighty. May Allāh bless our master Muḥammad, his family and his Companions, and may He grant them peace.

The Twenty-seventh Call

In the Name of Allāh, the All-Merciful, the All-Compassionate.
Bismi'llāhi 'r-Raḥmāni 'r-Raḥīm.

O you who truly believe,
do not choose unbelievers
yā ayyuha 'lladhīna āmanū lā tattakhidhu 'l-kāfirīna
for friends instead of believers.
awliyā'a min dūni 'l-mu'minīn:
Would you give Allāh a clear warrant against you?
a-turīdūna an taj'alū li'llāhi 'alai-kum sulṭānan mubīnā.

The hypocrites will surely be in the lowest depth of the Fire [of Hell],
inna 'l-munāfiqīna fi 'd-darki 'l-asfali mina 'n-nār:
and you will find no helper for them;
wa lan tajida la-hum naṣīrā:

Except those who repent and make amends,
illa 'lladhīna tābū wa aṣlaḥū
and hold fast to Allāh,
and devote their religion sincerely to Allāh.
wa ''taṣamū bi'llāhi wa akhlaṣū dīna-hum li'llāhi.
Those are with the believers.
fa-ulā'ika ma'a 'l-mu'minīn:
And Allāh will bestow on the believers
an immense reward.
wa sawfa yu'ti 'llāhu 'l-mu'minīna ajran 'aẓīmā.

What concern has Allāh for your torment
mā yaf'alu 'llāhu bi-'adhābi-kum
if you are thankful and believe?
in shakartum wa āmantum:
Allāh is All-Thankful, All-Knowing.
wa kāna 'llāhu Shākiran 'Alīmā. (4:144–47)

You must know that Allāh (Exalted is He) blamed the hypocrites for siding at one time with the unbelievers, and at another time with the Muslims, without committing themselves to either of the two parties. He did so in the preceding verses of Qur'ān, when He said (Exalted is He):

> The hypocrites seek to beguile Allāh
> *inna 'l-munāfiqīna yukhādiʿūna 'llāha*
> but it is He who beguiles them.
> *wa Huwa khādiʿu-hum.* (4:142)

> [They are] swaying between this [and that],
> *mudhabdhabīna baina dhālik:*
> belonging neither to these nor to those.
> *lā ilā hāʾulāʾi wa lā ilā hāʾulāʾ:*
> If Allāh causes someone to go astray,
> *wa man yuḍlili 'llāhu*
> you will not find a way for him.
> *fa-lan tajida la-hu sabīlā.* (4:143)

In the present Qurʾānic verse, He has forbidden the Muslims to act as the hypocrites act, for He has said (Exalted is He):

> O you who truly believe, do not choose unbelievers
> *yā ayyuha 'lladhīna āmanū lā tattakhidhu 'l-kāfirīna*
> for friends instead of believers.
> *awliyāʾa min dūni 'l-muʾminīn:*

There are two perspectives to be considered:

1. The occasion for this prohibition was that the Helpers [*Anṣār*] in Medina had a foster relationship [*riḍā*], an alliance and a bond of affection with the tribe of Banī Quraiẓa. They said to Allāh's Messenger (Allāh bless him and give him peace): "Whom should we choose for friends?" and he replied: "The Emigrants [*Muhājirūn*]." This Qurʾānic verse was then revealed.

2. According to the view expressed by al-Qaffāl (may Allāh bestow His mercy upon him), this prohibition is intended to keep the believers from befriending the hypocrites, since Allāh is saying: "I have shown you the characteristic features of the hypocrites, and their modes of conduct, so you must not choose them for friends."[469] Allāh (Exalted is He) has thus forbidden His believing servants to choose the unbelievers for friends, instead of the believers. This signifies the prohibition of

fellowship, friendship and confidential relations with them, harbouring strong feelings of affection for them, and disclosing to them the private situations of the believers. As Allāh (Exalted is He) has said:

> Do not let the believers take unbelievers
> *lā yattakhidhi 'l-mu'minūna 'l-kāfirīna*
> for friends instead of believers.
> *awliyā'a min dūni 'l-mu'minīn:*
> Whoever does that has no connection with Allāh,
> *wa man yaf'al dhālika fa-laisa mina 'llāhi fī shai'in*
> unless you are guarding yourselves against them, taking security.
> *illā an tattaqū min-hum tuqāh:*
> And Allāh warns you to beware of Himself.
> *wa yuḥadhdhiru-kumu 'llāhu Nafsa-h.* (3:28)

In other words, He is warning you to be on guard against His punishment for violating His prohibition, and that is why He has said here:[470]

> Would you give Allāh a clear warrant against you?
> *a-turīdūna an taj'alū li'llāhi 'alai-kum sulṭānan mubīnā.*

This means: "Do you wish to give Allāh an irrefutable argument in favour of your punishment, because of your friendship with the hypocrites?"[471] As reported by Ibn Abī Ḥātim, Ibn 'Abbās (may Allāh be well pleased with him and his father) once said, concerning Allāh's expression:

> a clear warrant
> *sulṭānan mubīnā.*

"Every warrant [*sulṭān*] in the Qur'ān is an irrefutable proof." (This report is based on a sound chain of transmission.)[472]

Allāh (Exalted is He) has then gone on to inform us:

> The hypocrites will surely be in the lowest depth of the Fire [of Hell].
> *inna 'l-munāfiqīna fī 'd-darki 'l-asfali mina 'n-nār.*

That is to say, on the Day of Resurrection, as a recompense for their obstinate unbelief. According to Ibn 'Abbās (may Allāh be well pleased with him and his father), *fī 'd-darki 'l-asfal* [in the lowest depth] is synonymous with *fī asfal* [at the very bottom]. Others maintain that the Fire of Hell consists of descending levels [*darakāt*], just as the Garden of Paradise consists of ascending levels [*darajāt*]. As reported by

Sufyān ath-Thawrī, it was Abū Huraira (may Allāh be well pleased with him) who said, concerning:

> The hypocrites will surely be in the lowest depth of the Fire [of Hell].
> *inna 'l-munāfiqīna fi 'd-darki 'l-asfali mina 'n-nār.*

"[They will be] in coffins, bolted over them." He is also reported as having said: "The lowest depth consists of boxes fitted with doors, which will be locked to contain them, then ignited beneath them and above them."[473]

Ibn Mas'ūd (may Allāh be well pleased with him) is reported as having said: "Coffins of iron, fitted with locks, will be bolted over them in the Fire." Ibn 'Umar said: "On the Day of Resurrection, the most terrible torment will be suffered by three sets of people: the hypocrites, those Companions of the Table [*Aṣḥāb al-Mā'ida*] who disbelieved, and the folk of Pharaoh. Confirmation of this can be found in the Book of Allāh (Exalted is He), for Allāh (Exalted is He) has said:

> The hypocrites will surely be in the lowest depth of the Fire [of Hell].
> *inna 'l-munāfiqīna fi 'd-darki 'l-asfali mina 'n-nār.*

—and He has said (Exalted is He), concerning the Companions of the Table [*Aṣḥāb al-Mā'ida*]:

> I will surely punish him with a torment
> *fa-innī u'adhdhibu-hu 'adhāban*
> such as I have never inflicted
> *lā u'adhdhibu-hu*
> on any of the peoples of the world.
> *aḥadan mina 'l-'ālamīn.* (5:115)

—and concerning the folk of Pharaoh, He has said (Exalted is He):

> Admit the folk of Pharaoh into the most terrible torment.
> *adkhilū āla Fir'awna ashadda 'l-'adhāb.* (40:46)"[474]

It was al-Laith who said: "The obvious conclusion is that Hell consists of several layers, and that the most terrible is the lowest of them all." According to aḍ-Ḍaḥḥāk: "The Arabic term *darj* is used when the levels are situated one above another, while the Arabic term *dark* is used when they come one below another."

Why should the hypocrite suffer torment more terrible than that of the unbeliever? Because he is like him in unbelief, but with an added dimension of unbelief, that being scorn for Islām and its people. Furthermore, since the hypocrites pretended to accept Islām, they were able to pry into the secrets of the Muslims, which they would then pass on the the unbelievers. The menace posed by those hypocrites was thereby multiplied. For these reasons, Allāh has made their torment greater than the torment of the unbelievers.[475]

The hypocrite is someone who makes an outward show of belief, while he is inwardly guilty of unbelief. According to one definition: "He is someone who professes Islām with his tongue, but does not put its legal requirements [*sharā'i'*] into practice, is not confined by its restraints, and does not conform to its regulations."

As for the application of the term "hypocrite [*munāfiq*]" to someone who is guilty of immoral conduct, it is a means of expressing harsh disapproval. Relevant in this context is the saying of the Prophet (Allāh bless him and give him peace):

> Three things, secreted within a person, make him a hypocrite, even if he keeps the fast, performs the ritual prayer, and insists that he is a Muslim. This applies to someone who, when he tells a tale, is telling a lie, and when he makes a promise, breaks it, and when he is trusted, betrays the trust.[476]

These vices are the attributes of the hypocrites, so anyone who is guilty of them deserves to be likened to the hyprocrites.[477]

> and you will find no helper for them.
> *wa lan tajida la-hum naṣīrā.*

That is to say: "[You will find no helper] to rescue them from their condition, and to deliver them from the painful torment."[478] This is a serious warning to them.[479] Then Allāh (Exalted is He) has informed them that, if any one of them repents in this world, He will relent towards him and accept his remorse, provided he is sincere in his repentance, corrects his behaviour, and holds fast to his Lord in all his business. Allāh (Exalted is He) has made this clear, for He has said:

> Except those who repent and make amends,
> *illa 'lladhīna tābū wa aṣlaḥū*
> and hold fast to Allāh,
> and devote their religion sincerely to Allāh.
> *wa 'ʿtaṣamū bi'llāhi wa akhlaṣū dīna-hum li'llāhi.*

In other words: "Those who replace pretentious display with sincere devotion," for righteous conduct will then prove beneficial to them, even if it is seldom practised. As reported by Ibn Abī Ḥātim, on the authority of Muʿādh ibn Jabal, Allāh's Messenger (Allāh bless him and give him peace) once said:

> Be sincerely devoted to your religion, for even a little active practice will then be sufficient for you.

> Those are with the believers.
> *fa-ulāʾika maʿa 'l-muʾminīn:*

That is to say: "They will be in their company on the Day of Resurrection."[480]

> And Allāh will bestow on the believers an immense reward.
> *wa sawfa yuʾti 'llāhu 'l-muʾminīna ajran ʿaẓīmā.*

This may indicate that He has postponed the reward of the believers till the future, because the hypocrites are presently associated with them. Allāh know best.[481]

As you must know, this Qurʾānic verse contains extremely harsh warnings for the hypocrites. That is because Allāh (Exalted is He) has laid down four conditions for removal of the torment:

1. Repentance.
2. Improvement of behaviour. Repentance means turning away from what is bad and ugly, while improvement of behaviour is an expression signifying progress towards that which is fine and good.
3. Holding fast to Allāh. This means that repentance and improvement of behaviour must be undertaken with the aim of acquiring the good pleasure of Allāh (Exalted is He), not for the sake of gaining temporal advantage. If his object were the procurement of benefits, and the repelling of disadvantages, there would be a rapid alteration in the person's commitment to repentance and improvement of behaviour. On the other hand, if his object is the good pleasure of Allāh (Exalted is He), the blissful happiness of the Hereafter, and close adherence to Allāh's religion, and if he keeps to this path, he will not experience any change in his commitment.
4. Sincere devotion. The point is that Allāh (Exalted is He) has commanded them in sequence: firstly, to abstain from what is bad and

ugly; secondly, to practise what is fine and good; thirdly, to ensure that their aim, in that abstinence and practise, is the good pleasure of Allāh (Exalted is He); and fourthly, to ensure that this aim, which is the acquistion of the good pleasure of Allāh (Exalted is He), is truly sincere, and that no other intention is mixed with it.

Once these four conditions have been fulfilled, He has said of those concerned:

> Those are with the believers.
> *fa-ulāʾika maʿa ʾl-muʾminīn:*

Note that He did not say: "Those are believers [*hum muʾminūn*]." Then He postponed the reward of the believers till the future, because the hypocrites are presently associated with them for He said:

> And Allāh will bestow on the believers an immense reward.
> *wa sawfa yuʾti ʾllāhu ʾl-muʾminīna ajran ʿaẓīmā.*

These connected points of evidence combine to prove that the condition of the hypocrites is terrible indeed, in the sight of Allāh (Exalted is He).[482]

I wish to make the following comment: Along with this terrible threat, expressed in His saying (Exalted is He):

> The hypocrites will surely be in the lowest depth of the Fire [of Hell].
> *inna ʾl-munāfiqīna fi ʾd-darki ʾl-asfali mina ʾn-nār.*

—Allāh (Exalted is He) has shown mercy for them, if they repent, in His words (Exalted is He):

> Those are with the believers.
> *fa-ulāʾika maʿa ʾl-muʾminīn:*

That is an expression of His tender kindness (Exalted is He) for His servants, despite the fact that they were secretly harbouring unbelief, while outwardly professing Islām. How, then, must it be for those believers who transgress the limit, in heedless neglect of their Creator, despite the existence of their faith? They will be entitled *a priori* to be covered by this promise, if Allāh, the All-Merciful and All-Generous, so wills, provided they repent. Then He (Exalted is He) has referred to His independence from everything apart from Him, and stated that He punishes His servants only for their sins, for He has said:

> What concern has Allāh for your torment
> *mā yafʿalu 'llāhu bi-ʿadhābi-kum*
> if you are thankful and believe?
> *in shakartum wa āmantum:*
> Allāh is All-Thankful, All-Knowing.
> *wa kāna 'llāhu Shākiran ʿAlīmā.*

That is to say: "If you improve your conduct and believe in Allāh and His Messenger."[483] What benefit can there be for Him (Glory be to Him) in your torment? Does it relieve Him of His rage, or does He take vengeance by it, or does He use it to drive away harm and procure benefit, when He is utterly Independent of you?[484]

It was Makḥūl who said: "Four things, inwardly concealed, are concealed to a person's credit, while three others, inwardly concealed, are concealed to a person's discredit. As for the four that are to his credit, they are: thankfulness [*shukr*], faith [*īmān*], supplication [*duʿāʾ*], and seeking forgiveness [*istighfār*]. Allāh (Exalted is He) has said:

> What concern has Allāh for your torment
> *mā yafʿalu 'llāhu bi-ʿadhābi-kum*
> if you are thankful and believe?
> *in shakartum wa āmantum.* (4:147)

> But Allāh would not punish them
> *wa mā kāna 'llāhu li-yuʿadhdhiba-hum*
> while you were with them, nor will Allāh punish them
> *wa anta fī-him: wa mā kāna 'llāhu muʿadhdhiba-hum*
> while they seek forgiveness.
> *wa hum yastaghfirūn.* (8:33)

> Say: "My Lord would not concern Himself with you at all,
> *qul mā yaʿbaʾu bi-kum Rabbī*
> if it were not for your prayer of supplication."
> *law lā duʿāʾu-kum.* (25:77)

"As for the three that are to his discredit, they are: deceitful conspiracy [*makr*], rebellion [*baghy*], and breach of contract [*nakth*]:

> So whoever breaks his oath,
> *fa-man nakatha*
> breaks it only to the detriment of his soul.
> *fa-inna-mā yankuthu ʿalā nafsi-h.* (48:10)

> And the evil plot encloses only the men who make it.
> *wa lā yaḥīqu 'l-makru 's-sayyiʾu illā bi-ahli-h.* (35:43)

> Your rebellion is only against yourselves.
> *inna-mā baghyu-kum ʿalā anfusi-kum.* (10:23)"[485]

Concerning the priority of thankfulness over faith, there are two possible explanations:

1. The reverse order is actually implied, in other words: "if you believe and are thankful," because faith takes precedence over all other acts of worshipful obedience.

2. If the human being looks inside himself, he will see the enormous grace [*ni*ʿ*ma*] inherent in his creation and his upbringing. He will thus feel a general sense of thankfulness. Then, if he completes the investigation, to the point of recognizing the Gracious Benefactor [*Mun*ʿ*im*], he will believe in Him, and will then give thanks with specific gratitude. That general sense of thankfulness is experienced before faith, and that is why Allāh has mentioned it first.[486]

> Allāh is Appreciative, All-Knowing.
> *wa kāna 'llāhu Shākiran* ʿ*Alīmā*.

That is to say: "If someone gives thanks, He will thank him, and if someone believes in his heart, He will teach him and reward him for that, with the most abundant reward."[487] When Allāh (Exalted is He) commanded them to be thankful, he named the reward for thankfulness, calling it appreciation of the request for forgiveness. The significance of the term *Shākir* [Appreciative], as it applies to Him (Exalted is He), is that He is One who rewards the giving of thanks. The significance of His being ʿ*Alīm* [All-Knowing] is that He is One who knows everything in minute detail, so it is absolutely impossible for Him to make a mistake. There can be no doubt, therefore, that He will deliver the reward to the thankful, and the punishment to the ungrateful.[488]

Thankfulness [*shukr*] is the opposite of unbelief [*kufr*], since unbelief is the concealment of gracious blessing, while thankfulness is its open manifestation.

Thankfulness on the part of the servant [of the Lord] means acknowledgment of the gracious blessing that he has received, expressed through all kinds of veneration. On the part of Allāh (Exalted is He) it means good pleasure. That is to say, He is well pleased with even a very little obedience from His servants. It also means the multiplication of the reward, from one to ten to seven hundred, and on to whatever multiple He wishes.

Concerning His words (Exalted is He):

> If you are thankful, I will surely give you more.
> *la-in shakartum la-azīdanna-kum* (14:7)

—it was al-Jurjānī who said: "That is to say: 'If you are thankful for nearness [*qurb*], I will surely grant you further intimacy [*uns*].'"

It is reported that ʿAlī (may Allāh be well pleased with him) once said: "When blessings reach you from all sides, you must not scare away the farthest of them, through paucity of thankfulness." By this he meant: "If someone is not thankful for the blessings he has already received, and those that are about to reach him, he will be deprived of those elusive blessings that are still far away from him."

Through thankfulness and faith, the servant [of the Lord] secures deliverance from the Fires of Hell. Otherwise, he has exposed himself to the torment, and he fully deserves that torment. The threat of chastisement reminds us that training in wisdom is a necessary duty. Allāh has created the Fire in order to teach His creatures the extent of His Majesty and Grandeur, so that they may be in awe and fear of the work of His Majesty, and use it to educate those who have not yet learned to follow the training of His Messengers to His creatures, and so that intelligent people may learn by contemplating that Fire in this world, and by hearing its roaring sound in the Hereafter.[489]

These are my own observations:

Allāh (Exalted is He and Magnificent is His Majesty) has said:

> The believers are nothing but brothers.
> *inna-ma 'l-mu'minūna ikhwatun.* (49:10)

—and the meaning of brotherhood is the brotherhood of faith and Islām, because they belong to the Community of the chief of the Messengers, our master Muḥammad (blessing and peace be upon him). If any self-professed believer is not content with this brotherhood, and with this Community, in spite of this categorical statement, and if he chooses the enemy of Allāh and the enemy of His Messenger for a friend, from desire for the vanities of this world, or from fear, or because they share the love of the Age of Ignorance, this faith of his does not go beyond his tongue. He is one of those who merely follow convention, and the faith of such uncritical imitators is the weakest of faith, in the sight of the Lord of All the Worlds. We must be fully convinced that the only Source of harm and benefit is Allāh, and that the Helper is Allāh.

> Do not fear them, but fear Me.
> *fa-lā takhāfū-hum wa khāfū-ni.* (3:175)
>
> Those to whom men said:
> *alladhīna qāla la-humu 'n-nāsu*
> "The people have gathered against you, so fear them."
> *inna 'n-nāsa qad jamaʿū la-kum fa-'khshaw-hum*
> But it increased them in faith and they cried:
> *fa-zāda-hum īmānā: wa qālū*
> "Allāh is sufficient for us! Most Excellent is the Custodian!"
> *ḥasbu-na 'llāhu wa niʿma 'l-Wakīl.* (3:173)

As for the case of the unbeliever:

> Many of the People of the Book would love to make you
> *wadda kathīrun min ahli 'l-Kitābi law yaruddūna-kum*
> unbelievers after your belief, through envy on their own account.
> *min baʿdi īmāni-kum kuffāran ḥasadan min ʿindi anfusi-him.* (2:109)
>
> And they say: "None enters the Garden
> *wa qālū lan yadkhula 'l-jannata*
> unless he be a Jew or a Christian."
> *illā man kāna Hūdan aw Naṣārā:*
> These are their own desires.
> *tilka amāniyyu-hum.* (2:111)

All of these texts point to their enmity towards you, their envy of you, and their rejection of your Qurʾān and your faith. The intelligent believer is therefore obliged to refrain from keeping them company. He must confine his friendship to the sincere and truthful believer, not only in the context of religion, but also in the worldly arena.

You must accept the advice of Allāh (Exalted is He and Magnificent is His Majesty). His advice to those of former and later times is true devotion to Allāh. One specimen of true devotion is fellowship with the truthful. for He has said:

> O you who truly believe, practise true devotion to Allāh,
> *yā ayyuha 'lladhīna āmanu 'ttaqu 'llāha*
> and be together with the truthful.
> *wa kūnū maʿa 'ṣ-ṣādiqīn.* (9:119)

O Allāh, grant us the ability to accomplish that. *Āmīn*. Peace be upon the Messengers, and praise be to Allāh, the Lord of All the Worlds. There is no might nor any power, except with Allāh, the All-High, the Almighty. May Allāh bless our master Muḥammad, his family and his Companions, and may He grant them peace.

The Twenty-eighth Call

In the Name of Allāh, the All-Merciful, the All-Compassionate.
Bismi'llāhi 'r-Raḥmāni 'r-Raḥīm.

O you who truly believe,
fulfil your contractual commitments.
yā ayyuha 'lladhīna āmanū awfū bi'l-ʿuqūd:
Permitted to you is the beast
of the grazing species,
uḥillat la-kum bahīmatu 'l-anʿāmi
except that which is now recited to you,
illā mā yutlā ʿalai-kum
game being unlawful while
you are in pilgrim consecration.
ghaira muḥilli 'ṣ-ṣaidi wa antum ḥurum:
Allāh decrees whatever He wishes.
inna 'llāhu yaḥkumu mā yurīd. (5:1)

The revelation of this Sūra coincided with the departure of Allāh's Messenger (Allāh bless him and give him peace) from al-Ḥudaibiyya. It contains a collection of legal rules [*aḥkām sharʿīyya*], because the Islāmic state [*dawla*] was then in the initial phase of its formation, and in need of the Lordly programme that would protect it from errors, and prescribe for it the method of construction and establishment.

It was Abū Maisara who said: "The Sūra of the Table [*al-Māʾida*] was the last part of the Qurʾān to be revealed. No element within it has been abrogated [*mansūkh*]. It contains eighteen obligatory religious duties [*farīḍa*]. As for the rules prescribed in the noble Sūra, we shall summarize them in the following list:

- The rules of contractual commitments [*ʿuqūd*].
- Sacrificial animals [*dhabāʾiḥ*].
- The hunting of game [*ṣaid*].

- The state of pilgrim consecration [*iḥrām*].
- Marriage with a woman of the pre-Qur'ānic scriptures [*nikāḥ kitābiyya*].
- Apostasy [*ridda*].
- The rules of ritual purity [*ṭahāra*].
- The penalty for theft [*ḥadd as-sariqa*].
- The penalty for rebellion [*ḥadd al-baghy*] and spreading corruption in the land [*ifsād fi 'l-arḍ*].
- The rules applied to strong drink [*khamr*] and games of chance [*maisir*].
- Expiation of the oath [*kaffārat al-yamīn*].
- The killing of game while in state of pilgrim consecration [*qatl aṣ-ṣaid fi 'l-iḥrām*].
- The testamentary bequest at the time of death [*waṣiyya 'inda 'l-mawt*].
- [The treatment of the she-camels known as] *al-baḥīra* and *as-sā'iba*.
- The legal status of someone who fails to act in accordance with the Sacred Law [*Sharī'a*] of Islām.
- Other rules of the Sacred Law."

In His saying (Exalted is He):

> O you who truly believe, fulfil your contractual commitments.
> *yā ayyuha 'lladhīna āmanū awfū bi'l-'uqūd:*

—the reference to belief is intended to confer dignity and respect. In other words: "O honourable company of the believers, fulfil your contractual commitments." The term *'uqūd* covers every contract [*'aqd*] and covenant [*'ahd*] between the human being and his Lord, and between one human being and another.

It was Ibn 'Abbās (may Allāh be well pleased with him and his father) who said: "Contractual commitments [*'uqūd*] are covenants [*'uhūd*], relating to what Allāh has made lawful and what He has made unlawful, and to all the legal obligations and rules that He has prescribed in the whole of the Qur'ān."

This opinion is the view preferred by aṭ-Ṭabarī and az-Zamakhsharī, and it is generally regarded as the most probable interpretation, since it means that the commandment to fulfil applies to every contractual commitment. It is the preference of the author of *al-Baḥr* [The Ocean], and of a group of the traditional commentators. According to Ibn Aslam: "Commitments are six in number: (1) the covenant of Allāh [*'ahdu 'llāh*]; (2) the contract of sworn alliance [*'aqd al-ḥilf*]; (3) the contract of partnership [*'aqd ash-sharika*]; (4) the contract of sale [*'aqd al-bai'*]; (5) the contract of marriage [*'aqd an-nikāḥ*]; (6) the contract of the oath [*'aqd al-yamīn*]." The same view is held by Ibn Kathīr.[490]

The term *īmān* [belief; faith] signifies intimate knowledge [*ma'rifa*] of Allāh (Exalted is He), in His Essence, His attributes, His ordinances and His workings. His ordinances include the obligation, incumbent on all people, to demonstrate obedience to Allāh in all His impositions, commandments and prohibitions. This commitment [*'aqd*] is one of the matters to be considered in ascertaining the true nature of belief, and this is why He said:

> O you who truly believe, fulfil your contractual commitments.
> *yā ayyuha 'lladhīna āmanū awfū bi'l-'uqūd:*

In other words: "O you who are committed, by virtue of your belief, to the various kinds of contracts and covenants, as a demonstration of obedience to Allāh, you must fulfil those contractual commitments." Allāh (Exalted is He) has called those obligations contractual commitments, in this Qur'ānic verse, for the simple reason that He (Exalted is He) has made them binding on His servants, just as one thing is bound to another with a dependable rope.

As you should also know, while Allāh (Exalted is He) sometimes calls these obligations contractual commitments [*'uqūd*], as [when He uses the corresponding verb *'aqqadtum*] in His saying (Exalted is He):

> But He will take you to task
> *wa lākin yu'ākhidhu-kum*
> for the oaths by which you make contractual commitments.
> *bi-mā 'aqqadtumu 'l-aimān.* (5:89)

—He sometimes calls them covenants [*'uhūd*], as [when He uses the singular form *'ahd*] in His saying:

> And fulfil your covenant with Me,
> *wa awfū bi-'ahdī*
> then I shall fulfil My covenant with you.
> *ūfi bi-'ahdi-kum.* (2:40)

—and when He said:

> Fulfil the covenant of Allāh when you make covenant,
> *wa awfū bi-'ahdi 'llāhi idhā 'āhadtum*
> and do not break your oaths.
> *wa lā tanquḍu 'l-aimāna.* (16:91)

The gist of what has been discussed, concerning the interpretation of this Qur᾿ānic verse, is that He has enjoined the discharging of obligations by performance [in the case of what is lawful] and by abstinence [in the case of what is unlawful].[491]

According to Ibn ῾Abbās (may Allāh be well pleased with him and his father): "It means: 'You must fulfil, O believers, the commitments which Allāh has made incumbent and binding upon you, in accordance with what He has made lawful or unlawful for you, and has imposed on you as an obligatory duty, and has shown you the limits thereof.'" We have maintained that this opinion, meaning the one expressed by Ibn ῾Abbās, is more likely to be correct, on the grounds that Allāh has gone on to explain what He has made lawful for His servants and what He has made unlawful for them.[492]

> Permitted to you is the beast of the grazing species,
> *uḥillat la-kum bahīmatu 'l-an῾āmi*
> except that which is now recited to you
> *illā mā yutlā ῾alai-kum*

That is to say: "It is permissible for you to eat the [flesh of] domestic animals, they being camels, cattle and sheep, after they have been duly slaughtered, with the exception of what has been declared unlawful for you in this Sūra: namely, carrion, blood, the meat of the pig, and so on."[493]

This is addressed to the believers specifically. The term *bahīma* [beast] is a name for every four-legged animal, but its strict definition excludes wild animals such as lions and predators.[494]

As related by Imām ash-Sha῾rānī, his Shaikh, ῾Alī al-Khawwāṣ (may Allāh sanctify his innermost being), maintained: "The reason for calling beasts [*bahā᾿im*, plural of *bahīma*] by that name, is simply that their speech and their natural states are unintelligible [*ubhima*] to the vast majority of human creatures, not that the word of command is unintelligible to them." He also mentioned evidence that points to their having intelligence and knowledge.[495] The erudite al-Ulūsī also reports: "The exotericists [*ahl aẓ-ẓāhir*] dismissed that idea with total rejection."[496]

Speaking for myself, the proper response to the opinion ascribed to Imām ash-Sha῾rānī, and its rejection by the exotericists, should be as follows: We may voice our opinions as long as speech is available to us.

As for the modes of verbal expression peculiar to plants, trees and other inanimate beings, by Allāh's permission and His will, they too may be recognized, after the softening of human nature and the progress of the spirit. This is an indisputable fact, according to those who can understand and hear, just as none of the Muslims would deny that the noble Qur'ān says:

> And your Lord inspired the bee.
> *wa awḥā Rabbu-ka ila 'n-naḥli.* (16:68)

There is also the case of the camel that complained to Allāh's Messenger (Allāh bless him and give him peace), as well as other instances of verbal utterance emanating from beasts. This serves to confirm what Shaikh ash-Sha'rānī said, and what he reported from his own Shaikh (may bestow His mercy upon them both).[497] Although there is no categorical proof of their assertions, their validity is established in the opinion of some of those believers who seek to ascertain the facts. While something may not appear to exist, and may not be generally recognized, and may not be noticed by some people, this does not necessarily mean that it does not exist, and that no one is aware of its existence.

According to az-Zajjāj: "The term *an'ām* is the plural form of *na'am*, and it applies to camels, cattle and sheep, but it does not apply to hoofed animals, in the opinion of all the expert linguists, so the scholars have disagreed over the meaning of the Qur'ānic verse."

According to al-Ḥasan and Qatāda: "The expression *bahīmat al-an'ām* applies to camels, cattle, sheep and goats." On the basis of this opinion, it is simply for the sake of emphasis that the term *bahīma* has been prefixed to *al-an'ām*.

According to al-Kalbī: "The expression *bahīmat al-an'ām* applies to beasts that graze in the wild, like gazelles, wild cattle and wild asses." On the strength of this opinion, Allāh prefixed the term *bahīma* to *al-an'ām* in order to identify the species of grazing animals, and those among them that are lawful, because, if He had used it by itself, and simply said *al-bahīma*, it would have included beasts that are lawful and those that are unlawful. This explains why He said:

> Permitted to you is the beast of the grazing species
> *uḥillat la-kum bahīmatu 'l-an'āmi*

According to Ibn ʿAbbās (may Allāh be well pleased with him and his father): "It applies to the foetuses that are found dead in the wombs of their mothers, when they are slaughtered or immolated." Most of the religious scholars have adopted the view that these are lawful, and such is the doctrine of ash-Shāfiʿī. It is supported by the traditional report from Ibn Saʿīd, according to whom the Prophet (Allāh bless him and give him peace) once said, concerning the foetus:

> Its ritual slaughter [*dhakāt*] is the ritual slaughter of its mother.

This version is reported by at-Tirmidhī and Ibn Māja. In the version related by Abū Dāwūd, he [Ibn Saʿīd] said: "Tell us, O Messenger of Allāh, if we immolate the she-camel and slaughter the cow and the sheep, and we find the foetus in her womb, should we discard it, or may we eat it?" To this he replied:

> Eat it, if you wish, for its ritual slaughter is the ritual slaughter of its mother.

As reported by aṭ-Ṭabarī, Ibn ʿUmar said, concerning His saying (Exalted is He):

> Permitted to you is the beast of the grazing species
> *uḥillat la-kum bahīmatu 'l-anʿāmi*

—"[It refers to] what is in the womb [of the slaughtered animal]." ʿAtiyya al-ʿAwfī said: "I asked: 'If it comes out dead, may I eat it?' He said: 'Yes, it is in the same category as its [mother's] lung and her liver."

Ibn ʿAbbās (may Allāh be well pleased with him and his father) is also reported as having said: "[It refers to] the foetus from the beast of the grazing species [*al-janīn min bahīmati 'l-anʿām*]." It is also reported that a cow was immolated, and a foetus was discovered in its womb, so Ibn ʿAbbās (may Allāh be well pleased with him and his father) took hold of the foetus by the tail, and said: "This is from the beast of the grazing species." Some of the scholars stipulate the presence of bristles of fur and complete development of the physical structure.

It was Ibn ʿUmar (may Allāh be well pleased with him and his father) who said: "The ritual slaughter of what is in its womb is its [the mother animal's] own ritual slaughter, provided that its physical structure is fully formed, and its fur has already grown." A similar statement is attributed to Saʿīd al-Musayyib. According to Abū Ḥanīfa (may Allāh be well pleased with him): "It is not permissible to eat the foetus, if it comes out dead after the ritual slaughter of the mother."

> except that which is now recited to you
> *illā mā yutlā ʿalai-kum*

That is to say: "except that which is declared unlawful in the Qurʾān." By this He was referring to His saying (Exalted is He):

> Forbidden to you are carrion, blood,
> *ḥurrimat ʿalai-kumu 'l-maitatu wa 'd-damu*
> the flesh of swine, what has been hallowed
> *wa laḥmu 'l-khinzīri wa mā uhilla*
> to other than Allāh, the beast strangled,
> *li-ghairi 'llāhi bi-hi wa 'l-munkhaniqatu*
> the beast beaten down, the beast fallen to death,
> *wa 'l-mawqūdhatu wa 'l-mutaraddiyatu*
> the beast gored, and that devoured by beasts of prey—
> *wa 'n-naṭīḥatu wa mā akala 's-sabuʿu*
> except what you have lawfully slaughtered—
> *illā mā dhakkaitum:*
> as well as whatever you have sacrificed to idols.
> *wa mā dhubiḥa ʿala 'n-nuṣubi.* (5:3)

—for this is part of what has been recited to the believer, and it lists what Allāh (Almighty and Glorious is He) has excepted from [the permissible category of] the beast of the grazing species [*bahīmat al-anʿām*].[498]

> game being unlawful while you are in pilgrim consecration.
> *ghaira muḥilli 'ṣ-ṣaidi wa antum ḥurum:*

That is to say: "These things have been made lawful for you, except that you must not consider it lawful to hunt game while you are in the state of pilgrim consecration."

> Allāh decrees whatever He wishes.
> *inna 'llāhu yaḥkumu mā yurīd.*

In other words: "He decides for His creatures as He wills, because He the All-Wise in His commandment and His prohibition."[499] He permits whatever He wishes to make lawful, and forbids whatever He wishes to make unlawful. He imposes whatever He wishes to impose upon them, in the form of His rules and His obligatory requirements, which are designed to secure the best interest of His servants.[500]

Suppose someone asked: "What is the reason for this detailed analysis and specification?" He would be given the answer: "Allāh (Exalted is He) is the Owner of all things, and their Creator, so there can be no objection to His judgment in any shape or form. This is what our colleagues have to say: 'The principle of good decorum is [the relationship between] Lordliness and servitude.'"[501] On this basis, they maintain that the essential elements of religion are four in number:

1. Genuineness in commitment.
2. Truthfulness in intention.
3. Fulfilment of the covenant.
4. Avoidance of the prescribed limit.

As the earlier reference to covenants [*ʿuhūd*] implies, the term *ʿaqd* [lit., knot] is used allegorically, in the sense of the covenant [*ʿahd*] that resembles the knotting of a rope. When commitments are described as binding, the concept is that the covenant is a binding knot between you and Allāh, as in the case of commandments and prohibitions. The fulfilment of commandments consists in their performance, while the fulfilment of prohibitions consists in their avoidance.

The expression "between [you and] Allāh" signifies that the covenant is also binding between the servant and Allāh's Messenger (Allāh bless him and give him peace), so it is incumbent on the human being to fulfil it, by believing in him, accepting the truth of what he has brought, treating him with reverence and profound respect, preferring him and giving him precedence over worldly concerns, and refraining absolutely from noncompliance with what he has commanded.

As for contracts between people, these are made in transactions such as buying and selling, marriage and divorce, the transfer of ownership, the granting of options, the emancipation of slaves, the settlement of debts, the entrusting of deposits, and treaties of peace. That also has to do with respectful and reverential treatment of the believers, and refraining from backbiting, insulting and slandering them, and from lying about them. It is also relevant to the fulfilment by disciples of their covenants with the Shaikhs.[502]

This Qurʾānic verse is remarkable for its eloquence and the many meanings it conveys, in very few words, to anyone endowed with insight into speech, for it contains five rulings:

1. The commandment to fulfil contractual commitments.
2. The declaration of the lawfulness of the beast of the grazing species.
3. The exception applied to what follows after that.
4. The exception applied to what may be hunted while in the state of pilgrim consecration.
5. The permission to hunt game, which is implicitly granted to someone who is not in the state of pilgrim consecration.

As related by an-Naqqāsh, the companions of al-Kindī said to him: "O wise one, show us how to act in accordance with this Qur'ān!" He said: "Yes, I shall act in accordance with some of it." He went into seclusion for many days, then he re-emerged and said: "By Allāh, I cannot do it, and nobody is capable of this. I opened the volume, and out came the Sūra of the Table [*al-Mā'ida*]. I looked at it, and lo and behold, He spoke of fulfilment, forbade breach of contract, and made a general declaration of lawfulness. Then He made one exception after another. Then He informed me of His power and His wisdom, in two lines of the text. No one is capable of putting all this into practice, except in story-books!"

Allāh's Messenger (Allāh bless him and give him peace) is reported as having said:

> In Allāh's heavenly kingdom, the Sūra of the Table [*al-Mā'ida*] is called the Saviour [*al-Munqidha*]. It will save its follower from the hands of the angels of torment.

This Sūra includes what was revealed during the Farewell Pilgrimage [*Ḥajjat al-Wadā'*], as well as what was revealed during the Year of Victory ['*Ām al-Fatḥ*], and His saying (Exalted is He):

> And when you call to prayer
> *wa idhā nādaitum ila 'ṣ-ṣalāti.* (5:58)

There is no mention of the call to prayer [*adhān*] in the Qur'ān, except in this Sūra. As for the call referred to in the Sūra of the Congregation [*al-Jumu'a*], that is peculiar to [the prayer on Friday] the Day of Congregation, whereas in this Sūra it applies to all the ritual prayers in general.

It is related that the Prophet (Allāh bless him and give him peace) recited the Sūra of the Table [*al-Mā'ida*] during the Farewell Pilgrimage, and that he said:

> O people, the Sūra of the Table is among the last of what has been revealed, so treat as lawful that which it makes lawful, and treat as unlawful that which it makes unlawful.[503]

ʿAbdu'llāh ibn ʿAmr ibn al-ʿĀṣ (may Allāh be well pleased with him) is reported as having said: "The Sūra of the Table [*al-Mā'ida*] was sent down to Allāh's Messenger (Allāh bless him and give him peace) while he was mounted on his riding animal, and the she-camel could not carry him, so he dismounted from her."[504]

These are my own remarks:

The symptom of compliance with Allāh's commandments, and avoidance of His prohibitions, is your fear and dread of Allāh (Exalted is He) when faced with the commandment and the prohibition. You must abase yourself before Him, and behave with humble modesty towards your fellow creatures, though without needing anything from them, and without coveting what they have at their disposal.

If you fail to exercise patience in tasks that have been commanded, and do not abstain from things that have been forbidden, you are not among those who submit to Allāh's command, because the real meaning of Islām is submissive obedience [*istislām*].

O Allāh, enliven our hearts with trust in You, with obedience to You, and with the remembrance of You. There is no might nor any power, except with Allāh, the All-High, the Almighty. May Allāh bless our master Muḥammad, his family and his Companions, and may He grant them peace.

The Twenty-ninth Call

In the Name of Allāh, the All-Merciful, the All-Compassionate.
Bismi'llāhi 'r-Raḥmāni 'r-Raḥīm.

O you who truly believe,
yā ayyuha 'lladhīna āmanū
do not profane the rites of Allāh
lā tuḥillū sha'ā'ira 'llāhi
nor the Sacred Month nor the offerings
nor the garlands,
wa la 'sh-shahra 'l-ḥarāma wa la 'l-hadya
wa la 'l-qalā'ida
nor those repairing to the Sacred House,
wa lā āmmīna 'l-baita 'l-ḥarāma
seeking grace and good pleasure from their Lord.
yabtaghūna faḍlan min Rabbi-him wa riḍwānā:

But once you have become unconsecrated,
wa idhā ḥalaltum
then go hunting.
fa-'ṣṭādū
And do not let your hatred of a folk
wa lā yajrimanna-kum shana'ānu qawmin
who denied you access to the Sacred Mosque
an ṣaddū-kum 'ani 'l-masjidi 'l-ḥarāmi
seduce you to transgress.
an ta'tadū

And help one another to practise piety
and dutiful devotion.
wa ta'āwanū 'ala 'l-birri wa 't-taqwā.
And do not help one another to practise
sin and enmity,
wa lā ta'āwanū 'ala 'l-ithmi wa 'l-'udwān:
and be careful to observe your duty to Allāh;
wa 'ttaqu 'llāh:

surely Allāh is Stern in retribution.
inna 'llāha Shadīdu 'l-ʿiqāb. (5:2)

As reported by Ibn ʿAbbās (may Allāh be well pleased with him and his father), this Qurʾānic verse was sent down for the following reason: The polytheists used to make pilgrimage to the House, bringing sacrificial offerings, venerating the sanctuaries and slaughtering [sacrificial animals]. The Muslims proposed to direct their zeal against them, so down came the revelation:

> O you who truly believe,
> *yā ayyuha 'lladhīna āmanū*
> do not profane the rites of Allāh.
> *lā tuḥillū shaʿāʾira 'llāhi*

That is to say: "Do not violate the sanctuaries of Allāh, and do not transgress His limits." According to al-Ḥasan: "He means those sanctuaries of His that He has declared off-limits to His servants." According to Ibn ʿAbbās, the meaning is: "[Do not profane] that which is unlawful to you in the state of pilgrim consecration [*iḥrām*]." The first opinion is preferable, and it is the choice of aṭ-Ṭābarī, on account of the generality of the Qurʾānic verse,[505] since it is in fact an address to the believers, meaning: "Do not transgress the limits of Allāh, in any context whatsoever."

The term *shaʿāʾir* is the plural of *shaʿīra*, which signifies the camel offered for sacrifice. Its marking [*ishʿār*] is performed by stabbing its hump until blood flows from it, so that it is recognizable as a sacrificial offering.

According to one opinion, the *shaʿāʾir* are those animals that are marked for shepherding to the House of Allāh. According to another opinion, maintained by Ibn ʿAbbās, the term applies to all the rites of the Pilgrimage [*Ḥajj*]. Mujāhid said: "[The sites of] aṣ-Ṣafā and al-Marwa, and the camels and other sacrificial animals, all of that is covered by the term *shaʿāʾir*." According to ʿAṭāʾ ibn Abī Ribāḥ: "The *shaʿāʾir* of Allāh are all those things that Allāh has commanded and forbidden."

According to al-Ḥasan, they signify the religion of Allāh, as in His saying (Exalted is He):

> And whoever magnifies the *shaʿāʾir* of Allāh,
> *wa man yuʿaẓẓim shaʿāʾira 'llāhi*
> it is surely from devotion of the hearts.
> *fa-inna-hu min taqwa 'l-qulūb.* (22:32)

This opinion is the one to be preferred, because of its universality.

The scholars have also disagreed concerning the marking [*ishʿār*] of sacrificial animals, though it is considered permissible by the majority. There is further disagreement as to which part of the body should be marked. According to ash-Shāfiʿī, Aḥmad and Abū Thawr, the mark should be on the right flank. According to a confirmed report from Ibn ʿAbbās, the Prophet (Allāh bless him and give him peace) marked his she-camel on the right side of its hump. This is reported by Muslim and others, and it is authentic.[506] For detailed study of this subject, the reader should consult the books of Islāmic jurisprudence [*fiqh*].

> nor the Sacred Month nor the offerings nor the garlands
> *wa la 'sh-shahra 'l-ḥarāma wa la 'l-hadya wa la 'l-qalāʾida*

That is to say: "Do not profane the Sacred Month by fighting in it (the Sacred Months being Dhu 'l-Qaʿda, Dhu 'l-Ḥijja, al-Muḥarram and Rajab), and do not profane the sacrificial offerings brought to the House of Allāh (such as a she-camel, or a cow, or a sheep), or that which is invested with a garland to indicate that it is a sacrificial offering, by interfering with it and its owners."[507] The garlands are fixed to the camel's neck. They are attached to the sacrificial offering as a way of emphasizing that it is the most noble kind of offering, as if to say that the garlands are its peculiar property. The prohibition of interference with the garlands is thus a way of emphasizing the prohibition of interference with the sacrificial offerings. The meaning is: "Do not profane their garlands, let alone the offerings themselves!"[508]

[The attaching of garlands] is a custom established by Abraham (on him and on our master Muḥammad be the finest blessing and the most perfect salutation of peace), which survived in the Time of Ignorance and was confirmed by Islām. It is not permissible to sell the sacrificial offering, nor to present it to someone as a gift, once it has been garlanded or marked, because it has been consecrated. If its consecrator dies, it cannot be inherited from him, and it must be duly sacrificed for his sake.[509]

> nor those repairing to the Sacred House,
> *wa lā āmmīna 'l-baita 'l-ḥarāma*
> seeking grace and good pleasure from their Lord.
> *yabtaghūna faḍlan min Rabbi-him wa riḍwānā.*

That is to say: "Do not consider it lawful to fight those who are heading towards the Sacred House of Allāh, to perform a Pilgrimage [*Ḥajj*] or a Visitation [*ʿUmra*]. Allāh (Exalted is He) has forbidden aggression against them, or barring them from the House, as the people of the Time of Ignorance used to do."[510]

> nor those repairing to the Sacred House
> *wa lā āmmīna 'l-baita 'l-ḥarāma*

In other words: "those who are heading towards it." The meaning is: "Do not obstruct the unbelievers who are heading towards the Sacred House for the purpose of worship and sacrifice. As for what these Qurʾānic verses contain, concerning the prohibition of excluding a polytheist [*mushrik*], or the need to respect his garlanded offering, or his right to repair to the House, it is said that all this has been abrogated by the Verse of the Sword [*Āyat as-Saif*], in His saying (Exalted is He):

> Then slay the polytheists wherever you find them.
> *fa-'qtulu 'l-mushrikīna ḥaithu wajadtumū-hum.* (9:5)

—and in His saying:

> So do not let them come near the Sacred Mosque
> *fa-lā yaqrabu 'l-Masjida 'l-Ḥarāma*
> after this year of theirs.
> *baʿda ʿāmi-him hādhā.* (9:28)

The polytheist is therefore not allowed to perform the Pilgrimage, nor is he granted security in the Sacred Months, even if he prepares a sacrificial offering, invests it with a garland, and sets out on the Pilgrimage.[511]

> seeking grace and good pleasure from their Lord.
> *yabtaghūna faḍlan min Rabbi-him wa riḍwānā.*

There are two interpretations of this reference to grace and good pleasure:

1. They are seeking gracious favour from their Lord, by pursuing the trade that is permissible for them during their Pilgrimage, in accordance with His saying:

> It is no sin for you
> *laisa ʿalai-kum junāḥun*
> that you seek bounty from your Lord.
> *an tabtaghū faḍlan min Rabbi-kum.* (2:198)

This is said to have been revealed in connection with their trading during the days of the festival season.

The meaning is: "Do not obstruct them, for their only purpose, in repairing to the House, is to improve their worldly life and their future prospects." The search for grace is related to this world, while the search for good pleasure is related to the Hereafter. According to the people of knowledge, the polytheists used to embark on their Pilgrimage in search of Allāh's good pleasure, even though they would not obtain it, so it is not too hard to imagine that, on account of this intention, they might receive some kind of respect.

2. What is meant by Allāh's grace is spiritual reward, and by good pleasure, that He might be well pleased with them. That is because the unbeliever, even though he could not obtain either grace or good pleasure, might still suppose that he was seeking them by his action. It is therefore permissible for that to be attributed to him, on the basis of his supposition. Allāh (Exalted is He) has said:

> Now look upon your god.
> *wa 'nẓur ilā ilāhi-ka.* (20:97)[512]

From an overall perspective, we have a clear indication of the relevance of the prohibition and the disapproval of that which is forbidden. This view is supported by the fact that the Qur'ānic verse was revealed, as stated by as-Suddī and others, in connection with a man from the Banī Rabī'a tribe, called al-Ḥaṭīm ibn Hind. The point is that he came to the Prophet (Allāh bless him and give him peace), all by himself, leaving his troop of horses outside Medina. He asked him: "To what do you summon the people?" The Prophet replied (Allāh bless him and give him peace):

> To bearing witness that there is no god but Allāh [*lā ilāha illa 'llāh*], to the performance of the ritual prayer [*ṣalāt*], and to payment of the alms-due [*zakāt*].

The man said: "That is fine, except that I have commanders, and I cannot make any decision without them. Perhaps I shall accept Islām, and bring them along." The Prophet (Allāh bless him and give him peace) said to his Companions:

> A man has entered your presence, speaking with a devil's tongue.

Then the man departed, and, as soon as he had left, Allāh's Messenger (Allāh bless him and give him peace) said:

> He came in with an unbeliever's face, and he went out with the heels of a traitor. The man is not a Muslim.

He passed by the cattle of Medina, rounded them up and herded them away with him. The Muslims tried to find him, but they could not trace his whereabouts. Then, when Allāh's Messenger (Allāh bless him and give him peace) went forth, in the year of making up for the Visitation [*ʿUmra*] from which he had been excluded, he heard the *talbiya* [the declaration: "Doubly at Your service, O Allāh"] of the pilgrims of al-Yamāma, so he said (Allāh bless him and give him peace):

> Here is al-Ḥaṭīm, with his companions, so catch him!

He had garlanded the cattle that he had plundered, and presented the herd as a sacrificial offering. Just as they were about to attack him, this Qurʾānic verse was sent down, so they withdrew.[513]

According to Abū Muslim al-Iṣfahānī: "The Qurʾānic verse refers to those unbelievers who entered into a treaty with the Prophet (Allāh bless him and give him peace). When the treaty was dissolved by the Sūra of Exemption [*Barāʾa*], the interdiction ceased to apply, and the import of His saying (Exalted is He):

> So do not let them come near the Sacred Mosque
> *fa-lā yaqrabu 'l-Masjida 'l-Ḥarāma*
> after this year of theirs.
> *baʿda ʿāmi-him hādhā.* (9:28)

—came into effect."[514]

> But once you have become unconsecrated, then go hunting.
> *wa idhā ḥalaltum fa-'ṣṭādū.* (5:2)

In other words: "As soon as you have left the state of consecration [*iḥrām*], hunting becomes permissible for you."[515] This interpretation of *wa idhā ḥalaltum* is indicated by His saying:

> while you are in pilgrim consecration.
> *wa antum ḥurum.* (5:1)

It is therefore no sin for you to engage in hunting, since the obstacle has been removed. The commandment grants permission after interdiction, as in a case like: "Do not enter the building until you have paid its fee," which means that once you have paid it, you may enter; in other words, entry will then be permissible for you.[516]

> And do not let your hatred of a folk
> *wa lā yajrimanna-kum shana'ānu qawmin*
> who denied you access to the Sacred Mosque
> *an ṣaddū-kum ʿani 'l-masjidi 'l-ḥarāmi*
> seduce you to transgress.
> *an taʿtadū.*

That is to say: "Do not let your hatred of certain people, who used to deny you access to the Sacred Mosque, incite you to transgress against them."[517] On the Day of al-Ḥudaibiyya, the people of Mecca had prevented Allāh's Messenger (Allāh bless him and give him peace) and the believers from performing the Visitation [ʿ*Umra*]. This Sūra was revealed after al-Ḥudaibiyya, and this denial of access was undoubtedly prior to the revelation of the verse.[518]

> And help one another to practise piety and dutiful devotion.
> *wa taʿāwanū ʿala 'l-birri wa 't-taqwā.*
> And do not help one another to practise sin and enmity.
> *wa lā taʿāwanū ʿala 'l-ithmi wa 'l-ʿudwān:*

In other words: "Help one another to perform good deeds, to abstain from things that are reprehensible, and to practise everything that brings you close to Allāh."[519] Allāh (Exalted is He) is commanding His believing servants to help one another in the performance of good deeds, which constitutes piety, and in abstinence from things that are reprehensible, which constitutes dutiful devotion. He is also forbidding them to assist one another in futility, and to help one another in the commission of sins and unlawful acts. As reported by Imām Aḥmad, on the authority of Anas ibn Mālik (may Allāh be well pleased with him), Allāh's Messenger (Allāh bless him and give him peace) once said:

> You must help your brother, whether he is a wrongdoer or a victim of wrongdoing.

Someone asked: "O Messenger of Allāh, I have helped this one as a victim, but how can I help him as a wrongdoer?" To this he replied:

> You must prevent him from doing wrong. That is how you can help him.[520]

> And help one another to practise piety and dutiful devotion.
> *wa taʿāwanū ʿala 'l-birri wa 't-taqwā.*

That is to say: "You must not transgress against those who approach the Sacred Mosque, because of their having denied you access to it. You must help one another to pardon and overlook, and to tolerate their offensive conduct." In the context of the Qur᾽ānic verse, the meaning of piety is absolute compliance with the commandment, while dutiful devotion means the shunning of passionate desire. Since the sentence is appended to all the preceding subjects in the verse, piety and dutiful devotion must apply to all the rites of the Pilgrimage.

And do not help one another to practise sin and enmity.
wa lā ta῾āwanū ῾ala 'l-ithmi wa 'l-῾udwān:

The prohibition embraces everything connected with wrongdoing and sinful acts of disobedience, and it includes the prohibition of mutual assistance in transgression and revenge.

It is reported Ibn ῾Abbās (may Allāh be well pleased with him and his father) interpreted sin [*ithm*] as the failure to do what Allāh has commanded them to do, and the commission of what He has forbidden them to do. He took enmity [*῾udwān*] to mean transgressing the limits set by Allāh (Glory be to him) for His servants in their religion, and violating His prescriptions for themselves. Embellishment has been preferred to conciseness, to accelerate the imposition of what is essentially intended.[521]

and be careful to observe your duty to Allāh;
wa 'ttaqu 'llāh:
surely Allāh is Stern in retribution.
inna 'llāha Shadīdu 'l-῾iqāb.

In other words: "You must fear His punishment, for He (Exalted is He) is Stern in retribution for those who disobey Him."[522] He has commanded dutiful devotion in all matters, for He is Stern in retribution for those who do not observe their duty to Him.[523]

You should also know that, in reality, the *sha῾ā᾽ir* of Allāh are the rites [*manāsik*] of passage to Allāh. They are the signposts of the religion and the Sacred Law [*Sharī῾a*], and the customary practices of the Spiritual Path [*Ṭarīqa*], as indicated by the masters of Reality [*Ḥaqīqa*]. The real meaning of piety is exclusive dedication to the Truth [*Ḥaqq*], while the real meaning of dutiful devotion is detachment from everything apart from Allāh (Exalted is He). Attainment [to Him] is impossible without these two, but they are steps that cannot be taken by the genuine seeker, except with the help of a Shaikh who is perfect and gives perfect training, who has access and provides access, for he is the guide of this path.

The Qur'ānic verse contains an implicit instruction, demanding reverence for all that Allāh has magnified, be it the time, the place, or one's brethren. He has distinguished certain months, days and moments above others, just as He has distinguished some of the Messengers and religious communities over others. He has done so in order that hearts may be quick to respect them, that spirits may yearn to be revived by serving them, and that creatures may long for their special virtues.

He has distinguished certain places above others, in order to magnify the reward for residing in them. Allāh has created human beings both fortunate and unfortunate, but what is important is the ultimate outcome. Every creature is good, by virtue of the fact that he is the creature of Allāh. The unbeliever must therefore be viewed from the standpoint of his being Allāh's creature, not from the standpoint of his unbelief, even though his unbelief does not meet with approval.

It is thus incumbent, on someone whose viewpoint is the affirmation of Oneness [*tawḥīd*], to see the best in everything, not to disparage any of Allāh's creatures, and not to preoccupy himself with enmity and hatred.

Consider one of the sayings of ['Alī] the Lion of Allāh (may Allāh ennoble his countenance): "Enmity is a distracting preoccupation, in the sense that preoccupation with enmity cuts one off from preoccupation with useful and valuable concerns, because the heart cannot cope with two preoccupations that are diametrically opposed."

The Prophet (Allāh bless him and give him peace) was endowed with noble traits of character and excellent modes of conduct. You are therefore obliged to follow his example. When Allāh extolled the Prophets (peace be upon them), and assigned a particular attribute to each Prophet, He said to him (Exalted is He):

> So follow their guidance.
> *fa-bi-hudā-humu 'qtadi-h.* (6:90)

—and he did so, and thus came to combine the perfection of all good qualities. Each of the Prophets was distinguished by a special virtue. In the case of Noah (peace be upon him), it was thankfulness [*shukr*]. In the case of Abraham (peace be upon him), it was forbearance [*ḥilm*]. In the case of Moses (peace be upon him), it was sincere devotion [*ikhlāṣ*]. In the case of Ishmael (peace be upon him), it was being true to the promise [*ṣidq bi'l-waʿd*]. In the case of Jacob and Job (peace be upon them both), it was patience [*ṣabr*]. In the case of David (peace be upon him), it was readiness to apologize [*iʿtidhār*]. In the case of Solomon (peace be upon him), it was humility [*tawāḍuʿ*]. In the case of Jesus (peace be upon him), it was pious abstinence [*zuhd*].

By following their example, he [our Prophet Muḥammad (Allāh bless him and give him peace)] became a combination of them all.

As for you, O believer, you belong to the Community of that Messenger (Allāh bless him and give him peace). You must therefore practise dutiful devotion to Allāh, and feel a sense of modesty before Allāh's Messenger (Allāh bless him and give him peace), so that you may escape the severe chastisement and the lengthy torment, so that you may attain to eternal life in everlasting bliss, and so that you may obtain what is obtained by the owner of a sound heart.[524]

Piety means doing what you have been commanded to do, while dutiful devotion means abstaining from what you have been forbidden to do. It is also said that piety means compliance with the Sacred Law, while dutiful devotion means opposition to passionate desire. As for helping one another to practise piety, this is said to be done by giving good advice and fine counsel to the believers. As for helping one another to practise dutiful devotion, this is a matter of restraining sinners, as the situation may require, by offering them fine admonition and eloquent reprimand, and preventing them completely, provided that can be achieved in accordance with religious knowledge. As for helping one another to practise sin and enmity, it means that you set an example of which the religion does not approve, by claiming that your conduct, which is followed by others, represents a traditional custom [*sunna*] that you are demonstrating, though you must bear the burden of sin involved. The exemplary aspect is likewise important in the case of helping one another to practise piety and dutiful devotion, in the sense that virtuous qualities should be presented as examples to be followed.[525]

These are my own observations:

You must exert yourself strenuously in seeking out the group that will help you to practise piety and dutiful devotion, because such people have become very rare at this time. As for those who will help you to sin and transgress, they constitute the vast majority. You must struggle with your lower self, while avoiding the company of this class of people, because they will damage your religion and your worldly interests, especially if they belong to the party of those who support their passionate desire with arguments based on the Sacred Law. You must seek out those who will help you to practise piety and dutiful devotion, for they will direct you, not to themselves but to Allāh (Almighty and Glorious is He).

Once Allāh has honoured you with their fellowship, you must stay in touch with them constantly. You must turn a deaf ear to the speech of their enemies. Do not say: "The righteous person has no enemies," but recite the words of Allāh (Exalted is He):

> Thus We have appointed to every Prophet
> *wa ka-dhālika ja'alnā li-kulli Nabiyyin*
> an opponent from among the guilty;
> *'aduwwan mina 'l-mujrimīn:*
> but your Lord suffices for a Guide and Helper.
> *wa kafā bi-Rabbi-ka Hādiyan wa Naṣīrā.* (25:31)

You must realize that companionship with these people calls for dedicated struggle against the lower self, because they are not at ease with self-centred desires and passions. By its very nature, the lower self loves those who applaud it, not those who admonish it.

We beg Allāh to show us our own faults, to inspire us with a sense of our right direction, and to enable us to make ourselves endure with patience,

> together with those who cry unto their Lord
> *ma'a 'lladhīna yad'ūna Rabba-hum*
> in the morning and the evening, seeking His countenance.
> *bi'l-ghadāti wa 'l-'ashiyyi yurīdūna Wajha-hu.* (18:28)

Āmīn. Peace be upon the Messengers, and praise be to Allāh, the Lord of All the Worlds. There is no might nor any power, except with Allāh, the All-High, the Almighty. May Allāh bless our master Muḥammad, his family and his Companions, and may He grant them peace.

The Thirtieth Call

In the Name of Allāh, the All-Merciful, the All-Compassionate.
Bismi'llāhi 'r-Raḥmāni 'r-Raḥīm.

O you who truly believe,
when you get ready for the ritual prayer,
yā ayyuha 'lladhīna āmanū idhā qumtum ila 'ṣ-ṣalāti
wash your faces, and your hands up to the elbows,
fa-'ghsilū wujūha-kum wa aidiya-kum ila 'l-marāfiqi
and rub your heads and [wash] your feet
up to the ankles.
wa 'msaḥū bi-ru'ūsi-kum wa arjula-kum ila 'l-ka'bain:
And if you are unclean, purify yourselves.
wa in kuntum junuban fa-'ṭṭaharū:
And if you are sick or on a journey,
wa in kuntum marḍā aw 'alā safarin
or one of you has come from the toilet,
aw jā'a aḥadun min-kum mina 'l-ghā'iṭi
or you have touched women,
aw lāmastumu 'n-nisā'a
and you have not found water,
fa-lam tajidū mā'an
then head for some fresh topsoil
fa-tayammamū ṣa'īdan ṭayyiban
and rub your faces and your hands
with some of it.
fa-'msaḥū bi-wujūhi-kum wa aidī-kum min-h:
Allāh does not wish to impose
any hardship on you
mā yurīdu 'llāhu li-yaj'ala 'alai-kum min ḥarajin
but He wishes to purify you
wa lākin yurīdu li-yuṭahhira-kum
and to perfect His grace upon you,
wa li-yutimma ni'mata-hu 'alai-kum
so that you may give thanks.
la'alla-kum tashkurūn. (5:6)

You must know that Allāh (Exalted is He) has opened the Sūra with His saying:

> O you who truly believe, fulfil your contractual commitments.
> *yā ayyuha 'lladhīna āmanū awfū bi'l-ʿuqūd:*

That is because the Lord and the servant are connected by the covenant of Lordship and the covenant of servanthood, so His saying (Exalted is He):

> fulfil your contractual commitments.
> *awfū bi'l-ʿuqūd:*

—is His requirement of His servants that they must fulfil the obligation of servanthood. It is as if the following conversation had taken place: "Our God," said the servants, "the covenant is twofold: the obligation of Lordship on Your part, and the obligation of servanthood on our part. It is more fitting that You should give precedence to fulfilling the obligation of Lordship and beneficence." "Yes," He replied (Exalted is He), "I shall first fulfil the obligation of Lordship and noble generosity."

It is well known that the benefits of this world are also of two kinds: the pleasures of dining and the pleasures of sexuality. Allāh (Glory be to Him) has therefore given a detailed explanation of what is lawful and what is unlawful, with regard to foodstuffs and sexual activities. Since the need for food is more important than the need for a sexual relationship, it is not surprising that He has discussed the former before the latter. On completion of this explanation, it is as if He is saying: "I have fulfilled the obligation of Lordship, by providing the benefits and pleasures that are sought in this world, so now it is your turn to concentrate on fulfilling the obligation of servanthood in this world." Since the ritual prayer [*ṣalāt*] is the most important act of worshipful obedience, after faith, and since the ritual prayer cannot be performed except in a state of ritual purity, it is not surprising that He has begun (Exalted is He) by stating the conditions of the ablution [*wuḍū'*],[526] for He has said:

> O you who truly believe, when you get ready for the ritual prayer,
> *yā ayyuha 'lladhīna āmanū idhā qumtum ila 'ṣ-ṣalāti*
> wash your faces, and your hands up to the elbows
> *fa-'ghsilū wujūha-kum wa aidiya-kum ila 'l-marāfiqi*

In other words: "When you intend to perform the ritual prayer, and you have voided excrement...."[527] This is reminiscent of His saying (Exalted is He):

> When you recite the Qur᾿ān, seek refuge with Allāh.
> *fa-idhā qara᾿ta 'l-qur᾿āna fa-'sta῾idh bi'llāhi.* (16:98)

That is to say: "When you intend to recite the Qur᾿ān, you must seek refuge with Allāh."

This saying stipulates the strict necessity of the ablution [*wuḍū᾿*] in preparation for every ritual prayer. Such is the obvious import of the Qur᾿ānic verse, and it is the doctrine of Dāwūd aẓ-Ẓāhirī. As for the majority of the scholars, among the Companions and those after them, they maintain that a number of ritual prayers can be covered by a single ablution. Since this does not tally with its obvious signification, they interpret the verse to mean: "When you get ready for the ritual prayer, and you are not in a state of purity...." They argue that this qualification has been omitted because the sense of it is clearly implied, and this is only one of the abbreviated expressions in the Qur᾿ān, of which there are very many indeed. Furthermore, on the Day of the Trench [*al-Khandaq*], the Prophet (Allāh bless him and give him peace) combined four ritual prayers with one ablution.

As reported by Abū Huraira (may Allāh be well pleased with him), Allāh's Messenger (Allāh bless him and give him peace) once said:

> Allāh will not accept the ritual prayer of any one of you, if he has voided excrement, until he performs the ablution.[528]

The verse has also been said to mean: "When you get ready for the ritual prayer after rising from sleep."

According to some, it is a strong recommendation, rather than a strict injunction. When someone is getting ready for the prayer, he is thereby urged to perform a new act of purification, even if he is already in a state of purity. This view is supported by a report from Ibn ῾Umar (may Allāh be well pleased with him and his father), relating that Allāh's Messenger (Allāh bless him and give him peace) once said:

> If someone performs the ablution in a state of purity, Allāh will record ten good deeds to his credit.[529]

The compulsory elements of the ritual ablution [*wuḍū᾿*] are four in number, as stated in this Qur᾿ānic verse:

1. The first is:

> wash your faces, and your hands up to the elbows.
> *fa-'ghsilū wujūha-kum wa aidiya-kum ila 'l-marāfiqi.*

According to ash-Shāfiʿī, this verse provides evidence that the intention [*niyya*] is necessary at the time of washing the face. His argument is that the ablution is commanded, and that everything that is commanded must be performed with explicit intent. Besides, it is related in the two *Ṣaḥīḥ*'s, among the reports attributed to ʿUmar ibn al-Khaṭṭāb, that the Prophet (Allāh bless him and give him peace) once said:

> [Religious] deeds are valued only by the intentions [*innama 'l-aʿmālu bi'n-niyyāt*].[530]

The ritual ablution is one of the [religious] deeds, so it must be performed with explicit intent.

When we say that the ritual ablution is commanded, and that it is one of the deeds of the religion, we are alluding to His saying (Exalted is He):

> They were commanded only to serve Allāh,
> *wa mā umirū illā li-yaʿbudu 'llāha*
> devoting the religion to Him sincerely.
> *mukhliṣīna la-hu 'd-dīn.* (98:5)

Sincere devotion is a synonym for genuine intention. So long as genuine intention is properly respected, proper respect will be paid to the principle of intention in all those deeds that bring one near to Allāh.

According to Abū Ḥanīfa, this verse provides evidence of the noncompulsory status of the intention, in the case of the ritual ablution. He said: "The intention is not a precondition for the validity of the ablution, because, in this verse, Allāh (Exalted is He) declared it compulsory to wash the four parts of the body, but He did not declare the intention compulsory. To make the intention compulsory, therefore, is to make an addition to the text. Adding to the text amounts to abrogation [*naskh*], and it is not permissible to abrogate the Qurʾān on the strength of one traditional report [*khabar*], or by analogical deduction [*qiyās*]."

Our response to this argument is as follows: In declaring the intention compulsory, in the case of the ritual ablution, we have drawn our evidence from no source but the Qur'ān itself, where He has said (Exalted is He):

> They were commanded only to serve Allāh,
> *wa mā umirū illā li-ya'budu 'llāha*
> devoting the religion to Him sincerely.
> *mukhliṣīna la-hu 'd-dīn.* (98:5)[531]

As for the definition of the face [*wajh*], it extends from the roots of the hair of the head to the tip of the chin, lengthwise, and from the ear to the ear in terms of width. That is because *wajh* is derived from *muwājaha* [facing; confrontation]. It is necessary to wash the whole of the face, in the ritual ablution. It is necessary to bring the water in contact with what is beneath the eyebrows, including the eyelashes, as well as both cheeks, the moustache, and the [skin beneath] the tuft of hair between the lower lip and the chin, even if the tuft is dense. As for the beard, if it is so thick that the skin beneath it is invisible, it is not necessary to wash what lies beneath it, though it is necessary to wash the skin beneath a slight beard.

2. The second compulsory element is:

> and your hands up to the elbows
> *wa aidiya-kum ila 'l-marāfiqi*

That is to say: "and wash your hands up to the elbows." Most of the scholars maintain that it is strictly necessary to include the elbows in the washing. The argument of the majority is that, in this context, the word *ilā* is used in the sense of *ma'a* [with; along with], as in His saying (Exalted is He):

> and do not consume their wealth "up to" your own wealth.
> *wa lā ta'kulū amwāla-hum ilā amwāli-kum.* (4:2)

In other words: "along with [*ma'a*] your own wealth."

This interpretation derives support from the Sunna, on the basis of an authentic report from Abū Huraira (may Allāh be well pleased with him). When he performed the ablution, he washed his face and did so very thoroughly, then he washed his right hand until he reached the upper arm, then his left hand until he reached the upper arm. Then he said: "That is how I used to see Allāh's Messenger (Allāh bless him and give him peace) perform his ablution."

The answer to the preceding argument [of the minority] is as follows: The limit is automatically included, if it is similar in nature to the object to which the limit is set, as in this Qur᾿ānic verse, because the elbow is similar in nature to the hand. If it is not similar in nature to the object to which the limit is set, it is not automatically included, as in His saying (Exalted is He):

> Then strictly observe the fast till nightfall.
> *thumma atimmu 'ṣ-ṣiyāma ila 'l-lail.* (2:187)

—because the day is different in kind from the night, and is therefore not included in it.

3. The third compulsory element is:

> and rub your heads
> *wa 'msaḥū bi-ru᾿ūsi-kum*

The scholars have disagreed concerning the extent to which it is necessary to rub the head. According to Mālik, it is strictly necessary to rub the head all over. The same opinion is attributed in Aḥmad, in one of two accounts. According the other account of his doctrine, it is strictly necessary to rub most of it. Abū Ḥanīfa said: "It is strictly necessary to rub a quarter of it," or, according to another report: "It is strictly necessary to rub an area of it corresponding to three fingers." According to ash-Shāfiʿī: "What is strictly required is to rub as much as the term *masḥ* [rubbing] would normally be understood to mean." Abū Ḥanīfa adopted the explanation provided by the Sunna, based on the report of al-Mughīra ibn Shuʿba, who said that, when the Prophet (Allāh bless him and give him peace) performed his ablution, he rubbed his forelock, and over his turban and boots.[532]

3. The fourth compulsory element is:

> and [wash] your feet up to the ankles.
> *wa arjula-kum ila 'l-kaʿbain:*

In the case of the feet, according to the majority of the scholars, among the Companions, the Successors and those after them, and the Four Imāms and their colleagues, the compulsory treatment is washing. This is also indicated by the conduct of the Prophet (Allāh bless him and give him peace), his Companions and the Successors.[533] According to az-Zamakhsharī: "The reason for specifying the limit:

up to the ankles.
ila 'l-ka'bain:

—is to dispel the notion of those who might suppose that they [the ankles] should merely be rubbed, because no limit to rubbing is specified in the Sacred Law. In the words of the Prophetic tradition [*ḥadīth*]:

Alas for the consequences from the Fire of Hell![534]

This refers to the [sectarians known as] the Imāmiyya, who maintain that rubbing, not washing, is the treatment required for the feet. The verse is explicit, however, since the noun *arjula* [feet] in

and your feet
wa arjula-kum

—is in the accusative case [instead of the genitive, which follows the preposition *bi-* after the Arabic verb meaning "rub"]. The feet are thus linked to the object of washing. The reference to rubbing is inserted between the objects of washing, in order to list the body parts in sequence.

And if you are unclean, purify yourselves.
wa in kuntum junuban fa-'ṭṭaharū:

That is to say: "And if you are in a state of major impurity [*janāba*], you must cleanse yourselves by washing the entire body."[535] That is made necessary for the man and the woman by one of two things: either (1) the emission of seminal fluid, in any manner whatsoever, including emission while dreaming, or (2) contact with the circumcisers, which must be followed by total ablution, even though it does not involve the emission of semen.[536]

And if you are sick or on a journey,
wa in kuntum marḍā aw 'alā safarin
or one of you has come from the toilet,
aw jā'a aḥadun min-kum mina 'l-ghā'iṭi
or you have touched women....
aw lāmastumu 'n-nisā'a....

That is to say: "If you are sick and water would be harmful to you, or you are on a journey and cannot find water, or one of you has come from the place of excretion, or you have had sexual intercourse with women."

and you have not found water, then head for some fresh topsoil
fa-lam tajidū mā'an fa-tayammamū ṣa'īdan ṭayyiban

In other words: "and if you have not found water after searching for it, then go to clean ground, in order to perform the dry ablution [*tayammum*] with it."

> and rub your faces and your hands with some of it.
> *fa-'msaḥū bi-wujūhi-kum wa aidī-kum min-h:*

In other words: "Rub your faces and your hands with the earth, with two strokes, as described by the Prophetic Sunna."[537] The practice has already been explained, and its rules set forth, in the Sūra of Women [*an-Nisā'*]. As indicated by His words (Exalted is He), the rubbing of the face and hands must be performed with *ṣa'īd*, which is topsoil [*turāb*].[538]

> Allāh does not wish to impose any hardship on you
> *mā yurīdu 'llāhu li-yaj'ala 'alai-kum min ḥarajin*

That is to say: "He does not wish to cause you serious inconvenience, by making it compulsory for you to perform the minor ablution [*wuḍū'*], the major ablution [*ghusl*] and the dry ablution [*tayammum*]."[539] The Qur'ānic verse proves that Allāh (Exalted is He) is One who wishes [*Murīd*], and this is generally agreed among the leading scholars, except that some of them have differed over the interpretation of his being One who wishes [*Murīd*]. According to our own colleagues, He is One who wishes with a sempiternal wish [*Murīd bi-irāda qadīma*].

You should know that this Qur'ānic verse represents a major principle in the Sacred Law, namely, the principle that harmful things are not legally prescribed. This is clearly indicated by this verse, for Allāh (Exalted is He) has also said:

> And He has not imposed upon you in the religion any hardship.
> *wa mā ja'ala 'alai-kum fi 'd-dīni min ḥaraj.* (22:78)

> Allāh desires ease for you;
> *yurīdu 'llāhu bi-kumu 'l-yusra*
> He does not desire hardship for you.
> *wa lā yurīdu bi-kumu 'l-'usr.* (2:185)

Further proof is contained in the Prophetic traditions [*aḥādīth*], for the Prophet (blessing and peace be upon him) once said:

> There is no harm [*ḍarar*] and no causing harm [*ḍirār*] in Islām.[540]

Evidence is also provided by the fact that the prevention of harm is intellectually commendable, so it must surely be likewise in the Sacred Law.

As for the assertion that the principle is permissibility [*ibāḥa*] in the case of things that are beneficial, the following points should be considered:

1. His saying (Exalted is He):

> He has created for you everything that the earth contains.
> *khalaqa la-kum mā fi 'l-arḍi jamīʿā.* (2:29)

2. His saying (Exalted is He):

> Good things are made lawful to you.
> *uḥilla la-kumu 'ṭ-ṭayyibāt.* (5:5)

As we have previously explained, the good things [*ṭayyibāt*] are sources of pleasure and delight, and things from which benefits are derived.

If these two principles are firmly established, there is absolutely no need for analogical deduction [*qiyās*] in the Sacred Law. For every incident that occurs, the appropriate ruling can be specified as follows: If it is mentioned in the Book and the Sunna, that will be all that is required. Otherwise, if it comes under the heading of things that are harmful, we must consider it unlawful, on the basis of all the evidence that, in the case of things that are harmful, the principle of unlawfulness applies. If it comes under the heading of things that are beneficial, on the other hand, we must consider it permissible, on the strength of all the evidence that proves the permissibility of things that are beneficial.[541]

> but He wishes to purify you and perfect His grace upon you,
> *wa lākin yurīdu li-yuṭahhira-kum wa li-yutimma niʿmata-hu ʿalai-kum*
> so that you may give thanks.
> *laʿalla-kum tashkurūn.*

That is to say: "[He wishes] to purify you by ridding you of sins and the defilement of errors, by means of the ritual ablution, either wet or dry, and to perfect His grace upon you, by expounding the laws of Islām, and so that you may give thanks to Him for His blessings, which are incalculable."[542]

As for the meaning of purification [*taṭhīr*], it relates to purity [*ṭahāra*] of the heart from the attitude of rebellion against worshipful obedience to Allāh (Exalted is He). That is because unbelief and sinful acts of disobedience constitute pollution for the spirits. Pollution is filth, because it is something that deserves to be discarded, done away with and banished. The same is true of unbelief and sinful acts of disobedience, for pollutants are also spiritual in nature. Just as the term purity [*ṭahāra*] is applied to the removal of physical pollutants, it is likewise applied to the removal of corrupt beliefs and futile attitudes. It was in this sense that Allāh (Exalted is He) said:

> The polytheists are nothing but filth.
> *inna-ma 'l-mushrikūna najasun.* (9:28)

—for He dismissed their opinion as a form of pollution.

He also said (Exalted is He):

> Allāh wishes only to remove uncleanness far from you,
> *inna-mā yurīdu 'llāhu li-yudhhiba ʿan-kumu 'r-rijsa*
> O People of the Household,
> *Ahla 'l-Baiti*
> and to cleanse you with a thorough cleansing.
> *wa yuṭahhira-kum taṭhīrā.* (33:33)

—thereby making their exemption from sinful acts of disobedience a state of purity [*ṭahāra*] for them.

With reference to Jesus (peace be upon him), He said:

> I am gathering you and causing you to ascend to Me,
> *innī mutawaffī-ka wa rāfiʿu-ka ilayya*
> and I am cleansing you of those who disbelieve.
> *wa muṭahhiru-ka mina 'lladhīna kafarū.* (3:55)

—thereby making his deliverance from their assault, and from their interference with him, a form of purification [*taṭhīr*] for him.[543]

If you understand this well, we may go on to say the following: When Allāh (Exalted is He) commands the servant to bring water in contact with these particular members of the body, even though these members are pure, the servant cannot recognize any intelligible benefit in this imposition. When he complies with that imposition, his compliance is simply a demonstration of servanthood and obedience to Lordship. This compliance rids his heart of all traces of rebellion, so that is a state of purity. Such is the valid reason for calling these actions "purification." This is also confirmed by the many traditional reports that have been handed down, to the effect that, when the believer washes his face, his sinful errors drop from his face. The same is said of his hands, his head and his feet.

You should also know that this basic principle, which we have established, is an important maxim in the legal doctrine of ash-Shāfiʿī. It may offer a solution to many of the disputed questions in the chapters concerning ritual purity. Allāh knows best, of course.

> and to perfect His grace upon you
> *wa li-yutimma niʿmata-hu ʿalai-kum*

There are two interpretations of this:

1. He was referring to the perfecting of the grace mentioned first, that being the grace of this world, and to the grace mentioned in second place, that being the grace of the religion.
2. The meaning is: "[He wishes] to perfect His grace upon you, by granting licence to perform the dry ablution [*tayammum*], and by lightening the imposition in the state of travel and sickness." Some take this as evidence that Allāh (Exalted is He) will treat you leniently on the Day of Resurrection, by pardoning your sins and overlooking your bad deeds.[544]

> so that you may give thanks.
> *laʿalla-kum tashkurūn.*

That is to say: "so that you may give thanks for Allāh's grace upon you, since He has cleansed you of defilements and sins, and has not imposed any hardship on you."

There are many Prophetic traditions concerning the excellent merit of the ritual ablution [*wuḍūʾ*]. For instance, as related by Muslim, on the authority of Abū Huraira (may Allāh be well pleased with him), Allāh's Messenger (Allāh bless him and give him peace) once said:

> When the Muslim or believing servant performs the ritual ablution, and so washes his face, every sinful error that he has seen with his eyes will depart from his face, along with the water, or, along with the last drop of water. When he washes his hands, every sinful error that his hands have touched will depart from his hands, along with the water, or, along with the last drop of water. When he washes his feet, every sinful error that his feet have trodden will depart from his hands, along with the water, or, along with the last drop of water. He will then depart [from his ablution] pure and free from sins.[545]

These are my own observations:

For the Muslim servant who is afraid of offending Allāh, it is essential to prepare for the ritual prayer [*ṣalāt*] before the arrival of its prescribed time, by thoroughly performing the ritual ablution [*wuḍū'*]. He should wait for the prayer in the place where he intends to perform it, and devote his attention to remembrance [*dhikr*], meaning the affirmation that there is no god but Allāh [*lā ilāha illa 'llāh*], so that his heart will be rid of the cares of this world. He must make his heart ready for intimate communion with his Lord (Glorious and Exalted is He), and present his heart to his Lord in his ritual prayer. His spirit must pray inside his outer form, then he will be one of those of whom Allāh (Exalted is He) has said:

> Successful indeed are the true believers
> *qad aflaḥa 'l-mu'minūn:*
> who are humble in their prayers.
> *alladhīna hum fī ṣalāti-him khāshi'ūn.* (23:1,2)

This is the kind of prayer that prevents its performer from committing indecency and reprehensible behaviour, as mentioned in His saying (Exalted is He):

> The ritual prayer helps to prevent
> *inna 'ṣ-ṣalāta tanhā*
> indecency and reprehensible behaviour.
> *'ani 'l-faḥshā'i wa 'l-munkar.*
> The remembrance of Allāh is greater;
> *wa la-dhikru 'llāhi akbar:*
> and Allāh knows the things you do.
> *wa 'llāhu ya'lamu mā taṣna'ūn.* (29:45)

If the servant wishes to comprehend the connection that exists between him and his Lord, he should examine his ritual prayer, for his portion is measured by the extent to which he understands his prayer. Enabling grace comes from Allāh, and Allāh guides to the straight path.

O Allāh, grant us the ability to accomplish all that. *Āmīn*. Peace be upon the Messengers, and praise be to Allāh, the Lord of All the Worlds. There is no might nor any power, except with Allāh, the All-High, the Almighty. May Allāh bless our master Muḥammad, his family and his Companions, and may He grant them peace.

The Thirty-first Call

In the Name of Allāh, the All-Merciful, the All-Compassionate.
Bismi'llāhi 'r-Raḥmāni 'r-Raḥīm.

O you who truly believe,
be steadfast witnesses for Allāh
yā ayyuha 'lladhīna āmanū kūnū qawwāmīna
li'llāhi shuhadā'a
in equity, and do not let hatred
of any people seduce you,
bi'l-qisṭi wa lā yajrimanna-kum shana'ānu qawmin
so that you do not deal justly.
'alā allā ta'dilū:
Deal justly, for that is nearer to true devotion.
i'dilū huwa aqrabu li 't-taqwā:
Observe your duty to Allāh.
Allāh is Aware of what you do.
wa 'ttaqu 'llāh: inna 'llāha Khabīrun bi-mā ta'malūn.

Allāh has promised, to those who believe
and do good works,
wa'ada 'llāhu 'lladhīna āmanū wa 'amilu 'ṣ-ṣāliḥāti
that theirs will be forgiveness
and immense reward.
la-hum maghfiratun wa ajrun 'aẓīm. (5:8,9)

Allāh (Exalted is He) has said:

O you who truly believe,
yā ayyuha 'lladhīna āmanū
be very steadfast witnesses for Allāh, in equity.
kūnū qawwāmīna li'llāhi shuhadā'a bi'l-qisṭi

In other words: "You must do your utmost* to ensure the probity and

*The intensive formation of the Arabic word *qawwām* [very steadfast] conveys the sense of "going to great lengths."[546]

correctness of your testimony for Allāh, and you must testify with fairness."

This is also connected with the preceding revelation, the purpose being to urge the believers to comply with the obligations imposed by Allāh (Exalted is He). You should know that those obligations, though they are very many, are subject to no more than a twofold classification: (1) The glorification of Allāh's commandment. (2) Compassion for Allāh's creatures.

His saying (Exalted is He):

> Be very steadfast for Allāh.
> *kūnū qawwāmīna li'llāhi.*

—is indicative of the first category, which is the glorification of Allāh's commandment. The meaning of steadfastness [*qiyām*] for Allāh is that the believer must steadily promote the truth, for Allāh's sake, in everything he is obliged to practise on a regular basis, in order to display servitude [*ʿubūdiyya*] and the glorification of Lordship [*Rubūbiyya*].

As for His words:

> witnesses for Allāh, in equity.
> *shuhadāʾa bi'l-qisṭi.*

—they are indicative of compassion for Allāh's creatures, since they signify: "In your testimony, you must not be biased in favour of those with whom you share loving affection and close kinship. Nor must you refuse to bear witness for your enemies and your adversaries."[547]

> And do not let hatred of any people seduce you,
> *wa lā yajrimanna-kum shanaʾānu qawmin*
> so that you do not deal justly.
> *ʿalā allā taʿdilū.*

That is to say: "Do not let the intensity of your hatred for your enemies prompt you to abandon fairness, where they are concerned, and cause you to treat them unjustly."

> Deal justly, for that is nearer to true devotion.
> *iʿdilū huwa aqrabu li 't-taqwā:*

In other words: "Justice in dealing with those you hate is nearer to your true devotion to Allāh."[548] Allāh has commanded justice for every individual, whether he be a close or a distant relative, and whether he be friend or foe.[549] He has explicitly commanded the believers to act justly, and He has made it clear that justice is on a par with true devotion. He has done so after forbidding them to act tyrannically, and making it clear that injustice is the product of passion.

Since this applies to justice in dealing with the unbelievers, can you have any idea of what it means to deal justly with the believers?![550] He has declared justice nearer to true devotion, because, when justice is obtained, the consequence is devout abstention from the cause of sin. True devotion is the cause of every noble virtue, because it is the head of those praiseworthy qualities that are conducive to everything good.[551]

> Observe your duty to Allāh. Allāh is Aware of what you do.
> *wa 'ttaqu 'llāh: inna 'llāha Khabīrun bi-mā taʿmalūn.*

That is to say: "He is Observant of your actions and He will recompense you for them." It was az-Zamakhsharī who said: "This contains an important notification, to the effect that justice is obligatory, even in dealing with the unbelievers, who are the enemies of Allāh. Since it is prescribed so emphatically in their case, it is hard to conceive how imperative it must be in dealing with the believers, who are His friends and His loved ones!"[552]

This is a promise, as it applies to those who are obedient, and a threat, as it applies to the sinful transgressors, because He is Aware of all that there is to be known, so nothing about their states of being can ever be hidden from Him.[553]

> Allāh has promised, to those who believe and do good works,
> *waʿada 'llāhu 'lladhīna āmanū wa ʿamilu 'ṣ-ṣāliḥāti*
> that theirs will be forgiveness and immense reward.
> *la-hum maghfiratun wa ajrun ʿaẓīm.*

That is to say: "Allāh has promised, to the obedient believers, that theirs will be forgiveness and an immense reward," meaning: "For them, in the Hereafter, there will be forgiveness of sins and a mighty reward, in the form of the Garden of Paradise."[554] Forgiveness means the elimination of evil deeds, as He has said:

> In their case, Allāh will change their evil deeds into good deeds.
> *fa-ulāʾika yubaddilu 'llāhu sayyiʾāti-him ḥasanāt.* (25:70)

This promise is specifically attributed to Allāh (Exalted is He), for He has said:

> Allāh has promised....
> *waʿada 'llāhu* ....

—and God [*al-Ilāh*] is the One who is Capable of all that can be done, Aware of all that can be known, Independent of all needs. This precludes any breach of His promise, because a breach could only result from ignorance, were He to forget his promise, or from inability, were He unable to fulfil His promise, or from stinginess, were stinginess to prevent Him from keeping His promise, or from need. Since God is completely untarnished by any deficiences, it is utterly inconceivable that any breach might affect His promise. The notification of this promise is even more certain and more potent than the notification of what is actually promised. Furthermore, since this promise reaches the believer before his death, it will enable him to experience joy in the throes of death, making those agonies easier to bear. It will also make things easier for him after death, in the darkness of the grave, and when he is exposed, on the field [*ʿarṣa*]*of the Resurrection, to the sight of all those dreadful terrors.[555]

After that [in the next verse of the Qurʾān], Allāh goes on to mention the threat to the unbelievers:

> And those who disbelieve and deny Our signs,
> *wa 'lladhīna kafarū wa kadhdhabū bi-āyāti-nā*
> such are rightful owners of Hell.
> *ulāʾika aṣḥābu 'l-jaḥīm*. (5:10)

Since He has mentioned the destination and final outcome of the truly devout believers, He also mentions the destination of the sinful unbelievers, and how they will dwell forever in the depths of Hell, suffering eternal torment.

It was Abū Ḥayyān who said: "The sentence referring to the believers begins with the verb *waʿada* [has promised] in the past tense, which indicates that something has already happened. In the case of the unbelievers, on the other hand, the Arabic sentence is a nominal construction, which indicates that this judgment definitely applies to

*The term *ʿarṣa* is applied to any wide space between houses, in which there is no building of any kind. The plural form is *ʿaraṣāt*.

them, and that they are the rightful owners of the Fire, since they will abide forever in the torment of Hell."[556] Such are those who deny the Uniqueness [*Waḥdāniyya*] of Allāh, and break their vows and their contracts, and refuse to believe in what the Messengers have brought from His presence.[557]

The expression: "Such are the rightful owners [*aṣḥāb*] of Hell" conveys the sense of confinement, since ownership implies permanent residence. (In Arabic, the inhabitants of the desert are called *aṣḥāb aṣ-ṣaḥrā᾽*.)

This Qur᾽ānic verse provides definite proof that eternal damnation is only for the unbelievers.[558] As for its principal content, it conveys the message that justice is, in fact, the praiseworthy middle ground [*wasaṭ*], which is appropriate to all action, speech and morality, and which has been commanded in His saying (Exalted is He):

> So tread the straight path, as you are commanded.
> *fa-'staqim ka-mā umirta.* (11:112)[559]

These are my own comments:

The fundamental principles for mankind are the rules of the noble Sacred Law [*Sharī῾a*], which have been available to them since the Prophet (Allāh bless him and give him peace) was sent on his mission. They are principles existing for all eternity and from all eternity [*abadiyya azaliyya*], and every responsible person will be held accountable for them in the Hereafter.

Our Lord (Magnificent is His Majesty) is the Knowledgeable One, from whose knowledge (Glory be to Him and Exalted is He) nothing escapes, whether it be past, present or future. He is Most Aware of the condition of His servants, from the outset to the final destination. It is therefore essential for the Muslim to observe all the following:

1. He must comply with the Divine judgment [*al-ḥukm al-Ilāhī*].
2. He must ensure that his enjoyment of this world is in harmony with the Divine law [*al-qānūn al-Ilāhī*], for that is the essence of true faith [*īmān*].
3. He must apply the sacred legal rules [*al-aḥkām ash-shar῾iyya*] to all his limbs and organs, just as the Companions of Allāh's Messenger (Allāh bless him and give him peace) applied them, in their day and age, to their good and pure selves.

This is a duty incumbent on every responsible person, until the advent of the Final Hour, wherever he happens to be. He must adorn himself with the Lordly qualities, they being the qualities of the Qur'ān, which are the essential qualities of the Prophet (Allāh bless him and give him peace). Consider, for instance, the words of Allāh (Exalted is He):

> Those who go in awe for fear of their Lord,
> *inna 'lladhīna hum min khashyati Rabbi-him mushfiqūn:*
>
> and those who believe in the signs of their Lord,
> *wa 'lladhīna hum bi-āyāti Rabbi-him yu'minūn:*
>
> and those who do not ascribe partners to their Lord.
> *wa 'lladhīna hum bi-Rabbi-him lā yushrikūn.* (23:57–59)

That is to say: "Those who do not make pretentious display in their worship."

> And those who give what they give with hearts afraid,
> *wa 'lladhīna yu'tūna mā ātaw wa qulūbuhum wajilatun*
> because they are about to return unto their Lord.
> *anna-hum ilā Rabbi-him rāji'ūn.*
>
> They are the ones who race for good things,
> *ulā'ika yusāri'ūna fi 'l-khairāti*
> and they shall win them in the race.
> *wa hum lā-hā sābiqūn.* (23:60, 61)

These splendid attributes are the attributes of the champions of truth [*ṣiddīqīn*], and there are many examples of these attributes in the Noble Qur'ān. You must adorn yourself with them, to fullest possible extent.

As for those who reject this advice, let them beware! Salvation from the tyranny of the lower self, and from its evil ways, can only be obtained through reliance on Allāh (Exalted is He) and strict adherence to Islām, for that is part of true faith.

We beg Allāh (Exalted is He and Glorious is His Majesty) to grant us the benefit of true faith and Islām, as they need to be constantly practised by His servant. *Āmīn.* Peace be upon the Messengers, and praise be to Allāh, the Lord of All the Worlds. There is no might nor any power, except with Allāh, the All-High, the Almighty. May Allāh bless our master Muḥammad, his family and his Companions, and may He grant them peace.

The Thirty-second Call

In the Name of Allāh, the All-Merciful, the All-Compassionate.
Bismi'llāhi 'r-Raḥmāni 'r-Raḥīm.

O you who truly believe,
remember Allāh's favour to you!
yā ayyuha 'lladhīna āmanu
'dhkurū ni'mata 'llāhi 'alai-kum
[Remember] how certain people proposed
idh hamma qawmun
to stretch out their hands against you,
an yabsuṭū ilai-kum aidiya-hum
but He withheld their hands from you;
fa-kaffa aidiya-hum 'an-kum
and practise true devotion to Allāh.
wa 'ttaqu 'llāh:
In Allāh let the believers put their trust.
wa 'ala 'llāhi fa-l'-yatawakkali 'l-mu'minūn. (5:11)

In the first phase of their conflict, the polytheists [*mushrikūn*] were triumphant, and the Muslims were conquered and defeated. The polytheists had always wanted to inflict misfortune, massacre and pillage on the Muslims, but Allāh (Exalted is He) prevented them from achieving their objective, while Islām gained strength and the Muslims came to represent a mighty force. He said (Exalted is He):

> O you who truly believe, remember Allāh's favour to you!
> *yā ayyuha 'lladhīna āmanu 'dhkurū ni'mata 'llāhi 'alai-kum*
> [Remember] how certain people proposed....
> *idh hamma qawmun....*

—those people being the polytheists:

> to stretch out their hands against you
> *an yabsuṭū ilai-kum aidiya-hum*

—in order to kill, and plunder, and drive you into exile, but Allāh (Exalted is He) withheld the hands of the unbelievers from you, O you Muslims, through His grace and His mercy. In exchange for such a tremendous favour, you are obliged to refrain from disobedience and opposition to Him.

This Qur'ānic verse was revealed in connection with a particular event, of which there are several traditional accounts:

1. According to Ibn ʿAbbās (may Allāh be well pleased with him and his father), al-Kalbī and Muqātil: "The Prophet (Allāh bless him and give him peace) dispatched a small expeditionary corps against the tribe of Banī ʿĀmir, and all but three of those troops were slain. One of the survivors was ʿAmr ibn Umayya aḍ-Ḍamrī, and he and another went together to the Prophet (Allāh bless him and give him peace), to give him a report of what had happened to their people. On their way, they encountered two men of the Banī Salīm, who had with them a guarantee of safe conduct from the Prophet (Allāh bless him and give him peace), but they killed them both, without realizing that they had a guarantee of safe conduct. The relatives of the two slain men then came to demand payment of the blood money [*diya*].

"The Prophet (Allāh bless him and give him peace) thereupon set out, accompanied by Abū Bakr, ʿUmar, ʿUthmān and ʿAlī (may Allāh be well pleased with them all), until they reached the tribe of Bani 'n-Naḍīr. The latter had contracted a treaty with the Prophet (Allāh bless him and give him peace), the terms of which required them to abstain from fighting, and to assist him in the settlement of blood-money claims. The Prophet (Allāh bless him and give him peace) said to them: 'One of my Companions has fatally attacked two men, who had with them a guarantee of safe conduct from me. I am therefore liable for their blood money, so I must ask you to help me.'

"They responded by saying: 'Sit down, while we feed you, and we shall give you what you are seeking.' It was then that they proposed to assassinate Allāh's Messenger (Allāh bless him and give him peace) and his Companions, so Gabriel (peace be upon him) came down with that message. Allāh's Messenger (Allāh bless him and give him peace) got up at once, together with his Companions, and they took their leave.[560] The Jews said: 'Our cooking pots are coming to the boil!' so the

Messenger told them that he had just received inspiration [*waḥy*], warning him of what they intended to do to him."

It was ʿAṭāʾ who said: "They plotted to throw a hand mill at him, or a slab of stone."

2. Others have said that Allāh's Messenger (Allāh bless him and give him peace) once stopped to make camp, and the people became separated from him. Allāh's Messenger (Allāh bless him and give him peace) had just hung his scabbard on a tree, when a desert Arab [*Aʿrābī*] came along, unsheathed the sword of Allāh's Messenger (Allāh bless him and give him peace), and then advanced towards him, saying: "Who can protect you from me?" The Messenger said: "Allāh!" He said that three times, whereupon Gabriel (peace be upon him) caused the sword to drop from the man's hand. Allāh's Messenger (Allāh bless him and give him peace) picked it up and said: "Who can protect you from me?" The man replied: "No one!" Then Allāh's Messenger (Allāh bless him and give him peace) cried out to his Companions, informing them of what had happened, but he declined to punish that man.[561]

3. It is related that the Muslims once gathered to perform the midday ritual prayer [*ṣalāt aẓ-ẓuhr*] in congregation, at a place called ʿAsfān. When they had prayed, the polytheists [*mushrikūn*] regretted having missed an opportunity. They said: "If only we had attacked them during their prayer!" They were told: "The Muslims will be holding another ritual prayer, which is dearer to them than their sons and their fathers," meaning the afternoon prayer [*ṣalāt al-ʿaṣr*]. The polytheists therefore proposed to attack them when they performed that prayer, so Gabriel (peace be upon him) brought down the revelation concerning the prayer in time of danger [*ṣalāt al-khawf*].[562]

As for His saying (Exalted is He):

> O you who truly believe, remember Allāh's favour to you!
> *yā ayyuha 'lladhīna āmanu 'dhkurū niʿmata 'llāhi ʿalai-kum*

—it means: "Remember the gracious favour that Allāh has bestowed upon you, by keeping you safe from your enemies."

> [Remember] how certain people proposed
> *idh hamma qawmun*
> to stretch out their hands against you,
> *an yabsuṭū ilai-kum aidiya-hum*

That is to say: "[They proposed] to afflict you with death and destruction."

> but He withheld their hands from you;
> *fa-kaffa aidiya-hum ʿan-kum:*

In other words: "He kept you safe from their wickedness, and turned their harmfulness away from you."

> And practise true devotion to Allāh.
> *wa 'ttaqu 'llāh.*

—by complying with His commandments and avoiding any violation of His prohibitions.

> In Allāh let the believers put their trust.
> *wa ʿala 'llāhi fa-l'-yatawakkali 'l-muʾminūn.*

That is to say: "Let the believers rely upon Allāh, for He is their Guardian [*Kāfī*] and their Helper [*Nāṣir*]."[563] This is because Allāh, and He alone, is the One who looks after them, by supplying all that is good and repelling all that is bad. He the One who provides benefit immediately, without any claim being made, and He is the One who grants the most perfect favour to those who put their trust in Him, to the exclusion of everything apart from Him.

Trust [*tawakkul*] is an expression signifying reliance on Allāh (Exalted is He) in all matters and concerns. It location is the heart. External activity is not incompatible with the trust of the heart, once the servant has been truly convinced that the outcome is predetermined by Allāh, so that, if something proves difficult, it is due to His predetermination.

The highest degree of trust is to be, in the presence of Allāh (Exalted is He), like a corpse in the presence of the ritual washer of the dead. When someone has that degree of trust, he is moved by the sempiternal power [*qudra azaliyya*], for he is someone whose conviction is really strong.

Consider the case of Abraham (peace be upon him), when Nimrod and his people proposed to stretch out their hands against him. They threw him into the fiery furnace, so Gabriel (peace be upon him) came to him and said, while hovering in the air: "Is there anything you need?" He replied: "As for needing anything of you, the answer is no!" Then he uttered the words: "Allāh is enough for me, and how excellent is the Custodian! [*ḥasbiya 'llāhu wa niʿma 'l-Wakīl*]."

Consider how real the trust of the Prophet (Allāh bless him and give him peace) must have been, since Allāh immediately withheld the hands of the polytheists from him and his Companions. Far from being able resist Him, they were afflicted, in most cases, with misfortunes they could not have imagined, in recompense for their evil intentions.

Trust is one of the highest degrees of those brought near [to the Lord]. It is therefore incumbent on the believer to embellish himself with praiseworthy attributes, and to travel the path of Truth in a seemly manner.

A wise man once paid someone a visit. He noticed a house that was newly restored and well furnished, but he also noticed that its owner was devoid of gracious virtues, so he hawked and spat in his face. The homeowner exclaimed: "What is this foolishness, O wise man?" The latter replied: "It is actually the essence of wisdom, because the spittle has stuck to the most contemptible object in the house, and I see nothing in your house that is more contemptible than you, on account of your complete lack of the inner virtues." He thereby drew attention to the inferiority and ugliness of his character, resulting from his addiction to his pleasures, and his total concentration on external appearance.

You must also understand that everything is subject to the decree of Allāh (Exalted is He), and that Allāh tests His servants with whatever He wishes. They are therefore obliged to rely on Him, in hardship and in ease, in what is pleasant and in what is repugnant.

Abū ʿUthmān is reported as having said: "Jesus (peace be upon him) was praying on the top of a mountain, when Iblīs came to him and said: 'Are you are the one who insists that everything is subject to Allāh's decree?' 'Yes,' he replied, so Iblīs said: 'Well then, throw yourself down from the mountain, and say: "My destiny is predermined!"' 'O accursed one,' replied Jesus, 'Allāh tests His servants. It is not for His servants to put Allāh to the test. Nothing is required of the servant except trust [*tawakkul*] and thankfulness [*shukr*] for gracious favours.'"

One of the gracious favours of Allāh (Exalted is He) is extraction from the darkness of nonexistence into the light of existence, by the commandment: "Be! [*kun*]." Allāh knows that the return of His servants to nonexistence is not brought about by them, and is not for them to determine, just as their emergence was not brought about by them. Their emergence was caused by the force of the commandment: "Be! [*kun*]," so their return can likewise only be brought about by the force of the commandments and prohibitions, which Allāh has laid down to guide them to the attractions of His providence and His grace.[564]

These are my own remarks:

You must rely entirely on your Patron, the Lord of All the Worlds. You must cling to His door with humble submission, supplication and weeping, through the watches of the night and the ends of the day, in the company of those who are humbly submissive. There is no escape from this situation of ours, except through the mercy of Allāh (Exalted is He). There is no safety from these troubles and temptations, except through His favourable attention, His enabling grace and His providential care. You must therefore wake up from the slumber of the heedless, and struggle with your lower self, for the sake of your Patron's good pleasure. Any request for help should be addressed to Allāh (Exalted is He), in every situation, for He is the Best Helper, and He (Exalted is He) is the Most Merciful of the merciful.

O Allāh, grant us the ability to accomplish all that. *Āmīn*. Peace be upon the Messengers, and praise be to Allāh, the Lord of All the Worlds. There is no might nor any power, except with Allāh, the All-High, the Almighty. May Allāh bless our master Muḥammad, his family and his Companions, and may He grant them peace.

The Thirty-third Call

In the Name of Allāh, the All-Merciful, the All-Compassionate.
Bismi'llāhi 'r-Raḥmāni 'r-Raḥīm.

O you who believe,
practise true devotion to Allāh,
yā ayyuha 'lladhīna āmanu 'ttaqu 'llāha
and seek the means of access to Him,
wa 'btaghū ilai-hi 'l-wasīlata
and strive in His way, so that you may succeed.
wa jāhidū fī sabīli-hi la'alla-kum tufliḥūn. (5:35)

Allāh (Exalted is He) had informed His Messenger (Allāh bless him and give him peace) that certain people, from among the Jews, were planning to stretch out their hands towards the Messenger, his brethren among the believers, and his Companions, in an act of treachery and deceit. Allāh (Exalted is He) prevented them from doing what they intended, and He then explained to the Messenger (Allāh bless him and give him peace) the intensity of their insolence towards the Prophets, and their unrelenting persistence in abusing them. The explanation was extended to this point, as if it had been said:

"You are well aware, by now, of the audacity with which the Jews commit acts of disobedience and sins, and of their remoteness from acts of worshipful obedience, which are the servant's means of access to the Lord. You must therefore represent, O believers, the very opposite of that. You must be devoutly on your guard against all forms of sinful disobedience to Allāh, while seeking access to Allāh through all forms of worshipful obedience to Allāh."[565]

He said (Exalted is He):

O you who believe, practise true devotion to Allāh,
yā ayyuha 'lladhīna āmanu 'ttaqu 'llāha

and seek the means of access to Him.
wa 'btaghū ilai-hi 'l-wasīlata

In other words: "You must be afraid of His punishment, and seek that which will bring you close to Him, meaning obedience and service to Him." According to Qatāda, this means: "You must draw close to Him through obedience to Him, and by performing that which is pleasing to Him."[566] Allāh (Glory be to Him) is saying, in effect: "O you who believe what Allāh and His Messenger have told you, about the reward He has promised you and the punishment He has threatened to inflict upon you."

Practise true devotion to Allāh
[-u] 'ttaqu 'llāha

He is saying: "Respond to Allāh in respect of His commandments and His prohibitions, by obeying Him therein, and verify your faith and your belief in your Lord and your Prophet, by the righteousness of your deeds."

and seek the means of access to Him.
wa 'btaghū ilai-hi 'l-wasīlata

In other words: "Seek nearness to Him by practising that which is pleasing to Him."

Ibn Zaid said: "The means of access is love. You must endear yourselves to Allāh," and he recited:

Those to whom they cry
ulā'ika 'lladhīna yad'ūna
seek the means of access to their Lord.
yabtaghūna ilā Rabbi-himu 'l-wasīlata. (17:57)[567]

The means of access is the means by which one arrives at the attainment of the goal. The means of access [*wasīla*] is also a signpost on the highest station in the Garden of Paradise, that being the station of Allāh's Messenger (Allāh bless him and give him peace), his abode in the Garden, and the nearest to the Heavenly Throne of all places in the Garden.

As recorded in the *Ṣaḥīḥ* of al-Bukhārī, on the authority of Jābir (may Allāh be well pleased with him), Allāh's Messenger (Allāh bless him and give him peace) once said:

> If someone says, when he hears the call [*nidā'*]: 'O Allāh, this is the perfect supplication and the proper benediction: Grant our master Muḥammad (Allāh bless him and give him peace) the means of access [*wasīla*] and special grace, and raise him up to a praiseworthy station, which You have promised him!'—he will be entitled to my intercession on the Day of Resurrection.

As recorded in the *Ṣaḥīḥ* of Muslim, Allāh's Messenger (Allāh bless him and give him peace) also said:

> When you hear the muezzin [*mu'adhdhin*], you must repeat what he says, then invoke blessing on me, for if someone invokes blessing on me, Allāh will bless him ten times. Then you must ask on my behalf for the means of access [*wasīla*], for that is a station in the Garden of Paradise. It is not appropriate to anyone except one of Allāh's servants, and I hope that I shall be he. If someone asks on my behalf for the means of access [*wasīla*], he will therefore be entitled to intercession.[568]

In his commentary on the Opening Sūra [*al-Fātiḥa*], al-Mawlā al-Fanārī said: "As for the means of access [*al-wasīla*], it is a very high level in the Garden of Eden, and it belongs to Allāh's Messenger (Allāh bless him and give him peace), bestowed upon him at the request of his Community. The Lord of Truth (Glory be to Him) did that for a wise reason, which He has kept secret. We have thereby obtained good fortune from Allāh. We have thus become the best community produced for humankind, and Allāh has made us the seal of the religious communities, just as He has made him the seal of the Prophets, he being a bringer of good tidings [*mubashshir*] (blessing and peace be upon him), as he was commanded to say.

"We have a special approach to Allāh (Exalted is He), from which we can converse with Him, and He converses with us. In like fashion, every creature has a special approach to its Lord. He [the Prophet (Allāh bless him and give him peace)] has therefore instructed us, on the strength of Allāh's commandment, to pray on his behalf for the means of access [*wasīla*], so that he may reside therein at the request of his Community. This comes under the heading of Divine solicitude [*ghaira Ilāhiyya*]."[569]

According to Ibn 'Abbās (may Allāh be well pleased with him and his father), *al-wasīla* signifies *al-ḥāja* [the need; what is needed], in which case the meaning is: "You must seek what you need by appealing to Allāh, for in His hand (Glorious is His Sublimity) are the keys of the heavens and the earth. You must not seek it by appealing to anyone other than Him."[570]

In this Qur'ānic verse, the believers are also told:

> and seek the means of access to Him.
> *wa 'btaghū ilai-hi 'l-wasīlata*

That is to say: "[Seek] that which will bring you near [to Him], meaning worshipful obedience, whether that act of obedience is obligatory [*farḍ*] or supererogatory [*nafl*]." In the words of the tradition [*ḥadīth*]:

> My servant does not cease to draw close to Me, through supererogatory acts of worship [*nawāfil*], until I love him. Then, when I love him, I become his hearing by which he hears.[571]

In this context, true devotion [*taqwā*] is the avoidance of all forms of disobedience, and seeking the means of access [*wasīla*] is the performance of all commandments. It is also correct to define true devotion [*taqwā*] as compliance with strict commandments, and avoidance of forbidden things that are strictly unlawful.

Seeking the means of access applies to absolutely everything that brings the seeker near to Him. That includes love for Allāh's Prophets and His saints [*awliyā'*], charitable gifts, visiting the friends of Allāh, frequent supplication, respect for family ties, frequent remembrance [*dhikr*], and so on. The meaning is, therefore: "Whatever brings you near to Allāh, you must adhere to it, and you must abandon everything that keeps you at a distance from Him."

If you acknowledge that, you are surely in plain error and obvious depravity, if you then accuse the Muslims of unbelief for visiting Allāh's saints, claiming that visiting them constitutes worship of other than Allāh. It is nothing of the kind, but rather an element of love for the sake of Allāh, to which Allāh's Messenger (Allāh bless him and give him peace) referred when he said:

> You cannot enter the Garden of Paradise until you truly believe, and you cannot truly believe until you love one another. Shall I show you something by which, if you do it, you will come to love one another? You must spread peace among you.[572]

He also said (Allāh bless him and give him peace):

> No indeed, no belief has he who has no love.

The means of access to Him, of which Allāh has said:

> and seek the means of access to Him.
> *wa 'btaghū ilai-hi 'l-wasīlata*

—is vitally important to the believers.[573]

You should know that all religious obligations can be assigned to either of two categories, with no need for a third:

1. The avoidance of things that are forbidden. This is implicitly indicated by His saying:

> Practise true devotion to Allāh
> *[-u] 'ttaqu 'llāha*

2. The performance of things that are commanded. This is implicitly indicated by His saying (Exalted is He):

> and seek the means of access to Him.
> *wa 'btaghū ilai-hi 'l-wasīlata*

Since the avoidance of things that are forbidden is essentially antecedent to the performance of things that are commanded, it is not surprising that Allāh (Exalted is He) has mentioned it first.

Avoidance and performance are concepts relevant to the outer aspect of actions, since what must be avoided are things that are unlawful, and what must be performed are the necessary duties. The two concepts are also relevant to moral characteristics, since what must be acquired are virtuous qualities, and what must be avoided are blameworthy qualities.

They are also relevant to the processes of thought, since that which must be performed is contemplation of the signs that point to the realization of Oneness [*tawḥīd*], Prophethood and the ultimate destination, while that which must be avoided is paying attention to dubious matters.

They are equally revelant to the station of [Divine] manifestation [*tajallī*], where performance means total immersion in Allāh (Exalted is He), and avoidance means paying attention to anything other than Allāh (Exalted is He).

Practitioners of spiritual exercise [*ahl ar-riyāḍa*] refer to performance and avoidance as divestment and adornment [*takhliya wa taḥliya*], as obliteration and consciousness [*maḥw wa ṣahw*], as negation and affirmation [*nafy wa ithbāt*], and as extinction and permanent survival [*fanā' wa baqā'*]. In each of the spiritual stations, the negation is expressed before the affirmation, and that is why, in our saying:

> There is no god but Allāh.
> *lā ilāha illa 'llāh.*

—the negation is stated before the affirmation.[574]

> and strive in His way, so that you may succeed.
> *wa jāhidū fī sabīli-hi laʿalla-kum tufliḥūn.*

That is to say: "You must strive for the exaltation of His religion, so that you may achieve the bliss of eternity."[575] The conjunction links a particular instruction to a general one, as an indication that the sacred struggle [*jihād*] is one of the most important acts of worshipful obedience. There are two parts to that:

1. A minor struggle. That is fighting the polytheists [*mushrikīn*].
2. A major struggle. That is detachment from passionate desire, the lower self and the devil.

Fighting the polytheists is a minor struggle [*jihād aṣghar*] because the enemy is present at one time, and absent at another. Besides, if the unbeliever kills you, you are a martyr [*shahīd*], and if you kill him, you become blissfully happy [*saʿīd*]. The lower self, by contrast, is never absent from you, and if it kills you, you become one of the wretched. We beg Allāh for safety![576]

As you should also understand, when He commanded the avoidance of what is improper, by His saying (Exalted is He):

> Practise true devotion to Allāh
> [-*u*] *'ttaqu 'llāha*

—and the performance of what is proper, by His saying (Exalted is He):

> and seek the means of access to Him.
> *wa 'btaghū ilai-hi 'l-wasīlata*

—both of these commandments are difficult, and weigh heavy on the lower self and the lustful appetite. The lower self summons to nothing but this world and sensual pleasures, while the intellect summons only to the service of Allāh, obedience to Him, and the shunning of things perceptible to the senses. The two cases are separated by mutual contradiction and incompatibility. That is why the scholars have coined various allegories, likening the quest for this world and the quest for the Hereafter to a pair of co-wives [*ḍarratain*], to a pair of adversaries, to the east and the west, and to the night and the day. Since that is the state of affairs, compliance with His instruction (Exalted is He):

> and seek the means of access to Him.
> *wa 'btaghū ilai-hi 'l-wasīlata*

—is one of the hardest things for the lower self, and one that weighs most heavily on the natural constitution. For this reason, He has immediately followed that instruction with His saying:

> and strive in His way, so that you may succeed.
> *wa jāhidū fī sabīli-hi la'alla-kum tufliḥūn.*

This noble Qur'ānic verse contains spiritual secrets, and we shall point to one of them here, by explaining that those who worship Allāh (Exalted is He) are divided into two groups: There are those who worship Allāh (Exalted is He) for no purpose other than Allāh, and there are those who worship Him for some other purpose.

The first rank is the noble and elevated rank, indicated by His saying:

> and strive in His way
> *wa jāhidū fī sabīli-hi*

That is to say: "in the way of servitude to Him, and the path of sincere devotion to awareness of Him and service to Him."

The second rank is below the first, and it is indicated by His saying:

> so that you may succeed.
> *la'alla-kum tufliḥūn.*

Success [*falāḥ*] is a collective term for deliverance from what is disliked and the attainment of that which is loved. In this Qur'ānic verse, as you should also know, Allāh (Exalted is He) has directed the believers to the stores of all good things, and to the keys of all sources of good fortune.[577]

The verse has explicitly issued the commandment to seek the means of access, and that is absolutely essential. Attainment to Allāh (Exalted is He) cannot be achieved without the means of access, and that is provided by the scholars of Reality [*Ḥaqīqa*] and the Shaikhs of the Spiritual Path [*Ṭarīqa*]. If work is motivated by the lower self, it thereby adds strength to its own existence. As for work in conformity with the instruction of the director [*murshid*], and with the guidance of the Prophets and the saints [*awliyā'*], such work rids the lower self of existence. It removes the veils and brings the seeker into contact with the Lord of lords.

Shaikh Abu 'l-Ḥasan ash-Shādhilī (may Allāh bestow His mercy upon him) has said: "A companion of mine and I repaired to a cave, in order to seek access to Allāh. We took shelter in it, saying: 'May He grant us an opening tomorrow, or after tomorrow.' Then, one day, a man of awesome dignity entered our presence. He informed us that he was one of Allāh's saints [*awliyā'*], so we asked him: 'How is your spiritual state?' He replied: 'How about the spiritual state of someone who says: "May He grant us an opening tomorrow, or after tomorrow"? O lower self, why do you not worship Allāh for Allāh's sake?' We came to our senses at that moment, and we repented to Allāh. After that, He opened the door for us. It is therefore essential to sever all attachment, so that the reality of the spiritual state may be disclosed."[578]

There is nothing to surpass what the noble traditional commentators have said (may Allāh bestow His mercy upon them), for it is unequivocal.

O Allāh, grant a good outcome to us, to our teachers, to our brethren and to all the Muslims, O Most Merciful of the merciful!

These are my own observations:

Shortcoming in the sacred struggle is a cause of the lack of intimate knowledge, because Allāh (Blessed and Exalted is He) has made access to the paths of His intimate knowledge dependent on the struggle with the lower self, for He has said (Blessed and Exalted is He):

> And as for those who strive in Our cause,
> *wa 'lladhīna jāhadū fī-nā*
> surely We shall guide them in Our ways.
> *la-nahdiyanna-hum subula-nā:*
> Allāh is surely with the good.
> *wa inna 'llāha la-maʿa 'l-muḥsinīn.* (29:69)

—and Allāh (Exalted is He) does not break His promise. If the human being is not steadfast in his struggle with his lower self, he will lapse into disobedience to Allāh. Lapsing into disobedience is the result of heedlessness, and that is the key to the gate of Hell, just as being present with Allāh (Exalted is He) is the key to the gate of the Garden of Paradise.

Allāh (Blessed and Exalted is He) has commanded us to struggle against our lower selves, to cut off our lustful appetites, and to kill them by adhering to the Sacred Law, so that the Garden of Paradise may be our final place of rest, for He has said (Exalted is He):

> But as for him who feared to stand before
> *wa ammā man khāfa maqāma Rabbi-hi*
> his Lord and restrained the self from passion,
> *wa naha 'n-nafsa ʿani 'l-hawā*
> surely the Garden of Paradise will be his final place of rest.
> *fa-inna 'l-jannata hiya 'l-maʾwā.* (79:40,41)

We beg Allāh to grant us safety from every sin, and the determination to practise every form of righteousness. O Allāh, grant us the ability to accomplish all that. *Āmīn.* Peace be upon the Messengers, and praise be to Allāh, the Lord of All the Worlds. There is no might nor any power, except with Allāh, the All-High, the Almighty. May Allāh bless our master Muḥammad, his family and his Companions, and may He grant them peace.

The Thirty-fourth Call

In the Name of Allāh, the All-Merciful, the All-Compassionate.
Bismi'llāhi 'r-Raḥmāni 'r-Raḥīm.

O you who truly believe,
yā ayyuha 'lladhīna āmanū
do not take the Jews and Christians for friends.
lā tattakhidhu 'l-Yahūda wa 'n-Naṣārā awliyā':
They are friends one to another.
ba'ḍu-hum awliyā'u ba'ḍ:
If one of you takes them for friends,
he is one of them.
wa man yatawalla-hum min-kum fa-inna-hu min-hum:
Allāh does not guide the wrongdoing folk.
inna 'llāha lā yahdi 'l-qawma 'ẓ-ẓālimīn. (5:51)

Allāh (Exalted is He) has already related, concerning the People of the Book, how they failed to put the Torah and the Gospel into practice, and He has declared them guilty of unbelief, wrongdoing and immorality. In these Qur'ānic verses, Allāh (Exalted is He) has warned against befriending the Jews and the Christians. Then He has enumerated the offences of the Jews, and the aspersions they have cast on the Divine Essence, by way of hideous statements and foul deeds.[579] He has now said (Exalted is He):

O you who truly believe,
yā ayyuha 'lladhīna āmanū
do not take the Jews and Christians for friends.
lā tattakhidhu 'l-Yahūda wa 'n-Naṣārā awliyā':

The traditional commentators have disagreed as to the occasion of the revelation of the verse, even though its ordinance applies to all the believers in general, because the specificity of the occasion is not incompatible with the generality of the ordinance.

According to one group: "This Qur'ānic verse was revealed in connection with 'Ubāda ibn aṣ-Ṣāmit (may Allāh be well pleased with him) and 'Abdu'llāh ibn Ubayy ibn Salūl, the chief of the hypocrites. These two engaged in a dispute, in which 'Ubāda said: 'I have friends among the Jews, many in number and remarkable in valour, but I now renounce their friendship in favour of Allāh and His Messenger, and I have no protecting friend except Allāh and His Messenger.' 'Abdu'llāh ibn Ubayy said: 'But I shall not renounce the friendship of the Jews, for I fear the vicissitudes (the accidents of fate and their unfortunate effects), and I cannot do without them.'

"The Prophet (Allāh bless him and give him peace) then said: 'O Abu'l-Ḥabbāb, whatever you seek from the friendship of the Jews, rather than 'Ubāda ibn aṣ-Ṣāmit, it will be yours, not his.' 'In that case,' he replied, 'I shall accept.' Allāh (Exalted is He) thereupon sent down this Qur'ānic verse."

According to 'Ikrima: "It was revealed in connection with Abū Lubāba ibn 'Abd al-Mundhir, when the Prophet (Allāh bless him and give him peace) dispatched him to the Banī Quraiẓa tribe. He besieged them, so they consulted him about surrender, saying: 'What will be done with us, if we surrender?' He replied by placing his finger on his throat, indicating slaughter and that he would kill them. Allāh (Exalted is He) thereupon sent down:

> O you who truly believe,
> *yā ayyuha 'lladhīna āmanū*
> do not take the Jews and Christians for friends.
> *lā tattakhidhu 'l-Yahūda wa 'n-Naṣārā awliyā':*

Allāh has thus addressed the prohibition to all the believers, and He has informed them that, if anyone chooses them [the Jews and Christians] for helpers, assistants and allies, instead of Allāh, His Messenger and the believers, he is one of them, and Allāh, His Messenger and the believers are relieved of responsibility for him.[580] Then he has explained the reason for the prohibition, by His saying:

> They are friends one to another.
> *ba'ḍu-hum awliyā'u ba'ḍ:*

That is to say: "They are hand in hand against the Muslims, because of their unity in unbelief and error, and the community of unbelief is a single entity."[581] In other words: "They are of one accord in their disagreement with you. They befriend one another because of their unity in religion, and their commonality in opposition to you."[582]

> If one of you takes them for friends, he is one of them.
> *wa man yatawalla-hum min-kum fa-inna-hu min-hum:*

This means: "If someone befriends the Jews and Christians, instead of the believers, and so helps them against the believers, he is one of the members of their religion and their community. He would not take anyone for a friend, unless he was pleased with him and with his religion, so, if he is pleased with him and with his religion, he becomes one of them." This is an admonition from Allāh (Exalted is He) and a stern warning to steer clear of the Jews, the Christians, and all those who contradict the religion of Islām.[583]

According to az-Zamakhsharī: "This is a harsh rebuke from Allāh, and a stern warning to avoid and stay away from anyone who is an opponent in the sphere of religion. As the Prophet (blessing and peace be upon him) once said:

> Do not let their two fires mount an ostentatious display."[584]

To mount an ostentatious display means to act in concert for the sake of attracting attention. Some people from Mecca accepted Islām, but they continued to reside in that city before the conquest, so the Prophet (blessing and peace be upon him) said:

> I am relieved of responsibility for every Muslim who is together with a polytheist [*mushrik*].

Someone asked him: "Why, O Messenger of Allāh?" so he said:

> Do not let their two fires mount an ostentatious display.

That is to say: "The two must be kept far apart, so that, if their two fires are kindled, one of them will not be aware of the other." The attribution of ostentatious display to fire is metaphorical.[585]

In the Qur'ānic verse, the expression:

> he is one of them.
> *fa-inna-hu min-hum:*

—signifies that hostility towards him is strictly required, just as hostility towards them is strictly required, and he is doomed to the Fire of Hell, just as they are doomed to it, since he has become one of them, meaning one of their companions.[586]

This applies to the case where he befriends them on account of their religion. As for the companionship involved in the business of purchasing something from them, or in getting them to do some job of work, despite the difference in belief and religious matters, this threat does not apply to it.

According to al-Mawlā Abū Saʿūd: "It also contains a stern reprimand for the believers, warning against showing the appearance of friendship for them, even if it is not friendship in reality."

> Allāh does not guide the wrongdoing folk.
> *inna 'llāha lā yahdi 'l-qawma 'ẓ-ẓālimīn.*

This is an explanation of the fact that he who befriends them is one of them. In other words: "He does not provide direction for those who wrong themselves, by abandoning their believing brothers and by befriending the enemies of Allāh. Instead, He leaves them to their own devices, so they lapse into unbelief and error."

O Allāh, do not entrust me to my lower self, not for the twinkling of an eye, and not for even less that that![587]

Abū Mūsā al-Ashʿarī is reported as having said: "I once said to ʿUmar ibn al-Khaṭṭāb (may Allāh be well pleased with him): 'I have a Christian clerk.' He said: 'What is wrong with you? May Allāh combat you! Could you not have chosen a righteous believer [*ḥanīf*]? Have you not heard the saying of Allāh (Exalted is He):

> O you who truly believe,
> *yā ayyuha 'lladhīna āmanū*
> do not take the Jews and Christians for friends.
> *lā tattakhidhu 'l-Yahūda wa 'n-Naṣārā awliyāʾ:*

"'I do not honour them, since Allāh has scorned them. I do not hold them in high esteem, since Allāh has abased them. I do not bring them close, since Allāh has set them at a distance.' I said: 'The business of al-Baṣra will not be completed without him.' To this he replied: 'Let the Christian die, and [offer the salutation of] peace [*wa 's-salām*]!'—meaning: 'Suppose that he has already died; how will you manage after he has gone? Whatever you would do after his death, you must do it now, and manage with someone else instead of him.'"'[588]

And you see those in whose heart is a disease
fa-tara 'lladhīna fī qulūbi-him maraḍun
racing towards them, saying:
yusāri'ūna fī-him yaqūlūna
"We fear that a change of fortune may befall us."
nakshā an tuṣība-nā dā'ira:
And it may happen that Allāh
will grant the victory,
fa-'asa 'llāhu an ya'tiya bi'l-fatḥi
or a commandment from His presence.
aw amrin min 'indi-hi
Then they will feel remorse
for their secret thoughts.
fa-yuṣbiḥū 'alā mā asarrū fī anfusi-him nādimīn. (5:52)

As for His saying (Exalted is He):

> And you see those in whose heart is a disease
> *fa-tara 'lladhīna fī qulūbi-him maraḍun*
> racing towards them, saying:
> *yusāri'ūna fī-him yaqūlūna*
> "We fear that a change of fortune may befall us."
> *nakshā an tuṣība-nā dā'ira:*

—this means: "You see, O Muḥammad, those in whose hearts there is doubt and hypocrisy."

> racing towards them
> *yusāri'ūna fī-him*

That is to say: "[You see them] racing towards the affection of the Jews, their friendship and their advice."[589]

> Those in whose heart is a disease
> [*-a*] *'lladhīna fī qulūbi-him maraḍun*

—are the hypocrites, like 'Abdu'llāh ibn Ubayy and his companions. They were racing towards the love of the Jews and Christians of Najrān, because they were in revolt, and they were helping them to obtain their supplies and providing them with loans. The hypocrites would say: "We associate with them only because we fear that a change of fortune [*dā'ira*] may befall us."

According to al-Wāḥidī: "The term *dā'ira* applies to one of the vicissitudes of fate, as does the term *dawla*. It is something that rotates [*tadūru*] from one set of people to another. The *dā'ira* is something that is feared, like being defeated and put to rout, and other dreadful misfortunes. The nouns *dawā'ir* [plural of *dā'ira*] and *dawā'il* [plural of *dā'ila*] are formed from the same roots [*d–w–r* and *d–w–l*, respectively] as the verbs *tadūru* and *tadūlu* [both meaning 'revolve, rotate; alternate; occur in cycles']."

According to az-Zajjāj: "That is to say: 'We fear that the power of command may not belong indefinitely to our master Muḥammad (Allāh bless him and give him peace), and that it may shift elsewhere, as happened in the past.'"[590]

In other words: "Fortune may turn against us, perhaps by inflicting scarcity, in which case they [the Muslims] will not supply our needs, and they will not be any better than we are. Then again, perhaps the Jews will triumph over the Muslims, in which case the power of command will not stay with our master Muḥammad (on him be the finest blessing and the most perfect salutation)."[591]

> And it may happen that Allāh will grant the victory,
> *fa-'asa 'llāhu an ya'tiya bi'l-fatḥi*
> or a commandment from His presence.
> *aw amrin min 'indi-hi*
> Then they will feel remorse for their secret thoughts.
> *fa-yṣbiḥū 'alā mā asarrū fī anfusi-him nādimīn.* (5:52)

According to the traditional commentators, when Allāh (Exalted is He) says:

> And it may happen that Allāh....
> *fa-'asa 'llāhu....*

—it is bound to happen. That is because, when the All-Generous holds out the prospect of something good, He will bring it about, since it is tantamount to a promise, due to His personal connection with it and His own wish to see it happen.

According to one interpretation, the meaning is: "It may happen that Allāh will grant the victory to Allāh's Messenger (Allāh bless him and give him peace) over his enemies, and the triumph of the Muslims over their enemies, or a commandment from His presence will dislocate the Jews, or expel them from their towns. The hypocrites will then feel remorse for the ideas they entertained within themselves." That is because they used to harbour doubts about the authority of Messenger (Allāh bless him and give him peace), saying: "We no not think that his power of command will last indefinitely. There will most likely be a turn of fortune in favour of his enemies."

It has also been said that:

> or a commandment from His presence.
> *aw amrin min ʿindi-hi*

—means that the Prophet (Allāh bless him and give him peace) may be commanded to disclose the secrets of the hypocrites, and to kill them, so they will feel remorse for their conduct. His saying:

> or a commandment from His presence.
> *aw amrin min ʿindi-hi*

—may also mean: "[or a situation] in which people have no freedom of action whatsoever, as in the case of the Banī Naḍīr. Allāh cast terror into their hearts, so they surrendered without waging war, and without gathering an army."[592]

> Then the believers will say: "Are these the ones
> *wa yaqūlu 'lladhīna āmanū a-hāʾulāʾi 'lladhīna*
> who swore by Allāh their most binding oaths
> *aqsamū bi'llāhi jahda aimāni-him*
> that they were surely with you?"
> *inna-hum la-maʿa-kum:*
> Their works have failed,
> *ḥabiṭat aʿmālu-hum*
> and they have come to be losers.
> *fa-aṣbaḥū khāsirīn.* (5:53)

In other words: "The believers will say, in astonishment at the state of the hypocrites, when Allāh has rent their veil: 'Are these the ones who swore to you the most serious oaths, O company of the Jews, that they were surely with you in support and assistance?'" As Allāh (Exalted is He) has related:

> [The hypocrites say]: "And if you are attacked,
> *wa in qūtiltum*
> we will surely help you."
> *la-nanṣuranna-kum*
> And Allāh bears witness that they are liars indeed.
> *wa 'llāhu yashhadu inna-hum la-kādhibūn.* (59:11)

As for His saying (Exalted is He):

> Their works have failed
> *ḥabiṭat aʿmālu-hum*

—this means: "Their works have been in vain, because of their hypocrisy, so they have come to be losers in this world and the Hereafter."[593]

The point that is emphasized, by the manner in which the believers express what they have to say about this, is their astonishment at the state of the hypocrites, since they had shown themselves inclined to befriend the Jews and the Christians: "They said that they that swore by Allāh their most binding oaths that they were with us, and among our helpers. So how can they have become allies to our enemies, fond of associating with them and trusting them?"

> Their works have failed,
> *ḥabiṭat aʿmālu-hum*
> and they have come to be losers.
> *fa-aṣbaḥū khāsirīn.* (5:53)

That is to say: "Their outward show of faith has departed, and every good deed of theirs has been annulled. They have now exposed their friendship for the Jews and the Christians, so they have come to be losers in this world and the Hereafter. Since their deeds have been annulled, they are left with nothing but the hardship experienced in performing those deeds. Far from obtaining any of their fruits and benefits, they have earned damnation in this world and torment in the Hereafter."[594]

These are my own comments:

You must renounce the fellowship of those pretenders [*aghyār*] whose words are at odds with their deeds. Do not put your trust in yourself, and do not lay claim to knowledge without practice. Your claim to knowledge is false without practice, for practice is the proof of knowledge. You must choose the fellowship of the good [*akhyār*], for they will give you sincere advice. You must accept their fellowship, for you will be directed aright by their instruction. There is no might nor any power, except with Allāh, the All-High, the Almighty.

You must also know, O brother in the religion, that our Prophet Muḥammad (Allāh bless him and give him peace) has described the time of seclusion, and explained its character and the character of its people. He commanded solitary isolation in it, and he was undoubtedly more conscious of its benefits and better equipped to recommend it than we ourselves. If you find your own time to be as he has described and explained, you must obey his commandment (Allāh bless him and give him peace) and accept his sound advice, without dubious hesitation, for he (Allāh bless him and give him peace) was more aware of what is useful to you in your own time. Do not offer lying pretexts, and do not deceive yourself, for otherwise you are doomed to destruction, and you will have no excuse on the Day of Resurrection.

The best account is given in the well-known report from ʿAbdu'llāh ibn ʿAmr ibn al-ʿĀṣ (may Allāh be well pleased with him and his father), who said: "While we were around Allāh's Messenger (Allāh bless him and give him peace), he mentioned corruption, for he said:

> When you see that people's compacts are spoilt'—that is to say, corrupted—'and their trusts are slight'—meaning insignificant—'and they are like this....' He intertwined his fingers, so I said: 'What should I do in that case? May Allāh make me your ransom!' He replied: 'You must stick to your house, control your tongue, accept what you know to be right, and forsake what you know to be wrong. You must adopt the business of the special few, and discard the business of the common folk.'"[595]

O Allāh, enable us to enjoy Your love to the fullest extent, and enable us to enjoy the fellowship of the truthful, through Your mercy, O Most Merciful of the merciful. Peace be upon the Messengers, and praise be to Allāh, the Lord of All the Worlds. There is no might nor any power, except with Allāh, the All-High, the Almighty. May Allāh bless our master Muḥammad, his family and his Companions, and may He grant them peace.

The Thirty-fifth Call

In the Name of Allāh, the All-Merciful, the All-Compassionate.
Bismi'llāhi 'r-Raḥmāni 'r-Raḥīm.

O you who truly believe,
yā ayyuha 'lladhīna āmanū
if one of you is guilty of apostasy,
man yartadda min-kum ʿan dīni-hi
Allāh will surely bring [in his stead]
a people whom He loves,
fa-sawfa yaʾti 'llāhu bi-qawmin yuḥibbu-hum
and who love Him, humble towards the believers,
wa yuḥibbūna-hu adhillatin ʿala 'l-muʾminīna
disdainful towards the unbelievers,
aʿizzatin ʿala 'l-kāfirīna
striving in the way of Allāh,
yujāhidūna fī sabīli 'llāhi
and not fearing the blame of any blamer.
wa lā yakhāfūna lawmatin lāʾim:
Such is Allāh's grace,
which He gives unto whom He will.
dhālika faḍlu 'llāhi yuʾtī-hi man yashāʾ:
Allāh is All-Embracing, All-Knowing.
wa 'llāhu Wāsiʿun ʿAlīm.

Your friend can only be Allāh, and His Messenger
inna-mā waliyyu-kumu 'llāhu wa Rasūlu-hu
and those who believe,
who perform the ritual prayer
wa 'lladhīna āmanū 'lladhīna yuqīmūna 'ṣ-ṣalāta
and pay the alms-due, and who bow down.
wa yuʾtūna 'z-zakāta wa hum rākiʿūn.

And whoever befriends Allāh
wa man yatawalla 'llāha
and His Messenger and those who believe:
wa Rasūla-hu wa 'lladhīna āmanū
the party of Allāh, surely they will be the victors.
fa-inna ḥizba 'llāhi humu 'l-ghālibūn. (5:54–6)

The Qur'ānic verse provides information about the apostasy [*irtidād*] of some of the believers, so it is a communication about the invisible future, before it came to pass and many sectarian groups apostasized from Islām.[596] According to the author of *al-Kashshāf*, eleven such groups were guilty of apostasy:

• Three in the lifetime of the Messenger (Allāh bless him and give him peace):

1. The Banū Mudlij. Their leader was al-Aswad ibn al-ʿAnsī, known as Dhu 'l-Ḥimār [the Owner of the Donkey]. He was a soothsayer who laid claim to Prophethood in Yemen, where he seized control of all the towns, and expelled the agents of Allāh's Messenger (Allāh bless him and give him peace). Allāh's Messenger (Allāh bless him and give him peace) wrote about him to Muʿādh ibn Jabal and the chieftains of Yemen, so Allāh caused him to perish at the hand of Fīrūz ad-Dailamī, who attacked him by night and killed him. Allāh's Messenger (Allāh bless him and give him peace) was informed of his slaying on the very night when he was slain, so the Muslims were delighted. Allāh's Messenger (Allāh bless him and give him peace) was taken [to his Lord] on the following day, and his news arrived [by ordinary channels] at the end of the month of Rabīʿ al-Awwal.

2. The Banū Ḥanīfa. They were the followers of Musailima, who laid claim to Prophethood and wrote to Allāh's Messenger (Allāh bless him and give him peace): "From Musailima, the Messenger of Allāh, to Muḥammad, the Messenger of Allāh. Half of the earth belongs to me, and half of it belongs to you." Allāh's Messenger (Allāh bless him and give him peace) replied to him: "From Muḥammad, the Messenger of Allāh, to Musailima, the liar. The earth belongs to Allāh; He bequeathes it to whom He will among His servants, and the ultimate outcome belongs to the truly devout."

Abū Bakr (may Allāh be well pleased with him) then waged war on him with the armies of the Muslims, and he was killed at the hand of Waḥshī, the murderer of Ḥamza. Waḥshī used to say: "I have killed the best of all people in the Time of Ignorance, and the worst of all people in Islām."

3. The Banū Asad. They were the followers of Ṭulaiḥa ibn Khuwailid. He laid claim to Prophethood, so Allāh's Messenger (Allāh bless him and give him peace) sent Khālid on an expedition against him, and he fled to Syria after the battle. Then he accepted Islām, and his Islām was excellent.

• Seven during the Caliphate of Abū Bakr (may Allāh be well pleased with him):

1. Fazāra, the followers of ʿUyaina ibn Ḥisn.
2. Ghaṭafān, the followers of Qurra ibn Salama al-Qushairī.
3. The Banū Sulaim, the followers of al-Fajjāʾa ibn ʿAbd Yābīl.
4. The Banū Yarbūʿ, the followers of Mālik ibn Nuwaira.
5. Some of the Banū Tamīm, the followers of Sajjāj bint al-Mundhir, who laid claim to Prophethood and gave herself in marriage to Musailima the Liar.
6. Kinda, the followers of al-Ashʿath ibn Qais.
7. The Banū Bakr ibn Wāʾil in Baḥrain, the followers of al-Ḥaṭm ibn Zaid.

Allāh put a stop to their business at the hand of Abū Bakr, the Champion of Truth (may Allāh be well pleased with him).

• One group during the Caliphate of ʿUmar ibn al-Khaṭṭāb (may Allāh be well pleased with him):

Ghassān, the followers of Jubulla ibn Aiham. Jubulla had accepted Islām at the hand of ʿUmar ibn al-Khaṭṭāb (may Allāh be well pleased with him). He was walking about one day, trailing his cloak on the ground. A man trod on the edge of his cloak, so he flew into a rage and punched him. The man complained to ʿUmar (may Allāh be well pleased with him), who judged him entitled to retaliation, unless he chose to pardon his assailant, so Jubulla said: "I shall pay a thousand [coins] in compensation." The man refused this offer, so Jubulla kept raising the figure till it reached ten thousand, but the man would only accept retaliation. Jubulla then asked ʿUmar to grant him a postponement, and ʿUmar (may Allāh be well pleased with him) granted his request, so he fled to Byzantium and became an apostate.[597]

When the Prophet (Allāh bless him and give him peace) was taken [to his Lord], most of the Arabs apostatized, except the people of Mecca, the people of Medina, and the people of Baḥrain, members of the tribe of ʿAbd al-Qais. The apostates said: "As for the ritual prayer [*ṣalāt*], we shall perform it. As for the alms-due [*zakāt*], however, our possessions may not be misappropriated." When Abū Bakr was told about that, he declared: "By Allāh, I shall not separate what Allāh (Exalted is He) has linked together, by His saying:

> And perform the ritual prayer, and pay the alms-due.
> *wa aqīmu 'ṣ-ṣalāta wa ātu 'z-zakāta.* (2:43)

"By Allāh, if they withhold from me a yearling goat, out of what they paid to Allāh's Messenger (Allāh bless him and give him peace), I shall surely do battle with them over it." Allāh (Almighty and Glorious is He) thereupon dispatched troops with Abū Bakr (may Allāh be well pleased with him), so he fought over what the Prophet (Allāh bless him and give him peace) had fought over, until they agreed to pay the obligatory alms-due.

According to al-Ḥasan: "But for what Abū Bakr did, people would have refused to pay the alms-due till the Day of Resurrection."[598]

As for His saying (Exalted is He):

> O you who truly believe,
> *yā ayyuha 'lladhīna āmanū*
> if one of you is guilty of apostasy,
> *man yartadda min-kum ʿan dīni-hi*
> Allāh will surely bring [in his stead]
> *fa-sawfa ya'ti 'llāhu*
> a people whom He loves, and who love Him.
> *bi-qawmin yuḥibbu-hum wa yuḥibbūna-hu.*

—this address conveys a warning and a threat. That is to say: "O company of the believers, if one of you turns back from his true religion, and replaces it with another religion, and if he reverts from belief to unbelief, Allāh will surely bring in his stead believing people, whom Allāh loves and who love Allāh."[599] In other words: "O you who truly believe, if one of you befriends the unbelievers, and so becomes an apostate from his religion, let him know that Allāh (Exalted is He) will bring other peoples, who will support this religion to the utmost extent."

According to al-Ḥasan (may Allāh bestow His mercy upon him): "Allāh knew that some people would renounce Islām, after the death of their Prophet, so He has informed them that He will bring a people whom He loves, and who love Him." On the basis of this interpretation, this Qurʾānic verse is a communication about the invisible future, and, since what was communicated did indeed occur, exactly as predicted, it constitutes a miracle [*muʿjiz*].[600]

According to ʿAlī ibn Abī Ṭālib, al-Ḥasan, Qatāda, aḍ-Ḍaḥḥāk and Ibn Juraij (may Allāh be well pleased with them): "They [whom Allāh loves and who love Him] are Abū Bakr (may Allāh be well pleased with him) and his companions, because they are the ones who fought the people guilty of apostasy and of withholding the alms-due."

As for the meaning of love [*maḥabba*], one may say: "I love so-and-so," in the sense of: "I have committed my heart to loving him." To love someone also means thinking well of him. The love of Allāh (Exalted is He) for His servant means His gracious favour towards him, His enabling him and guiding him towards worshipful obedience to Him, and towards conduct worthy of His good pleasure. It means that He will grant him the finest reward for his worshipful obedience, and that He will bestow His commendation and approval upon him.

As for the servant's love for Allāh (Almighty and Glorious is He), it means that he is quick to obey Him and seek His good pleasure, that he does nothing to cause His displeasure and necessitate His punishment, and that he endears himself to Him by behaving with the politeness that is appropriate in His presence. May Allāh include us among those whom He loves, and who love Him, through His grace and noble generosity![601]

Allāh (Exalted is He) has put His love for them ahead of their love for Him, and this is right and proper, because, if Allāh had not loved them, He would not have enabled them to become lovers of Him.[602]

> humble towards the believers,
> *adhillatin ʿala 'l-muʾminīna*
> disdainful towards the unbelievers
> *aʿizzatin ʿala 'l-kāfirīna*

That is to say: "compassionate and modest towards the believers, stern and haughty towards the unbelievers."

According to Ibn Kathīr: "These are the attributes of the perfect believers: that one of them is modestly humble towards his brother, and haughty towards his enemy."[603] They are among the attributes of those believers whom Allāh (Exalted is He) has preferred, and whom He has described by His saying:

> whom He loves, and who love Him.
> *yuḥibbu-hum wa yuḥibbūna-hu.*

—meaning that they are tender and compassionate towards the people of their religion and their brethren among the believers. According to Ibn ʿAbbās (may Allāh be well pleased with him and his father): "You regard them as the son regards his father, and the servant his master."[604]

In this context, humility means kindness and mercy.[605] Compare His saying (Exalted is He):

> Hard against the unbelievers, merciful among themselves.
> *ashiddāʾu ʿala 'l-kuffāri ruḥamāʾu baina-hum.* (48:29)

One token of the believer's love for Allāh (Exalted is He) is that he is gentle and modestly humble towards his believing brethren, but clad in haughty disdain when relating to the unbelievers and the hypocrites.[606] In depicting them as humble towards the believers, the intention is not to suggest that they are insignificant and contemptible in the eyes of the believers. It is rather to explain that they, despite the loftiness of their status and their superiority, are modestly unassuming in relating to the believers.[607]

In His expression (Exalted is He):

> humble towards the believers
> *adhillatin ʿala 'l-muʾminīna*

—He has used the preposition *ʿalā* [lit., over], to indicate the loftiness of their status, their superiority and their nobility, so it is clear that their being humble is not because of their being lowly in themselves. That humility is simply due to the fact that they wish to add, to the loftiness of their status, the virtue of humble modesty.[608]

> striving in the way of Allāh,
> *yujāhidūna fī sabīli 'llāhi*
> and not fearing the blame of any blamer.
> *wa lā yakhāfūna lawmatin lā'im:*

That is to say: "They are striving to exalt the Word of Allāh, and they do not care who blames them, for they are firmly committed to Allāh's religion, fearing no one but Allāh Himself."[609]

To this I would add: Their lack of fear and their indifference to creatures are signs of their rootedness in faith, their sound conviction, and their presence with Allāh in spirit, heart and awareness.

The hypocrites used to be wary of the unbelievers and fearful of their blame, so Allāh (Exalted is He) has explained, in the verse, that if someone is strongly committed to the religion, he will support Allāh's religion with his hand and his tongue, without fearing the blame of any critic.[610]

> Such is Allāh's grace, which He gives unto whom He will.
> *dhālika faḍlu 'llāhi yu'tī-hi man yashā':*

That is to say: "If someone matches these praiseworthy descriptions, he owes that to the favour bestowed upon Him by Allāh, and to His enabling grace."[611]

To this I would add: As the noble verse indicates, when virtues accrue to the believer, he must understand that they are due to His gracious favour (Blessed and Exalted is He), and that he must keep himself out of the picture, so that the feeble servant is not deluded by his own lower self.

His use of the word *dhālika* [that; such] is a means of reference to what has been mentioned previously, in describing people in terms of love, humility, disdain, striving, and not fearing any blame. Allāh (Exalted is He) has thus explained that all of that is due to His gracious favour and beneficence. It is an explicit statement that His servants' acts of obedience are created by Allāh (Exalted is He).[612]

> Allāh is All-Embracing, All-Knowing.
> *wa 'llāhu Wāsi'un 'Alīm.*

In other words: "He is the All-Embracing Source of gracious favour and beneficence, fully Aware of those who are truly deserving thereof."[613]

> Not an atom's weight escapes Him.
> *lā ya'zubu 'an-hu mithqālu dharratin.* (34:3)

"All-Embracing" is an indication of the perfection of power, while "All-Knowing" is an indication of the perfection of knowledge. After letting it be known that He will bring other people of this nature and character, Allāh (Exalted is He) has reinforced that by describing Himself as Perfect in capability, so He is not incapable of fulfilling this promise, and as Perfect in knowledge, so there can be no contradiction of his information and his promises.[614]

Having forbidden the believers to befriend the unbelievers, Allāh (Exalted is He) has now gone on to mention those who are worthy of friendship, for He has said:

> Your friend can only be Allāh, and His Messenger
> *inna-mā waliyyu-kumu 'llāhu wa Rasūlu-hu*
> and those who believe
> *wa 'lladhīna āmanū*

In other words: "The Jews and the Christians are not your friends. Your only friends are Allāh, His Messenger and the believers."[615]

To this I would add: Such is the character of those loved ones who have abandoned expectation, desire, and fear of the Fire of Hell, and who worship Allāh for no reason except that they are servants to Him (Glorious and Exalted is He).

There are two opinions concerning His saying:

> and those who believe
> *wa 'lladhīna āmanū*

1. It refers to the believers in general. That is because, when 'Ubāda ibn aṣ-Ṣāmit washed his hands of the Jews, saying: "I declare to Allāh that I am rid of allegiance to Quraiẓa and an-Naḍīr, and I befriend Allāh and His Messenger," this Qur'ānic verse was revealed in keeping with his statement.

2. It is related that 'Abdu'llāh ibn Salām said: "O Messenger of Allāh, our people have forced us to emigrate, and they have sworn that they will not keep us company, but we cannot join your Companions, because of the distance involved." This verse was thereupon revealed, so he said: "We are well pleased with Allāh, His Messenger and the believers as friends."

This means that the verse applies generally to all the believers, for everyone who is a believer is the friend of all the believers. Compare His saying (Exalted is He):

> And the believers, men and women,
> *wa 'l-mu'minūna wa 'l-mu'minātu*
> are friends of one another.
> *ba'ḍu-hum awliyā'u ba'ḍ.* (9:71)

On this basis, His saying:

> who perform the ritual prayer
> *[-u] 'lladhīna yuqīmūna 'ṣ-ṣalāta*
> and pay the alms-due, and who bow down.
> *wa yu'tūna 'z-zakāta wa hum rāki'ūn.*

—is a description of all the believers, and the mention of these attributes is intended to distinguish the believers from the hypocrites, because they used to lay claim to faith, yet they were not regular in performing the prayers and paying the alms-due. Allāh (Exalted is He) has said of their attitude to the ritual prayer:

> And they do not perform the ritual prayer except as idlers.
> *wa lā ya'tūna 'ṣ-ṣalāta illā wa hum kusālā.* (9:54)

—and He has said of their attitude to the alms-due:

> [They are] greedy for wealth.
> *ashiḥḥatan 'alā 'l-khair.* (33:19)

There are two interpretations of His saying:

> and who bow down.
> *wa hum rāki'ūn.*

1. Bowing down refers to humble submissiveness, so the meaning is: "They perform the ritual prayer and pay the alms-due, and they are submissively compliant with all of Allāh's commmandments and prohibitions."

2. The act of bowing down is an element in their performance of the ritual prayer, and He has singled it out for special mention as a mark of honour, as in His saying:

> and bow down with those who bow down.
> *wa 'rka'ū ma'a 'r-rāki'īn.* (2:43)[616]

To this I would add: Those who prefer and give priority and precedence to Allāh's commandment and His Sacred Law, and to the commandment of His Messenger, over their own selves and over everything, they are the believers, in actual fact. O Allāh, include us among those for whom providential care has been predestined, and for whom special enabling grace and guidance have been foreordained. *Āmīn*, O Lord of All the Worlds!

> Your friend can only be....
> *inna-mā waliyyu-kumu....*

According to the author of *at-Tas'hīl*: "Allāh (Exalted is He) has used the word *waliyyu* [friend] in the singular, to assign singularity to Himself (Exalted is He). Then He has linked the Messenger (Allāh bless him and give him peace) and the believers to His Name (Exalted is He), by way of sequel. If He had used the plural form *awliyā'u-kum* [your friends], the sentence would not have contained a basic element and a sequel.

> And whoever befriends Allāh
> *wa man yatawalla 'llāha*
> and His Messenger and those who believe:
> *wa Rasūla-hu wa 'lladhīna āmanū*
> the party of Allāh, surely they will be the victors.
> *fa-inna ḥizba 'llāhi humu 'l-ghālibūn.*

That is to say: "If someone befriends Allāh and His Messenger and the believers, he belongs to the party of Allāh, and they are the victorious conquerors of their enemies."[617]

The commentators offer several interpretations of His expression (Exalted is He):

> the party of Allāh
> *fa-inna ḥizba 'llāhi*

According to al-Ḥasan, it means "the army of Allāh." According to Abū Rawq: "the friends of Allāh." Some say: "the helpers of Allāh." According to al-Akhfash: "The party of Allāh are those who profess His religion and obey Him, so He helps them."[618]

This brings us to the following conclusions: Befriending Allāh entails hostility towards everything apart from Allāh. In the words of [Abraham] the Bosom Friend [*al-Khalīl*] (peace be upon him):

"They are all an enemy to me,
fa-inna-hum ʿaduwwun lī
except the Lord of All the Worlds."
illā Rabba 'l-ʿālamīn. (26:77)

Befriending the Messenger (Allāh bless him and give him peace) entails hostility towards the lower self, and opposition to passionate desire, as he once said (Allāh bless him and give him peace):

> None of you will truly believe, until his passionate desire is in compliance with what I have brought.[619]

He also said (Allāh bless him and give him peace):

> None of you will truly believe, until I am dearer to him than himself, his property, his children and all other people.[620]

Befriending the believers entails brotherhood with with them in the religion, as He has said (Exalted is He):

The believers are nothing but brothers,
inna-ma 'l-muʾminūna ikhwatun. (49:10)

The Prophet (blessing and peace be upon him) once said:

> None of you will truly believe, until he loves for his brother what he loves for himself.[621]

The point is to distinguish the sincere believer from someone who pretends to believe, but is a hypocrite, because sincerity can only be recognized through his diligence in performing the prayer and paying the alms-due, while in the state of "bowing down," meaning the state of humility and submissiveness to Allāh (Exalted is He).

Whoever befriends these, well, they are the party of Allāh, and the party of Allāh will surely be the victors. A man's *ḥizb* [party] consists of his companions. A party is a group of people who rally to support their party's cause. As you should also know, victory over Allāh's enemies, both external and internal, like passionate desire, the lower self and the devil, can only be achieved with the help of Allāh (Exalted is He). He has said (Exalted is He):

If you help Allāh, He will help you.
in tanṣuru 'llāha yanṣur-kum. (47:7).

If someone follows the passionate desire of the lower self, and does not attend to its purification, he is striving to attach himself to the troop of the enemies, so he will not be helped at all, since recklessness [*jasāra*] leads to nothing but loss [*khasāra*]. Passionate desire is the dictate of the lower self, and the lower self is tenebrous, and nothing but darkness [*ẓulma*] results from tenebrosity [*ẓulmāniyya*]. That is why you see the Prophets and the saints [*awliyā'*] in receipt of help.[622]

These are my own remarks:

There are two kinds of apostasy [*irtidād*]:

1. Total departure from the religion. (Let us seek refuge with Allāh!)
2. Departure from the moral and ethical standards of Islām. This is widespread in our own day and age. Just as He has forbidden us to commit outright apostasy, Allāh (Exalted is He) has also forbidden us to depart from the praiseworthy norms of conduct, in favour of those that are blameworthy, such as wasteful extravagance, lack of self-respect, lying, cheating, lack of humility in the ritual prayer, lack of concern for depositions in trust, and other such violations.

As Allāh (Exalted is He) has said:

> And let those who conspire to evade his orders beware,
> *fa-l'-yaḥdhari 'lladhīna yukhālifūna ʿan amri-hi*
> lest grief or painful torment afflict them.
> *an tuṣība-hum fitnatun aw yuṣība-hum ʿadhābun alīm.* (24:63)

That is to say: "Let them beware, those who conspire to evade the commandment of the Messenger (Allāh bless him and give him peace), and who abandon his path, his procedure and his Sunna, in case they are afflicted by a tremendous trial in this world, or by a terrible torment in the Hereafter."

O believer, you must call yourself to account. You must weigh your conduct in the balance of the Qur'ān, and reach a verdict after that. Then tell the truth, even against yourself.

I wish to convey to you, O noble reader, the observation of Abu 'l-Ḥasan ash-Shādhilī (may Allāh bestow His mercy upon him). It was he who said: "The most splendid of Allāh's gifts include contentment [*riḍā*] with the vicissitudes of fate, patience [*ṣabr*] in the face of tribulation, trust [*tawakkul*] in Allāh in the presence of adversities, and returning to Him in times of misfortune. If these four treasures emerge for someone from the stores of his deeds, on the rug of earnest endeavour, compliance with the Sunna and following the Imāms, he is surely genuine in his friendship for Allāh, for His Messenger and for the believers.

> And whoever befriends Allāh
> *wa man yatawalla 'llāha*
> and His Messenger and those who believe:
> *wa Rasūla-hu wa 'lladhīna āmanū*
> the party of Allāh, surely they will be the victors.
> *fa-inna ḥizba 'llāhi humu 'l-ghālibūn.*

"If they emerge for him from the treasuries of gracious favours, on the carpet of love, Allāh's friendship for him is surely complete, in view of His saying:

> And He befriends the righteous.
> *wa Huwa yatawalla 'ṣ-ṣāliḥīn.* (7:196)

"He has thus distinguished between the two kinds of friendship, for there is a servant who befriends Allāh, and a servant whom Allāh befriends. These are two forms of friendship, a lesser and a greater...."[623]

We beg Allāh to grant us steadfastness in this world and the Hereafter. There is no might nor any power, except with Allāh, the All-High, the Almighty. He is All-Hearing, Ever-Near. *Āmīn.* Peace be upon the Messengers, and praise be to Allāh, the Lord of All the Worlds. May Allāh bless our master Muḥammad, his family and his Companions, and may He grant them peace.

The Thirty-sixth Call

In the Name of Allāh, the All-Merciful, the All-Compassionate.
Bismi'llāhi 'r-Raḥmāni 'r-Raḥīm.

O you who truly believe, do not choose
yā ayyuha 'lladhīna āmanū
lā tattakhidhu 'lladhīna 'ttakhadhū
those who adopt your religion
as a joke and for fun,
dīna-kum huzuwan wa la'iban
such as those who received the Book before you,
and the unbelievers.
[Do not choose them] for friends,
mina 'lladhīna ūtu 'l-Kitāba min qabli-kum
wa 'l-kuffāra awliyā':
but practise true devotion to Allāh,
if you are believers.
wa 'ttaqu 'llāha in kuntum mu'minīn.

And when you call to prayer
they adopt it as a joke and for fun.
wa idhā nādaitum ila 'ṣ-ṣalāti 'ttakhadhū-hā
huzuwan wa la'ibā:
That is because they are a folk
who do not understand.
dhālika bi-anna-hum qawmun lā ya'qilūn. (5:57,58)

In the preceding Qur'ānic verse, Allāh (Exalted is He) has forbidden the believers to take the Jews and Christians for friends. He has reiterated that prohibition, to stress its importance, then He has stated the general prohibition of befriending the unbelievers,[624] for He has said:

> O you who truly believe, do not choose those who adopt
> *yā ayyuha 'lladhīna āmanū lā tattakhidhu 'lladhīna 'ttakhadhū*
> your religion as a joke and for fun.
> *dīna-kum huzuwan wa la'iban*

This is a disparagement of friendship with the enemies of Islām, who adopt the pure and established laws of Islām, which comprise every worldly and Otherworldly benefit, but only to make a jest and a sport of them, for they are merely a kind of game, as viewed through their corrupt vision and considered with their inane thinking.[625] They adopt the religion of the Muslims as a source of amusement, professing it with their tongues while persisting in unbelief in their hearts.

The prohibition of befriending them is linked to their adoption of your religion as a joke and for fun, in order to explain the reason for the prohibition, and to let it be known that such people deserve to be treated with hostility, so friendship with them is out of the question.[626]

Concerning the occasion on which this Qur᾽ānic verse was revealed, it is said that Rifā῾a ibn Zaid and Suwaid ibn al-Ḥarth made a show of faith, but then acted hypocritically. Some Muslim men were still very fond of them, however, so Allāh (Exalted is He) revealed this verse in connection with them.[627]

> such as those who received the Book...and the unbelievers.
> *mina 'lladhīna ūtu 'l-Kitāba...wa 'l-kuffāra*

[In the terminology of the Arab grammarians] the word *mina* is used here *li-bayāni 'l-jins* [to explain the genus], as it is also used in His saying:

> So shun filthy stuff such as idols.
> *fa-'jtanibu 'r-rijsa mina 'l-awthāni.* (22:30)

Those referred to here as "the unbelievers [*kuffār*]" are the polytheists [*mushrikīn*].[628] They are mentioned specifically because of the twofold nature of their unbelief. The prohibition applies to befriending those who do not conform to the Truth, as a matter of principle, whether they profess a religion, but follow desire and deviate from the correct path, like the People of the Book, or whether they do not [profess a religion], like the polytheists.[629]

This Qur᾽ānic verse [5:57] requires a distinction to be drawn between the People of the Book and the unbelievers, because the grammatical conjunction necessarily indicates a difference. However, in His saying:

> Those who disbelieve, such as the People of the Book, would not....
> *lam yakuni 'lladhīna kafarū min Ahli 'l-Kitābi....* (98:1)

—it is explicitly stated that they are unbelievers. In order to reconcile the two statements, it may be sufficient to note that the unbelief of the polytheists is greater and more outrageous, so we apply the term "unbelief [*kufr*]" to them in particular, for that reason. Allāh knows best, of course![630]

> but practise true devotion to Allāh, if you are believers.
> *wa 'ttaqu 'llāha in kuntum mu'minīn.*

That is to say: "Beware of offending Allāh by choosing these enemies of you and your religion for friends, if you are believers in the Sacred Law of Allāh, which these folk have adopted as a joke and for fun." As He has also said (Exalted is He):

> Do not let the believers choose the unbelievers
> *lā yattakhidhi 'l-mu'minūna 'l-kāfirīna*
> for friends instead of the believers.
> *awliyā'a min dūni 'l-mu'minīn.* (3:28)[631]

According to one interpretation, the meaning is: "You must be afraid of offending Allāh, O believers, by choosing them for friends and helpers. You must be in dread of His penalty for doing that, if you do it after He has presented you with the prohibition that forbids it, and if you have faith in Allāh and believe in the truth of His threat against disobedience to Him."[632]

He has then gone on to mention one example of their mockery, for He has said (Exalted is He):

> And when you call to prayer they adopt it as a joke and for fun.
> *wa idhā nādaitum ila 'ṣ-ṣalāti 'ttakhadhū-hā huzuwan wa la'ibā:*
> That is because they are a folk who do not understand.
> *dhālika bi-anna-hum qawmun lā ya'qilūn.*

In other words: "They act like that when you give the call to the ritual prayer [*ṣalāt*], which is the most excellent of deeds for intelligent people who know and understand. They adopt it [*-i' ttakhadhū-hā*], but only as a joke and for fun."

> That is because they are a folk who do not understand.
> *dhālika bi-anna-hum qawmun lā ya'qilūn.*

They do not understand the true significance of worshipful service to Allāh, nor that of His laws. Their attributes are symptomatic of the influence of Satan, who turns away when he hears the call to prayer, then comes forward as soon as the call is concluded. When spiritual reward is bestowed for the prayer, he turns away, and when the bestowal of reward is concluded, he comes forward. He sows distractions between a man and his heart, by saying: "Remember such-and-such, and remember such-and-such," when those things would otherwise not occur to him, until the man loses count of how many cycles of prayer he has performed. If one of you has that experience, he must perform two acts of prostration [*sajdatain*] before the final salutation [*salām*], as stated in the two *Ṣaḥīḥ*'s.

According to az-Zuhrī: "Allāh has mentioned the call to prayer [*ta᾽dhīn*] is His Book, for He has said:

> And when you call to prayer they accept it as a joke and for fun.[633]
> *wa idhā nādaitum ila 'ṣ-ṣalāti 'ttakhadhū-hā huzuwan wa laʿibā:*

"In other words: 'When you proclaim the call to prayer and summon people to perform it, they make fun of you and of your prayer.'"

As we are told in *al-Baḥr* [The Ocean]: "The Jews were envious of the Messenger (Allāh bless him and give him peace), when they heard the call to prayer [*adhān*], and they said: 'You have invented something that was not practised by the Prophets. Where did you get this braying noise, like the braying of the wild ass? There is no sound more disgusting!' It was then that Allāh (Exalted is He) sent down this Qur᾽ānic verse, to serve notice that, if someone ridicules the ritual prayer [*ṣalāt*], far from being chosen for a friend, he must be shunned and rejected."

This verse came as a confirmation of the verse before it, and to explain that their behaviour was due to their being dissolute types, who could not understand the wisdom of the ritual prayer, and who could not comprehend its value for the purification of the lower selves. Lack of intelligence is ascribed to them because they have made no use of that faculty in the sphere of religion, even if they have minds with which they grasp the benefits of this world.[634]

It was as-Suddī who remarked, concerning His saying (Exalted is He):

> And when you call....
> *wa idhā nādaitum....*

"When a certain man, one of the Christians in Medina, heard the caller proclaim: 'I bear witness that Muḥammad is the Messenger of

Allāh,' he said: 'May the liar be burned!' Then, one night, his maidservant came in with a shovel of fire, while he and his family were all asleep. A spark was dropped, and it set the house ablaze, so that man and his family were all consumed by fire."[635]

The Qur᾿ānic verse proves that the call to prayer [*adhān*] is established by the explicit text of the Book, not by the [traditionally reported] dream alone.[636]

In the *Sīra* [Biography of the Prophet (Allāh bless him and give him peace)], Muḥammad ibn Isḥāq gives the following account:

"In the Year of Victory, Allāh's Messenger (Allāh bless him and give him peace) entered the Ka῾ba, accompanied by Bilāl, whom he instructed to give the call to prayer. Abū Sufyān ibn Ḥarb, ῾Attāb ibn Usaid and al-Ḥārith ibn Hishām were sitting in the courtyard of the Ka῾ba, so ῾Attāb ibn Usaid exclaimed: 'May Allāh grant Usaid the privilege of not hearing this, for the sound of it annoys him intensely!' Then al-Ḥārith ibn Hishām said: 'By Allāh, even if I knew him to be telling the truth, I would not follow him.' Abū Sufyān then said: 'I shall not say anything. If I were to speak, these pebbles would inform against me.' The Prophet (Allāh bless him and give him peace) thereupon emerged to confront them, and he told them: 'I know what you have been saying!' Then he recounted that to them, so al-Ḥārith said: 'We bear witness that you are Allāh's Messenger. There was no one with us to overhear our conversation, so we can only say that He must have informed you.'"

As reported by Imām Aḥmad: "῾Abdu'llāh ibn Muḥairīz, who was an orphan in the care of Abū Maḥdhūra, once told me: 'I said to Abū Maḥdhūra: 'O my uncle, I am leaving for Syria, and I feel embarrassed about asking whether you know how to give the call to prayer.' He then went on to tell me that Abū Maḥdhūra said: 'Yes! I had gone out as one of a group, and we were somewhere along the road to Ḥunain. The caravan of Allāh's Messenger (Allāh bless him and give him peace) was returning from Ḥunain, so we encountered Allāh's Messenger (Allāh bless him and give him peace) at some point on the road.

"'The muezzin [*mu᾿adhdhin*] of Allāh's Messenger (Allāh bless him and give him peace) gave the call to prayer in the presence of Allāh's Messenger (Allāh bless him and give him peace). While listening to the muezzin's voice, having turned aside from the road, we made a loud noise, as we mimicked him and made fun of him. Allāh's Messenger (Allāh bless him and give him peace) could hear us, so he sent someone over, to invite us to present ourselves before him. Allāh's Messenger (Allāh bless him and give him peace) then said:

"""Which of you is the one whose voice I heard so loud and clear?" Everyone in the group pointed at me, and they were telling the truth, so he sent the rest of them away and kept only me behind. "Stand up," he said to me, "and give the call to prayer!" I promptly stood up, though there was nothing more hateful to me than Allāh's Messenger (Allāh bless him and give him peace), nor than what he was commanding me to do. I stood in front of Allāh's Messenger (Allāh bless him and give him peace), and Allāh's Messenger himself (Allāh bless him and give him peace) taught me how to give the call to prayer. He told me to say:

Allāh is Supremely Great!
Allāh is Supremely Great!
Allāhu Akbar: Allāhu Akbar:
I bear witness that there is no god but Allāh.
ashhadu an lā ilāha illa 'llāh:
I bear witness that there is no god but Allāh.
ashhadu an lā ilāha illa 'llāh:
I bear witness that Muḥammad
is the Messenger of Allāh.
ashhadu anna Muḥammadar Rasūlu 'llāh:
I bear witness that Muḥammad
is the Messenger of Allāh.
ashhadu anna Muḥammadar Rasūlu 'llāh:
Come to the prayer! Come to the prayer!
ḥayy ʿala 'ṣ-ṣalāt: ḥayy ʿala 'ṣ-ṣalāt:
Come to salvation! Come to salvation!
ḥayy ʿala 'l-falāḥ: ḥayy ʿala 'l-falāḥ:
Allāh is Supremely Great!
Allāh is Supremely Great!
Allāhu Akbar: Allāhu Akbar:
There is no god but Allāh.
lā ilāha illa 'llāh.

"'Then, as soon as I had finished giving the call to prayer, he beckoned me to him and gave me a purse containing some silver. Then he placed his hand on Abū Maḥdhūra's forelock, then moved it down over his face, then between his breasts, then over his liver, until the hand of Allāh's Messenger (Allāh bless him and give him peace) reached Abū Maḥdhūra's navel. Then Allāh's Messenger (Allāh bless him and give him peace) said: "May Allāh bless you, and may He bestow grace upon you!" I said: "O Messenger of Allāh, command me to give the call to prayer in Mecca." He said: "I have already commanded you to do so."

"'All the dislike I had felt towards Allāh's Messenger (Allāh bless him and give him peace) simply vanished away, and all such feelings were replaced by love for Allāh's Messenger (Allāh bless him and give him peace). I was then approached by ʿAttāb ibn Usaid, the agent of Allāh's Messenger (Allāh bless him and give him peace), so I joined him in giving the call to prayer, in compliance with the command of Allāh's Messenger (Allāh bless him and give him peace).'

"I also heard that report from members of my family, who knew Abū Maḥdhūra, and their version was similar to the account I heard from ʿAbdu'llāh ibn Muḥairīz." This is how it was related by Imām Aḥmad, and it is recorded by Muslim in his *Ṣaḥīḥ*, as well as by the compilers of the four *Sunan*.[637]

There are many nuggets of wisdom in the call to prayer, including: the hoisting of the banners of Islām; the affirmation of Divine Oneness [*Tawḥīd*]; the announcement of the arrival of the time prescribed [for performance of the prayer], and of its place; and the summons to the congregation.

The call to prayer conveys a real signal of the invitation to Allāh, for the caller is the Muḥammadan inheritor [*al-wārith al-Muḥammadī*]. He summons the heedless and the separated to the station of nearness and the place of direct address. If someone is too deaf to hear the Truth, he will make fun of the caller and his summons, due to the completeness of his ignorance. If, on the other hand, he is one of those who lend an ear, and he is a true witness, he will respond to the invitation of Allāh, the Almighty, the Praiseworthy, and he will be attracted to the presence of the Lord of Might and Glory.[638]

These are my own observations:

The heart is not capable of more than one love, so it may either contain the love of Allāh (Exalted is He)—which entails the love of those who love Allāh (Exalted is He), and whom Allāh (Exalted is He) loves—or something apart from that. A man is together with the one he loves, so congratulations to someone whose heart no longer contains any love except for Allāh (Glory be to Him and Exalted is He), and who seeks nothing but His Countenance (Exalted and Sanctified is He), for he is together with Allāh the Exalted (Magnificent is His Authority), even if he is still together with his fellow creatures, and involved with them in outward appearance.

So long as the servant is not entirely detached from his self-centred desire, his Lord is not his sole objective, and his heart cannot contain the love of Allāh (Blessed and Exalted is He). His heart is attached to others, and he may even befriend His enemies, because of the exteme heedlessness that reigns over his heart. If someone wishes for Allāh (Exalted is He), and for the friendship of the saints [*awliyā*ʾ] and the righteous, he must therefore practise frequent remembrance of Allāh (Exalted is He), together with contemplative recitation of the noble Qurʾān. He must then engage in combat with the lower self, and cut off its roots entirely.

We beg Allāh (Exalted is He) to enable us, through His gracious favour and His noble generosity, to remember Him and to enjoy the protective friendship of His saints [*awliyā*ʾ]. He is indeed Capable of all things, and He is Competent to grant such requests. *Āmīn*. Peace be upon the Messengers, and praise be to Allāh, the Lord of All the Worlds. There is no might nor any power, except with Allāh, the All-High, the Almighty. May Allāh bless our master Muḥammad, his family and his Companions, and may He grant them peace.

The Thirty-seventh Call

In the Name of Allāh, the All-Merciful, the All-Compassionate.
Bismi'llāhi 'r-Raḥmāni 'r-Raḥīm.

O you who truly believe,
do not forbid the pleasant things
yā ayyuha 'lladhīna āmanū lā tuḥarrimū ṭayyibāti
that Allāh has made lawful for you,
and do not transgress.
mā aḥalla 'llāhu la-kum wa lā ta'tadū:
Allāh does not love the transgressors.
inna 'llāha lā yuḥibbu 'l-mu'tadūn.

Eat of what Allāh has provided for you
as lawful and pleasant food,
wa kulū mimmā razaqa-kumu 'llāhu ḥalālan ṭayyibā:
and practise true devotion to Allāh,
in Whom you are believers.
wa 'ttaqu 'llāha 'lladhī antum
bi-hi mu'minūn. (5:87,88)

Following a detailed presentation of the controversy with the Jews and the Christians, Allāh (Exalted is He) has now resumed His exposition of the rules [of the Sacred Law]. He has mentioned several of these, with particular reference to the lawfulness of footstuffs, beverages and sensual delights, for He has said:

> O you who truly believe, do not forbid the pleasant things
> *yā ayyuha 'lladhīna āmanū lā tuḥarrimū ṭayyibāti*
> that Allāh has made lawful for you.
> *mā aḥalla 'llāhu la-kum:*

Those pleasant things are the delights that excite the appetites of our lower selves. It is related that the Prophet (Allāh bless him and give him peace) once described the Day of Resurrection to his Companions, in the home of ʿUthmān ibn Maẓʿūn. He went to great lengths, and expressed himself most emphatically, in warning and urging precaution, so they resolved to reject this world. They decided to make pleasant foodstuffs and delicious drinks unlawful for themselves, to fast by day and keep vigil through the night, to refrain from sleeping on comfortable beds, to have themselves castrated, to wear hair shirts, and to wander about in the land.

The Prophet (Allāh bless him and give him peace) was informed of this, so he said to them: "I have not commanded anything of that kind. Your lower selves have a rightful claim on you, so fast and break fast, and keep vigil and sleep, for I keep vigil and I sleep, I fast and I break fast, I eat meat and fat, and I have sexual intercourse with women. If anyone does not wish to follow my example, he is not one of mine."[639]

According to a report from Ibn ʿAbbās (may Allāh be well pleased with him and his father), a man once came to the Prophet (blessing and peace be upon him) and said: "O Messenger of Allāh, whenever I ate this meat, I would go looking for women, and my lustful desire would take hold of me, so I have made meat unlawful for me." Allāh thereupon sent down:[640]

> O you who truly believe, do not forbid the pleasant things
> *yā ayyuha 'lladhīna āmanū lā tuḥarrimū ṭayyibāti*
> that Allāh has made lawful for you.
> *mā aḥalla 'llāhu la-kum:*

As related by aṭ-Ṭabarī, it was ʿIkrima who said: "Some of the Companions of the Prophet (Allāh bless him and give him peace) were planning on castration and abstinence from meat and women, so this Qurʾānic verse was sent down. It conveyed the message: 'Do not deny yourselves those pleasures, saying: "We have made them unlawful for ourselves," and going to extremes in abstaining from them and in practising mortification and asceticism.'"[641]

Suppose someone says: "What is the wisdom in this prohibition? It is well known that the love of this world exerts a controlling influence over the natural instincts and the emotions. The more a human being indulges in pleasures and delights, the stronger his inclination towards them becomes, and the more his desire for them intensifies. Whenever those bounties multiply and become longer-lasting, that inclination grows stronger and more serious. Whenever the inclination increases in strength and eagerness, there is a corresponding increase in the person's greedy appetite for the benefits of this world, and in his preoccupation with their procurement. That prevents him from being preoccupied with the intimate knowledge of Allāh, and with obedience to Him. It also prevents him from seeking the blissful joys of the Hereafter.

"If, on the other hand, he shuns the pleasures and delights of this world, then, the more complete and permanent that rejection becomes, the weaker the inclination will be, and the less eager the desire. The self will then be free to pursue the intimate knowledge of Allāh, and to concentrate on His service. This being the case, what is the wisdom in Allāh's prohibition of monasticism?"

The answer to this includes several important points:

1. Extreme monasticism, and complete abstinence from all pleasures and delights, are among the causes of weakness in the principal organs, meaning the heart and the brain. When weakness affects them, thinking becomes disordered, and the mind becomes confused. Beyond any doubt, the most perfect of all forms of happiness, and the most sublime of all intimate experiences, is the direct knowledge of Allāh (Exalted is He). If intense monasticism is among the causes of deficiency in that respect, for the reason we have explained, it must surely be subject to prohibition.

2. The gist of your argument is that a person is prevented, by the preoccupation of the lower self with sensory pleasures, from achieving the full enjoyment of intellectual benefits. This must be conceded, but only in the case of those whose lower selves are feeble. As for those whose lower selves are perfectly developed, their engaging in sensory activities does not prevent them from achieving the full enjoyment of intellectual benefits. In the case of those whose lower selves are feeble, their condition is apparent to us, since we notice how, when they are preoccupied with one concern, it is impossible for them to pay attention to another concern.

The stronger the lower self, the more perfect a person's overall state can become. This being the case, unadulterated monasticism must be a sign of some kind of weakness and deficiency. Perfection depends on complete development in both [the sensory and the intellectual] aspects, and the quest for perfection is inherent in human beings.

3. If someone takes his full share of the sensory pleasures, with the intention of using them to assist the fulfilment of the intellectual pleasures, his exertion and his striving are more complete than the exertion of someone who shuns the sensory pleasures. That is because accepting the share of the lower self, and turning it in the direction of obedience, is a far more painful and difficult task than rejecting the share of the lower self entirely. Perfection in the former case is therefore more complete.

To this I would add: The point made here is relevant only to the élite. As for the common folk, it never occurs to them to turn their energies, acquired in the pursuit of sensory pleasures, in the direction of worshipful obedience, so that their habits could become a form of obedience by virtue of their intentions. Allāh is the only Source of help!

4. Complete monasticism requires isolation in the wilderness, and abstinence from sowing one's seed and producing offspring. As for the rejection of monasticism, accompanied by dedication to direct experience, love, and acts of worshipful obedience, that is conducive to the cultivation of this world and the Hereafter, so it represents a more perfect approach.[642]

That explains why abstinence from the pleasures and lustful delights of this world—with total dedication to Allāh and concentration on worshipful service, without doing violence to the lower self, and without neglecting the rights of other people—is not merely an unobjectionable virtue, but something that is positively commanded.[643]

> And do not transgress.
> *wa lā taʿtadū:*
> Allāh does not love the transgressors.
> *inna 'llāha lā yuḥibbu 'l-muʿtadūn.*

That is to say: "Do not transgress the limits of what Allāh has made lawful for you, by going beyond the lawful into the unlawful. Allāh hates those who go beyond the limit, and Islām calls for moderation, with neither shortcoming nor excess."[644]

> And do not transgress.
> *wa lā taʿtadū:*

—also means: "Do not follow any other path, apart from the Sunna of the Muslims."[645] There are several other interpretations:

1. Allāh (Exalted is He) has declared it a transgression and a misdeed to declare pleasant things unlawful, so he has forbidden transgression, to include it under the prohibition of declaring those things unlawful.

2. After declaring pleasant things permissible, He declared it unlawful to indulge in them extravagantly, by saying:

> And do not transgress.
> *wa lā taʿtadū:*

This is comparable to His saying:

> And eat and drink, but do not be extravagant.
> *wa kulū wa 'shrabū wa lā tusrifū.* (7:31)

3. It means: "Since pleasant things have been made lawful for you, be satisfied with these lawful things, and do not transgress into what has been made unlawful for you."[646]

> Eat of what Allāh has provided for you
> *wa kulū mimmā razaqa-kumu 'llāhu*
> as lawful and pleasant food,
> *ḥalālan ṭayyibā:*
> and practise true devotion to Allāh,
> *wa 'ttaqu 'llāha 'lladhī*
> in Whom you are believers.
> *antum bi-hi muʾminūn.*

That is to say: "Eat what is lawful and pleasant for you, from that which Allāh has provided for you." According to the author of *at-Tas'hīl*: "The meaning is: 'Enjoy lawful foodstuffs, women, and so on.' When He mentioned eating explicitly, He did so because it is the most important of all human needs."

> and practise true devotion to Allāh....
> *wa 'ttaqu 'llāha....*

This summons to true devotion is expressed in the most subtle fashion, as if He is saying: "Do not waste your faith by falling short in obedience to Allāh (Almighty and Glorious is He), for then you would suffer the most terrible distress. Faith in Allāh (Exalted is He) demands the utmost exertion in true devotion to Allāh."[647]

As the Qur'ānic verse implies, Allāh (Almighty and Glorious is He) has taken it upon Himself to provide for each and every one of His servants, for if He (Exalted is He) had not assumed that responsibility, He would not have said:

> Eat of what Allāh has provided for you.
> *wa kulū mimmā razaqa-kumu 'llāhu.*

Since He has assumed responsibility for the servant's provision, the servant is obliged to refrain from extravagance in seeking and desiring the benefits of this world. He must rely on that which Allāh has promised, and for which He (Exalted is He) has made Himself responsible, for He (Exalted is He) is far too Noble to go back on His promise. That is why the Prophet (blessing and peace be upon him) once said:

> You must surely practise true devotion to Allāh, and conduct yourselves decently in the quest [for what you seek].[648]

One of the marks of good fortune is stopping at the limit set by the commandment. If the Lord of Truth has made something permissible, one should accept it, and approach it with humility. If He has forbidden something, one must stop, and not run the risk of denial.[649]

These are my own comments:

When your lower self demands drink, and food, and rest, you must give it enough to sustain it, and equip it with sufficient strength for obedience to Allāh (Almighty and Glorious is He). Far from treating it indulgently in response to every demand, you must give it no more than what the noble Sacred Law allows you. Otherwise, you will fall from the level of humanity to the level of bestiality. The only refuge is with Allāh!

The consumption of food is an affliction for the believer, from one point of view, and an act of obedience, from another. If it strengthens him in disobedience to Allāh, it is an affliction where he is concerned, but if it strengthens him in obedience to Allāh, it is an act of worshipful obedience. For his eating to be in conformity with the commandment, he must take a sufficient amount of food, neither too much nor too little, after first making sure that it is lawful. He must abstain from taking what belongs to other people. The human being must realize that, if something belongs to him, it will surely reach him, and if it belongs to someone else, it will never reach him. This means that he should not abase himself before any of his fellow creatures, because the One who brought him from nonexistence into being has said:

> There is no beast on the earth for which Allāh does not provide.
> *wa mā min dābbatin fi 'l-arḍi illā ʿala 'llāhi rizqu-hā.* (11:6)

Where are the faculties of understanding? That is why it is necessary for us to cling to the coat-tails of those who know Allāh by direct experience, so that they may bring us into contact with Allāh, and enable us to achieve this objective. *Āmīn.* Peace be upon the Messengers, and praise be to Allāh, the Lord of All the Worlds. There is no might nor any power, except with Allāh, the All-High, the Almighty. May Allāh bless our master Muḥammad, his family and his Companions, and may He grant them peace.

The Thirty-eighth Call

In the Name of Allāh, the All-Merciful, the All-Compassionate.
Bismi'llāhi 'r-Raḥmāni 'r-Raḥīm.

O you who truly believe, strong drink
yā ayyuha 'lladhīna āmanū inna-ma 'l-khamru
and games of chance and idols and divining arrows
wa 'l-maisiru wa 'l-anṣābu wa 'l-azlāmu
are only a foul abomination of Satan's handiwork,
rijsun min ʿamali 'sh-shaiṭāni
so leave it aside, in order that you may succeed.
fa-'jtanibū-hu laʿalla-kum tufliḥūn.

Satan only seeks to cast among you enmity
inna-mā yurīdu 'sh-shaiṭānu an yūqiʿa
baina-kumu 'l-ʿadāwata
and hatred by means of strong drink
and games of chance,
wa 'l-baghḍāʾa fi 'l-khamri wa 'l-maisiri
and to turn you from remembrance of Allāh
and from worship.
wa yaṣudda-kum ʿan dhikri 'llāhi wa ʿani 'ṣ-ṣalāh:
Will you therefore have done?
fa-hal antum muntahūn.

Obey Allāh and obey the Messenger.
wa aṭīʿu 'llāha wa aṭīʿu 'r-Rasūla
And beware! But if you turn away,
wa 'ḥdharū: fa-in tawallaitum
know that the duty of Our Messenger
is only plain communication.
fa-'ʿlamū anna-mā ʿalā Rasūli-nā
balāghun mubīn. (5:90–92)

In a previous revelation, Allāh (Exalted is He) said:

> Do not forbid the good things that Allāh has made lawful for you....
> *lā tuḥarrimū ṭayyibāti mā aḥalla 'llāhu la-kum....*
> Eat of what Allāh has bestowed on you
> *wa kulū mimmā razaqa-kumu 'llāhu*
> as food that is lawful and good.
> *ḥalālan ṭayyibā.* (5:87,88)

Then, since strong drink and games of chance are among those things that may be considered good, Allāh (Exalted is He) explained that, far from being included among those things that are lawful, they are actually among those that are unlawful.[650] He said (Exalted is He):

> O you who truly believe, strong drink
> *yā ayyuha 'lladhīna āmanū inna-ma 'l-khamru*
> and games of chance and idols and divining arrows
> *wa 'l-maisiru wa 'l-anṣābu wa 'l-azlāmu*
> are only a foul abomination of Satan's handiwork, so leave it aside.
> *rijsun min ʿamali 'sh-shaiṭāni fa-'jtanibū-hu.*

According to Ibn ʿAbbās and Mujāhid:

> strong drink
> *al-khamru*

—means all drinks that cause intoxication, while:

> and games of chance
> *wa 'l-maisiru*

—refers to gambling [*qimār*], as it was practised in the Age of Ignorance, and His words:

> and idols and divining arrows
> *wa 'l-anṣābu wa 'l-azlāmu*

—refer to the statues that were erected as objects of worship, and to the large bowls [containing divining arrows] that were kept by the custodians of the Sacred House and the servants of the idols.

Ibn ʿAbbās and Mujāhid also said: "The idols were stones, beside which they used to slaughter their sacrificial offerings, and the divining arrows were [kept in] large bowls, for the purpose of drawing lots."

> a foul abomination
> *rijsun*

—means: "something filthy and polluted, which our minds find disgusting," and "something vile and repulsive, which is part of Satan's fancy make-believe."[651] A foul abomination is the kind of deed that merits the highest degree of infamy, and that ranks in the top class of shamefulness. It is part:

> of Satan's handiwork
> *min ʿamali 'sh-shaiṭāni*

—because Satan is filthy and vile, since he is an unbeliever [*kāfir*], and the unbeliever is filthy, as He has said:

> The polytheists are filthy.
> *inna-ma 'l-mushrikūna najasun*. (9:28)

—and the vile does not appeal to anyone but the vile.[652]

> So leave it aside, in order that you may succeed.
> *fa-'jtanibū-hu laʿalla-kum tufliḥūn*.

That is to say: "Abandon it, and be in a different situation, far removed from these defilements, so that you may succeed in gaining the mighty reward."[653] The pronoun *hu* [it] in *fa-'jtanibū-hu* [so leave it aside] refers to this foul abomination. The term *rijs* [foul abomination] applies to the four things mentioned [strong drink, games of chance, idols and divining arrows], so the commandment to "leave aside" must apply to them all.[654]

> Satan only seeks to cast among you enmity
> *inna-mā yurīdu 'sh-shaiṭānu an yūqiʿa baina-kumu 'l-ʿadāwata*
> and hatred by means of strong drink and games of chance,
> *wa 'l-baghḍā'a fi 'l-khamri wa 'l-maisiri*
> and to turn you from remembrance of Allāh and from worship.
> *wa yaṣudda-kum ʿan dhikri 'llāhi wa ʿani 'ṣ-ṣalāh:*
> Will you therefore have done?
> *fa-hal antum muntahūn*.

That is to say: "Satan's only purpose, in promoting these depravities, is to cast enmity and hatred among the believers, through their indulgence in strong drink and their gambling games. By means of strong drink and games of chance, he seeks to keep you from the remembrance of Allāh, which is the source of righteousness in your worldly and Otherworldly lives, and from the ritual prayer [*ṣalāt*], which is the pillar of your religion.

It was Abū Ḥayyān who said: "In connection with strong drink and games of chance, Allāh (Exalted is He) has mentioned two corrupting influences. One of them pertains to this world, and the other to religion:

- As for the worldly aspect, strong drink excites bad feelings and resentments, and its consumption leads to the breaking of relationships. Where games of chance are concerned, a man will not stop gambling until he is stripped of all he possesses, and he may even stake his wife and children as bets.
- As for the religious aspect, strong drink can be the source of so much pleasure and delight, that the drinker is utterly distracted from the remembrance of Allāh and from the ritual prayer [*ṣalāt*]. Games of chance, regardless of whether the gambler wins or loses, can also distract from the remembrance of Allāh."

> Will you therefore have done?
> *fa-hal antum muntahūn.*

This is framed as an enquiry, but it is meant to be a command; in other words: "Have done!" According to the author of *al-Baḥr* [The Ocean]: "This interrogative expression is one of the most effective ways of delivering a negative command. It conveys the impact of: "You are being controlled by the depravities in which you indulge, and which ought to come to an end, so will you have done with them, or will you remain in your present state?""[655]

It is related that, when His words (Exalted is He):

> O you who believe,
> *yā ayyuha 'lladhīna āmanū*
> do not approach the ritual prayer when you are intoxicated.
> *lā taqrabu 'ṣ-ṣalāta wa antum sukārā.* (4:43)

—were revealed, ʿUmar (may Allāh be well pleased with him) had said: "O Allāh, grant us an unequivocal pronouncement on the subject of strong drink!" Then, when this Qurʾānic verse [5:91] was sent down, ʿUmar (may Allāh be well pleased with him) exclaimed: "We have done, O Lord, we have done!"[656]

> Obey Allāh and obey the Messenger. And beware!
> *wa aṭīʿu 'llāha wa aṭīʿu 'r-Rasūla wa 'ḥdharū.*

That is to say: "Obey the commandment of Allāh and the commandment of His Messenger (Allāh bless him and give him peace), and beware of contradicting them.

> But if you turn away, know that the duty of Our Messenger
> *fa-in tawallaitum fa-'ʿlamū anna-mā ʿalā Rasūli-nā*
> is only plain communication.
> *balāghun mubīn.*

In other words: "But if you turn aside, and do not act upon the commandment of Allāh and His Messenger, he is not charged with your right guidance. His duty is only to convey the message to you, and your recompense is Our responsibility."[657] This is a threat from Allāh, addressed to those who turn away from His command and His prohibition. He is telling them (Exalted is His remembrance): "If you turn aside from My command and My prohibition, you must anticipate My punishment, and beware of My displeasure!"[658] Abū Ḥayyān has noted: "The import of this serious threat is unmistakable, since it clearly implies that your punishment is entirely the business of the Sender [*Mursil*], not of the Messenger [*Rasūl*]."[659]

If someone stays on the right course, and refrains from random wandering [*iʿtisāf*],* he obviously understands that this Qurʾānic verse is an explicit text [*naṣṣ*], [containing the legal ruling] that every intoxicant is unlawful.[660]

The Qurʾānic verse serves notice that Allāh (Exalted is He) has linked strong drink and games of chance together with idols, so their prohibition is very emphatic. The saying of the Prophet (blessing and peace be upon him):

> The consumer of strong drink is like the worshipper of idols.[662]

—may well have been based on this Qurʾānic verse. The following sayings are also to be found in records of the Prophetic tradition [*ḥadīth*]:

> If someone consumes strong drink in this world, Allāh will make him drink the poison of snakes and scorpions. As soon as he sips it, the flesh will start peeling off his face and falling into the vessel, before he has swallowed the drink. Then, when he swallows it, his flesh will shrivel like that of a corpse, to the horror of the local inhabitants. If someone dies before repenting the consumption of strong drink, Allāh will be obliged to make him drink, for every gulp he took in this world, a draught of the pus of Hell.

*The related Arabic expression *huwa yarkabu 't-taʿāsīf* [he rides the random roads] is used of someone who has not travelled the straight path.[661]

> May Allāh curse strong drink, the person who drinks it, the person who offers it to others, the person who sells it, the person who buys it, the person who distils it and the distillery he uses, the person who transports it and the shop to which it is transported, and the person who consumes its price.[663]

As for His words (Exalted is He):

> O you who truly believe!
> *yā ayyuha 'lladhīna āmanū.*

—they implicitly refer to a genuine belief, derived from the inscribing of the Truth in their hearts, with the pen of providential care.

> Strong drink and games of chance
> *inna-ma 'l-khamru wa 'l-maisiru*
> and idols and divining arrows are only....
> *wa 'l-anṣābu wa 'l-azlāmu....*

As for strong drink, it causes fermentation in the intellect, which is a superior spiritual light among the prime elements of created beings, and which is naturally disposed towards obedience, loyalty and humble submission to its Lord, like the angel. Its opposite is passionate desire, which is dark, selfish, and the lowest of the most inferior elements of created beings, and which is naturally disposed towards rebellion, contrariness, disdain and arrogant refusal to worship its Lord, like the devil. When strong drink causes fermentation in the light of the intellect, the latter becomes incapacitated, so it cannot find guidance to the Truth and its path. Then strong drink also seizes control of the darkness of passionate desire, so the lower self becomes an instigator of evil [*ammāra bi's-sū'*]. It draws support from passionate desire, so that all its selfish appetites and base animal lusts are stimulated by the lowest kind of desire. Then Satan conquers it, and plunges it into the deadly perils of disbodience in all its forms. This explains why the Prophet (Allāh bless him and give him peace) has said:

> Strong drink is the mother of all forms of wickedness [*al-khamru ummu 'l-khabā'ith*].[664]

As for games of chance, they provide stimulation for most of the blameworthy attributes, such as greed, stinginess, arrogance, irascibility, animosity, hatred, spitefulness, envy and the like, all of which cause the servant [of the Lord] to stray from the path.[665]

These are my own remarks:

The fruit of every act of sinful disobedience is bad moral character, most of which results from keeping indecent company. Whenever the source of fruit is praiseworthy, the fruit is also worthy of praise.

It is therefore essential for you, O truly believing brother, to love for the sake of Allāh, and to hate for the sake of Allāh. If you love someone for Allāh's sake, on account of that person's obedience to Allāh and love for Allāh, but then he or she disobeys Allāh, you are obliged to hate the offender, because he or she has become a sinner, abhorrent to Allāh (Almighty and Glorious is He). If someone loves for a reason, he must inevitably hate for the opposite reason. These two are inextricably linked, so that neither can be separated from the other, and love and hate are like two sides of a coin.

Since love and hate are deeply embedded in the heart, they can only be developed when they are brought under strict control. They are trained by the actions of those who love and hate, through the experience of closeness and remoteness. For someone to be a lover of Allāh (Glory be to Him and Exalted is He) and of His Messenger (Allāh bless him and give him peace), that person must be together with those who love them both, otherwise he cannot be their lover.

Difficult problems are bound to arise, so long as obedience is mixed with acts of disobedience, and you are still wondering: "How can I combine hate with love, when they are mutually exclusive?" It is therefore essential to act in accordance with the demands of true belief [*īmān*], and that means abstinence from things that are forbidden and compliance with things that are commanded. Allāh is the only source of help!

O Allāh, grant us the ability to accomplish all that. *Āmīn*. Peace be upon the Messengers, and praise be to Allāh, the Lord of All the Worlds. There is no might nor any power, except with Allāh, the All-High, the Almighty. May Allāh bless our master Muḥammad, his family and his Companions, and may He grant them peace.

The Thirty-ninth Call

In the Name of Allāh, the All-Merciful, the All-Compassionate.
Bismi'llāhi 'r-Raḥmāni 'r-Raḥīm.

O you who truly believe,
Allāh will surely try you with something
yā ayyuha 'lladhīna āmanū la-yabluwanna-kumu 'llāhu bi-shai'in
of the game you take with your hands
and your spears,
mina 'ṣ-ṣaidi tanālu-hu aidī-kum wa rimāḥu-kum
so that Allāh may know who fears Him in secret.
li-ya'lamu 'llāhu man yakhfā-hu bi'l-ghaib:
Whoever transgresses after this,
for him there is a painful torment.
fa-mani 'ʿtadā baʿda dhālika
fa-la-hu ʿadhābun alīm. (5:94)

You should know that this represents another modification of the legal rules [*aḥkām*]. In a previous instance of such modification, Allāh (Exalted is He) said:

> Do not forbid the good things that Allāh has made lawful for you.
> *lā tuḥarrimū ṭayyibāti mā aḥalla 'llāhu la-kum.* (5:87)

—but then He excepted wine and gambling from that licence. In similar fashion, He has now excepted this kind of hunted game from things declared lawful, and has announced its inclusion among those declared unlawful, for He has said:

> O you who truly believe, Allāh will surely try you with something
> *yā ayyuha 'lladhīna āmanū la-yabluwanna-kumu 'llāhu bi-shai'in*
> of the game you take with your hands and your spears.
> *mina 'ṣ-ṣaidi tanālu-hu aidī-kum wa rimāḥu-kum.*

In other words, Allāh will put you to the test, in your state of consecration for the Pilgrimage [*Ḥajj*] or the Visitation [*ʿUmra*], with something of the game you catch, by taking the small creatures with your hands and the big ones with your spears.[666]

This Qurʾānic verse was revealed in the year of al-Ḥudaibiyya. When Allāh (Glory be to Him and Exalted is He) tried them with game, the wild animals would descend upon them at night, in their camps. This gave them the opportunity to treat those animals as game, by catching them with their hands and stabbing them with their spears, while they [the campers] were in a state of consecration.[667]

The year of al-Ḥudaibiyya was the year [A.H.] 6, and "while they were in a sate of consecration" means "for the Visitation [*ʿUmra*]." The murder of ʿUthmān (may Allāh be well pleased with him) had been rumoured. The Prophet (blessing and peace be upon him) therefore took the pledge of allegiance from his Companions beneath the tree, with the stipulation that they would enter Mecca in martial combat. Then came the peace treaty between the unbelievers and Allāh's Messenger (Allāh bless him and give him peace), and he ordered the Muslims to mark the end of consecration for the Visitation with the shaving of their heads and the slaughter of sacrificial offerings.[668]

According to the author of *al-Baḥr* [The Ocean]: "For the Arabs, game was part of their diet. They delighted in the hunting of it, and they had poems and beautiful descriptions to celebrate it."[669]

His saying (Exalted is He):

> [Allāh] will surely try you
> *la-yabluwanna-kum*

—means: "He will surely test your obedience, to see how it compares with your disobedience." In other words, He will treat you in the manner referred to in His saying:

> with something of the game
> *bi-shaiʾin mina ʾṣ-ṣaidi*

The reference to a small amount means that He does not regard this as one of those major tests, which are experienced as very hard and troublesome, like the trial involving the expenditure of spiritual energies and material possessions. This is quite an easy trial, for Allāh (Exalted is He) has tested the Community of our master Muḥammad (Allāh bless him and give him peace) with the game of the land, just as

He tested the Children of Israel with the game of the sea, that being the catching of fish.[670]

The word *min* [from; of] is used to indicate particularization. In this instance, it signifies that the term "game [*ṣaid*]" refers specifically to the game of the land, and does apply not apply to game in general, because the sea also has a kind of game.

His saying (Exalted is He):

> [that] you take with your hands and your spears
> *tanālu-hu aidī-kum wa rimāḥu-kum*

—makes it clear that the rule applies to small game animals as well as to big ones. It was al-Mujāhid who said: "The hands grab the hens and the eggs, and whatever cannot easily escape, while the spears reach the big game animals."[671]

> so that Allāh may know who fears Him in secret.
> *li-ya'lamu 'llāhu man yakhfā-hu bi'l-ghaib.*

That is to say: "So that He may distinguish someone who fears Allāh in a way that remains invisible, due to the strength of his faith, from someone who does not fear Allāh at all, due to the weakness of his faith."[672] It has also been said to mean: "We shall treat you as someone seeking to know would treat you," or, "in order that what is known—the fear of the fearful, that is—may became apparent." The implication may be: "so that the saintly friends [*awliyā'*] of Allāh may know who fears Him in secret." There are two possible interpretations to be considered:

1. "[So that Allāh may know] who fears Him because of his belief in the Unseen," as mentioned in His saying (Exalted is He):

> They believe in the Unseen.
> *yu'minūna bi'l-ghaibi.* (2:3)

2. "[So that Allāh may know] who fears Him in secret;" in other words, who fears Him with sincere devotion and as a real experience, and whose state does not alter because of the presence of someone or his absence, as in the case of the hypocrites, of whom He has said:

> And when they fall in with those who believe, they say:
> *wa idhā laqu 'lladhīna āmanū qālū*

"We believe." But when they go apart to their devils they declare:
āmannā wa idhā khalaw ilā shayāṭīni-him qālū
"We are indeed with you; of course we were only mocking."
innā maʿa-kum inna-mā naḥnu mustahziʾūn. (2:14)[673]

Let us now consider His words (Exalted is He):

Whoever transgresses after this, for him there is a painful torment.
fa-mani 'ʿtadā baʿda dhālika fa-la-hu ʿadhābun alīm.

That is to say: "If someone goes hunting game after this notification and warning, for him there will be a painful and agonizing torment."[674] What is meant is both the torment of the Hereafter and chastisement [*taʿzīr*] in this world. It was Ibn ʿAbbās who said: "This torment should be an agonizing beating, inflicted on his belly and his back, while his clothing is stripped off."

According to al-Qaffāl: "This is interpretation is permissible, because the term *ʿadhāb* is applied to beating, as when the flogging of the adulterous couple is referred to as *ʿadhāb*, in His saying (Exalted is He):

And let a party of the believers witness their flogging.
wa 'l-yashhad ʿadhāba-humā ṭāʾifatun mina 'l-muʾminīn. (24:2)"

He said, when telling the story of Solomon and the hoopoe:

I will surely chastise him with a terrible torment.
la-uʿadhdhibanna-hu ʿadhāban shadīdan. (27:21)[675]

The errant hunter of game should therefore be subjected to an agonizing beating, applied separately to each part of his body, except the face, the head and the sexual organ. He should also be commanded to make amends, because transgression after that is a flagrant offence on a major scale. It signifies indifference to Allāh's direction, departure from obedience to Him, and totally discarding the fear and dread of offending Him. The Qurānic verse indicates that Allāh has caused the test of loyalty to resemble the furnace for refining gold, for He has said:

O you who truly believe,
yā ayyuha 'lladhīna āmanū

—with the faith of the lovers who have detached themselves from the pleasures of this world, even from the satisfaction of lawful appetites, and have consecrated themselves for the Pilgrimage of direct contact [*Ḥajj al-wuṣūl*] and the Visitation of communion [*ʿUmrat al-wiṣāl*].

Allāh will surely try you
la-yabluwanna-kumu 'llāhu

—in the course of the spiritual journey:

with something of the game
bi-shai'in mina 'ṣ-ṣaidi

—namely, the temptations posed by the desires of the animal nature and the designs of worldly lustfulness.

[that] you take with your hands
tanālu-hu aidī-kum

In other words, that which is linked to the appetites of your lower selves and the pleasures of your physical bodies.

and your spears,
wa rimāḥu-kum

In other words, that which relates to wealth and prestige.

so that Allāh may know who fears Him in secret.
li-ya'lamu 'llāhu man yakhfā-hu bi'l-ghaib:

Since He knows and sees [everything and always], this must mean: "so that Allāh may show you the distinctive features of someone who fears Him in secret, forsaking all other objects of desire and purpose in the quest for the Truth, practising detachment, and being on guard against paying attention to anything other than Him."

Whoever transgresses after this,
fa-mani ''tadā ba'da dhālika

That is to say, whoever becomes attached to the objects of desire, after embarking on the quest:

for him there is a painful torment.
fa-la-hu 'adhābun alīm.

It is incumbent on the genuine seeker to endure the hardships of spiritual exercises, to purify himself of lustful appetites, and to be on guard against consuming whatever lawful food he may find, let alone whatever Allāh, the Exalted Sovereign, has forbidden. As for the improvement of the natural disposition and the lower self, it must be ascribed to the grace of Allāh and His providence, but fasting and reduced intake of food are undoubtedly among the potent contributory factors.

The venerable Mawlawī [Jalāl ad-Dīn Rūmī] was once asked: "Does the Ṣūfī ever disobey?" He replied: "No, unless he eats food before experiencing a genuine appetite, for then it is a poison for him and a sickness. O Allāh, help us to improve this instigating self [*an-nafs al-ammāra*]!"[676]

These are my own comments:

You must wake up from heedlessness and slumber. See how Allāh (Almighty and Glorious is He) has tested the noble Prophet (Allāh bless him and give him peace), despite his impeccable virtue [*ʿiṣma*], and the noble Companions, despite Allāh's good tidings to them, assuring them of the Garden of Paradise in this world.

You must adhere to the Sacred Law of Allāh and the Sunna of His Messenger (Allāh bless him and give him peace). This is the end of the age, for the market of hypocrisy has appeared, along with the market of falsehood. So beware of the companionship of the lying reprobates, and do not befriend your own lower self, for it is an enemy to you, hypocritical, lying and immoral, which only strives to destroy you. How can you side with it? You must oppose it and refuse to comply with its wishes. You must restrict it and not set it free. You must imprison it and give it nothing but its basic due, to which it is strictly entitled. You must make every dedicated effort to render it virtually nonexistent.

As for passionate desire, you must ride it and not let it ride you. You must seek help from Allāh, and be constant in the remembrance of Allāh, so the spirit will be nourished, and obedience will become easy for you. You must be sincere in your all your work, so that even a little of it will be highly beneficial to you.

O Allāh, grant us the ability to accomplish all that. *Āmīn*. Peace be upon the Messengers, and praise be to Allāh, the Lord of All the Worlds. There is no might nor any power, except with Allāh, the All-High, the Almighty. May Allāh bless our master Muḥammad, his family and his Companions, and may He grant them peace.

The Fortieth Call

In the Name of Allāh, the All-Merciful, the All-Compassionate.
Bismi'llāhi 'r-Raḥmāni 'r-Raḥīm.

O you who truly believe, kill no wild game
yā ayyuha 'lladhīna āmanū lā taqtulu 'ṣ-ṣaida
while you are in the state of consecration.
wa antum ḥurum:
Whoever of you kills it wilfully,
there shall be recompense
wa man qatala-hu min-kum muta'ammidan fa-jazā'un
equivalent to what he has killed,
consisting of domestic animals,
mithlu mā qatala mina 'n-na'ami
as decided by two men among you
known for justice,
yaḥkumu bi-hi dhawā 'adlin min-kum
an offering fit to reach the Ka'ba;
or, for expiation,
hadyan bāligha 'l-Ka'bati aw kaffāratun
food for poor persons,
or the equivalent of that in fasting,
ṭa'āmu masākīna aw 'adlu dhālika ṣiyāman
so that he may taste the grave discomfort
of his situation.
li-yadhūqa wabāla amri-h:
Allāh has pardoned what is past,
'afa 'llāhu 'ammā salaf:
but if anyone relapses,
Allāh will take vengeance on him.
wa man 'āda fa-yantaqimu 'llāhu min-h:
Allāh is Almighty, Capable of taking vengeance.
wa 'llāhu 'Azīzun Dhu 'ntiqām.

Made lawful for you is the game of the sea,
uḥilla la-kum ṣaidu 'l-baḥri
and its food is a provision for you
and for travellers;
wa ṭa'āmu-hu matā'an la-kum wa li's-sayyāra:
but unlawful for you is the game of the land,
wa ḥurrima 'alai-kum ṣaidu 'l-barri
so long as you remain in the state of consecration.
mā dumtum ḥurumā:
Practise true devotion to Allāh,
to Whom you will be gathered.
wa 'ttaqu 'lladhī ilai-hi tuḥsharūn. (5:95,96)

O you who truly believe,
yā ayyuha 'lladhīna āmanū
kill no wild game while you are in the state of consecration.
lā taqtulu 'ṣ-ṣaida wa antum ḥurum:

That is to say: "You must not kill wild game while you are in a state of consecration for the Pilgrimage [*Ḥajj*] or the Visitation [*'Umra*]."[677]

According to Abū Ḥanīfa, the term *ṣaid* [wild game] applies to all animals that are wild and inaccessible, whether or not their meat is edible. In this context, however, it applies to all wild animals and birds except vermin, meaning the scorpion, the snake, the raven, the rat, the dog, the beast with a savage bite, the kite, and the aggressive predator. These may be killed at any time, even by someone who is in the state of pilgrim consecration.

while you are in the state of consecration.
wa antum ḥurum:

The word *ḥurum* is the plural of *ḥarām*, meaning someone who is *muḥrim* [person in a state of consecration].[678] The corresponding verb *aḥrama* is used to state that someone has made the commitment to *iḥrām* [the state of consecration]. The same verb *aḥrama* is also used to state that the subject has entered the *Ḥaram* [Sanctuary]. Both meanings are intended in this Qur'ānic verse, it has been said, so the killing of wild game is permissible neither for the *muḥrim* [person in a state of consecration], nor inside the *Ḥaram* [Sanctuary].[679]

Whoever of you kills it wilfully...
wa man qatala-hu min-kum muta'ammidan...

That is to say: "while conscious of his state of consecration," or: "knowing that what he is killing is one of those creatures the killing of which is unlawful." The prohibitions imposed during the state of consecration are equally applicable to deliberate acts and to mistakes, but the Qur'ānic verse is aimed emphatically at those who act with deliberate intent. According to a traditional report, a wild ass strayed into the presence of those performing the Visitation [*'Umra*] [in the year] of al-Ḥudaibiyya, so Abu 'l-Yusr attacked it and killed it. He was told: "You have killed wild game, while you are in the state of consecration [*muḥrim*]," and the Qur'ānic verse was thereupon revealed.

The principal target is the deliberate act, and the mistake is appended to it, for the sake of stressing the seriousness of the prohibition. According to az-Zuhrī: "The Book has specified the deliberate act, and the Sunna has included the mistake."[680]

When He says:

> of you...
> *min-kum...*

—Allāh (Exalted is He) is referring to the believers. The purpose of the qualification may be to rebuke the believer for his failure to act in accordance with the requirement of his faith.[681]

> there shall be recompense equivalent to what he has killed,
> *fa-jazā'un mithlu mā qatala*
> consisting of domestic animals.
> *mina 'n-na'ami*

That is to say: "If someone kills wild game while in the state of consecration, he must pay a recompense, equivalent to what he has killed, in the form of domestic animals, meaning camels, cattle, and sheep or goats."[682]

It was the jurist Abū Ja'far who said: "When He spoke of killing, rather than slaughtering, He did so in order to declare it subject to the rule of carrion [*maita*]. Whatever wild game is killed by someone in the state of consecration, it cannot be ritually immolated [as a sacrificial offering], and if it has not been ritually immolated, eating it is not permissible."

As for His expression:

> equivalent to what he has killed
> *mithlu mā qatala*

—in other words: "comparable to what he has killed," this is a description of the recompense. According to Abū Ḥanīfa and Abū Yūsuf, the equivalence refers to the monetary value, not to the physical nature and form [of the animals concerned].[683]

> as decided by two men among you known for justice
> *yaḥkumu bi-hi dhawā ʿadlin min-kum*

That is to say: "The equivalent should be decided by two fair judges from among the Muslims."

> an offering fit to reach the Kaʿba
> *hadyan bāligha 'l-Kaʿbati*

In other words: "Its condition should be that of a sacrificial offering, ritually slaughtered and presented as a charitable gift to the poor." In the case of wild game that has no equivalent among the domestic animals, such as the sparrow and the locust, he must pay its monetary value.[684]

The sacrificial offering is a domestic animal that is led to the House [the Kaʿba], as a mark of dedication to Allāh (Exalted is He). The least significant is a sheep, at the mid-point is a cow, and the highest on the scale is a she-camel."[685] The Kaʿba is called a *kaʿba* [cubic structure] because of its loftiness and its quadrilateral dimensions. In the present context, it stands for the Sanctuary as a whole, because slaughtering and immolation do not take place in the Kaʿba itself, and it has no additional structure attached to it. This Qurʾānic verse is reminiscent of another, namely:

> Then their lawful place of sacrifice is by the Ancient House.
> *thumma maḥillu-hā ila 'l-Bait al-ʿAtīq.* (22:33)[686]

> or, for expiation, food for poor persons
> *aw kaffāratun ṭaʿāmu masākīna*

That is to say: "If the consecrated person cannot find an equivalent to what he has killed, in the form of domestic animals, he should ascertain the monetary value of the game killed, then use it to purchase food, a measure of which should be distributed to every needy individual."

> or the equivalent of that in fasting,
> *ṭaʿāmu masākīna aw ʿadlu dhālika ṣiyāman*
> so that he may taste the grave discomfort of his situation.
> *li-yadhūqa wabāla amri-h:*

In other words: "For each measure of that equivalent amount of food, he must devote a day to fasting, so that he may taste the bad consequence of his violation of the sanctity of the state of consecration." According to the author of *at-Tas'hīl*: "Allāh (Exalted is He) has enumerated the consequences of the killing of wild game, committed by someone in the state of consecration. First of all, He has mentioned the recompense consisting of domestic animals, then the provision of food, and then fasting. According to the doctrine of Mālik and the majority [of the Islāmic jurists], these are presented as optional alternatives, since they are linked by the particle *aw* [or]. According to Ibn ʿAbbās (may Allāh be well pleased with him), however, they are listed in order of priority."[687]

As for His saying:

> that he may taste the grave discomfort of his situation.
> *li-yadhūqa wabāla amri-h:*

—it is linked to His statement:

> there shall be recompense
> *fa-jazāʾun*

—to convey the meaning: "The offender must make recompense or expiation, so that he may taste the bad consequence of his violation of the sanctity of consecration." The term *wabāl* [grave discomfort] applies to the inconvenience and detriment he will suffer as the result of misconduct, because of all the trouble it will cause him. The corresponding adjective *wabīl* occurs in:

> so We seized him [Pharaoh] with a heavily oppressive grip.
> *fa-akhadhnā-hu akhdhan wabīlā.* (73:16)

Food is described as *wabīl* when it weighs heavily on the stomach, so that it cannot be digested in comfort.[688]

> Allāh has pardoned what is past
> *ʿafa 'llāhu ʿammā salaf:*

In other words: "[He has pardoned] those who killed wild game before the prohibition was announced."

> but if anyone relapses, Allāh will take vengeance on him.
> *wa man ʿāda fa-yantaqimu 'llāhu min-h:*

That is to say: "If anyone reverts to killing wild game, while he is in the state of consecration, Allāh will take vengeance on him in the Hereafter."[689] Vengeance [*intiqām*] is a deliberately exaggerated reference to punishment.

This threat does not preclude the imposition of recompense on the second occasion, and the third. If the killing of wild game is committed repeatedly by someone in the state of consecration, recompense will also be demanded of him repeatedly. Such is the majority opinion of the religious scholars.[690]

> Allāh is Almighty, Capable of taking vengeance.
> *wa 'llāhu ʿAzīzun Dhu 'ntiqām.*

In other words: "He is All-Prevailing over His business, Vengeful against those who disobey Him,[691] Severe with those who persist in disobedience and hostility." [According to a Sacred Tradition] Allāh (Exalted is He) once addressed these words to His Bosom Friend [*Khalīl*]:

> O Abraham, you must be afraid of Me, just as you are afraid of the savage beast of prey!

What this signifies is that, when Allāh (Exalted is He) intends to carry out His judgment on someone, He does not differentiate between a Prophet, a friend, and an enemy, just as the beast of prey does not distinguish between someone who is beneficent and someone who causes harm. Allāh (Exalted is He) is Severe in the wielding of power, so how can sinful offenders escape from the hand of His coercion and His vengeance? The intelligent person must beware of opposition and disobedience, to the full extent of his ability and capacity, wherever he may be, for the human being reaps only what he sows. It is amazing how the feeble human being can disobey Allāh, the Strong. This can only be attributed to preoccupation with carnal desires, and to heedless disregard of Allāh (Exalted is He).[692]

Made lawful for you is the game of the sea
uḥilla la-kum ṣaidu 'l-baḥri

That is to say: "Made lawful for you, O human beings, is the game of the sea, whether or not you are in the state of consecration."[693]

the game of the sea
ṣaidu 'l-baḥri

—is whatever is fished from any waters, whether those of an ocean or sea, or those of a river or stream, or those of a lake or pond. It is that which lives only in water, whether it is edible or inedible. As for that which lives both on land and in the sea (like the duck and the frog), it is not called "the game of the sea." All such creatures are included among the game of the land, and recompense is incumbent on someone who kills them. This subject is treated in detail in the books of Islāmic jurisprudence [*fiqh*].[694]

and its food is a provision for you and for tavellers
wa ṭaʿāmu-hu matāʿan la-kum wa li's-sayyāra:

That is to say: "Of the game of the sea, that which serves as food, like fish and other edible creatures, is a benefit and a source of nourishment for you, and a provision for travellers, who supply themselves with it on their journeys."

but unlawful for you is the game of the land,
wa ḥurrima ʿalai-kum ṣaidu 'l-barri
so long as you remain in the state of consecration.
mā dumtum ḥurumā:

In other words: "The game of the land has been made unlawful for you, so long as you remain *muḥrimīn*." [As explained above, the Arabic term *ḥurum* is synonymous with the more familiar *muḥrimīn*.]

Practise true devotion to Allāh, to Whom you will be gathered.
wa 'ttaqu 'lladhī ilai-hi tuḥsharūn.

That is to say: "You must be afraid of offending Allāh, to Whom you will be brought forth on the Day of Resurrection, for He will recompense you for your deeds." This is both a threat and a warning.[695] It is intended to ensure that a man will be diligent in worshipful obedience, carefully on guard against all forms of sinful disobedience. Since the killing of wild game, while in the state of consecration, is subject to very serious prohibition, the point is repeated four times in this Sūra:

1. In His saying (Exalted is He):

> Wild game is unlawful while you are in the state of consecration.
> *ghaira muḥilli 'ṣ-ṣaidi wa antum ḥurum:* (5:1)

2. In His saying (Exalted is He):

> Allāh will surely try you with something of the wild game.
> *la-yabluwanna-kumu 'llāhu bi-shai'in mina 'ṣ-ṣaidi.* (5:94)

3. In His saying (Exalted is He):

> Kill no wild game while you are in the state of consecration.
> *lā taqtulu 'ṣ-ṣaida wa antum ḥurum.* (5:95)

4. In His saying (Exalted is He):

> but unlawful for you is the game of the land.
> *wa ḥurrima ʿalai-kum ṣaidu 'l-barri.* (5:96)[696]

> Practise true devotion to Allāh, to Whom you will be gathered.
> *wa 'ttaqu 'lladhī ilai-hi tuḥsharūn.*

That is to say: "[You will be gathered to Him] and to no other, with whom you might think of taking refuge, in order to escape from His grasp (Exalted is He)." As He has said (Exalted is He):

> Towards your Lord that day will be the herding.
> *ilā Rabbi-ka yawma'idhini 'l-masāq.* (75:30)

In other words: "The destination and the point of return, for the herding conducted by the angels, will be as Allāh has commanded them, either towards the Garden of Paradise, or towards the Inferno of Hell." According to the Prophetic tradition [*ḥadīth*]:

> If someone yearns for the Garden of Paradise, let him make haste to perform good deeds. If someone dreads the torment of Hell, let him restrain himself from things that are unlawful. If someone is detached from this world, misfortunes will consider him unworthy of their notice.

If someone wishes for an easy death, he should therefore set to work on good deeds without delay. If someone fails to abstain from carnal lust, his Lord will not be pleased with him on account of his worshipful obedience. If someone fails to practise true devotion to Allāh in his innermost being, he will derive no benefit from his outward display of true devotion.[697]

These are my own comments:

For the intelligent person who is a genuine seeker, it is essential to stop paying attention to anything other [than his Lord], and to attain to the One who holds all goodness in His hand. Allāh is the Enabler and the Helper!

O believer, you must feel a sense of shame before Allāh (Almighty and Glorious is He), for you are included in this general and universal address to the believers. You must remember that you are standing in the presence of your Lord, here in this world, before your journey to the Day when no remorse will be any use to you. What you say is right and proper, but you do not act upon it. You must hear the stern rebuke delivered to those who enjoin what they do not practise. For example, listen to His words (Exalted is He):

> Do you enjoin righteousness on other people,
> *a-taʾmurūna 'n-nāsa bi'l-birri*
> while you forget [to practise it] yourselves?
> *wa tansawna anfusa-kum.* (2:44)
>
> It is most hateful in the sight of Allāh
> *kabura maqtan ʿinda 'llāhi*
> that you say what you do not do.
> *an taqūlū mā lā tafʿalūn.* (61:2)

Our religious scholars have cited these texts to prove the stipulation of integrity in commanding what is right and fair, and forbidding what is wrong and unfair. They maintain that the profligate is not qualified to enforce moral standards. They also quote the saying attributed to the Prophet (Allāh bless him and give him peace):

> On the night of my Heavenly Journey, I passed by a group of people whose lips were being clipped with scissors of fire, so I said to them: 'Who are you?' They replied: 'We used to enjoin good conduct, but we did not practise it, and we used to forbid wicked conduct, but we did not act accordingly.'[698]

You must turn to Allāh, repenting every sin, and apologize to Him, for He is the Most Merciful of the merciful. Allāh (Exalted is He) has told us:

> And ask forgiveness of Allāh.
> *wa 'staghfiru 'llāh:*
> Allāh is indeed Forgiving, Merciful.
> *inna 'llāha Ghafūrun Raḥīm.* (2:199)

There is no might nor any power, except with Allāh, the All-High, the Almighty.

> Our Lord, give us in this world that which is good,
> *Rabba-nā āti-nā fi 'd-dunyā ḥasanatan*
> and in the Hereafter that which is good,
> *wa fi 'l-ākhirati ḥasanatan*
> and guard us against the torment of the Fire [of Hell].
> *wa qi-nā ʿadhāba 'n-nār.* (2:201)

Āmīn. Peace be upon the Messengers, and praise be to Allāh, the Lord of All the Worlds. May Allāh bless our master Muḥammad, his family and his Companions, and may He grant them peace.

The Forty-first Call

In the Name of Allāh, the All-Merciful, the All-Compassionate.
Bismi'llāhi 'r-Raḥmāni 'r-Raḥīm.

O you who truly believe, do not ask about things
yā ayyuha 'lladhīna āmanū lā tas'alū 'an ashyā'a
which, if they were made known to you,
would trouble you,
in tubda la-kum tasu'-kum:
but if you ask about them while the Qur'ān
is being revealed,
wa in tas'alū 'an-hā ḥīna yunazzalu 'l-Qur'ānu
they will be made known to you.
tubda la-kum:
Allāh pardons this, for Allāh
is All-Forgiving, All-Forbearing.
'afa 'llāhu 'an-hā wa 'llāhu Ghafūrun Ḥalīm.

A folk before you asked for them,
but then disbelieved therein.
qad sa'ala-hā qawmun min qabli-kum
thumma aṣbaḥū bi-hā kāfirīn. (5:101,102)

With regard to the connection between this Qur'ānic verse and what was revealed before it, the following points deserve consideration:

1. When Allāh (Exalted is He) said:

> The Messenger has no other charge than to convey.
> *mā 'ala 'r-Rasūli illa 'l-balāghu.* (24:54)

—He was presumably saying, in effect: "Whatever the Messenger conveys to you, accept it, and be his faithful followers. As for what he does not convey to you, do not ask about it, and do not wallow in it.

If you become engrossed in matters that do not concern you, that idle curiosity may confront you with weighty and difficult problems."

2. When He said (Exalted is He):

> The Messenger has no other charge than to convey.
> *mā ʿala 'r-Rasūli illa 'l-balāghu.* (24:54)

—He thereby enabled him to lay claim to Messengership, but then, after the manifestation of miracles [*muʿjizāt*], the unbelievers kept demanding other miracles from him, in a stubbornly annoying manner. Allāh (Exalted is He) was referring to them when He said:

> And they say: "We will not put faith in you
> *wa qālū lan nuʾmina la-ka*
> till you cause a spring to gush forth from the earth for us;
> *ḥattā tafjura la-nā mina 'l-arḍi yanbūʿā:*
>
> "Or you have a garden of date palms and grapes,
> *aw takūna la-ka jannatun min nakhīlin wa ʿinābin*
> and cause rivers to gush forth therein abundantly;
> *fa-tufajjira 'l-anhāra khilāla-hā tafjīrā.*
>
> "Or you cause the heaven to fall on us piecemeal,
> *aw tusqiṭa 's-samāʾa*
> as you have pretended,
> *ka-mā zaʿamta ʿalai-nā kisafan*
> or bring Allāh and the angels as a warrant;
> *aw taʾtiya bi'llāhi wa 'l-malāʾikati qabīlā:*
>
> "Or you have a house of gold; or you ascend up into heaven,
> *aw yakūna la-ka baitun min zukhrufin aw tarqā fi 's-samāʾ:*
> and even then we will put no faith in your ascension
> *wa lan nuʾmina li-ruqiyyi-ka*
> till you bring down for us a book that we can read."
> *ḥattā tunazzila ʿalai-nā kitāban naqraʾū-h:* (17:90–93)

To this He added (Exalted is He):

> Say: "Glory be to my Lord!
> *qul subḥāna Rabbī*
> I am nothing but a mortal Messenger!"
> *hal kuntu illā basharan Rasūlā.* (17:93)

—meaning: "I am a Messenger who has been commanded to convey to you the Message, the Sacred Laws [*Sharāʾiʿ*] and the rules of proper conduct. Allāh (Exalted is He) has provided evidence of the validity of my claim, through the manifestation of many kinds of miracles. To demand more after that amounts to arbitrariness. In any case, that is not within my capacity. Perhaps their manifestation would cause you harm. For example, suppose that everyone who remained in opposition, after they appeared, would be condemned to chastisement in this world."

Furthermore, when the Muslims heard the unbelievers demanding these miracles from the Messenger (Allāh bless him and give him peace), their hearts were infected with a desire for their manifestation. They were therefore given to understand, in this Qur'ānic verse, that it was not appropriate for them to look for that, since their manifestation might cause them to suffer harmful consequences.[699] He told them (Exalted is He):

> O you who truly believe, do not ask about things
> *yā ayyuha 'lladhīna āmanū lā tas'alū 'an ashyā'a*
> which, if they were made known to you, would trouble you.
> *in tubda la-kum tasu'-kum:*

In other words: "Do not ask the Messenger about things of which you have no need. If they became apparent to you, they would only cause you trouble." According to az-Zamakhsharī: "That is to say: 'You must not bother Allāh's Messenger (Allāh bless him and give him peace) with too many questions, in case you end up asking him about matters that will subject you to painful obligations. If he gives you a formal pronouncement on them, and imposes them on you as binding duties, they will cause you grief and agony, and you will regret having asked about them.'"[700]

This is an edification from Allāh to His believing servants, and a prohibition forbidding them to ask about things that do not warrant their inquiry and investigation. If those matters were disclosed to them, the hearing of them might prove troubling and disturbing to them. As reported in the tradition [*ḥadīth*], Allāh's Messenger (Allāh bless him and give him peace) once said:

> Let no one tell me anything about any of my Companions! When I go out to meet you, I love to have a good feeling in my breast.[701]

As reported by al-Bukhārī, it was Anas ibn Mālik who said: "Allāh's Messenger (Allāh bless him and give him peace) once delivered a sermon, the like of which I had never heard. In the course of it he said:

> If you knew what I know, you would surely laugh a little, and you would surely weep a lot.

"On hearing this, the Companions of Allāh's Messenger (Allāh bless him and give him peace) covered their faces, as they uttered a gentle cry of tender emotion. A man asked: 'Who is my father?' He told him: 'So-and-so.' This Qur᾽ānic verse was thereupon revealed."

As reported on the authority of Ibn ʿAbbās (may Allāh be well pleased with him and his father), and likewise from Abū Huraira (may Allāh be well pleased with him), while the Prophet (blessing and peace be upon him) was delivering a sermon one day, he was angry at the great number of questions people asked, about matters that did not concern them, so he said: "'I must not be asked about anything, unless I have already answered [the previous question].'

"A man asked: 'Where is my father?' so he told him: 'In the Fire of Hell!' ʿAbdu'llāh ibn Ḥudhāfa as-Sahmī then stood up and said: 'Who is my father?' so he replied: 'Your father is Ḥudhāfa,' though he used to claim someone else [as his father]. ʿUmar ibn al-Khaṭṭāb (may Allāh be well pleased with him) then stood up and said: 'We are well pleased with Allāh as a Lord, with Islām as a religion, with Muḥammad (Allāh bless him and give him peace) as a Prophet, and with the Qur᾽ān as a leader. O Messenger of Allāh, we have just recently emerged from an age of ignorance and idolatry, and Allāh knows best who our fathers really are.' His anger thereupon subsided, and he received the revelation:

> O you who truly believe, do not ask.... "[702]
> *yā ayyuha 'lladhīna āmanū lā tas᾽alū....*

Ibn ʿAbbās (may Allāh be well pleased with him and his father) is reported as having said: "Certain people used to put questions to the Prophet (Allāh bless him and give him peace) in a mocking fashion. A man would ask: 'Who is my father?' and another would say: 'My she-camel has gone astray. Where is my she-camel?' Allāh therefore sent down the revelation:

> O you who truly believe, do not ask about things
> *yā ayyuha 'lladhīna āmanū lā tas᾽alū ʿan ashyā᾽a*
> which, if they were made known to you, would trouble you.[703]
> *in tubda la-kum tasu᾽-kum:*

As related by ʿUkkāsha ibn Miḥṣan, Surāqa ibn Mālik once said: "O Messenger of Allāh, must we perform the Pilgrimage [*Ḥajj*] every year?"

Allāh's Messenger (Allāh bless him and give him peace) ignored him, until he repeated the question two or three times, then he said (blessing and peace be upon him):

> Woe unto you! What assurance do you have against my saying yes? By Allāh, if I did say yes, you would be under an obligation, and if you were under an obligation, you would not comply, and if you did not comply, you would be guilty of unbelief. Leave me alone, for I have not abandoned you. Your people before you were destroyed by asking too many questions. When I command you to do something, perform it to the best of your ability, and when I forbid you to do something, avoid it.

Asking about things may sometimes lead to the disclosure of hidden conditions, the disclosure of which is unpleasant. It may sometimes result in the imposition of difficult and painful obligations. For the intelligent person, therefore, the best course is to keep silent about matters that need not concern him. It was Abū Tha'laba al-Khashanī who said: "Allāh has prescribed certain obligatory religious duties [*farā'iḍ*], so you must not fail to discharge them. He has forbidden certain things, so you must not violate those prohibitions. He has set certain limits, so you must not transgress them. He has also exempted certain things from regulation, though not because of forgetfulness, so do not inquire about them."[704]

> but if you ask about them while the Qur'ān is being revealed,
> *wa in tas'alū 'an-hā ḥīna yunazzalu 'l-Qur'ānu*
> they will be made known to you.
> *tubda la-kum:*

That is to say: "If you ask about these difficult impositions, at the time of the descent of inspiration [*waḥy*], those troublesome obligations will be disclosed to you, so do not ask about them!" It was Ibn 'Abbās (may Allāh be well pleased with him and his father) who said, when commenting on the Qur'ānic verse:

> do not ask about things....
> *lā tas'alū 'an ashyā'a....*

—"There is trouble in store for you, in being informed about them. It may take the form of a legal obligation imposed upon you, or it may be an item of news that will trouble you, as in the case of the man who asked: 'Where is my father?' If the Qur'ān brings down some revelation, however, and your Lord presents a new commandment, if you ask at that time for an explanation of its meaning, it will be explained and made clear to you."[705]

In order to interpret the Qur᾽ānic verse correctly, one should understand that there are two types of inquiry:

1. Asking about something to which no reference has been made in the Book and the Sunna, from any point of view. Such inquiry has been forbidden by His saying:

> Do not ask about things which,
> *yā ayyuha 'lladhīna āmanū lā tas᾽alū ῾an ashyā᾽a*
> if they were made known to you, would trouble you.
> *in tubda la-kum tasu᾽-kum:*

2. Asking about something which the Qur᾽ān has revealed, but which the hearer has not properly understood. In this case, inquiry is a necessary duty, in accordance with His saying:

> but if you ask about them while the Qur᾽ān is being revealed,
> *wa in tas᾽alū ῾an-hā ḥīna yunazzalu 'l-Qur᾽ānu*
> they will be made known to you.
> *tubda la-kum:*

The benefit in mentioning this second type is that, when He barred questioning at the beginning of the verse, He gave the impression that all kinds of inquiry were forbidden. He therefore went on to distinguish the second type from the first.[706]

> Allāh pardons this, for Allāh is All-Forgiving, All-Forbearing.
> *῾afa 'llāhu ῾an-hā wa 'llāhu Ghafūrun Ḥalīm.*

That is to say: "Allāh has pardoned your previous questionings, which were unnecessary, and He has waived your Otherworldly punishment, so do not repeat the same mistake. Allāh is All-Embracing in forgiveness, Splendid in gracious favour and beneficence. That is why He has pardoned you, and has not subjected you to immediate punishment."[707] It was ῾Aṭā᾽ who said: "'All-Forgiving [*Ghafūr*]' means 'of what happened in the Age of Ignorance.' 'All-Forbearing [*Ḥalīm*]' means 'with regard to your punishment, since you have believed and accepted the truth.'"

According to one of the religious scholars: "As for those things about which it is permissible to ask questions, they are matters relating to the best interests, both religious and worldly, of the servants [of the Lord]. As for whatever lies beyond that, it is not permissible to ask about it."[708]

> A folk before you asked for them,
> *qad sa'ala-hā qawmun min qabli-kum*
> but then disbelieved therein.
> *thumma aṣbaḥū bi-hā kāfirīn.*

That is to say: "A people before you asked questions like these, but then, when they received the answers and the corresponding obligations were imposed on them, they disbelieved in them." That is why He said:

> but then disbelieved therein.
> *thumma aṣbaḥū bi-hā kāfirīn.*

In other words: "They became unbelievers, by failing to put them into practice." The Children of Israel used to ask their Prophets for legal rulings on various things, but then, when they were commanded to act accordingly, they failed to comply, and so they perished.[709]

According to the traditional commentators: "The folk referred to were the people of Ṣāliḥ (peace be upon him). They asked for the she-camel, but then they hamstrung the creature. Then there were the people of Moses (peace be upon him). They said: 'Let us see Allāh in open view,' but that was an affliction for them. Then there were the Children of Israel, who said to a Prophet of theirs: 'Raise up a king for us, and we shall fight in the cause of Allāh.' He said (Exalted is He):

> Yet when fighting was prescribed for them,
> *fa-lammā kutiba 'alai-himu 'l-qitālu*
> they turned away, all but a few of them.
> *tawallaw illā qalīlan min-hum.*
>
> Their Prophet said to them:
> *wa qāla la-hum Nabiyyu-hum*
> "Allāh has raised up Saul to be a king for you."
> *inna 'llāha qad ba'atha la-kum Ṭālūta*
> They said: "How can he have a kingdom over us
> *malikā: qālū annā yakūnu la-hu 'l-mulku 'alai-nā*
> when we are more deserving of the kingdom than he is?"
> *wa naḥnu aḥaqqu bi'l-mulki min-hu.* (2:246,247)

"They made their request, but then, when it was granted, they disbelieved. There were also the people of Jesus (peace be upon him).

They asked for the table [*mā'ida*], but then disbelieved in it. It is as if He is saying (Exalted is He): 'Those people asked, but then, when their requests were granted, they found that troublesome. So do not ask about things, in case you have that same unfortunate experience!'"

Someone might say: "Allāh (Exalted is He) said, first of all:

> Do not ask about things.
> *lā tas'alū 'an ashyā'a.*

—"then He went on to say:

> A folk before you asked for them
> *qad sa'ala-hā qawmun min qabli-kum*

—"although it would have been most proper for Him to say: 'A folk asked **about** them [*sa'ala* ***'an-hā*** *qawmun*].' What is the reason for that?"

The answer to this would be: "As for the people of former times, they asked Allāh to bring the she-camel forth from the desert, and to send the table down from the sky, so they asked for the thing itself [not about it]. As for the Companions of our master Muḥammad (Allāh bless him and give him peace), they did not ask in that sense. They only asked about the conditions and attributes of things. Since the two kinds of asking are different, there is a corresponding difference in the grammatical expression [used in Arabic]. Nevertheless, the two types do share one common characteristic, that being the element of excessive curiosity and interest in what is not only unnecessary, but potentially dangerous."[710]

As the two Qur'ānic verses [5:101,102] indicate, Allāh (Exalted is He) has forbidden the people of faith to study the esoteric sciences [*'ulūm laduniyya*], and the realities [*ḥaqā'iq*] of things, by the method of asking questions. That is because they are not included among the sciences of verbal sophistry [*'ulūm al-qāl*], but only among the sciences of the spiritual state [*'ulūm al-ḥāl*]. You cannot find guidance to the realities through verbal explanation, for your muddled minds will fall into suspicions and doubts, under the damaging influence of passionate desire, imagination and fantasy. You will thus become exhausted from wandering in their valleys. You will share the fate of the philosophical sects, who tried to pursue the sciences of the realities by the method of verbal sophistry and intellectual proofs. Satan caused them to stumble in their research, so they slipped from the straight path. He caused them to fall into the valleys of doubts and perils, so they were ruined. They also brought ruination to a great many people, through their literary compositions.

The Prophet (blessing and peace be upon him) once said:

> Show things to us as they are!

Such was the state of the Community in the company of the Prophet (blessing and peace be upon him). He used to teach them the Book by means of speech, and wisdom (the Sunna) by means of the spiritual state, using the method of fellowship and the purification of their lower selves, in order to rid them of the serious flaws and tendencies of the lower self [*nafs*]. As He has said (Exalted is He):

> [A Messenger who] recites to them His signs,
> *yatlū ʿalai-him āyāti-hi*
> and purifies them,
> *yatlū ʿalai-him āyāti-hi wa yuzakkī-him*
> and teaches them the Book and wisdom.
> *wa yuʿallimu-humu 'l-Kitāba wa 'l-ḥikmata.* (3:164)[711]

(Wisdom means loyal adherence to the Sunna.)

These are my own remarks:

O believing brother, the study of the sciences of the realities must be conducted through true devotion to Allāh (Almighty and Glorious is He):

> Practise true devotion to Allāh,
> *wa 'ttaqu 'llāh:*
> and Allāh will teach you.
> *wa yuʿallimu-kumu 'llāh:*
> Allāh is Aware of all things.
> *wa 'llāhu bi-kulli shaiʾin ʿAlīm.* (2:282)

True devotion is practised by abstaining from sinful acts of disobedience, and by performing righteous work. The righteousness of work is not determined by the number of deeds performed, but only by its exclusive dedication to the Countenance of Allāh (Almighty and Glorious is He). The crucial factor is not the frequency and amount of the work performed. The crucial factor is keeping the work detached from all worldly interests and carnal desires, and ensuring that it is dedicated purely to the Countenance of Allāh (Almighty and Glorious is He).

> They were commanded only to serve Allāh,
> *wa mā umirū illā li-ya'budu 'llāha*
> devoting the religion to Him sincerely, as men of pure faith,
> *mukhliṣīna la-hu 'd-dīn: ḥunafā'a*
> and to perform the ritual prayer, and pay the alms-due.
> *wa yuqīmu 'ṣ-ṣalāta wa yu'tu 'z-zakāta*
> That is the religion of true worth.
> *wa dhālika dīnu 'l-qayyima.* (98:5)

The outward performance of work, however much and however frequent, is of no avail in the absence of sincere devotion. The crucial point is sincerity, not frequency and quantity. As the saying goes: "A single jewel is better than a thousand pearls, and one seldom finds many kernels in a large pile of walnuts. It so often happens that you crack a heap of walnuts, but only get a few kernels for your trouble."

We beg Allāh (Exalted is He) to endow us with that of which only He is Capable, through His gracious favour and His kindness. *Āmīn*. Peace be upon the Messengers, and praise be to Allāh, the Lord of All the Worlds. There is no might nor any power, except with Allāh, the All-High, the Almighty. May Allāh bless our master Muḥammad, his family and his Companions, and may He grant them peace.

The Forty-second Call

In the Name of Allāh, the All-Merciful, the All-Compassionate.
Bismi'llāhi 'r-Raḥmāni 'r-Raḥīm.

O you who truly believe,
you must take charge of your own selves.
yā ayyuha 'lladhīna āmanū ʿalai-kum anfusa-kum:
Those who err cannot injure you,
if you are rightly guided.
lā yaḍurru-kum man ḍalla idha 'htadaitum:
To Allāh you must all return;
and then He will inform you
ila 'llāhi marjiʿu-kum jamīʿan fa-yunabbiʾu-kum
of what you used to do.
bi-mā kuntum taʿmalūn. (5:105)

O you who truly believe, you must take charge of your own selves.
yā ayyuha 'lladhīna āmanū ʿalai-kum anfusa-kum:

Allāh (Exalted is He) is speaking as One who is commanding His servants to improve themselves, and to do what is good, through their dedicated effort and worshipful obedience. He is also informing them that, if someone corrects his own condition, he will not be injured by the depravity of people whose behaviour is corrupt, whether he be close to home or far afield.

Ibn ʿAbbās (may Allāh be well pleased with him and his father) was commenting on this Qurʾānic verse, when he said: "Allāh (Exalted is He) is saying: 'Provided the servant obeys Me in all that I have enjoined upon him as lawful [*ḥalāl*], and in all that I have forbidden to him as unlawful [*ḥarām*], no harm can come to him from those who have gone astray, as long as he does what I have commanded him to do.'" Muqātil ibn Ḥayyān said likewise.

As reported by at-Tirmidhī, it was Abū Umayya ash-Shaʿyānī who said: "I once approached Abū Thaʿlaba al-Khashanī, and asked him: 'What do you make of this Qurʾānic verse?' He said: 'Which Qurʾānic verse?' so I said: 'The one in which Allāh (Exalted is He) says:

> O you who truly believe, you must take charge of your own selves.'
> *yā ayyuha 'lladhīna āmanū ʿalai-kum anfusa-kum.*

"He replied: 'By Allāh, you have put your question about it to a well-informed person! I once asked Allāh's Messenger (Allāh bless him and give him peace) about it, and he said:

> You must command one another to observe what is right and fair [*maʿrūf*], and forbid one another to do what is wrong and unfair [*munkar*], until the time comes when you see avarice obeyed, passion followed, worldly interest preferred, and every holder of an opinion infatuated with his own opinion. You must then take charge of yourself exclusively, and leave the common people to their own devices. Lurking behind you, there are days when the patient person is like someone holding live coals, and the worker is entitled to the reward of fifty men, all of them doing the work you are doing.

According one report, he was asked: "O Messenger of Allāh, does that mean the reward of fifty of our men, or fifty of theirs?." He said: "It means the reward of fifty of you!"[712]

As for his expression "avarice obeyed," avarice [*shuḥḥ*] is the ultimate degree of stinginess, while "obeyed" means that the person concerned is obedient to it. As for "passion [*hawā*]," that is the inclination of the lower self [*nafs*] towards shameful abominations, while "followed" means that the person concerned goes along with it. As for "worldly interest preferred," this is a way of saying that the person concerned gives this world priority over the Hereafter. As for "every holder of an opinion infatuated with his own opinion," it signifies that he is not impressed by someone else's opinion, and does not accept his advice.[713] As for the words of Allāh (Exalted is He):

> You must take charge of your own selves.
> *ʿalai-kum anfusa-kum.*

—that is to say: "You must preserve them from the contamination of acts of disobedience, and the persistent commission of sins, and you must be dedicated to their improvement."

Those who err cannot injure you if you are rightly guided.
lā yaḍurru-kum man ḍalla idha 'htadaitum:

In other words: "You cannot be harmed by the error of people of who go astray, as long as you are rightly guided." According to az-Zamakhsharī: "The Muslims used to wear themselves out with distress, through longing to see the unbelievers enter Islām, so they were told: "You must take charge of your own selves, by improving them, and walking with them on the path of right guidance. Their straying from your religion cannot harm you, provided you are rightly guided." As Allāh (Exalted is He) said to His Prophet (Allāh bless him and give him peace):

So do not let your soul expire in sighings for them.
fa-lā tadhhab nafsu-ka ʿalai-him ḥasarāt. (35:8)

It was Abu 's-Saʿūd who said: "Let no one suppose there to be any licence, in this Qurʾānic verse, for abandoning the duty to enjoin what is right and fair [*al-amr bi'l-maʿrūf*] and forbid what is wrong and unfair [*an-nahy ʿani 'l-munkar*], because criticism is an element of right guidance."

It is related of [Abū Bakr] the Champion of Truth (may Allāh be well pleased with him) that he said one day, from the pulpit: "O people, you read this verse, but you take it out of its proper context. I once heard Allāh's Messenger (Allāh bless him and give him peace) say:

If people see something wrong and unfair, and they do not change it, Allāh will include them in His chastisement."[714]

This is supported by the [previously quoted] Prophetic tradition [*ḥadīth*]:

When you see avarice obeyed....[715]

The most convincing of these statements, and the soundest of these interpretations, in our view of this verse, is this saying attributed to Abū Bakr aṣ-Ṣiddīq [the Champion of Truth]: "It calls for active obedience to Allāh, and the necessary performance of enjoining what is right and fair, forbidding what is wrong and unfair, and restraining the hand of the wrongdoer, because Allāh (Exalted is He) says:

And help one another to practise piety and true devotion.
wa taʿāwanū ʿala 'l-birri wa 't-taqwā. (5:2)

—and helping one another to practise piety and true devotion includes enjoining what is right and fair, forbidding what is wrong and unfair, and restraining the hand of the wrongdoer, until he desists from his wrongdoing."[716]

Concerning the reasons for the revelation of this Qur'ānic verse, there are several traditional accounts to be considered:

1. According to a report from al-Kalbī, on the authority of Ibn ʿAbbās (may Allāh be well pleased with him and his father): "When the Prophet (Allāh bless him and give him peace) accepted the tribute-tax [*jizya*] from the People of the Scripture, but accepted only Islām or the sword from the Arabs, the hypocrites reproached the believers for accepting the tribute-tax from some of the unbelievers, but not from others. This verse was therefore sent down, turning the blame against the critics, and giving the assurance:

> Those who err cannot injure you
> *lā yaḍurru-kum man ḍalla*

—if you are following right guidance."

2. The believers were sorely distressed by the persistence of the unbelievers in their unbelief and error, so they were told:

> You must take charge of your own selves.
> *ʿalai-kum anfusa-kum.*

They were thus assured that: "So long as you are committed to the improvement of your own selves, and to making them walk on the path of right guidance, the error of those in error:

> cannot injure you.
> *lā yaḍurru-kum.*

—nor can the ignorance of the ignorant."

3. They used to grieve for their kinsfolk, when they died in a state of unbelief, so they were forbidden to do that. The most plausible explanation is that of the commentator who said: "The unbelievers had been told:

> Come to what Allāh has revealed and to the Messenger!
> *taʿālaw ilā mā anzala 'llāhu wa ila 'r-Rasūli*

—but they said:

> Enough for us is that wherein we found our fathers.
> *ḥasbu-nā mā wajadnā ʿalai-hi ābā'a-nā.* (5:104)

—so Allāh (Exalted is He) then issued this verse." Its purpose is to make clear that the believers must not imitate them in this corrupt persuasion. They must be fully committed to their religion, and know that they cannot be harmed by the ignorance of those ignorant folk, so long as they are firmly rooted and established in their religion.[717]

It may be said: "From the obvious meaning of the Qur'ānic verse, one might assume that it is no longer necessary to enjoin what is right and fair, and to forbid what is wrong and unfair." There are several possible responses to this:

1. According to the majority opinion, that is not what the verse conveys. It simply requires, of the servant obedient to his Lord, that he should abstain from censuring the sins of the disobedient. As for the duty to enjoin what is right and fair, and to forbid what is wrong and unfair, that is firmly established by all the evidence.[718] Right guidance is not complete without the enjoining of what is right and fair, and the forbidding of what is wrong and unfair, so the abandonment thereof, when the ability is present, amounts to going astray.[719]

2. The verse is exclusively relevant to the case of those unbelievers who, as the believer well knows, are impervious to admonition and will never abandon their unbelief.

3. The verse is relevant to a particular situation, in which a person is afraid of the consequences for himself, or his merchandise, or his property, if he should engage in enjoining what is right and fair, and forbidding what is wrong and unfair. In a case like this, he must take charge of himself, knowing that no harm can come to him from the error of those in error, nor from the ignorance of the ignorant.[720]

To this I would add: Your responsibility is not to ensure right guidance, but simply to discharge your duty, as long as you have reason to think that sound advice will be accepted, rather than criticized. You must not invite contempt for the truth, because speaking the truth, in the presence of someone who does not acknowledge the truth, is tantamount to negative criticism of the truth.

> To Allāh you must all return;
> *ila 'llāhi marji'u-kum jamī'an*
> and then He will inform you of what you used to do.
> *fa-yunabbi'u-kum bi-mā kuntum ta'malūn.*

That is to say: "You are inevitably destined, as all creatures are inevitably destined, to return to Allāh, so that He may recompense you for your deeds."[721] This is a promise and a threat, aimed at the two parties concerned, and it serves notice that one person must not censure the sin of another.[722]

As for His injunction (Exalted is He):

> You must take charge of your own selves.
> *ʿalai-kum anfusa-kum.*

—it signifies: "You must concentrate on their purification and development," for:

> Successful indeed is he who causes it to grow in purity,
> *qad aflaḥa man zakkā-hā.*
> and a failure indeed is he who stunts its growth.
> *wa qad khāba man dassā-hā.* (91:9,10)

You must not become preoccupied, before attending to the purification of your own self, with the purification of the selves of your fellow creatures. You must not be misled by the wishes of other creatures, by what they say, by their good opinion of you, and by their currying favour with you. For the seeker, that is the poison of the present moment. As Allāh (Exalted is He) has said:

> And for every folk there is a guide.
> *wa li-kulli qawmin hād.* (13:7)

In our own day and age, this has escaped the people of authority, to the point where someone claims to be a Shaikh, though he has never been a pupil. He speaks as a Shaikh to the ignorant and the erring, from his own ignorance and error, eagerly desiring the spread of his fame and reputation, and seeking to attract large numbers of disciples. It is vital to beware of anyone like this. Allāh is the only Source of help![723]

These are my own comments:

As for the duty to enjoin what is right and fair, and to forbid what is wrong and unfair, it can only be neglected on account of sheer incapacity, because it is a form of worshipful service. The *muḥtasib* [someone who does his public duty] can feel the benefit thereof, just as he feels the benefit of physical worship. This benefit is received in proportion to the sincere devotion involved, the degree of dedication, and the extent of sympathetic concern for the Community. The *muḥtasib* is thus obliged to observe the rules of the Sacred Law, and to practise personal detachment, so that he may perfect his sincere devotion, and obtain his credentials and his spiritual reward.

O Allāh, grant us the ability to accomplish all that, for the sake of our master Muḥammad (Allāh bless him and give him peace). *Āmīn*. Peace be upon the Messengers, and praise be to Allāh, the Lord of All the Worlds. There is no might nor any power, except with Allāh, the All-High, the Almighty. May Allāh bless our master Muḥammad, his family and his Companions, and may He grant them peace.

The Forty-third Call

In the Name of Allāh, the All-Merciful, the All-Compassionate.
Bismi'llāhi 'r-Raḥmāni 'r-Raḥīm.

O you who truly believe,
let there be witnesses between you
yā ayyuha 'lladhīna āmanū shahādatu baini-kum
when death draws near to one of you,
idhā ḥaḍara aḥada-kumu 'l-mawtu
at the time of bequest—two [witnesses],
ḥīna 'l-waṣiyyati 'thnāni
just men from among you, or two others
dhawā ʿadlin min-kum aw ākharāni
from those who are not your own,
min ghairi-kum
in case you are travelling in the land
in antum ḍarabtum fi 'l-arḍi
and the calamity of death befalls you.
fa-aṣābat-kum muṣībatu 'l-mawt:
You shall empanel them both after the prayer,
taḥbisūna-humā min baʿdi 'ṣ-ṣalāti
and, if you doubt,
they shall be made to swear by Allāh:
fa-yuqsimāni bi'llāhi ini 'rtabtum
"We will not take a bribe,
lā nashtarī bi-hi thamanan
even if it were [offered by] a near kinsman,
wa law kāna dhā qurbā
nor will we hide the testimony of Allāh,
wa lā naktumu shahādata 'llāhi
for then we should be among the sinful."
innā idhan mina 'l-āthimīn.

But then, if it is ascertained
that both of them are guilty of sin,

fa-in ʿuthira ʿalā anna-huma ʾstaḥaqqā ithman
let two others take their place,
of those nearly concerned,
and let them swear by Allāh:
fa-ākharāni yaqūmāni
maqāma-humā mina ʾlladhīna ʾstaḥaqqa
ʿalai-himu ʾl-awlayāni fa-lʾ-yuqsimāni biʾllāhi
"Our testimony is truer
than their testimony
and we have not transgressed,
la-shahādatu-nā aḥaqqu min shahādati-himā
wa ma ʾʿtadainā
for then indeed we should be among the unjust."
innā idhan la-mina ʾẓ-ẓālimīn.

Thus it is more likely
that they will bear true witness
dhālika adnā an yaʾtū biʾsh-shahādati ʿalā wajhi-hā
or fear that after their oath
the oath [of others] will be taken.
aw yakhāfū an turadda aimānun baʿda aimāni-him:
So practise true devotion to Allāh, and listen.
wa ʾttaqu ʾllāha wa ʾsmaʿū:
Allāh does not guide the corrupt folk.
wa ʾllāhu lā yahdi ʾl-qawmi ʾl-fāsiqīn. (5:106–8)

You should know that Allāh (Exalted is He), having commanded personal responsibility by His saying:

> You must take charge of your own selves.
> *ʿalai-kum anfusa-kum.*

—has now commanded the responsible management of property, by His saying:

> O you who truly believe, let there be witnesses between you,
> *yā ayyuha ʾlladhīna āmanū shahādatu baini-kum*
> when death draws near to one of you, at the time of bequest.
> *idhā ḥaḍara aḥada-kumu ʾl-mawtu ḥīna ʾl-waṣiyyati.*

The experts are unanimously agreed that this Qurʾānic verse was revealed in the following context:

Tamīm ad-Dārī and his brother ʿAdī were both Christians. They set out for Syria, accompanied by Budail, the client of ʿAmr ibn al-ʿĀṣ, who was a Muslim Emigrant [*Muhājir*]. They set out on a trading expedition, but when they arrived in Syria, Budail fell ill, so he wrote a letter containing a list of everything he had with him. He placed it among the wares, and did not tell his companions about it. Then he gave them his last bequest, and instructed them to hand his property over to his family, on their return. Budail died, so they took from his possessions a flask made of silver, ornamented with gold and weighing three hundred *mithqāl*, and handed the rest of his property over to his family, as soon as they reached home. The members of his family conducted a search, and they discovered the document. It included a reference to the flask, so they said to Tamīm and ʿAdī: "Where is the flask?" They replied: "We do not know. Whatever he entrusted to us, we have handed it over to you." The family then brought the incident to the notice of Allāh's Messenger (Allāh bless him and give him peace), and Allāh (Exalted is He) promptly sent down this Qurʾānic verse.[724]

O you who truly believe, let there be witnesses between you
yā ayyuha 'lladhīna āmanū shahādatu baini-kum

That is to say: "O believers, when one of you is on the verge of death, and its symptoms are apparent, it is necessary for his testament to be witnessed."[725] In other words: "Witnessing must take place between you, for the simple reason that evidence is needed when litigation and quarrelling ensue."[726]

when death draws near to one of you
idhā ḥaḍara aḥada-kumu 'l-mawtu

This proves the strict necessity of the final bequest, and it serves notice that the bequest must not be regarded as a trivial matter. Since the time of death's approach is mentioned as the time of the bequest, it is clearly indicated that the bequest must be made at that time. The bequest is like death, in that neither can be postponed. Just as the person's death is inevitable, there can be no question of evading the bequest.[727]

two [witnesses], just men from among you,
[i] 'thnāni dhawā ʿadlin min-kum
or two others from those who are not your own
aw ākharāni min ghairi-kum

That is to say: "Let the bequest be witnessed by two just individuals from among the Muslims, or two from among the non-Muslims, if you cannot find two witnesses among yourselves."[728]

just men from among you
dhawā ʿadlin min-kum

The two must share both attributes. In other words: "They must be endowed with trustworthiness and intelligence, and they must also be from among your close relatives." That is because they are most aware of the circumstances of the deceased, most sincerely devoted to him, and most likely to consider what is in his best interest. Or the meaning may be: "from among the people of your religion, O company of the believers." This is part of a complete sentence, which includes the rule of witnessing the bequest both at home and on a journey.

or two others from those who are not your own
aw ākharāni min ghairi-kum

That is to say: "or the witnessing of two other just men, from among the strangers who are not your own relatives," or, "who are not from among the people of your religion, but from among the *ahl adh-dhimma* [non-Muslims protected by treaty]." Such was the rule at the beginning of Islām, when the very existence of the Muslims was at stake, especially on a journey, but then it was abrogated by His saying (Exalted is He):

and call to witness two just men among you.
wa ashhidū dhawai ʿadlin min-kum. (65:2)

—so the evidence of the *dhimmī* [protected non-Muslim] cannot be accepted against the Muslim, because of his lack of loyal friendship for the latter, since witnessing comes under the heading of loyal friendship.[729]

in case you are travelling in the land
in antum ḍarabtum fi 'l-arḍi
and the calamity of death befalls you.
fa-aṣābat-kum muṣībatu 'l-mawt:

That is to say: "if your final term draws near while you are on a journey, and death descends upon you,[730] and you have no close relatives or fellow Muslims with you to deal with the business of witnessing, as is usually the case during journeys, the witnessing between you may involve the witnessing of two others."[731]

In this Qur'ānic verse, Allāh (Exalted is He) has called death a calamity [*muṣība*]. While it is true that death is a terrible calamity and a major disaster, our religious scholars maintain that there is something even more serious. That is heedlessness of death, reluctance to remember it, failure to contemplate it, and failure to act in preparation for it. In death and its inevitability there is an admonition for those who take heed, and a lesson for those who take thought. The Prophet (Allāh bless him and give him peace) is reported as having said:

> If the beasts of the field knew what you know about death, you would not find one of them fat enough for you to eat.[732]

It is related that an Arab nomad was travelling on a camel of his, when the camel suddenly dropped down dead. The Bedouin dismounted from the corpse and started circling around it. Wondering what was wrong with it, he kept saying: "What is the matter with you? Why don't you get up? Why don't you start moving again? These limbs of yours are perfect, and all your organs are healthy. What is your problem? What used to get you up and going? What has brought you to the ground? What has stopped you from moving?" Then he left it and went away, pondering what had happened and wondering about his situation.[733]

> You shall empanel them both after the prayer
> *taḥbisūna-humā min ba'di 'ṣ-ṣalāti*

That is to say: "You shall appoint them both in the wake of the afternoon prayer [*ṣalāt al-'aṣr*], because that is the time when people gather together." That was the practice of Allāh's Messenger (Allāh bless him and give him peace), who exacted the oath from 'Adī and Tamīm in the wake of the afternoon prayer, beside the pulpit.[734]

> You shall empanel them both
> *taḥbisūna-humā*

The beginning of this sentence comes like an answer to the question: "What shall we do, if we have misgivings about the two witnesses?"[735]

> after the prayer
> *min ba'di 'ṣ-ṣalāti*

In other words: "in the wake of the afternoon prayer, which is the appropriate time for swearing them in, because it is the time when people gather together, and when the angels of the night encounter the angels of the day. It is also the time when the people of faith are most solemnly disposed to shun the false oath." It is related that the Prophet (Allāh bless him and give him peace) chose to administer the oath at that particular time of day.[736]

> and, if you doubt, they shall be made to swear by Allāh
> *fa-yuqsimāni bi'llāhi ini 'rtabtum*

That is to say: "They must be made to swear by Allāh, if you are suspicious and have misgivings about their testimony." According to Abu 's-Sa'ūd: "In other words, if the heir among you has misgivings about the two of them, suspecting treachery or that something may be taken from the legacy, you must detain them and make them swear by Allāh."[737] This only applies if they are both unbelievers. If they are both believers, no oath is required of them, because exacting an oath from a Muslim witness is not in accordance with the Sacred Law.[738]

> "We will not take a bribe,
> *lā nashtarī bi-hi thamanan*
> even if it were [offered by] a near kinsman."
> *wa law kāna dhā qurbā*

That is to say: "The two of them must swear by Allāh, saying: 'We will not be partial to anyone in our testimony, nor will we exchange the oath by Allāh for any worldly property.' In other words: 'We would not swear by Allāh falsely, for the sake of material gain, even if the person in whose favour we were swearing happened to be a close relative of ours.'"[739] The two of them are saying, in effect: "We would not accept any wealth for ourselves, as a substitute for the honour of His Name (Exalted is He), even if it involved consideration for our close relatives, since it involves something even more compelling than that, and of greater incentive to swearing falsely, that being our own self-preservation."[740]

> "nor will we hide the testimony of Allāh,
> *wa lā naktumu shahādata 'llāhi*
> for then we should be among the sinful."
> *innā idhan mina 'l-āthimīn.*

In other words: "nor will we hide the testimony that Allāh (Exalted is He) has commanded us to present. If we did that, we should be included among the sinful."[741] The testimony is ascribed to Him, for the simple reason that He has commanded its presentation and forbidden its concealment.[742]

> But then, if it is ascertained that both of them are guilty of sin
> *fa-in ʿuthira ʿalā anna-huma 'staḥaqqā ithman*

That is to say: "But if it is discovered, after they have sworn, that they are guilty of deceit or lying in their testimony...."[743]

It is related that, when the first verse was revealed, Allāh's Messenger (Allāh bless him and give him peace) performed the afternoon prayer, then summoned Tamīm and ʿAdī. He made them swear, beside the pulpit: "By Allāh—there is no god but He—we will not be found guilty of deceit concerning this article of wealth." Then, as soon as they had sworn, Allāh's Messenger (Allāh bless him and give him peace) let them go on their way. They concealed the flask for a certain period, but then it came to light.

On this point the experts have disagreed. According to some: "It was discovered in Mecca. After a long time had gone by, the two of them revealed the flask, and the news reached the tribe of Banī Sahm, who claimed it back from them. When the two of them said: 'We bought it from him,' the others said: 'Surely we asked you: "Did our companion sell you anything?" and you both said no.' The pair replied: 'We had no proof [of the purchase] and we did not want to be detected, so we resorted to concealment.' The story was then related to Allāh's Messenger (Allāh bless him and give him peace), so Allāh sent down:

> But then, if it is ascertained....
> *fa-in ʿuthira....*

"ʿUmar ibn al-ʿĀṣ and al-Muṭṭalib ibn Abī Rifāʿa, the two Sahmīs, thereupon stood up and swore by Allāh, in the wake of the afternoon prayer. The Messenger (Allāh bless him and give him peace) presented the flask to these two, and to the guardians of the deceased. Tamīm ad-Dārī used to say, after he had accepted Islām: 'Allāh and His Messenger have told the truth. I did take the flask, so I repent to Allāh (Exalted is He).'"

As reported by Ibn ʿAbbās (may Allāh be well pleased with him and his father): "That event remained hidden until Tamīm ad-Dārī accepted Islām. Then, when he became a Muslim, he told Allāh's Messenger (Allāh bless him and give him peace) about it. He said: 'I swore a false oath. My companion and I sold the flask for a thousand [coins] and shared the price.' He then handed over five hundred dirhams [silver coins] from his own pocket, took another five hundred from his companion, and presented the thousand to the guardians of the deceased."[744]

This is the import of the Qur'ānic verse: "If it is detected and established that the two witnesses have committed perjury, and that they are guilty of sin because of the false oath...."

> let two others take their place,
> *fa-ākharāni yaqūmāni maqāma-humā*
> of those nearly concerned
> *mina 'lladhīna 'staḥaqqa ʿalai-himu 'l-awlayāni*

That is to say: "Two other men, from among the heirs entitled to the legacy, should take the place of the two perjurious witnesses, and they should be two of those best qualified among those entitled to claim the inheritance."

> and let them swear by Allāh:
> *fa-l'-yuqsimāni bi'llāhi*
> "Our testimony is truer than their testimony
> *la-shahādatu-nā aḥaqqu min shahādati-himā*

In other words: "Let them swear by Allāh that their testimony is more truthful, and more worthy of being heard and considered, than their testimony, because they committed perjury."

> and we have not transgressed,
> *wa ma 'ʿtadainā*
> for then indeed we should be among the unjust."
> *innā idhan la-mina 'ẓ-ẓālimīn.*

That is to say: "and we have not transgressed in accusing the two of them of perjury. If we accused them falsely, we should be included among the unjust."[745]

According to al-Baiḍāwī, in his Qur'ānic commentary: "That is to say: 'We have not overstepped the truth in our testimony. If that were the case, and we had indeed transgressed, we should be included among those who substitute falsehood for the truth, or those who wrong themselves.' The two verses signify that, when the dying person wishes to make his bequest, he must call two just witnesses, members of his family or his religion, to witness his bequest. Alternatively, as a precaution, he may bequeath his property to the two of them directly. If he cannot find such a pair, due to being on a journey, two others of a different type [should be appointed]. Then, if any dispute and doubt should arise, the two must swear to the truthfulness of what they say, with the solemnity appropriate to the occasion.

"If it subsequently becomes apparent, by some symptom and suspicious indication, that they have lied, two others should swear an oath, from among the guardians of the diseased. This rule is abrogated if the two are witnesses, because the witness is not required to swear, and his oath is not contradicted by the oath of the heir. The rule is established, however, if the two are legal custodians. The oath is referred to the heirs, either because of evidence of perjury on the part of the legal custodians, or because of alteration to the claim."[746]

> Thus it is more likely that they will bear true witness
> *dhālika adnā an ya᾽tū bi'sh-shahādati ʿalā wajhi-hā*
> or fear that after their oath the oath [of others] will be taken.
> *aw yakhāfū an turadda aimānun baʿda aimāni-him:*

In other words: "That rule is more conducive to their bearing witness to the true facts, without alteration or substitution.[747] It makes them more likely to fear the torment of the Hereafter, on account of the false oath, or to fear public disgrace through the invalidation of their oaths, and the implementation of the oaths of the heirs. They will thus be dissuaded from committing the perjury that would result in such invalidation, since either kind of fear will have the desired effect, which is the bearing of true witness."[748]

> So practise true devotion to Allāh
> *wa 'ttaqu 'llāha*

In other words: "Be afraid of offending your Lord, and obey His commandment:[749] in your testimony, so that you do not distort it; in your oaths, so that you do not swear false oaths; in your trusts, so that you do not betray them; and in observing the rules prescribed by Allāh, so that you do not violate His legislation."

and listen
wa 'sma'ū

—to the admonitions you are receiving, with the ear of obedience and acceptance.

Allāh does not guide the corrupt folk
wa 'llāhu lā yahdi 'l-qawmi 'l-fāsiqīn.

—who depart from worshipful obedience. That is to say: "If you do not practise true devotion, and do not listen, you are corrupt, and Allāh does not guide the corrupt folk to the path of the Garden of Paradise, or to that in which your benefit resides."

You should know that bearing witness, in accordance with the Sacred Law, means giving information about a situation where the witnesses were present, and where they witnessed what occurred, either with their eyesight, in the case of actions, such as murder and adultery or fornication, or with their hearing, in cases like verbal contracts and confessions. It is not permissible, therefore, for a person to testify to something, unless he was present when it occurred, and understood it and heard it. This is why it is not permissible for him to provide testimony until he clearly recalls the event concerned. In the words of the Prophetic tradition [*ḥadīth*]:

You must treat your witnesses with great respect, for Allāh will use them to establish legal rights.

When someone is charged with the responsibility [of testifying], he is not allowed to refuse, if he is asked about something involving the forfeiture of legal rights, unless the right is upheld by some other means, such as documentary evidence produced by the person whose right is at issue. It is then permissible for him to refuse, because the right will not be forfeited because of his refusal. Where legal penalties [*ḥudūd*] are involved, he is free to choose between bearing witness and concealment, because, while the enforcement of legal penalties is a discretionary duty [*ḥisba*], concealment [of faults] is also a discretionary duty, and concealment is more meritorious. To quote another Prophetic tradition [*ḥadīth*]:

If someone veils the faults of a Muslim, Allāh will veil his faults in this world and the Hereafter.[750]

These are my own observations:

The subject of testimony [*shahāda*] is an extensive topic, which the religious scholars (may Allāh the Exalted bestow His mercy upon them) have discussed at length in the books of jurisprudence [*fiqh*]. As far as we are concerned, the most important point is truthfulness in word and deed, in all our transactions, wherever we may be. That is an essential requirement of faith, for the fulfilment of which our Lord (Blessed and Exalted is He) has made us a sure promise, for He has said:

> And [the Qur᾿ān] gives tidings to the believers
> *wa yubashshiru 'l-mu᾿minīna 'lladhīna*
> who do good works that theirs will be a great reward.
> *ya῾malūna 'ṣ-ṣāliḥāti anna la-hum ajran kabīrā.* (17:9)

In other words: "Give good tidings to those who believe in the Qur᾿ān, and who act in accordance with the rules and the requirement of faith, by letting them know that they will have a Garden of Paradise, whoever they may be, in whatever time and place." As He has said (Exalted is He):

> This is a day when their truthfulness profits the truthful.
> *qāla 'llāhu hādhā yawmu yanfa῾u 'ṣ-ṣādiqīna ṣidqu-hum.* (5:119)

—[meaning their truthfulness] in word and deed.

May Allāh preserve us, and all of you, from failure to comply with His commandment. We beg Him not to include us among those who waste the breaths of their lives. He is indeed the Enabling Helper, the Guide and the Ever-Giving One. Peace be upon the Messengers, and praise be to Allāh, the Lord of All the Worlds. There is no might nor any power, except with Allāh, the All-High, the Almighty. May Allāh bless our master Muḥammad, his family and his Companions, and may He grant them peace.

The Forty-fourth Call

In the Name of Allāh, the All-Merciful, the All-Compassionate.
Bismi'llāhi 'r-Raḥmāni 'r-Raḥīm.

O you who truly believe,
yā ayyuha 'lladhīna āmanū
when you meet those who disbelieve,
idhā laqītumu 'lladhīna kafarū
in a creeping advance,
zaḥfan
do not turn your backs on them.
fa-lā tuwallū-humu 'l-adbār.

Whoever on that day turns his back on them,
wa man yuwalli-him yawma'idhin dubura-hu
unless manoeuvering for battle
illā mutaḥarrifan li-qitālin
or joining forces with a company,
aw mutaḥayyizan ilā fi'atin
he has incurred wrath from Allāh,
fa-qad bā'a bi-ghaḍabin mina 'llāhi
and his habitation will be Hell,
wa ma'wā-hu Jahannam:
an awful journey's end.
wa bi'sa 'l-maṣīr.

You did not slay them, but Allāh slew them.
fa-lam taqtulū-hum wa lākinna 'llāhu qatala-hum
And it was not you who did the throwing,
wa mā ramaita
when you threw, but Allāh did the throwing,
idh ramaita wa lākinna 'llāha ramā.
that He might test the believers
by a fair test from Him.
wa li-yubliya 'l-mu'minīna min-hu balā'an ḥasanā:
Allāh is All-Hearing, All-Knowing.
inna 'llāha Samī'un 'Alīm. (8:15–17)

The Sūra of the Spoils [*al-Anfāl*] is one of the Medinan Sūras, which are concerned with legislation, particularly in connection with military campaigns [*ghazawāt*] and the sacred struggle [*jihād*] for Allāh's cause. It has dealt with some of the military perspectives that appeared in the wake of some of the campaigns, and it contains many legal rulings relating to warfare, as well as the Divine directives that must be followed by the believers in fighting their enemies. It covers both peace and war, including the rules of captivity and booty. In the course of the account of the events at Badr, Divine calls to the believers occur six times, referring to them specifically in terms of belief:

> O you who truly believe!
> *yā ayyuha 'lladhīna āmanū.*

—like an inducement for them to be patient and steadfast in their struggle with Allāh's enemies, and like a reminder that these obligations, which they have been commanded to fulfil, are the necessary requirements of the faith they have adopted, and that the victory they achieved was due to faith, not the multitude of weapons and men.

As for the first call [*nidā'*], it conveys the warning against fleeing from the battlefield, and the verses have threatened those who turn in flight before the enemy with the most dreadful torment, for He has said (Exalted is He):

> O you who truly believe,
> *yā ayyuha 'lladhīna āmanū*
> when you meet those who disbelieve,
> *idhā laqītumu 'lladhīna kafarū*
> in a creeping advance....
> *zaḥfan....*

In other words: "When you meet your unbelieving enemies massed together, as if, because of their great number, they are creeping [*yazḥfūna*] like a single body...."[751] (That is to say: "They are creeping on their buttocks, like a young boy moving along on his backside.") This is a sweeping instruction to the believers, applicable to all future battles and wars. It is inserted between the lines of the story [of Badr], in order to draw attention to it, and to urge its careful observance.

The term *zaḥf* [lit., creeping] means simply "advancing to the fight," regardless of whether the number involved is great or small. The movement is so called because it is usual at the encounter of the two parties, when each moves slowly towards the other. The meaning is: "When you meet the unbelievers, advancing to fight them, moving forward to combat them, or, each one of you walking towards his opposite number, do not turn your backs." The prohibition is aimed at that specifically, to make it clear that the encounter is the point at issue, and to express disgust at the very idea of retreating, since it is incompatible with that situation. To put it in a nutshell: "When you advance, you must not retreat."[752]

> do not turn your backs on them.
> *fa-lā tuwallū-humu 'l-adbār.*

That is to say: "Do not flee in front of them, but stand firm and be patient."[753] The overall meaning is: "O you who truly believe, when you meet your unbelieving enemies in battle, and they are a great host, while you are few in number, you must not turn your backs on them, let alone retreat in flight. You must face them squarely and fight them, even if you are very few, let alone when you are close or equal to them in number.[754] You must not expose your backs to them at close range."

Having forbidden this retreat in flight, Allāh (Exalted is He) has then declared that such retreat is unlawful, except in two cases:

1. When it is a combat manoeuvre, designed to make the enemy believe it is a rout, which then swings back against him. This is one of the techniques and stratagems of military deception.
2. When it is covered by His saying (Exalted is He):

> or joining forces with a company
> *aw mutaḥayyizan ilā fi'atin*

The point is that a company [*fi'a*] is a group [*jamā'a*], so, if the person joining it is a solitary individual, and the unbelievers are many, it stands to reason that, if he stays by himself, he will be killed to no avail. If he joins the group, on the other hand, he can hope to survive and tackle the enemy in force. Joining this company may therefore be strictly incumbent on him, let alone permissible. In short, retreat from the enemy is unlawful, except in these two cases.[755]

> Whoever on that day turns his back on them....
> *wa man yuwalli-him yawma'idhin dubura-hu....*

That is to say: "Whoever turns his back on them, taking flight on the day of the encounter...."

> unless manoeuvering for battle
> *illā mutaḥarrifan li-qitālin*

In other words: "except in the case of changing direction in order to fight another company, or retreating in preparation for a surprise attack, as a cunning stratagem to deceive the enemy." This is comes under the heading: "War is a deception."

> or joining forces with a company
> *aw mutaḥayyizan ilā fi᾽atin*

That is to say: "linking up with a group of Muslims, seeking salvation with them."

> he has incurred wrath from Allāh
> *fa-qad bā᾽a bi-ghaḍabin mina 'llāhi*

In other words: "he has incurred a terrible displeasure."

> and his habitation will be Hell
> *wa ma᾽wā-hu Jahannam:*

That is to say: "His abode and dwelling, to which he will finally arrive, will be the Fire of Hell."

> an awful journey's end.
> *wa bi᾽sa 'l-maṣīr.*

In other words: "That is an awful destination,[756] for he will incur a terrible wrath, of immeasurable dimensions.

As reported by the two Shaikhs [al-Bukhārī and Muslim] and others, on the authority of Abū Huraira (may Allāh be well pleased with him), the Prophet (Allāh bless him and give him peace) once said:

> Avoid the seven deadly sins!

When they asked: "O Messenger of Allāh, and what are they?" he replied:

> Associating partners [*shirk*] with Allāh (Exalted is He); witchcraft [*siḥr*]; taking a life that Allāh (Exalted is He) has made sacrosanct, except with legal right; the consumption of usury [*ribā*]; consuming the wealth of the orphan; and turning in flight on the day of the advance [*zaḥf*].

(It [turning in flight on the day of the advance] is listed in many of the Prophetic traditions [*aḥādīth*] concerning the major sins.)[757]

The religious scholars have disagreed on this subject. According to Abū Sa'īd al-Khudrī: "This refers specifically to the people of Badr, since it was not permissible for them to retreat on the Day of Badr, because the Prophet (Allāh bless him and give him peace) was with them, and they had no company to join, except the Prophet (Allāh bless him and give him peace). If they had withdrawn, they would have withdrawn to join the polytheists. Besides, it was the first military campaign undertaken by the Messenger himself (Allāh bless him and give him peace), and the Muslims were with him, so Allāh made retreat a very serious matter for them, and He declared it unlawful for them on the Day of Badr. As for occasions after that day, the Muslims formed separate companies, so a person in retreat could be joining a company, in which case his retreat would not be a major sin."

This is also the opinion of al-Ḥasan, Qatāda and aḍ-Ḍaḥḥāk. According to Yazīd ibn Abī Ḥabīb: "Allāh ordained the Fire for anyone who fled on the Day of Badr. Then, when it came to the Day of Uḥud, Allāh (Exalted is He) said:

> Satan alone it was who caused them to backslide,
> *inna-ma 'stazalla-humu 'sh-shaiṭānu*
> because of some of what they have earned.
> *bi-ba'ḍi mā kasabū*. (3:155)

Then came the Day of Ḥunain, so He said (Glory be to Him and Exalted is He):

> Then you turned back in flight!
> *thumma wallaitum mudbirīn*. (9:25)

Then:

> Then Allāh will relent towards whomever He will.
> *thumma yatūbu 'llāhu min ba'di dhālika 'alā man yashā'*. (9:27)

It was 'Abdu'llāh ibn 'Umar who said: "We were in an army, and Allāh's Messenger (Allāh bless him and give him peace) sent us on an expedition. The people beat a retreat, so we withdrew. We said: 'O Messenger of Allāh, we are the deserters [*farrārūn*],' but he replied: 'No, you are the attackers [*karrārūn*]. I am the company of the Muslims.'"[758]

According to ʿAṭāʾ ibn Abī Rubbāḥ: "This verse has been abrogated by His saying (Exalted is He):

> Now Allāh has lightened your burden.
> *al-āna khaffafa 'llāhu ʿan-kum* (8:66)"

A group of people may not flee from twice their own number, so it has been abrogated by that, except where this number is concerned. Most of the people of knowledge accept this opinion: If the Muslims are half as many as their enemy, it is not permissible for them to flee from them and turn their backs on them, but if the enemy is more than twice their number, it is permissible for them to flee from them. According to Ibn ʿAbbās: "If someone flees from three, he has not fled, but if someone flees from two, he has fled."[759]

> You did not slay them, but Allāh slew them.
> *fa-lam taqtulū-hum wa lākinna 'llāhu qatala-hum*

That is to say: "You did not kill them at Badr, O Muslims, with your own strength and power, but Allāh killed them by making you victorious over them, and by casting terror into their hearts."

> And it was not you who did the throwing, when you threw
> *wa mā ramaita idh ramaita*

In other words: "You did not throw, in actual fact. You, O Muḥammad, did not throw a handful of dust in the eyes of the people, because a handful of dust would not fill the eyes of a great army." It was Ibn ʿAbbās (may Allāh be well pleased with him and his father) who said: "Allāh's Messenger (Allāh bless him and give him peace) took a handful of dust, threw it in the faces of the polytheists, and said: 'May the faces be disfigured!' Not one of them escaped being struck in his eye and his nostrils by that throw, so they turned in retreat."

> but Allāh did the throwing.
> *wa lākinna 'llāha ramā.*

That is to say: "by causing that dust to reach them, so the matter in reality was from Allāh."[760]

This Qurʾānic verse was revealed when the Muslims boasted after their return from Badr. One of them would say: "I killed so-and-so, and I took so-and-so prisoner." Allāh therefore taught them proper behaviour, by His saying:

> You did not slay them
> *fa-lam taqtulū-hum*

The wisdom of His saying:

> You did not slay them
> *fa-lam taqtulū-hum*

—is that it serves as a lesson for some of the believers. As for the wisdom of His saying:

> And it was not you who did the throwing, when you threw
> *wa mā ramaita idh ramaita*

—it establishes that the throwing was a miraculous gift [*muʿjiza*] from Allāh to His Prophet, to be remembered as one of His many miracles, the telling of which He has commanded, for He has said (Exalted is He):

> And as for the blessing of your Lord, tell of it!
> *wa ammā bi-niʿmati Rabbika fa-ḥaddith.* (93:11)

Regarding the reason for the revelation of this Qurʾānic verse, there are several opinions:

1. Most of the commentators maintain that it was revealed on the Day of Badr, when the Prophet (Allāh bless him and give him peace) took a handful of gravel and threw it in the faces of the enemy, and that act of throwing was a cause of their defeat.

2. It was revealed on the Day of Khaibar. It is related that the Prophet (peace be upon him) took a bow, when he was at the gate of Khaibar, and shot an arrow. The arrow flew until it killed the son of Abu'l-Ḥaqīq, who was on his horse at the time, so down came the revelation:

> And it was not you who did the throwing [or shooting],
> *wa mā ramaita*
> when you threw [or shot]
> *idh ramaita*

3. It was revealed on the Day of Uḥud, in connection with the killing of Ubayy ibn Khalaf. Ubayy came to the Prophet (Allāh bless him and give him peace) with a decayed bone, and said: "O Muḥammad, who can revive this rotten bone?" He replied (blessing and peace be upon him):

> Allāh will revive it, then He will cause you to die. Then He will revive you, and then He will cause you to enter the Fire of Hell.

Ubayy was taken captive on the Day of Badr, then, when he was ransomed, he said to Allāh's Messenger (Allāh bless him and give him peace): "I have a horse, which I feed every day with a portion of grain, so that I may ride it when I come to kill you." To this he replied (blessing and peace be upon him):

> Oh no! I shall kill you, if Allāh so wills.

When the Day of Uḥud arrived, Ubayy advanced, riding that horse, until he drew near to the Messenger (Allāh bless him and give him peace). Some Muslim men opposed him, intending to kill him, but the Prophet (blessing and peace be upon him) said: "Wait!" He then threw a spear at him, and broke one of his ribs. Ubayy was carried away, and he died somewhere along the road. It was about this incident that the Qur'ānic verse was revealed. The soundest opinion, however, is that this verse was revealed on the Day of Badr.

On the strength of this verse, our colleagues, the people of the Sunna and the Community, have argued that the actions of His servants are creations of Allāh. The argument is centred on His saying (Exalted is He):

> You did not slay them, but Allāh slew them.
> *fa-lam taqtulū-hum wa lākinna 'llāhu qatala-hum*

It is known that they inflicted wounds, so this goes to prove that the occurrence of those actions came only from Allāh. Furthermore, His saying:

> And it was not you who did the throwing, when you threw
> *wa mā ramaita idh ramaita*

—has both established that he (Allāh bless him and give him peace) was a thrower, and denied that he was a thrower. The conclusion must therefore be that he did the throwing as an acquired act, not as an act of his own creativity.

As for His saying:

> You did not slay them, but Allāh slew them.
> *fa-lam taqtulū-hum wa lākinna 'llāhu qatala-hum*

—the following points may be raised:

1. The slaying of the unbelievers was only made easy by Allāh's help, assistance and support, so this qualification is valid.

2. They were responsible for the wounding, but the extraction of the spirit was Allāh's responsibility, so the inference is: "You did not cause them to die, but Allāh caused them to die." As for His saying:

> And it was not you who did the throwing, when you threw
> *wa mā ramaita idh ramaita*

—according to al-Qāḍī: "This raises several points, one of them being that a single throw would not cause the dust to reach their eyes, and only Allāh could cause the particles of dust to reach their eyes. Another is that the dust he threw was a very small amount, so it would be impossible for that quantity to reach all their eyes. This proves that Allāh (Exalted is He) must have added extra particles of dust, and caused them to reach their eyes. Yet another point is that, at the moment of his throwing, Allāh (Exalted is He) cast terror into their hearts, so the meaning of His saying:

> but Allāh did the throwing.
> *wa lākinna 'llāha ramā.*

—is that He (Exalted is He) threw that terror into their hearts.

The answer to these points is as follows: Everything that you have mentioned is inconsistent with the obvious meaning, and the basic principle in speech is the statement of fact. They have said: "For intellectual reasons, it is impossible to say that the action of the servant is a creation of Allāh (Exalted is He)." To this we object: "How absurd! From our point of view, both intellectual arguments and traditional proofs support the validity of our opinion, so we cannot deviate from the obvious meaning in favour of the metaphorical interpretation. Allāh knows best, of course."[761]

> that He might test the believers by a fair test from Him.
> *wa li-yubliya 'l-mu'minīna min-hu balā'an ḥasanā:*

That is to say: "He did that in order to defeat the unbelievers, and to bless the believers with the reward, the victory and the booty."

> Allāh is All-Hearing, All-Knowing.
> *inna 'llāha Samī'un 'Alīm.*

In other words: "He is All-Hearing of their spoken words, All-Seeing of their intentions and their spiritual states."[762]

The test [*balā'*] refers to both the blessing and the trial, because its root meaning is examination. In the case of the trial, it is designed to demonstrate patience, and in the case of the blessing, to demonstrate thankfulness. The examination by Allāh (Exalted is He) is designed to demonstrate what He knows, as He already knows, not to obtain knowledge of what He does not know, because lack of knowledge can never be attributed to Him (Exalted is He).

As the verse implies, the effect is from Allāh (Exalted is He), while the servant is merely an intermediate instrument. It is therefore improper for the believing man to take pride in himself and his work, and he is obliged to keep himself out of the picture. That is why He has said (Exalted is He):

> You did not slay them
> *fa-lam taqtulū-hum*

He has demonstrated His gracious treatment of them, and it is vain conceit to magnify righteous work, without mentioning His enabling grace [*tawfīq*].[763]

These are my own remarks:

If you contemplate the universe, you will discover the source of every disorder, outrage and sin afflicting Allāh's creatures, from the beginning of creation till the Day of Resurrection. You will find that source to be this lower self [*nafs*].

The very first act of disobedience to Allāh came from Iblīs, and its cause, after the primordial decree of destiny, was the passion of the lower self in its arrogance and envy. Then came the sin of Adam and Eve (peace be upon them). They succumbed to the desire of the lower self, and to their greed for perpetuity and life. That serves to prove that the lower self is the hardest thing to contend with, and the most hostile enemy. It can be resisted and controlled by three things only:

1. Curbing the carnal appetites, for the obstinate beast becomes tame when its fodder is in short supply.
2. Making it accustomed to worshipful service, because worshipful service makes the lower self humble.
3. Turning to Allāh (Exalted is He) for help, and humbly entreating Him to assist you, for otherwise there is no salvation:

> Surely the self is always inciting to evil,
> *inna 'n-nafsa la-ammāratun*
> except inasmuch as my Lord has mercy.
> *bi's-sū'i illā mā raḥima Rabbī.* (12:53)

You must remember that you stand before Allāh (Exalted is He), and He sees you, so appeal to Him for help, for He is the Most Merciful of the merciful. He has said in His clear Book:

> And as for those who strive in Our cause,
> *wa 'lladhīna jāhadū fī-nā*
> surely We shall guide them in Our ways.
> *la-nahdiyanna-hum subula-nā:*
> Allāh is surely with those who are active in goodness.
> *wa inna 'llāha la-ma'a 'l-muḥsinīn.* (29:69)

There is no power nor any strength except with Allāh, the All-High, the Almighty.

You must therefore beware of neglecting your lower self, and do not let it indulge in sinful acts of disobedience. This is necessary to secure salvation and triumph on the Day of Resurrection, as the Prophet (blessing and peace be upon him) once said:

> We have returned from the lesser struggle [*al-jihād al-aṣghar*] to the greater struggle [*al-jihād al-akbar*].[764]

Our Lord (Glorious and Exalted is He) has constantly forbidden us to flee and turn our backs towards the unbelievers. This relates to worldly affairs, though it is also relevant to the affairs of the Hereafter, such as bearing witness and exalting the Word of Allāh.

Hostility and resistance to the lower self, and waging war on the devil, are likewise a cause of everlasting good fortune for the believer. By means of that combat and resistance, the servant acquires the truthfulness on which Allāh confers His good pleasure. He has said (Exalted is He):

> Allāh is well pleased with them,
> *raḍiya 'llāhu 'an-hum*
> and they are well pleased with Him.
> *wa raḍū 'an-h:*
> That is the mighty triumph.
> *dhālika 'l-fawzu 'l-'aẓīm.* (5:119)

Its significance is mighty indeed, since He has described it as "the mighty triumph." He has also said (Exalted is He):

> Their recompense is with their Lord:
> *jazā'u-hum 'inda Rabbi-him*
> Gardens of Eden, beneath which rivers flow,
> *jannātu 'Adnin tajrī min taḥti-ha 'l-anhāru*
> dwelling therein forever.
> *khālidīna fī-hā abadā:*
> Allāh is well pleased with them,
> *raḍiya 'llāhu 'an-hum*
> and they are well pleased with Him.
> *wa raḍū 'an-h:*
> That is for anyone who fears his Lord.
> *dhālika li-man khashiya Rabba-h.* (98:8)

This description applies to those humble servants whose humble submission results in Allāh's good pleasure. We must adhere to the Book and the Sunna, since the fear of Allāh is established in the Book and the Prophetic Sunna. We beseech Allāh to include us among those described by Allāh in His saying:

> Successful indeed are the true believers
> *qad aflaḥa 'l-mu'minūn.*
> who are humble in their prayers.
> *alladhīna hum fī ṣalāti-him khāshi'ūn.* (23:1,2)

—and to preserve us from acts of sinful disobedience, through His grace, His safekeeping and His noble generosity. Weakness is our natural characteristic. Except through Him, we lack the power and the strength to observe His commandments and to avoid His prohibitions. Peace be upon the Messengers, and praise be to Allāh, the Lord of All the Worlds. May Allāh bless our master Muḥammad, his family and his Companions, and may He grant them peace.

The Forty-fifth Call

In the Name of Allāh, the All-Merciful, the All-Compassionate.
Bismi'llāhi 'r-Raḥmāni 'r-Raḥīm.

O you who truly believe,
obey Allāh and His Messenger,
yā ayyuha 'lladhīna āmanū aṭī'u 'llāha wa Rasūla-hu
and do not turn away from him when you hear.
wa lā tawallaw 'an-hu wa antum tasma'ūn.

Do not be like those who say: "We hear,"
wa lā takūnū ka-'lladhīna qālū sami'nā
though they do not hear.
wa hum lā yasma'ūn:

The worst of beasts in Allāh's sight
inna sharra 'd-dawābbi
are the deaf, the dumb, who have no sense.
'inda 'llāhi 'ṣ-ṣummu 'l-bukmu 'lladhīna lā ya'qilūn.

If Allāh had known of any good in them
wa law 'alima 'llāhu fī-him khairan
He would have made them hear,
la-asma'a-hum:
but if He had made them hear,
wa law asma'a-hum
they would have turned away, averse.
la-tawallaw wa hum mu'riḍūn. (8:20–3)

In this, the second call [*nidā'*] from the Sūra of the Spoils of War [*al-Anfāl*], comes the order to hear and to obey the commandment of Allāh and the commandment of His Messenger. Just as other noble Qur'ānic verses have depicted the unbelievers as grazing cattle, who do not hear, do not pay attention, and do not respond to the summons of the Lord of Truth,[765] Allāh (Exalted is He) has now said:

O you who truly believe, obey Allāh and His Messenger,
yā ayyuha 'lladhīna āmanū aṭī'u 'llāha wa Rasūla-hu
and do not turn away from him when you hear.
wa lā tawallaw 'an-hu wa antum tasma'ūn.

—with the elision of one of the two *tā*'s [from the regular form of the verb ***tata**wallaw*]. In other words: "Do not turn away [*lā tatawallaw*]:

from him
'an-hu

—that is to say, from the Messenger (blessing and peace be upon him)." He did not say: "from them both [*'an-humā*]," because obedience to Allāh can only be through obedience to His Messenger.

when you hear.
wa antum tasma'ūn.

In other words: "when the situation is such that you are hearing the Qur'ān pronounce the necessity of obedience to him, and the stern admonitions against opposing him, with the hearing of understanding and belief."[766]

Allāh (Exalted is He) has already said, in the preceding Qur'ānic verse:

If you are seeking victory,
in tastaftiḥū
victory has already come to you.
fa-qad jā'a-kumu 'l-fatḥ:
And if you cease it will be better for you,
wa in tantahū fa-huwa khairun la-kum:
but if you return, We also shall return,
wa in ta'ūdū na'ūd:
and your host will avail you nothing,
wa lan tughniya 'an-kum fi'atu-kum shai'an
however numerous it may be.
wa law kathurat
And [know] that Allāh is with the believers.
wa anna 'llāha ma'a 'l-mu'minīn. (8:19)

Abū Jahl said, on the Day of Badr: "O Allāh, whoever of us has been most immoral, and most disruptive of the ties of kinship, destroy him today!" Allāh then sent down:

If you are seeking victory,
in tastaftiḥū
victory has already come to you.
fa-qad jā'a-kumu 'l-fatḥ:

—so Abū Jahl was the one seeking victory.

> And if you cease it will be better for you
> *wa in tantahū fa-huwa khairun la-kum:*

That is to say: "And if you make amends, O tribe of Quraish, for waging war against the Messenger and treating him with hostility, and for disbelieving in Allāh and His Messenger, it will be better for you in your worldly and your Otherworldly life."

> but if you return, We also shall return
> *wa in taʿūdū naʿūd:*

In other words: "If you return to waging war against him and fighting him, We shall help him to triumph over you."

> and your host will avail you nothing,
> *wa lan tughniya ʿan-kum fiʾatu-kum shaiʾan*
> however numerous it may be.
> *wa law kathurat*

That is to say: "Your combined force, on which you rely for support, will not afford you any protection from the torment of this world, however numerous your assistants and helpers may be."

> And [know] that Allāh is with the believers.
> *wa anna 'llāha maʿa 'l-muʾminīn.* (8:19)

In other words: "Allāh (Glory be to Him and Exalted is He) is with the believers in providing help, assistance and support." He has said:

> O you who truly believe, obey Allāh and His Messenger
> *yā ayyuha 'lladhīna āmanū aṭīʿu 'llāha wa Rasūla-hu*

—meaning: "Persist in obedience to Allāh and obedience to His Messenger, for then you will continue to enjoy the might and glory achieved at Badr."

> and do not turn away from him
> *wa lā tawallaw ʿan-hu*

In other words: "Do not reject him by opposing his command."

> when you hear
> *wa antum tasmaʿūn.*

—the Qurʾān and the admonitions.[767]

The sacred struggle [*jihād*] involves two things: (1) putting oneself at risk, and (2) the sacrifice of possessions. Putting oneself at risk is extremely painful for everyone, and forsaking material wealth, after having the power to obtain it, is also extremely painful. Allāh (Exalted is He) has undoubtedly gone to great lengths in imposing discipline in this context, for He has said:

> Obey Allāh and His Messenger
> *aṭīʿu 'llāha wa Rasūla-hu*

—in compliance with the demands of the sacred struggle, and in compliance with the abandonment of wealth, when Allāh commands its abandonment. The purpose is to confirm what we have mentioned in the commentary on His saying (Exalted is He):

> Say: "The spoils belong to Allāh and the Messenger."
> *quli 'l-anfālu li'llāhi wa 'r-Rasūl.* (8:1)

The question may be asked: "Why has He said:

> and do not turn away from him
> *wa lā tawallaw ʿan-hu*

—using the singular pronoun, when He has just mentioned both Allāh and His Messenger?" Our response to this will be: "Allāh (Exalted is He) has commanded obedience to Allāh and obedience to His Messenger, then He has said:

> and do not turn away...
> *wa lā tawallaw...*

—because turning away is meaningful only in relation to the Messenger (Allāh bless him and give him peace), in the sense that they may reject him, refuse to accept his word, and refrain from assisting him in the sacred struggle."[768]

> Do not be
> *wa lā takūnū*

—in noncompliance with the commandment and the prohibition:

> like those who say: "We hear"
> *ka-'lladhīna qālū samiʿnā*

—as an expression of acceptance:

> though they do not hear
> *wa hum lā yasmaʿūn:*

—for the purpose of acceptance, but only for the purpose of denial and rejection, like the unbelievers who said: "We hear and we disobey," and like the hypocrites who claim hearing and acceptance with their tongues, while secretly harbouring unbelief and refutation.[769]

In other words: "Do not be like the unbelievers, who hear with their ears, but not with their hearts. Their hearing is like not hearing, because the purpose of hearing is to reflect and take advice."[770] The point is that the human being is incapable of accepting the imposition of responsibility, and assuming it as a duty, unless he has first heard it. Allāh has therefore used hearing as a metonym for acceptance. This is reminiscent of the expression [uttered in the course of the ritual prayer]:

> Allāh hears anyone who praises Him.[771]
> *samiʿa 'llāhu li-man ḥamida-h.*

> The worst of beasts
> *inna sharra 'd-dawābbi*

That is to say: "The worst of that which crawls [*dabba*] upon the earth," assuming that the term *dābba* [singular of *dawābb*] is used in its strict linguistic sense, or: "The worst of beasts [*bahā'im*]," if it is meant to be understood in its colloquial sense. The term *bahīma* [singular of *bahā'im*] applies to any four-legged animal of the land or the sea.

> in Allāh's sight
> *ʿinda 'llāhi*

In other words: "in His judgment and His decree."

> the deaf
> [*i*] 'ṣ-ṣummu

—are those who do not hear the truth.

> the dumb
> [*u*] *'l-bukmu*

—are those who do not speak the truth.

> [those] who have no sense.
> [*u*] *'lladhīna lā yaʿqilūn.*

—are those who do not understand the truth.

Allāh has counted them among the beasts, and He has also called them the worst thereof, because they have wantonly squandered their potential for distinction and superiority. He has described them as devoid of intelligence because the deaf and the dumb, if they have any sense, can sometimes understand certain matters and explain them to others in sign language, thereby achieving some of their goals. As for those who are also senseless, nothing could be worse than their condition.[772]

The verse was revealed in connection with a group from the Banī ʿAbd ad-Dār, who used to say: "We are 'deaf, dumb, blind,' according to Muḥammad." They were bent on fighting the Messenger (Allāh bless him and give him peace), together with Abū Jahl.

The verse contains the utmost blame for the unbelievers, since it describes them as worse than dogs, pigs and donkeys, because they have not availed themselves of their faculties, and have thus become more contemptible than every vile creature.[773]

> If Allāh had known of any good in them
> *wa law ʿalima 'llāhu fī-him khairan*

That is to say: "[If He had recognized] anything of the kind of goodness that would have included their making efforts to discover the truth and follow right guidance."

> He would have made them hear
> *la-asmaʿa-hum*:

—with the hearing of understanding and reflection. They would then have grasped the true significance of the Messenger (Allāh bless him and give him peace), and they would have obeyed him and believed in him.[774] The conjunctive particle *wa* [in *wa law ʿalima*] conveys the sense of: "But there is no good in them, so He did not make them understand."[775]

The point is that, for anything to be extant, Allāh must know of it, so the absence of Allāh's knowledge of its existence is a necessary cause of its non-existence. Its non-existence *per se* is therefore undoubtedly well expressed in terms of the absence of Allāh's knowledge of its non-existence.

The import of the statement is as follows: "If any good had been extant in them, Allāh would have made them hear the convincing arguments and the admonitions, with the hearing of education and instruction. If He had made them hear, after He knew that there was no good in them, they would have derived no benefit thereby, and:

> they would have turned away, averse."[776]
> *la-tawallaw wa hum muʿriḍūn.*

To this I would add: This rather clumsy interpretation hinges on the precise signification of the conditional particle *law* [if], as defined by the grammarians, because it is used when the condition is impossible. If you wish for a detailed explanation, you will need to study the books of Qurʾānic exegesis [*tafsīr*].

> but if He had made them hear
> *wa law asmaʿa-hum*

—with the hearing of comprehension, while they were in this state, entirely bereft of goodness:

> they would have turned away
> *la-tawallaw*

—from the truth that they heard, and they would never have derived any benefit from it; or else they would have apostasized after having believed, and would have come to be as if they had not heard it at all.

> [they being] averse.
> *wa hum muʿriḍūn.*

That is to say: "They would have turned their backs, since they were averse in their hearts to what they heard, and because of their obstinacy."[777] In other words: "Supposing that Allāh made them hear, even though He knew that there was no good in them, they would have turned away, being averse to Him, in disbelief and stubbornness."[778] This contains some consolation for the Prophet (blessing and peace be upon him), to relieve his concern over the unbelievers' lack of faith.[779] It also indicates that, if someone is doomed to misfortune, he will turn away from following the spiritual path, shunning Allāh and the quest for Him, and devoting himself to this world and its vanities.

You should know that the human being was created:

> in fairest stature
> *fī aḥsani taqwīm.* (95:4)

—susceptible to training and development, equipped for a perfection that cannot be attained by the angel brought near. At the outset, his natural constitution is below the angelic and above the animal level, but then, through the training of the Sacred Law, he comes to be superior to the angels, and thus becomes the best of all creatures. On the other hand, through noncompliance with the Sacred Law, and following passionate desire, he comes to be lower than the animals, and so becomes the worst of all creatures. The state of someone who is better than the angels may thus be converted into that of the worst of the beasts.

The intelligent person must therefore refrain from disobeying the commandment of the Messenger (Allāh bless him and give him peace) and his Sacred Law. The animals are submissive to his command, so how can it be otherwise in the case of the human being? It is related that a man came to him, during one of his travels (Allāh bless him and give him peace), and said: "O Messenger of Allāh, I once had a compound in which I and my dependants lived our lives. I also kept two camels there, of the kind employed in drawing water, but they have denied me access to themselves, and to my enclosure and everything in it. We simply cannot approach the pair of them."

The Prophet (Allāh bless him and give him peace) and his Companions promptly set out. When they reached the compound, he said to its owner: "Open up!" The man said: "They are a terrible menace," but he said again: "Open up!" As soon as he moved the gate, the two beasts came towards it, making a tumultuous commotion. Then, when the gate stood ajar, they looked at the Prophet (Allāh bless him and give him peace) and knelt down, then bowed in prostration. Allāh's Messenger (Allāh bless him and give him peace) took hold of their heads, then handed them over to their owner, saying: "Put them to work, and treat them well!" The people present said: "The beasts prostrate themselves before you, so will you not permit us to make prostration before you, too?" He replied (Allāh bless him and give him peace):

> Prostration [*sujūd*] is appropriate only before the Ever-Living, the Self-Sustaining One [*al-Ḥayy al-Qayyūm*]. If I were to command anyone to bow in prostration before anyone else, I would command the wife to prostrate herself before her husband.

In whatever the Prophet (peace be upon him) commanded or forbade, there is a wisdom and a benefit. You are not commanded to inquire about it, but simply obliged to obey and comply.[780]

Where obedience to Allāh is concerned, people are of several types: One type is obedient for fear of His chastisement. One type is obedient in hope of His reward. Another is obedient to prove his servitude to Him, and yet another to show reverence for His Lordship. How great is the difference between one obedient type and another![781]

How can you feel satisfied with yourself? If a physician said to you: "If you eat salt, it will do you harm, so you must give it up," you would believe what he told you, but you do not believe the master of humankind (Allāh bless him and give him peace), with regard to the information he gives you. Laziness makes you sluggish in performing what he has commanded you to do, though you must realize that he (blessing and peace be upon him) is able to disclose all the secrets and all the wisdom in the universe, as he has said of himself:

> I have mastered the knowledge of the ancients and the moderns.

When Allāh extracted you from the loins of Adam, at the station of "Am I not [your Lord]?" you were reduced to the lowest of the low. Then you were summoned from it, by the faith bestowed upon you through the gracious favour of Allāh, so that you might ascend, through your effort and your endeavour, to the highest of the high. It all depends on your capability, and two things are necessary to make that possible:

1. Love for Allāh's Messenger (Allāh bless him and give him peace), and giving his love priority over yourself, your family and your material wealth.

2. Loyal obedience to him (Allāh bless him and give him peace) in all that he has commanded and forbidden. Your fitness will be established thereby, and, through the perfection of your loyal obedience, you will obtain promotion to the pinnacle of perfection. The symptoms of love include fondness for the Qur'ān and fondness for its recitation. If these are lacking in a person, he is one of those who are averse to travelling his path (Allāh bless him and give him peace). The completeness of love for him includes preference for poverty and abstinence from this world.[782]

O Allāh, preserve us from the dangers of destruction, and include us among those who embark upon the best of courses!

These are my own remarks:

O believing brother, it is incumbent upon you to obey the commandment of Allāh and His Messenger (Allāh bless him and give him peace), and to adhere to the Prophetic Sunna and the Muḥammadan Law, so that you may be distinguished by their blessed grace from the animals and the beasts.

Many of the believing people are equipped with preparedness, but they do not activate their preparedness. Instead, their lower selves remain attached to their personal pleasures and the vanities of this world. They neglect this preparedness, which Allāh has installed within them to ready them for the reception of good benefits and Lordly directions. They will be questioned about this preparedness on the Day of Resurrection. It is incumbent upon us to cling to the means of access, which is obedience and compliance with the commandment of Allāh and the commandment of His Messenger (on him be the most excellet blessing and the most perfect salutation). Even if we do not progress to the stations of the consummate saints [*awliyā'*], let us at least be secure from the tribulation of this world and the torment of the Hereafter. Allāh (Exalted is He) has said:

> The day when neither wealth nor sons will avail [any man],
> *yawma lā yanfa'u mālun wa lā banūn:*
> except one who comes to Allāh with a whole heart.
> *illā man ata 'llāha bi-qalbin salīm.* (26:88,89)

O Allāh, grant us the ability to accomplish all that. *Āmīn.* Peace be upon the Messengers, and praise be to Allāh, the Lord of All the Worlds. There is no might nor any power, except with Allāh, the All-High, the Almighty. May Allāh bless our master Muḥammad, his family and his Companions, and may He grant them peace.

The Forty-sixth Call

In the Name of Allāh, the All-Merciful, the All-Compassionate.
Bismi'llāhi 'r-Raḥmāni 'r-Raḥīm.

O you who truly believe,
respond to Allāh and the Messenger
yā ayyuha 'lladhīna āmanu 'stajībū li'llāhi wa li'r-Rasūli
when he calls you to that which brings you to life.
idhā da'ā-kum li-mā yuḥyī-kum:
And know that Allāh comes in between the man
wa ''lamū anna 'llāha yaḥūlu baina 'l-mar'i
and his own heart,
wa qalbi-hi
and that it is He to whom you will be gathered.
wa anna-hu ilai-hi tuḥsharūn.

And guard yourselves against a chastisement
wa 'ttaqū fitnatan
which cannot fall on those
lā tuṣībanna 'lladhīna
of you who are wrongdoers exclusively,
ẓalamū min-kum khāṣṣa:
and know that Allāh is Severe in punishment.
wa ''lamū anna 'llāha Shadīdu 'l-'iqāb. (8:24,25)

As Allāh has explained in this, the third Call from the Sūra of the Spoils [*al-Anfāl*], that to which the Messenger (Allāh bless him and give him peace) summons the believers is their life, their honour and glory, and their good fortune in this world and the Hereafter.[783]

Allāh (Exalted is He) has already described the unbelievers, likening them to roaming cattle, because they have refused to accept the summons of Allāh. He has now commanded the believers to respond to Allāh and the Messenger, and to accept his summons, in which there is life for their hearts, and the prospect of perfect happiness in this world and the Hereafter, for He has said:[784]

> O you who truly believe, respond to Allāh and the Messenger
> *yā ayyuha 'lladhīna āmanu 'stajībū li'llāhi wa li'r-Rasūli*
> when he calls you to that which brings you to life.
> *idhā daʿā-kum li-mā yuḥyī-kum.*

That is to say: "Answer the call of His Messenger (Allāh bless him and give him peace), when he calls you to the faith by which souls are enlivened, and by which you will live the life everlasting." According to al-Qatāda: "This refers to the Qur'ān, in which there is life, confidence, salvation and safekeeping in this world and the Hereafter."[785]

The repetition of the call, combined with their depiction in terms of belief, is intended to encourage them to comply with the commandments that are about to follow, and to alert them to the fact that it is in their own interest to do so.

> O you who truly believe, respond to Allāh and the Messenger
> *yā ayyuha 'lladhīna āmanu 'stajībū li'llāhi wa li'r-Rasūli*

—with the best of worshipful obedience:

> when he calls you
> *idhā daʿā-kum*

That is to say: "When the Messenger (Allāh bless him and give him peace) calls you," since he is the conveyer of the summons of Allāh (Exalted is He), as we have indicated above.

> to that which brings you to life.
> *li-mā yuḥyī-kum.*

In other words: "to that which will cause you to inherit everlasting life in permanent bliss," meaning the religious doctrines and practices, or the sacred struggle, by which Allāh (Exalted is He) has honoured you after abasement, strengthened you after weakness, and protected you from your enemy after defeat." Abū Muslim said: "[It means] the Garden of Paradise."[786]

In support of this interpretation of this Qur'ānic verse, we may cite the following report of Abū Huraira (may Allāh be well pleased with him):

"The Prophet (Allāh bless him and give him peace) once passed by the door of Ubayy ibn Kaʿb, so he gave him a call. Ubayy was performing his ritual prayer, so he made haste to conclude it, then came to the door. When the Prophet asked: 'What kept you from answering me?' he replied: 'I was praying.' The Prophet then said: 'Have you not been informed of what was conveyed to me by inspiration: "Respond to Allāh and the Messenger"?' Ubayy said: 'Whenever you summon me, I shall certainly answer you!'"[787]

The relevant point is that, when the Prophet (Allāh bless him and give him peace) summoned Ubayy, and he did not answer him, he blamed him for his failure to respond, and he justified that blame by quoting this Qur'ānic verse. If this verse did not prove the strict necessity [of responding], that justification would be invalid.

When does an imperative expression impose a strict obligation? According to some legal experts, this is a matter requiring categorical proof, so it is not permissible to draw a definitive conclusion from a single traditional report [*khabar*]. This argument is weak, however, because we do not concede that that categorical proof is required, in order to determine that an imperative expression imposes a strict obligation. In our opinion, it is a matter of reasonable conjecture, because the object here is a course of action, and reasonable proofs are sufficient, where practical requirements are concerned.[788]

As for His saying (Exalted is He):

> when he calls you to that which brings you to life.
> *idhā daʿā-kum li-mā yuḥyī-kum.*

—this refers to several kinds of vitalizing factors:

1. The religious sciences, for they are the life of the heart, whereas ignorance is its death. As we are told in the traditional report [*khabar*], Allāh (Exalted is He) will surely bring the dead heart to life, just as He revives the dead earth with the downpour of rain. The lawful religious sciences are Qur'ānic commentary [*tafsīr*], the Prophetic tradition [*ḥadīth*], the sources [*uṣūl*], jurisprudence [*fiqh*], and the obligatory duties [*farā'iḍ*].

2. Religious beliefs and practices, for they bequeath eternal life in everlasting bliss.

3. The sacred struggle [*jihād*], for it is the means of survival, since, if

they were to abandon it, the enemy would overwhelm them and kill them. As Allāh (Exalted is He) has said:

> And there is life for you in retaliation.
> *wa la-kum fi 'l-qiṣāṣi ḥayātun.* (2:179)[789]

And know that Allāh comes in between the man
wa 'ʿlamū anna 'llāha yaḥūlu baina 'l-marʾi
and his own heart.
wa qalbi-hi

That is to say: "Allāh (Exalted is He) is the Manager of all things. He manages the heart however He will, in ways of which its owner is incapable. He may cancel his decisions, alter his objectives, and inspire him with His guidance, or He may cause his heart to swerve aside from the right path." In the words of the Prophetic tradition [*ḥadīth*]:

> O Transformer of hearts, make my heart firmly committed to Your religion![790]

It was Ibn ʿAbbās (may Allāh be well pleased with him and his father) who said: "He intervenes between the believer and unbelief, and between the unbeliever and belief."[791]

To this I would add: If you pay attention to your heart, O believer, you will find that it is not committed, for less than an instant, to a particular state, whether of worshipful service or anything else. How, then, can you trust and rely on yourself, when you are in this condition of weakness? You must seek refuge with your Lord, and leave your own power and strength.

In short, the fortunate person is he whom Allāh blesses with good fortune, while the unhappy wretch is he whom Allāh sends astray. All hearts are in Allāh's hand; He controls them however He will. This is reported on the authority of Ibn ʿAbbās and aḍ-Ḍaḥḥāk (may Allāh be well pleased with them).[792] According to Abū Ḥayyān: "That contains an inducement to vigilant awareness, fear of Allāh (Exalted is He), and alacrity in responding to Him (Glorious and Exalted is He)."[793]

> And know that Allāh comes in between the man
> *wa 'ʿlamū anna 'llāha yaḥūlu baina 'l-marʾi*
> and his own heart.
> *wa qalbi-hi*

This is an allegorical depiction of His extreme nearness to His servant, comparable to His saying:

> And We are nearer to him than the jugular vein.
> *wa Naḥnu aqrabu ilai-hi min ḥabli 'l-warīd.* (50:16)

It is a reminder that He is Aware of the hidden contents of all hearts, including things of which their owners may be heedless. It may also be an incentive to hastening the dedication and purification of the heart, before Allāh brings death or something else between a person and his heart.[794] In this poor beggar's opinion, it is closer to the meaning:

> and that it is He to whom you will be gathered.
> *wa anna-hu ilai-hi tuḥsharūn.*

In other words: "and that it is He (Glory be to Him) who is your point of return and your journey's end, so He will recompense you for your actions,[795] and He will reward you in keeping with the soundness of your hearts and the sincerity of your worshipful obedience."[796]

> And guard yourselves against a chastisement
> *wa 'ttaqū fitnatan*
> which cannot fall on those of you who are wrongdoers
> *lā tuṣībanna 'lladhīna ẓalamū min-kum*
> exclusively.
> *khāṣṣa:*

That is to say: "And beware of the onslaught of Allāh and His vengeance, if you disobey His commandment. Beware of a chastisement which, if it descends upon you, will not be confined to the wrongdoer exclusively, but will affect you all. You will be linked to the righteous and the unrighteous, because the wrongdoer will perish because of his wrongdoing and his sinful disobedience, while the non-wrongdoer will perish because of his failure to restrain the wrongdoer, and his failure to speak out against him." In the words of the Prophetic tradition [*ḥadīth*]:

> If people notice the wrongdoer, but do not grab hold of his hands, it is likely that Allāh will include them in his torment.[797]

According to Ibn al-ʿAbbās (may Allāh be well pleased with him and his father): "Allāh has commanded the believers not to let reprehensible conduct continue behind their backs, for Allāh will include them in the torment, which will afflict both the wrongdoer and the non-wrongdoer."

Tradition tells us that, when sinful error is common in the land, if someone is present when it is committed, and he expresses disapproval of it, he is like someone who is absent from it. As for someone who is absent when it is committed, but approves of it, he is like someone who is present when it is committed. We know of several traditions to the same effect. If you are aware of that, you will not see any contradiction with His saying (Exalted is He):

> And one burdened soul does not bear the burden of another.
> *wa lā taziru wāziratun wizrā ukhrā.* (6:164)

—since you will understand that, when someone is silent in the face of reprehensible conduct, he will be chastised for his own burden of sin, not for the burden of the immediate offender.[798]

Suppose you raise the question: "It is clear that His saying (Exalted is He):

> And guard yourselves against a chastisement
> *wa 'ttaqū fitnatan*
> which cannot fall on those of you who are wrongdoers
> *lā tuṣībanna 'lladhīna ẓalamū min-kum*
> exclusively.
> *khāṣṣa:*

—applies to the wrongdoer and the non-wrongdoer, as previously explained, but how can it be compatible with the mercy of Allāh, and His noble generosity, for Him to inflict chatisement on someone who has not sinned?"

This will be my reply: "Allāh (Exalted is He) is the Sovereign of sovereignty and the Creator of all creatures. They are His servants, and in His sovereignty He deals with them as He will.

> He shall not be questioned as to what He does,
> *lā yus'alu 'ammā yaf'alu*
> but they shall be questioned.
> *wa hum yus'alūn.* (21:23)

"That is appropriate for Him, therefore, in the exercise of sovereign power, or because He (Exalted is He) knows that it contains various kinds of benefit. Allāh knows best what His purpose is, of course!"[799]

To this answer I would add: Allāh (Exalted is He) is fully Aware of what is in the hearts of the believers, whether it be approval of that wrongdoing, or disapproval thereof. If someone is afflicted by worldly temptation and surrounded by corruption, but he adheres to the Book and the Sunna and practises true devotion to Allāh, while remaining constant in his aversion to those evils and his disapproval of them, even though he cannot prevent them, he will enjoy the reward of those who patiently endure, in the belief that Allāh is the Sovereign of sovereignty and that they are His servants. It does not befit His mercy and His justice (Glorious and Exalted is He), that He should chastise him in the Hereafter for the wrongdoing of the wrongdoers, despite his aversion to that wrongdoing and his disapproval of it. Far from being chastised, he will be rewarded and recompensed for his patient endurance of these tribulations:

1. In this world, [he will be rewarded] with Allāh's togetherness [*maʿiyya*] and His help, in accordance with His saying (Exalted is He):

> Surely Allāh is together with those who are patient.
> *inna 'llāha maʿa 'ṣ-ṣābirīn.* (2:153)

2. In the Hereafter, in the Garden of Paradise, he will obtain the reward of those who patiently endure, in accordance with His saying (Exalted is He):

> Surely the patiently enduring will be paid their wages in full,
> *innamā yuwaffa 'ṣ-ṣābirūna ajra-hum*
> without reckoning.
> *bi-ghairi ḥisāb.* (39:10)

As viewed by the people of certainty and understanding, this affliction is the very essence of mercy for this servant. It is actually more in keeping with His mercy and His justice, that He should put His servant to the test, so that he may practise patience and true devotion to Allāh, for he may thus obtain, by passing his test, the mighty reward referred to in His saying:

> their wages in full, without reckoning.
> *ajra-hum bi-ghairi ḥisāb.* (39:10)

Umm Salama (may Allāh be well pleased with her), the wife of the Prophet (Allāh bless him and give him peace), is reported as having said: "I once heard Allāh's Messenger (Allāh bless him and give him peace) say:

> 'When sinful acts of disobedience appear in my Community, Allāh will include all its members in the torment of those beside them.'

"So I said: 'O Messenger of Allāh, are there no righteous people among them?' 'Yes, indeed!' he replied.'" She then asked: "So how will those folk be treated?" He said:

> They will be afflicted with that which afflicts the rest of the people, but then they will eventually attain to Allāh's forgiveness and His good pleasure.[800]

It was Ibn Masʿūd (may Allāh be well pleased with him) who said: "There is not one of you who is not subject to temptation. Allāh (Exalted is He) says:

> Your wealth and your children are merely a temptation.
> *innamā amwālu-kum wa awlādu-kum fitna.* (64:15)

"You must therefore seek refuge, so one must appeal to Allāh for refuge from the errors caused by temptations."[801] As for the opinion that this admonition includes the Companions, as well as others to whom it is addressed, that opinion is correct.[802]

> and know that Allāh is Severe in punishment.
> *wa 'ʿlamū anna 'llāha Shadīdu 'l-ʿiqāb.*

This is a severe threat. In other words: "[He is] Severe in the torment He inflicts on those who disobey Him."[803] The purpose of it is to urge adherence to the right path, from fear of Allāh's punishment.[804] That is why the torment will also afflict those who are not directly responsible for it. (In other words, it applies in general, to the wrongdoer and the non-wrongdoer alike). There is also a warning of the severity of the punishment for anyone who stirs temptations. According to one of the traditional reports [*akhbār*]:

> Temptation is asleep. May Allāh curse anyone who wakes it up![805]

You must beware of committing a sinful error that is bound to bring punishment upon you all, not only its actual perpetrator, because its unfortunate consequence will affect both those who are directly involved in its commission and those who are not involved in it directly.

The non-offender is not charged with the offence of the person who commits it. It may happen, however, that someone commits an offence all by himself, and then certain people come to share the burden of guilt, through their involvement with the perpetrator of this offence. For instance, they may take sides with him when he is found guilty of that offence, so that, after not having been wrongdoers, they come to be wrongdoers, by helping and stubbornly supporting this wrongdoer. Chatisement is therefore not confined to a wrongdoer in the immediate present. It will also be inflicted on someone who becomes a wrongdoer subsequently, by taking sides with this wrongdoer, agreeing with him and approving of him.

As for His saying (Exalted is He):

> respond to Allāh and the Messenger
> [*u*] *'stajībū li'llāhi wa li'r-Rasūli*

—it has been noted that "responding" must be understood in the positive sense, since it must be an expression of obedient acceptance, not of rejection. There is also a difference between someone who responds out of fear or desire, and someone who responds without expecting anything in return, and without any ulterior motive.

To give a true response, you must respond absolutely and completely, without the slightest trace of reservation.[806]

The scholars have disagreed concerning the permissibility of interrupting the ritual prayer [*ṣalāt*] for the sake of responding to anyone else, because interruption causes its annulment, and the annulment of an act of worship is unlawful. According to some, it is permissible for any worshipper to interrupt his ritual prayer, to deal with a matter that cannot be delayed. For instance, if he has reason to fear that someone may fall from a roof, or be scorched by fire, or drown in water, it is permissible for him to interrupt his ritual prayer, even in the case of an obligatory observance [*farīḍa*]. This is stated in *Ghunyat al-Fatāwā* [Sufficient Provision of Legal Opinions].

In the case of a supererogatory observance [*nāfila*], he should respond to the call of his mother, but not to the summons of his father, because the mother's distress will cause her to weary of bearing more children. According to one of the Shaikhs, however, the father should receive precedence over the mother, out of respect, for the mother is in a state of service. According to aṭ-Ṭaḥāwī: "If someone is performing a supererogatory prayer, and one of his parents summons him, knowing that he is engaged in prayer, there is no harm in his not responding. If the parent is not aware of his situation, he should respond. In the case of someone who is performing the obligatory ritual prayer, if one of his parents summons him, he should not respond until he has finished his prayer, unless he is asked for help with something urgent, since interrupting the ritual prayer is permissible only in an emergency."

By way of implication, as you should also understand, responding to the Messenger (Allāh bless him and give him peace) includes responding to the learned, refined and trustworthy saints [*awliyā'*], because they are his inheritors, and their spiritual path is the Spritual Path of the Prophet (blessing and peace be upon him). If someone wishes to attain to Allāh (Exalted is He), he cannot dispense with the fellowship of a perfect guide, one whose knowledge of the stations and degrees of spiritual progress is based on experience, and he must accept his direction, provided that his method is compatible with the Book and the Sunna.

The people of the Spiritual Path [*Ṭarīqa*] are three: worshipful servants [*'ubbād*], seekers [*murīdūn*], and those who know by experience [*'ārifūn*].

1. The technique of the worshipful servants [*'ubbād*] is the frequent performance of religious practices, and the careful avoidance of sinful lapses and erroneous conduct.
2. The technique of the seekers [*murīdūn*] is the purification of the inner being, by ridding it of flaws, and detachment from distracting preoccupations.
3. The technique of those who know by experience [*'ārifūn*] is the dedication of the heart to Allāh, and the sacrifice of this world and the Hereafter in the quest for His good pleasure.

O Allāh, include us among those who respond to the summons of the Truth![807]

These are my own comments:

This injunction has been imposed on everyone endowed with firm resolve and aspiration, who believes in Allāh and the Last Day: He must not neglect to call his lower self to account, and he must keep it under tight control, in all its active and passive modes and in its risky situations—for every breath of life is an irreplaceable jewel—so that he can hold it by the reins and return it to Allāh and His Messenger. He must not allow it to offer any resistance. He must be firmly committed to the reality of the belief that Allāh sees him, as He has said (Exalted is He):

> Is he not aware that Allāh sees?
> *a-lam yaʿlam bi-anna 'llāha yarā.* (96:14)
>
> Allāh is always Watchful over you.
> *inna 'llāha kāna ʿalai-kum Raqībā.* (4:1)

Provided the servant matches this description, his heart will be vigilantly aware of the Watcher, preoccupied with Him, attentive to Him and heedful of Him.

The fruit of this state is the knowledge that Allāh is Observing our consciences, Aware of our innermost beings, Watchful over the actions of His servant.

If someone matches this description, it will be easy for him to practise obedience and compliance, with Allāh's help, if such be the will of Him who holds the matter in His hand. He will be endowed with tremendous good fortune, as Allāh (Exalted is He) has said in His noble Book:

> Those who believe and do good works,
> *inna 'lladhīna āmanū wa ʿamilu 'ṣ-ṣāliḥāti*
> their Lord guides them by their faith.
> *yahdī-him Rabbu-hum bi-īmāni-him:*
> Rivers will flow beneath them in the Gardens of Delight.
> *tajrī min taḥti-himu 'l-anhāru fī jannāti 'n-naʿīm.*
>
> Their prayer therein will be: "Glory be to You, O Allāh!'
> *daʿwā-hum fī-hā subḥāna-ka 'llāhumma*
> and their greeting therein will be: "Peace!"
> *wa taḥiyyatu-hum fī-hā salām:*
> and the conclusion of their prayer will be:
> *wa ākhiru daʿwā-hum*
> "Praise be to Allāh, Lord of the Worlds!"
> *ani 'l-ḥamdu li'llāhi Rabbi 'l-ʿālamīn.* (10:9,10)

O Allāh, guide us to Your straight path, through Your gracious favour, O Most Noble of the most noble. *Āmīn.* Peace be upon the Messengers, and praise be to Allāh, the Lord of All the Worlds. There is no might nor any power, except with Allāh, the All-High, the Almighty. May Allāh bless our master Muḥammad, his family and his Companions, and may He grant them peace.

The Forty-seventh Call

In the Name of Allāh, the All-Merciful, the All-Compassionate.
Bismi'llāhi 'r-Raḥmāni 'r-Raḥīm.

O you who truly believe, do not betray Allāh
yā ayyuha 'lladhīna āmanū lā takhūnu 'llāha
and the Messenger,
nor knowingly betray your trusts.
wa 'r-Rasūla wa takhūnū amānāti-kum
wa antum ta'lamūn.

And know that your possessions
and your children are a test,
wa ''lamū anna-mā amwālu-kum
wa awlādu-kum fitnatun
and that with Allāh there is immense reward.
wa anna 'llāha 'inda-hu ajrun 'aẓīm. (8:27,28)

In this, the fourth call from the Sūra of the Spoils of War [*al-Anfāl*], Allāh (Exalted is He) has served notice to the believers that divulging the secrets of the Community to the enemies constitutes betrayal of Allāh, as well as of the Messenger (Allāh bless him and give him peace), for He has said:

> O you who truly believe,
> *yā ayyuha 'lladhīna āmanū*
> do not betray Allāh and the Messenger.
> *lā takhūnu 'llāha wa 'r-Rasūla.*

As for the occasion on which this Qur'ānic verse was revealed, the following account is related by Ibn Jubair, on the authority of az-Zuhrī:

"When Allāh's Messenger (Allāh bless him and give him peace) laid siege to the Jews in the tribe of Banī Quraiẓa, they appealed for a truce, so he commanded them to yield to the authority of Sa'd ibn Mu'ādh, but they said: 'Send us Abū Lubāba Hārūn ibn 'Abd al-Mundhir, the

Helper [*Anṣārī*].'[808] He was favourably disposed towards them, because his property, his children and his dependants were in their midst.[809] Allāh's Messenger (Allāh bless him and give him peace) agreed to send him, and, when they saw him, the men approached him. The women and children were terrified, however, and they were weeping at the sight of him, so he felt pity for them.[810]

"They said: 'O Abū Lubāba, what do you think? Should we yield to the authority of Sa'd?' He said: 'Yes,' and he pointed to his throat, meaning that he was the sacrificial animal.'

"Abū Lubāba said later: 'By Allāh, my feet had not left their place, before I realized that I had betrayed Allāh and His Messenger.' He thereupon said: 'No, by Allāh, I shall taste neither food nor drink, until I die or until Allāh relents towards me,'[811] and he fastened himself to one of the columns of the mosque.[812]

"When the news of him reached Allāh's Messenger (Allāh bless him and give him peace), and he considered it too slow in arriving, he said: 'If he had come to me, I would have sought forgiveness on his behalf, but since he has done what he has done, I am not the one to release him from his place, until Allāh relents towards him.' Abū Lubāba then stayed tied to the pillar for six nights (some say about ten nights), until he lost his hearing and almost lost his sight. His wife would come to him at the time of a ritual prayer [*ṣalāt*], unfasten him for the prayer, then tie him up again.

"Then it was revealed to Allāh's Messenger (Allāh bless him and give him peace) in the apartment of Umm Salama, shortly before daybreak, that Allāh had accepted his repentance. He got up laughing, so Umm Salama said: 'What are you laughing at? May Allāh make you laugh!' He said: 'Forgiveness has been granted to Abū Lubāba.' She said: 'Shall I give him the good news, O Messenger of Allāh?' He said: 'Yes indeed, if you wish,' so she stood at the door of her room—this was before the revelation of the Qur'ānic verse concerning the veil—and cried: 'O Abū Lubāba, rejoice, for Allāh has relented towards you!' People rushed to set him loose, but he said: 'No, by Allāh, not unless Allāh's Messenger is the one to unfasten me with his own hand.' As soon as the day had dawned, he set him free.[813]

"Then Abū Lubāba said: 'For my repentance to be complete, I must move away from the abode of my people, in which I committed the sin, and divest myself of my property.' Allāh's Messenger (Allāh bless him and give him peace) responded to this by saying: 'It will be sufficient compensation for you to give a third [of your property] as a charitable donation.'"[814]

> O you who truly believe,
> *yā ayyuha 'lladhīna āmanū*
> do not betray Allāh and the Messenger
> *lā takhūnu 'llāha wa 'r-Rasūla.*

That is to say: "Do not betray your religion and your Messenger by making the polytheists privy to the secrets of the believers."

> nor knowingly betray your trusts.
> *wa takhūnū amānāti-kum wa antum ta'lamūn.*

In other words: "[Do not knowingly betray] the legal obligations with which I have entrusted you." Compare His saying (Exalted is He):

> We offered the trust to the heavens
> *innā 'araḍna 'l-amānata 'ala 's-samāwāti*
> and the earth and the hills.
> *wa 'l-arḍi wa 'l-jibāli.* (33:72)[815]

The root meaning of betrayal [*khawn*] is deficiency, just as the root meaning of loyalty [*wafā'*] is completeness. It is used to signify the opposite of trust [*amāna*] because it implicitly conveys that meaning. If you have betrayed a man, you have afflicted deficiency upon him.[816]

The import of the Qur'ānic verse, therefore, is the imposition of the duty to fulfil all obligations, in a complete and perfect manner, with no deficiency and no infringement. As for the points that have been mentioned above, concerning the immediate reason for the revelation of the verse, they are included in it, but the verse should not be confined to them, because the injunction is expressed in general terms, not with specific reference to the immediate occasion.[817]

It was Ibn 'Abbās (may Allāh be well pleased with him and his father) who said: "Betrayal of Allāh (Glory be to him) is committed by abandoning His obligatory religious duties [*farā'iḍ*]. Betrayal of the Messenger consists in the abandonment of his Sunna [exemplary practice] and the commission of disobedience towards him. Trusts [*amānāt*] are those actions which Allāh has charged his servants to perform."[818] This means that you must not make an outward show of the Truth, designed to win approval for you, but then contradict it in private, for the sake of someone other than Him, since that amounts to destruction for your trusts and to betrayal for yourselves.[819]

Qatāda said: "You should understand that Allāh's religion is a trust, so you must discharge for Allāh what He has entrusted to you, meaning His obligatory religious duties and His legal rules. If someone is charged with a trust, he must carry it out for the sake of the person who charged him with it."[820]

> knowingly
> *wa antum taʿlamūn.*

That is to say: "When you know that it is a betrayal, and you are aware of the evil consequences thereof."[821] In other words: "The betrayal emanates from you by deliberate intent, not due to absent-mindedness." Having forbidden betrayal, He has indicated that its motivation is nothing but the love of property and children. Notice how, in the case of Abū Lubāba, his action was prompted by his property, his family and his children, who were among the Banī Quraiẓa, because it was only for their sake that he advised them as he did, and it was because of them that he betrayed the Muslims.[822] Allāh (Exalted is He) has said:

> And know that your possessions and your children are a test.
> *wa 'ʿlamū anna-mā amwālu-kum wa awlādu-kum fitnatun*

In other words: "They are a trial from Allāh, designed to test how well you observe His rules while dealing with them."[823] Then, since it is the love of wealth and children that motivates the commission of betrayal, Allāh (Exalted is He) has served notice that the intelligent person is obliged to be on his guard against the harmful effects of that love, for He has said:

> And know that your possessions and your children are a test.
> *wa 'ʿlamū anna-mā amwālu-kum wa awlādu-kum fitnatun*

That is because they keep the heart preoccupied with this world, and become an obstacle to the service of the Master.[824]

The term *fitna* may be applied to disaster and affliction, and it may also be applied to trial and testing. The first meaning is appropriate in that:

> your possessions and your children
> *anna-mā amwālu-kum wa awlādu-kum*

—are causes that lead to falling into the disaster that is the commission of sinful disobedience in this world, and to falling into the punishment of the Hereafter. The second meaning is also appropriate, since they are causes of the servant's falling into the trial of Allāh (Exalted is He) and His tests, by which those who follow passion are distinguished from those who prefer the Master's good pleasure.[825]

It is therefore incumbent upon you to abstain from this world and everything connected with it, and to focus your aspirations on that which is conducive to lasting spiritual blessings.

The Qur'ānic verse can also be construed as an explanation that preoccupation with supererogatory acts of worship [*nawāfil*] is conducive to immense reward in the presence of Allāh, and is therefore of greater merit than preoccupation with marriage.[826] Marriage produces children, and necessitates the acquisition of property, and that is a test. Preoccupation with something that leads to the immense reward, in the presence of Allāh, is obviously better than preoccupation with something that results in being put to the test,[827] for He has said:

> and [know] that with Allāh there is immense reward.
> *wa anna 'llāha ʿinda-hu ajrun ʿaẓīm.*

In other words: "His reward and His gifts are better for you than your possessions and your children, so concentrate your efforts on obedience to Allāh."[828]

> There is immense reward.
> *ajrun ʿaẓīm.*

—for those who accord priority to Allāh's good pleasure, and who carefully observe His rules concerning them. You must therefore attach your aspirations to that which leads you to His good pleasure, and not let the love of them [possessions and children] prompt you to betrayal.[829]

According to the authentic tradition, the Messenger (Allāh bless him and give him peace) is reported as having said:

> There are three people who experience the ecstasy of the sweetness of faith: (1) someone to whom Allāh and His Messenger are dearer than everything apart from them; (2) someone who, when he loves a man, loves him only for the sake of Allāh; and (3) someone who would prefer to be cast into the Fire of Hell, rather than revert to unbelief, after Allāh has delivered him from it.[830]

The love of Allāh's Messenger (Allāh bless him and give him peace) should take precedence over children, possessions and personal interests, as he said (Allāh bless him and give him peace), according to the authentic tradition:

> By the One in whose Hand my soul is held, not one of you truly believes, until I am dearer to him than himself, his family, his property, and all other people.[831]

The Qur'ānic verse may be interpreted as follows:

> O you who truly believe,
> *yā ayyuha 'lladhīna āmanū*

That is to say: "O spirits and hearts, illuminated by the light of faith, prepared by the blessings of direct knowledge!"

> do not betray Allāh
> *lā takhūnu 'llāha*

—in connection with the gifts that He has brought you, by treating them as the snare of this world and the game of its hunters.

> and the Messenger
> *wa 'r-Rasūla.*

—by abandoning the Sunna and practising heretical innovation [*bid'a*].

> nor betray your trusts
> *wa takhūnū amānāti-kum*

—for the trust is the love of Allāh, and its betrayal means replacing it with the love of creatures. This is directed at the lords of hearts and the masters of the spiritual journey, since they have reached the highest degrees of all forms of worshipful obedience and proximity, but have then turned their attention to some aspect of this world and its allurement. They have betrayed Allāh by some kind of affectation, and betrayed the Messenger by heretical innovation. They have abandoned loyal adherence by transgressing into betrayal and its damaging effect on the trust, which means love. It is thus stripped from them, by a gradual process, so they come to be reliant on this world, and dependent on all forms of material wealth, due to their passionate interest in children.

> knowingly
> *wa antum ta'lamūn.*

—selling the religion for this world, and the Patron for what is considered most important [*al-Mawlā bi'l-awlā*].

And know that your possessions and your children
wa 'ʿlamū anna-mā amwālu-kum wa awlādu-kum

—for the sake of which you turn away from Allāh:

are a test
fitnatun

—by which Allāh examines you, so that the compliant [*muwāfiq*] will be distinguished from the hypocrite [*munāfiq*], and the champion of truth [*ṣiddīq*] from the atheist [*zindīq*], for, if someone rejects this world and all that it contains, he is sincere in the quest for the Patron.

and [know] that with Allāh there is immense reward.
wa anna 'llāha ʿinda-hu ajrun ʿaẓīm.

—so, if someone abandons what he has at his disposal, in search of what is at Allāh's disposal, he will find it in His presence.[832]

These are my own remarks:

You must heed the Qur'ānic admonitions, for Allāh's good pleasure resides in compliance with His commandments and loyal obedience to His Prophet (Allāh bless him and give him peace), whereas Allāh's displeasure resides in the following of passion.

You must therefore dress in the clothing of true devotion, for the raiment of true devotion is best in the sight of Allāh:

But the raiment of true devotion, that is best.
wa libāsu 't-taqwā dhālika khair. (7:26)

You must evict the love of this world from your heart, so that you may be counted among those of whom Allāh has said:

Is he whose breast Allāh has expanded to receive Islām...?
a-fa-man sharaḥa 'llāhu ṣadra-hu li'l-islāmi.... (39:22)

That is to say: "He has expanded his breast to receive Islām, faith, worshipful obedience, the love of Allāh and His Messenger, and the illumination of his heart with His Light, so that he may distinguish between love for Allāh and His Messenger, on the one hand, and that which excites the instigating self [*an-nafs al-ammāra*], on the other."

The scope of the ruling hinges on divestment [*takhliya*] and embellishment [*taḥliya*], and divestment takes precedence over embellishment.

You must not succumb to the delusion of fame and reputation, nor take pride in that which is fleeting, at the risk of losing what your Lord has promised, in His saying (Exalted is He):

> Allāh is well pleased with them,
> *raḍiya 'llāhu ʿan-hum*
> and they are well pleased with Him.
> *wa raḍū ʿan-h:*
> That is for anyone who fears his Lord.
> *dhālika li-man khashiya Rabba-h.* (98:8)

You must be one of those who are just and fair. Are you immersed in the love of Allāh (Almighty and Glorious is He) and loyal obedience to His Messenger, or is your heart controlled by the love of this world, children and money? You will be judged by what is in your conscience, for Allāh is an Observer of consciences and a Supervisor of innermost beings.

May Allāh preserve us, and all of you, from obstinate disobedience. *Āmīn*. Peace be upon the Messengers, and praise be to Allāh, the Lord of All the Worlds. There is no might nor any power, except with Allāh, the All-High, the Almighty. May Allāh bless our master Muḥammad, his family and his Companions, and may He grant them peace.

The Forty-eighth Call

In the Name of Allāh, the All-Merciful, the All-Compassionate.
Bismi'llāhi 'r-Raḥmāni 'r-Raḥīm.

O you who truly believe,
if you practise true devotion to Allāh,
yā ayyuha 'lladhīna āmanū in tattaqu 'llāha
He will give you a criterion, and He will rid you
yaj'al la-kum furqānan wa yukaffir 'an-kum
of your evil ways and deeds,
and He will forgive you.
sayyi'āti-kum wa yaghfir la-kum:
Allāh is of infinite bounty.
wa 'llāhu Dhu 'l-faḍli 'l-'aẓīm. (8:29)

In this call, the fifth from the Sūra of the Spoils of War [*Sūrat al-Anfāl*], Allāh has directed the believers' attention towards the fruit of true devotion. He has reminded them that it forms the basis of all goodness, and that one of the fruits of true devotion is that Lordly light, which Allāh casts into the heart of the believer, and by which He distinguishes between proper conduct and error, right guidance and wandering astray.

O you who truly believe, if you practise true devotion to Allāh,
yā ayyuha 'lladhīna āmanū in tattaqu 'llāha
He will give you a criterion.
yaj'al la-kum furqānan.

That is to say: "If you obey Allāh and refrain from sinning against Him, He will provide you with guidance and a light within your hearts, by which you can discriminate between the true and the false." As He has said (Exalted is He):

He will provide you with a light by which to walk.
wa yaj'al la-kum nūran tamshūna bi-hi. (57:28)

The Qur᾽ānic verse implies that true devotion illuminates the heart, expands the breast, and leads to an increase in knowledge and real understanding.[833]

The term *furqān* [criterion] is a verbal noun from the same root as *farq* [discrimination]. It is applied to that which serves as a means of discrimination and differentiation. When Allāh (Exalted is He) issued a warning against preoccupation with worldly possessions and children, He awakened interest in true devotion to Allāh, through the avoidance major sins and the constant practice of all forms of worshipful obedience. If someone persists in obedience, Allāh will give him the means to distinguish himself from the profligates and the sinful rebels, in this world and in the Hereafter.

In this world, He will do so by guiding his heart, and illuminating it with the light of direct experience and certainty. The fountains of wisdom will then flow from his heart onto his tongue, and nothing will emanate from him except that which is true and correct. This guidance is therefore a criterion [*furqān*], by which the truly devout servant is distinguished from his opposites.

The fact that he receives assistance is likewise a criterion that distinguishes him from the liars, by enabling him to succeed, while causing the liars to fail; by supplying him with irrefutable proofs, which relieve him of doubts in the sphere of religion; by delivering him from all that he fears in this world and the Hereafter; and by revealing his value and exalting his worth. Just as these factors constitute a criterion by which the truly devout servant is distinguished from others, they also represent a criterion by which he can distinguish between the true and the false. The same applies to success, since it marks the distinction that, while he is on the side of truth, the one against whom he is helped to succeed is on the side of falsehood. It also applies to deliverance and salvation, since they distinguish between him and the person who is beset with doubts and fears.[834]

The meaning of true devotion [*taqwā*] has previously been explained. Allāh already knows whether they will practise true devotion, or will not practise it. When He uses the conditional expression ["if..."], He does so because He is addressing His servants in the way they address one another. If the servant is truly devoted to his Lord—and that means compliance with His commandments and nonviolation of His prohibitions; avoidance of things that are of dubious legality, for fear of trespassing into things that are strictly unlawful; filling his heart with sincere intention, and his limbs and organs with righteous deeds; guarding against the flaws of polytheistic association [*shirk*], both covert and overt, due to consideration for anyone but Allāh in his actions; and keeping this world in its place, through abstinence from material wealth—his Lord will give him a criterion, by which to distinguish between the true and the false, and He will empower him to accomplish all his good intentions.

It was Ibn Wahb who said: "I once asked Mālik about His saying (Glory be to Him and Exalted is He):

> If you practise true devotion to Allāh,
> *yā ayyuha 'lladhīna āmanū in tattaqu 'llāha*
> He will give you a criterion.
> *yaj'al la-kum furqānan.*

—and he replied: '[A criterion] is a way out [*makhraj*].' Then he recited:

> And if someone practises true devotion to Allāh,
> *wa man yattaqi 'llāha*
> He will give him a way out.
> *yaj'al la-hu makhrajā.* (65:2)"[835]

> and He will rid you of your evil ways and deeds
> *wa yukaffir 'an-kum sayyi'āti-kum*

That is to say: "He will eradicate from you all your previous sins."

> and He will forgive you.
> *wa yaghfir la-kum:*

In other words: "He will pardon you for them, and He will not take you to task for them,[836] so He will not disgrace you in this world or the Hereafter."[837]

> Allāh is of infinite bounty.
> *wa 'llāhu Dhu 'l-faḍli 'l-'aẓīm.*

That is to say: "He is the Source of abundant grace, Prodigious in bestowing generous gifts."[838] This is an explanation of what precedes it. It is also a notification that Allāh's promise to them, in return for true devotion, is a gracious favour and a benefaction—not an automatic and inevitable consequence of true devotion—as when a master promises his servant a special favour for doing a job.[839]

This criterion may therefore be considered either in the context of this world, or in the context of the Hereafter. Within the context of this world, it may be relevant to the conditions of the heart, meaning the inner states of being, or to the outer states. As for the conditions of the heart, there are several interpretations to consider:

1. That Allāh (Exalted is He) will endow the believers with guidance and intimate knowledge.
2. That He will confer expansion on their hearts and their breasts, as He has said (Exalted is He):

> Is he whose breast Allāh has expanded to receive Islām,
> *a-fa-man sharaḥa 'llāhu ṣadra-hu li'l-islāmi*
> so that he is guided by a light from his Lord...?
> *fa-huwa ʿalā nūrin min Rabbi-h.* (39:22)

3. That He will eliminate malice, spite and envy from their hearts, and remove deceitfulness and treachery from their breasts, whereas the heart of the hyprocrite and the unbeliever will be filled with these despicable vices and blameworthy characteristics.

In each of these cases, the point is that, when the heart becomes enlightened through obedience to Allāh, all of these darknesses vanish from it, because direct experience of Allāh is a radiant light. These vices are dark shadows, and, when the light appears, darkness is bound to vanish away.

As for the external context, Allāh (Exalted is He) will endow the Muslims with exaltation, victory, success and triumph, as mentioned in His sayings (Exalted is He):

> Glory belongs to Allāh, and to His Messenger and the believers.
> *wa li'llāhi 'l-ʿizzatu wa li-rasūli-hi wa li'l-muʾminīna.* (63:8)

> That He may cause it [Islām] to prevail over all religion.
> *li-yuẓhira-hu ʿala 'd-dīni kulli-h.* (48:28)

The condition of the profligate and the unbeliever is the opposite of that.

As for the context of the Hereafter, there will be spiritual reward, everlasting benefits, and enormous respect from Allāh and His angels. The criterion is relevant in all of these contexts.[840]

The intelligent person is therefore obliged to make every effort, till the end of his life, to ensure that Allāh will rid him of the evils of his transitory existence, and that He will shield him with the radiant lights of His Beauty and His Majesty.

> Allāh is of infinite bounty.
> *wa 'llāhu Dhu 'l-faḍli 'l-ʿaẓīm.*

—for anyone who transcends his personal situation, seeking what is is in the presence of Allāh. The infinite bounty is eternity with Allāh, after extinction for His sake.[841]

These are my own remarks:

After Allāh (Exalted and Glorious is He) has addressed the believers with:

> O you who truly believe
> *yā ayyuha 'lladhīna āmanū*

—He has added the condition:

> if you practise true devotion to Allāh,
> *yā ayyuha 'lladhīna āmanū in tattaqu 'llāha*
> He will give you a criterion.
> *yajʿal la-kum furqānan.*

—and He has made this criterion contingent on true devotion. Once true devotion has arrived, the criterion will be forthcoming, and the ridding of evils will follow in the wake of the criterion.

There is yet another subtle implication here: If true devotion becomes an atonement for sins, but remains without pardon, and if Allāh does not pardon the sinner, He will disgrace him among His servants on the Day of Resurrection. This does not befit His Majesty, His Perfection and His Mercy, however, so He has graciously added:

> and He will forgive you.
> *wa yaghfir la-kum.*

Forgiveness is therefore a gracious favour from Him, and a pardon for His servant. It will be as if he had never sinned, and had never tried to make amends for his evil ways among his fellow creatures. Even though that really happened, within the knowledge of Allāh (Glorious and Exalted is He), He will graciously refrain from disgracing him among the people, and He will pardon him.

We are thus obliged, O companies of the believers, to feel a humble sense of shame, in the presence of this noble generosity and this gracious favour, bestowed upon us without any claim to entitlement on our part. If any ordinary person is given something of material value, he becomes a captive of its owner. He feels too ashamed to oppose or contradict him, since he is acutely conscious of the gracious treatment he received from him. How, then, can we fail to feel a humble sense of shame, in the presence of the Most Generous of the most generous, the Most Merciful of the merciful, the Forgiver of sins, the Almighty, when He pardons us in this world and the Hereafter, to preserve our dignity through the absence of disgrace?

You need to remember your origin. Your point of origin is in nonexistence, and you are approaching eternity. Between this eternity and that nonexistence, you must focus on the present moment, the second in which you are living. You must not be deluded by your lower self, nor by your material wealth, not by your children. You must be truly devoted to Allāh:

> For Allāh loves those who are truly devoted.
> *fa-inna 'llāha yuḥibbu 'l-muttaqīn.* (3:76)

> And know that Allāh is with those who are truly devoted.
> *wa ' 'lamū anna 'llāha maʿa 'l-muttaqīn.* (9:36)

Practise true devotion to Allāh, for then, by the grace of Allāh, you will be resurrected together with all the truly devout. O Allāh, include us among the truly devout, and resurrect us together with those who practise true devotion. Enfold us in Your mercy, through Your grace and noble generosity, together with Your righteous servants.

O Allāh, grant us Your enabling grace. *Āmīn*. Peace be upon the Messengers, and praise be to Allāh, the Lord of All the Worlds. There is no might nor any power, except with Allāh, the All-High, the Almighty. May Allāh bless our master Muḥammad, his family and his Companions, and may He grant them peace.

The Forty-ninth Call

In the Name of Allāh, the All-Merciful, the All-Compassionate.
Bismi'llāhi 'r-Raḥmāni 'r-Raḥīm.

O you who truly believe, when you meet an army,
yā ayyuha 'lladhīna āmanū idhā laqītum fi'atan
hold firm and remember Allāh frequently,
fa-'thbutū wa 'dhkuru 'llāha kathīran
so that you may be successful.
la'alla-kum tufliḥūn.

And obey Allāh and His Messenger,
wa aṭī'u 'llāha wa Rasūla-hu
and do not dispute one with another,
wa lā tanāza'ū
lest you falter and your wind depart from you.
fa-tafshalū wa tadhhaba rīḥu-kum
Endure with patience.
wa 'ṣbirū:
Allāh is with the patiently enduring.
inna 'llāha ma'a 'ṣ-ṣābirīn. (8:45,46)

This is the sixth call [*nidā'*] from the Sūra of the Spoils [*al-Anfāl*]. It is also the final call, in which Allāh (Exalted is He) has described for them the path of glory and the basis of victory, that being steadfastness in front of the enemy; patience at the time of the encounter; evoking the might of Allāh, which has no limit, and His strength, which is insuperable; and reliance on the spiritual support that will help them to hold firm—in other words, remembering Allāh frequently.[842] He has said (Exalted is He):

> O you who truly believe, when you meet an army,
> *yā ayyuha 'lladhīna āmanū idhā laqītum fi'atan*
> hold firm and remember Allāh frequently.
> *fa-'thbutū wa 'dhkuru 'llāha kathīran*

That is to say: "when you fight an unbelieving troop," because the meeting presumably occurs in war and battle, and they did not wage war on any but the unbelievers.

His expression:

> hold firm
> *fa-'thbutū*

—means: "At the time of meeting them and fighting them, hold firm and do not retreat in disarray."[843]

This contains instruction from Allāh to His believing servants, concerning the modes of conduct appropriate to military confrontation, and the kind of courage required in facing their enemies. According to confirmed reports in the two *Ṣaḥīḥ*'s, on some of the days on which Allāh's Messenger (Allāh bless him and give him peace) confronted the enemy, he waited until the sun had waned, then he stood up and said:

> O people, do not be too eager to meet the enemy. Ask Allāh for well-being. Then, when you meet them, be patient, and know that the Garden of Paradise lies beneath the swords.

The Prophet (Allāh bless him and give him peace) then stood up and said:

> O Allāh, the Revealer of the Book, the Mover of the clouds, the Vanquisher of the parties, vanquish them and make us victorious over them!

According to one report, he said (Allāh bless him and give him peace):

> When you meet them, be firm and remember Allāh. If they bellow and shout, you must remain silent.

As reported by Zaid ibn Arqam, the Prophet (Allāh bless him and give him peace) once said:

> Allāh loves silence on three occasions: during the recitation of the Qur'ān, during the approach to battle, and during the funeral service.[844]

When he forbade great eagerness to meet the enemy, he did so because it implies conceit and overconfidence, and because it involves too little attention to the enemy. Such underestimation of them is at odds with due precaution. As the experts have said about the good manners of debate: "The debater must not regard his adversary as insignificant, because disparagement of the adversary may lead to a weak argument from the debater, due to careless indifference. This may result in his defeat by the weak adversary, so the weak becomes strong, and the strong becomes weak."

> and remember Allāh frequently
> *wa 'dhkuru 'llāha kathīran*

That is to say: "[Remember Him] in the episodes of battle and the scenes of violence, with *takbīr* [proclaiming: *Allāhu Akbar* (Allāh is Supremely Great!)] and *tahlīl* [declaring: *Lā ilāha illa 'llāh* (There is no god but Allāh!)] and similar affirmations, and appeal to Him for the victory of the believers and the defeat of the unbelievers."[845]

In the Qur'ānic verse:

> O you who truly believe, when you meet an army, hold firm
> *yā ayyuha 'lladhīna āmanū idhā laqītum fi'atan fa-'thbutū*

—there is guidance to the path of victory, in combat with the enemies. In other words: "When you meet a troop of the unbelievers, hold firm to fight them and do not retreat in disarray."

> and remember Allāh frequently
> *wa 'dhkuru 'llāha kathīran*

That is to say: "Make a frequent practice of remembering Allāh, in order to invoke His help and His assistance, and so gain victory over them."[846]

Having mentioned the various blessings that He bestowed upon the Messenger (Allāh bless him and give him peace) and the believers on the Day of Badr, Allāh (Exalted is He) has now taught them to observe two kinds of good conduct, when they meet the army of their warrior foes:

1. Holding firm, which means that they must steady themselves for the encounter, and not talk themselves into turning in retreat.
2. They must remember Allāh frequently. In other words, they must remember Allāh with their hearts, and mention Allāh with their tongues.

According to Ibn ʿAbbās: "Allāh has commanded His friends to remember Him in the most difficult of their situations, serving notice that it is not permissible for the human being to detach his heart and his tongue from the remembrance of Allāh. If one man travelled all the way from the east to the west, spending wealth in a generous manner, and another man travelled all the way from the west to the east, wielding his sword in support of Allāh's cause, the one who remembered Allāh would earn the greater reward."[847]

> so that you may be successful.
> *la'alla-kum tufliḥūn.*

In other words: "so that you may obtain your wish and triumph in your purpose, by gaining victory and the spiritual reward."[848]

Suppose you say: "The obvious meaning of the verse requires holding firm in every situation, and that seems to suggest that it abrogates the verse of manoeuvering and repositioning [*āyat at-taḥarruf wa 't-taḥayyuz*]:

> unless manoeuvering for battle
> *illā mutaḥarrifan li-qitālin*
> or joining forces with a company.
> *aw mutaḥayyizan ilā fi'atin.* (8:16)"

My reply will be: "In this context, what is meant by 'holding firm' is holding firm during combat and fighting in general, and the verse of manoeuvering and repositioning does not conflict with this instruction to hold firm in combat. As a matter of fact, holding firm is sometimes impossible without that manoeuvering and repositioning."[849]

The verse admonishes the servant to let nothing distract him from remembering Allāh, to seek refuge with Him in difficult situations, and to dedicate himself to Him completely, free of concern, confident that His grace will not desert him under any circumstance. It assures him that the remembrance of Allāh is tremendously effective in dispelling injuries and procuring benefits.

In the words of the Prophetic tradition [*ḥadīth*]:

> Allāh has a band of angels patrolling in search of the circles of remembrance. When they come upon them they surround them, then they send their leader heavenwards to the Lord of Glory (Blessed and Exalted is He)—though He already knows everything—and they say: 'Our Lord, we have come upon some servants of Yours, who are magnifying Your bounties, reciting Your Book, invoking blessing upon Your Prophet Muḥammad (Allāh bless him and give him peace), and appealing to You for the benefit of their lives in the Hereafter and this world.' Allāh (Blessed and Exalted is He) then says: 'Cover them with My mercy, for they are the companions whose companion in their gathering is not unhappy with them.'[850]

According to one of the wise: "Allāh has a Garden of Paradise in this world, and those who enter it enjoy a pleasant life. That Garden consists of the sessions of remembrance."

As we are told in *Anwār al-Mashāriq* [Lights of the Points of Sunrise]: "Just as remembrance itself is recommended, it is also recommendable to sit in the circles of its practitioners. It is customary for circles of remembrance to be conducted publicly, since there is no known instance, in the course of the ages, of a circle of remembrance in which its members kept their remembrance to themselves. Remembrance in an audible voice is more effective in curbing the feelings rooted in the heart of the novice. Besides, through the open display of religion, the blessed grace of remembrance can be enjoyed by people within hearing, in neighbouring buildings and houses, and every moist and dry tongue will bear witness, on the Day of Resurrection, to having heard its sound. This is especially important in crowded places among the heedless common folk, in order to alert the negligent and provide guidance for the sinful."

It is forbidden for anyone to attend a session in which Allāh is not remembered, and blessing is not invoked upon His Prophet Muḥammad (Allāh bless him and give him peace). If he does attend it, that session will be an affliction for him on the Day of Resurrection. In the words of the Prophetic tradition [*ḥadīth*]:

> If someone attends a session in which he makes a lot of noise, but then he says, before getting up to leave that session: 'Glory be to You, O Allāh, and with Your praise! I bear witness that there is no god but You. I seek Your forgiveness and I repent to You,' Allāh will forgive him for what happened in that session of his.[851]

The intelligent person must therefore keep his tongue constantly moist with remembrance, supplication and begging forgiveness, especially at blessed times. Frequent remembrance—provided that it is performed with purity of heart—is the Garden of Paradise in this world for the spiritually aware. Through the remembrance of Allāh (Exalted is He), one passes beyond the hell of the instigating self [*an-nafs al-ammāra*] and its bottomless pit, and progresses to the bliss of present awareness.

It was Abū Bakr al-Farghānī who said: "I had dropped out of the caravan one day, so I said: 'O my Lord, if only You had taught me the

Supreme Name!' Two men approached me, and one of them said to the other: 'To utter the Supreme Name is to say: "O Allāh!" with a feeling of joy,' but the other man said: 'It is not as you say, but rather with a genuine plea for refuge and a sense of urgent need, as when the speaker is in the depth of the sea, and has no refuge but Allāh.'"

You should know that the sacred struggle [*jihād*] is one of the most important acts of worshipful obedience. That is why the dust of the sacred warrior [*mujāhid*] does not mingle with the smoke of Hell. With one step taken by the sacred warrior, a sin is forgiven, and with another, a good deed is recorded. It is essential, however, for his intention to be sound, and for him to hold firm on the battlefields. It is by firmness of heart and foot that men's true worth is demonstrated, as in the case of [Abū Bakr] the Champion of Truth (may Allāh be well pleased with him), when he was stricken with grief at the death of Allāh's Messenger (Allāh bless him and give him peace), and he said: "Whoever worships Muḥammad (Allāh bless him and give him peace), well, Muḥammad (Allāh bless him and give him peace) has died. Whoever worships the Lord of Muḥammad (Allāh bless him and give him peace), well, He is Living and will never die!"

Victory over the enemies is won by Holy strength and Divine support, not by physical strength and force of numbers.[852]

In connection with His saying (Exalted is He):

> To Allāh belong the Most Beautiful Names.
> *wa li'llāhi 'l-Asmā'u 'l-Ḥusnā.* (7:180)

—the following commentary has been offered: "That which causes entry into Hell is neglect of the remembrance of Allāh, while that which provides salvation from the torment of Hell is the remembrance of Allāh (Exalted is He). The masters of direct experience and perception will discover, from their spirits, that this is the truth of the matter. If someone's heart neglects the remembrance of Allāh (Exalted is He), and he concentrates on this world and its pleasures, he will fall through the gate of greed and into the bitter cold of deprivation. He will never stop shifting from one craving to another, from one desire to another, and from one darkness to another. On the other hand, if his heart receives an opening to the remembrance of Allāh and direct experience of Allāh, he will be delivered from the fires of disasters and the woes of casualties, and he will experience intimate knowledge of the Lord of the earth and the heavens."[853]

Sahl once said: "I know of no worse sin than forsaking the remembrance of this Lord." According to Abu 'l-Ḥasan ash-Shādhilī (may Allāh be well pleased with him): "One symptom of hypocrisy is the heaviness of remembrance on the tongue. Repent to Allāh (Exalted is He), then He will make remembrance light and easy on your tongue!"[854]

According to al-Junaid (may Allāh bestow His mercy upon him): "When someone remembers and mentions this Name (Allāh), he is transcending his own self, gaining contact with his Lord, fulfilling his duty to Him, beholding Him with his heart. The lights of direct witnessing have burnt away the attributes of his merely human condition."[855]

As you should also know, the rebel army is outwardly like the unbelieving troop and the immoral gang, while inwardly it is like the troop of the carnal appetites and the gang of the self that is always instigating evil [*an-nafs al-ammāra bi'-sū'*]. Just as the believer has been commanded to hold firm at the appearance of the external rebel army, he has likewise been commanded to hold firm at the appearance of the internal rebel army, by waging the necessary struggles.

The struggle with the unbelievers is a minor struggle [*jihād aṣghar*], while the struggle with the lower self is a major struggle [*jihād akbar*]. That is why someone who is slain in the major struggle is a champion of the truth [*ṣiddīq*], whereas someone who is slain in the minor struggle is a martyr [*shahīd*]. The champion of the truth is above the martyr, as Allāh (Exalted is He) has said:

> They are in the company of those
> *fa-ulā'ika ma'a 'lladhīna*
> to whom Allāh has granted gracious favour:
> *an'ama 'llāhu 'alai-him*
> the Prophets, the champions of truth and the martyrs.
> *mina 'n-Nabiyyīna wa 'ṣ-ṣiddīqīna wa 'sh-shuhadā'i.* (4:69)

Escape from the gloom and darkness of the realm of creation, and gaining the lights of remembrance, which ought to be one's sole preoccupation—these are among the greatest kinds of sacred struggle, and the quickest route to contact with the Lord of the servants. We beg Allāh (Exalted is He) to let us truly experience the realities of remembrance [*dhikr*] and the affirmation of Oneness [*tawḥīd*].[856]

Let us now consider His saying (Exalted is He):

> And obey Allāh and His Messenger,
> *wa aṭīʿu 'llāha wa Rasūla-hu*
> and do not dispute one with another,
> *wa lā tanāzaʿū*
> lest you falter and your wind depart from you.
> *fa-tafshalū wa tadhhaba rīḥu-kum*
> Endure with patience. Allāh is with the patiently enduring.
> *wa 'ṣbirū: inna 'llāha maʿa 'ṣ-ṣābirīn.*

Allāh (Exalted is He) has commanded steadfastness in fighting the enemies, and patience in confronting them, so the believers must not flee, they must not be rashly self-confident, and they must not be cowardly. He has commanded them (Exalted is He) to remember Allāh in that situation, and not to forget Him, but to seek His help, to put their trust in Him, and to appeal to Him for victory over their enemies. He has also commanded them (Exalted is He) to obey Allāh and His Messenger in that situation of theirs. They must therefore comply with what Allāh (Exalted is He) has commanded them to do, and steer clear of what He has forbidden them to do. They must also refrain from quarrelling among themselves, and so becoming divided, for that would result in their lack of cohesion and loss of courage.

> and your wind depart from you.
> *wa tadhhaba rīḥu-kum*

In other words: "your strength and your unity, and the forward thrust in which you were engaged."

> Endure with patience. Allāh is with the patiently enduring.
> *wa 'ṣbirū: inna 'llāha maʿa 'ṣ-ṣābirīn.*

When it came to courage, compliance with whatever Allāh and His Messenger commanded, and conformity with the guidance He gave them, the Companions (may Allāh be well pleased with them) set a unique example. There was no one to match them in the communities and generations before them, and there will be none in those to come after them. Through the blessed grace of the Messenger (Allāh bless him and give him peace), and their obedience to him in whatever he commanded them, they conquered hearts and whole countries, east and west, in the shortest period of time. Few as they were in number, in comparison with the armies of other countries, they defeated them all, so that the Word of Allāh was exalted and His religion triumphed over all other religions. Allāh was therefore well pleased with them, and He made all of them well pleased. May He resurrect us in their company, for He is surely Generous, Ever-Relenting![857]

> And obey Allāh and His Messenger
> *wa aṭī'u 'llāha wa Rasūla-hu*

That is to say: "in everything else that He commands you to do," because the sacred struggle is of no avail, unless accompanied by strict adherence to all other acts of worshipful obedience."[858]

> and do not dispute one with another
> *wa lā tanāza'ū*

In other words: "Do not disagree, for argument and disagreement will result in hesitation, weakness and cowardice."

> lest you falter and your wind depart from you.
> *fa-tafshalū wa tadhhaba rīḥu-kum*

Your wind [*rīḥ*] means your strength, or, according to Mujāhid, your support. He said: "The *rīḥ* of the Companions of Muḥammad (Allāh bless him and give him peace) departed when they quarrelled on the Day of Uḥud."

In this context, *rīḥ* is an allusion to the execution of the command, and its implementation in accordance with the intended purpose. The Arabs say: "So-and-so's wind [*rīḥ*] has blown," when he accomplishes his business as he wishes. According to Qatāda and Ibn Zaid: "It means the wind of victory, for there has never been a victory without a wind sent by Allāh (Exalted is He) to smite the faces of the enemy." This fits with the saying of the Prophet (Allāh bless him and give him peace):

> I was helped to victory by an east wind [*ṣabā*], and 'Ād were destroyed by a west wind [*dabūr*].[859]

It is reported that an-Nu'mān ibn Muqarrin said: "I noticed that Allāh's Messenger (Allāh bless him and give him peace), when he did not fight from the beginning of the day, would postpone the battle till the sun was setting and the winds were gusting, and victory would then be won."[860]

Endure with patience.
wa 'ṣbirū:

That is to say: "[Endure with patience] at the time of meeting your enemies, and do not retreat from them in disarray."

Allāh is with the patiently enduring.
inna 'llāha maʿa 'ṣ-ṣābirīn.

In other words: "[He is with them] in assistance and support."[861] The word *maʿa* [with] should not be understood to mean that He is with them in their personal identity, but only inasmuch as they are practising patience, so they are accompanied from that standpoint. His *maʿiyya* ["with-ness"] (Exalted is He) is simply an indication of support and assistance.[862]

The Qurʾānic verse contains two admonitions:

1. Harmony among the Muslims is the root of the religion, while disharmony is the beginning of corruption and the starting point of errors. Just as harmony is necessary in religious practice and doctrine, it is equally necessary in the process of considering opinions and making decisions. Allāh (Exalted is He) has said of the unbelievers:

You think of them as a whole,
taḥsabu-hum jamīʿan
whereas their hearts are diverse.
wa qulūbu-hum shattā. (59:14)

If the resolutions of the Muslims are to be unanimous, it can only be because all of them agree on detachment from their own power and strength, dedicate themselves entirely to their return to Allāh, and recognize what this entails, so that they become united in this single state of being. As for those who are deluded by their own ideas, so that they make mistakes in their calculations, and try to manage affairs on the basis of their subjective opinion, everything is constructed on what occurs to them as preferable. Then, when they dispute with one another, their opinions cause them to split up, and they head in different directions, so they become weak and their paths are divided.

Just as obedience to Allāh's Messenger (Allāh bless him and give him peace) is necessary in the context of religion, obedience to those in command is also necessary. This is why, in every period of time, it is necessary to appoint a leader for the Muslims, and it is then impermissible to oppose him. The Prophet (blessing and peace be upon him) once said:

> You must obey him, even if he is a slave who has had both his ears cut off.[863]

When Allāh's Messenger (Allāh bless him and give him peace) dispatched a military squadron, he would appoint a commander in charge of them, and he would say:

> Rely on the great majority![864]

The consensus of the Muslims is a convincing proof, and the prayer of the congregation [*ṣalāt al-jamāʿa*] is an established custom [*sunna*]. Loyal adherence [*ittibāʿ*] is praiseworthy, whereas heretical innovation [*ibtidāʿ*] is erroneous.

What is commanded by His saying (Exalted is He):

> Endure with patience.
> *wa 'ṣbirū:*

—is the kind of patience that is exercised against your passionate desire.

> Allāh is with the patiently enduring.
> *inna 'llāha maʿa 'ṣ-ṣābirīn.*

That is to say: "He will take satisfactory care of them, provided they demonstrate firm steadfastness and excellent commitment."[865]

2. Holding firm can only be achieved through strength of heart and intense conviction, and that cannot be without acute discernment, serious commitment to Allāh, and the recognition that all happenings emanate from Him. The believer must therefore surrender to Allāh, be content with His judgements, and be ready to receive the best of help from Him. This is why He has directed them towards remembrance, for He has said:

> and remember Allāh frequently
> *wa 'dhkuru 'llāha kathīran*

It is said that all good things reside in steadfastness of heart, and that is how men's virtues are brought to light. Suppose a disturbing idea occurs to someone, or an unpleasant thought upsets him. If he is endowed with insight, he will pause until the true significance of the notion becomes clear to him, thereby maintaining his composure, keeping his heart calm and his mind pure. That is a fair description of those who are preeminently distinguished.[866]

These are my own comments:

You must not forget your share of this worshipful service. You must accept what your Lord has promised, and have confidence in Him (Glorious and Exalted is He). You are a believer, if Allāh wills.

Your Lord (More Glorious is He than any other speaker) has said:

> Those who believe and whose hearts have rest
> *alladhīna āmanū wa taṭma'innu qulūbu-hum*
> in the remembrance of Allāh,
> *bi-dhikri 'llāh:*
> it is truly in the remembrance of Allāh
> *a-lā bi-dhikri 'llāhi*
> that hearts feel comfortably at rest.
> *taṭma'innu 'l-qulūb.* (13:28)

You must hear what Allāh (Magnificent is His Majesty) has said, and what the Most Splendid Messenger (Allāh bless him and give him peace) has said, and what the religious scholars, the Qur'ānic commentators and others have said. You must not follow your lower self and its passionate desire, for they are hostile to you. We shall not bore you by going on at length, for the best kind of speech is brief and to the point.

O Allāh, grant us the ability to accomplish all that. *Āmīn*. Peace be upon the Messengers, and praise be to Allāh, the Lord of All the Worlds. There is no might nor any power, except with Allāh, the All-High, the Almighty. May Allāh bless our master Muḥammad, his family and his Companions, and may He grant them peace.

The Fiftieth Call

In the Name of Allāh, the All-Merciful, the All-Compassionate.
Bismi'llāhi 'r-Raḥmāni 'r-Raḥīm.

O you who truly believe,
do not choose your fathers
yā ayyuha 'lladhīna āmanū lā tattakhidhū ābā'a-kum
and your brothers for friends,
wa ikhwāna-kum awliyā'a
if they take pleasure in unbelief rather than faith.
ini 'staḥabbu 'l-kufra 'ala 'l-īmān:
If any of you takes them for friends,
such are wrongdoers.
wa man yatawalla-hum min-kum
fa-ulā'ika humu 'z-zālimūn.

Say: "If your fathers, and your sons,
and your brothers,
qul in kāna ābā'u-kum wa abnā'u-kum
wa ikhwānu-kum
and your wives, and your tribe,
wa azwāju-kum wa 'ashīratu-kum
and wealth you have acquired, and merchandise
wa amwāluni 'qtaraftumū-hā wa tijāratun
for which you fear that there will be no sale,
takhshawna kasāda-hā
and dwellings you find pleasing,
wa masākinu tarḍawna-hā
are dearer to you than Allāh
aḥabba ilai-kum mina 'llāhi
and His Messenger and striving in His way,
wa Rasūli-hi wa jihādin fī sabīli-hi
then wait till Allāh brings His command to pass.
fa-tarabbaṣū ḥattā ya'tiya 'llāhu bi-amri-h:
Allāh does not guide the dissolute folk aright."
wa 'llāhu lā yahdi 'l-qawma 'l-fāsiqīn. (9:23,24)

Allāh (Exalted is He) has already described the vices of the polytheists, and commended the believing Emigrants [*Muhājirīn*], who migrated from their houses and their homelands for the love of Allāh and His Messenger. He has now gone on to give warning against befriending the unbelievers, and He has declared it necessary to sever relations with fathers and close relatives, on the grounds of unbelief.

According to al-Kalbī: "When Allāh's Messenger (Allāh bless him and give him peace) was commanded to migrate to Medina, a man would say to his father, his brother and his wife: 'He has commanded us to migrate.' One of them would please him by being quick to do so, while another would be held back by his wife and his children, for they would say: 'We implore you by Allāh! If you leave us without anything, we shall perish.' He would then take pity, so he would stay at home with them and refrain from the Migration [*Hijra*]."[867] The Qur'ānic verse was therefore revealed to reprimand them.

Imām al-Fakhr ar-Rāzī said: "According to the correct opinion, this Sūra was not revealed until after the conquest of Mecca, so how can it be construed in the context of the obligation to perform the Migration [*Hijra*]? The fact is that the Migration was necessary only before the conquest of Mecca, and this verse most probably concerns the obligation to disown their polytheistic relatives, and to refrain from treating them as intimates and friends, since that would mean sharing their secrets with them, and preferring their companionship to migration to the abode of Islām."[868]

When He issued the call (Exalted is He):

> O you who truly believe, do not choose your fathers
> *yā ayyuha 'lladhīna āmanū lā tattakhidhū ābā'a-kum*
> and your brothers for friends
> *wa ikhwāna-kum awliyā'a*

—the reference to belief was intended as a mark of honour, and to arouse the aspiration to make haste in complying with the commandments of Allāh. It was Ibn Mas'ūd (may Allāh be well pleased with him) who said: "When you hear Allāh (Exalted is He) say: 'O you who truly believe,' you must pay very close attention, for there is something good that you are being commanded to do, or something bad that you are being forbidden to do." The meaning is: "Do not choose your unbelieving fathers and brothers for helpers and assistants, feeling love and affection for them."

> if they take pleasure in unbelief rather than faith.
> *ini 'staḥabbu 'l-kufra ʿala 'l-īmān:*

That is to say: "If they prefer unbelief, choose it instead of faith, and persist in it stubbornly."

> If any of you takes them for friends, such are wrongdoers.
> *wa man yatawalla-hum min-kum fa-ulāʾika humu 'ẓ-ẓālimūn.*

According to Ibn ʿAbbās: "He is a polytheist [*mushrik*] just like them, because anyone who approves of polytheism [*shirk*] must be a polytheist."[869] The obvious interpretation of the verse is that it is an address to all the believers, without distinction, and that it will remain in force till the Day of Resurrection, insisting on the severance of friendship between the believers and the unbelievers.

Allāh (Glory be to Him and Exalted is He) has singled out fathers and brothers, since there is no closer relationship than with them. He has disallowed friendship between them, just as He has disallowed it between them and the people mentioned in His saying (Exalted is He):

> O you who truly believe,
> *yā ayyuha 'lladhīna āmanū*
> do not take the Jews and Christians for friends.
> *lā tattakhidhu 'l-Yahūda wa 'n-Naṣārā awliyāʾ.* (5:51)

—in order to explain that closeness means the closeness of religions, not the closeness of physical bodies. He has not mentioned sons in this Qurʾānic verse, since human nature is such that sons are most likely to be their fathers' followers. It should also be noted that good treatment and gifts are excluded from [the prohibition of] friendship. Asmāʾ (may Allāh be well pleased with her) once said: "O Messenger of Allāh, if my mother approaches me with a request, she being a polytheist, should I give her something?" To this he replied (Allāh bless him and give him peace): "Give to your mother!"[870]

> Say: "If your fathers, and your sons, and your brothers,
> *qul in kāna ābāʾu-kum wa abnāʾu-kum wa ikhwānu-kum*
> and your wives, and your tribe,
> *wa azwāju-kum wa ʿashīratu-kum*
> and wealth you have acquired, and merchandise
> *wa amwāluni 'qtaraftumū-hā wa tijāratun*

for which you fear that there will be no sale,
takhshawna kasāda-hā
and dwellings you find pleasing,
wa masākinu tarḍawna-hā
are dearer to you than Allāh
aḥabba ilai-kum mina 'llāhi
and His Messenger and striving in His way, then wait....
wa Rasūli-hi wa jihādin fī sabīli-hi fa-tarabbaṣū....

You should know that this Qur'ānic verse is a confirmation of the answer He gave in the preceding verse, in response to a group of the believers who said: "O Messenger of Allāh, how can it be possible to disavow them entirely? Such disavowal is bound to result in our separation from our fathers, our brothers and our social connections, the loss of our merchandise, the destruction of our properties and the ruination of our houses, and our permanent destitution." He therefore explained (Exalted is He) that it is necessary to endure all these worldly hardships, in order to keep the religion safe and sound. "If the cultivation of these worldly interests of yours is more important to you," he told them, "than obedience to Allāh and obedience to His Messenger (Allāh bless him and give him peace), then wait for what you love so dearly, until Allāh brings His command to pass." That is to say, until He inflicts a worldly or an Otherworldly punishment, for the purpose is to deliver a threat.[871]

Say
qul

—O Muḥammad (Allāh bless him and give him peace), to those who abstained from the Migration [*Hijra*]:

"If your fathers, and your sons, and your brothers,
in kāna ābā'u-kum wa abnā'u-kum wa ikhwānu-kum
and your wives, and your tribe...."
wa azwāju-kum wa 'ashīratu-kum...

The term *'ashīra* [tribe] signifies one's closest relatives,[872] in other words, the collection of people to whom you appeal for help.[873]

and wealth you have acquired
wa amwāluni 'qtaraftumū-hā

That is to say: "[The wealth] you have acquired and gained in Mecca."

and merchandise
wa tijāratun

In other words: "commodities that you have bought for the purpose of trading and making profit."

for which you fear that there will be no sale
takhshawna kasāda-hā

—due to missing the time of their marketability on the days of seasonal festivities.

and dwellings you find pleasing
wa masākinu tarḍawna-hā

In other words: "dwellings in which you are pleased to reside, consisting of houses and gardens."

are dearer to you than Allāh and His Messenger
aḥabba ilai-kum mina 'llāhi wa Rasūli-hi

That is to say: "[dearer to you] than obeying Allāh and obeying His Messenger (Allāh bless him and give him peace), by undertaking the Migration [*Hijra*] to Medina."

and striving in His way....
wa jihādin fī sabīli-hi....

In other words: "and dearer to you than the sacred struggle in obedience to Allāh." The expression "dearer [*aḥabba*] to you" alludes to voluntary fondness [*ḥubb ikhtiyārī*] (accompanied by a deliberate intent, which may or may not weigh heavily on the lower self, depending on whether it is in compliance with Allāh's commandment), of which the desired effect is close attachment and inseparableness, as opposed to natural fondness [*ḥubb jibillī*] (in which the servant has no wilful intent, and for which he is not held responsible), from which no human being is exempt, since it is not subject to the constraint imposed in the sphere of obedience.[874]

You should also know that Allāh (Exalted is He) has mentioned the factors that are conducive to association with the unbelievers. These are four in number:

1. The association of close relatives, of which He has mentioned four types in detail, namely: fathers, sons, brothers and wives. He has then referred to the rest with a single term, covering them all, that term being *al-ʿashīra* [the tribe].

2. The inclination to keep a tight hold on acquired wealth.
3. The desire to gain wealth by means of trading.
4. The desire for dwellings.

There can be no doubt that this is an excellent arrangement in sequence, for, of all the factors conducive to association, the most important is close kinship. That association facilitates not only the retention of wealth already acquired, but also the obtainment of wealth that has not yet been acquired. At the end of the list comes the desire for the construction of buildings in the homelands, and houses erected for residential purposes. Allāh (Exalted is He) has mentioned these things in this necessary order, and He has concluded by explaining that attending to the religion is better than attending to all of these matters put together,[875] for He has said:

> then wait till Allāh brings His command to pass.
> *fa-tarabbaṣū ḥattā yaʾtiya 'llāhu bi-amri-h:*

That is to say: "[until He inflicts] a worldly or an Otherworldly punishment." This a threat, directed at anyone who gives priority to his selfish interests, instead of to the welfare of his religion.

> Allāh does not guide the dissolute folk aright.
> *wa 'llāhu lā yahdi 'l-qawma 'l-fāsiqīn.*

That is to say: "[He does not guide] those who forsake obedience by befriending the polytheists." In other words: "He does not direct them towards that which is best for them,"[876] referring to those who forsake worshipful obedience to Him in favour of sinful disobedience to Him. This is also a dire warning. As this Qurʾānic verse implies, if there is ever a conflict between any of the interests of the religion, on the one hand, and all the concerns of this world, on the other, the Muslim is obliged to accord the religion preference over this world.[877]

To this I would add: This preference is established in hearts that are enlightened, in the spirit that is exalted, and in the intelligence that is holy, divinely inspired and consciously aware, through detachment from the love of this world, and constant devotion to the service of the Master. By Allāh, we beg for enabling grace and right direction. O Allāh, do not let this world be our greatest concern!

The Qurʾānic verse contains a very stern threat, from which only the fewest of the few can be secure. If you followed the brethren of our own time, among the pious ascetics, you would find them confused and sad, regretting the loss of the slightest of all worldly things, and indifferent to the loss of the most splendid of all religious benefits. The import of the Qur᾿ānic verse is that, if someone prefers these worldly objects of desire, instead of worshipful obedience to the All-Merciful, he must prepare for the descent of a punishment, either worldly or Otherworldly. He must consider the immediate luxuries that he prefers, and ask himself whether he can escape the pending terrors and disasters. O Allāh, grant us Your pardon and Your forgiveness, O Most Merciful of the merciful!

In the words of the noble Prophetic tradition [*ḥadīth*]:

> Not one of you truly believes, until I am dearer to him that his wealth, his children and all people whomsoever.[878]

According to Ibn Malik: "The intention is to deny the perfection of belief, while 'dearer [*aḥabb*]' alludes to voluntary fondness [*ḥubb ikhtiyārī*]. For instance, if Allāh's Messenger (Allāh bless him and give him peace) commanded a believer to fight the unbeliever, so that he might become a martyr, or if he commanded him to kill his unbelieving parents and children, he would dearly love to make that choice voluntarily, because of his knowledge that salvation resides in compliance with his command (blessing and peace be upon him). He would also know that the choice does not come naturally, just as the invalid instinctively recoils from the course of treatment, but he accepts it nevertheless, and puts it into practice, because he thinks that his health and well-being depend on it.

"How, then, could we fail to do likewise, when our Prophet (Allāh bless him and give him peace) is more kindly disposed towards us than ourselves, our fathers and our children, because he (blessing and peace be upon him) exerts himself for our sake, not for any ulterior motive, and love for him (blessing and peace be upon him) includes support for his Sunna and the defence of his Sacred Law?"

The basis of the religion is the love of Allāh (Exalted is He), and the neglect of preparedness for the love of Allāh is due to these things that have been mentioned. They include dissolute conduct, which means deserting the love of the Creator in favour of the love of what has been created. If someone prefers the love of what has been created to the love of the Creator, he has cancelled his innate readiness to accept the divine emanation of grace. He has made deprivation inevitable, and defeat and disappointment have overtaken him.

> then wait till Allāh brings His command to pass.
> *fa-tarabbaṣū ḥattā yaʾtiya 'llāhu bi-amri-h:*

That is to say: "His all-prevailing command."

> Allāh does not guide the dissolute folk aright.
> *wa 'llāhu lā yahdi 'l-qawma 'l-fāsiqīn.*

In other words: "[He does not guide] those who depart from the good state of preparedness, in the sense that He does not guide them to the presence of His Majesty and the acceptance of the emanation of His Beauty, after they have rendered the good state of preparedness null and void."[879]

As related by al-Ḥāfiẓ, it was ʿAbdu'llāh ibn Shawdhab who said: "The father of Abū ʿUbaida ibn al-Jarrāḥ started describing the gods [*āliha*] to him on the Day of Badr, and Abū ʿUbaida tried to get away from him. Then, when al-Jarrāḥ continued more and more, his son Abū ʿUbaida attacked and killed him. It was then that Allāh (Exalted is He) sent down this Qurʾānic verse:

> You will not find folk who believe
> *lā tajidu qawman yuʾminūna*
> in Allāh and the Last Day
> *bi'llāhi wa 'l-yawmi 'l-ākhiri*
> loving those who oppose Allāh and His Messenger,
> *yuwāddūna man ḥādda 'llāha wa Rasūla-hu*
> even if they are their fathers or their sons
> *wa law kānū ābāʾa-hum aw abnāʾa-hum*
> or their brothers or their clan.
> *aw ikhwāna-hum aw ʿashīrata-hum*
>
> As for such, He has written faith upon their hearts,
> *ulā'ika kataba fī qulūbi-himu'l-īmāna*
> and strengthened them with a Spirit from Him,
> *wa ayyada-hum bi-Rūḥin min-h:*
> and He will bring them into Gardens
> *wa yudkhilu-hum jannātin*
> underneath which rivers flow, wherein they will abide.
> *tatjrī min taḥti-ha 'l-anhāru khālidīna fī-hā*
>
> Allāh is well pleased with them,
> *raḍiya 'llāhu ʿan-hum*

> and they are well pleased with Him.
> *wa raḍū ʿan-h.*
> They are Allāh's party. Is it not Allāh's party
> *ulāʾika ḥizbu 'llāh: a-lā inna ḥizba 'llāhi*
> who are the ones who will prosper?
> *humu 'l-mufliḥūn.* (58:22)[880]

Bishr ibn al-Ḥārith (may Allāh be well pleased with him) is reported as having said: "I once saw the Prophet (Allāh bless him and give him peace) in a dream, and he said to me:

> 'O Bishr, do you realize why Allāh (Exalted is He) has promoted you above your peers?'

"When I said: 'No, O Messenger of Allāh,' he said:

> Because of your loyal adherence to my Sunna, your service to the righteous, your sincere advice to your brethren, and your love for my Companions and the people of my household, it is He who has caused you to reach the stations of the devout."

To this I would add: Love is an enormous doorway, which is opened only for the people of sound hearts. Its influence is extraordinary and its power is amazing. We beseech Allāh (Glory be to Him and Exalted is He) to include us among those who prefer the love of Allāh and the love of His Messenger to the love of anything apart from them. *Āmīn.*[881]

These are my own comments:

If a person has reflected on the import of this Qurʾānic verse, considering how our Lord (Glorious and Exalted is He) has instructed us to let go of children, wives and so on, and to attach more importance to Allāh's commandment than to [the pain of] separation from them, and if he does not act accordingly, let us take refuge with Allāh! Those who are commanded by this verse will depart from the religion, and join the unbelievers, if they do not act as they have been commanded.

What about our own condition? For the sake of the rubbish of this world, we prefer falsehood to the requirement of faith. We do not tell the truth. We do not give charitable gifts. We accumulate material wealth, by legal or by illegal means. If you are admonished, you say: "I am considering the interest of my children, so that poverty will not afflict them." I must ask: "What is the state of our belief in these matters?"

It is essential for us, O company of the believers, to believe in the Qur᾽ān and in the rules that we have been commanded to obey, so that we may be included among the genuine believers.

Allāh has pledged Himself to guarantee your sustenance, but He is not a guarantor of your pardon. If you quote His words:

> Allāh is All-Forgiving, All-Compassionate.
> *wa 'llāhu Ghafūrun Raḥīm.* (5:74)

—I shall say: "Allāh forgives whomever He will, not whomever we will. You must not be misled into expecting the forgiveness of Allāh (Glorious and Exalted is He), despite the absence of work in accordance with faith. The believer works and hopes for His forgiveness, while the sinner does not work, yet relies on forgiveness. Our Lord (Glorious and Exalted is He) has told us:

> And I am indeed All-Forgiving
> *wa innī la-Ghaffārun*
> toward anyone who repents and believes,
> *li-man tāba wa āmana*
> and does righteous work, and then is rightly guided.
> *wa ʿamila ṣāliḥan thumma 'htadā.* (20:82)

—and stays on the right path. We must not be deluded, and we must not heedlessly ignore the commandment of Allāh.

O Allāh, grant us the ability to accomplish all that. *Āmīn.* Peace be upon the Messengers, and praise be to Allāh, the Lord of All the Worlds. There is no might nor any power, except with Allāh, the All-High, the Almighty. May Allāh bless our master Muḥammad, his family and his Companions, and may He grant them peace.

The Fifty-first Call

In the Name of Allāh, the All-Merciful, the All-Compassionate.
Bismi'llāhi 'r-Raḥmāni 'r-Raḥīm.

O you who truly believe,
the polytheists are nothing but filth.
yā ayyuha 'lladhīna āmanū
inna-ma 'l-mushrikūna najasun
So do not let them come near the Sacred Mosque
fa-lā yaqrabu 'l-Masjida 'l-Ḥarāma
after this year of theirs. If you fear indigence,
baʿda ʿāmi-him hādhā: wa in khiftum ʿailatan
Allāh will suffice you from His bounty,
if He so wishes.
fa-sawfa yughnī-kumu 'llāhu min faḍli-hi in shāʾ:
Allāh is All-Knowing, All-Wise.
inna 'llāha ʿAlīmun Ḥakīm. (9:28)

Allāh's Messenger (Allāh bless him and give him peace) had commanded ʿAlī to recite the first part of the Sūra of Absolution [*Barāʾa*] to the polytheists of Mecca, informing them that their treaty was dissolved, and that Allāh was exempt from collusion with the polytheists [*mushrikīn*], as was His Messenger. This had prompted some folk to say: "O people of Mecca, you are about to learn what calamity awaits you, due to highway robbery and the loss of caravan shipments!" This Qurʾānic verse was then sent down, in order to dispel this alarming suspicion. Allāh (Exalted is He) responded to it by saying:

If you fear indigence
wa in khiftum ʿailatan

—meaning poverty or need,

Allāh will suffice you from His bounty.
fa-sawfa yughnī-kumu 'llāhu min faḍli-hi.

Such is the context of this well-arranged sequence.[882] Let us now consider His saying:

> O you who truly believe, the polytheists are nothing but filth.
> *yā ayyuha 'lladhīna āmanū inna-ma 'l-mushrikūna najasun*

In other words: "They are nothing but impurity, due of the rottenness of their inner condition." Ibn ʿAbbās said: "They are filthy by nature, like dogs and pigs." It was al-Ḥasan who said: "If someone shakes hands with a polytheist, let him perform the ritual ablution [*wuḍūʾ*]!" According to the majority opinion, this is a comparison, indicating that they are on the level of filth, or like filth. Due to the rottenness of their persuasion and their disbelief in Allāh, they are represented as if they were filthy pollution itself. Such descriptive exaggeration also occurs, for instance, in the expression: "ʿAlī is a lion," meaning "like a lion."[883] As for the Islāmic jurists [*fuqahāʾ*], they are generally agreed on the attribution of cleanliness to the physical bodies of the polytheists.[884]

> So do not let them come near the Sacred Mosque
> *fa-lā yaqrabu 'l-Masjida 'l-Ḥarāma*
> after this year of theirs.
> *baʿda ʿāmi-him hādhā.*

That is to say: "So do not let them enter the Sanctuary [*Ḥaram*]." While mentioning the Sacred Mosque specifically, He intended it to mean the Sanctuary as a whole.

According to Abū Saʿūd: "What this signifies, it has also been said, is prohibition from the Pilgrimage [*Ḥajj*] and the Visitation [*ʿUmra*]." In other words: "They must not perform the Pilgrimage, nor must they perform the Visitation, after this year of theirs, which is the year Nine of the Hijra." This is supported by the Prophetic tradition [*ḥadīth*]:

> And no polytheist may perform the Pilgrimage after this year.[885]

That is the year in which the Sūra of Absolution [*Barāʾa*] was sent down, and ʿAlī recited it as a proclamation in the seasons of Pilgrimage.[886]

According to ash-Shāfiʿī (may Allāh be well pleased with him): "The unbelievers are barred from the Sacred Mosque in particular." According to Mālik: "They are barred from all the mosques." According to Abū

Ḥanīfa (may Allāh bestow His mercy upon him): "They are not barred from the Sacred Mosque, nor from the rest of the mosques." By its very wording, however, the verse negates the statement of Abū Ḥanīfa (may Allāh bestow His mercy upon him). By its implicit meaning, it also negates the statement of Mālik. We may put it like this: "While the basic assumption is the absence of preclusion, we contradict it in the case of the Sacred Mosque, on account of this explicitly definitive text. In all other cases, however, the basic assumption must apply."[887]

According to a traditional report, Ibn ʿUmar (may Allāh be well pleased with him) once heard Allāh's Messenger (Allāh bless him and give him peace) say:

> I will surely expel the Jews and the Christians from the Arabian Peninsula [*Jazīrat al-ʿArab*], so that I leave in it no one who is not a Muslim.[888]

He bequeathed this task, for he said:

> You must expel the polytheists [*mushrikīn*] from the Arabian Peninsula.[889]

Abū Bakr (may Allāh be well pleased with him) did not attend to that, but ʿUmar (may Allāh be well pleased with him) cleared them out during his Caliphate.

According to another traditional report, Jābir (may Allāh be well pleased with him) said: "I once heard Allāh's Messenger (Allāh bless him and give him peace) say:

> Satan has despaired of being worshipped by those who perform their prayers in the Arabian Peninsula, but not of sowing discord amongst them."[890]

According to the religious scholars, the areas of Islām, as far as the unbelievers are concerned, are three:

1. The [Meccan] Sanctuary [*Ḥaram*]. It is not permissible for the unbelievers to enter this area under any circumstance.

2. The Ḥijāz. It is not permissible for the unbelievers to enter this territory, except with special permission. Even then, they may not stay in it for more than three days, because of what is stated in the Prophetic tradition [*ḥadīth*], namely:

> Two religions must not coexist in the Arabian Peninsula.[891]

3. The other territories of Islām. It is permissible for the unbelievers to reside in them, subject to a covenant of protection [*dhimma*] or an official warrant of security [*amān*]. They may not enter the mosques, however, except with permission from a Muslim, granted because of some emergency.[892]

> If you fear indigence,
> *wa in khiftum ʿailatan*
> Allāh will suffice you from His bounty.
> *fa-sawfa yughnī-kumu 'llāhu min faḍli-hi.*

That is to say: "In case you are afraid, O believers, of suffering some poverty, as a result of their being barred from entering the Sanctuary, or from performing the Pilgrimage, Allāh (Glory be to Him) will make you independent of them by some other means, from His gracious favour and generous giving."

According to the traditional commentators: "When the Muslims were prevented from enabling the polytheists to enter the Sanctuary, although the polytheists used to procure foodstuffs and merchandise for them during the seasons of Pilgrimage and Visitation, Satan instilled anxiety in their hearts, by saying to them: 'Where are you going to find something to eat? How are you going to survive, when you have been prevented from obtaining sustenance and things you need to acquire?' Allāh therefore assured them against poverty and indigence, and provided them with the spoils of war [*ghanāʾim*] and the tribute-tax [*jizya*]."[893]

In this Qurʾānic verse, there is evidence that the heart's attachment to the means of sustenance is permissible, and is not incompatible with trust [*tawakkul*]. While it is true that sustenance is decreed by destiny, and Allāh's decree and His allotment must be carried out, He has linked it to the material means. He has done so as an act of wisdom, so that He may distinguish the hearts that depend on the material means, from the hearts that place all their trust in the Lord of lords. As mentioned above, however, attachment to the means is not totally incompatible with trust. The Prophet (Allāh bless him and give him peace) once said:

> If you trust in Allāh with all the trust He deserves, He will surely sustain you, just as He sustains the birds. They start the day on empty stomachs, but they settle down to rest with their stomachs full.[894]

The correct approach is the one prescribed by the Sunna, which is considered obvious by the Islāmic jurists: namely, work with all the worldly means available, such as farming, trade in the markets, the cultivation of properties, and the planting of fruit-trees.

That is what the Companions (may Allāh be well pleased with them) used to do, and the Prophet (Allāh bless him and give him peace) was among the most outstanding of them in this respect. According to Abu'l-Ḥasan ibn Baṭṭāl: "In several Qur'ānic verses, Allāh (Glory be to Him) has commanded His servants to spend [on worthy causes] some of the good things they have acquired. He has also said:

> But he who is driven by necessity,
> *fa-mani 'ḍṭurra*
> neither craving nor transgressing, it is no sin for him.
> *ghaira bāghin wa lā ʿādin fa-lā ithma ʿalai-h.* (2:173)

"He has thus made lawful, to someone driven by necessity, that which He has made unlawful to him in its absence, in order to ensure the nourishment that He has commanded him to acquire and use for sustenance. He has not commanded him to wait for food to descend upon him out of the sky. Besides, if he were to abstain from what he needs for nourishment, he would be committing suicide. Allāh's Messenger (Allāh bless him and give him peace) used to wriggle and squirm from hunger, when he could find nothing to eat, but no food ever descended upon him out of the sky. He used to keep a year's supply of basic foodstuffs in store for his family, until Allāh granted him victories."

As related by Anas ibn Mālik (may Allāh be well pleased with him), a man once brought a camel to the Prophet (Allāh bless him and give him peace). "O Messenger of Allāh," he said, "should I hobble it with a cord, and then have trust [in the Lord], or should I leave it untied, and then have trust?" He received the reply: "Hobble it, and then have trust!"

No argument can be based on the special case of the People of the Bench [*Ahl aṣ-Ṣuffa*], for they were paupers who used to sit in the mosque. They did not engage in farming or trade, and they had no earned income or property. They were the guests of Islām, at a time when its territories were narrowly confined. Nevertheless, they used to gather firewood by day, and carry water to the home of Allāh's Messenger (Allāh bless him and give him peace). They used to recite the Qur'ān by night, and perform the ritual prayer. That is how they are described by al-Bukhārī and others, so they obviously dealt with the material means. When the Prophet (Allāh bless him and give him peace) received a sacrificial animal, he would eat it with them, and if he received a charitable gift, he would make a point of bestowing it on them. Then, when victory came in abundance, and Islām spread far and wide, they emerged and assumed positions of authority (like Abū Huraira—may Allāh be well pleased with him—and others), and did not stay seated [on the Bench].

Concerning the various means by which sustenance can be sought, they are said to be of six kinds:

1. At the highest level is the means referred to by our Prophet Muḥammad (Allāh bless him and give him peace), when he said:

> He has laid my sustenance beneath the shadow of my spear, and He has laid humiliation and belittlement upon anyone who opposes my command.[895]

Allāh has thus placed the sustenance of His Prophet (Allāh bless him and give him peace) where he can readily acquire it, because of his special merit, and He has favoured him uniquely with the best of all kinds of acquisition.

2. The food a man earns by the work of his hand. The Prophet (Allāh bless him and give him peace) once said:

> The tastiest food is what a man earns by the work of his hand. Allāh's Prophet David (peace be upon him) used to eat from what he earned by the work of his hand.[896]

As Allāh said [of David (peace be upon him)]:

> And We taught him the art of making garments to protect you.
> *wa ʿallamnā-hu ṣanʿata labūsin la-kum* (21:80)

It is also related that Jesus (peace be upon him) used to eat from what his mother earned by spinning.

3. Trade. This was the work of the majority of the Companions (may they enjoy Allāh's good pleasure), especially the Emigrants [*Muhājirīn*]. The Qurʾānic revelation refers to them in more than one instance.

4. Ploughing the land and planting crops.

5. Teaching the art of Qurʾānic recitation, and providing instruction in the chanting of religious incantations [*ruqā*].

6. Borrowing, when really necessary, with the intention of paying

back. The Prophet (Allāh bless him and give him peace) once said:

> If someone borrows other people's possessions, intending to repay them, Allāh will repay on his behalf. On the other hand, if someone borrows them with the intention of ruining them, Allāh will ruin him.[897]

> if He so wishes.
> *in shā'*.

He has qualified the assertion "He will suffice you" with this condition, making it dependent on the wish to do so. Although this qualification appears to be incompatible with the object of the Qur'ānic verse, which is to dispel their fear of indigence, it actually teaches several lessons of great value:

1. That the heart must not be attached to the actualization of what has been promised. It must rather be attached to the noble generosity of the One who has made that promise. It must be humbly submissive to Him, in the receipt of all provisions and the dispelling of all disasters and misfortunes.
2. The notification that the promised sufficiency is not incumbent on Allāh (Exalted is He). He is freely conferring His gracious favour, which He does not confer except by His wish and His will.
3. The notification that what is promised is not promised in relation to all individuals, nor in relation to all places and times.

> Allāh is All-Knowing, All-Wise.
> *inna 'llāha 'Alīmun Ḥakīm*.

He is All-Knowing where your best interests are concerned, and He is All-Wise with respect to what He gives and withholds.

The Qur'ānic verse implies that Allāh (Exalted is He) has removed the pen of imposition from the human being, until he reaches complete maturity of the outer mould [*qālab*]. During that span of time, the lower self and its attributes are circumambulating the Ka'ba of the heart [*qalb*], supported by the intellectual and spiritual energies. They are thus reinforced by their appetites for this world and its pleasure, until the worship of this world becomes their normal habit, and the attribution of partners to Allāh becomes their natural inclination. The outer mould is thereby brought to completion, and the characteristics of humanity come to match those of animality, with the manifestation of carnal desire in its maturity. As soon as that point is reached, Allāh causes the pen of imposition to flow upon them. He forbids the heart to follow the lower self [*nafs*], and commands it to kill it. He forbids the lower self to wander around, in case it contaminates the Kaʿba of the heart with the filthy pollution of polytheistic association [*shirk*] and blameworthy attributions. Then, once the lower self has been barred from wandering around the precincts of the heart, the heart feels afraid of losing the means of satisfying its appetites, which it used to obtain by following the lower self. Allāh therefore makes it independent of those means of satisfaction, by providing it with the gracious favour of His gifts, consisting of Lordly inspirations, direct visions, and merciful disclosures.

His saying (Exalted is He):

> if He so wishes.
> *in shā'.*

—also signifies that what is in the presence of Allāh cannot be obtained except by Allāh's wish.[898]

These are my own remarks:

You must abandon whatever you may wish, in favour of whatever He wishes. You must beware of your own preference. Once you have experienced complete submission, in the heart and the core of the innermost being, not in speech alone, then, and only then, will you be a servant to your Lord. Self-centered concerns will no longer be with you, ordinary human nature will have vanished from you, and whatever benefit comes to you, or emanates from you, it will be because of Him, not because of you. You must contemplate what your Creator (Glory be to Him) has said:

> if He so wishes.
> *in shā':*

—for Reality [*Ḥaqīqa*] will then become apparent to you.

O Allāh, join us to the people who specialize in real experience! If someone loves on the basis of Reality, nothing wields any power over his heart, except his Beloved, and he has no wish apart from His wish.

O Allāh, grant us the ability to accomplish all that. *Āmīn.* Peace be upon the Messengers, and praise be to Allāh, the Lord of All the Worlds. There is no might nor any power, except with Allāh, the All-High, the Almighty. May Allāh bless our master Muḥammad, his family and his Companions, and may He grant them peace.

The Fifty-second Call

In the Name of Allāh, the All-Merciful, the All-Compassionate.
Bismi'llāhi 'r-Raḥmāni 'r-Raḥīm.

O you who truly believe,
many of the [Jewish] rabbis
yā ayyuha 'lladhīna āmanū inna kathīran mina 'l-aḥbāri
and the [Christian] monks
devour the wealth of mankind
wa 'r-ruhbāni la-ya'kulūna amwāla 'n-nāsi
wantonly, and debar [men] from the way of Allāh.
bi-'l-bāṭili wa yaṣuddūna ʿan sabīli 'llāh:
They who hoard up gold and silver
and do not spend it
wa 'lladhīna yaknizūna 'dh-dhahaba
wa 'l-fiḍḍata wa lā yunfiqūna-hā
in the way of Allāh, to them give tidings
of a painful torment.
fī sabīli 'llāhi fa-bashshir-hum bi-ʿadhābin alīm.

On the Day when it will be heated
in the Fire of Hell,
yawma yuḥmā ʿalai-hā fī nāri Jahannama
and with it will be branded
fa-tukwā bi-hā
their foreheads and their flanks and their backs:
jibāhu-hum wa junūbu-hum wa ẓuhūru-hum
"This is what you hoarded for yourselves.
hādhā mā kanaztum li-anfusi-kum
Now taste what you used to hoard!"
fa-dhūqū mā kuntum taknizūn. (9:34,35)

O you who truly believe,
yā ayyuha 'lladhīna āmanū
many of the rabbis and the monks....
inna kathīran mina 'l-aḥbāri wa 'r-ruhbāni....

That is to say: "O you who believe in Allāh and His Messenger, many of the scholars of the Jews [*al-aḥbār*] and the scholars of the Christians [*ar-ruhbān*]":

> devour the wealth of mankind wantonly,
> *la-ya'kulūna amwāla 'n-nāsi bi-'l-bāṭili*
> and debar [men] from the way of Allāh.
> *wa yaṣuddūna ʿan sabīli 'llāh:*

In other words: "They take people's wealth by unlawful means, and prevent them from entering the religion of Islām."

According to Ibn Kathīr: "The purpose is to warn against the scholars of evil and the worshippers of error."

According to Ibn ʿUyaina: "In those of our own scholars who are corrupt, there is some resemblance to the Jews, and in those of our worshippers who are corrupt, there is some resemblance to the Christians."[899]

As you should know, Allāh (Exalted is He) has already described the leaders of the Jews and the Christians as guilty of arrogance, haughtiness, laying claim to lordship, and exalting themselves above their fellow creatures. In this Qur'ānic verse, He has further described them as guilty of greed and the avaricious desire to seize people's wealth. As He has thereby pointed out, the purpose of that display of lordship, haughtiness and vainglory is to acquire people's wealth under false pretences,[900] and by degrading their importance and belittling their intelligence. That is because they have adopted the religion as a means of obtaining this world, and that is the ultimate ignominy and disgrace.[901]

By my life, if anyone considers the states of the people of sly deceit [*nāmūs*]—meaning corruption and falsification—in this time of ours, it will seem to him that these verses must have been revealed in connection with their situation, and to explain their states of being. You will notice how one of them claims that he attaches no importance to this world, that he is utterly disinterested in all created things, and that, in purity and splendour, he is like the angels brought near.

In fact, however, if it comes to the matter of a single loaf of bread, you will see him desperate to obtain it, and ready to go to the utmost length of shame and disgrace in order to acquire it. All of these characteristics abound in our own time, and this is the method used by most of the ignorant and counterfeiting types, in order to misappropriate the possessions of the common folk and the simpletons among their fellow creatures.[902] They misappropriate them by means of bribery and corruption. In order to change the rules and the laws, and to limit and reduce their application, they deceive people into thinking that they are skilled professionals in the interpretation of the Qur᾽ānic verse, and the explanation of what Allāh (Exalted is He) intended by it.[903]

> and [they] debar [men] from the way of Allāh.
> *wa yaṣuddūna ʿan sabīli 'llāh:*

That is because they used to kill to maintain their own following, and they used to put obstacles in the way of following of the best of creatures. The scholars of the time, as in the time of our master Muḥammad (Allāh bless him and give him peace), would go to extreme lengths in order to prevent people from following him, using all types of deception and duplicity.

The compiler (may Allāh be well pleased with him) has said: "For creatures in this world, the ultimate objects of desire are wealth and high rank. In describing the rabbis and the monks, Allāh (Exalted is He) has therefore made it plain that they are infatuated with these two ambitions. Wealth is referred to in His saying:

> [They] devour the wealth of mankind wantonly
> *la-ya᾽kulūna amwāla 'n-nāsi bi-'l-bāṭili*

"As for high rank, it is implicitly referred to in His saying:

> and [they] debar [men] from the way of Allāh."[904]
> *wa yaṣuddūna ʿan sabīli 'llāh:*

❧ ❧

> They who hoard up gold and silver
> *wa 'lladhīna yaknizūna 'dh-dhahaba wa 'l-fiḍḍata*

That is to say: "They accumulate possessions and store up riches."

> and do not spend it in the way of Allāh
> *wa lā yunfiqūna-hā fī sabīli 'llāhi*

In other words: "They do not pay the alms-due [*zakāt*] on it, and they do not spend any of it on good causes." According to Ibn ʿUmar (may

Allāh be well pleased with him): "A treasure, on which the alms-due has not been paid, is not a treasure."

> to them give [good] tidings of a painful torment.
> *fa-bashshir-hum bi-ʿadhābin alīm.*

This is a sarcastic expression, signifying: "Inform them of the painful torment in the abode of the Inferno." According to az-Zamakhsharī: "Allāh has made the connection between the hoarders and the Jews and Christians for the simple purpose of rebuking them harshly, and to indicate that any of them who takes ill-gotten property, and any Muslim who fails to share the benefit of his wealth, he is equally entitled to the 'good tidings' of the painful torment."

[The following Prophetic tradition is recorded] in the *Ṣaḥīḥ* of Muslim:

> If any man fails to pay the alms-due [*zakāt*] on his wealth, pages of fire will be assigned to him on the Day of Resurrection. His side and his forehead and his back will be scorched thereby, on a day that lasts as long as fifty thousand years, until judgment is decreed among the servants [of the Lord]. Then he will see his path, leading either to the Garden of Paradise or to the Fire of Hell.

It is related that an Arab of the desert said to Ibn ʿUmar (may Allāh be well pleased with him and his father): "Tell me about the saying of Allāh (Exalted is He):

> They who hoard up gold and silver."
> *wa 'lladhīna yaknizūna 'dh-dhahaba wa 'l-fiḍḍata*

Ibn ʿUmar (may Allāh be well pleased with him and his father) replied: "If somone hoards them, and does not pay the alms-due on them, woe unto him! This was before the [law concerning the] alms-due was revealed. When that revelation came down, Allāh made the alms-due a purification for material possessions. I don't mind! If I had gold like someone, I would purify it, and I would put it to good use in obedience to Allāh (Exalted is He)."[905]

As reported by Imām Aḥmad, ʿAlī (may Allāh be well pleased with him) said: "Allāh's Messenger (Allāh bless him and give him peace) once said:

> Perish gold! Perish silver!"

"He said this three times, and that was disturbing to the Companions of Allāh's Messenger (Allāh bless him and give him peace). They said: 'What form of wealth should we adopt?' ʿUmar (may Allāh be well pleased with him) said: 'I shall let you know about that.' Then he said:

'O Messenger of Allāh, your Companions are disturbed. They have asked: "What form of wealth should we adopt?"' He replied:

> A tongue that expresses remembrance, a heart that is thankful, and a wife who makes you concentrate on your religion![906]

> On the Day when it will be heated in the Fire of Hell
> *yawma yuḥmā ʿalai-hā fī nāri Jahannama*

That is to say: "On the Day when it will be heated in the blazing Fire, until it becomes hot enough for branding."

> and with it will be branded
> *fa-tukwā bi-hā*
> their foreheads and their flanks and their backs
> *jibāhu-hum wa junūbu-hum wa ẓuhūru-hum*

In other words: "Their foreheads, flanks and backs will be scorched by the branding imprinted upon them."[907]

It was Ibn Masʿūd who said: "By the One apart from Whom there is no god, a servant will not be branded by a pile of treasure, with one dīnār [gold coin] on top of another dīnār, nor with one dirham [silver coin] on top of another dirham. What will happen is that his skin will be stretched, for each dīnār and dirham will be placed on it separately. These parts of the body have been singled out for branding, because, when the miser sees the poor beggar approaching, he knits his forehead in a scowl, and then, when he comes up to him, he turns his side towards him, and then, when he appeals to him for charity, he turns his back on him."[908]

Branding on the face is more conspicuous and more hideous, while on the back and the flank it is more painful and more excruciating. That is why He has mentioned them in particular, singling them out from the other parts of the body.[909]

> "This is what you hoarded for yourselves.
> *hādhā mā kanaztum li-anfusi-kum*
> Now taste what you used to hoard!"
> *fa-dhūqū mā kuntum taknizūn.*

That is to say: "You will be told, reproachfully and scoldingly: 'This is what you hoarded for yourselves, so taste the evil consequence of what you used to hoard!'"[910]

You should know that the Way of the Truth requires this to be said: "The best course, for the man in quest of religious experience, is not to accumulate much wealth, unless the outer aspect of the Sacred Law presents no obstacle to his doing so. The first course is predicated on true devotion [*taqwā*], while the second is predicated on the outward appearance of true devotion." As for the assertion that the best course is to refrain from seeking much wealth, there are several factors to consider:

1. When the human being loves something, the more often he gains access to it, and the more he takes pleasure in it, the more intense his love for it becomes, and the stronger his inclination towards it. If a person is poor, it seems that he cannot taste the pleasure of having wealth at his disposal, and that he is unaware of that pleasure. Then, if he comes to possess a little wealth, he experiences a corresponding degree of pleasure, so his inclination is intensified. Then, whenever his wealth increases, his enjoyment of it will be all the greater, and his greed for its pursuit and his urge to acquire it will be even more intense. It is well established that the multiplication of wealth is a cause of the multiplication of greed in its pursuit. Greed is wearisome to the spirit, the soul and the heart, and its harmful effects are severe. The intelligent person is therefore obliged to take precautions against doing himself harm.

As we have also explained, whenever wealth increases, the greed for it intensifies. If we could assume that the search for wealth would reach a certain limit, at which point the search would come to an end, and greed would disappear, we could expect a person to strive to reach that limit. The facts prove, however, that the more wealth is acquired, the greater the harm resulting from greed, and that there is no end to this harm and to this search. The human being is therefore obliged to abandon it at the outset.

2. The acquisition of material wealth is a very hard task, and preserving it after its acquisition is even harder, more exacting and more problematic. A person must devote the whole of his life, sometimes to the quest for obtainment, and at other times to the exhausting effort of preservation. This leaves him with little time to

enjoy the benefits, which he must eventually forgo altogether, with heavy sighs and groans, and:

> That is the sheer loss.
> *dhālika huwa 'l-khusrānu 'l-mubīn.* (22:11)

3. Great wealth and high rank give rise to exceeding the proper limits, as He has said (Exalted is He):

> No indeed! The human being does overstep the bounds,
> *kallā inna 'l-insāna la-yaṭghā*
> in that he regards himself as self-sufficient.
> *an ra'ā-hu 'staghnā.* (96:6,7)

Transgression prevents the servant from reaching the station of the good pleasure of the All-Merciful, and makes him fall into loss and disappointment.

4. Allāh (Exalted is He) has imposed the alms-due [*zakāt*] as an obligatory duty, and that represents an endeavour to diminish material wealth. If increasing that wealth had been a virtue, the Sacred Law would hardly have endeavoured to diminish it!

Suppose someone asks: "Why did the Prophet (blessing and peace be upon him) say:

> The upper hand is better than the lower hand?"[911]

We shall reply: "The upper hand has awarded him [who has paid the alms-due] the attribute of superiority because he has given that small amount. Because of that small reduction in his wealth, he has acquired superiority, and because the pauper has obtained that small increase, preponderance has come about."

Many traditional reports have reached us, concerning the threat that is levelled at the withholder of the alms-due. As for the withholding of the monetary alms-due, its consequence is mentioned in this Qur'ānic verse:

> On the Day when it will be heated in the Fire of Hell
> *yawma yuḥmā 'alai-hā fī nāri Jahannama*

As for the alms-due payable in the form of livestock, it is related in the tradition [*ḥadīth*] that Allāh (Exalted is He) will subject the owners of livestock to torment, if they do not pay the appropriate alms-due, by herding the biggest of those beasts towards them, so that they stampede over their masters, trampling them with their cloven hoofs and goring them with their horns. As soon as the last of the animals is exhausted, the first will return to them, and they will carry on like that, until the people have finished undergoing the reckoning.[912]

These are my own observations:

The best of wealth is that which you employ for lawful purposes. If you cling to your wealth, you belong to it, and if you spend it wisely, it belongs to you. The most lawful wealth is that which comes to you without your asking. The average person concentrates his attention on this world, in order to avoid depending on anyone else, so he works night and day to avoid becoming a pauper. This class of people has a very large membership. As for those who devote their attention to preparing for the life to come, in order to avoid being poor in the Hereafter, they represent a tiny fraction of humankind.

In actual fact, this world is guaranteed to its inhabitants, each one of them being entitled to the amount of sustenance that Allāh has foreordained for him. As for the Hereafter, it is not guaranteed to anyone, except those for whom Allāh has vouchsafed a fine conclusion, such as the Prophets and those who received glad tidings of the Garden of Paradise. These used to do the kind of work that is done by someone who fears his Lord (Blessed and Exalted is He).

As for those who have entered into sainthood [*wilāya*] for the sake of Allāh (Almighty and Glorious is He), they have entered through the door of their opposition to their lower selves. Since everything vile has its source in the instigating self [*an-nafs al-ammāra*], it is essential to gain knowledge of its secrets, and call it to account with every breath, so that it cannot cheat.

We beg Allāh to ensure our safety and success in all our actions, both outwardly and inwardly. He is All-Hearing, Ever-Responsive. O Allāh, grant us the ability to accomplish all that. *Āmīn*. Peace be upon the Messengers, and praise be to Allāh, the Lord of All the Worlds. There is no might nor any power, except with Allāh, the All-High, the Almighty. May Allāh bless our master Muḥammad, his family and his Companions, and may He grant them peace.

The Fifty-third Call

In the Name of Allāh, the All-Merciful, the All-Compassionate.
Bismi'llāhi 'r-Raḥmāni 'r-Raḥīm.

O you who truly believe, what ails you
yā ayyuha 'lladhīna āmanū mā la-kum
that when it is said to you: "Go forth
idhā qīla la-kumu 'nfirū
in the way of Allāh,"
you are weighed down to the ground?
fī sabīli 'llāhi 'ththāqaltum ila 'l-arḍ:
Are you content with the life of this world,
a-raḍītum bi-'l-ḥayāti 'd-dunyā
rather than that of the Hereafter?
mina 'l-ākhira:
Yet the enjoyment of the life of this world,
fa-mā matā'u 'l-ḥayāti 'd-dunyā
compared with that of the Hereafter,
is merely a trivial thing.
fi 'l-ākhirati illā qalīl.

If you do not go forth,
He will afflict you with a painful torment,
illā tanfirū yu'adhdhib-kum 'adhāban alīman
and He will choose instead of you
a folk other than you.
wa yastabdil qawman ghaira-kum
You cannot harm Him at all.
wa lā taḍurrū-hu shai'ā:
Allāh is Capable of all things.
wa 'llāhu 'alā kulli shai'in Qadīr. (9:38,39)

Having described the faults and vices of these unbelievers, Allāh (Exalted is He) has returned to arousing enthusiasm for fighting them,[913] and He has said:

O you who truly believe, what ails you
yā ayyuha 'lladhīna āmanū mā la-kum
that when it is said to you: "Go forth
idhā qīla la-kumu 'nfirū
in the way of Allāh," you are weighed down to the ground?
fī sabīli 'llāhi 'ththāqaltum ila 'l-arḍ:

This is phrased as a question for the purpose of censure and rebuke. It is a reproach for the abandonment of the sacred struggle [*jihād*], and a reprimand for those who stayed behind from the military expedition of Tabūk. It signifies: "What is wrong with you, O believers, that when you are told: 'Go forth to combat the enemies of Allāh,' you are sluggish and drag your feet, inclining towards this world and its lustful desires, and recoiling from the hardships of the journey and its pursuit?"[914]

In the preceding verses, Allāh (Exalted is He) has mentioned many factors that make it necessary to fight them. He has also mentioned many advantages to be gained by fighting them, as in His saying:

Allāh will chastise them at your hands,
yu'adhdhibu-humu 'llāhu bi-aidī-kum
and He will lay them low and give you victory over them.
wa yukhzi-him wa yanṣur-kum 'alai-him. (9:14)

He has mentioned their reprehensible utterances and their foul deeds, in the sphere of religion and the context of this world. Given this state of affairs, no obstacle can remain to keep the individual from fighting them, except that he is afraid of being killed and dearly loves this world. Allāh (Exalted is He) has therefore explained that this obstacle is contemptible, because the happiness of this world, in relation to the bliss of the Hereafter, is like a drop from the ocean, and forsaking much goodness for the sake of a little evil is sheer ignorance and folly.

According to traditional report, Ibn 'Abbās (may Allāh be well pleased with him and his father) related that this Qur'ānic verse was revealed in connection with the expedition of Tabūk. When the Prophet (blessing and peace be upon him) returned from aṭ-Ṭā'if, he stopped in Medina and commanded the campaign against the Byzantines.

That was during the season of intense heat, when the fruits of Medina became ripe and mellow, so they regarded the Byzantine expedition as a colossal burden, and they viewed it with dread. In was then that the Qurʾānic verse came down.

According to the experts, the people found that burdensome for several reasons:

1. The hardship experienced in the season of summer and lack of rain.
2. The remoteness of the distance involved, and the need for preparations far exceeding those usually required for other military expeditions.
3. That was the fruit-gathering season in Medina.
4. The intensity of the heat at that time.
5. Dread of the army of the Byzantines.

These many factors combined to produce the sluggish attitude of the people towards that expedition. Allāh knows best, of course.[915]

> Are you content with the life of this world,
> *a-raḍītum bi-'l-ḥayāti 'd-dunyā*
> rather than that of the Hereafter?
> *mina 'l-ākhira:*
> Yet the enjoyment of the life of this world,
> *fa-mā matāʿu 'l-ḥayāti 'd-dunyā*
> compared with that of the Hereafter,
> *fī 'l-ākhirati*
> is merely a trivial thing.
> *illā qalīl.*

That is to say: "Are you content with the bounty of this world and its transitory enjoyment, instead of the bounty of the Hereafter and its permanent reward? Yet the enjoyment of the pleasures of this world, by comparison with the Hereafter, is merely a despicable and trivial thing, without any value.[916]"

Is it not true that your Master is commanding you to fight them, and you know that obedience to your Master entails the tremendous reward in the Hereafter? Does it make any sense for the intelligent person to forgo the tremendous reward in the Hereafter, for the sake of the insignificant benefit available in this world? The proof that the enjoyment of this world, compared with that of the Hereafter, is merely a trivial thing, is that the pleasures of this world are undoubtedly contemptible in themselves, mixed with disasters and afflictions, cut off from every close and meaningful relationship. The benefits of the Hereafter, on the other hand, are noble, lofty, free from all disasters, and everlastingly enduring. That necessitates the conclusion that the enjoyment of this world is trivial, mean and contemptible.[917]

As reported by ath-Thawrī, it was al-Aʿmash who said, concerning His saying (Exalted is He):

> Yet the enjoyment of the life of this world,
> *fa-mā matāʿu 'l-ḥayāti 'd-dunyā*
> compared with that of the Hereafter,
> *fi 'l-ākhirati*
> is merely a trivial thing.
> *illā qalīl.*

—"It is like the rider's provision for the journey." According to ʿAbd al-ʿAzīz ibn Abī Ḥāzim, his father told him: "When death approached ʿAbd al-ʿAzīz ibn Marwān, he said: 'Bring me my shroud, in which I shall be wrapped for burial.' He looked at it, and then, when it was placed in front of him, he looked at it again and said: 'Have I nothing more significant than this, to leave behind as a relic of this world?' He turned his back and wept, saying [to this world]: 'Fie on you! A wretched abode are you! Much of you is too little, and a little of you is too much, and we have been in a state of delusion about you.'[918]

Allāh has rebuked them for preferring comfort in this world over comfort in the Hereafter, since the comfort of the Hereafter can only be acquired through the stressful exertion of this world. The Prophet (blessing and peace be upon him) once said to ʿĀʾisha, when she was riding around [the Kaʿba]:

> Your reward corresponds to the amount of your exertion.[919]

> If you do not go forth,
> *illā tanfirū*
> He will afflict you with a painful torment
> *yuʿadhdhib-kum ʿadhāban alīman*

That is to say: "If you do not set out to wage the sacred struggle, together with Allāh's Messenger (Allāh bless him and give him peace), Allāh will afflict you with an acutely painful torment, by giving the enemy control over you in this world, and with the blazing Fire of Hell in the Hereafter." According to Ibn ʿAbbās (may Allāh be well pleased with him and his father): "[The torment will be inflicted by] depriving them of rain."[920]

As you should understand, the threat may refer to the torment of this world, or it may refer to the torment of the Hereafter. It was Ibn ʿAbbās (may Allāh be well pleased with him and his father) who said: "Allāh's Messenger (Allāh bless him and give him peace) ordered the people to go to war, but they were sluggish about it, so they were deprived of rain." According to al-Ḥasan: "Allāh knows best what kind of torment He will inflict upon them." According to some, the torment must be that of the Hereafter, since the adjective *alīm* [painful] is appropriate only in that case. According to others, it holds out the threat of torment in all its forms: the torment of this world, the torment of the Hereafter, deprival of the benefits of this world, and deprival of the benefits of the Hereafter.[921]

> and He will choose instead of you a folk other than you.
> *wa yastabdil qawman ghaira-kum*

In other words: "He will destroy you, and in your place He will choose other people, better than you, who will be quicker to respond to His Messenger (Allāh bless him and give him peace), and more obedient."[922]

Allāh (Glory be to Him and Exalted is He) has served notice that He has guaranteed support for His Prophet (Allāh bless him and give him peace), and the strengthening of His religion. If they set out with him quickly, as they have been instructed to go forth, they will therefore receive support, and their reward will be incumbent on Allāh (Almighty and Glorious is He). If they are sluggish, however, and hang back from the fray, victory will be achieved by means of others. The reproof has been delivered to them, in case they imagine that the reinforcement of Allāh's Messenger (Allāh bless him and give him peace), and his triumph, can only come about through them. In His saying (Exalted is He):

> You cannot harm Him at all.
> *wa lā taḍurrū-hu shaiʾā:*

—the pronoun refers to Allāh (Exalted is He), so the meaning is: "You cannot harm Allāh at all, because He is Independent of all the worlds. You can only harm yourselves, by your failure to wage the sacred struggle together with Allāh's Messenger (Allāh bless him and give him peace)." According to some, the pronoun refers to Allāh's Messenger (Allāh bless him and give him peace), so the meaning is: "You cannot harm Muḥammad (Allāh bless him and give him peace) at all, for Allāh is his Helper against his enemies, and He will not leave him in the lurch."

> Allāh is Capable of all things.
> *wa 'llāhu ʿalā kulli shaiʾin Qadīr.*

That is to say: "He is Capable of all things, so He will support His Prophet and fortify His religion."

According to the majority of the experts: "This Qurʾānic verse is immune to abrogation, because it is addressed to a set of people who were ordered to go forth by Allāh's Messenger (Allāh bless him and give him peace), but who did not go forth."[923]

You must know that idleness hardens the heart, so activity is essential. There are blessings in activities, both at home and while travelling. There are two kinds of travel: the travel of this world and the travel of the Hereafter. Both of them involve hardship, although the second is more exacting. In the words of the Prophetic tradition [*ḥadīth*]:

> Travel is a portion of the torment.[924]

A man must therefore use the days of his life to good advantage, and strive to obtain the good pleasure of his Lord.

The Prophet (blessing and peace be upon him) compared the responsible person to the merchant, and in his saying:

> There are two blessings which many people fail to appreciate: health and leisure.

—he likened health and leisure to financial capital, because these two are among the assets available to human spirits, and among the principal means of achieving success, for, if someone relates to Allāh (Exalted is He) in compliance with His commandments, he will prosper, as He has said (Exalted is He):

> Shall I show you a commerce
> *hal adullu-kum ʿalā tijāratin*
> that will save you from a painful torment?
> *tunjī-kum min ʿadhābin alīm.*
>
> You must believe in Allāh and His Messenger,
> *tuʾminūna bi'llāhi wa Rasūli-hi*

and strive for Allāh's cause
wa tujāhidūna fī sabīli 'llāhi
with your wealth and your own selves.
bi-amwāli-kum wa anfusi-kum:
That is better for you, if you did but know.
dhālikum khairun la-kum in kuntum ta'lamūn. (61:10,11)

If someone relates to Satan by following him, he will lose his capital, and remorse will not avail him. In compliance with the commandment of Allāh, on the other hand, there is a praiseworthy outcome, since many a thing is disliked by the lower self, such as the sacred struggle [*jihād*], though it is lovable in the sight of Allāh. By the renunciation of comfort, therefore, and the choice of hardship, the servant may obtain both his worldly and his Otherworldly desires. The grace to enable that must come from Allāh (Exalted is He). It is not for everyone who does not care about the diminution of his worldly interest, since complete fulfilment resides in the sphere of his religion.

This you must understand: Just as Allāh (Exalted is He) replaces substances with other substances, he likewise replaces attributes with other attributes. If someone tags along behind his lustful appetites, and follows his passionate desire in all his active and passive modes, he will perish in the valley of the natural constitution and the lower self. He will never attain to the stations of the men of the realm of sanctity and intimate friendship. He will not experience fellowship with them in their speech, their station and their spiritual state.

There is a vast distance between him and them, since his attributes are the attributes of the lower self and its states, and the states of the natural constitution, whereas their attributes are the attributes of the spirit, and their standards are the standards of Allāh. That is why many people will be gathered [at the Resurrection] in the shape of their dominant and blameworthy attributes of character, unless Allāh (Exalted is He) corrects them by His gracious favour, and clothes them with the clothing of human existence, as it should be in reality.[925]

These are my own remarks:

You must take notice, be on the alert, and prepare for the Day of Resurrection:

A day when the trumpet is blown,
yawma yunfakhu fi 'ṣ-ṣūri
and you will come in multitudes.
fa-ta'tūna afwājā. (78:18)

We beseech Allāh to exclude us from the ten groups about whom Allāh's Messenger (Allāh bless him and give him peace) was questioned, while he was among his Companions. Muʿādh (may Allāh be well pleased with him) is reported as having said: "I once asked: 'O Messenger of Allāh, what do you make of Allāh's saying (Exalted is He):

> A day when the trumpet is blown,
> *yawma yunfakhu fi 'ṣ-ṣūri*
> and you will come in multitudes.
> *fa-ta'tūna afwājā.* (78:18)?'

"The Prophet (Allāh bless him and give him peace) replied: 'O Muʿādh ibn Jabal, you have asked about a tremendously important subject!' Then he flooded his eyes with tears, before going on to say:

> Ten groups from my Community will be resurrected separately. Allāh will differentiate them from the general congregations of the Muslims, and He will transform their shapes. Some of them will appear in the form of monkeys, and some of them in the form of pigs. Some of them will be turned upside down, with their legs above them, and with their faces stretched over their feet. Some of them will be wandering about in blindness. Some of them will be deaf and dumb, incapable of comprehending. Some of them will be chewing their tongues, which will be dangling over their breasts, while pus drivels out of their mouths, and the people in the gathering will shun them as unclean. Some of them will have their hands and feet cut off. Some of them will be crucified on stumps of fire. Some of them will be more foul-smelling than rotten corpses. Some of them will be clothed in flowing garments of tar, sticking to their skins.
> As for those in the shape of monkeys, they are those who sow discord among the people (meaning the scandalmongers).
> As for those in the shape of pigs, they are the holders of ill-gotten gains, unlawful property and dues collected by fraud.
> As for those whose heads and faces are turned upside down, they are the consumers of usurious profit [*ribā*].
> The blind are those who act tyrannically in government.
> The deaf and dumb are those who take vain pride in their actions.
> As for those who chew their tongues, they are those scholars and narrators whose words are at odds with their deeds.
> As for those whose hands and feet have been amputated, they are those who harm their neighbours.
> As for those who are crucified on stumps of fire, they are those who slanderously denounce other people to the ruler.
> As for those who are more foul-smelling than rotten corpses, they are those who indulge in carnal lusts and pleasures, and withhold what is due to Allāh from their possessions.
> As for those who are clothed in flowing gowns [of tar], they are the people who are guilty of arrogance, vainglory and conceitedness."

We beg Allāh for salvation from the torment of Allāh. There can be no salvation for us, except through Allāh. O Allāh, make that possible for us! *Āmīn*. Peace be upon the Messengers, and praise be to Allāh, the Lord of All the Worlds. There is no might nor any power, except with Allāh, the All-High, the Almighty. May Allāh bless our master Muḥammad, his family and his Companions, and may He grant them peace.

The Fifty-fourth Call

In the Name of Allāh, the All-Merciful, the All-Compassionate.
Bismi'llāhi 'r-Raḥmāni 'r-Raḥīm.

O you who truly believe,
practise true devotion to Allāh,
yā ayyuha 'lladhīna āmanu 'ttaqu 'llāha
and be together with the truthful.
wa kūnū ma'a 'ṣ-ṣādiqīn. (9:119)

O you who truly believe, practise true devotion to Allāh
yā ayyuha 'lladhīna āmanu 'ttaqu 'llāha

That is to say: "Be keenly aware of Allāh in all that you say and do."

and be together with the truthful.
wa kūnū ma'a 'ṣ-ṣādiqīn.

In other words: "Be together with the people of truthfulness and certainty, meaning those who are true to the religion in intention, in speech and in active practice."[926]

Having decreed the repentance of those three [who lagged behind] to be acceptable, Allāh (Exalted is He) has gone on to explain what should serve as an impediment to that which was done in the past, meaning lagging behind Allāh's Messenger (Allāh bless him and give him peace) in the sacred struggle, for He has said:

O you who truly believe, practise true devotion to Allāh
yā ayyuha 'lladhīna āmanu 'ttaqu 'llāha

—by refraining from disobedience to the Messenger (Allāh bless him and give him peace)—

and be together with the truthful.
wa kūnū ma'a 'ṣ-ṣādiqīn.

—meaning: "Be together with the Messenger (Allāh bless him and give him peace) in the military campaigns, and do not be truants from them, staying at home in the company of the hypocrites."

Allāh (Exalted is He) has commanded the believers to be together with the truthful, and, since being with the truthful is a necessary duty, the existence of the truthful is essential at all times. That prevents the whole proposition from resting on a false foundation, and, since the whole proposition is prevented from resting on a false foundation, those who affirm it must be telling the truth. This indicates that the consensus of the Community is a compelling proof.

The Qur'ānic verse also points to the excellent merit of truthfulness, and the perfection of its degree. This is reinforced by the saying attributed to Ibn Mas'ūd (may Allāh be well pleased with him): "You must make a practice of truthfulness, for it brings one close to righteousness, and righteousness brings one close to the Garden of Paradise. If the servant is always truthful, he will be recorded in the sight of Allāh as a champion of truth [*ṣiddīq*]. You must beware of lying, for lying brings one close to iniquity, and iniquity brings one close to the Fire of Hell. If a man is always telling lies, he will eventually be recorded in the sight of Allāh as a liar. You must surely be familiar with the expression: 'I have told the truth, and nothing but the truth [*ṣadaqtu wa barartu*].'"

Concerning the meaning of His injunction:

> and be together with the truthful.
> *wa kūnū ma'a 'ṣ-ṣādiqīn.*

—the question may be asked: "Why is not permissible to understand this in the sense of: 'Be on the path of the truthful'?" The answer is that His saying: "and be together with the truthful" is an injunction demanding harmony with the truthful, and a prohibition forbidding alienation from them.

One of the special merits of truthfulness is that true belief depends on it, and not on any other forms of worshipful obedience. One of the grievous faults of lying is that unbelief stems from it, and not from any other sins. People have disagreed as to what makes lying so utterly vile. According to our colleagues: "What makes lying so utterly vile is the fact that it is damaging to the interests of society as a whole, as well as to the interests of the individual."[927]

The truthful, it has also been said, are those who fulfil their covenants. This is based on His saying (Exalted is He):

> Men who are true to what they covenanted with Allāh.
> *rijālun ṣadaqū mā ʿāhadu 'llāha ʿalai-h:*
> Some of them have paid their vow by death,
> *fa-min-hum man qaḍā naḥba-hu*
> and some of them are still waiting;
> *wa min-hum man yantaẓir:*
> and they have not altered in the least.
> *wa mā baddalū tabdīlā.* (33:23)

They are those whose outer beings exactly match their inner beings. This quality precludes hypocrisy in belief and disobedience in action.

When someone understands and comprehends Allāh, it becomes his duty to practise truthfulness in all his utterances, sincerity in all his actions, and honesty in all his states of being. If someone fits this description, he will join the righteous and attain to the good pleasure of the All-Forgiving [*al-Ghaffār*]. Lying is a disgrace, and its practitioners are deprived of the right to testify, for the Prophet (Allāh bless him and give him peace) rejected a man's testimony because he had told a lie.

Muʿammar said: "I do not know whether he lied about Allāh, or lied about His Messenger, or lied about one of the people." ʿAbdu'llāh ibn Masʿūd is reported as having said: "No good can come from telling lies, whether in earnest or in jest, nor from promising something and then failing to carry it out. Read, if you will:

> O you who truly believe, practise true devotion to Allāh
> *yā ayyuha 'lladhīna āmanu 'ttaqu 'llāha*
> and be together with the truthful.
> *wa kūnū maʿa 'ṣ-ṣādiqīn.*

"Do you see any licence there for lying?"[928]

Concerning His injunction (Exalted is He):

> and be together with the truthful.
> *wa kūnū maʿa 'ṣ-ṣādiqīn.*

—it was Ibn ʿAbbās (may Allāh be well pleased with him and his father) who said: "[This means]: 'Together with those whose intentions were genuine, whose feelings and actions were honest, and who went forth with Allāh's Messenger (Allāh bless him and give him peace) to Tabūk with sincerity of intention.' [It also means]: 'Together with those who truthfully confessed their sin, and did not offer false and lying excuses, they being the three who were left behind, but then repented, whereupon Allāh relented towards them.'"[929]

Ibn Shaiba and Aḥmad have stated, on the authority of a report from Asmāʾ bint Zaid, that the Prophet (Allāh bless him and give him peace) once said:

> Every lie is recorded against the human being concerned, except a man who lies for the purpose of deception in warfare, or for the sake of reconciling a couple, or a man who tells his wife a yarn, in order to please her.[930]

This call is addressed to all the believers, and its full significance is expressed in His words (Exalted is He):

> It is not piety, that you turn your faces to the East and to the West.
> *laisa 'l-birra an tuwallū wujūha-kum qibala 'l-mashriqi wa 'l-maghribi*
> True piety is [that of] one who believes in Allāh and the Last Day
> *wa lākinna 'l-birra man āmana bi-'llāhi wa 'l-yawmi 'l-ākhiri*
> and the angels and the Book and the Prophets;
> *wa 'l-malāʾikati wa 'l-kitābi wa 'n-nabiyyīn:*
> one who gives his wealth, for love of Him, to kinsfolk and to orphans
> *wa āta 'l-māla ʿalā ḥubbi-hi dhawi 'l-qurbā wa 'l-yatāmā*
> and the needy and the wayfarer and to those who beg,
> *wa 'l-masākīna wa 'bna 's-sabīli wa 's-sāʾilīna*
> and to set slaves free; one who duly performs the ritual prayer,
> *wa fi 'r-riqāb : wa aqāma 'ṣ-ṣalāta*
> and pays the alms-due.
> *wa āta 'z-zakāh:*
> [It is the piety of] those who fulfil their covenant
> *wa 'l-mūfūna bi-ʿahdi-him*
> when they have committed themselves to a covenant,
> *idhā ʿāhadū:*
> and who are patient in tribulation and adversity and in time of stress.
> *wa 'ṣ-ṣābirīna fi 'l-baʾsāʾi wa 'ḍ-ḍarrāʾi wa ḥīna 'l-baʾs:*
> Such are those who are truthful. Such are the truly devout.
> *ulāʾika 'lladhīna ṣadaqū: ulāʾika humu 'l-muttaqūn.* (2:177)[931]

The truthful referred to in His saying:

> and be together with the truthful.
> *wa kūnū maʿa 'ṣ-ṣādiqīn.*

—are those who were truthful in the commitment they made, in response to Allāh's question:

> "Am I not your Lord?" They said: "Yes indeed."
> *a-lastu bi Rabbi-kum qālū balā.* (7:172)

They are those who told Allāh the truth, when they vowed to Him that they would worship none but Allāh, that they would not associate anything with Him, from among the objects of this world and the Hereafter, and that they would keep themselves detached from every novel phenomenon.[932]

The Qur᾽ānic verse implicitly extols the honour and high degree of those who practise truthfulness. Notice how Iblīs himself was too ashamed to lie, when he mentioned the exception in his saying:

> "Then, by Your might, I shall surely beguile them every one,
> *qāla fa-bi῾Izzati-ka la-ughwiyanna-hum ajma῾īn:*
> except Your sincerely devoted servants among them."
> *illā ῾ibāda-ka min-humu 'l-mukhlaṣīn.* (38:82,83)

Had he not mentioned the exception, he would have been a liar in claiming to beguile them all. If lying is something that even the accursed Iblīs is ashamed of, there is all the more reason for the Muslim to be ashamed of it.

It is related that someone came to Allāh's Messenger (Allāh bless him and give him peace) and told him: "I wish to believe in you, but I love strong drink, fornication, stealing and lying, and people say that you have made these things unlawful. I lack the ability to give them all up, but if you can be satisfied with my abstinence from one of them, I shall believe." The Messenger (Allāh bless him and give him peace) replied: "You must give up lying!" He agreed to that, and then accepted Islām.

As soon as he had left the presence of the Messenger (Allāh bless him and give him peace), they offered him strong drink, so he said: "If I drink, and the Messenger (Allāh bless him and give him peace) asks me whether I have done so, and I tell a lie, I shall have broken my vow. If I tell the truth, on the other hand, he will inflict the penalty [of flogging] on me." He therefore abstained from the strong drink.

Then they offered him an opportunity to fornicate, but the same line of thinking occurred to him again, so he abstained. He reacted likewise in the case of stealing. Then he went back to Allāh's Messenger (Allāh bless him and give him peace) and said: "You did a really fine job! As soon as you prevented me from lying, the doors of all sins were bolted to shut me out." He repented, there and then, of all his former vices.[933]

The truthful are also those who show the way to the path of

attainment, so, if the spiritual traveller is counted among their friends, and included among the servants at the threshold of their doorway, he will surely attain—through their love, their training and the strength of their custodianship—to all the stages of the journey to Allāh, and he will abandon everything apart from Him.

His excellency, the Greatest Shaikh [Ibn ʿArabī] (may Allāh bestow His mercy upon him), once said: "If your actions do not conform to anyone's wish but your own, you could never achieve detachment from your passionate desire, even if you spent your whole life struggling with your lower self. If you find someone who inspires you with a feeling of respect for him, you must therefore serve him faithfully. You must be like a corpse in his hands, so that he may direct you as he wishes, while you exercise no control over yourself in his company. You will then live a happy and blessed life, through compliance with his commands and prohibitions. You must therefore spare no effort, O my dear son, in the quest for a Shaikh to direct you and curb your wild ideas, so that your essence may be perfected in the Divine Presence."

You must practise truthfulness absolutely, in both intention and action. It depends very much on sincere devotion, which means that the servant must be motivated by nothing whatsoever, whether in active or in passive states, except by Allāh (Exalted is He). If he mixes it with some ingredient of self-interest, truthfulness is rendered null and void, and he may justly be called a liar. There is no end to the degrees of truthfulness. The servant may possess it in certain areas, though not in others. If he is truthful in everything, he is really and truly the champion of truth [*ṣiddīq*].[934]

These are my own observations:

The degrees of truthfulness are many. The least of them requires conformity between how you are in private and how you are in public. It requires you to be truthful in complying with your Lord's command and prohibition, obediently following your Messenger (Allāh bless him and give him peace), until you are truly established in servitude to Allāh (Exalted is He). That is the aspiration of the spiritual wayfarers. If someone is keenly aware of Allāh (Exalted is He), in active and passive states alike, and believes that He knows the secret and what is more deeply hidden still, he is bound to be on guard against the abomination of lying. We beg Allāh for protection!

The believer does not become truthful through simple belief alone. He must act in accordance with belief, and one of the essential demands of belief is truthfulness. Allāh (Exalted is He) tells us:

> And those who believe in Allāh and His Messengers,
> *wa 'lladhīna āmanū bi'llāhi wa Rusuli-hi*
> they are the champions of truth.
> *ulā'ika humu 'ṣ-ṣiddīqūna.* (57:19)

As the Qur'ānic verse indicates, belief in Allāh and His Messengers sets him who believes among the champions of truth, but action in accordance with belief remains vital. How can he tell a lie, when he is one of the champions of truth? How can he consume usurious interest [*ribā*], when he is one of the champions of truth? How can he persist in committing acts of disobedience, when he is one of the champions of truth? It is obviously essential to act in accordance with belief. To be acceptable in the sight of Allāh, one must be truthful, and the truthful person must be endowed with several distinctive characteristics:

1. He must be truthful in his intention, seeking nothing but Allāh's good pleasure.
2. He must be truthful with his tongue, and observe the same standard in private and in public.
3. He must be truthful in the discharge of commitment, and his reliance must be entirely on Allāh (Exalted is He).
4. He must be truthful in his determination to fulfil his good intention, so he must not be distracted or procrastinate.
5. He must be truthful in his spiritual stations, from fear and hope, and love and longing.
6. He must be truthful in his intimate conversations with his Lord (Blessed and Exalted is He).

The human being will come to know for himself, as Allāh (Blessed and Exalted is He) already knows, whether or not he is truthful. He must not be deluded, therefore, by the praise he receives from people, and by their gathering around him. He must be content with the knowledge of Allāh (Almighty and Glorious is He) and the reality of His existence, and the fact that:

He knows the treachery of the eyes,
yaʿlamu khāʾinata ʾl-aʿyuni
and what the breasts conceal.
wa mā tukhfi ʾṣ-ṣudūr. (40:19)

There is no might nor any power, except with Allāh, the All-High, the Almighty. Peace be upon the Messengers, and praise be to Allāh, the Lord of All the Worlds. May Allāh bless our master Muḥammad, his family and his Companions, and may He grant them peace.

The Fifty-fifth Call

In the Name of Allāh, the All-Merciful, the All-Compassionate.
Bismi'llāhi 'r-Raḥmāni 'r-Raḥīm.

O you who truly believe,
yā ayyuha 'lladhīna āmanū
fight those of the unbelievers who are near to you,
qātilu 'lladhīna yalūna-kum mina 'l-kuffāri
and let them find harshness in you,
wa l'-yajidū fī-kum ghilẓa:
and know that Allāh is with those
who are truly devout.
wa 'ʿlamū anna 'llāha maʿa 'l-muttaqīn. (9:123)

O you who truly believe,
yā ayyuha 'lladhīna āmanū
fight those of the unbelievers who are near to you.
qātilu 'lladhīna yalūna-kum mina 'l-kuffāri.

That is to say: "Fight those who are close to you, and purify your surroundings by ridding them of the filth of the polytheists [*mushrikīn*], then move on to fight other foes." The aim is to direct the believers towards the most proper and correct procedure, which requires them to start with the nearest, then advance step by step, until they gradually reach the most distant.[935] The same approach is called for in missionary work [*daʿwa*], as Allāh (Exalted is He) has said:

And warn the nearest of your kinsfolk.
wa andhir ʿashīrata-ka 'l-aqrabīn. (26:214)

This gradual procedure is likewise appropriate in the conduct of military campaigns, because the Prophet (Allāh bless him and give him peace) first waged war against his own tribe, then moved on to engage the rest of the Arabs in combat. He had no practical alternative, since it was impossible to tackle them all in one fell swoop.[936]

As for His saying (Exalted is He):

> and let them find harshness in you.
> *wa l'-yajidū fī-kum ghilẓa*

—the meaning is: "Let these unbelievers experience severe treatment from you."[937] Since this Qur'ānic verse implies the commandment to treat them harshly, it is comparable to His injunctions (Exalted is He):

> Be harsh with them,
> *wa 'ghluẓ ʿalai-him.* (9:73)
> and do not go easy.
> *wa lā tahinū.* (3:139)

—and His description of the Companions (may Allāh be well pleased with them), of whom He said:

> [They are] hard on the unbelievers.
> *aʿizzatin ʿala 'l-kāfirīna.* (5:54)

You must know that harshness, which is the opposite of gentleness, refers to severity in the inflicting of retribution. While it can be beneficial, inasmuch as it effectively discourages and prevents bad behaviour, it cannot be applied as a general rule in all cases. There are times when sternness needs to be offset by other qualities, such as gentleness and kindness. That is why He used the expression:

> and let them find harshness in you.
> *wa l'-yajidū fī-kum ghilẓa*

—as a reminder that it is not permissible to resort to harshness absolutely, since it alienates people and causes them to scatter. His saying:

> and let them find harshness in you.
> *wa l'-yajidū fī-kum ghilẓa*

—actually suggests the infrequent use of harshness. It is as if He had said: "They [the unbelievers] must realize that, if they were to scrutinize your characters and your natural inclinations, they would discover an element of harshness in you." This statement is applicable only to someone whose feelings are mostly those of compassion and kindliness, though he is not entirely devoid of harshness.[938]

He then goes on to say (Exalted is He):

> and know that Allāh is with those who are truly devout.
> *wa 'ʿlamū anna 'llāha maʿa 'l-muttaqīn.*

—meaning: "[He is with them] to provide safekeeping and assistance." He has used the noun [*muẓhar*] instead of the pronoun [*muḍmar*]—that is, [He has used the Arabic noun *al-muttaqīn*, meaning "the truly devout,"] instead of *maʿa-kum* [with you]—to draw attention to the cause of divine help, which is true devotion. He has said, in effect: "You must know that Allāh's help is with you, because of your true devotion, practised through the affirmation of My Oneness [*tawḥīd*], surrender to My Will [*islām*], faith [*īmān*], and obedience in the rejection of polytheistic association [*ishrāk*], unbelief [*kufr*], hypocrisy [*nifāq*], and sinful rebellion in the realm of the Sacred Law [*Sharīʿa*].

By Allāh, you must also be with Him in the realm of Reality [*Ḥaqīqa*], to the exclusion of everything apart from Allāh, and not with the unbelievers, the polytheists, the hypocrites and the sinfully disobedient. If He has given them the means to fight, He has done so as a cunning stratagem and a lure to destruction, just as He has given them to you out of noble generosity and beneficence.

To the extent of your devotion to the Lord of Truth [*Ḥaqq*], to the exclusion of mere creatures [*khalq*], Allāh will make His creatures subservient to you. To the extent that you make your natural faculties subservient to Allāh, Allāh will make the unbelievers subservient to you. To the extent that you make your spiritual faculties subservient to Allāh, Allāh will make the believers subservient to you.

The Greatest Shaikh [Ibn al-ʿArabī] (may Allāh be well pleased with him) once said, concerning the orbits of the stars: "You must know, my dear son, that when Allāh wishes (Glorious be His praise) to promote His special servant to the stations on high, He brings his enemies close to him, so that he must concentrate on his struggle with them, and preoccupy himself with waging war on them, first and foremost, before doing battle with other enemies, who are more remote from him.

"Allāh (Exalted is He) has said:

> O you who truly believe,
> *yā ayyuha 'lladhīna āmanū*
> fight those of the unbelievers who are near to you,
> *qātilu 'lladhīna yalūna-kum mina 'l-kuffāri*
> and let them find harshness in you,
> *wa l'-yajidū fī-kum ghilẓa:*
> and know that Allāh is with those who are truly devout.
> *wa ʿlamū anna 'llāha maʿa 'l-muttaqīn.*

—and this Qur'ānic verse provides every Ṣūfī, indeed everyone blessed with good fortune, with the opportunity to examine his lower self [*nafs*], the self that is always instigating evil [*ammāra bi's-sū'*], the self that prompts him to commit whatever is forbidden and reprehensible, and turns him away from everything that is obligatory and commendable, in accordance with the contrary disposition instilled in it by Allāh. It is the closest to him of all the unbelievers and hostile foes, so if he struggles with it and kills it, or takes it captive, he will then be in a position to consider other matters, commensurate with the requirements of his station and appropriate to his rank."

The lower self is the most stubborn of all enemies in its obstinacy, and the strongest in its determination, so the struggle with it is the greatest struggle [*al-jihād al-akbar*]. That struggle involves opposition to its passionate desire, the transformation of its characteristics, and its conversion to obedience to Allāh.

The lower self has two swords, with which it severs the necks of even the most valiant and distinguished heroes. Those swords are the appetites of the belly and the sexual organ. The appetite of the belly is even stronger and more intense than the appetite of the sexual organ, because it depends for support on no one but the owner of the appetite of the belly. There is no full container worse than a belly stuffed with lawful food. This is true when the food is lawful [*ḥalāl*], so what if it is unlawful [*ḥarām*]?! The consumption of food, especially too much and too often, forms an obstacle to the spiritual path. The same can be said of talking. The same can also be said of taking offence, in reaction to the insulting behaviour of one's fellow human beings. The believer must practise patience, and not find them offensive. Because he is a *muwaḥḥid* [a person committed to the affirmation of Oneness], the badly behaved and the well behaved should be on an equal footing, as far as he is concerned. Better still, he should regard the badly behaved as positively beneficial.

One of the religious scholars has said: "If someone spends forty whole nights in wakeful vigil, it will be proclaimed in the dominion of the heavens: 'Allāh has awakened us, and you, from the slumber of heedlessness. He is indeed Responsive to supplication!'"[939]

These are my own comments:

All of us truly believe, and we have long avowed our hostility towards the instigating self [*an-nafs al-ammāra*], recognizing that it is the enemy of Allāh and an enemy to us. In spite of that, it is still dear to us, and we defend it instead of opposing it. Our hostility towards it is therefore confined to our tongues, and we do not put it into practice. We remain as effective as the suckling child. Is it possible for him to do any writing, for instance? Well, if he gains the strength and receives the necessary instruction, it will become possible for him to write. Allāh (Exalted is He) has said:

> Say: "Act! Allāh will behold your actions,
> *wa quli 'ʿmalū fa-sa-yara 'llāhu ʿamala-kum*
> and so will His Messenger and the believers."
> *wa Rasūlu-hu wa 'l-muʾminūn.* (9:105)

The wording of the command conveys the threat. He did not say: "Know!" because knowledge without action is not merely useless; it is positively harmful.

Approval and disapproval are dependent on action, not on knowledge, just as a debt is not settled by mere words, but only by the act of payment. This matter is self-evident, not mysterious, to any intelligent person. The same is true of pretentious display, and the love of prestige, this world, and charismatic wonders [*karāmāt*], as well as other blameworthy features.

O Allāh, guide us to that wherein our righteousness resides. *Āmīn.* Peace be upon the Messengers, and praise be to Allāh, the Lord of All the Worlds. There is no might nor any power, except with Allāh, the All-High, the Almighty. May Allāh bless our master Muḥammad, his family and his Companions, and may He grant them peace.

The Fifty-sixth Call

In the Name of Allāh, the All-Merciful, the All-Compassionate.
Bismi'llāhi 'r-Raḥmāni 'r-Raḥīm.

O you who truly believe, bow down
yā ayyuha 'lladhīna āmanu 'rkaʿū
and prostrate yourselves, and worship your Lord,
wa 'sjudū wa 'ʿbudū Rabba-kum
and do good, so that you may prosper.
wa 'fʿalu 'l-khaira laʿalla-kum tufliḥūn.

And strive for Allāh's sake
wa jāhidū fi 'llāhi
with all the effort He deserves.
ḥaqqa jihādi-h:
He has chosen you
and has not laid upon you in religion
Huwa 'jtabā-kum wa mā jaʿala ʿalai-kum fi 'd-dīni
any hardship; the faith of your father Abraham.
min ḥaraj: millata abī-kum Ibrāhīm:
He has named you Muslims of old time
and in this,
Huwa sammā-kumu 'l-muslimīn: min qablu wa fī hādhā
so the Messenger may be a witness against you,
li-yakūna 'r-Rasūlu shahīdan ʿalai-kum
and so you may be witnesses against humankind.
wa takūnū shuhadāʾa ʿala 'n-nās:
So perform the ritual prayer and pay the alms-due,
fa-aqīmu 'ṣ-ṣalāta wa ātu 'z-zakāta
and hold fast to Allāh.
wa 'taṣimū bi'llāh:
He is your Protecting Friend.
Huwa Mawlā-kum:
A blessed Patron and a blessed Helper!
fa-niʿma 'l-Mawlā wa niʿma 'n-Naṣīr. (22:77,78)

You should understand that Allāh (Glory be to Him and Exalted is He) has already spoken about the attributes of Divinity [*Ilāhiyyāt*] and the attributes of Prophethood [*Nubuwwāt*], and that He has now gone on to speak about the Sacred Laws [*Sharā'i'*], from four points of view: (1) Identification of those subject to the commandment. (2) Classification of what is commanded. (3) What necessitates the acceptance of those commandments. (4) Confirmation of that imposition of duty.

1. As for the identification of those subject to the commandment, it occurs in His saying (Exalted is He):

> O you who truly believe....
> *yā ayyuha 'lladhīna āmanu....*

—about which there are two opinions: (a) It refers to every responsible adult, whether believer or unbeliever, because the obligation in these matters is imposed on all responsible adults, so it does not make sense to apply that to the believers exclusively. (b) It refers to the believers only, for two reasons: (i) The wording is explicit to that effect. (ii) He has gone on to say:

> He has chosen you...
> *Huwa 'jtabā-kum...*
>
> He has named you Muslims...
> *Huwa sammā-kumu 'l-muslimīn...:*
>
> and so you may be witnesses against humankind.
> *wa takūnū shuhadā'a 'ala 'n-nās:*

—and all of that is applicable only to the believers. Allāh (Exalted is He) has referred to them specifically in this address, so that it will be like a stimulus for them to be diligent in accepting it, and it will be like a mark of honour for them to receive that specific recognition.

2. As for that which is commanded, Allāh has mentioned four points:

a. The ritual prayer [*ṣalāt*]. This is what is meant by His saying (Exalted is He):

> bow down and prostrate yourselves
> [*-u*] *'rka'ū wa 'sjudū*

That is because bowing [*rukū'*] and prostration [*sujūd*] are the most noble of the basic elements [*arkān*] of the ritual prayer. These two basic elements are distinctive features of the ritual prayer, so mentioning them is tantamount to mentioning the ritual prayer itself. In other words: "Pray to your Lord submissively." According to Ibn ʿAbbās (may Allāh be well pleased with him and his father): "At the beginning of their Islām, people used to bow down, but they did not prostrate themselves until this Qur'ānic verse was revealed."

b. His saying (Exalted is He):

> and worship your Lord
> *wa 'ʿbudū Rabba-kum*

This may be interpreted in several ways:

- "Worship Him and do not worship any other."
- "Worship your Lord by observing all things that have been commanded and prohibited."
- "Perform the acts of bowing and prostration, and all other acts of obedience, in the spirit of worshipful service, because mere performance is not sufficient. Unless they are performed with the conscious intention to worship Allāh (Exalted is He), they are of no avail with regard to spiritual reward." That is why He has appended this sentence to the mention of bowing and prostration.

c. His saying (Exalted is He):

> and do good
> *wa 'fʿalu 'l-khaira*

According to Ibn ʿAbbās (may Allāh be well pleased with him and his father): "This is a reference to the cultivation of family ties and moral virtues."[940]

> and do good
> *wa 'fʿalu 'l-khaira*

That is to say: "Perform the kinds of good works that will bring you near to Allāh (Exalted is He), like the cultivation of family ties, taking good care of the orphans, praying at night while people are asleep, and dedication to the frequent remembrance of Allāh, until the heart comes to feel His nearness (Exalted is He) and awakens from heedlessness to present awareness."[941]

Someone said: "Doing good can be subdivided into service of the Master in the sense of revering the commandment of Allāh, and beneficent conduct in the sense of treating the creatures of Allāh (Exalted is He) with gentle kindness. It includes filial piety, fairness, charity for the poor, and saying good things to people. It is as if Allāh (Glory be to Him and Exalted is He) has said: "I have charged you with the ritual prayer. Indeed, I have charged you with something more general, and that is worship. I have also charged you with something more general than worship, and that is the performance of good works."

As for His saying (Exalted is He):

> so that you may prosper.
> *la'alla-kum tufliḥūn.*

—it signifies triumphant success and attainment of the bliss of the Hereafter. According to Imām Abū Qāsim al-Anṣārī: "The word *la'alla* [lit., perhaps] is used to indicate expectation. In the performance of an obligatory religious duty, a person is seldom free from shortcoming, so he cannot know for certain whether his performance is acceptable in the sight of Allāh (Exalted is He), and the ultimate consequences are also concealed." Allāh's Messenger (Allāh bless him and give him peace) once said:

> Everyone is made ready for the purpose for which he was created.[942]

That is to say: "If someone turns towards Allāh, to the full extent of his capacity and ability, we may expect Allāh (Glorious and Exalted is He) to pardon his shortcoming, to include him in His gracious favour, and to honour him together with those who are successful." In other words: "Do all this, while hoping to achieve success thereby, though not certain of it, relying on your deeds."[943]

d. His saying (Exalted is He):

> And strive for Allāh's sake with all the effort He deserves.
> *wa jāhidū fi 'llāhi ḥaqqa jihādi-h:*

According to the author of *al-Kashshāf*: "The expression *fi 'llāhi* means *fī dhāti 'llāhi* [for the essence of Allāh], or rather *fī wajhi 'llāhi* [for Allāh's countenance], because our minds cannot attain to direct knowledge of Allāh's essence, and *min ajli-hi* [for His sake]."[944]

> And strive for Allāh's sake
> *wa jāhidū fi 'llāhi*

That is to say: "[against] your external and internal enemies." The external foes are the sects of error and unbelief. The nature of the struggle with them is well known, and it is called the minor struggle [*al-jihād al-aṣghar*]. The internal foes are the lower self, passionate desire and the devil, and the struggle with them is waged by refusing to satisfy their lustful appetites, bit by bit. It is called the the major struggle [*al-jihād al-akbar*]. As reported in the tradition [*ḥadīth*], when the Prophet (Allāh bless him and give him peace) returned from the campaign of Tabūk, he said:

> We have returned from the minor struggle to the major struggle.[945]

It has been said: "By the minor one he meant the struggle against the unbelievers, and by the major one he meant the struggle against the lower self. He called it *akbar* [major, greater] because the external enemies are present at one time, while at another they are absent and offering to make peace. Whether a person kills them, or they kill him, he is in the Garden of Paradise. The internal enemies, by contrast, are never absent, and it is impossible to make peace with them. If they kill their owner and gain control of him, he is in the Fire of Hell.[946]

> with all the effort He deserves.
> *ḥaqqa jihādi-h*:

In other words: "For the sake of Allāh, the believer must not fear the blame of any critic." According to ʿAbdu'llāh ibn al-Mubārak: "The expression *ḥaqqa jihādi-h* refers to the struggle with the lower self and passionate desire." The best interpretation is that it applies to all responsibilities, since the careful observance of what one has been commanded and forbidden to do involves a struggle,[947] waged to the full extent of one's capacity and ability.

3. The third element concerns the factors that necessitate acceptance of these commandments, and they are three in number:

a. His saying (Exalted is He):

> He has chosen you
> *Huwa 'jtabā-kum*

In other words: "He has selected you from among the communities to support His religion, and He has specially favoured you with the most perfect Law and the most noble Messenger (our master Muḥammad

[Allāh bless him and give him peace])."[948] This means that the imposition of duty is a bestowal of honour from Allāh (Exalted is He) to the servant. He has singled you out for the greatest of all marks of honour, and chosen you for His service and dedicated obedience to Him. What rank is higher than this? What good fortune is above this? His choosing you also implies that He has selected you for guidance, assistance and facilitation.[949]

> and has not laid upon you in religion any hardship
> *wa mā jaʿala ʿalai-kum fi 'd-dīni min ḥaraj:*

That is to say: "In this religion, He has not laid upon you any narrow constraint or painful difficulty, and He has not imposed upon you that of which you are incapable." It is indeed the truly magnanimous religion, and this is why He has said:

> the faith of your father Abraham.[950]
> *millata abī-kum Ibrāhīm:*

What is meant by religion [*dīn*] is its roots and its branches, which He has not made difficult for them, as He made them difficult for those before them. That includes His readiness to accept their repentance, provided they are contrite and renounce their sin. He does not require them to repent by committing suicide. If one of them is guilty of a sin, Allāh shields him and does not put him to shame in this world, so he does not find it inscribed on his forehead, or on the door of his house, as used to happen to those before them. He has also decreed the removal of impurity by water, instead of the amputation of its spot, and so on.

Suppose you say: "How can there be no hardship in religion, when the hand is amputated for the theft of four dīnārs [gold coints], and when the otherwise chaste man is stoned to death for committing adultery on one occasion, not to mention other such penalties?"

To this I shall reply: The removal of hardship is for the benefit of those who adhere to the path of the Sacred Law. As for thieves and others who incur the legal penalties [*ḥudūd*], they have violated the prohibition of the Sacred Law, and transplanted themselves from ease to difficulty, because Allāh has not forbidden property absolutely, nor sexual intercourse absolutely. He has made certain things lawful, and He has made certain things unlawful, so the penalty for someone who transgresses the limits is simply to impress that upon him.[951]

b. His saying (Exalted is He):

> the faith of your father Abraham.
> *millata abī-kum Ibrāhīm:*
> He has named you Muslims of old time and in this,
> *Huwa sammā-kumu 'l-muslimīn: min qablu wa fī hādhā*

That is to say: "Your religion, in which their is no hardship, is the religion of Abraham (peace be upon him), so adhere to it, because it is the right religion, as He has said (Exalted is He):

> a right religion,
> *dīnan qayyiman*
> the faith of Abraham, the upright.
> *millata Ibrāhīma ḥanīfā.* (6:161)"

He has called you the Muslims in the previous Books, as well as in this Qur'ān:

> And I have approved Islām for you as religion.
> *wa raḍītu la-kumu 'l-Islāma dīnā.* (5:3)[952]

This gives rise to several questions:

- Why has He said:

> the faith of your father Abraham.
> *millata abī-kum Ibrāhīm:*

—and why has He included the believers who lived in the time of the Messenger (Allāh bless him and give him peace), though he was not one of his children?

The answer is twofold: (i) Since most of them were his offspring, like the Messenger (Allāh bless him and give him peace) and his clan, and all the Arabs, that is permissible. (ii) According to al-Ḥasan, Allāh (Exalted is He) has imposed reverence for Abraham (peace be upon him) upon the Muslims, just as He has imposed reverence for the father upon his children. Consider His saying (Exalted is He):

> The Prophet is closer to the believers than their own selves.
> *an-Nabiyyu awlā bi'l-mu'minīna min anfusi-him.* (33:6)

He has thus made reverence for him like the reverence owed to the father by his children, and reverence for his wives like the reverence owed to the mother, for He has also said (Exalted is He)

> and his wives are their mothers.
> *wa azwāju-hu ummahātu-hum.* (33:6)

• Does this mean that the religion of our master Muḥammad (Allāh bless him and give him peace) is exactly like the religion of our master Abraham (blessing and peace be upon them both), so the Messenger (Allāh bless him and give him peace) cannot have a Sacred Law peculiar to himself? Is that confirmed by His saying (Exalted is He):

> Follow the faith of Abraham, as one by nature upright.
> *ani 'ttabiʿ millata Ibrāhīma ḥanīfā.* (16:123)?

Answer: This expression is relevant only in connection with the worshippers of idols. It is as if He has said (Exalted is He): "The worship of Allāh and the forsaking of idols, that is the religion of Abraham (peace be upon him)." As for the detailed prescriptions of the Sacred Law, they are not at issue in this context.

• What is the meaning of His saying (Exalted is He):

> He has named you Muslims of old time?
> *Huwa sammā-kumu 'l-muslimīn: min qablu*

The answer is threefold:

i. The pronoun *huwa* [he] refers to Abraham (peace be upon him), for every Prophet has had a supplication answered, as when Abraham (peace be upon him) said:

> Our Lord, and make us both submissive unto You
> *Rabba-nā wa 'jʿal-nā muslimaini la-ka*
> and of our seed a community submissive unto You.
> *wa min dhurriyyati-nā ummatan muslimatan la-k.* (2:128)

Allāh (Exalted is He) responded to his supplication, for He made that community the Community of our master Muḥammad (Allāh bless him and give him peace). It is related that Abraham (blessing and peace be upon him) announced that Allāh (Almighty and Glorious is He) would send our master Muḥammad (Allāh bless him and give him peace) with the like of his religion, and that his Community would be called the Muslims [*al-muslimīn*, the ones submissive to His will].

ii. The pronoun refers to Allāh (Exalted is He), as in His saying:

> He has chosen you
> *Huwa 'jtabā-kum*

As reported by ʿAṭāʾ, it was Ibn ʿUmar (may Allāh be well pleased with him and his father) who said: "Allāh is the subject of the sentence:

> He has named you Muslims
> *Huwa sammā-kumu 'l-muslimīn:*

"The expression:

> of old time
> *min qablu*

"—means: 'in all the Books,' while:

> and in this
> *wa fī hādhā*

"—means: 'in the Qur'ān.'" This is the most likely interpretation, because Allāh (Exalted is He) has gone on to say:

> so the Messenger may be a witness against you,
> *li-yakūna 'r-Rasūlu shahīdan ʿalai-kum*
> and so you may be witnesses against humankind.
> *wa takūnū shuhadāʾa ʿala 'n-nās:*

He has thus explained that He has called them by that name for this purpose, and this can only apply to Allāh.

The meaning is: "In all the earlier Books, as well as in the Qur'ān, Allāh (Glory be to Him) has declared your superiority over all other religious communities, and He has called you by this most noble name, for the sake of the testimony referred to. Since Allāh has singled you out by this honour, you must worship Him and not reject the duties He has imposed."[953]

iii. In His saying (Exalted is He):

> so the Messenger may be a witness against you,
> *li-yakūna 'r-Rasūlu shahīdan ʿalai-kum*
> and so you may be witnesses against humankind.
> *wa takūnū shuhadāʾa ʿala 'n-nās:*

—the expression:

> so the Messenger may be
> *li-yakūna 'r-Rasūlu*

—means that our Master Muḥammad (Allāh bless him and give him peace) will be present on the Day of Resurrection:

> [as] a witness against you
> *shahīdan ʿalai-kum*

—by testifying that he delivered the message to you. This implies that his testimony will be in his own favour, on the strength of his impeccability, or to prove the obedience of those who obey and the disobedience of those who disobey.

and so you may be witnesses against humankind.
wa takūnū shuhadā'a 'ala 'n-nās:

—by testifying that the Messengers did deliver the message.[954]

That is to say: "We have made you a community that is moderate, equitable, exemplary, recognized for your impartiality in the sight of all the communities, so that you may be, on the Day of Resurrection:

witnesses against humankind.
shuhadā'a 'ala 'n-nās:

—because, on that Day, all the communities will acknowledge its leadership and its superiority over every other community. This is why your testimony will be accepted against them on the Day of Resurrection, when you bear witness that the Messengers did deliver to them the message of their Lord. The Messenger (Allāh bless him and give him peace) will also testify against this community that he did deliver the message to it, as stated in His saying (Exalted is He):

Thus We have appointed you a moderate community,
wa ka-dhālika ja'alnā-kum ummatan
so that you may be witnesses against humankind,
wasaṭan li-takūnu shuhadā'a 'ala 'n-nāsi
and so the Messenger may be a witness against you.
wa yakūna 'r-Rasūlu 'alai-kum shahīdā. (2:143)

4. The fourth element is the explanation of what serves to confirm what has gone before. It is contained in His saying (Exalted is He):

So perform the ritual prayer and pay the alms-due,
fa-aqīmu 'ṣ-ṣalāta wa ātu 'z-zakāta
and hold fast to Allāh.
wa 'taṣimū bi'llāh:
He is your Protecting Friend.
Huwa Mawlā-kum:
A blessed Patron and a blessed Helper!
fa-ni'ma 'l-Mawlā wa ni'ma 'n-Naṣīr.

So perform the ritual prayer and pay the alms-due
fa-aqīmu 'ṣ-ṣalāta wa ātu 'z-zakāta

That is to say: "You must acknowledge this enormous blessing by demonstrating thankfulness, so discharge Allāh's rightful claim over you, by performing the duties that He has prescribed, obeying what He has ordained, and refraining from what He has declared unlawful. The most important elements in that are performance of the ritual prayer [*ṣalāt*] and payment of the alms-due [*zakāt*]. The latter confers upon Allāh's creatures the benefit of what He has obliged the rich man to do for the pauper, by subtracting a trifling portion from his wealth, once a year, and making it available to the poor and the needy."[955] The prayer and the alms-due are mentioned specifically, because of their excellent merit. The former is a sign of reverence for Allāh's commandment, while the latter is a sign of compassion for His creatures.[956]

> and hold fast to Allāh.
> *wa 'taṣimū bi'llāh:*

In other words: "Rely on Him in all your affairs, and do not seek help and support from anyone but Him."

> He is your Protecting Friend.
> *Huwa Mawlā-kum:*

He is your Helper and the Manager of your affairs.

> A blessed Patron and a blessed Helper!
> *fa-niʿma 'l-Mawlā wa niʿma 'n-Naṣīr.*

That is to say: "There is none like Him in providing protection and support. Indeed, there is really no friend and no helper apart from Him (Exalted is He)."

A man once complained to his brother about the need and hardship he was suffering, so his brother told him: "O my brother, do you wish for something other than the management of your Lord? Do not beg from people. Beg from the One to whom you belong."

Sulaimān ibn ʿAbd al-Malik once entered the Kaʿba, where he said to Sālim ibn ʿAbdi'llāh: "Tell me your needs!" "By Allāh," he replied, "I shall not ask anyone for anything in the House of Allāh, except Allāh."

It is thus incumbent upon the servant, as one who seeks the protection of Allāh (Exalted is He), to hold fast to Him in all situations, and to strive for His approval in private and in public. He must not say:

"This problem is difficult," because that is easy for Allāh, for He is the Patron, and He is:

> A blessed Patron and a blessed Helper![957]
> *fa-niʿma 'l-Mawlā wa niʿma 'n-Naṣīr.*

It should be sufficient for us to quote the saying of Allāh (Exalted is He):

> And as for those who strive for Our sake,
> *wa 'lladhīna jāhadū fī-nā*
> surely We shall guide them in Our ways.
> *la-nahdiyanna-hum subula-nā*
> Allāh is surely with those who are active in goodness.
> *wa inna 'llāha la-maʿa 'l-muḥsinīn.* (29:69)

That is to say: "As for those who adorn their outer beings with dedicated strivings, their innermost beings are beautified with direct perceptions. As for those who occupy their outer beings with the diligent performance of duties, We shall bestow gracious favours on their innermost beings. As for those who tire themselves out for Our sake, by performing the ritual prayers, We shall reward them with the rapturous delight of direct contacts."

Striving for His sake is said to mean: First of all, abstaining from things that are unlawful. Then abstaining from things that are dubious. Then abstaining from things that are superfluous. Then severing attachments and ridding oneself of worldly preoccupations, at all times. It is also said to mean guarding the senses for the sake of Allāh, and counting one's breaths in the presence of Allāh.

The following sayings are worthy of note:

"He made worship various for them, and commanded them to perform it, then He made it all one single worship, and promised for it a reward so great, that faculties are incapable of comprehending it."

"He knew that the loved ones love to hear His speech, so He prolonged it for them to the end of the Qur'ānic verse, so that, while listening, they could experience intimate friendship upon intimate friendship, and refreshment upon refreshment. The repetition of speech to the loved ones is the refreshment [*rawḥ*] of their spirit [*rūḥ*] and the perfection of their comfort [*rāḥa*]."

"There are several kinds of striving: striving with the lower self, striving with the heart, and striving with wealth. Striving with the lower self means that the servant must be content with nothing, unless he acquires it through his submissiveness in worshipful obedience, by enduring hardships and seeking no dispensations or special favours. Striving with the heart means preserving it from bad tendencies, like heedlessness, involvement in disputes, and dwelling on former days of slackness and idleness. Striving with wealth means charitable spending and generous donation, then munificence and altruism.[958]

These are my own observations:

The light of Allāh (Magnificent is His Majesty) is shining without ever ceasing, and human spirits are never deprived of those radiant beams, except because of the veil. That veil is nothing but preoccupation with something other than Allāh (Almighty and Glorious is He). To the extent that the veil is removed, manifestation is sure to occur. It all depends on the servant's readiness to seek, for, if the servant does not seek, he will not be given anything. There is one sort who does not seek his Lord because he is attached to his lower self, and his devil combines forces with his lower self. That explains why this type does not make any spiritual progress.

Be earnest, therefore, in your dedication, for Allāh is the Protecting Friend of the righteous. Peace be upon the Messengers, and praise be to Allāh, the Lord of All the Worlds. There is no might nor any power, except with Allāh, the All-High, the Almighty. May Allāh bless our master Muḥammad, his family and his Companions, and may He grant them peace.

The Fifty-seventh Call

In the Name of Allāh, the All-Merciful, the All-Compassionate
Bismi'llāhi 'r-Raḥmāni 'r-Raḥīm.

O you who truly believe,
do not follow the footsteps of the devil,
yā ayyuha 'lladhīna āmanū lā tattabiʿū
khuṭuwāti 'sh-shaiṭāni
for, if anyone follows the devil's footsteps,
wa man yattabiʿ khuṭuwāti 'sh-shaiṭāni
he will surely command indecency
and reprehensible behaviour.
fa-inna-hu yaʾmuru bi'l-faḥshāʾi wa 'l-munkar:

But for the grace of Allāh and His mercy to you,
wa law lā faḍlu 'llāhi ʿalai-kum wa raḥmatu-hu
not one of you would ever have grown pure.
mā zakā min-kum min aḥadin abadan
But Allāh causes whom He will to grow in purity.
wa lākinna 'llāha yuzakkī man yashāʾ:
Allāh is All-Hearing, All-Knowing.
wa 'llāhu Samīʿun ʿAlīm. (24:21)

After mentioning the story of the incident of the Lie [*ifk*], and describing the state of slanderers and their victims, Allāh (Glory be to Him and Exalted is He) has gone on to explain the precepts and admonitions that are appropriate in this context. These are of several kinds:

1. The first kind is referred to in His saying (Exalted is He):

> When you heard it, why did the believers, men and women,
> *law lā idh samiʿtumū-hu ẓanna 'l-muʾminūna wa 'l-muʾminātu*
> not think well of themselves, and say: "This is an obvious lie!"?
> *bi-anfusi-him khairan wa qalū hādhā ifkun mubīn.* (24:12)

2. The second kind is referred to in His saying (Exalted is He):

> Why did they not produce four witnesses?
> *law lā jā'ū ʿalai-hi bi-arbaʿati shuhadā'.* (24:13)

These behavioural precepts are set forth in verses 12–21 of this Sūra, so this verse is one of a series concerning the rules of conduct enjoined on the believers.

The Commander of the Believers, ʿUmar ibn al-Khaṭṭāb (may Allāh be well pleased with him), wrote to the people of Kūfa, telling them: "You must teach your women the Sūra of Light [*an-Nūr*]." It is called the Sūra of Light because of the rays of Lordly light contained within it, which illuminate the enactment of the legal rules, the standards of behaviour, and the human virtues that are a torch from the Light of Allāh (Glory be to Him), shining upon His servants, and an emanation of His mercy and His generosity.

Allāh (Exalted is He) has clearly addressed this to the believers in particular, because he has warned them against following his footsteps, by His saying:

> for, if anyone follows the devil's footsteps....
> *wa man yattabiʿ khuṭuwāti 'sh-shaiṭāni....*

—and that obviously implies that they have not yet followed him. It could hardly have been intended for the unbelievers, since they were following him already. It seems that Allāh (Glory be to Him), after having explained the threat that is levelled at the People of the Lie, has also instructed the believers, by mentioning them specifically, to be unrelenting in the abandonment of sinful disobedience, to ensure that their condition will not resemble that of the People of the Lie.[959] He has said:

> O you who truly believe,
> *yā ayyuha 'lladhīna āmanū*
> do not follow the footsteps of the devil
> *lā tattabiʿū khuṭuwāti 'sh-shaiṭāni*

In other words: "O you who honestly believe in Allāh and His Messenger, do not follow the tracks of the devil, and do not imitate his habits, by spreading obscenity and by listening to the Lie and repeating it."

for, if anyone follows the devil's footsteps...
wa man yattabiʿ khuṭuwāti 'sh-shaiṭāni...

That is to say: "If anyone follows the course of the devil and his path..."

he will surely command indecency and reprehensible behaviour.
fa-inna-hu ya'muru bi'l-faḥshā'i wa 'l-munkar:

In other words: "The devil will surely lead the human being astray, and seduce him, because he will command him to commit indecency, which is extremely disgusting, and reprehensible behaviour, meaning that which is condemned by the Sacred Law, and from which all sound minds recoil."[960]

This sounds an alarm and a warning against all that, couched in the most eloquent, fluent, succinct and fitting terms. As reported by ʿAlī ibn Abī Ṭalḥa, it was Ibn ʿAbbās (may Allāh be well pleased with them) who said: "The 'footsteps' of the devil are his work." According to ʿIkrima, they are his insinuations, while Qatāda said: "Every sinful act of disobedience is one of the 'footsteps' of the devil."[961]

he will surely command indecency and reprehensible behaviour.
fa-inna-hu ya'muru bi'l-faḥshā'i wa 'l-munkar:

That is to say: "[He will surely command] foul words and deeds, and everything that Allāh (Almighty and Glorious is He) despises." The Qur'ānic verse applies generally, to every individual case, because every responsible person is forbidden to do what it prohibits.[962] Reprehensible behaviour is that which is not in keeping with the Sacred Law, nor with the Sunna.[963]

for, if anyone follows the devil's footsteps,
wa man yattabiʿ khuṭuwāti 'sh-shaiṭāni
he will surely command indecency and reprehensible behaviour.
fa-inna-hu ya'muru bi'l-faḥshā'i wa 'l-munkar:

That is to say: "He will acquire the peculiar disposition of the devil, which is to command those two vices," or: "[He will do so] because, having gone astray himself, he will be inclined to lead others astray." According to Abu 's-Saʿūd's interpretation: "The follower of the devil will enjoin those two vices on other people, for the devil's business is misguidance. If someone follows him, that person will advance from the stage of personal error and corruption to the stage of misguiding and corrupting others."[964]

> But for the grace of Allāh and His mercy to you...
> *wa law lā faḍlu 'llāhi ʿalai-kum wa raḥmatu-hu...*

In other words: "But for Allāh's bestowal of grace upon you, O believers, by enabling the repentance that erases sins, and prescribing the rules of atonement for sinful mistakes...."

> not one of you would ever have grown pure.
> *mā zakā min-kum min aḥadin abadan*

That is to say: "Not one of you would have become pure and free from the burdens of sin, not for all eternity."

> But Allāh causes whom He will to grow in purity.
> *wa lākinna 'llāha yuzakkī man yashāʾ:*

In other words: "But Allāh purifies whomever He wishes, by His grace and His mercy, and by making sincere repentance both possible and acceptable."[965] The point is that His causing you to grow, and His purification and His guidance, depend entirely on His grace, not on your own actions.[966]

As for the People of the Lie, just as they are subject to punishment for what they manifested outwardly, they are likewise deserving of chastisement for what they inwardly concealed, meaning the love of propagating indecency among the believers. That also goes to prove that soundness of heart is just as necessary, for the believers, as restraining their limbs and speech from what is harmful to them.

For someone to be pure [*zakī*], as you should also understand, he must have attained, in obedience to Allāh, to the ultimate degree of approval. It will then be said of him: "The seed has grown pure [*zakiya 'z-zarʿ*]." Once the believer has attained to righteousness in the religion, to the point where Allāh (Exalted is He) is well pleased with him, he may be called pure. He cannot be called pure unless he is actually pure at the time, just as, in the case of someone who has abandoned right guidance, it cannot be said, without qualification: "Allāh (Exalted is He) guided him aright," for what must then be said is: "Allāh guided him aright, but he did not follow right guidance."[967]

To put it briefly, some of the traditional commentators maintain that the Qurʾānic verse is general in its application. They say: "Allāh (Exalted is He) has let it be known that, but for His grace and His mercy in granting immunity, not one of you would be righteous." According to some, the verse is addressed to those who plunged into the Lie,[968] and this implies that they repented and were purified. That is indeed how they were, with the exception of ʿAbdu'llāh ibn Ubayy, for he persisted in hypocrisy until he died as an unbeliever.[969]

> Allāh is All-Hearing, All-Knowing.
> *wa 'llāhu Samīʿun ʿAlīm.*

This signifies that He hears whatever you say in calumny, and whatever you say in confirmation of innocence. He is Aware of what your hearts contain, whether it be the love of spreading indecency, or the hatred thereof. That being the case, it is necessary to be on one's guard against disobeying Him.[970]

The Qurʾānic verse draws attention to several points, including the following:

- While the footsteps of the devil are many, they can be summed up as indecency and reprehensible behaviour. These headings cover such vices as calumny, vilification, lying, and exploring people's faults. Let us quote some relevant Prophetic traditions:

> Congratulations to anyone whose own fault keeps him too busy to notice the faults of other people.[971]
>
> As for the speech of the human being, all of it is counted against him, not to his credit, with the exception of a command to do something that is right and fair, or a prohibition of something that is wrong and unfair, or the remembrance of Allāh.
>
> Great is the extent of the betrayal involved, if you tell your brother a tale, when he believes you to be telling the truth, though you are actually lying to him.[972]

- Purification is strictly Allāh's business, for it depends on His grace and His mercy. He has granted the servant access to acts of worshipful obedience and to the material means, but the servant cannot dispense with a teacher, from whom he can learn the nature of purification, in accordance with Allāh's wish. The most valuable agent of instruction is the Prophet (Allāh bless him and give him peace), then whoever can direct him towards Allāh (Exalted is He).

It was Shaikh al-Islām ʿAbdu'llāh al-Anṣārī (may Allāh sanctify his innermost being) who said: "In the science of Tradition [*Ḥadīth*] and the science of the Sacred Law [*Sharīʿa*], my Shaikhs are numerous. As for my Shaikh in the Spiritual Path [*Ṭarīqa*], he is Shaikh Abu 'l-Ḥasan al-Kharaqānī. But for his insight, I would not have experienced Reality [*Ḥaqīqa*]. The people who provide direction are the guides of the path of the religion, and the keys to the doors of certainty. The discovery of the perfect human being is therefore a splendid prize, and to sit in his company is a tremendous blessing."

When purification is truly experienced, it cleanses the heart by ridding it of all attachments to others [apart from Allāh], after cleansing it of the inclination towards acts of disobedience and serious sins.

As for His expression:

> whom He will
> *man yashāʾ*:

—it is simply a reminder that not everyone is worthy of purification, such as the hypocrites and those who are addicted to filth and frivolity.

• The implication that forgiveness has been granted to those among the People of Badr who plunged into telling the Lie, like Miṣṭaḥ. This is alluded to in the next Qurʾānic verse, and it has been established that Allāh viewed the People of Badr with the gaze of mercy and forgiveness, for He said [in a Sacred Tradition]:

> Do whatever you wish, for I have already forgiven you.[973]

This was intended as a demonstration of providential care for them, and an elevation of their rank, not as a licence for them in every action whatsoever. It is comparable to the way a loved one may be told: "Do whatever you wish!"

When the heart is untainted by devilish insinuations, and free from misgivings, the lights of brilliant notions appear within it. Then, when the servant is ready to rise beyond that, those notions fall away, and the sayings [*aḥādīth*] of the Lord of Truth (Glory be to Him) appear within him, as he [the Prophet (Allāh bless him and give him peace)] said in the traditional report [*khabar*]:

> There have been *muḥaddathūn* [recipients of Divine communications] in the [earlier] communities, so, if there is one in my Community, long may he live![974]

Since the saying is from Him, it will be a communication that remains with the servant, and it will contain no ambiguity, no obscurity and no disturbance. It recipient must be worthy of trust, not someone who reveals the secret content of what is disclosed to him.

> But for the grace of Allāh and His mercy to you,
> *wa law lā faḍlu 'llāhi ʿalai-kum wa raḥmatu-hu*
> not one of you would ever have grown pure.
> *mā zakā min-kum min aḥadin abadan*

He has thus referred them, in all their states of being, to the contemplation of what the Lord of Truth has bestowed upon them, in the two categories of the procurement of benefit and the repulsion of harm, and the two conditions of hardship and ease, for purity is from Allāh, and felicity is from Allāh, and blessings are from Allāh. He has said (Exalted is He):

> And whatever blessing you enjoy, it is from Allāh.
> *wa mā bi-kum min niʿmatin fa-mina 'llāhi.* (16:53)[975]

These are my own comments:

Beware, beware! Beware of following the footsteps of the devil, for he will come between you and your Lord, between you and your Prophet, between you and your Shaikh, and between you and your brethren. When he puts you into a tricky situation, you will not be able to argue with him and resist him, because he will simply tease you, and move you from one tricky situation to another. You must rather seek refuge from him with Allāh (Exalted is He):

> And if a slander from the devil wounds you,
> *wa immā yanzaghanna-ka mina 'sh-shaiṭāni nazghun*
> seek refuge with Allāh.
> *fa-'staʿidh bi'llāh.* (7:200)

In this situation, you are instructed to seek refuge, not to engage in argument and contention with him.

We take refuge with Allāh from the devils of humankind and of the jinn. *Āmīn*. Peace be upon the Messengers, and praise be to Allāh, the Lord of All the Worlds. There is no might nor any power, except with Allāh, the All-High, the Almighty. May Allāh bless our master Muḥammad, his family and his Companions, and may He grant them peace.

The Fifty-eighth Call

In the Name of Allāh, the All-Merciful, the All-Compassionate.
Bismi'llāhi 'r-Raḥmāni 'r-Raḥīm.

O you who truly believe,
yā ayyuha 'lladhīna āmanū
do not enter houses other than your own
lā tadkhulū buyūtan ghaira buyūti-kum
without seeking permission
ḥattā tasta'nisū
and saluting their inhabitants
with the greeting of peace.
wa tusallimū 'alā ahli-hā:
That is better for you, so that you may be heedful.
dhālikum khairun la-kum la'alla-kum tadhakkarūn.

And if you find no one therein, still do not enter
fa-in lam tajidū fī-hā aḥadan fa-lā tadkhulū-hā
until permission has been given to you.
ḥattā yu'dhana la-kum:
And if it is said to you: "Go away again,"
wa in qīlā la-kumu 'rji'ū
then go away, for it is purer for you.
fa-'rji'ū huwa azkā la-kum:
Allāh is Aware of what you do.
wa 'llāhu bi-mā ta'malūna 'Alīm.

It is no sin for you to enter uninhabited houses
laisa 'alai-kum junāḥun an tadkhulū
buyūtan ghaira maskūnatin
in which there is comfort for you.
fī-hā matā'un la-kum:
Allāh knows what you proclaim
and what you hide.
wa 'llāhu ya'lamu mā tubdūna wa mā taktumūn.
(24:27–9)

You should understand that Allāh (Exalted is He) has moved on from the subject of calumny and slander, and the legal ruling applicable to them, to an account of the behaviour that is appropriate in this context. The People of the Lie [*Ahl al-Ifk*] depended on sly intrusion of privacy, in order to spread their false accusation, so this came to be like the path of suspicion. Allāh (Exalted is He) therefore made it incumbent on a man to refrain from entering the home of another, without first seeking permission and offering the greeting of peace [*salām*]. To enter in any other manner would entail suspicion, and the harm involved in that is quite obvious.[976] That is why He said (Exalted is He):

> O you who truly believe,
> *yā ayyuha 'lladhīna āmanū*
> do not enter houses other than your own....
> *lā tadkhulū buyūtan ghaira buyūti-kum....*

Allāh (Exalted is He) has already warned against the slandering of virtuous women [*muḥṣanāt*], and made the punishment for it extremely severe. Suspicious allegations used to arise because the men would mingle freely with the women, and would even enter their presence during times of private retreat. Allāh (Exalted is He) has therefore drawn attention to the legal modes of conduct [*ādāb shar'iyya*] that must be observed when entering other people's houses, for He has commanded the seeking of permission before entry, and the salutation of peace after it:

> without seeking permission
> *ḥattā tasta'nisū*
> and saluting their inhabitants with the greeting of peace.
> *wa tusallimū 'alā ahli-hā:*

That is to say: "You must not enter the houses of other people, without seeking permission and saluting the occupants of the dwelling with greeting of peace."[977]

> without seeking permission
> *ḥattā tasta'nisū*

That is because, if they seek permission and offer the greeting of peace, the people of the house will be friendly, whereas, if they entered without consent, they would be alienated and disturbed. The Qur'ānic verse gives rise to several questions:

1. What is the wisdom in demanding the request for permission, as a precondition for entry?

Answer: The wisdom is that which Allāh (Exalted is He) has indicated in His saying:

> It is no sin for you to enter uninhabited houses.
> *laisa ʿalai-kum junāḥun an tadkhulū buyūtan ghaira maskūnatin*

—for He has thereby implicitly explained why entry is forbidden, unless this precondition is met, when the houses concerned are inhabited. The point is that, if someone bursts in on them without seeking permission, he cannot be sure that he is not trespassing on something unlawful for him to see, such as a private part of the body, or intruding into some matters the people would not like him and others to know about. This comes under the heading of reasons that are expounded by the authorative text [*naṣṣ*]. Furthermore, [permission is necessary] because he is operating within the domain of someone else's property, so it is essential for his doing so to meet with that person's approval, otherwise it resembles illegal usurpation [*ghaṣb*].

2. How should the request for permission be expressed?

Answer: A man once asked permission of Allāh's Messenger (Allāh bless him and give him peace), by saying: "May I pop in [*a aliju*]?" He responded (Allāh bless him and give him peace) by telling a woman called Rawḍa: "Go and teach this fellow, for he does not know the proper way to ask permission. Tell him to say: 'Peace be upon you! May I come in? [*as-salāmu ʿalai-kum—a adkhulu*]?'" The man listened to her, and said what she told him to say, so the Prophet (Allāh bless him and give him peace) said: "Come in!" The man entered at once, and asked Allāh's Messenger (Allāh bless him and give him peace) about certain things. He answered all his questions, so the man said: "Is there anything, in the whole of knowledge, that you do not know?" To this he replied (Allāh bless him and give him peace): "Allāh has given me much good, but there is a part of knowledge that no one knows except Allāh." Then he recited:

> Allāh! With Him is knowledge of the Hour.
> *inna 'llāha ʿinda-hu ʿilmu 's-Sāʿa:*

> He sends down rain, and knows what is in the wombs.
> *wa yunazzilu 'l-ghaitha wa ya'lamu mā fi 'l-arḥām:*
> No soul knows what it will earn tomorrow,
> *wa mā tadrī nafsun mā-dhā taksibu ghadā:*
> and no soul knows in what land it will die.
> *wa mā tadrī nafsun bi-ayyi arḍin tamūt:*
> Allāh is All-Knowing, Ever-Aware.
> *inna 'llāha 'Alīmun Khabīr.* (31:34)[978]

The point is that seeking permission, and offering the greeting of peace, is better for you than intruding without permission, and better than entering people's presence unexpectedly, or with the greeting of the Age of Ignorance. In those days, when a man entered someone else's house, he would say: "Good morning!" or "Good evening!" Then he would go straight in, sometimes to find the man of the house in a blanket with his wife.

It is related that a man once said to the Prophet (Allāh bless him and give him peace): "Should I seek permission from my own mother?" When he said yes, the man went on to say: "She has no servant apart from me. Must I seek her permission every time I enter?" To this he replied: "Would you like to see her naked?" The man said no, so he told him: "Well then, you must seek her permission!"[979]

3. How many times must permission be requested?

Answer: As reported by Abū Huraira (may Allāh be well pleased with him), Allāh's Messenger (Allāh bless him and give him peace) once said:

> The request for permission should be made three times. The first time, they will wonder if they heard it. The second time, they will make sure that they heard it correctly. The third time, they will either grant permission or refuse it.

Jundub is reported as having said: "I once heard Allāh's Messenger (Allāh bless him and give him peace) say:

> If one of you seeks permission three times, but he does not receive permission, he should go away."[980]

It is also important to note that the three requests should not be linked together. There must be an interval between each one and the next. As for knocking violently at the door, and yelling for the owner of the house, that is unlawful, because it entails offence and alienation. There should be enough to serve as a deterrent in the story of the Banī

Asad tribesmen, and the reference to it in His saying (Exalted is He):

> Those who call you from behind the private apartments,
> *inna 'lladhīna yunādūna-ka min warā'i 'l-ḥujurāti*
> most of them have no sense.
> *aktharu-hum lā ya'qilūn.* (49:4)

4. How should the visitor stand at the door?

Answer: It is related that Abū Sa'īd once asked permission of Allāh's Messenger (Allāh bless him and give him peace), while directly facing the door, so he said (Allāh bless him and give him peace):

> You must not ask permission [to enter] while you are directly facing the door.[981]

It is also related that, when the Prophet (Allāh bless him and give him peace) came to some people's door, he would not approach the door with his face directly towards it, but looking over his right shoulder, or the left, and he would say: "Peace be upon you [*as-salāmu 'alai-kum*]!"[982]

5. Finally, what is the verdict on someone who inspects another person's house, without his permission?

Answer: According to ash-Shāfi'ī (may Allāh bestow His mercy upon him): "If his eye is gouged out, he will not be entitled to retaliation."[983]

Allāh (Glory be to Him) has singled human beings out for special favour, honouring them and endowing them with dwellings, in which He has concealed them from curious eyes, and which He has empowered them to enjoy in privacy. He has barred other people from inspecting their contents from outside, or taking refuge in them without their owner's permission. He has therefore instructed them [in this Qur'ānic verse] concerning the precautions needed to preserve their privacy, so that none of them will catch sight of an exposed pudendum. According to a report from Abū Huraira (may Allāh be well pleased with him), recorded in the *Ṣaḥīḥ* of Muslim, the Prophet (Allāh bless him and give him peace) once said:

> If someone inspects a house belonging to other people, without their permission, it is lawful for them to gouge out his eye.

The experts have differed as to how this should be interpreted.

According to some of the scholars, it is not be taken literally, for the owner will be liable [to retaliation] if he gouges out the intruder's eye. They maintain that this traditional report [*khabar*] has been abrogated, since it antedates the revelation of His saying (Exalted is He):

> If you punish, punish with the like
> *wa in ʿāqabtum fa-ʿāqibū*
> of that with which you were afflicted.
> *bi-mithli mā ʿūqibtum bi-h.* (16:126)

—and that it was probably intended as a threat, not as a legal ruling. In any case, when a traditional report contradicts the Book of Allāh, it is not permissible to act on the strength of it.[984]

> That is better for you, so that you may be heedful.
> *dhālikum khairun la-kum laʿalla-kum tadhakkarūn.*

In other words: "Making that request for permission, and giving the greeting of peace, is better for you than entering by surprise, so that you may heed advice, and act in accordance with these rightly guided modes of conduct."[985] Entering with permission is one of those refined manners and pleasing forms of behaviour that lead to happiness in the two abodes [this world and the Hereafter].

You should know that the greeting of peace is part of the Sunna [traditional custom] of the Muslims. It is the salutation of the people of the Garden of Paradise, conducive to loving affection and an antidote to resentment. As reported by Abū Huraira (may Allāh be well pleased with him), the Prophet (blessing and peace be upon him) once said:

> The Muslim is entitled to six things from the Muslim.

When someone asked him: "What are they, O Messenger of Allāh?" he replied:

> When you meet him, you must salute him with the greeting of peace. When he appeals to you, you must answer him. When he asks you for advice, you must advise him sincerely. When he sneezes, and then praises Allāh, you must sympathize with him. When he is ill, you must visit him, and when he dies, you must follow him [in his funeral procession].[986]

According to the author of *al-Kashshāf*: "People view many a chapter of the religion as abrogated law, so they have ceased to act upon it, and the request for permission is one of those chapters."

And if you find no one therein...
fa-in lam tajidū fī-hā aḥadan...

That is to say: "If you do not find anyone in the houses to give you permission to enter them..."

And if you find no one therein, still do not enter
fa-in lam tajidū fī-hā aḥadan fa-lā tadkhulū-hā
until permission has been given to you.
ḥattā yu'dhana la-kum:

In other words: "You must be patient, and do not enter them until you receive permission to go inside, because houses are endowed with sanctity, and it is not lawful to enter them without their owners' consent.

And if it is said to you: "Go away again," then go away...
wa in qīlā la-kumu 'rji'ū fa-'rji'ū...

That is to say: "And if permission is not granted to you, and you are asked to go away, then go away, and do not be obstinate."

for it is purer for you.
huwa azkā la-kum:

In other words: "Going away is purer and more honourable for yourselves, since it is better for you than stubborn insistence and waiting at the doors."

Allāh is Aware of what you do.
wa 'llāhu bi-mā ta'malūna 'Alīm.

That is to say: "Allāh (Exalted is He) is Aware of your hidden thoughts and intentions, and of all your actions, so He will recompense you for them." This also contains a warning threat for those who indulge in spying on the houses.

Next, after mentioning the rule that applies to inhabited houses, Allāh (Exalted is He) has mentioned the rule that applies to uninhabited houses, for He has said:

It is no sin for you...
laisa 'alai-kum junāḥun...

In other words: "It is no sin or offence on your part..."

to enter uninhabited houses.
an tadkhulū buyūtan ghaira maskūnatin

That is to say: "for you to enter houses, without seeking permission, when they are not designed for the residential use of a particular individual, such as caravansarais, hotels and inns." Mujāhid said: "They are those hotels, situated along the public roads, which no one permanently inhabits, but which are established so that any traveller can come to them."

> in which there is comfort for you.
> *fī-hā matāʿun la-kum:*

In other words: "in which there is some benefit for you, or something to meet a certain need, such as shelter from the heat, and accommodation for merchandise and luggage."

> Allāh knows what you proclaim and what you hide.
> *wa 'llāhu yaʿlamu mā tubdūna wa mā taktumūn.*

That is to say: "He knows what you openly display and what you keep secret inside yourselves, so He will recompense you for it." According to Abū Saʿūd: "This is also a threat, directed at anyone who enters a place for some corrupt purpose, or to gaze at private parts."

The Qur'ānic verse also refers, by implication, to abstinence from entering and settling in those transitory metaphorical houses that are our physical bodies, and to abstinence from feeling comfortably at home in them. In order to obtain salvation, it is necessary to salute them with the farewell greeting of peace [*salām al-wadāʿ*]. Once the servant has abandoned reliance on this fleeting world and its pleasures, and turned away from houses that can never be a permanent abode, he has returned to the real home, which is his love of the faith.[987]

To this I would add: "This world is the home of the homeless. It is merely the sowing field of the Hereafter, and the site of testing. We entreat Allāh (Exalted is He) to preserve us from this world, so that it cannot play games with us."

The special few do not regard themselves as the sole owners of any property, neither of movable goods nor of fixed dwellings, because these can be entered into. If someone claims anything of the kind from them, there will be no resistance on their part, no rebuke, no objection and no prohibition. This applies to what they have at their own disposal. As for things they need, but which are at the disposal of others, they do not pester those who have possession of them, not by a demonstration of desire, not by way of begging, and not by cajoling. If the immediate situation demands something of the kind, the Lord of Truth will coerce the person who has the thing in his possession, compelling him to deliver it with an attitude of humble submission and a sense of closeness to Him. The saint [*walī*] will then receive that thing as a mark of honour. This interpretation is appropriate only to this special case, in other words, to the masters of the Ṣūfī path.[988]

These are my own comments:

Adherence to the Sacred Law is good for your interests in both this world and the Hereafter, while acts of noncompliance are damaging to those interests, so the intelligent believer cannot afford to waste his moments of opportunity. He must not forget his point of return. He must remember where he stands before the power of his Lord. He must not rely on his own work, because the value of work is dependent on two preconditions: compatibility with the Sacred Law, and sincere devotion, but the servant is never free from some kind of inadequacy. If you are in any doubt on this score, just consider your ritual prayer [*ṣalāt*], which is one of the pillars of your religion. When you see the extent of your present awareness in that, you will realize the extent of your intimate converse with your Lord.

We beg Allāh to grant us pardon for our shortcomings. Peace be upon the Messengers, and praise be to Allāh, the Lord of All the Worlds. There is no might nor any power, except with Allāh, the All-High, the Almighty. May Allāh bless our master Muḥammad, his family and his Companions, and may He grant them peace.

The Fifty-ninth Call

In the Name of Allāh, the All-Merciful, the All-Compassionate.
Bismi'llāhi 'r-Raḥmāni 'r-Raḥīm.

O you who truly believe,
yā ayyuha 'lladhīna āmanū
let those seek permission from you
li-yasta'dhin-kumu 'llādīna
whom your right hands possess,
malakat aimānu-kum
and also those of you
who have not reached puberty,
wa 'lladhīna lam yablughu 'l-ḥuluma min-kum
at three times:
thalātha marrāt:
Before the prayer of dawn,
min qabli ṣalāti 'l-fajri
and when you lay aside your clothing
wa ḥīna taḍa'ūna thiyāba-kum
because of the heat of noon,
and after the prayer of night.
mina 'z-ẓahīrati wa min ba'di ṣalāti 'l-'ishā':
Three times of privacy for you.
thalāthu 'awrātin la-kum:
It is no sin for them or for you at other times,
laisa 'alai-kum wa lā 'alai-him junāḥun ba'da-hunn:
when some of you go round
attendant upon others.
ṭawwāfūna 'alai-kum ba'ḍu-kum 'alā ba'ḍ:
Thus Allāh makes clear the signs for you.
ka-dhālika yubayyinu 'llāhu la-kumu 'l-āyāt:
Allāh is All-Knowing, All-Wise.
wa 'llāhu 'Alīmun Ḥakīm.

And when the children among you reach puberty,
wa idhā balagha 'l-aṭfālu min-kumu 'l-ḥuluma
let them seek permission,
fa-l'-yasta'dhinū
just as those before them used to seek it.
ka-ma 'sta'dhana 'lladhīna min qabli-him:
Thus does Allāh make His signs clear for you.
ka-dhālika yubayyinu 'llāhu la-kum āyāti-h:
Allāh is All-Knowing, All-Wise.
wa 'llāhu 'Alīmun Ḥakīm. (24:58,59)

These noble Qur'ānic verses deal with the need for close relatives to seek permission, before entering one another's presence. In the preceding fifty-eighth call [*nidā'*], also from the Sūra of Light [*an-Nūr*], the subject was the need for strangers to seek permission from one another. Allāh (Exalted is He) has now commanded their slaves, and also their children who have not reached puberty, to seek permission [at certain times].[989]

O you who truly believe,
yā ayyuha 'lladhīna āmanū
let those seek permission from you
li-yasta'dhin-kumu 'llādīna
whom your right hands possess
malakat aimānu-kum

Concerning the occasion on which this verse was revealed, it was Ibn 'Abbās (may Allāh be well pleased with him and his father) who said: "Allāh's Messenger (Allāh bless him and give him peace) sent an attendant, one of the Helpers [*Anṣār*], to invite 'Umar to come to him. He found him asleep in his house, so he pushed the door ajar and uttered the greeting of peace. Since 'Umar did not wake up, the attendant said: 'O Allāh, make him wake up for me!' He pushed the door again, then called out to him. 'Umar awoke and sat up, and the attendant came inside.

"Some part of 'Umar was uncovered, and 'Umar realized that the attendant had noticed that about him, so he said: 'I dearly wish that Allāh (Exalted is He) had forbidden our children, our womenfolk and our servants to enter our presence at these hours, except with permission.' Then he went with him to Allāh's Messenger (Allāh bless him and give him peace), and discovered that he had just received the revelation:

> O you who truly believe,
> *yā ayyuha 'lladhīna āmanū*
> let those seek permission from you
> *li-yasta'dhin-kumu 'llādīna*
> whom your right hands possess
> *malakat aimānu-kum*

"'Umar (may Allāh be well pleased with him) thereupon gave praise to Allāh (Exalted is He), so the Prophet (blessing and peace be upon him) said: 'What is that about, O 'Umar?' When he told him what the attendant had done, Allāh's Messenger (Allāh bless him and give him peace) was pleasantly surprised at his conduct, so he took note of his name and commended him, and he said:

> "Allāh surely loves the mild-tempered, the modest, the chaste, the decent, and He hates the obscene, the insolent, the importunate beggar.

"This is therefore one of the Qur'ānic verses that were revealed on account of 'Umar (may Allāh be well pleased with him)."

According to some, it was revealed in connection with Asmā', the daughter of Abū Marthad. She said: "We invade the privacy of a man and wife, even though the pair may be together in a single blanket!" It is said that an adult manservant of hers once entered her presence, at a time when she disapproved of his intrusion, so she came to Allāh's Messenger (Allāh bless him and give him peace) and told him: "Our servants and our attendants intrude upon us in a manner we dislike." The Qur'ānic verse was thereupon revealed.[990]

> O you who truly believe,
> *yā ayyuha 'lladhīna āmanū*
> let those seek permission from you
> *li-yasta'dhin-kumu 'llādīna*
> whom your right hands possess
> *malakat aimānu-kum*

That is to say: "O believers, you who accept Allāh and His Messenger as true, and who are convinced of the rightness of the Sacred Law [*Sharī'a*] of Islām, as a system, an authority and a method, your male and female slaves, whom you own as 'property of the right hand [*milk al-yamīn*],' must be required to ask you for permission to enter your presence."[991]

As for the precise meaning of His saying (Exalted is He):

> O you who truly believe,
> *yā ayyuha 'lladhīna āmanū*
> let those seek permission from you
> *li-yasta᾿dhin-kumu 'llādīna*
> whom your right hands possess
> *malakat aimānu-kum*

—it was al-Qāḍī who said: "While the verse apparently refers to men [because of the masculine forms used in the Arabic], it actually refers to both men and women, because a grammatically masculine expression normally includes the corresponding feminine. Since no distinction is made, His saying:

> O you who truly believe,
> *yā ayyuha 'lladhīna āmanū*
> let [those] seek permission from you
> *li-yasta᾿dhin-kumu*

—applies to both genders, and that is made clear by His saying:

> whom your right hands possess
> [*u*] *'llādīna malakat aimānu-kum*

—because that expression is used with reference to both men and women."

In my own opinion, the rule must apply to women *a fortiori*, by clear analogical deduction. That is because, where protection of the private anatomy is concerned, the situation of women is more precarious than that of men. Since this rule is established with regard to men, its application to women must therefore be established *a fortiori*.

As for the obvious meaning of His expression (Exalted is He):

> whom your right hands possess
> [*u*] *'llādīna malakat aimānu-kum*

—it includes both adults and minors. If it is meant to refer to male and female slaves when they become adults, there is nothing to prevent it from being a commandment to them, in actual fact. On the other hand, if what is meant by it is: "those who have not reached puberty," it is not permissible for it to be a commandment to them. It must be a commandment to us, requiring us to instruct them in that behaviour, and to encourage them to practise it, just as we have been commanded to instruct an immature youngster to perform the ritual prayer [*ṣalāt*], once he has understood it. This is not a matter of strict obligation for them, but it is a strict obligation for us, because of the benefit we can derive from it, and which they will be enjoy after puberty.

As for His saying (Exalted is He):

> let [those] seek permission from you
> *li-yasta'dhin-kumu*

—it may amount to an exhortation and a recommendation. Some maintain, however, that it is a strict injunction, and this is a better interpretation, since it is well established that an imperative expression imposes a necessary duty.

According to Ibn ʿAbbās (may Allāh be well pleased with him and his father): "It applies to both men and women. They must seek permission in every circumstance, at night and during the day." The correct opinion is that this rule must be applicable to women, because, just as a person dislikes having males become privy to his personal conditions, he also dislikes having females become privy to them. It must be noted, however, that the application of the rule to women is based on analogical deduction [*qiyās*], not on the explicit wording, as we have previously explained.[992]

> and also those of you who have not reached puberty
> *wa 'lladhīna lam yablughu 'l-ḥuluma min-kum*

That is to say: "and those children who have not reached the age of maturity of free men, they—meaning those who are free—must also seek permission."[993]

The jurists have agreed that puberty [*iḥtilām*] marks the attainment of legal maturity. The Prophet (Allāh bless him and give him peace) is reported as having said:

> The pen is withheld from [recording the misdeeds of] three people: from the sleeper until he wakes up, from the lunatic until he comes to his senses, and from the youngster until he reaches puberty.[994]

The reference is not to those of them who have not acquired knowledge of the private parts of women, but rather to those who are well aware of the condition of women, although they have not yet reached puberty. That is the age of discernment, rationality, and so on.

The experts are in disagreement concerning the case of someone who has reached the age of fifteen, but has not experienced sexual maturity. According to Abū Ḥanīfa (may Allāh bestow His mercy upon him): "The boy does not become an adult until he reaches and completes his eighteenth year, and the girl her seventeenth year." According to ash-Shāfi'ī, Abū Yūsuf, Muḥammad and Aḥmad (may Allāh bestow His mercy upon them): "The boy and the girl become legally responsible at the age of fifteen, and the rules of law then apply to him, even if he has not experienced sexual maturity."[995]

According to Abū Bakr ar-Rāzī: "The Qur'ānic verse implies that someone who has not reached puberty, but who is capable of rational understanding, should be commanded to act in accordance with the Sacred Law, and should be forbidden to commit foul deeds. Allāh has commanded them to seek permission at these times, and the Prophet (blessing and peace be upon him) has said:

> You must instruct them to perform the ritual prayer [*ṣalāt*], when they are seven years old, and compel them to do so when they are ten years of age."[996]

Ibn Mas'ūd is reported as having said: "Once the boy reaches the age of ten, good deeds will be recorded in his favour, while bad deeds will not be recorded against him until he reaches puberty." Abū Bakr ar-Rāzī said, however: "He should be instructed to do that by way of teaching, and so that he will become accustomed to it. He should be well trained in its performance, for then it will be easier for him after puberty, and he will be less inclined to shy away from it. He should also be forbidden to violate any prohibitions, because, if he is not prevented from committing minor offences, it will be hard for him the refrain from major offences. Allāh (Exalted is He) has said:

> Guard yourselves and your families against a Fire.
> *qū anfusa-kum wa ahlī-kum nāran.* (66:6)"[997]

As for His saying (Exalted is He):

> at three times:
> *thalātha marrāt:*

—the three times are specified as follows:

> Before the prayer of dawn
> *min qabli ṣalāti 'l-fajri*

—in other words: "during the night, in the time of your sleep and your comfortable repose."

> and when you lay aside your clothing
> *wa ḥīna taḍaʿūna thiyāba-kum*
> because of the heat of noon
> *mina 'ẓ-ẓahīrati*

—in other words: "at the time of noon, when you take off your clothes for the midday nap."

> and after the prayer of night.
> *wa min baʿdi ṣalāti 'l-ʿishāʾ:*

—in other words: "at the time when you intend to sleep, and are getting yourself ready to do so."

> Three times of privacy for you.
> *thalāthu ʿawrātin la-kum:*

That is to say: "They are three times when your covering is discarded, your private parts are visible, and exposure is usual." You must therefore inform your slaves, your servants and your young folk not to enter your presence at these times, except after seeking permission.

> It is no sin for them or for you at other times
> *laisa ʿalai-kum wa lā ʿalai-him junāḥun baʿda-hunn:*

In other words: "It is no offence on your part, nor on the part of your slaves and your young folk, if they enter your presence without seeking permission after these three times."

> when some of you go round attendant upon others.
> *ṭawwāfūna ʿalai-kum baʿḍu-kum ʿalā baʿḍ:*

That is to say: "because they, your servants, move around you in providing service and suchlike." According to Abū Ḥayyān: "In other words, they pass to and fro, and enter your presence in your houses, in the morning and in the evening, without requiring permission except at those particular times."[998] The noun *ṭawāf* [corresponding to the intensive adjective *ṭawwāfūna*] means circulating around something.

> some of you [attendant] upon others.
> *baʿḍu-kum ʿalā baʿḍ:*

In other words: "They are circulating around you in order to provide service, while you are going around in order to obtain service." If He obliged them to seek permission at every turn, meaning at these three times and others, the situation would be very awkward for them. That is why He has allowed you to refrain from seeking permission at all times apart from these.[999]

> Thus Allāh makes clear the signs for you.
> *ka-dhālika yubayyinu 'llāhu la-kumu 'l-āyāt:*

That is to say: "With that kind of clarification and explanation, Allāh has made the rules of the Sacred Law clear for you, so that you may be educated by them, adhere to them, and act in accordance with them. Your faces will thus be bright on that Day of dread and awful terror."

> Allāh is All-Knowing, All-Wise.
> *wa 'llāhu ʿAlīmun Ḥakīm.*

In other words: "He is Aware of the affairs of His creatures, Wise in His management on their behalf."[1000] He prescribes for you what is in your best interest, for this life and for the life to come.[1001] That is why He has said (Exalted is He):

> And follow what is inspired in you from your Lord.
> *wa 'ttabiʿ mā yūḥā ilai-ka min Rabbi-k:*
> Allāh is surely Aware of what you do.
> *inna 'llāha kāna bi-mā taʿmalūna Khabīrā.* (33:2)

That is to say: "Follow, and do not concoct heretical innovations. Be led by what We command you to do, and do not be guided by your own choice, instead of what We choose for you. Do not pursue a zigzag course in the lands of laziness. Do not deviate in the direction of negligence. Be for Us, not for you, and stand for Us, not for you."

Allāh has narrowed the commandment in one respect, and widened it in another. He has commanded the cultivation of prudence, good administration of the rules of the religion, scrupulous attention to what is unlawful, and avoidance of the perils of discord. If all sides are well protected, the points of danger are rendered secure.[1002]

It was ʿUmar (may Allāh be well pleased with him) who said: "Since Allāh treats you generously, you should be generous towards yourelves!" It is also said that affluence has a corrupting influence on women, due to the control exerted by their carnal appetite over their faculties of reason. As we are told in the Prophetic tradition [*ḥadīth*]:

> Allāh loves to see the effect His gracious favour has upon His servant.[1003]

That is to say: "When Allāh grants His servant one of the benefits of this world, he should let it be visibly apparent, by dressing smartly in a manner befitting his situation. He should choose his clothing with the intention of displaying the gracious favour Allāh has bestowed upon him, so that those in need will approach him to request the alms-due [*zakāt*] and charitable gifts [*ṣadaqāt*]. The wearing of old rags, in spite of affluence, does not constitute humility."[1004]

> And when the children among you reach puberty
> *wa idhā balagha 'l-aṭfālu min-kumu 'l-ḥuluma*

In other words: "[When they reach] sexual maturity." The reference is to those free men who have arrived[1005] at the stage of manhood, and have reached the age of responsibility.[1006]

> let them seek permission,
> *fa-l'-yasta'dhinū*

That is to say: "They must seek permission at all times, before entering your presence."

> just as those before them used to seek it.
> *ka-ma 'sta'dhana 'lladhīna min qabli-him:*

In other words: "those who reached maturity before them, they being the adult men, or those mentioned before them in His saying (Exalted is He):

> O you who truly believe,
> *yā ayyuha 'lladhīna āmanū*
> do not enter houses other than your own
> *lā tadkhulū buyūtan ghaira buyūti-kum*
> without first announcing your presence
> *ḥattā tasta'nisū*
> and invoking peace on their inhabitants.
> *wa tusallimū 'alā ahli-hā.* (24:27)"[1007]

The meaning is that the children are allowed to enter without seeking permission, except during the three times of privacy. If the children are accustomed to that, but then they reach puberty or the age [of maturity], it is necessary for them to be weaned from that habit. They must adopt the practice of seeking permission at all times, like those adult men who have not been accustomed to entering your presence except with permission. People are heedless of this, however.

> Thus does Allāh make His signs clear for you.
> *ka-dhālika yubayyinu 'llāhu la-kum āyāti-h:*
> Allāh is All-Knowing, All-Wise.
> *wa 'llāhu 'Alīmun Ḥakīm.*

That is to say: "He gives you a detailed exposition of all matters pertaining to the Sacred Law and the religion, and Allāh is All-Knowing with regard to His creatures, All-Wise in His legislation." He has repeated this statement, for the sake of confirmation and emphasis concerning the commandment to seek permission.[1008]

These are my own observations:

The sword of the pure Sacred Law [*Sharī'a*] is poised over the believer's shoulder. If he does not comply with the commandments and prohibitions of the Sacred Law, its sword will sever his honour and deliver him to his lower self, which is always instigating evil [*al-ammāra bi's-sū'*].—Let us take refuge with Allāh (Exalted is He)!—His life will thus be wasted on contradictions, and his likeness will be that of those animals that eat and graze in the pasture, then return to the barn. The Divine constitution [*al-qānūn al-Ilāhī*] on this earth is the noble Qur'ān, so it is not permissible for the Muslim to challenge the articles of this constitution, just as worldly governments will not allow any individual to challenge the articles of their legal constitution.

Adherence to the Sacred Law is a guarantee of a fine conclusion, if Allāh (Exalted is He) so wills, because it is the heavenly inspiration [*waḥy*] that arrived on the tongue of the Chieftain of the Messengers (blessing and peace be upon him). We have no means more excellent for drawing close to Allāh (Almighty and Glorious is He) and following the conveyer of the Sacred Law (Allāh bless him and give him peace). May Allāh reward our master Muḥammad (Allāh bless him and give him peace), for our sake, with the reward he truly deserves.

O Allāh, assemble us beneath his banner, O Lord of All the Worlds. Peace be upon the Messengers, and praise be to Allāh, the Lord of All the Worlds. There is no might nor any power, except with Allāh, the All-High, the Almighty. May Allāh bless our master Muḥammad, his family and his Companions, and may He grant them peace.

The Sixtieth Call

In the Name of Allāh, the All-Merciful, the All-Compassionate.
Bismi'llāhi 'r-Raḥmāni 'r-Raḥīm.

O you who truly believe,
remember Allāh's favour to you
yā ayyuha 'lladhīna āmanu 'dhkurū
ni'mata 'llāhi 'alai-kum
when armies came against you,
and We sent against them
idh jā'at-kum junūdun fa-arsalnā 'alai-him
a great wind and armies you could not see.
rīḥan wa junūdan lam taraw-hā:
And Allāh is All-Seeing of what you do.
wa kāna 'llāhu bi-mā ta'malūna Baṣīrā.

When they came upon you from above you
and from below you,
idh jā'ū-kum min fawqi-kum wa min asfala min-kum
and when eyes grew wild
and hearts reached the throats,
wa idh zāghati 'l-abṣāru
wa balaghati 'l-qulūbu 'l-ḥanājira
and you were imagining vain thoughts
about Allāh.
wa taẓunnūna bi'llāhi 'ẓ-ẓunūnā.

There were the believers sorely tried,
hunālika 'btuliya 'l-mu'minūna
and they were shaken with a mighty shock.
wa zulzilū zilzālan shadīdā.

And when the hypocrites,
wa idh yaqūlu 'l-munāfiqūna
and those in whose hearts is a sickness
were saying:
wa 'lladhīna fī qulūbi-him maraḍun

**"Allāh and His Messenger
have promised us nothing but delusion."**
mā waʿada-na 'llāhu wa Rasūlu-hu illā ghurūrā.
(33:9–12)

This Sūra provides a detailed account of the Raid of the Trench [*Ghazwat al-Khandaq*], which is also called the Raid of the Confederates [*Ghazwat al-Aḥzāb*]. It gives a vivid description of how the forces of injustice and evil arrayed themselves against the believers. It discloses the secrets of the hypocrites, and warns against their methods of deception, betrayal and obstruction, leaving them with no screen of concealment and nowhere to hide their cunning plots. It reminds the believers of the most enormous favour that Allāh bestowed upon them, by sending the angels and the wind to ward off the stratagem of their enemies. It also tells of the Raid of the Banī Quraiẓa, and how the Jews broke their treaty with the Messenger (Allāh bless him and give him peace).[1009]

When Allāh (Exalted is He) embarked on His account of the Raid of the Confederates, He began by mentioning the abundant blessings and brilliant signs that flowed from it, to the benefit of the believers, for He said:

> O you who truly believe, remember Allāh's favour to you
> *yā ayyuha 'lladhīna āmanu 'dhkurū niʿmata 'llāhi ʿalai-kum.*

In other words: "Remember His grace and His blessed kindness towards you,"

> when armies came against you,
> *idh jāʾat-kum junūdun*

That is to say: "At the time when the armies of the Confederates [*Aḥzāb*] arrived on the scene, and arrayed themselves against you."

According to Ibn Masʿūd: "The armies referred to are the Confederates [*Aḥzāb*], they being Quraish, Ghaṭafān, and the Jews of Quraiẓa and Bani 'n-Naḍīr. They were approximately twelve thousand strong. When Allāh's Messenger (Allāh bless him and give him peace) heard of their approach, he had the Trench [*Khandaq*] constructed to defend Medina, on the advice of Salmān al-Fārisī (may Allāh be well pleased with him). Then he sallied forth with three thousand of the Muslims, and pitched his camp with the Trench between him and the polytheists [*mushrikīn*]. Fear grew intense, the believers harboured every kind of suspicion, and hypocrisy reared its head among the hypocrites, to the point where Muʿattib ibn Qashīr said: 'Muḥammad is preparing us to receive the treasures of Chosroes and Caesar, and we cannot go to the toilet!'"

and We sent against them
fa-arsalnā ʿalai-him
a great wind and armies you could not see.
rīḥan wa junūdan lam taraw-hā:

In other words: "We sent against the Confederates a violent wind and armies of angels, invisible to you, about a thousand strong."

According to the traditional Qurʾānic commentators: "Allāh sent against them a violent wind, that being the east wind, on a night that was extremely cold and dark. Their tents were blown away, their cooking pots were overturned, and men were thrown to the ground. Allāh sent the angels, who shook them so badly that they could not fight. They instilled such terror in their hearts,[1010] that one of them would cling to another, from fear of the horses in the depth of the night. The story is well known."[1011]

And Allāh is All-Seeing of what you do.
wa kāna 'llāhu bi-mā taʿmalūna Baṣīrā.

That is to say: "Allāh (Exalted is He) is Observing what you are doing, from the hollow of the Trench." This is confirmation of the assistance given to the Prophet (Allāh bless him and give him peace) at that time.[1012] It conveys the implicit message: "Allāh knew that you were seeking refuge with Him, and hoping for His gracious favour, so We helped you against your enemies, as soon as the appeal for help was made." This underlines the necessesity of fear [of Him], and the impermissibility of fearing anything other than Allāh, for He has said:

and We sent against them
fa-arsalnā ʿalai-him
a great wind and armies you could not see.
rīḥan wa junūdan lam taraw-hā:

In other words: "Allāh satisfies your need, though you do not see how. The prospect of safety may not be apparent to you, but you must not be disconcerted by its lack of visibility, because there are things you cannot see. You must not be afraid of anything other than Allāh, and never say: 'We are doing something that He cannot see.'"

> Surely He is One who sees all things.
> *inna-hu bi-kulli shai'in Baṣīr*. (67:19)

In the immediately preceding verse, Allāh (Exalted is He) has said:

> That He may ask the truthful about their truthfulness.
> *li-yas'ala 'ṣ-ṣādiqīna 'an ṣidqi-him:*
> And He has prepared a painful doom for the unbelievers.
> *wa a'adda li'l-kāfirīna 'adhāban alīmā*. (33:8)

In other words: "He has sent the Messengers [to test the truthfulness of the truthful], and the ultimate outcome, for those those charged with responsibility, will be either a reckoning or a torment, because the truthful person is one who is called to account, while the unbeliever is subject to torment." This is how 'Alī (may Allāh be well pleased with him) expressed it: "In this world, that which is lawful is a reckoning, while that which is unlawful is a torment." This is something that ought to inspire a general fear [of offending Allāh], in view of His imperative statement:

> O Prophet, you must practise true devotion to Allāh.
> *yā ayyuha 'n-Nabiyyu 'ttaqi 'llāha*. (33:1)

It confirmed the previous commandment to practise true devotion to Allāh, so that no fear of anyone else would remain with him. That was because of the dire situation, in which the Confederates had assembled, and the Companions were beset with serious difficulties. The polytheists had combined all their forces, and so had the Jews. They had descended upon Medina, and the Prophet (Allāh bless him and give him peace) had constructed the Trench [*Khandaq*]. The situation was extremely dangerous, and fear was mounting to the utmost degree, but then Allāh (Exalted is He) repelled the people from them, without any fighting, and He made them secure from fear.

This means that the servant must not be afraid of anything other than his Lord, for He is Competent to deal with his situation. It means that the servant must not feel secure from His craftiness, for He is Capable of every possibility, as He was Capable of causing the unbelievers to defeat the Muslims, even though they were weak, and as He caused the believers to defeat the unbelievers, in spite of their strength and might.[1013]

The remembrance of:

> Allāh's favour
> *niʿmata 'llāhi*

—is expressed by receiving it with grateful thanks. If you remembered what He kept you from suffering in former times, you would barely notice the hardship of tribulation in the present. If you remembered how well He treated you in the past, your heart would feel confident of receiving what it hopes for in the future. Of all the things of which He has reminded them, one is mentioned in His saying (Exalted is He):

> when armies came against you
> *idh jāʾat-kum junūdun*

How many a trial He has deflected from His servant, without his being aware! How many a problem was heading his way, but He prevented it from reaching him, without his knowing! How many a project He has blocked, despite the servant's noisy complaint, because He knows (Glory be to Him) that its facilitation would be deadly for the servant! He has prevented him from carrying it out, as a mercy from Him, though the servant is suspicious and tight in his feelings because of that.[1014] O Allāh, grant us contentment and submission, combined with love and patient perseverance therein!

> When they came upon you from above you
> *idh jāʾū-kum min fawqi-kum*

That is to say: "When the Confederates came to you from above the valley, meaning from its highest part, towards the east, from whence came Asad and Ghaṭafān."

> and from below you,
> *wa min asfala min-kum*

That is to say: "From below the valley, meaning its lowest part, towards the west, from whence came Quraish, Kināna, and the riff-raff of the Arabs." The significance of this is that the polytheists came to them from both directions, from the east and the west, and surrounded the Muslims as tightly as an armband surrounds the wrist. The Jews of Banī Quraiẓa assisted them, for they broke their treaty with the Messenger (Allāh bless him and give him peace) and joined forces with the polytheists. Fear became intense, and misfortune loomed large.

> and when eyes grew wild
> *wa idh zāghati 'l-abṣāru*

That is to say: "When eyes began to wander and lose their focus in bewilderment, and started glazing over, due to the violence of the terror and alarm."[1015]

> and hearts reached the throats
> *wa balaghati 'l-qulūbu 'l-ḥanājira*

In other words: "They left their places in the breasts, until they almost reached the throats." This is a metaphor, indicating the intensity of the alarm and panic that afflicted them, until it seemed that someone's heart had reached his throat, due to the violence of the terror that was striking him. That is the gist of a report from ʿIkrima. The most obvious interpretation is that it refers to the agitation of the heart and its pounding, until it seems to have reached the throat, due to the intensity of its agitation.[1016] That is because the heart becomes disturbed in the presence of danger, and constricted in the presence of fear, so it cleaves to the throat. It may even reach the point where it blocks the flow of breath, so the man cannot breathe at all, and he dies from fear. This is reminiscent of His saying (Exalted is He) about the spirit:

> Why then, when it comes up to the throat....
> *fa-law lā idhā balaghati 'l-ḥulqūm......* (56:83)[1017]

> and you were imagining vain thoughts about Allāh.
> *wa taẓunnūna bi'llāhi 'ẓ-ẓunūnā.*

In other words: "While you were in that terrifying situation, you were thinking those muddled thoughts."

It was al-Ḥasan al-Baṣrī (may Allāh be well pleased with him) who said: "The hypocrites thought that the Muslims were being annihilated, while the believers thought that they were being helped to win, so the believers thought a good thought, while the hypocrites thought an evil one." According to Ibn ʿAṭiyya: "The believers became so confused, that they were on the point of saying: 'What is this breach of the promise?'" This is a way of describing the notions that occurred to the believers, and it is impossible for the human being to repel them. As for the hypocrites, they wasted no time in expressing their thoughts, and they said:

> "Allāh and His Messenger have promised us nothing but delusion."
> *mā waʿada-na 'llāhu wa Rasūlu-hu illā ghurūrā.*

> There were the believers sorely tried
> *hunālika 'btuliya 'l-muʾminūna*

That is to say: "At that time at place, the believers were severely tried and tested, in order to distinguish the sincerely truthful from the hypocrite."[1018] This trial was by fear, fighting, hunger, encirclement and assault."[1019]

> and they were shaken with a mighty shock.
> *wa zulzilū zilzālan shadīdā.*

In other words: "They were violently moved about by the impact of what befell them, until it seemed as if an earthquake was shaking them and unsettling the ground beneath their feet." As Ibn Jazī explained: "The basic meaning of *zalzala* [earthquake] is violent movement. In this context it signifies the agitation and convulsion of their hearts."

> And when the hypocrites,
> *wa idh yaqūlu 'l-munāfiqūna*
> and those in whose hearts is a sickness were saying:
> *wa 'lladhīna fī qulūbi-him maraḍun*

That is to say: "Remember when the hypocrites, and those in whose hearts is the sickness of hyprocrisy, were saying..., because faith had no place in their hearts."

> "Allāh and His Messenger have promised us nothing but delusion."
> *mā waʿada-na 'llāhu wa Rasūlu-hu illā ghurūrā.*

In other words: "Allāh and His Messenger have promised us nothing but falsehood and betrayal." The actual speaker of these words, Muʿaṭṭil ibn Qushair, was the one who said: "Muḥammad is promising us the victory of the Persians and the Romans, yet not one of us can empty his bowels from fright. This is nothing but an illusory promise, by which Muḥammad is trying to delude us."[1020]

These are my own remarks:

The truthfulness of the truthful, like the lying of the liars, does not become apparent until it is cast into the fire of trial and tribulation. Allāh (Exalted is He) has said:

> Alif–Lām–Mīm.
> *Alif–Lām–Mīm.*
> Do men imagine that they will be left because they say:
> *a-ḥasiba 'n-nāsu an yutrakū an yaqūlū*
> "We believe," and will not be tested with affliction?
> *āmannā wa hum yuftanūn.* (29:1,2)

Once it is cast into the fire of trial and tribulation, the fragrant scents of patience emerge from the essence of the truthful, while the foul odours of ingratitude for blessings emanate from the liars. The believer must therefore understand that the test of affliction is like the furnace for testing gold. He must understand that Allāh is Good, and accepts nothing but the good. There is no greater proof, of all that we have said, than what was experienced by the Companions of our master Muḥammad (Allāh bless him and give him peace)

We beg Allāh to grant us safekeeping and security, and to establish us, in accordance with His indubitable word, in the life of this world and in the Hereafter, for the sake of His Chosen Prophet (Allāh bless him and give him peace), and for the sake of his perfect inheritors. *Āmīn.* Peace be upon the Messengers, and praise be to Allāh, the Lord of All the Worlds. There is no might nor any power, except with Allāh, the All-High, the Almighty. May Allāh bless our master Muḥammad, his family and his Companions, and may He grant them peace.

The Sixty-first Call

In the Name of Allāh, the All-Merciful, the All-Compassionate.
Bismi'llāhi 'r-Raḥmāni 'r-Raḥīm.

O you who truly believe, remember Allāh
yā ayyuha 'lladhīna āmanu 'dhkuru 'llāha
with frequent remembrance.
dhikran kathīrā:

And glorify Him at the dawn and in the evening.
wa sabbiḥū-hu bukratan wa aṣīlā

He is the One who blesses you, as do His angels,
Huwa 'lladhī yuṣallī ʿalai-kum wa malāʾikatu-hu
so that He may bring you forth
from darkness into light;
li-yukhrija-kum mina 'ẓ-ẓulumāti ila 'n-nūr:
and to the believers He has been Compassionate.
wa kāna bi'l-muʾminīna Raḥīmā. (33:41–43)

O you who truly believe, remember Allāh
yā ayyuha 'lladhīna āmanu 'dhkuru 'llāha
with frequent remembrance.
dhikran kathīrā:

Allāh (Exalted is He) has commanded His servants to remember Him and give thanks to Him, and to do so frequently, for all that He has graciously bestowed upon them. He has enjoined that without a precise definition (Exalted is He), to make compliance easier for the servant, and to magnify the reward assigned to it.

It was Ibn ʿAbbās who said: "No one has any excuse for failing to remember Allāh, unless his mind is completely deranged." As reported by Abū Saʿīd, the Prophet (Allāh bless him and give him peace) once said:

> You must practise the remembrance of Allāh with great frequency, to the point where they call you a lunatic [*majnūn*].[1021]

It has been said that frequent remembrance is consistent with sincere devotion of the heart, while too little of it is symptomatic of hypocrisy, like remembrance with the tongue.[1022]

Allāh (Exalted is He) commands His believing servants to behave as He commands His Prophetic Messengers to behave. He has thus instructed His servants, just as He has trained His Prophet, in the reverence due to Him, for He has said:

> O you who truly believe, remember Allāh
> *yā ayyuha 'lladhīna āmanu 'dhkuru 'llāha*
> with frequent remembrance.
> *dhikran kathīrā*:

—just as He said to His Prophet:

> O Prophet, you must practise true devotion to Allāh.
> *yā ayyuha 'n-Nabiyyu 'ttaqi 'llāha.* (33:1)

There is a subtle point to be noted here: The believer may sometimes forget to remember Allāh, so he has been commanded to be constant in remembrance. As for the Prophet (blessing and peace be upon him), due to the fact that he is one of those brought near, he does not forget, but one who is brought near to the Sovereign may be dazzled by his nearness to Him, and his sense of fear may thus be diminished. He has therefore said (Exalted is He):

> You must practise true devotion to Allāh.
> *[u] 'ttaqi 'llāha.* (33:1)

—for, when someone is sincerely committed to righteousness, he is in a state of grave peril, and the virtue of the saints [*awliyā'*] is the vice of the Prophets [*Anbiyā'*].

To this I would add: In everything relating to the Prophet (Allāh bless him and give him peace) in the noble Qur'ānic verses, there is a lesson for the Community, because the Messenger (Allāh bless him and give him peace) is a mirror for his Community. He is the impeccable example, the one who is firmly committed to true devotion. Consider, for instance, His saying (Exalted is He) [to the Messenger (Allāh bless him and give him peace)]:

> So know that there is no god but Allāh.
> *fa-'ʿlam anna-hu lā ilāha illa 'llāhu.* (47:19)

Remember Allāh
[u] 'dhkuru 'llāha

—with all that He deserves, in the way of *tahlīl* [the affirmation that there is no god but Allāh (*lā ilāha illa 'llāh*)], and *taḥmīd* [saying: "Praise be to Allāh (*al-ḥamdu li'llāh*)"], and *takbīr* [proclaiming: "Allāh is Supremely Great (*Allāhu Akbar*)!"], and so on. Remembrance means causing something to be present in the heart or in speech, when it is a question of recollection after forgetfulness, as in His saying (Exalted is He):

And remember your Lord when you forget.
wa 'dhkur Rabba-ka idhā nasīta. (18:24)

This applies to the condition of the common folk. Remembrance may also signify the maintenance of constant awareness and retention of memory, as in the case of the special few, since they experience no forgetfulness at all, and they are absolutely present with the One they remember.[1023]

with frequent remembrance.
dhikran kathīrā:

In many of the instances where Allāh (Exalted is He) has mentioned remembrance, He has described it in terms of frequency, since there is nothing to prevent remembrance in all situations, as we have explained.[1024] That is to say, [there is nothing to prevent it] at all times, by night and by day, in summer and in winter, and likewise in all locations, on land and at sea, on level ground and in the mountains, as well as in all situations, at home and on a journey, in health and in sickness, in private and in public, while standing and while sitting, and while reclining on one's side, and when performing an act of worshipful obedience, by performing it with sincere devotion and begging for acceptance and enabling grace, and when involved in sinful disobedience, by refraining from it and repenting and seeking forgiveness, and when blessed with gracious favour, by giving thanks, and when in a state of hardship, by enduring with patience.

The states of those who remember [*dhākirīn*] are as varied as their ways of practising remembrance [*adhkār*]:

1. The remembrance of one type of person is merely with the tongue. He does not use his mind to contemplate the One remembered by him,

nor to reflect on His works. His heart is devoid of the presence and disclosures of the One remembered by him. He does not experience the intimate friendship of the One remembered by him, nor does he witness His radiant lights with his spirit. He does not experience personal extinction in the One remembered by him, nor does he behold His secrets with his innermost being. This should be rejected absolutely.

(In my opinion, this judgment is unacceptable, because remembrance with the tongue should not be abandoned, since it may possibly move from the tongue to the heart.)

2. The remembrance of one type is with the tongue and the mind. He remembers with his tongue, while using his mind to contemplate the One remembered by him, and to reflect on His works, but he does not experience the presence and the intimate friendship of the One remembered by him, nor does he experience personal extinction in Him. This is the remembrance of the piously devout, and it is acceptable in contrast to the first.

3. The remembrance of one type is only with the tongue, the mind and the heart. He experiences neither the intimate friendship of the One remembered by him, nor personal extinction in Him. This is the remembrance of the novices among those who are drawn near, and it is more acceptable than the remembrance of the piously devout and what is inferior thereto.

4. The remembrance of another type is with the tongue, the mind, the heart, the spirit and the innermost being, all together. This is the remembrance of the masters of the final stage among those drawn near, such as the Prophets and the Messengers and the most perfect saints [*awliyāʾ*]. It is absolutely acceptable.

In order to point the way to these progressive stages of development, the Prophet (blessing and peace be upon him) once said:

> These hearts become rusty, just as iron becomes rusty.

When someone asked: "O Messenger of Allāh, what is their polish?" he replied:

> The recitation of Allāh's Book, and frequent remembrance of Him.

By the frequent practice of remembrance, therefore, the spiritual traveller should progress from the stage of the tongue to the high stages above it. He must polish the mirror of the heart, to rid it of its darkness and its filthy stains. While the remembrance of Allāh includes the performance of the ritual prayer [*ṣalāt*], Qur'ānic recitation [*tilāwa*], religious study, and so on, the most excellent of all forms of remembrance is the affirmation: "There is no god but Allāh [*lā ilāha illa 'llāh*]." Preoccupation with this, both in isolation and together with the congregation, while carefully observing the rules of good conduct, both outwardly and inwardly, is quite unlike preoccupation with anything else.[1025]

In His saying (Exalted is He):

> And glorify Him at the dawn and in the evening.
> *wa sabbiḥū-hu bukratan wa aṣīlā*

—those two times are mentioned specifically, not to restrict the glorification to them, as distinct from all other times, but rather to emphasize their special merit, since they are attended by the descent of the angels. Glorification [*tasbīḥ*] is similarly singled out from all other forms of remembrance, despite its inclusion among them, for the simple reason that it is the basic element in them all.[1026] When you remember Him, your remembrance of Him must be an expression of reverence and dissociation from everything bad, and that is the meaning of glorification.[1027]

> He is the One who blesses you, as do His angels.
> *Huwa 'lladhī yuṣallī 'alai-kum wa malā'ikatu-hu*

Concerning the circumstances of the revelation of this noble Qur'ānic verse, Ibn 'Abbās (may Allāh be well pleased with him and his father) is reported as having said: "When His saying (Exalted is He):

> Allāh and His angels shower blessings on the Prophet.
> *inna 'llāha wa malā'ikata-hu yuṣallūna 'ala 'n-Nabiyy.* (33:56)

—was revealed, the Emigrants [*Muhājirūn*] and the Helpers [*Anṣār*] said: 'This is for you exclusively, O Messenger of Allāh. There is nothing in it for us.' It was then that Allāh (Exalted is He) revealed this verse."

This is a gracious favour, bestowed by Allāh on this Community, and it is one of the greatest of all favours. It is a proof of its superiority over all other communities, confirmed by His saying (Exalted is He):

> You are the best community that has ever
> *kuntum khaira ummatin*

> been brought into being for the sake of mankind.
> *ukhrijat li-'n-nāsi.* (3:110)

The blessing conferred by Allāh upon His servant is His compassion for him, and His bestowal of gracious favour. The blessing conferred by the angels is their supplication on behalf of the believers, and their seeking forgiveness for them, as He has said (Exalted is He):

> And they ask forgiveness for those who believe.
> *wa yastaghfirūna li'lladhīna āmanū.* (40:7)[1028]

The overall meaning is: "Allāh (Magnificent is His Majesty) will always treat you mercifully, attending to your situation and ensuring your best interest and your prosperity."

> as do His angels.
> *wa malā'ikatu-hu*

They also shower blessings upon you, by offering supplication, seeking forgiveness and appealing for mercy on your behalf. It was Ibn Kathīr who said: "The blessing from Allāh (Glory be to Him) is His commendation of His servant in the presence of the angels."[1029] Allāh bestows blessings and mercy upon you, but you do not remember Him, so the mention of His blessing is intended to spur the believers on to remembrance.[1030]

> so that He may bring you forth from darkness into light
> *li-yukhrija-kum mina 'ẓ-ẓulumāti ila 'n-nūr:*

In other words: "So that Allāh (Exalted is He) may bring you forth through this blessing and providential care." He did not say: "So that both [Allāh and the angels] may bring you forth [*li-yukhrijā-kum*]," for the simple reason that the angels have not been endowed with the capacity to bring forth. They are incapable of that, because Allāh is the Guide in reality, and no other.

> from darkness into light
> *mina 'ẓ-ẓulumāti ila 'n-nūr:*

Darkness is the absence of light, and it is used as a metaphor for ignorance, polytheism [*shirk*], immorality, sinful disobedience, error, and humanity and its attributes.

> into
> *ilā*

—the light of knowledge, the affirmation of Oneness [*tawḥīd*], worshipful obedience, certainty, guidance, spirituality and its attributes, and Lordliness [*Rubūbiyya*], through the attractions of the manifestation of His Essence and His attributes. The meaning is: "Through the mercy of Allāh, and because of the supplication of the angels and their plea for forgiveness, you will achieve the goal, you will obtain the vision, you will be illumined by the light of the Sacred Law [*Sharīʿa*], and you will truly experience the secret of Reality [*Ḥaqīqa*]."[1031]

> and to the believers He has been Compassionate.
> *wa kāna bi'l-muʾminīna Raḥīmā.*

That is to say: "Generous in compassionate treatment of the believers, since He accepts their few good deeds, and pardons their many sins, on account of their sincerity in their belief."[1032] In the expression:

> and He has been
> *wa kāna*

—the use of the past tense signifies: "in eternity-without-beginning [*al-azal*], before the creation of the angels drawn near [*al-malāʾikat al-muqarrabīn*]."

> to the believers
> *bi'l-muʾminīna*

—to all of them, before their individual existences.

> Compassionate.
> *Raḥīmā.*

That is why He has treated them as He has treated them, by attending to their best interest both directly and by means of the angels. His merciful compassion never changes with the changing of the states of those who have been blessed in sempiternity.[1033]

To this I would add: Those who understand what Allāh says (Exalted is He and Magnificent is His Majesty) are afraid of eternity-without-beginning, because Allāh's Knowledge and His Will do not change. That was before the existence of the outer forms. Then, after the entry of the spirit, they do not know if what has been predestined for them is sempiternal mercy and providential care, or misfortune and seeking refuge with Allāh. This sempiternal knowledge places the servant in terror and dread of the Lord of lords, thereby urging him to set to work.

The important point is that sempiternal Divine care [*ʿināya Ilāhiyya azaliyya*] is an unknown factor, as far as we are concerned. We therefore remain subject to the obligations of the Sacred Law, and we must adhere to them strictly. If sempiternal care has predestined good fortune for us, then all is well. Even if this is not the case, we shall have adhered to the Sacred Law, while performing the duty of servitude. We have no right to say: "Why is this like this, and why is that like that?" because the Creator administers His servants as He wishes. In the words of the Prophetic tradition [*ḥadīth*]:

> Everyone is made ready for the purpose for which he was created.[1034]

He has said (Exalted is He):

> Allāh erases what He will, and establishes [what He will],
> *yamḥu 'llāhu mā yashāʾu wa yuthbitu*
> and with Him is the original source of the Book.
> *wa ʿinda-hu ummu'l-Kitāb.* (13:39)

That is to say: "Allāh erases misfortune, if its erasure accords with Allāh's Will, and it is not sempiternal [*azaliyya*]. If the misfortune is sempiternal, and its erasure is not in accordance with His Will, it remains established." The Will is not attached to temporality [*ḥudūth*], whereas erasure and establishment are both connected with temporality. The attributes of the Essence of the Lord of Truth (Glory be to Him), such as His speech, His knowledge, His word and His judgment, are not subject to erasure and establishment. Erasure and establishment are merely some of the attributes of His action. Erasure refers to extinction, and establishment to invention.

From the hearts of the abstinent He erases the love of this world, and in its place He establishes pious abstinence. According to the traditional report [*khabar*], Ḥāritha once asked the Prophet (Allāh bless him and give him peace): "For every matter of fact there is a reality [*li-kulli ḥaqq ḥaqīqa*], so what is the reality of your faith [*īmān*]?" To this he replied: "My soul has shunned this world."

We felt constrained to write about this theme relating to eternity-without-beginning [*azaliyya*]. Please consider leaving it alone, if you find it incomprehensible.

These are my own comments:

Allāh's Messenger (Allāh bless him and give him peace) once said:

> Not one of you will truly believe, until he wishes for his brother what he wishes for himself.[1035]

The servant of the believers says: "This is because it should be natural for us, and we have been trained accordingly." If someone wishes to be on good terms with his Lord (Glorious and Exalted is He), it is incumbent upon him, after correctly performing the obligatory acts of worship, such as the ritual prayer [*ṣalāt*] and other duties, to remember Allāh (Glorious and Exalted is He) with the heart and the mind, in a state of complete awareness, and with his innermost being and his conscience, until he truly experiences the light of the commandment of the most glorious Messenger (Allāh bless him and give him peace):

> You must worship Allāh as if you could see Him.

Once you have firmly grasped the true significance of this, through the blessed grace of the most glorious Messenger (Allāh bless him and give him peace), all will be well, for then you will acknowledge that the people [of the Lord] are telling the truth. If you have not yet firmly grasped it, you must hold the correct conviction and the indirect belief [*īmān ghaibī*] that Allāh sees you.

In either case, you will taste the import of the saying of the most glorious Messenger (Allāh bless him and give him peace), when he was asked about active goodness [*iḥsān*], for he said:

> [It means] that you must worship Allāh as if you could see him, for, even if you do not see him, He surely sees you.

Once you have tasted that experience, nothing but the love of Allāh will be established in your heart, through servitude. The jewel and the stone will be equally important in your sight. This does not come without a price, however. People may accuse you of insanity, in which case you must accept the charge. People may also accuse you of ignorance, so you must accept the charge, because you are indeed ignorant.

You must not be deluded by your lower self, nor must you be attached to it. You must be for Allāh and because of Allāh, and obtain deliverance from its evil through Allāh. You must accept the Sacred Law [*Sharīʿa*]. You must depart before you depart [from this world], and contemplate that journey, after the return. In this connection, you must work as Allāh (Exalted is He) has said:

> For the like of this, let the workers work.
> *li-mithli hādhā fa-l'-yaʿmali 'l-ʿāmilūn.* (37:61)

—and as He has said (Exalted is He):

> So after this let the strivers strive.
> *wa fī dhālika fa-l'-yatanāfasi 'l-mutanāfisūn.* (83:26)

O Allāh, direct our hearts towards You, through our loyalty to Your most noble friend (on him be the most excellent blessing and peace). Turn the Muslims back to their religion in fine style, so that You may be well pleased with them, through the Sacred Law and loyal obedience to the Messenger (Allāh bless him and give him peace). We hope for Your good pleasure. Peace be upon the Messengers, and praise be to Allāh, the Lord of All the Worlds. There is no might nor any power, except with Allāh, the All-High, the Almighty. May Allāh bless our master Muḥammad, his family and his Companions, and may He grant them peace.

The Sixty-second Call

In the Name of Allāh, the All-Merciful, the All-Compassionate.
Bismi'llāhi 'r-Raḥmāni 'r-Raḥīm.

O you who truly believe,
if you marry believing women,
yā ayyuha 'lladhīna āmanū idhā
nakaḥtumu 'l-mu'mināti
and then divorce them before
you have touched them,
thumma ṭallaqtumū-hunna min qabli an tamassū-hunna
no waiting period is required of them,
that you would have to reckon.
fa-mā la-kum ʿalai-hinna min ʿiddatin taʿtaddūna-hā
So compensate them,
and release them in fine style.
fa-mattiʿū-hunna wa sarriḥū-hunna sarāḥan jamīlā.
(33:49)

O you who truly believe, if you marry believing women....
yā ayyuha 'lladhīna āmanū idhā nakaḥtumu 'l-mu'mināti....

There is a close connection between this Qur'ānic verse and the preceding revelations, for, in this Sūra, Allāh (Exalted is He) has expounded the most noble moral standards. He has instructed His Prophet (Allāh bless him and give him peace) in the manner we have described, but Allāh (Exalted is He) has also commanded His believing servants to behave as He has commanded the Messenger to behave. Whenever He has mentioned a noble standard to the Prophet (Allāh bless him and give him peace), and taught him a mode of good conduct, He has told the believers about something corresponding to it.

Allāh has thus begun the training of the Prophet (blessing and peace be upon him) by mentioning what is important in relation to Allāh, in His words:

> O Prophet, you must practise true devotion to Allāh.
> *yā ayyuha 'n-Nabiyyu 'ttaqi 'llāha.* (33:1)

Secondly, He has mentioned what is important in relation to the wives who are at his disposal, in His subsequent saying:

> O Prophet, say to your wives....
> *yā ayyuha 'n-Nabiyyu qul li-azwāji-ka....* (33:28)

Thirdly, He has mentioned what is important in relation to the common folk, in His saying:

> O Prophet, We have sent you as a witness.
> *yā ayyuha 'n-Nabiyyu innā arsalnā-ka shāhidan.* (33:45)

In similar fashion, He has begun the instruction of the believers by mentioning what is important in relation to Allāh, for He has said:

> O you who truly believe, remember Allāh
> *yā ayyuha 'lladhīna āmanu 'dhkuru 'llāha*
> with frequent remembrance.
> *dhikran kathīrā.* (33:41)

Then, secondly, He has mentioned what is important in relation to the wives at their disposal:

> O you who truly believe, if you marry believing women....
> *yā ayyuha 'lladhīna āmanū idhā nakaḥtumu 'l-mu'mināti....*

Then, just as He treated the Prophet's relationship to the Community as the third point in his training, He treated the relationship of the believers to their Prophet as the third point relevant to them, for He said after this:

> O you who truly believe,
> *yā ayyuha 'lladhīna āmanū*
> do not enter the dwellings of the Prophet.
> *lā tadkhulū buyūta 'n-Nabiyyi.* (33:53)

Allāh (Exalted is He) has chosen to make special mention of those divorcées who have been divorced before physical contact, since their case directs attention to the highest standards of conduct, and thus provides an instructive example.

When the woman is divorced before physical contact has occurred, the marriage contract has not been consummated. This explains why He has said (Exalted is He), in reference to the woman who has been touched:

How can you take it, after one of you has gone in to the other,
wa kaifa ta'khudhūna-hu wa qad afḍā ba'ḍu-kum ilā ba'ḍin
and they have taken from you a solemn covenant?
wa akhadhna min-kum mīthāqan ghalīẓā. (4:21)

Since Allāh has commanded compensation and good treatment, even though there is no love between him and her, what should you expect of a man who has fallen in love with her, or whose connection with her has been reinforced by their common parentage of a child?

The Noble Qur'ān may be small in physical size, but if all its meanings were to be spelled out, there would be a shortage of pens, and too few sheets of paper for the task. For instance, consider His saying:

Do not say 'Ugh!,' to them [your parents].
fa-lā taqul la-humā uffin. (17:23)

Many meanings can be deduced from that brief expression, and the same is true in this case. From the fact that He has commanded good treatment of a woman, despite the absence of love from the relationship, it can be inferred that good treatment is essential in relating to a wife who has been touched, to one who has not been divorced after that, and to one who has given birth to her husband's child, while married to him.[1036]

In His saying (Exalted is He):

if you marry believing women....
idhā nakaḥtumu 'l-mu'mināti....

—He has made specific mention of believing women, even though women of the scriptural religions [*kitābiyyāt*] are included in the ruling. This is a way of serving notice that, for the Muslim, it is most appropriate to choose the best receptacle for his seed, and to marry none but a virtuous believing woman.[1037]

and then divorce them before you have touched them.
thumma ṭallaqtumū-hunna min qabli an tamassū-hunna.

This may be cited as proof that it is not correct to make divorce conditional on the sexual consummation of marriage, because, if that were the case, divorce could only take place after sexual consummation. Allāh (Exalted is He) has prefaced his mention of it [divorce] with the word *thumma* [then], which indicates a lack of immediacy.[1038]

before you have touched them.
min qabli an tamassū-hunna.

That is to say: "before you have engaged in sexual intercourse with them." According to the Ḥanafī scholars, genuine privacy with the woman is synonymous with touching. Such privacy means that he is alone with her, in a situation where neither of the two spouses is subject to any legal impediment [to sexual intercourse], such as pilgrim consecration [*iḥrām*], obligatory fasting, or menstruation, nor to any physical impediment, such as illness, nor to any mental impediment, such as inhibition felt by the wife on account of the nearby presence of an intimidating individual. If he is alone with her in this kind of privacy, and then divorces her before penetrating her, the husband is obliged to provide the complete marriage dower, and she must observe the *ʿidda* [prescribed waiting period before remarriage], as a precaution [in case she has in fact become pregnant].

On the other hand, if he is alone with her in the presence of one of the impediments mentioned above, and then divorces her before penetrating her, he is obliged to provide half of the marriage dower, and she must observe the *ʿidda* as a precaution.[1039]

no waiting period is required of them,
fa-mā la-kum ʿalai-hinna min ʿiddatin
that you would have to reckon.
taʿtaddūna-hā.

That is to say: "They are not required to wait [before they are free to remarry] for a certain number of days, which you would have to count."[1040] In other words: "You have no right to make them observe the *ʿidda*, because you have not cohabited with them. Since pregnancy is out of the question, you have no reason to confine the woman for the purpose of safeguarding your lineage."[1041]

So compensate them, and release them in fine style.
fa-mattiʿū-hunna wa sarriḥū-hunna sarāḥan jamīlā.

That is to say: "Compensate the divorced woman, if you do not owe her a legal due [stipulated in the marriage contract]." If he does owe her a stipulated due, he is obliged to pay her half of that due, without the compensatory gift [*mutʿa*], although the latter is customary [*sunna*].[1042]

If she is not owed a stipulated due, the injunction is understood in terms of strict entitlement. In the case of a woman for whom no marriage dower has been specified, and only in her case, the compensatory gift [*mut*ʿ*a*] is strictly required. Ibn ʿAbbās (may Allāh be well pleased with him and his father) is reported as having said: "In the case where no marriage dower has been named, the compensatory gift [*mut*ʿ*a*] is due to her, if he divorces her before physical contact. If a dower has been stipulated for her, she is entitled to half of the dower, and no compensatory gift is due to her."[1043]

It is permissible to interpret the instruction to compensate as a combined reference to strict entitlement and strong recommendation, since the compensatory gift [though not obligatory] is customary [*sunna*] in the case of a woman who is owed a stipulated due.[1044] The commandment to provide compensation is not made conditional on her not being owed a stipulated due. It is actually delivered, without qualification, in reference to a woman who is divorced before sexual penetration, whether or not her dower has been named. His saying (Exalted is He):

> So compensate them.
> *fa-matti*ʿ*ū-hunna.*

—may be interpreted in the sense of giving them something for them to enjoy, since that would cover the ordinary, non-technical meaning of the term *mut*ʿ*a* [enjoyment], as well as half of the stipulated due. The force of the commandment may also be construed as a combination of strict injunction and strong recommendation, for, in the case of a woman whose dower has been named at the time of the marriage contract, and who is then divorced before intercourse, it is considered commendable to compensate her with something extra, in addition to half of the specified dower.

As mentioned in the books of the Ḥanafī scholars, divorced women fall into four different categories:

1. A divorcée whose marriage was not sexually consummated, and for whom no dower was specified. She is strictly entitled to the compensatory gift [*mut*ʿ*a*], consisting of a chemise, a veil and a shawl.

2. A divorcée whose marriage was not sexually consummated, but for whom a dower was specified. The compensatory gift [*mut*ʿ*a*] is not recommended in her case, but she is strictly entitled to half of the specified dower.

3. A divorcée whose marriage was sexually consummated, but for whom no dower was specified.

4. A divorcée whose marriage was sexually consummated, and for whom a dower was specified. In each of these last two cases, the compensatory gift [*mutʿa*] is recommended.

The main points are the following:

• If the husband has had intercourse with her, the compensatory gift [*mutʿa*] is recommended in her case, whether or not a marriage dower was specified for her. This is because he has left her in the lurch, through divorce, after she had submitted to him what was promised in the marriage contract, that being her genitalia. It is therefore considered commendable for him to give her something extra, in addition to what is strictly required, the latter being the stated amount [of the dower], in a case where the amount was specified, or the dower appropriate to a woman like her [*mahr al-mithl*], in a case of non-specification.

• If he has not had intercourse with her, then, in a case of specification, she must take only half of the stated amount, to allow for the absence of genital submission, and nothing else is recommended for her. In a case of non-specification, the compensatory gift [*muʿta*] is strictly required, because she would otherwise receive nothing at all.[1045]

> and release them
> *sarriḥū-hunna*

That is to say: "Let them leave their houses, since you have no reason to make them observe a waiting period [*ʿidda*]."

> in fine style.
> *sarāḥan jamīlā.*

In other words: "without any inconvenience, and without denying any just claim."[1046] To release a divorced wife in fine style, a man must refrain from demanding the return of anything that he has given her.

These are my own comments:

What is called for by Allāh (Glory be to Him and (Exalted is He) is release in fine style, without hurt or offence or infringement of their rights, so how can there be any question of mutual maltreatment?! That is why our Lord has told us, in a Sacred Tradition [*Ḥadīth Qudsī*]:

> O My servants, I have made maltreatment unlawful for Myself, and I have also made it unlawful between you, so do not treat one another wrongfully![1047]

This text provides proof of the unlawfulness of both kinds of maltreatment, since there is maltreatment of oneself and there is maltreatment of others. Maltreatment of oneself is inflicted by sinful acts of disobedience, the most serious of which is attributing partners to Allāh (Exalted is He). He has said (Exalted is He):

> Attributing partners [to Allāh] is a tremendous wrong.
> *inna 'sh-shirka la-ẓulmun ʿaẓīm.* (31:13)

> And We did not wrong them,
> *wa mā ẓalamnā-hum*
> but they used to wrong themselves.
> *wa lākin kānū anfusa-hum yaẓlimūn.* (16:118)

The maltreatment of others is inflicted by word and deed. Both kinds of maltreatment are referred to in the saying of the Prophet (Allāh bless him and give him peace), reported by Abū Mūsā al-Ashʿārī (may Allāh be well pleased with him):

> Allāh (Exalted is He) will surely grant respite to the wrongdoer, but then, when He grabs him, He will not let him slip away.

Then [according to this same report] he recited:

> Such is the grasp of your Lord when He grasps the townships
> *wa ka-dhālika akhdu Rabbi-ka idhā akhadha 'l-qurā*
> while they are doing wrong. His grasp is painful, very intense.
> *wa hiya ẓālima: inna akhdha-hu ʿalīmun shadīd.* (11:102)[1048]

This applies to the person who wrongs himself, by committing sinful acts of disobedience in their various degrees, and it also applies to the person who wrongs others. Such is the state of the people of the townships, some of whom wrong themselves, while some of them do wrong to others.

As for the Day of Resurrection, it is a day on which there will be a perfect manifestation of Divine Justice. A believer will not enter the Garden of Paradise, even though he is one of its people, so long as any servant [of the Lord] has a rightful claim against him, even if this servant is one of the people of the Fire of Hell. In the Sacred Tradition related by Aḥmad, on the authority of ʿAbdu'llāh ibn Anīs, we are told:

> No one from among the people of the Fire should be made to enter the Fire, if he has a rightful claim on someone from among the people of the Garden, until he has settled his account with him. Nor should anyone from among the people

of the Garden be allowed to enter the Garden, so long as someone from among the people of the Fire has a rightful claim on him, until he settles his account with him, even if it involves no more than a slap on the face.

You must therefore beware of wrongdoing. You must do no wrong to any one of the creatures of Allāh (Exalted is He), for wrongdoing [*ẓulm*] will assume the form of ominous dark shadows [*ẓulumāt*] on the Day of Resurrection:

And do not think that Allāh is unaware of what the wicked do.
wa lā taḥsabanna 'llāha ghāfilan ʿammā yaʿmalu 'ẓ-ẓālimūn:
He merely gives them respite till a day when eyes will stare.
inna-mā yu'akhkhiru-hum li-yawmin tashkhaṣu fī-hi 'l-abṣār. (14:42)

You must not be someone who does wrong to himself and to others, for Allāh (Exalted is He) has said:

Until, when death comes to one of them,
ḥattā idhā jā'a aḥada-humu 'l-mawtu
he says: "My Lord, send me back,
qāla Rabbi 'rjiʿū-n.
that I may do right in what I have left behind!"
laʿallī aʿmālu ṣāliḥan fī-mā taraktu
Oh no, it is merely a word that he speaks, and behind them
kallā inna-hā kalimatun huwa qā'ilu-hā wa min warā'i-him
there is a barrier until the day when they are resurrected.
barzakhun ilā yawmi yubʿathūn. (23:99,100)

This request, at that late hour, will not avail the wrongdoer, just as his repentance will not be accepted. Allāh (Exalted is He) has said:

Repentance is not for those who do evil deeds
wa laisati 't-tawbatu li'lladhīna yaʿmalūna 's-sayyi'āti
until, when death presents itself to one of them,
ḥattā idhā ḥaḍara aḥada-humu 'l-mawtu
he says: "I now repent."
qāla innī tubtu 'l-āna. (4:18)

We beg Allāh to keep us safe from the wickedness of the evildoers, and to include us among those endowed with grace and providential care, for the sake of His Chosen Prophet (Allāh bless him and give him peace). Peace be upon the Messengers, and praise be to Allāh, the Lord of All the Worlds. There is no might nor any power, except with Allāh, the All-High, the Almighty. May Allāh bless our master Muḥammad, his family and his Companions, and may He grant them peace.

The Sixty-third Call

In the Name of Allāh, the All-Merciful, the All-Compassionate.
Bismi'llāhi 'r-Raḥmāni 'r-Raḥīm.

O you who truly believe,
yā ayyuha 'lladhīna āmanū
do not enter the dwellings of the Prophet
lā tadkhulū buyūta 'n-Nabiyyi
unless you are granted permission, for a meal,
illā an yu'dhana la-kum ilā ṭa'āmin
without waiting for its preparation.
ghaira nāẓirīna inā-hu

But if you are invited, enter.
wa lākin idhā du'ītum fa-'dkhulū
Then, when you have finished eating, disperse,
fa-idhā ṭa'imtum fa-'ntashirū
and do not linger for conversation.
wa lā musta'nisīna li-ḥadīth:

That would cause annoyance to the Prophet,
inna dhālikum kāna yu'dhi 'n-Nabiyya
and he would be shy of you,
fa-yastaḥyī min-kum
but Allāh is not shy of the truth.
wa 'llāhu lā yastaḥyī mina 'l-ḥaqq:

And when you ask them [his wives]
for some utensil,
wa idhā sa'altumū-hunna matā'an
ask it of them from behind a veil.
fa-'s'alū-hunna min warā'i ḥijāb:
That is purer for your hearts and for their hearts.
dhālikum aṭharu li-qulūbi-kum wa qulūbi-hinn:

And it is not for you
wa mā kāna la-kum

to cause annoyance to Allāh's Messenger,
an tu'dhū Rasūla 'llāhi
nor that you should ever marry
his wives after him.
wa lā an tankiḥū azwāja-hu min ba'di-hi abadā:
That in Allāh's sight would be an enormity.
inna dhālikum kāna 'inda 'llāhi 'aẓīmā. (33:53)

O you who truly believe,
yā ayyuha 'lladhīna āmanū
do not enter the dwellings of the Prophet
lā tadkhulū buyūta 'n-Nabiyyi
unless you are granted permission.
illā an yu'dhana la-kum

After having issued this third call [to the Prophet (Allāh bless him and give him peace) in this Sūra]:

O Prophet, We have sent you as a witness.
yā ayyuha 'n-Nabiyyu innā arsalnā-ka shāhidan: (33:45)

—in order to explain his relationship with his Community in general, Allāh (Exalted is He) has now said to the believers, in this call [*nidā'*]: "Do not enter...," as an instruction to them and as an explanation of their relationship with the Prophet (blessing and peace be upon him) in terms of due respect. There are actually two aspects to the relationship of the Community with the Prophet (blessing and peace be upon him):

1. In the state of privacy, when it is strictly necessary for him to be undisturbed. Allāh has stated this clearly in His saying:

Do not enter the dwellings of the Prophet.
lā tadkhulū buyūta 'n-Nabiyyi

2. In the context of public assembly. In this case it is strictly necessary to show reverence, as He has said:

O you who truly believe, invoke blessings upon him
yā ayyuha 'lladhīna āmanū ṣallū 'alai-hi
and salute him with a worthy salutation.
wa sallimū taslīmā. (33:56)[1049]

The reduplication [in *sallimū taslīmā*] is meant to emphasize the expression of honour and respect. The Qur᾽ānic verse is an instruction to the believers, pointing them towards this noble and elevated mode of conduct. It signifies: "Do not enter the dwellings of the Prophet under any circumstances, except in the case where you have his permission (blessing and peace be upon him), out of respect for the rights of his womenfolk, and an eager desire to avoid offending him and causing him inconvenience."

> for a meal, without waiting for its preparation.
> *ilā ṭaʿāmin ghaira nāẓirīna inā-hu*

That is to say: "Except when he invites you to a meal, without waiting for it to be properly cooked."[1050] In other words: "Do not enter the dwellings of the Prophet for a meal, unless he gives you permission."[1051]

> But if you are invited, enter.
> *wa lākin idhā duʿītum fa-'dkhulū*
> Then, when you have finished eating, disperse.
> *fa-idhā ṭaʿimtum fa-'ntashirū*

That is to say: "But if you are invited, and you have permission to enter, then enter. As soon as you have finished the meal, disperse to your homes, and do not linger."

> and do not linger for conversation.
> *wa lā mustaʾnisīna li-ḥadīth:*

This is linked with:

> without waiting
> *ghaira nāẓirīna*

In other words: "Do not enter his dwellings while waiting for the meal, nor while engaging in conversation with one another." According to Abū Ḥayyān: "They were forbidden to prolong the session, by entertaining one another with conversation."[1052]

After having depicted the rôle of the Prophet (Allāh bless him and give him peace) as that of a summoner to Allāh, in His saying:

> And as one who summons unto Allāh.
> *wa dāʿiyan ila 'llāhi.* (33:46)

—Allāh (Exalted is He) has now gone on to say: "Do not enter unless you are summoned." In other words: "Just as you did not enter the religion except in response to his summons, you must not enter his presence except after having received his summons."[1053]

Two topics are dealt with in this Qur'ānic verse:

1. Proper behaviour in the context of the meal and the time spent sitting [in the presence of the Messenger (Allāh bless him and give him peace)].
2. The matter of the veil [*ḥijāb*].

As for the first topic, most of the commentators maintain that this verse was revealed in connection with the wedding banquet [*walīma*] of Zainab, the daughter of Jaḥsh, when Allāh's Messenger (Allāh bless him and give him peace) consummated his marriage with her. According to a generally accepted report, Anas ibn Mālik was ten years old when the Prophet (Allāh bless him and give him peace) arrived in Medina. He said: "Umm Hāni' used to keep me busy in the service of Allāh's Messenger (Allāh bless him and give him peace), so I served him for ten years. When Allāh's Messenger (Allāh bless him and give him peace) completed his earthly life, I was twenty years of age. I was the person most aware of the matter of the veil, at the time when [the verse concerning] it was sent down. It was first revealed in connection with the consummation of the marriage of Allāh's Messenger (Allāh bless him and give him peace) to Zainab bint Jaḥsh. When the Prophet (Allāh bless him and give him peace) became her bridegroom, he invited the people, so they partook of the meal, then [most of them] departed.

"A group remained with the Prophet (Allāh bless him and give him peace), and they prolonged their stay, so the Prophet (Allāh bless him and give him peace) stood up and went out, and I went out with him, to encourage them to leave. The Prophet (Allāh bless him and give him peace) took a stroll, and I walked with him, until he came to the threshold of the room belonging to 'Ā'isha (may Allāh be well pleased with her). He then assumed that they had left, so he went back, and I went back with him, until he entered the presence of Zainab, only to find that they were still sitting there.

"Since they did not get up and leave, the Prophet (Allāh bless him and give him peace) retraced his steps, and I went along with him, until, when he reached the threshold of ʿĀʾisha's room, he assumed that they must have left. He went back again, and I went back with him, and they had indeed departed. The Prophet (Allāh bless him and give him peace) then drew the screen between me and him, and [the verse concerning] the veil was sent down."

In a fuller version of this report, which is also generally accepted as authentic, Anas ibn Mālik said: "He—meaning the Prophet (Allāh bless him and give him peace)—went into the house and lowered the screen, and there I was in the room, while he was reciting:

> O you who truly believe,
> *yā ayyuha 'lladhīna āmanū*
> do not enter the dwellings of the Prophet
> *lā tadkhulū buyūta 'n-Nabiyyi*
> unless you are granted permission...
> *illā an yuʾdhana la-kum ilā ṭaʿāmin...*

—up to His words:

> but Allāh is not shy of the truth."
> *wa 'llāhu lā yastaḥyī mina 'l-ḥaqq:*

According to a report from ʿĀʾisha, the wives of the Prophet (Allāh bless him and give him peace) used to go out at night, making their way to the toilets, which were situated on a broad stretch of ground. ʿUmar (may Allāh be well pleased with him) would say to the Prophet (blessing and peace be upon him): "You should keep your women veiled from sight," but Allāh's Messenger (Allāh bless him and give him peace) did not act on his advice. Then Sawda bint Zamaʿa, the wife of the Prophet (Allāh bless him and give him peace), who was a tall woman, went out one night after dark, so ʿUmar called out to her: "We can easily recognize you, O Sawda!" His motive was to bring down the veil, so Allāh sent down the veil.

As reported on the authority of Anas and Ibn ʿUmar (may Allāh be well pleased with them), ʿUmar (may Allāh be well pleased with him) once said: "I was in harmony with my Lord on three counts: (1) I said: 'O Messenger of Allāh, if only you would take the Station of Abraham as a place of prayer,' so down came the revelation:

> And take the Station of Abraham as a place of prayer.
> *wa 'ttakhidhū min Maqāmi Ibrāhīma muṣallā.* (2:125)

"(2) I said: 'O Messenger of Allāh, both the pious and the immoral enter the presence of your womenfolk, so if only you would command them to veil themselves!' The verse of the veil [*āyat al-ḥijāb*] was thereupon sent down. (3) The wives of the Prophet (Allāh bless him and give him peace) were all involved in jealousy, so I said: 'Perhaps, if he divorces you, his Lord will give him better wives instead of you,' and down came a revelation to that effect [Q. 66:5]."[1054]

That would cause annoyance to the Prophet
inna dhālikum kāna yu᾿dhi 'n-Nabiyya

In other words: "This conduct of yours will annoy the Messenger (Allāh bless him and give him peace). It will cause him inconvenience and trouble, and prevent him from fulfilling many of his beneficial tasks and occupations."

and he would be shy of you
fa-yastaḥyī min-kum:

That is to say: "He will feel too shy to send you out, and his shyness will prevent him from ordering you to go away, on account of his noble character and his sympathetic heart."

but Allāh is not shy of the truth.
wa 'llāhu lā yastaḥyī mina 'l-ḥaqq:

In other words: "Allāh (Glorious and Exalted is He) does not refrain from declaring the truth, and nothing can prevent Him from showing you the truth and explaining it to you."[1055]

This is a mode of conduct in which Allāh has disciplined the dim-witted sluggards. In the book of ath-Thaʿlabī we read: "As for the dim-witted sluggards, it is enough for you to know that the Sacred Law does not tolerate them."[1056] In other words: "Allāh does not tolerate them."[1057] Allāh is not too shy to be forthright with them, for He has said:

Then, when you have finished eating, disperse.
fa-idhā ṭaʿimtum fa-'ntashirū

As for His saying (Exalted is He):

And when you ask them [his wives] for some utensil,
wa idhā sa᾿altumū-hunna matāʿan
ask it of them from behind a veil.
fa-'s᾿alū-hunna min warā᾿i ḥijāb:

—since Allāh has barred people from entering the private quarters of the Prophet (blessing and peace be upon him), that would make it difficult for them to obtain the utensils [needed for the meal to which they have been invited]. He has therefore explained that there is no objection to their asking for such things, provided they make their request from behind a veil or curtain.

> That is purer for your hearts and for their hearts.
> *dhālikum aṭharu li-qulūbi-kum wa qulūbi-hinn:*

That is because the eye is the window of the heart, which means that the heart is influenced by what the eye sees. If the eye does not see, the heart does not become excited with desire. If the eye does see, the heart may or may not become excited with desire. The heart is therefore purer in the absence of sight, and the absence of temptation is then more obvious.[1058]

This indicates that it is improper for anyone to trust himself in private, in the company of a woman who is not lawful to him. The avoidance thereof is better for his spiritual state, safer for his lower self, and more perfect for his chastity.[1059]

To this I would add: Suppose someone asks: "How could bad thoughts be entertained about the Companions of Allāh's Messenger (Allāh bless him and give him peace)?" The answer will be:

The Lord of Truth (Blessed and Exalted is He) has transferred them from the usage of custom to the propriety of the Sacred Law and the duty of worshipful service. He has explained that human beings are no more than human, even if they are Companions of the Prophet (Allāh bless him and give him peace). The dignity of Allāh's Messenger (Allāh bless him and give him peace) is greater than the dignity of the Companions (may Allāh be well pleased with them), and their dignity is greater than the dignity of other human beings, after the Prophets (blessing and peace be upon them). The zealous self-respect of Allāh's Messenger (Allāh bless him and give him peace) is alluded to in the tradition [*ḥadīth*] of al-Bukhārī, in which it is reported, on the authority of our master Sa'd ibn 'Ubāda (may Allāh be well pleased with him), that Allāh's Messenger (Allāh bless him and give him peace) once said:

> You are amazed at the zealous self-respect of Sa'd. By Allāh, I am more zealously self-respectful than he is, and Allāh is more zealously Self-respectful than I am.

As a mark of respect for Allāh's Messenger (Allāh bless him and give him peace), Allāh (Exalted is He) instructed the Companions of Allāh's Messenger (Allāh bless him and give him peace) to refine their behaviour, by His saying:

> And when you ask them [his wives] for some utensil,
> *wa idhā sa'altumū-hunna matā'an*
> ask it of them from behind a veil.
> *fa-'s'alū-hunna min warā'i ḥijāb:*

—even though they were the purest and the best, the people of true devotion, as He said (Exalted is He):

> And He imposed on them the word of true devotion,
> *wa alzama-hum kalimata 't-taqwā*
> for they were worthy of it and deserving of it.
> *wa kānū aḥaqqa bi-hā wa ahla-hā.* (48:26)

He taught them that refinement so that they would be a righteous model for all mankind, setting the standard of zealous self-respect in people's characters. Allāh's Messenger (Allāh bless him and give him peace) once said:

> While I was asleep, I saw myself in the Garden of Paradise. I noticed that a woman was performing her ablution beside a palace, so I said: 'To whom does this palace belong?' They said: 'It belongs to 'Umar ibn al-Khaṭṭāb (may Allāh be well pleased with him).' I recalled his zealous sense of honour, so I turned and moved away.

When 'Umar (may Allāh be well pleased with him) heard this, he burst into tears and said: "Would I direct my self-respecting zeal against you, O Messenger of Allāh?"[1060]

Since this is relevant to the pure Companions (may Allāh be well pleased with them), what should we make of our own condition? It is clearly necessary that none of us, men and women alike, should have confidence in our own instincts. That is why the commandment has been stated emphatically in the Sacred Law, to the effect that a man should never be alone with a woman, unless they are [married to each other, or] related in a degree of consanguinity precluding marriage.

As reported by al-Bukhārī and Muslim, on the authority of 'Uqba ibn 'Āmir (may Allāh be well pleased with him), Allāh's Messenger (Allāh bless him and give him peace) once said:

> Beware of entering the presence of women!

A man from among the Helpers [*Anṣār*] then asked: "What if I go to see the in-laws [*ḥamū*]?" To this he replied:

> The in-laws are death!

The in-laws [*ḥamū*] are the close relatives of one's spouse, and his expression: "The in-laws are death," is a way of saying: "You may as well die, so don't do that!" This applies to such close relatives of the spouse as a brother, a paternal uncle and a paternal cousin, so how about a distant relative?

In another tradition [*ḥadīth*], likewise reported by al-Bukhārī and Muslim, on the authority of ʿAbdu'llāh ibn ʿAbbās (may Allāh be well pleased with him and his father), we are told that Allāh's Messenger (Allāh bless him and give him peace) once said:

> None of you should ever be alone with a woman, except with one who is too closely related to be a potential partner in marriage.

ʿUmar (may Allāh be well pleased with him) was extremely fond of drawing the veil over them, and he would often mention the subject. He longed for a revelation about it to be sent down, and he used to say: "If I had my way, where you are concerned, no eye would ever see you!"

Allāh (Exalted is He) has gone on to say:

> And it is not for you
> *wa mā kāna la-kum*
> to cause annoyance to Allāh's Messenger.
> *an tu'dhū Rasūla 'llāhi*

In other words: "It is neither fitting nor proper for you to annoy your Messenger, by whom Allāh has guided you during his life."[1061] That is to say: "It is neither correct nor right for you to do anything that he finds unpleasant, and that is a nuisance to him, such as lingering and indulging in conversation, and other such habits of yours."[1062]

The Qur'ānic verse contains a repetition of the point at issue, and a confirmation of the rule that applies to it. Rules are reinforced by such emphasis on the reasons for their enactment.

As for His saying (Exalted is He):

> nor that you should ever marry his wives after him.
> *wa lā an tankiḥū azwāja-hu min baʿdi-hi abadā:*

—Ismāʿīl ibn Isḥāq has reported that Qatāda said: "A man once said: 'If Allāh's Messenger (Allāh bless him and give him peace) were to die, I would marry ʿĀʾisha.' Allāh (Exalted is He) thereupon sent down:

> And it is not for you
> *wa mā kāna la-kum*
> to cause annoyance to Allāh's Messenger."
> *an tuʾdhū Rasūla 'llāhi*

In another revelation, He said (Exalted is He):

> and his wives are their mothers.
> *wa azwāju-hu ummahātu-hum.* (33:6)

—thereby applying to them the rule that applies to mothers. This is one of his unique peculiarities, conferred to distinguish his nobility and draw attention to his rank (Allāh bless him and give him peace).

According to ash-Shāfiʿī (may Allāh bestow His mercy upon him): "As for those of his wives (Allāh bless him and give him peace) whom he left as widows, it is not lawful for anyone to marry them. If anyone considers that to be lawful, he is an unbeliever. It has been said that He banned marriage to his wives for the simple reason that they are his wives in the Garden of Paradise, and that a woman in the Garden belongs to the last of her husbands. The Prophet (blessing and peace be upon him) once said:

> My wives in this world are my wives in the Hereafter."[1063]

The meaning of His saying (Exalted is He):

> That in Allāh's sight would be an enormity.
> *inna dhālikum kāna ʿinda 'llāhi ʿaẓīmā.*

—is that offending him, and marrying his wives, would be an enormous sin. It also contains an expression of reverence from Allāh (Exalted is He) for His Messenger (Allāh bless him and give him peace), and an insistence on respect for him, both living and dead. That is why He has underlined the threat so heavily.[1064]

These are my own observations:

Through your conscious awareness of the Sublime Glory of Allāh (Blessed and Exalted is He), a veil will be drawn between you and acts of sinful disobedience to Him. The abandonment of acts of sinful disobedience is a prerequisite for the performance of acts of worshipful obedience. Once you have refrained from acts of sinful disobedience, you will behave in accordance with the demands of faith. The requirements of faith include reverence for Allāh's Messenger (Allāh bless him and give him peace), and reverence for him (Allāh bless him and give him peace) includes loyal adherence to him, both outwardly and inwardly. There is nothing more burdensome for the lower self than following him in what he has commanded. You must therefore be on your guard against the temptation posed by this world and by women.

The ultimate goal of travelling the spiritual path, together with the heirs of Allāh's Messenger (Allāh bless him and give him peace), is adherence to the noble Sacred Law. That which cuts you off from the straight path is the consumption of people's wealth, wantonly and with the sword of shame, as well as ogling women and consorting with them. You must focus your attention on the Sacred Law of Allāh's Messenger (Allāh bless him and give him peace), and adhere to it strictly, while begging the Patron to grant us, and you, an excellent conclusion.

O Allāh, grant us the blessing of following in his footsteps (Allāh bless him and give him peace) and refraining from passionate desire, through Your mercy, O Most Merciful of the merciful. Peace be upon the Messengers, and praise be to Allāh, the Lord of All the Worlds. There is no might nor any power, except with Allāh, the All-High, the Almighty. May Allāh bless our master Muḥammad, his family and his Companions, and may He grant them peace.

The Sixty-fourth Call

In the Name of Allāh, the All-Merciful, the All-Compassionate.
Bismi'llāhi 'r-Raḥmāni 'r-Raḥīm.

Allāh and His angels
shower blessings on the Prophet.
inna 'llāha wa malā'ikata-hu yuṣallūna 'ala 'n-Nabiyy:
O you who truly believe,
invoke blessings upon him
yā ayyuha 'lladhīna āmanū ṣallū 'alai-hi
and salute him with a salutation [of peace].
wa sallimū taslīmā. (33:56)

Allāh and His angels shower blessings on the Prophet.
inna 'llāha wa malā'ikata-hu yuṣallūna 'ala 'n-Nabiyy:

When Allāh commanded the believers to request permission [to enter the presence of the Prophet (Allāh bless him and give him peace)], and not to look at the faces of his womenfolk, as a mark of reverent respect, He completed the explanation of his sanctity. That is because there are two aspects to his situation:

1. His state of privacy. Allāh has indicated the reverence he deserves while in that situation, by His saying:

Do not enter the dwellings of the Prophet.
lā tadkhulū buyūta 'n-Nabiyyi. (33:53)

2. His situation in council [*mala'*]. The council may be either the Highest Council or the lower council. As for the Highest Council, it is sanctified, for Allāh and His angels shower blessings upon him [while it is in session]. As for the lower council, that must also be treated with the utmost respect, because of His saying (Exalted is He):

O you who truly believe, invoke blessings upon him
yā ayyuha 'lladhīna āmanū ṣallū 'alai-hi

> and salute him with a salutation [of peace].
> *wa sallimū taslīmā.*[1065]

This signifies that Allāh (Glorious and Exalted is He) bestows His mercy on His Prophet, magnifies his dignity, and exalts his station, and that His righteous angels pray for the Prophet and seek forgiveness on his behalf. They entreat Allāh to venerate His servant and His Messenger, and to endow him with the highest of all degrees.[1066] The blessing comes from Allāh, as do His mercy and His good pleasure, while from the angels come the prayer of supplication and the plea for forgiveness, and from the Community come the prayer of supplication and the veneration of his authority.[1067] This Qur'ānic verse is the most compelling proof that he is the receptacle of mercies, and the most excellent of the first and the last. This is true absolutely, since the blessing and mercy from Allāh to His Prophet are combined with veneration, whereas it is mercy pure and simple that Allāh confers on anyone other than the Prophet. As He has said (Exalted is He):

> He is the One who blesses you, as do His angels.
> *Huwa 'lladhī yuṣallī ʿalai-kum wa malā'ikatu-hu.* (33:43)

Notice the distinction between the two blessings, and the relative excellence of the two stations. That is how he became the fountain of mercies and the fountain of manifestations.[1068]

> O you who truly believe, invoke blessings upon him
> *yā ayyuha 'lladhīna āmanū ṣallū ʿalai-hi*
> and salute him with a salutation [of peace].
> *wa sallimū taslīmā.*

That is to say: "You must make it your frequent practice, O believers, to invoke blessings upon him and salute him with the greeting of peace." His claim on you is enormous, for he has been the one to deliver you from error into right guidance, and to bring you out of the darkness into the light. Whenever his noble name is mentioned, you must therefore say: 'O Allāh, bless our master Muḥammad and his family, and salute them often with the greeting of peace.'"

As reported by Kaʿb ibn ʿUjra: "We once said: 'O Messenger of Allāh, we know how to salute you with the greeting of peace, but how should blessings be invoked upon you?' He replied: 'Say: "O Allāh, bless Muḥammad and the family of Muḥammad, as You blessed Abraham."'"[1069]

The angels and the believers have good reason to invoke blessings on the Prophet (Allāh bless him and give him peace), for they honour themselves thereby, since they are following the example of Allāh (Glorious and Exalted is He) in blessing and venerating him. It is also a recompense for some of his claims on his fellow creatures, because he is the supreme channel for every benefit that has reached them, and it is a duty, for anyone who receives a benefit, to recompense the person through whom it reaches him. Since mere creatures are incapable of recompensing the Messenger (Allāh bless him and give him peace), they must entreat Allāh, the Omnipotent Sovereign, to recompense him. This is the secret meaning implicit in their saying: "O Allāh, bless our master Muḥammad (Allāh bless him and give him peace)."[1070]

This Qur᾿ānic verse gives rise to several intricate points of discussion:

1. Allāh (Exalted is He) has commanded His servants to invoke blessings on His Prophet Muḥammad (Allāh bless him and give him peace), rather than on all His Prophets, as a way of honouring him. There is no disagreement over the fact that invoking blessings on him is an obligatory religious duty [*farḍ*], once in a lifetime. At all other times, it is one of the necessary duties, as strictly required as all those firmly established customs [*sunan*] that no one abandons or neglects, unless he is devoid of all goodness.

It was az-Zamakhsharī who said: "If you ask me whether the invocation of blessings on Allāh's Messenger (Allāh bless him and give him peace) is strictly necessary, or simply recommended, I shall say: 'It is strictly necessary, of that I am certain.'"

The experts have disagreed over the extent to which it is necessary. Some maintain that it is strictly required whenever the Messenger (Allāh bless him and give him peace) is mentioned. This view is supported by the Prophetic tradition [*ḥadīth*]:

> If I am mentioned in someone's presence, and he fails to invoke blessings on me, may Allāh banish him!

It is reported that he was once asked: "O Messenger of Allāh, how do you understand the words of Allāh (Almighty and Glorious is He):

> Allāh and His angels shower blessings on the Prophet?"
> *inna 'llāha wa malā᾿ikata-hu yuṣallūna ʿala 'n-Nabiyy:*

To this the Prophet (Allāh bless him and give him peace) replied:

> That is an item of hidden knowledge. Even if you asked me about it, I could not tell you anything. Allāh (Exalted is He) has appointed two angels in charge of me, so that, whenever I am mentioned in the presence of a Muslim, and he invokes blessings upon me, those two angels will say: 'May Allāh forgive you your sins!' In response to those two angels, Allāh and His other angels will then say: '*Āmīn*.' But whenever I am mentioned in the presence of a Muslim servant [of the Lord], and he fails to invoke blessings upon me, those two angels will say: 'May Allāh not forgive you!' Allāh and His other angels will then say '*Āmīn*' to those two angels.

According to one of the experts: "It is strictly necessary in every session, though only once, even if he is mentioned repeatedly. This is in keeping with what he himself said, concerning the Qur᾿ānic verse of prostration [*āyat as-sajda*] and the expression of sympathy for the sneezer. It is likewise required in every prayer of supplication [*du῾ā᾿*], once at the beginning and once at the end."

Another maintained that it is strictly required only once in a lifetime. He held a similar view concerning the declaration of the two testimonies of belief [*shahādatain*], and he said: "Caution must be exercised when it comes to the invocation of blessings at every mention [of the Prophet (Allāh bless him and give him peace)], because of all the reports that have been transmitted on that subject."

2. Concerning the merit of invoking blessings on the Prophet (Allāh bless him and give him peace), he himself said (Allāh bless him and give him peace), according to a well-attested report:

> If someone pronounces a single invocation of blessing upon me, Allāh will bless him for it, ten times over.[1071]

It was Sahl ibn ῾Abdi'llāh who said: "The invocation of blessings on our master Muḥammad (Allāh bless him and give him peace) is the most meritorious of all forms of worshipful service, because Allāh (Exalted is He) made a practice of it, He and His angels, then He enjoined it on the believers. The other forms of worship are not like that."

According to Abū Sulaimān ad-Dārānī: "If someone intends to ask Allāh to satisfy a need, he should begin by invoking blessings on the Prophet (Allāh bless him and give him peace). He should then present his need to Allāh, then conclude his plea with the invocation of blessings on the Prophet (Allāh bless him and give him peace). Allāh

(Exalted is He) will surely accept those two invocations, and He is far too Noble and Generous to reject what is between them."

As reported by Saʿīd ibn al-Musayyib, ʿUmar ibn al-Khaṭṭāb (may Allāh be well pleased with him) once said: "The supplication [*duʿāʾ*] is prevented from reaching heaven, until the supplicant invokes blessings on the Prophet (blessing and peace be upon him). Then, as soon as the invocation of blessings on the Prophet (blessing and peace be upon him) arrives, the supplication is raised aloft."

The Prophet (Allāh bless him and give him peace) once said:

> If someone invokes blessings upon me in a book, the angels will not cease invoking blessings upon him, as long as my name is still in that book.

3. The religious scholars have held differing views concerning the invocation of blessings on the Prophet (Allāh bless him and give him peace) in the ritual prayer [*ṣalāt*]. According to the great majority, however, that is one of the customary elements [*sunan*] of the ritual prayer, and one of the most highly recommended. Ibn al-Mundhir said: "It is recommended that no one should perform a ritual prayer, without including in it the invocation of blessings on Allāh's Messenger (Allāh bless him and give him peace)."

4. Concerning His words (Exalted is He):

> and salute him with a salutation [of peace].
> *wa sallimū taslīmā.*

—it was al-Qāḍī Abū Bakr ibn Bukair who said: "This Qurʾānic verse was revealed to the Prophet (blessing and peace be upon him), so he instructed his Companions to salute him with the greeting of peace. Those who came after them were likewise commanded to salute him with the greeting of peace, when they were in the presence of his tomb, and whenever he was mentioned."

As related by an-Nasāʾī, ʿAbdu'llāh ibn Abī Ṭalḥa reported that his father had told him: "Allāh's Messenger (Allāh bless him and give him peace) came along one day, and joy was showing in his face, so I said: 'We can see the good news in your face!' He responded by saying:

> 'The angel came to me and said: "O Muḥammad, your Lord is saying: 'It will surely please you to know, that if someone invokes blessings upon you, I shall bless him ten times, and if someone salutes you, I shall salute him ten times.'"'

According to an-Nasāʾī, ʿAbdu'llāh said that Allāh's Messenger (Allāh bless him and give him peace) once said:

> Allāh has angels travelling about in the land, to bring me the greeting of peace from my Community.

It was al-Qushairī who said: "The salutation [*taslīm*] is your greeting: Peace be upon you! [*salāmun ʿalaik*]."[1072]

These are my own comments:

It well befits you never to forsake the invocation of blessings on the Prophet (Allāh bless him and give him peace). You must try hard to make a constant practice of invoking blessings upon him (Allāh bless him and give him peace), a thousand times by day and by night, for he (Allāh bless him and give him peace) is:

> closer to the believers than their own selves.
> *awlā bi'l-muʾminīna min anfusi-him* (33:6)

He is fully entitled (Allāh bless him and give him peace) to expect this of us, because, through frequent invocation of blessings and peace upon him, combined with being completely present with him (Allāh bless him and give him peace), we can grasp something from His words:

> Say: "If you love Allāh, follow me;
> *qul in kuntum tuḥibbūna 'llāha fa-'ttabiʿū-nī*
> Allāh will love you and forgive you your sins."
> *yuḥbib-kumu 'llāhu wa yaghfir la-kum dhunūba-kum.* (3:31)

This is quite miraculous, that Allāh (Exalted is He) should make His love for His servants dependent on following one man, he being Allāh's Messenger (Allāh bless him and give him peace), and that He should make following him a proof of the genuineness of the servant's love for Allāh. If following him (Allāh bless him and give him peace) is not practised by the servants, they will have deprived themselves of the love of Allāh (Exalted is He). They will have been false in claiming to love Allāh (Exalted is He), and likewise in claiming to love Allāh's Messenger (Allāh bless him and give him peace).

We beg Allāh, through His gracious favour and His noble generosity, to bestow much blessing and peace upon Allāh's Messenger (Allāh bless him and give him peace), and to enable us to follow him at heart, in spirit, in private, and both outwardly and inwardly. Allāh is indeed Capable of whatever He wills. Peace be upon the Messengers, and praise be to Allāh, the Lord of All the Worlds. There is no might nor any power, except with Allāh, the All-High, the Almighty. May Allāh bless our master Muḥammad, his family and his Companions, and may He grant them peace.

The Sixty-fifth Call

In the Name of Allāh, the All-Merciful, the All-Compassionate.
Bismi'llāhi 'r-Raḥmāni 'r-Raḥīm.

O you who truly believe,
do not be like those who maligned Moses,
yā ayyuha 'lladhīna āmanu lā
takūnū ka-'lladhīna ādhaw Mūsā
but Allāh proved his innocence
of what they alleged,
fa-barraʾa-hu 'llāhu mimmā qālū:
and he was well esteemed in Allāh's sight.
wa kāna ʿinda 'llāhi wajīhā. (33:69)

When Allāh (Exalted is He) clearly stated that, if anyone maligns Allāh and His Messenger, he will be cursed and tormented, He was referring to a malevolence that is tantamount to unbelief [*kufr*]. He has also directed the believers to refrain from a less serious kind of slander, which does not entail unbelief. An example of the latter is provided by someone who expressed dissatisfaction with the allotment made by the Prophet (Allāh bless him and give him peace), with his awarding the booty to a certain person, and so on.[1073]

Thus He has said (Exalted is He):

> O you who truly believe, do not be like those who maligned Moses.
> *yā ayyuha 'lladhīna āmanu lā takūnū ka-'lladhīna ādhaw Mūsā.*

—but people have disagreed over what kind of slander gave offence to our master Muḥammad (Allāh bless him and give him peace) and to our master Moses (blessing and peace be upon him). According to the report of an-Naqqāsh, their way of slandering our master Muḥammad (Allāh bless him and give him peace) was to speak of [his freedman as] "Zaid ibn Muḥammad [Muḥammad's son Zaid]." It was Abū Wāʾil who said: "He was maligned (Allāh bless him and give him peace) when he allotted a share [of the booty], and a man from among the Helpers [*Anṣār*] protested, saying: 'This allotment is not calculated to please Allāh.' When this remark was mentioned to the Prophet (Allāh bless him and give him peace), he became angry and said:

> May Allāh treat Moses with compassion, for he was maligned with much more than that!"[1074]

Allāh (Exalted is He) has mentioned this subject in His pronouncement:

> Those who malign Allāh and His Messenger,
> *inna 'llāhīna yu'dhūna 'llāha wa Rasūla-hu*
> Allāh has cursed them in this world and the Hereafter,
> *la'ana-humu 'llāhu fi 'd-dunyā wa 'l-ākhirati*
> and He has prepared for them a shameful doom.
> *wa a'adda la-hum 'adhāban muhīnā.* (33:57)

The religious scholars have disagreed as to what constitutes the maligning of Allāh. In the view of the majority, it signifies: unbelief; attributing a female consort, a son, or a partner to Him; and describing Him improperly. The Jews are guilty of this:

> The Jews say: "Allāh's hand is fettered."
> *wa qālati 'l-Yahūdu yadu 'llāhi maghlūla.* (5:64)

—as are the Christians:

> And the Christians say: "The Messiah is the son of Allāh."
> *wa qālati 'n-Naṣāra 'l-Masīḥu 'bnu 'llāh.* (9:30)

—and so are polytheists [*mushrikūn*], who say: "The angels are the daughters of Allāh, and the idols are His partners."

As for the maligning of Allāh's Messenger (Allāh bless him and give him peace), it consists of all those words and deeds that are intended to slander and insult him.

These are examples of slanderous words: sorcerer [*sāḥir*]; poet [*shā'ir*]; soothsayer [*kāhin*]; madman [*majnūn*].

Malignant actions include: the breaking of his lateral incisor tooth [*rubā'iyya*] and the gashing of his face, one day, and the throwing of the placenta [*salā*]* against his back (Allāh bless him and give him peace), in Mecca, while he was bowing down in prostration [during the ritual prayer].[1075]

*The Arabic term *salā* signifies a skin containing a human or animal foetus. The term *mashīma* is also applied to the human placenta.

As for the words of Allāh (Exalted is He):

> like those who maligned Moses.
> *ka-'lladhīna ādhaw Mūsā.*

—there are differences of opinion concerning the kind of slander those people uttered against Moses. According to one account, they maligned him by alleging the existence of a defect in his physical body. Others maintain that Qārūn associated with a harlot, until he persuaded her to say, in the presence of the Children of Israel: "Moses has committed fornication with me." Then, when Qārūn assembled the people to hear the woman, Allāh instilled in her heart the urge to tell the truth, and she did not say what she had been instructed to say.

Be that as it may, the slander mentioned in the Qur'ān is slander enough, for they said to him, among other things:

> So go, you and your Lord, and fight!
> *fa-'dhhab anta wa Rabbu-ka fa-qātilā.* (5:24)

> We shall not believe in you until we see Allāh plainly.
> *lan nu'mina la-ka ḥattā nara 'llāha jahratan.* (2:55)

> We are weary of one kind of food.
> *lan naṣbira ʿalā ṭaʿāmin wāḥidin.* (2:61)

Allāh therefore told the believers: "You must not be like them, when the Messenger (Allāh bless him and give him peace) calls on you to fight." In other words: "You must not say:

> So go, you and your Lord, and fight!
> *fa-'dhhab anta wa Rabbu-ka fa-qātilā.* (5:24)

—and you must not ask for that which has not been permitted to you. When the Messenger commands you to do something, you must do it to the best of your ability."[1076]

As reported by al-Bukhārī, on the authority of Abū Huraira (may Allāh be well pleased with him), Allāh's Messenger (Allāh bless him and give him peace) once said:

> Moses was a modest and bashful man. His modesty prevented him from showing any part of his skin, so some of the Children of Israel maligned him by saying: 'This bashfulness can only mean that he has some skin defect to hide. Maybe it is a form of leprosy, or maybe a scrotal hernia, or maybe some kind of plague.' Allāh wished to prove Moses innocent of what they alleged, so this is what happened:

Moses was all alone one day, so he laid his clothes on a rock and then took a bath. As soon as he had finished, he went to recover his clothes, but the rock had rolled away with his clothes. Moses therefore took his staff in hand, and went looking for that rock. He took to saying: 'My clothing has been turned to stone! My clothing has been turned to stone!' He eventually passed by the Council of the Children of Israel, and they saw that, in his nakedness, he was the finest of all that Allāh had created. Allāh had indeed proved him innocent of what they were alleging.[1077]

The significance of:

but Allāh proved his innocence of what they alleged.
fa-barra'a-hu 'llāhu mimmā qālū.

—is that Allāh (Exalted is He) intended not only to prove Moses innocent, but also to broadcast his innocence (blessing and peace be upon him) and the fact that they were lying, when they charged him with those faults. The consequence of their slander was the manifestation of his innocence, not his innocence itself, because the latter had already been conferred upon him.

As for the expression:

and he was well esteemed in Allāh's sight.
wa kāna 'inda 'llāhi wajīhā.

—this is a way of saying: "Moses was endowed with dignity and high rank in His sight (Almighty and Glorious is He)." As reported by Ibn Ḥātim, al-Ḥasan said: "The adjective *wajīhā* [well esteemed] is applied to someone whose prayer of supplication is sure to be answered." Someone added: "He never asked for anything without his request being granted, except the vision [of his Lord] in this world. It is no secret that the acceptance of supplication is among the branches of elevated status."[1078]

These are my own remarks:

The proof of your love for Allāh's Messenger (Allāh bless him and give him peace) is the fact that you follow him (Allāh bless him and give him peace), both outwardly and inwardly, with complete submission, and that you abandon your passionate desire. You must follow the Prophet (Allāh bless him and give him peace), because following passionate desire is one of the gravest dangers for the true believer. The most serious peril is that you may reinforce your passionate desire with pretexts, supposedly based on Islāmic law. Once you have abandoned your passionate desire, and followed the Prophet (Allāh bless him and give him peace), you must not seek rank or prestige in the sight of your fellow creatures. If you do that, you will consume this world at the expense of your religion. The only refuge is with Allāh!

You must seek acceptance from Allāh, for, if Allāh (Exalted is He) accepts you, you will be well esteemed [*wajīhā*] in His sight, and He will grant you acceptance on earth and in heaven. We beg Allāh to honour us with the station of worshipful servitude. He is indeed Capable of whatever He wills, and He is Competent to grant such requests. Peace be upon the Messengers, and praise be to Allāh, the Lord of All the Worlds. There is no might nor any power, except with Allāh, the All-High, the Almighty. May Allāh bless our master Muḥammad, his family and his Companions, and may He grant them peace.

The Sixty-sixth Call

In the Name of Allāh, the All-Merciful, the All-Compassionate.
Bismi'llāhi 'r-Raḥmāni 'r-Raḥīm.

O you who truly believe,
you must practise true devotion to Allāh,
yā ayyuha 'lladhīna āmanu 'ttaqu 'llāha
and use speech that gets straight to the point.
wa qūlū qawlan sadīdā.

He will improve your works for you
and He will forgive you your sins.
yuṣliḥ la-kum a'māla-kum
wa yaghfir la-kum dhunūba-kum
Whoever obeys Allāh and His Messenger,
wa man yuṭi'i 'llāha wa Rasūla-hu
he has truly won a mighty triumph.
fa-qad fāza fawzan 'aẓīmā. (33:70,71)

The author of *al-Kashshāf* has said: "This Qur'ānic revelation, from:

> O you who truly believe, you must practise true devotion to Allāh,
> *yā ayyuha 'lladhīna āmanu 'ttaqu 'llāha*
> and use speech that gets straight to the point.
> *wa qūlū qawlan sadīdā.*

—to the end [of the next verse], is a confirmation of that which precedes it. While the preceding revelation is based on the prohibition of anything intended to malign Allāh's Messenger (Allāh bless him and give him peace), this one is based on the commandment to practise true devotion to Allāh (Exalted is He), in the matter of guarding the tongue. This is meant to ensure that the prohibition and the commandment will have a cumulative impact on the believers. Since the commandment closely follows the prohibition, it implicitly contains the threat from the story of our master Moses (blessing and peace be upon him). This is because his characterization, in terms of his high esteem in the sight of Allāh (Exalted is He), implies that He (Exalted is He) will exact vengeance for him from those who malign him. The commandment is immediately followed by the eloquent promise:

> He will improve your works for you and He will forgive you your sins.
> *yuṣliḥ la-kum aʿmāla-kum wa yaghfir la-kum dhunūba-kum.*

—to encourage anyone who turns away from slander, and anyone who summons others to refrain from it. So do not fail to take notice!"[1079]

Allāh (Exalted is He) has instructed the believers concerning the words and deeds that ought to emanate from them. In the case of deeds, the standard is goodness, and in the case of words, the standard is truth. This is because, if someone does what is good, and refrains from what is bad, he is practising true devotion to Allāh, and if someone speaks the truth, he is using speech that gets straight to the point.[1080] In other words, you must be conscious of Allāh in all your words and deeds, and use accurate speech that is pleasing to Allāh,[1081] speech that is direct and not unfair, that is true and not false.[1082]

Concerning His expression (Exalted is He):

> and use speech that gets straight to the point.
> *wa qūlū qawlan sadīdā.*

—the following explanations have been offered:

• Ibn ʿAbbās (may Allāh be well pleased with him and his father) is reported as having said: "[It means speech that is] right and proper [*ṣawāb*]."

• Qatāda and Muqātil said: "[It means]: 'Use speech that gets straight to the point on the subject of Zainab and Zaid, and do not link the Prophet (blessing and peace be upon him) to that which is not lawful.'"

• According to ʿIkrima and Ibn ʿAbbās (may Allāh be well pleased with them): "The most accurate speech is the affirmation: 'There is no god but Allāh [*lā ilāha illa 'llāh*].'"

• "It is that of which the outward expression coincides with the inner meaning."

• "It is that which is meant to please Allāh, and no one other than Him."
• "It is [the speech that brings about] the reconciliation of two parties in dispute."
• "The term *sadīd* is derived from *tasdīd*, which means the aiming of an arrow to hit the target."

Accurate speech embraces all good things, so it applies to everything that has been mentioned, and more besides.[1083]

You must practise true devotion to Allāh
[u] 'ttaqu 'llāha

—through scrupulous observance of His rights and the rights of His servants. The former include compliance with His command, while the latter include the abandonment of hurtfulness, especially where Allāh's Messenger (Allāh bless him and give him peace) is concerned.

It was al-Wāsiṭī who said: "True devotion [*taqwā*] must be considered from four points of view:

1. For the ordinary people, it means the abandonment of attributing partners to Allāh [*shirk*], that is to say, of ostentatious display [*riyā'*] in the performance of good works, as mentioned in His words (Exalted is He):

> So whoever hopes for the meeting with his Lord,
> *fa-man kāna yarjū liqā'a Rabbi-hi*
> let him do righteous work, and let him give no one any share at all
> *fa-'l-ya'mal 'amalan ṣāliḥan wa lā yushrik*
> in the worship due unto his Lord.
> *bi-'ibādati Rabbi-hi aḥadā.* (18:110)

2. For the special few, it means being on guard against sinful acts of disobedience.
3. For the élite of the saints [*awliyā'*], it means being on guard against relying on their own actions to achieve results.
4. For the Prophets [*Anbiyā'*], it means their taking refuge from Him with Him."[1084]

Allāh (Exalted is He) is speaking as One who is commanding His servants to practise true devotion to Him, to worship Him as if they could actually see Him, and to use speech that gets straight to the point, speech that is right and proper, free from distortion and obliquity.

Abū Mūsā al-Ashʿarī is reported as having said: "Allāh's Messenger (Allāh bless him and give him peace) had led us in the performance of the midday prayer [*ṣalāt aẓ-ẓuhr*]. When he was about to leave, he signalled to us with his hand, so we sat down, and he said: 'Allāh has commanded me to instruct you to practise true devotion to Allāh, and to use speech that gets straight to the point.' Then the women arrived, so he said [using the feminine forms of the relevant Arabic words]: 'Allāh has commanded me to instruct you to practise true devotion to Allāh, and to use speech that gets straight to the point.'"[1085]

In *Kitāb at-Taqwā* [The Book of True Devotion], Ibn Abi 'd-Dunyā states that ʿĀʾisha (may Allāh be well pleased with her) said: "Not once did Allāh's Messenger (Allāh bless him and give him peace) mount the pulpit [*minbar*], without my hearing him say:

> O you who truly believe, you must practise true devotion to Allāh,
> *yā ayyuha 'lladhīna āmanu 'ttaqu 'llāha*
> and use speech that gets straight to the point. "[1086]
> *wa qūlū qawlan sadīdā.*

In His statement (Exalted is He):

> He will improve your works for you and He will forgive you your sins.
> *yuṣliḥ la-kum aʿmāla-kum wa yaghfir la-kum dhunūba-kum:*

—Allāh has promised the believers two things, in exchange for the two things He has commanded in His words:

> O you who truly believe, you must practise true devotion to Allāh,
> *yā ayyuha 'lladhīna āmanu 'ttaqu 'llāha*
> and use speech that gets straight to the point.
> *wa qūlū qawlan sadīdā.*

1. In exchange for their good endeavours, He has promised to improve their works. It is thus through true devotion to Allāh that work becomes righteous, and righteous work is elevating and perpetuating, so those who perform it will enjoy perpetual life in the Garden of Paradise.

2. In exchange for speech that gets straight to the point, He has promised the forgiveness of sins;[1087] in other words, He will pardon you for your sins.[1088] Just as He forgives them for sins committed in the past, He will inspire the believers to repent of those that may occur in the future.[1089]

In this Qur᾽ānic revelation, there is an indication that, when Allāh grants someone His enabling grace, the recipient will surely be righteous in his actions. This is a clear sign that his sins have been forgiven.

Let us now consider His words (Exalted is He):

> Whoever obeys Allāh and His Messenger,
> *wa man yuṭiʿi 'llāha wa Rasūla-hu*
> he has truly won a mighty triumph.
> *fa-qad fāza fawzan ʿaẓīmā.*

Obedience to Allāh is synonymous with obedience to the Messenger (Allāh bless him and give him peace), but He has mentioned the two in combination, in order to highlight the noble nature of the obedient servant's conduct. If someone acts obediently, he receives a promise in the presence of Allāh, and a helping hand in the presence of the Messenger, so:

> he has truly won a mighty triumph.
> *fa-qad fāza fawzan ʿaẓīmā.*

That is to say, he has triumphed mightily in two respects:

1. He has escaped the mighty torment [of Hell]. Escape from the mighty torment is properly described as mighty, because the torment in question is so mighty. If one person was about to strike another with a whip, but the intended victim escaped, he would not be said to have "won a mighty triumph," because the "torment" from which he escaped would not have been terribly serious, even if it had been inflicted.

2. He has attained to a considerable reward, since that is the eternal, everlasting reward.[1090] He has won the mightiest favour from Allāh.[1091] He is worthy of praise in the life of this world, and of bliss in the Hereafter. He has been saved from everything he might fear, and has attained to everything he might hope to achieve.[1092] That is because he enjoys protection from the Fire of Hell, and is on his way towards everlasting bliss.[1093]

You should understand that obedience to Allāh (Exalted is He) is the process of obtaining the degrees of the affirmation of Oneness [*Tawḥīd*], in deeds, attributes and essence, while obedience to the Messenger (Allāh bless him and give him peace) is practised by clinging to the rope of the Sacred Law [*Sharīʿa*]. Salvation from the ocean of denial [*juḥūd*] and the darkness of polytheism [*shirk*] comes either by the light of spiritual illumination, or aboard the ship of the Sacred Law.

As for the former, it means that the seeker takes refuge with Allāh in his search, so that he is guided towards Him by His light, and Allāh grants Him knowledge from His presence.

As for the latter, it means that he is content with the affirmation of Singularity [*Waḥdāniyya*], conventional belief [*īmān taqlīdī*], and acting in accordance with the external rules of the Sacred Law.

It is related that, when Imām Aḥmad ibn Ḥanbal (may Allāh be well pleased with him) observed [the modesty required by] the Sacred Law, in the midst of a group of people who exposed their private parts in the public steam bath, he was told in a dream: "Allāh has appointed you to serve as a leader for the people, because of your scrupulous observance of the Sacred Law."[1094]

These are my own remarks:

Keep your eyes focused on the Sacred Law. Take the Book of Allāh in one hand, and the Sunna of Allāh's Messenger (Allāh bless him and give him peace) in the other hand. Keep your tongue moist with the remembrance [*dhikr*] of Allāh (Exalted is He). Attach no importance to praise or blame from your fellow creatures. You will then be well esteemed in the sight of Allāh, so He will improve your work for you, and He will forgive you your sin. If Allāh (Exalted is He) so wills, you will ensure for yourself a good conclusion.

You must also beware of deviating from following Allāh's Messenger (Allāh bless him and give him peace), because if someone deviates, he is so deprived that he cannot smell the scent of Reality [*Ḥaqīqa*]. There is no degree higher than adherence to the Sacred Law. You must practise true devotion. Through frequent remembrance you will experience good fortune, if Allāh (Exalted is He) so wills.

O Allāh, grant us the ability to accomplish all that, for the sake of the Chosen Prophet (Allāh bless him and give him peace), and for the sake of his noble heirs. *Āmīn*. Peace be upon the Messengers, and praise be to Allāh, the Lord of All the Worlds. There is no might nor any power, except with Allāh, the All-High, the Almighty. May Allāh bless our master Muḥammad, his family and his Companions, and may He grant them peace.

The Sixty-seventh Call

In the Name of Allāh, the All-Merciful, the All-Compassionate.
Bismi'llāhi 'r-Raḥmāni 'r-Raḥīm.

O you who truly believe, if you help Allāh,
yā ayyuha 'lladhīna āmanū in tanṣuru 'llāha
He will help you
and He will make your foothold firm.[1095]
yanṣur-kum wa yuthabbit aqdāma-kum. (47:7)

This Qur'ānic verse has clearly shown the way to glory and victory. It has also laid down the preconditions attached to Allāh's help for His believing servants: namely, strict adherence to His Sacred Law [*Sharī'a*] and support for His religion,[1096] for He has said:

> O you who truly believe, if you help Allāh....
> *yā ayyuha 'lladhīna āmanū in tanṣuru 'llāha....*

The summons to help Allāh may be understood in several ways:

1. It means that you must support Allāh's religion and His path (His Sacred Law [*Sharī'a*], in other words).
2. It means that you must support the party [*ḥizb*] of Allāh and His brigade [*farīq*].
3. It signifies that Allāh's victory is a reality [*ḥaqīqa*], as we shall now explain:

Victory is the realization [*taḥqīq*] of the objective of one of the two opponents in the struggle, and the effort to confirm his standard. Satan, the enemy of Allāh, is striving to achieve the confirmation of unbelief [*kufr*] and the defeat of the people of faith [*īmān*]. Allāh, on the other hand, is seeking the suppression of unbelief, the destruction of its people, and the annihilation of those who choose to attribute partners [to Him] in their ignorance. If someone realizes the victory of Allāh, he has thereby realized His objective [*maṭlūb*].

You should not say, "he has realized His purpose [*murād*]," since Allāh's purpose cannot be realized by anyone other than Him. According to the people of the Sunna and the Community, His objective is something other than His purpose, since Allāh (Exalted is He) has demanded belief from the unbeliever, but He has not purposed it, otherwise it would certainly have happened.

Let me offer an explanatory example: Suppose that a servant disobeys his master, so his master beats him, and the servant complains to the judge, saying: "My master has beaten me for no offence." The judge then summons the master, and asks him about that beating for no offence. The master tells the magistrate: "He will surely disobey me, even if I give him an order while standing here before you. If he does comply with my command, he is entitled to judgment in his favour." Then he gives an order to the servant: "Saddle my horse," for example. The servant refuses, but the master's objective is not that he should comply with his command; his objective is that he should not accept his instruction. If the servant did comply with his master's command, the judge would find the master guilty of wrongdoing, and that is not the master's purpose. Even though his actual intention [*irāda*] is absent from it, he nevertheless gives the order. That is the difference between his objective and [what is apparently required in response to] his command.

The believer helps Allāh by going out to fight, and by demonstrating his courage. Allāh helps him by giving him strength, confirming his courage, and sending the protecting angels to support him, from behind him and in front of him.[1097]

You should understand that help is of two kinds:

1. The help provided by the servant [of the Lord]. This is supplied by clearly stating the proofs of the religion, and removing the doubt of the immature, by explaining its rules [*aḥkām*], its obligatory duties [*farā'iḍ*], its customary practices [*sunan*], what it considers lawful [*ḥalāl*] and what it declares unlawful [*ḥarām*], and how to act in accordance with its prescriptions. Such help is also provided by engaging in military campaigns, and in the sacred struggle [*jihād*] to exalt the Word of Allāh. In order to defeat the enemies of the religion, help may be supplied directly, through personal engagement in warfare, for instance. It may

also be provided indirectly, by standing beneath the flags of the warriors [*mujāhidīn*] to increase their multitude, or by offering a prayer of supplication [*duʿāʾ*] for the victory of the Muslims and the disappointment of the unbelievers. There is also the greater sacred struggle [*al-jihād al-akbar*], since this is a means of helping Allāh against the lower self [*nafs*], in order to throw it down and kill it, so that no trace of its passionate desire will survive.

2. The help provided by Allāh (Exalted is He). This is supplied by the sending of the Messengers, the revelation of the Book, the manifestation of signs and miracles [*muʿjizāt*], and the clarification of the ways that lead to the bliss of Paradise, to the Inferno, and to the presence of the Noble One. It is provided by the commandment to engage in both the lesser and the greater sacred struggle, and by the grace that makes it possible to strive therein, in pursuit of His good pleasure, not in obedience to the promptings of the servant's own desire. It is also provided by rendering the servant victorious over the enemies of the religion, and ensuring their defeat, through the exaltation of Allāh's Word Most High. By offering right guidance, it directs him towards the extinction of his transitory existence, in the existence that is everlasting, through the manifestation of the attributes of His Beauty [*Jamāl*] and His Majesty [*Jalāl*].[1098]

> He will help you and He will make your foothold firm.
> *yanṣur-kum wa yuthabbit aqdāma-kum.*

That is to say: "He will help you against the unbelievers." It was Quṭrub who said: "If you help Allāh's Prophet, Allāh will help you and He will make your foothold firm, meaning "in the fighting." It has also been said to mean: "[He will make your foothold firm] in Islām." According to another interpretation, it signifies the establishment of hearts in security, since the establishment of firm footholds is an expression of support and assistance in the context of warfare. It has also been said to mean: "[He will make your foothold firm] on the Bridge [over Hell]."[1099] This is based on the Prophetic tradition [*ḥadīth*]:

> If someone brings another's need to the attention of one who is capable of meeting it, when the needy person cannot communicate it himself, Allāh will set his feet firmly on the Bridge [*Ṣirāṭ*] on the Day of Resurrection.[1100]

To quote yet another interpretation: "Apart from the obvious meaning: 'He will establish you firmly on the battlefield,' there is reason to understand His expression *aqdāma-kum* [your feet] in a figurative sense, as referring to all essential elements. These are represented by the feet, because it is in them that steadiness and unsteadiness are most clearly apparent."[1101]

According to one of the distinguished scholars: "Three things cause the feet to slip, namely:

1. Idolatrous worship [*shirk*] of the gifts of Allāh (Exalted is He), committed by the innermost being [*sirr*].
2. Being afraid of anything other than Allāh (Almighty and Glorious is He).
3. Pinning one's hope on anything other than Allāh (Glory be to Him and Exalted is He).

"Steadiness of the feet is likewise due to three causes, namely:

1. Constant recognition of the Benefactor [*Mufḍil*], gratitude for gracious favours, and recognition of one's own shortcoming in all conditions and circumstances.
2. Being afraid of offending Him (Blessed and Exalted is He).
3. Reliance on Allāh's guarantee, in all that He has guaranteed, without any discomfort or sense of need. It is incumbent on the intelligent person to support the religion, in accordance with the firm commitment he has undertaken."[1102]

As explained by another source, the meaning is: "He will make your foothold firm, through the constant provision of enabling grace, so that there can be no question of retreat from the onslaught of the enemies of the religion."[1103]

These are my own comments:

You must apply the rules of the Sacred Law to all your limbs and organs, both the outer and the inner. You must triumph and prevail victoriously over your lower self [*nafs*], so that its passionate desire will die. You must be a loyal servant to your Lord, and be with Him in speech, in spiritual state, and in action. You must be supportive of the religion, so that the believers derive benefit from your state of being. They will then say: "His state is that of one man in a thousand," or better still: "He is a thousand men in one."

The Muslim is an investor in eternity, and he is therefore obliged to acquire the equipment needed for eternal life, that equipment being nothing less than true devotion [*taqwā*]. He is like the ordinary traveller, who must equip himself with money and food, in preparation for his journey from one place to another in this world.

You must not be deluded by this transitory life. You must treat your worldly existence as a farm, to be cultivated for the sake of the Hereafter. You must put it to good use, in order to acquire provision for the Hereafter, by practising true devotion and making dedicated efforts. If a person cannot conquer his own lower self, he will not be able to help others. If he does not conquer his own lower self, and fails to improve it, how can he be of help to anyone else? It is through victory over the lower self that support for the religion becomes a reality, and that real benefit is conferred on the servants of Allāh.

In other words, if someone is able to conquer his lower self, and to improve it, he will then be capable of supporting the religion of Allāh, by steering the believers towards Allāh's religion, and in the direction of obedience to Allāh's Messenger (Allāh bless him and give him peace), with honesty and sincerity.

We beg Allāh to grant us the ability to accomplish all that. *Āmīn*. Peace be upon the Messengers, and praise be to Allāh, the Lord of All the Worlds. There is no might nor any power, except with Allāh, the All-High, the Almighty. May Allāh bless our master Muḥammad, his family and his Companions, and may He grant them peace.

The Sixty-eighth Call

In the Name of Allāh, the All-Merciful, the All-Compassionate.
Bismi'llāhi 'r-Raḥmāni 'r-Raḥīm.

O you who truly believe,
yā ayyuha 'lladhīna āmanū
obey Allāh and obey the Messenger,
aṭīʿu 'llāha wa aṭīʿu 'r-Rasūla
and do not render your actions vain.
wa lā tubṭilū aʿmāla-kum. (47:33)

O you who truly believe, obey Allāh and obey the Messenger.
yā ayyuha 'lladhīna āmanū aṭīʿu 'llāha wa aṭīʿu 'r-Rasūla.

That is to say: "You must comply with the commandments of Allāh, and with the commandments of the Messenger (Allāh bless him and give him peace),[1104] in everything pertaining to religious beliefs [*ʿaqāʾid*] and the rules of law [*sharāʾiʿ*]." You must not contradict Allāh and His Messenger in any aspect of their commandments,[1105] since obedience to Allāh is contingent on obedience to the Messenger:

Whoever obeys the Messenger, obeys Allāh.
man yuṭiʿi 'r-Rasūla fa-qad aṭāʿa 'llāh. (4:80)

This points implicitly to the active practice that must follow the acquisition of knowledge. It is as if He had said (Exalted is He): "O you who have come to know the Truth, you must now do what is best."[1106] That is because, when Allāh (Exalted is He) described the conditions of the unbelievers, and their opposition to Allāh's Messenger (Allāh bless him and give him peace), in the preceding verses [of this Sūra], He also commanded the believers to obey Him and to obey His Messenger (Allāh bless him and give him peace). This Sūra therefore contains an overall account of the qualities of the believers and the unbelievers, set forth in a most excellent arangement.

As for His saying (Exalted is He):

> and do not render your actions vain.
> *wa lā tubṭilū aʿmāla-kum.*

—the implied meaning is: "by committing sinful acts of disobedience." Some examples of these are:

• Apostasy [*ridda*], since it renders all righteous actions vain, from their very root.
• Arrogant conceit [*ʿujb*] and hypocritical display [*riyāʾ*], since both of them annul the spiritual reward of good deeds.
• Taunting [*mann*] and hurtfulness [*adhā*], since they annul the spiritual reward of charitable gifts. Taunting [by reminding people of favours bestowed] is blameworthy, except when Allāh does it to His servants.[1107]

In other words: "You must not render your actions vain, by being guilty of things for which I shall annul them, such as unbelief [*kufr*], hypocrisy [*nifāq*], arrogant pride, pretentious display, taunting, hurtfulness, and so on."

There is no indication, in this Qurʾānic verse, that what is meant is the invalidation of obedient acts by major sins.[1108] In other words, there is nothing to indicate that they are rendered vain by the loss of their spiritual reward, due to the commission of major sins. That is because His expression:

> and do not render your actions vain.
> *wa lā tubṭilū aʿmāla-kum.*

—is linked to the two forms of obedience. If this is an instance of linking the result to the cause, as when you say: "Sit down and take a rest," or, "Get up and take a walk," it can be understood from it that obedience is a cause of the absence of the invalidation of actions, and that noncompliance is a cause of their invalidation. There is no evidence in this, however, to prove that noncompliance, through the commission of major sins, is an absolute cause of their invalidation. The point is confirmed by His statement (Exalted is He):

> Allāh does not forgive that anything be associated with Him;
> *inna 'llāha lā yaghfiru an yushraka bi-hi*

> all else He forgives to whom He will.
> *wa yaghfiru mā dūna dhālika li-man yashā'.* (4:48)

From this it is clear that action is not necessarily invalidated by anything less than *shirk* [the association of partners with Allāh]. Indeed, the whole matter is conditional on the will of Allāh (Exalted is He), so there can be no question of insisting that the commission of major sins is an absolute cause of the invalidation of action. The power to invalidate can only be attributed, with certainty, to that which can be proved to possess it, on the basis of irrefutable Qur'ānic texts [*nuṣūṣ*] and sound traditional reports [*āthār*]. Such proof applies only to unbelief [*kufr*] and hypocrisy [*nifāq*], though it has also been reported that arrogant pride [*'ujb*] devours good deeds, just as fire consumes dry wood.

In the Sacred Tradition [*Ḥadīth Qudsī*] concerning the pursuit of undeserved fame [*sum'a*] and pretentious display [*riyā'*], Allāh (Exalted is He) is reported as having said:

> Of all "partners," I am the Most Independent from association.
> *Ana Aghna 'sh-shurakā'i 'ani 'sh-shirk:*
> If someone associates anything other than Me with Me,
> *fa-man ashraka bī ghairī*
> in an action he performs for My sake,
> *fī 'amalin 'amala-hu lī*
> I have nothing to do with him and his associating.
> *taraktu-hu wa shirka-h.*

It is thereby established that sincerity [*ikhlāṣ*] is a precondition for the acceptance of the action, and that, if any deed is motivated by ostentatiousness and the pursuit of undeserved fame, it will be thrown back at its perpetrator. If something is not accepted at the outset, it does not constitute an action, so how can it be subject to invalidation?!

It has been reported, concerning taunting and hurtfulness, that they annul the charitable gift [*ṣadaqa*], since it is as if the taunter is saying, while bestowing his favour: "I have done this for your sake, and for the purpose of improving your condition, otherwise I would not have done it." This is amounts to the negation of sincerity, so he will not be rewarded for his act of charity. He will be told: "You must seek your recompense from the person for whose sake you performed it, for Allāh (Exalted is He) will only accept what is sincerely devoted to Him."

Muqātil is reported as having said: "[The tribes of] Asad and Khuzaima came to the Prophet (Allāh bless him and give him peace), for they had accepted Islām. They said: 'We have come to you with our children, and we have left our goods and our kinsfolk behind. [The rest of] the Arabs will not believe in you, except after they have fought you, but we have not fought you, so you owe us a favour." It was then that Allāh (Exalted is He) sent down His warning:

> and do not render your actions vain.
> *wa lā tubṭilū aʿmāla-kum.*

—that is to say: "by taunting reference to the favour you have bestowed."

According to [the sectarian doctrine of] the Muʿtazila: "The major sin invalidates all good deeds. Even if they were like the foam on the sea [in their abundance], it would still invalidate them." On the basis of this doctrine, az-Zamakhsharī interpreted this Qurʾānic verse to mean: "Do not invalidate acts of obedience by committing major sins."

The people of the Sunna maintain that if any action, emanating from a competent individual, is in conformity with all its basic requirements and preconditions, the commission of major sins will not invalidate it, nor remove its spiritual reward, for:

> Allāh does no wrong, not even as little as the weight of an atom.
> *inna 'llāha lā yaẓlimu mithqāla dharra.* (4:40)

> And anyone who has ever done an atom's weight of evil will see it then.
> *wa man yaʿmal mithqāla dharratin sharran yara-h.* (99:8)

The action will not be invalidated after the complete fulfilment of its basic requirements, and after the preconditions of its correctness and its acceptance have been met. There is no evidence to the contrary, neither rational nor traditional, though the following argument may be offered in support of the invalidation of the good deed by the major sin:

The believer may view the spiritual reward of his good deeds as he views the punishment of his bad deeds, unless the bad deeds outnumber the goods deeds in the balance, so that he has too few good deeds left to offset the weight of those bad deeds, and the reward of his good deeds is not enough to counter the punishment of the bad deeds. In that case, it can truthfully be said: "His bad deeds have invalidated the reward of his good deeds," in the sense that he too little left, from the reward of the good deeds, to dispel the punishment of the bad deeds.

With this we must agree, since it contains nothing controversial.[1109] It means that you must not render your actions vain, by imagining that anything is required of them, apart from the gracious favour of Allāh.[1110]

The Qur'ānic verse indicates, by implication, that if any deed or act of obedience is not in accordance with the commandment of Allāh and the Sunna of His Messenger, it is vain and fruitless. That is because it has emanated from the natural instinct, and the natural instinct is related to darkness [*ẓulmānī*]. The Sacred Law, which is related to light [*nūrānī*], has come for the sole purpose of dispelling the gloom of the natural instinct with the radiance of the Sacred Law. It is fruitful, and its fruit is that you may exit from the darkness into the light, that is to say, from the darkness of the natural instinct into the light of the Truth. You must therefore practise obedience, and act in accordance with the Sacred Law. Beware of noncompliance and neglect![1111]

These are my own comments:

The head of all forms of worshipful service is sincere devotion [*ikhlāṣ*]. Whatever is built on genuineness is genuine, and whatever is built on corruption is corrupt. Sincere devotion is located in the heart, so it is essential to examine the heart most thoroughly, to determine its intention completely. If it is found to contain the opposite of sincere devotion, its contents must be discarded. This is because the servant may be performing acts of worship, and they may appear to be in conformity with the Sacred Law, and we may say: "He has prayed, and fasted, and practised remembrance, and enjoined [what is right] and forbidden [what is wrong]," but what is the use of all that, if the proper spirit is missing from those actions?

Their proper spirit is the secret presence of sincere devotion within them. It is therefore essential for you, O pious one, to make friends with the truthful, so that their secret may be transmitted to you, for the close companion is influenced by his close companion. If that were not the case, our Lord (Glorious and Exalted is He) would not have said:

> O you who truly believe, you must practise true devotion to Allāh,
> *yā ayyuha 'lladhīna āmanu 'ttaqu 'llāha*
> and be with the truthful.
> *wa kūnū ma'a 'ṣ-ṣādiqīn*. (9:119)

We beg Allāh (Exalted is He) to include us among those who cling to the coat-tails of the genuine champions of truth, so that we may attain to blissful happiness in the two abodes [of this world and the Hereafter]. He is indeed Capable of all things. Peace be upon the Messengers, and praise be to Allāh, the Lord of All the Worlds. There is no might nor any power, except with Allāh, the All-High, the Almighty. May Allāh bless our master Muḥammad, his family and his Companions, and may He grant them peace.

The Sixty-ninth Call

In the Name of Allāh, the All-Merciful, the All-Compassionate.
Bismi'llāhi 'r-Raḥmāni 'r-Raḥīm.

O you who truly believe, do not presume
yā ayyuha 'lladhīna āmanū lā tuqaddimū
in the presence of Allāh and His Messenger,
baina yadayi 'llāhi wa Rasūli-hi
and practise true devotion to Allāh.
wa 'ttaqu 'llāh:
Allāh is All-Hearing, All-Knowing.
inna 'llāha Samī'un 'Alīm. (49:1)

This noble Sūra is Medinan. In spite of its brevity, it is a splendidly copious Sūra, containing the eternal facts of education, and the ideal principles of civilization. Some of the traditional commentators have actually called it the Sūra of Ethical and Moral Standards [*Sūrat al-Akhlāq*].

The noble Sūra begins with the refined manner in which Allāh has taught the believers to conduct themselves, with respect to the Sacred Law [*Sharī'a*] of Allāh and the authority of His Messenger. This means that, in the presence of the Messenger (Allāh bless him and give him peace), they must not presume to settle a matter, or to pronounce a definitive opinion, or to pass a final judgment, until they have consulted him and paid close attention to his wise advice,[1112] for Allāh has said:

O you who truly believe, do not presume
yā ayyuha 'lladhīna āmanū lā tuqaddimū
in the presence of Allāh and His Messenger.
baina yadayi 'llāhi wa Rasūli-hi

Allāh (Exalted is He) has used the expression:

O you who truly believe!
yā ayyuha 'lladhīna āmanū.

—five times in this Sūra, as a way of arousing the believers' interest in the commandments and prohibitions. In similar fashion, Luqmān used to address his son with the expression:

> O my dear son!
> *yā bunayya.* (31:13,16,17)

The purpose is also to dispel any supposition that the words are addressed to someone else, and not to the person for whom they are directly intended. In one instance, He uses the expression:

> O humankind!
> *yā ayyuha 'n-nāsu.* (49:13)

—to indicate that His following statement (Exalted is He):

> We have created you male and female.
> *innā khalaqnā-kum min dhakarin wa unthā.* (49:13)

—is generally applicable, to both the believer and the unbeliever.

This Sūra deals with proper modes of conduct in every aspect, external and internal, public and private, including the Ṣūfī path [*ṭarīqa*], which is reached by those who strictly adhere to them. Then He has followed the call with the commandment.[1113] The reason for prefacing the address with the call, is to notify the believers that its contents are a matter of very great importance, demanding their utmost attention and their most careful consideration. As for the reference to their true belief, it is meant to stimulate their interest, and to serve notice that He is summoning them to keep their belief intact, and deterring them from violating it.[1114]

As for His expression:

> Do not presume
> *lā tuqaddimū*

—it signifies: "O you who are distinguished by true faith, and who have believed in the Book of Allāh, you must not take things for granted, or act in a forward manner, in the presence of Allāh and His Messenger." The grammatical object of the transitive verb *tuqaddimū* is omitted, for the purpose of generalization, so that the mind of the hearer will contemplate everything that could possibly be the object of presumption [*taqdīm*], whether in speech or in action. For instance, if a question was raised at his meeting (Allāh bless him and give him peace), they should not presume to answer it ahead of him; if food was served, they should not presume to start eating before him; if they accompanied him to some place, they should not presume to walk in front of him, and so on and so forth.[1115]

It was Ibn ʿAbbās (may Allāh be well pleased with him and his father) who said: "[It means that] they were forbidden to talk in the presence of Allāh and His Messenger." According to aḍ-Ḍaḥḥāk, it means: "You must not decide a matter, connected with the laws of your religion, without consulting Allāh and His Messenger."[1116]

If someone speaks or acts presumptuously in relation to Allāh's Messenger (Allāh bless him and give him peace), he has done so in relation to Allāh (Exalted is He), because the Messenger (Allāh bless him and give him peace) commands him only in accordance with the commandment of Allāh (Almighty and Glorious is He).[1117] That is because forwardness in the presence of a man is a departure from the state of obedience, and a show of independence in the matter concerned. Forwardness in the presence of Allāh and His Messenger (Allāh bless him and give him peace) is therefore incompatible with true belief.

This prohibition calls for strict adherence to the Book and the Sunna, so that a man will carefully observe the limits set by Allāh, and obediently follow His Messenger (Allāh bless him and give him peace).[1118] You must therefore refrain from thrusting yourselves and your opinions to the fore in His presence.[1119]

According to Ibn ʿAbbās (may Allāh be well pleased with him and his father), the meaning of the Qurʾānic verse is: "Do not speak in contradiction of the Book and the Sunna." The spiritual pauper (*viz.*, al-Burūsawī) says: "Perhaps this is an instance of rhetorical omission, and the meaning also includes: 'And do not act in contradiction of thereof,' since each of the two [contradictory speech and contradictory action] is a kind of presumptuousness in relation to the rules of Allāh and the rules of His Messenger. I received this interpretation of this verse by way of inspiration, while in a state between sleep and wakefulness. Allāh knows best, of course!"

This Qurʾānic verse also contains an expression of Allāh's tender kindness for His servants, since He has called them the believers, in spite of their sinful disobedience, for He has said:

> O you who truly believe!
> *yā ayyuha 'lladhīna āmanū.*

—and He has not said: "O you who have sinfully rebelled." This call is a commendation, as stated in the commentary of Abu 'l-Laith.[1120]

Concerning His words (Exalted is He):

> in the presence of Allāh and His Messenger,
> *baina yadayi 'llāhi wa Rasūli-hi*

—there are several points worth noting, for instance:

1. To say that so-and-so is *baina yadai* [lit., between the hands of] so-and-so, is way of saying that one of them is present [*ḥāḍir*] with the other, and it implies that one of them holds high rank, while the other is at the level of servants and attendants. This is because, if someone sits at a person's side, he must take the trouble to turn his gaze towards him, and move his head towards him, when speaking and giving instructions. If someone sits "between his hands," however, he does not suffer that inconvenience. Because the hands are symbolic of power, the statement that so-and-so is "between the hands [*baina yadai*]" of so-and-so, is also a way of saying that he can manipulate him as he wishes, just as a person can deal with any material object that is placed between his hands. That expression emphasizes the need to beware of presumptuousness and pushing oneself to the fore. If someone is liable to be manipulated like a material object, in the hands of a certain person, how will it be for him if he thrusts himself forward in that person's presence?

2. Allāh has indicated the necessity of reverence for the Messenger (Allāh bless him and give him peace), and compliance with his commands. That is because reverence for the Messenger (Allāh bless him and give him peace) might be neglected, on the assumption of the Sender's remoteness, and His lack of awareness of what is being done by His Messenger, so He has said:

> "between the hands" of Allāh....
> *baina yadayi 'llāhi....*

—meaning: "You are in a state of presence in relation to Allāh (Exalted is He), and He is watching you." In a situation like this, reverence for His Messenger (Allāh bless him and give him peace) is strictly required.

> And practise true devotion to Allāh.
> *wa 'ttaqu 'llāh:*

—because, if someone in the presence of another is like a material object placed between his hands, so that he can do with him whatever he wishes, it is surely appropriate for him to treat that other person with devout respect. The meaning is: "Do not behave in a presumptuous manner in His presence. What is more, even if you have refrained from such forwardness, you must not be content with that, and you must not try to take advantage of it. In addition to maintaining that restraint, and treating Him with reverence, you must be truly devoted to Allāh, and fearful of offending Him. Otherwise, you will not be paying Him the kind of respect that is strictly required.[1121] You must therefore practise true devotion to Allāh in everything you do, or refrain from doing, in every sphere of action and speech in which We are involved."

> Allāh is All-Hearing, All-Knowing.
> *inna 'llāha Samīʿun ʿAlim.*

He is All-Hearing [*Samīʿ*] in the sense that He hears everything there is to be heard, including all the words you utter. He is All-Knowing [*ʿAlīm*] in the sense that He knows everything there is to be known, including your actions, your intentions and your states of being. It is therefore the believer's duty to practise true devotion and vigilant awareness.[1122]

He hears their speech, and He knows what they do and what their hearts contain, whether it be true devotion or betrayal. It is therefore important to ensure that your words, your deeds and your consciences are not at odds with one another. What is required, indeed, is perfect compatibility between that which is in His hearing, when you say: "We believe, and we hear and obey [*āmannā wa samiʿnā wa aṭaʿnā*]," and that which is in His knowledge, pertaining to your external conduct, which should mean the absence of forwardness, and also to the inner content of your hearts, which should mean true devotion.[1123]

The Qurʾānic verse also contains a threat, aimed at someone who judges on the basis of a random notion, without knowledge of the difference between genuine inspiration [*ilhām*] and satanic insinuation [*waswās*]. He says: "It is the truth, so you must conform to it," but his intention is to put on a show, and to earn a reputation.

To meet the standard of a true believer, a person must not regard his own opinions, ideas and preferences, as superior to the view presented by the Book and the Sunna. The prohibition:

> Do not presume
> *lā tuqaddimū*

—extends to walking in front of the religious scholars, for they are the heirs of the Prophets. There is traditional evidence for this, since Abu 'd-Dardā' (may Allāh be well pleased with him) is reported as having said: "Allāh's Messenger (Allāh bless him and give him peace) once saw me walking in front of Abū Bakr (may Allāh be well pleased with him), so he said:

> "You are walking in front of someone who is better than you, in this world and the Hereafter!"[1124]

These are my own observations:

The watchfulness of Allāh (Exalted is He) has been exercised over His servants from the most ancient times:

> Allāh has always been Watchful over you.
> *inna 'llāha kāna ʿalai-kum Raqībā.* (4:1)

You must therefore stay on constant guard duty at the door of your heart, to make sure that your conscience is matched by your public behaviour. You must practise truthfulness, because truthfulness necessitates [Divine] approval. As for the approval of mere creatures, it does not depend on your truthfulness, so, if what is in your heart is in harmony with that which flows from your tongue, you are sure to benefit in both your religious and your worldly life. It cannot be otherwise, except by Allāh's decree. The proof is for you to provide, and you must not expect others to pass judgment on your truthfulness, because they are not privy to what is in your heart. All that you need is Allāh's knowledge about you:

> Allāh is All-Hearing, All-Knowing.
> *inna 'llāha Samīʿun ʿAlim.*

O Allāh, grant us the ability to follow faithfully. Keep us away from heretical innovation, and endow us with truthfulness and sincere devotion, through Your mercy, O Most Merciful of the merciful. Peace be upon the Messengers, and praise be to Allāh, the Lord of All the Worlds. There is no might nor any power, except with Allāh, the All-High, the Almighty. May Allāh bless our master Muḥammad, his family and his Companions, and may He grant them peace.

The Seventieth Call

In the Name of Allāh, the All-Merciful, the All-Compassionate.
Bismi'llāhi 'r-Raḥmāni 'r-Raḥīm.

O you who truly believe, do not raise your voices
yā ayyuha 'lladhīna āmanū lā tarfaʿū aṣwāta-kum
above the voice of the Prophet, and do not shout
fawqa ṣawti 'n-Nabiyyi wa lā tajharū
when speaking to him
as you shout to one another,
la-hu bi'l-qawli ka-jahri baʿḍi-kum li-baʿḍin
lest your works be rendered vain
while you do not notice.
an taḥbaṭa aʿmālu-kum wa antum lā tashʿurūn.

Those who subdue their voices
inna 'lladhīna yaghuḍḍūna aṣwāta-hum
in the presence of the Messenger of Allāh,
ʿinda Rasūli 'llāhi
those are they whose hearts
Allāh has tested for true devotion.
ulāʾika 'lladhīna 'mtaḥana 'llāhu qulūba-hum li't-taqwā
Theirs will be forgiveness and immense reward.
la-hum maghfiratun wa ajrun ʿaẓīm.

Those who call you from
behind the private apartments,
inna 'lladhīna yunādūna-ka min warāʾi 'l-ḥujurāti
most of them have no sense.
aktharu-hum lā yaʿqilūn.

And if they had been patient
wa law anna-hum ṣabarū
till you came out to meet them,
ḥattā takhruja ilai-him

it would have been better for them.
la-kāna khairan la-hum
And Allāh is All-Forgiving, All-Compassionate.
wa 'llāhu Ghafūrun Raḥīm. (49:2–5)

This is the second call from the Sūra of the Private Apartments *[al-Ḥujurāt]*. It deals with another item of good conduct, that being the lowering of the voice when you converse with Allāh's Messenger (Allāh bless him and give him peace), to show reverence for his noble worth and respect for his lofty station. He is not like the ordinary mass of people, for he is Allāh's Messenger (Allāh bless him and give him peace), and the duty of the believers requires them to be well-mannered in his presence, by speaking with deference, exaltation and veneration.[1125]

Allāh (Exalted is He) has said:

> O you who truly believe, do not raise your voices
> *yā ayyuha 'lladhīna āmanū lā tarfaʿū aṣwāta-kum*
> above the voice of the Prophet
> *fawqa ṣawti 'n-Nabiyyi*

In other words: "Do not let your speech be raised above the speech of the Prophet (Allāh bless him and give him peace), during the conversation." That is because raising the voice is a symptom of insufficient modesty and respect.[1126]

In His saying (Exalted is He):

> O you who truly believe, do not be forward.
> *yā ayyuha 'lladhīna āmanū lā tuqaddimū.* (49:1)

—there is a prohibition against acting in a way that shows them to be assigning to themselves, in the presence of Allāh and Allāh's Messenger (Allāh bless him and give him peace), any weight and importance in relation to these two, or any influence on their commandments and prohibitions. As for His saying:

> do not raise....
> *lā tarfaʿū....*

—it is a prohibition against speaking in a way that displays that same attitude, because, if someone raises his voice in the presence of another person, he is assigning significance and importance to himself.

What useful lesson is there, it may be asked, in the repetition of the call, and what is the point of the two injunctions:

> O you who truly believe, do not be forward in the presence of Allāh.
> *yā ayyuha 'lladhīna āmanū lā tuqaddimū baina yadayi 'llāh.* (49:1)

—and:

> do not raise your voices?
> *lā tarfaʿū aṣwāta-kum*

Our response to this will be: There are several useful lessons in the repetition of the call; for instance, it demonstrates how extra care is devoted to the seeker of right guidance, as in Luqmān's advice to his son:

> "O my dear son, ascribe no partners to Allāh."
> *yā bunayya lā tushrik bi'llāh.* (31:13)

> "O my dear son, though it be but the weight of a mustard-seed...."
> *yā bunayya inna-hā in taku mithqāla ḥabbatin....* (31:16)

> "O my dear son, perform the ritual prayer."
> *yā bunayya aqimi 'ṣ-ṣalāta.* (31:17)[1127]

The repetition of the call is intended to invite additional reflection, to intensify awareness, and to indicate the need for increased consideration of the subject of the call.[1128] In each case, the purpose is to induce the listener to pay very careful attention. Since the import of both is one and the same, as when you say: "O Zaid, do not tell lies," and, "O Zaid, tell nothing but the truth," it is not appropriate for anything to intervene between the two, as may be appropriate when each has a different purpose.[1129]

In other words: "When you speak to Allāh's Messenger (Allāh bless him and give him peace), lower your voices and do not raise them above the voice of the Prophet (Allāh bless him and give him peace).[1130] Do not pitch your voices beyond a level to which the Prophet (Allāh bless him and give him peace) pitches his voice."[1131] If someone deserves great respect, so that voices must be lowered in his presence, out of reverence for him and his exalted dignity, there should not be much talking in his presence.[1132]

The reason for the revelation of the noble Qur'ānic verse was as follows, according to Abū Malīka (may Allāh be well pleased with him):

"The excellent pair almost perished. Abū Bakr and ʿUmar (may Allāh be well pleased with them) raised their voices in the presence of the Prophet (Allāh bless him and give him peace). When a mounted troop of the Banī Tamīm arrived on the scene, one of the two pointed at al-Aqraʿ ibn Ḥābis, while the other pointed at another man. (Nāfiʿ said: 'I do not remember his name.') Abū Bakr said to ʾUmar (may Allāh be well pleased with them both): 'You only wanted to contradict me,' but he replied: "I did not want to contradict you.' Their voices were raised in the process, so Allāh (Almighty and Glorious is He) sent down:

> O you who truly believe, do not raise your voices
> *yā ayyuha 'lladhīna āmanū lā tarfaʿū aṣwāta-kum*
> above the voice of the Prophet, and do not shout
> *fawqa ṣawti 'n-Nabiyyi wa lā tajharū*
> when speaking to him as you shout to one another,
> *la-hu bi'l-qawli ka-jahri baʿḍi-kum li-baʿḍin*
> lest your works be rendered vain while you do not notice."
> *an taḥbaṭa aʿmālu-kum wa antum lā tashʿurūn.*

According to Ibn az-Zubair: "After this verse was revealed, ʿUmar (may Allāh be well pleased with him) would not speak in the hearing of Allāh's Messenger (Allāh bless him and give him peace), unless he asked him to do so."[1133]

As reported in the two *Ṣaḥīḥ*'s, on the authority of Anas ibn Mālik (may Allāh be well pleased with him), the Prophet (Allāh bless him and give him peace) once inquired about Thābit ibn Qais. A man said: "O Messenger of Allāh, I shall find out about him for you." He then went and found him sitting in his house, with his head bowed low, so he asked him: "How are you?" "In a bad way," said Thābit, "I was someone who raised his voice above the voice of the Prophet (Allāh bless him and give him peace), so my work was in vain, and I am one of the people of the Fire." The man went back to the Prophet (Allāh bless him and give him peace), and told him that Thābit had said such-and-such and such-and-such. (According to Mūsā, the man was Ibn Anas, one of the transmitters of the Prophetic tradition.) Then he paid Thābit a final visit, bearing wonderful news, for he had been told: "Go to him and tell him: 'You are not one of the people of the Fire of Hell, but you are one of the people of the Garden of Paradise!'"

This Thābit is Thābit ibn Qais ibn Shammās al-Khazrajī. Three sons of his were killed on the Day of al-Ḥarra [the Stony Tract]: Muḥammad, Yaḥyā and ʿAbdu'llāh. He was so renowned as an eloquent orator [*khaṭīb*], that he was called the Orator of Allāh's Messenger (Allāh bless him and give him peace), just as Ḥassān was called the Poet of Allāh's Messenger (Allāh bless him and give him peace). When the delegation of Tamīm approached Allāh's Messenger (Allāh bless him and give him peace), and they sought to compete in glory, their orator stood up and spoke in boastful terms. Then Thābit ibn Qais stood up and delivered a remarkably eloquent oration, by which he got the better of them. Their poet, al-Aqraʿ ibn Ḥābis, stood up and recited, then Ḥassān ibn Thābit took his turn to utter some poetic verses. They said: "Their orator is more eloquent than our orator, and their poet is more poetic than our poet!" Their voices were raised in the process, so Allāh (Exalted is He) sent down the revelation:

> do not raise your voices
> *lā tarfaʿū aṣwāta-kum*

As for His saying:

> and do not shout when speaking to him
> *wa lā tajharū la-hu bi'l-qawli*
> as you shout to one another
> *ka-jahri baʿḍi-kum li-baʿḍin*

—that is to say: "Do not address him with: 'O Muḥammad!' and 'O Aḥmad!' but rather: 'O Prophet of Allāh!' and 'O Messenger of Allāh!' out of reverence for him."[1134] You must keep your voices lower than his voice, and be careful to address him in a gentle tone akin to whispering, as is customary in addressing someone who inspires awe and veneration. You must cultivate respect for the grandeur of Prophethood, its majesty and its noble worth.

It was Abū Bakr aṣ-Ṣiddīq [the Champion of Truth] (may Allāh be well pleased with him) who said, after the revelation of this Qurʾānic verse: "By the One who has revealed the Book to you, O Messenger of Allāh, I shall not speak to you except as my brother, in secret whispers, until I meet Allāh (Exalted is He)."[1135]

They have been forbidden to practise a particular kind of shouting, that being the kind of shouting to which they have been accustomed among themselves, not shouting under any circumstances, to the point where they are not allowed to speak except in whispers and undertones. As we understand from *al-Kashshāf*, concerning the difference between the two prohibitions in His saying:

> do not raise your voices above the voice of the Prophet,
> *lā tarfaʿū aṣwāta-kum fawqa ṣawti 'n-Nabiyyi*
> and do not shout when speaking to him
> *wa lā tajharū la-hu bi'l-qawli*

—the meaning of the first prohibition is as follows: "When the Prophet speaks (blessing and peace be upon him) and you speak too, you must not pitch your voices above the level to which he pitches his voice (blessing and peace be upon him). You must lower your voices, so that his voice sounds louder than your voices."

This is the meaning of the second prohibition: "When you speak to him (blessing and peace be upon him), while he is silent, you must not express yourselves with the kind of shouting that is usual among you. Instead, you must soften your speech to the near whisper that is the opposite of shouting.[1136]

As for His saying (Exalted is He):

> lest your works be rendered vain while you do not notice.
> *an taḥbaṭa aʿmālu-kum wa antum lā tashʿurūn.*

—the expression "lest your works rendered vain" is a warning that, if you raise your voices and behave in a presumptuous manner, these vices may take control of you, resulting in contempt and leading to the isolation and rejection of the person whose works are rendered vain.

The expression: "while you do not notice" indicates that rudeness can take control of the lower self, to the point where the person concerned is unaware of what has happened. If someone commits a sin that he has never committed in his life, you will see him suffering extreme remorse, experiencing the most extreme fear. If he commits it many times, however, his fear and his remorse will diminish. It becomes such a habit that he does not realize that he has lost control. His saying (Exalted is He):

> while you do not notice.
> *wa antum lā tashʿurūn.*

—is thus a reinforcement of the prohibition. In other words: "Do not say: 'It only happened once, so it will be pardoned and will not result in rejection,' because the matter is not known for certain, so you had better lock the door."[1137]

From the obvious meaning of the verse, it might be inferred that works are rendered vain by all sins, absolutely. According to the doctrine of the people of the Sunna, however, the only sin that renders them vain is unbelief [*kufr*], not any other.

By general agreement, the preferred maxim is that offending the Prophet (blessing and peace be upon him) is tantamount to the unbelief that annuls good work. As for shouting, it is also generally agreed that some forms of it are not subject to the prohibition, namely, shouting in a battle, or in a fierce dispute, or in frightening an enemy, or in other such cases, where there is no question of offending or belittling the Prophet (blessing and peace be upon him).

According to the Prophetic tradition [*ḥadīth*], the Prophet (blessing and peace be upon him) said to ʿAbbās ibn ʿAbd al-Muṭṭalib, when the Muslims fled on the Day of Ḥunain: "Summon the companions of as-Samura!" ʿAbbās cried out at the top of his voice: "Where are the companions of as-Samura?"[1138] He was very loud-voiced man. It is related that a raiding party came upon them one day, so al-ʿAbbās yelled: "O morning raid [*yā ṣabāḥāh*]!" The attackers' legs collapsed, because of the violent impact of his voice.[1139]

In my own opinion, the expression:

> while you do not notice.
> *wa antum lā tashʿurūn.*

—really signifies a lack of awareness as to whether or not the annulment of works will actually happen. This may be viewed from two perspectives:

1. From the standpoint of the Messenger (Allāh bless him and give him peace). If what is understood, from the way the speaker speaks, is disdain for Allāh's Messenger (Allāh bless him and give him peace), the annulment will undoubtedly happen, for that amouts to unbelief [*kufr*].

2. From the standpoint of the speaker. If his way of speaking is an expression of stubborn resistance, or criticism of the Prophet's tremen-

dous dignity (Allāh bless him and give him peace), each is sufficient cause for the annulment of work. If the speaker is naturally endowed with a high-pitched voice, and his conviction is sound, with no lack of respect for the Prophet (Allāh bless him and give him peace), the annulment will not happen in his case.

Lowering the voice is a necessary obligation, for the simple reason that it is consistent with respect for superiors. When voices are raised, the relationship becomes obscure. [Where annulment is concerned] no distinction can be made between one particular case and another. In other words, there is nothing here to indicate that the work to be annulled can be distinguished from any other, though Allāh knows best what is correct. This rule must therefore apply to general politeness in speech, between the common folk and those of superior rank.

The case of Thābit ibn Qais serves as proof that the raising of his voice did not result in annulment, while he did not notice. Indeed, Allāh's Messenger (Allāh bless him and give him peace) gave him the good news that he was one of the people of the Garden of Paradise, as his story is told between the lines of the Qur'ānic verse.

This general politeness is something with which the believer ought to adorn himself. If he speaks with a high-pitched voice because that is his natural condition, the person addressed should not be offended. On the other hand, if he is motivated by stubborn contrariness, criticism and arrogance, and the person addressed is aware of that, and takes it as a sign of contempt, this is what has been prohibited. (O Allāh, make us true to the Islāmic standards of behaviour!) Similarly, if a person contravenes the Sunna of the Prophet (Allāh bless him and give him peace), but does so unintentionally and without conscious disrespect, no penalty will be imposed upon him. If he does so deliberately, however, he should heed the Prophetic tradition [*ḥadīth*]:

> If someone dislikes my Sunna, he will be deprived of my intercession.

Those who subdue their voices
inna 'lladhīna yaghuḍḍūna aṣwāta-hum
in the presence of the Messenger of Allāh,
'inda Rasūli 'llāhi

> those are they whose hearts Allāh has tested for true devotion.
> *ulā'ika 'lladhīna 'mtaḥana 'llāhu qulūba-hum li't-taqwā*

In other words: "Those who lower their voices in the presence of the Messenger (Allāh bless him and give him peace), those are they whose hearts Allāh has caused to be sincere in their devotion to duty, and trained them in it, and fixed it in them as a firmly rooted attribute." According to Ibn Kathīr: "That is to say: 'He has made them sincere in their devotion to duty, and He has made them competent and clever.'"[1140]

Allāh already knew what devotion to Him was in their hearts, and He tested their hearts because of the devotion they contained. If their hearts had not been filled with devotion, he would not have commanded them to treat His Messenger (Allāh bless him and give him peace) with reverence, and to prefer His Prophet to themselves. No indeed, He would have told them: "Believe in My Messenger, and do not offend him and call him a liar," for, when the unbeliever first comes to believe, he must acknowledge the fact that the Prophet (Allāh bless him and give him peace) is truthful. There is a vast difference between someone who is told: "Do not deride the Messenger of Allāh, do not call him a liar, and do not offend him," and someone who is told: "Do not raise your voice in his presence, do not attach importance to yourself before him, and do not shout your truthful speech in front of him."

As you should also understand, to the extent that you give precedence to the Prophet (Allāh bless him and give him peace) over yourself, in this world, the Prophet (Allāh bless him and give him peace) will accord you priority in the Hereafter, for no one will enter the Garden of Paradise, so long as Allāh has not admitted the devout members of his Community to the Garden.[1141]

As for His saying (Exalted is He):

> Theirs will be forgiveness and immense reward.
> *la-hum maghfiratun wa ajrun ʿaẓīm.*

—that is to say: "Theirs in the Hereafter will be pardon for their sins, and an immense reward in the Gardens of Bliss."[1142] Forgiveness means the elimination of the bad deeds committed by the lower self in this world, while the immense reward refers to the life to come, after the separation of this world from the self. Allāh will eliminate the ugly vices of animality, and clothe His servant in the beautiful virtues of angelic nature.[1143] Allāh (Exalted is He) has then blamed the uncouth Arab nomads, who used to behave improperly when calling for the Messenger (blessing and peace be upon him), for He has said:

> Those who call you from behind the private apartments....
> *inna 'lladhīna yunādūna-ka min warā'i 'l-ḥujurāti*

In other words: "They summon you from behind the private apartments of your pure wives (may Allāh be well pleased with them)."[1144] This indicates that such behaviour is at odds with proper conduct in his presence, and a cause of inconvenience to him.[1145]

> most of them have no sense.
> *aktharu-hum lā ya'qilūn.*

That is to say: "Most of these folk are unintelligent, since intelligence insists on good behaviour, and on respect for the great when addressing them, especially for someone of this momentous importance."[1146]

It is said that those who called him were 'Uyaina ibn Ḥuṣain and al-Aqra' ibn Ḥābis. They came to visit Allāh's Messenger (Allāh bless him and give him peace) in a delegation of seventy men from the tribe of Banī Tamīm. They arrived at the time of high noon, when he was taking a rest, so they said: "O Muḥammad, come out to meet us!"[1147]

> And if they had been patient till you came out to meet them,
> *wa law anna-hum ṣabarū ḥattā takhruja ilai-him*
> it would have been better for them.
> *la-kāna khairan la-hum*

In other words: "And if these callers had not disturbed the Messenger (Allāh bless him and give him peace) with their call, and if they had been patient till he came out to meet them, that patience would have been better for them, and more meritorious in the sight of Allāh and in the sight of the people, because it would have constituted polite respect for the station of Prophethood."

> And Allāh is All-Forgiving, All-Compassionate.
> *wa 'llāhu Ghafūrun Raḥīm.*

That is to say: "He is the Forgiver of His servants' sins, the One who is Compassionate in His treatment of the believers, since He has confined Himself to advising them and scolding them, and has not inflicted punishment upon them."[1148] That is a confirmation of two things:

1. The badness of their acting in haste. If a person commits an outrage, and the king or the master does not punish him, people will say: "How tolerant is his master!"—not to proclaim his tolerance, but to proclaim the enormity of the servant's offence.

2. The goodness of patience. That is to say: "Because of their doing what is better, Allāh will forgive them for their bad deeds, and He will treat this good deed as an atonement for many bad deeds, just as the runaway slave will be told, when he returns to his master's door: 'You have done well by returning, and your master is compassionate.'" In other words: "He will not punish you for your previous sin, because of the good deed you have now performed."

> All-Forgiving, All-Compassionate.
> *Ghafūrun Raḥīm.*

That is to say: "He will forgive his bad deeds, then He will look at him and see that he is naked and needy, so He will invest him with the clothing of noble generosity. He may see him immersed in bad deeds, so He will forgive his bad deeds, then He will treat him with compassion, after forgiveness." The emphasis is sometimes on the compassion that follows forgiveness, so [in some verses of the Qur'ān] He mentions forgiveness first, and sometimes on the compassion that precedes forgiveness, so He mentions forgiveness in second place.[1149]

These are my own observations:

The honour of our master Muḥammad (Allāh bless him and give him peace) is tremendous in the sight of Allāh (Exalted is He). If someone faithfully respects his noble dignity (Allāh bless him and give him peace), and follows his Sunna after surrendering to his authority, he will therefore receive a beam of that light. If someone strengthens that radiant thread, through loyal obedience in both his outer and his inner life, he will never fall from the providence of Allāh (Almighty and Glorious is He). In the maintenance of due respect for the Prophet (blessing and peace be upon him), one element is proper conduct in the company of his heirs (may Allāh be well pleased with them), because good behaviour with the legatee is part of good behaviour with his legator.

We beg Allāh to endow us with uprightness, and with proper conduct in the company of our master, the Messenger of Allāh (Allāh bless him and give him peace), and in the company of our spiritual leaders (may Allāh be well pleased with them all, while they are still alive and after their departure from this world). He is indeed Capable of all things. Peace be upon the Messengers, and praise be to Allāh, the Lord of All the Worlds. There is no might nor any power, except with Allāh, the All-High, the Almighty. May Allāh bless our master Muḥammad, his family and his Companions, and may He grant them peace.

The Seventy-first Call

In the Name of Allāh, the All-Merciful, the All-Compassionate.
Bismi'llāhi 'r-Raḥmāni 'r-Raḥīm.

O you who truly believe,
if a corrupt person brings you some news,
yā ayyuha 'lladhīna āmanū in jā'a-kum
fāsiqun bi-naba'in
you must verify it,
in case you attack a group of folk in ignorance
fa-tabayyanū an tuṣībū qawman bi-jahālatin
for then you will feel remorse for what you did.
fa-tuṣībū 'alā mā fa'altum nādimīn. (49:6)

The Sūra now moves on from proper conduct in private to proper conduct in public, in order to establish the pillars of the excellent society. It commands the believers to turn a deaf ear to rumours, and to verify all news and reports, especially if the information comes from an untrustworthy individual, or one who deserves to be treated with suspicion. How many a statement, transmitted by a brazen liar, has been a cause of serious distress! How many an item of news, unverified by its listener, has resulted in bad feelings and broken relations!

> O you who truly believe, if a corrupt person brings you some news,
> *yā ayyuha 'lladhīna āmanū in jā'a-kum fāsiqun bi-naba'in*
> you must verify it, in case you attack a group of folk in ignorance.
> *fa-tabayyanū an tuṣībū qawman bi-jahālatin*

That is to say: "If a man brings you a report of some kind, and that man is corrupt, unreliable and untrustworthy, you must verify the accuracy of his report."[1150]

This Sūra contains guidance for the believers, directing them to cultivate the noble virtues, whether in the company of Allāh (Exalted is He), or in the company of the Messenger (Allāh bless him and give him peace), or in the company of others, among their fellow members of the human race. The latter fall into two categories, because they are either on the path of the believers, at the level of obedience, or outside of that, in which case they are corrupt. As for someone who belongs to the party of the believers, and is a follower of their path, he may either be present in their midst, or absent from them.

These five categories must therefore be distinguished :

1. That which relates to Allāh (Exalted is He).
2. That which relates to Allāh's Messenger (Allāh bless him and give him peace).
3. That which relates to the corrupt person.
4. That which relates to the believer who is present.
5. That which relates to the believer who is absent.

Allāh (Exalted is He) has mentioned them all in this Sūra, in five stages:

1. In the first instance:

> O you who truly believe, do not be forward
> *yā ayyuha 'lladhīna āmanū lā tuqaddimū*
> in the presence of Allāh and His Messenger.
> *baina yadayi 'llāhi wa Rasūli-hi.* (49:1)

—the reference to the Messenger is an explanation of the duty to obey Allāh, because it is only made known through the speech of Allāh's Messenger (Allāh bless him and give him peace).

2. The second instance:

> O you who truly believe, do not raise your voices
> *yā ayyuha 'lladhīna āmanū lā tarfaʿū*
> above the voice of the Prophet.
> *aṣwāta-kum fawqa ṣawti 'n-Nabiyyi.* (49:2)

—is an explanation of the duty to honour and respect the Prophet (blessing and peace be upon him).

3. The third instance:

> O you who truly believe,
> *yā ayyuha 'lladhīna āmanū*
> if a corrupt person brings you some news, you must verify it.
> *in jāʾa-kum fāsiqun bi-nabaʾin fa-tabayyanū.* (49:6)

—explains the need to beware of accepting what they say as true, since they intend to sow discord among you.

4. The fourth instance:

> O you who truly believe, one group of people
> *yā ayyuha 'lladhīna āmanū lā yaskhar*
> should not scoff at another group people.
> *qawmun min qawmin.* (49:11)

—explains the duty to refrain from abusing the believers in their presence, and from slighting their condition and their dignity.

5. The fifth instance:

> O you who truly believe, avoid a great deal of suspicion.
> *yā ayyuha 'lladhīna āmanu 'jtanibū kathīran mina 'ẓ-ẓann.* (49:12)

—explains the need to beware of defaming the believer in his absence.

While this sequence is arranged in a most excellent manner, the question could be raised: "Why was the believer not mentioned before the corrupt person, so that the stages would proceed in regular descending order, beginning with Allāh and His Messenger, then down to the believer who is present, then to the believer who is absent, and then to the corrupt person?"

To this our reply would be: "Allāh has placed that which is most important ahead of that which is next in importance. He has therefore mentioned the honour of Allāh, then the honour of the Messenger (Allāh bless him and give him peace). Then He has mentioned what leads to conflict between the parties of the Muslims, as a result of listening to the speech of the corrupt, and taking its credibility for granted. He has thus mentioned each point in sequence, according to the relative force of its impact on the feelings."

As for the believer, whether he is present or absent, the believer must not give offence to the point where killing results. You must surely be aware that Allāh (Exalted is He) has followed this Qur'ānic verse, concerning news conveyed by the corrupt, with the verse concerning fighting, for He has said:

> And if two parties of believers fall to fighting....
> *wa in ṭā'ifatāni mina 'l-mu'minīna 'qtatalū....* (49:9)

This Qur'ānic verse [49:6] was revealed on the following occasion: The Prophet (Allāh bless him and give him peace) sent al-Walīd ibn

ʿUqba, the maternal brother of ʿUthmān, on a mission to the tribe of Bani 'l-Muṣṭaliq, as a friend and trustworthy delegate. They came out to meet him, but he suspected them of being ready for a fight, so he returned to the Prophet (Allāh bless him and give him peace) and said: "They held themselves aloof, and refused to cooperate." The Messenger (Allāh bless him and give him peace) considered launching an attack against them, so this Qurʾānic verse was revealed, and the Prophet (Allāh bless him and give him peace) understood that they were doing nothing of the kind.

As for His saying (Exalted is He):

> If a corrupt person brings you some news....
> *in jāʾa-kum fāsiqun bi-nabaʾin....*

—it contains a subtle implication, to the effect that the believer is typically stern and harsh towards the unbeliever, so the corrupt person would hardly be capable of conveying information to him, and if he could do so at all, it would be a rare exception.[1151]

It was al-Ḥasan who said: "By Allāh, it may have been revealed in connection with those folk in particular, but [this Qurʾānic verse] will apply in general till the Day of Resurrection. Nothing has abrogated it, and the message is addressed comprehensively to the Prophet (Allāh bless him and give him peace) and the believing member of his Community."

The corrupt person [*fāsiq*] is someone who leaves the fold of the Sacred Law [*Sharʿ*]. The term *fāsiq* is most often applied to someone who adheres to the rule of the Sacred Law, and affirms it, but then infringes all or some of its provisions. If the absolute unbeliever [*kāfir*] is also called a *fāsiq*, it is because he has violated the rule that intelligence has imposed, and that nature [*fiṭra*] has decreed.[1152]

According to Qatāda, Allāh's Messenger (Allāh bless him and give him peace) used to say:

> Caution is from Allāh, and haste is from Satan.[1153]

The rule contained in the Qurʾānic verse must therefore be of general application. It has come to emphasize the need for cautious verification, and the abandonment of uncritical reliance on what the corrupt person has to say. This makes better sense than applying the rule to one man in particular, because corruption [*fusūq*] means total departure from the truth, and al-Walīd is not suspected of that. He did suspect and imagine something, but he was mistaken, and that is all there was to it.

In view of His saying (Exalted is He):

> in case you attack a group of folk in ignorance.
> *an tuṣībū qawman bi-jahālatin.*

—the Qurʾānic verse clearly signifies: "If a corrupt person brings you news, meaning some kind of information, you must verify; in other words, you must investigate, you must check. You must seek an explanation of the matter, and full disclosure of the facts. You must not take the word of the corrupt person at face value,[1154] to avoid the horror of attacking a group of people, while ignorant of their true condition. That would leave you with an incurable feeling of distress, wishing it had never happened.[1155]

This implies that the ignorant person is bound to feel remorse for what he has done, long after the time of his action. He will constantly regret what came to pass because of him, while wishing it had never happened.[1156]

If a corrupt person brings you a report, of the kind that has disturbing implications, you must therefore conduct a thorough and frank enquiry, until it is perfectly clear to you that what he has brought you is true, or that he is a liar. You must not simply take his statement at face value, because, if someone fails to be on guard against the whole genus of corruption, he will not be on guard against outright lying, which is a particular species thereof.[1157] If you neglect this precaution, you may attack a group of people while ignorant of the true facts of the case.

As for His words (Exalted is He):

> for then you will feel remorse for what you did.
> *fa-tuṣībū ʿalā mā faʿaltum nādimīn.*

—that is to say: "for then you will come to regret your behaviour, with an acute sense of remorse."[1158] Two points deserve to be noted here:

1. The very strong emphasis placed on taking precaution. When Allāh (Exalted is He) said:

> in case you attack a group of folk in ignorance.
> *an tuṣībū qawman bi-jahālatin.*

—He went on to say, in effect: "That is not something to be disregarded, nor is it permissible for the intelligent person to say: 'Supposing I did attack a group of folk, why should that bother me?' That would indeed affect you, for you would suffer enduring grief and permanent sorrow, and it is strictly necessary to be on your guard against anything like that!"

2. The commendation of the believers, who are implicitly being told: "You are not among those who, if they committed an evil deed, would think nothing of it. No indeed, you would become remorseful."[1159]

This Qur'ānic verse also contains an allusion to the seductive temptations of the corrupt lower self [*nafs*], which is always instigating evil [*ammāra bi's-sū'*], and to the fact that it comes at every moment with news of some lustful worldly attraction. You must therefore check the profit and the loss involved, before attacking a set of hearts and their characters, in ignorance of whether their contents are healing and life for souls, or sickness and death for hearts. Otherwise, when the Resurrection dawns, you will find yourselves regretting what you have done.[1160]

These are my own remarks:

When you have dealings with your fellow human beings, you must not tell anything but the truth. You must not let any speech flow from your tongue, if Allāh (Blessed and Exalted is He) knows that what is in your heart is the very opposite. In their ways of talking, human beings are of three types:

1. The type who converses with his fellow creatures, while fearing no one but Allāh (Exalted is He), and considering nothing but the noble Sacred Law. He therefore tells nothing but the truth, seeking only the good pleasure of Allāh (Almighty and Glorious is He), regardless of whether people approve or disapprove.

2. The type who converses with his fellow creatures, and treats them honestly, not from fear of offending Allāh, but because he would feel ashamed if people knew him for a liar. He is afraid of offending his fellow creatures, and seeks to gain prestige in their sight.

3. The type who is familiar with the truth, but not with speaking it, so he tells lies and cultivates the art of lying. He ignites the fire of

enmity among the Muslims, and feels no shame before Allāh (Exalted is He). If someone feels no shame before Allāh (Exalted is He), it follows *a priori* that he feels no shame before his fellow creatures.

O believers, you must not forget His words (Exalted is He):

> Allāh is always Watchful over you.
> *inna 'llāha kāna ʿalai-kum Raqībā.* (4:1)

We beseech Allāh to endow us with uprightness of heart and tongue, as well as with uprightness in all the limbs and organs of the body, in keeping with the example set by the Prophet (Allāh bless him and give him peace). Allāh is indeed Capable of whatever He wills, and He is Competent to grant such requests. Peace be upon the Messengers, and praise be to Allāh, the Lord of All the Worlds. There is no might nor any power, except with Allāh, the All-High, the Almighty. May Allāh bless our master Muḥammad, his family and his Companions, and may He grant them peace.

The Seventy-second Call

In the Name of Allāh, the All-Merciful, the All-Compassionate.
Bismi'llāhi 'r-Raḥmāni 'r-Raḥīm.

O you who truly believe,
yā ayyuha 'lladhīna āmanū
one [group of] people should not scoff
lā yaskhar qawmun
at another [group of] people,
min qawmin
who may be better than they,
ʿasā an yakūnū khairan min-hum
and do not let their women [deride] women
wa lā nisā'u-hum min nisāʾin
who may be better than they are.
ʿasā an yakunna khairan min-hunn:

Do not defame one another,
wa lā talmizū anfusa-kum
and do not taunt one another with nicknames.
wa lā tanābazū bi 'l-alqāb:
An evil name is depravity after faith.
biʾsa 'l-ismu 'l-fusūqu baʿda 'l-īmān:
And those who do not repent,
such are the wrongdoers.
wa man lam yatub fa-ulāʾika humu 'ẓ-ẓālimūn.
(49:11)

This Sūra has warned against mockery, taunting and defamation. It has aroused repugnance for backbiting, spying, and thinking ill of the believers. It has urged the cultivation of noble traits of character, and of the social virtues. When it warned against backbiting, the prohibition was couched in a startling and terrifying allegory, entirely unique to the Qurʾān: the picture of a man sitting beside a dead brother of his, tearing at his body with his teeth, and eating his flesh. What a frightfully alarming impression that image makes!

Allāh (Exalted is He) has now said:

> O you who truly believe,
> *yā ayyuha 'lladhīna āmanū*
> one [group of] people should not scoff
> *lā yaskhar qawmun*
> at another [group of] people, who may be better than they.[1161]
> *min qawmin ʿasā an yakūnū khairan min-hum*

As we have already explained, the Sūra provides direction after direction. It has directed attention to what is required of the believer in relation to Allāh (Exalted is He), then in relation to the Prophet (Allāh bless him and give him peace), and then in relation to someone who opposes these two and disobeys them, meaning the depraved offender [*fāsiq*]. After that, it has explained what is required of the believer in relation to his fellow believer.

We have mentioned that the believer is either present or absent, and that, if he is present, it is not proper to scoff at him, nor to treat him in any way that is incompatible with full respect. The Qurʾānic verse refers to three offences in descending order of seriousness, namely: (1) mockery or scoffing [*sukhriyya*], (2) defamation [*lamz*], and lastly, (3) taunting with derisive nicknames [*nabaz*].[1162]

1. As for mockery or scoffing [*sukhriyya*], it means that a person disparages his brother, belittles him, undervalues him, and counts him among those who are quite unworthy of notice.

2. Defamation [*lamz*] means that a person's faults are mentioned in his absence. This is less serious than the first offence, because the scoffer has no regard whatsoever for the person who is the object of his mockery. He does not count him as anything at all, and does not like to say anything about him, apart from attributing some fault or other to him. He reduces him to the level of ridicule at which he is represented as entirely unworthy of consideration. The defamer [*lāmiz*], by contrast, does attach some importance to the person he defames, so he assigns something to him, then criticizes him for it.

3. Taunting [*nabaz*] means that a person calls someone by a bad nickname. This is less serious than the second offence, because

taunting is simply a matter of name-calling, in contrast with defamation. Since the defamer assigns a clearly stated description to the person he defames, designed to prove his inferiority and lower his standing, defamation is not mere labelling.[1163]

There are differences of opinion concerning the reasons for the revelation of this Qurʾānic verse:

• According to aḍ-Ḍaḥḥāk: "It was revealed in connection with the delegates from the tribe of Banī Tamīm. They ridiculed the paupers among the Companions, like ʿAmmār, Khabbāb, Ibn Fuhaira, Bilāl, Ṣuhaib, Salmān, Sālim, the client of Abū Ḥudhaifa, and others, when they noticed the raggedness of their condition. [The verse] was therefore revealed for the benefit of those among them who believed."

• According to Mujāhid: "It refers to the mockery of the poor by the rich."

• According to Ibn Zaid, it means: "If Allāh has screened a person's sins, he must not scoff at someone whom Allāh has exposed, for the exposure of his sins in this world may be better for him in the Hereafter."

Briefly stated, it is improper for anyone to have the audacity to ridicule someone he happens to notice, if he sees that his condition is shabby, or that he has some physical infirmity, or that he is not coherent in his speech. That person may actually be more sincere in conscience, and purer in heart, than someone who is his very opposite in outward appearance. The scoffer will therefore wrong himself, by disparaging someone who is honoured by Allāh (Exalted is He), and by ridiculing someone who is highly respected by Allāh. According to ʿAbdu'llāh ibn Masʿūd: "The test is entrusted to speech. If I were to scoff at a dog, I would be afraid of being transformed into a dog."[1164]

> One people...at another people
> *qawmun min qawmin*

That is to say: "One group [*jamāʿa*]...at another group." The choice of the collective expression is not intended to exclude mockery by a single individual, but rather to address what usually happens. The fact is that, while mockery may involve two people, it generally occurs in the presence of a group, who find it amusing and laugh because of it, instead of observing their duty to forbid and disapprove. They thus become partners of the scoffer in bearing the burden of sin. They are in the legal category of scoffers, so they have been forbidden to act like that.

The Qurʾānic verse was revealed in connection with Thābit ibn Qais ibn Shammās. He had a cavity in his ear, so, when he attended the public meeting of Allāh's Messenger (Allāh bless him and give him peace), and others had arrived before him, they made room for him, so that he could sit by his side (Allāh bless him and give him peace) to hear what he had to say. When he arrived one day, he had missed a cycle [*rakʿa*] of the dawn prayer [*ṣalāt al-fajr*]. As soon as the Prophet (Allāh bless him and give him peace) had moved away from the ritual prayer, his Companions took their seats. On this occasion, each man hoarded his own sitting space, leaving hardly any room for another. When someone else came along, he could not find any place to sit, so he had to stand there on his feet.

As soon as Thābit had finished performing the ritual prayer, he moved towards Allāh's Messenger (Allāh bless him and give him peace), stepping on the necks of the people, while saying: "Make room, make room!" They started to make room for him, until he almost reached Allāh's Messenger (Allāh bless him and give him peace). There was still one man between them, so he said: "Make room," but the man did not move. When he asked: "Who is this?" the man told him: "I am so-and so," but he said: "No, you are the son of the woman so-and-so [*ibn fulāna*]," attributing to him a mother who was reviled in the Time of Ignorance. Allāh's Messenger (Allāh bless him and give him peace) was embarrassed by this, and he bowed his head low. It was then that Allāh (Exalted is He) sent down this Qurʾānic verse.[1165]

> who may be better than they
> *ʿasā an yakūnū khairan min-hum*

The one who is scoffed at may be better in the sight of Allāh than the scoffer. In the words of the authentic Prophetic tradition [*ḥadīth ṣaḥīḥ*]:

> There is many a person with dishevelled hair, covered in dust, possessing only a couple of rags, whose oath, if he solemnly swore by Allāh, would surely be fulfilled by Him.[1166]

As for His saying (Exalted is He):

> and do not let their women [deride] women
> *wa lā nisā'u-hum min nisāʾin*
> who may be better than they are.
> *ʿasā an yakunna khairan min-hunn:*

—He has mentioned the women specifically, because mockery is more frequent where they are concerned. According to Anas and Ibn Zaid: "[The verse] was revealed in connection with the wives of the Prophet (Allāh bless him and give him peace). They derided Umm Salama for being very short." Some say it was revealed in connection with ʿĀʾisha, who pointed her hand at Umm Salama, saying: "O Prophet of Allāh, she is so very short!" As reported by ʿIkrima, it was Ibn ʿAbbās (may Allāh be well pleased with him and his father) who said:

"Ṣafiyya, the daughter of Ḥuyayy ibn Akhṭab, once came to the Messenger (Allāh bless him and give him peace) and said: 'O Messenger of Allāh, the women are deriding me. They keep saying to me: "O Jewess, daughter of two Jews!"' When Allāh's Messenger (Allāh bless him and give him peace) heard this, he said: 'Have you not told them: "My father is Aaron [*Hārūn*], my paternal uncle is Moses [*Mūsā*], and my husband is Muḥammad"?' May Allāh bless you, O my master, O Messenger of Allāh! It was then that Allāh sent down this Qurʾānic verse."

As recorded in the *Ṣaḥīḥ* of Muslim, on the authority of Abū Huraira (may Allāh be well pleased with him), Allāh's Messenger (Allāh bless him and give him peace) once said:

> Allāh does not look at your outer forms and your possessions, but He does look at your hearts and your deeds.

This is a momentous Prophetic tradition [*ḥadīth*]. It proves that one cannot decide, for certain, whether or not a person is at fault, solely on the basis of his apparent acts of obedience or disobedience. While someone is meticulous in observing the external practices, it may be that Allāh recognizes, from his heart, a blameworthy quality that invalidates those actions. It is also possible that, while we regard someone as guilty of negligence or sinful disobedience, Allāh recognizes, from his heart, a praiseworthy quality because of which He forgives him.

Actions are hypothetical indications, not definitive proofs, and they justify neither excessive admiration for someone we deem responsible for righteous actions, nor contempt for a Muslim we consider guilty of bad deeds. Contempt and blame should be directed towards that bad state of affairs, not towards the offending individual. You must reflect on this with care, for it is a subtle point, and Allāh is the source of enabling grace.

As for His saying (Exalted is He):

> Do not defame one another [lit., your own selves]
> *wa lā talmizū anfusa-kum*

—defamation [*lamz*] means finding fault [*ʿaib*]. According to aṭ-Ṭabarī: "Defamation may be with the hand, the eye and the tongue, and also by innuendo. This Qurʾānic verse is reminiscent of His saying:

> And do not kill your own selves.
> *wa lā taqtulū anfusa-kum.* (4:29)

"That is to say: 'Do not kill one another,' because the believers are like one single soul, so killing one's brother is like committing suicide. The meaning of the expression: 'Do not defame your own selves,' is therefore: 'Do not defame one another.'" According to Ibn ʿAbbās, Mujāhid, Qatāda and Saʿīd ibn Jubair, it signifies: "Do not assault one another verbally."

In His expression (Exalted is He):

> one another [lit., your own selves]
> *anfusa-kum.*

—there is an admonition to the effect that the intelligent person does not find fault with himself, so it is not appropriate for the believer to find fault with another, because he is like himself. Allāh's Messenger (Allāh bless him and give him peace) once said:

> The believers are like a single body. If one of its members complains, the rest of the body will rally to it with insomnia and fever.[1167]

It was Bakr ibn ʿAbdi'llāh al-Mazanī who said: "If you wish to see faults in abundance, you should contemplate a fault-finder, for he only finds fault with other people on account of the faults in himself."

Allāh's Messenger (Allāh bless him and give him peace) also said:

> One of you will notice the speck in his brother's eye, but ignore the tree stump in his own eye.

Part of a man's good fortune, it has been said, is that he pays attention to his own faults, to the exclusion of the faults of others.[1168]

As for His saying (Exalted is He):

> and do not taunt one another with nicknames.
> *wa lā tanābazū bi 'l-alqāb:*

—it signifies: "Do not call one another by the nickname of evil."[1169] This Qur'ānic verse was revealed in connection with a group of people who had certain names in the Time of Ignorance, but then, when they accepted Islām, they were forbidden to call one another by them. That applied in cases where particular names, by which they had been called in the Time of Ignorance, were offensive to the people concerned. Allāh then generalized His prohibition of that, and did not apply it to certain nicknames but not to others. It is not permissible, therefore, for any of the Muslims to taunt his brother with a name he dislikes, or with an attribute he finds repugnant.[1170]

As for His saying (Exalted is He):

> An evil name is depravity after faith.
> *bi'sa 'l-ismu 'l-fusūqu ba'da 'l-īmān:*

—it means: "It is bad to refer to the believers in a way that reminds them of depravity, after they have entered the faith and acquired the corresponding reputation." The point may be either:

- To censure the linking of unbelief and depravity to the believers, since it is related that the Qur'ānic verse was revealed in connection with Ṣafiyya, the daughter of Ḥuyayy (may Allāh be well pleased with her), who came to Allāh's Messenger (Allāh bless him and give him peace) and said: "The women keep calling me a Jewess, the daughter of two Jews...," as mentioned in the Prophetic tradition [*ḥadīth*].
- Or, to emphasize the fact that mutual taunting is a form of depravity, and that connecting it with faith is ignominious.[1171]

The meaning is also: "It is bad to name someone by saying to him: 'O Jew,' or, 'O Christian,' after he has accepted Islām, or, 'O depraved sinner,' after he has repented." According to some, the meaning is that, if someone does what he has been forbidden to do, in the way of scoffing, defamation and taunting, he is a depraved sinner, and:

> An evil name is depravity after faith.
> *bi'sa 'l-ismu 'l-fusūqu ba'da 'l-īmān:*

In other words: "So you must not do that, for, if you do, you will deserve the name of depravity."[1172]

As for His saying (Exalted is He):

> And those who do not repent,
> *wa man lam yatub*
> such are the wrongdoers.
> *fa-ulā'ika humu 'ẓ-ẓālimūn.*

—it means: "And those who fail to repent of what they have been forbidden to do, such are they who do wrong, by substituting sinful disobedience for worshipful obedience, and exposing the soul to the torment." The wrongdoer is more common than the depraved sinner, and the depraved sinner is more common than the unbeliever.

In the work entitled *at-Ta'wīlāt an-Najmiyya* [The Starry Interpretations], we are told: "'And those who do not repent' refers to those who fail to turn in repentance from the speech and actions of Iblīs [the Devil], by regarding themselves with vain conceit, and viewing other people with contempt. Such are the wrongdoers, so they are doomed to the path of damnation and rejection, along with Iblīs, as Allāh (Exalted is He) has said:

> Surely the curse of Allāh is upon the wrongdoers.
> *a-lā la'natu 'llāhi 'ala 'ẓ-ẓālimīn.* (11:18)"

His saying (Exalted is He) also contains a clear indication that, by abstaining from repentance, a man enters into the lobby of the wicked offenders. It is therefore essential to turn in sincere repentance from all shameful deeds and sinful acts of disobedience.[1173] Allāh (Glory be to Him and Exalted is He) has forbidden the slighting of other people, and backbiting, and disregard for legal rights, and the failure to pay due respect.

> Do not defame one another [lit., your own selves].
> *wa lā talmizū anfusa-kum*

That is to say: "Do not find fault with one another." Compare His saying:

> And do not kill one another [lit., your own selves].
> *wa lā taqtulū anfusa-kum.* (4:29)

It is also said: "No one ever belittles someone, without that person being given authority over him."

Conclusions should not be drawn from the outer aspect of people's states of being, for there are secrets in the nooks and crannies, and the Lord of Truth conceals His saints [*awliyā'*] in the veil of lowliness:

> There is many a person with dishevelled hair, covered in dust, possessing only a couple of rags, whose oath, if he solemnly swore by Allāh, would surely be fulfilled by Him.[1174]

These are my own remarks:

If you are going to love Allāh and His Messenger (Allāh bless him and give him peace), you must first love the Community of our master Muḥammad (Allāh bless him and give him peace), because its members are like the children of Allāh's Messenger (Allāh bless him and give him peace). When you love his Community (Allāh bless him and give him peace), he will be delighted with you, so, through your love for them, you will gain the love of Allāh's Messenger (Allāh bless him and give him peace). The believer's love for the believer is not devoid of divine reverence.

You must beware of attacking anyone who attacks you with violence. You must hold your tongue, entrust your situation to Allāh (Almighty and Glorious is He), and beware of harming anyone.

O Allāh, endow us with the moral characteristics of our master Muḥammad (Allāh bless him and give him peace). *Āmīn*. Peace be upon the Messengers, and praise be to Allāh, the Lord of All the Worlds. There is no might nor any power, except with Allāh, the All-High, the Almighty. May Allāh bless our master Muḥammad, his family and his Companions, and may He grant them peace.

The Seventy-third Call

In the Name of Allāh, the All-Merciful, the All-Compassionate.
Bismi'llāhi 'r-Raḥmāni 'r-Raḥīm.

O you who truly believe,
avoid a great deal of suspicion.
yā ayyuha 'lladhīna āmanu
'jtanibū kathīran mina 'ẓ-ẓann:
Some suspicion is a sin.
inna ba'ḍa 'ẓ-ẓanni ithmun.
And do not spy, and do not backbite one another.
wa lā tajassasū wa lā taghtab ba'ḍu-kum ba'ḍā:

Would one of you love to eat the flesh
a-yuḥibbu aḥadun min-kum an ya'kula laḥma
of his dead brother?
akhī-hi maitan
You would consider that disgusting!
fa-karihtumū-h:
And practise true devotion to Allāh.
wa 'ttaqu 'llāh:
Allāh is Ever-Relenting, All-Compassionate.
inna 'llāha Tawwābun Raḥīm. (49:12)

Allāh (Glory be to Him and Exalted is He) is telling His believing servants that He forbids them to indulge in a great deal of suspicion, meaning doubt and mistrust, of the family and close relatives, as well as people outside one's immediate circle. Some of that is a downright sin, so a great deal of it must be scrupulously avoided,[1175] for He has said (Exalted is He):

O you who truly believe, avoid a great deal of suspicion.
yā ayyuha 'lladhīna āmanu 'jtanibū kathīran mina 'ẓ-ẓann:
Some suspicion is a sin.
inna ba'ḍa 'ẓ-ẓanni ithmun.

The verse was revealed in connection with two men who slandered their companion behind his back. When Allāh's Messenger (Allāh bless him and give him peace) went on a military expedition or a journey, he used to assign a needy man to a pair of affluent men, to act as their servant. He would go ahead of them to the campsite, and prepare suitable food and drink for the two of them. On one of his journeys, the Prophet (Allāh bless him and give him peace) assigned Salmān to two such men, so he went ahead of them to the campsite. His eyes got the better of him, however, so he fell asleep and prepared nothing for them. When they arrived, they said to him: "Have you not done anything?" He said: "No, my eyes got the better of me," so they told him: "Go to Allāh's Messenger (Allāh bless him and give him peace) and ask him to provide us with some food."

Salmān then came to Allāh's Messenger (Allāh bless him and give him peace) and asked him for some food. Allāh's Messenger (Allāh bless him and give him peace) told him: "Go to Usāma ibn Zaid, and tell him to give you some food and condiments, if he has any to spare." Usāma was the keeper of food supplies for Allāh's Messenger (Allāh bless him and give him peace). Salmān came to him, but he said: "I have nothing with me," so Salmān went back to the two men and told them the news. They said: "Usāma did have something, but he was stingy." They then sent Salmān to a group of the Companions, but he found nothing with them. When he returned, they said: "If we had sent you to Biʾr Samḥa (a copious well in Medina), its water would have dried up!"

The pair then went to spy on Usāma, to see if he really did have what Allāh's Messenger (Allāh bless him and give him peace) had told him to give them. Then, when they came to Allāh's Messenger (Allāh bless him and give him peace), he said to them: "How is it that I see the green colour of meat in your mouths?" They said: "By Allāh, O Messenger of Allāh, this day of ours has brought us no meat." He said (blessing and peace be upon him): "You have done wrong, by eating the flesh of Salmān and Usāma." Then down came the revelation:

> O you who truly believe, avoid a great deal of suspicion.
> *yā ayyuha 'lladhīna āmanu 'jtanibū kathīran mina 'ẓ-ẓann:*
> Some suspicion is a sin.[1176]
> *inna baʿḍa 'ẓ-ẓanni ithmun.*

According to a confirmed report in the two *Ṣaḥīḥ*'s, transmitted on the authority of Abū Huraira (may Allāh be well pleased with him), the Prophet (Allāh bless him and give him peace) once said:

> Beware of suspicion [*ẓann*], for suspicion is the most untruthful account. Do not probe and do not spy. Do not overvalue by bidding up the price. Do not envy one another. Do not hate one another. Do not turn your backs on one another. Be Allāh's servants, as brothers.

Both here and in the Qur'ānic verse, according to our scholars, the term *ẓann* means *tuhma* [suspicion]. The warning and the prohibition are applicable only to suspicion without cause, as when someone is suspected of fornication or of drinking alcoholic liquor, for example, although there is nothing about him to justify that suspicion. Evidence that *ẓann* is used here in the sense of *tuhma* [suspicion] is furnished by His saying (Exalted is He):

> And do not spy
> *wa lā tajassasū*

That is because it may happen that suspicion occurs to someone, first of all, and he then resorts to spying in order to investigate the matter. He keeps looking and listening for evidence to prove the truth of that suspicion, so the Prophet (Allāh bless him and give him peace) has forbidden that.

If you wish, you may say: "As for what makes those suspicions that must be avoided distinct from other kinds, it is as follows: Whenever there is no valid evidence and no obvious reason for it, suspicion is unlawful and must be avoided. That applies when the person suspected is someone who shows every sign of discretion and righteousness, and who is obviously worthy of trust. It is unlawful to suspect such a person of corruption and deception, in stark contrast with someone who is notorious for his perfidious behaviour and flagrant atrocities."

The Prophet (Allāh bless him and give him peace) is reported as having said:

> Allāh has made it unlawful to shed the blood of a Muslim, to violate his honour, and to harbour a bad suspicion of him.[1177]

The Commander of the Believers, ʿUmar ibn al-Khaṭṭāb (may Allāh be well pleased with him), is reported as having said: "You must think nothing but good of a statement made by your believing brother, so long as you can find a good way of construing it." It was Abū ʿAbdi'llāh who said: "ʿAbdu'llāh ibn ʿUmar (may Allāh be well pleased with him and his father) told us: 'I once saw the Prophet (Allāh bless him and give him peace) circumambulating the Kaʿba, while saying:

> How fine you are, and how fine is your perfume! How splendid you are, and how splendid is your honour! By the One in whose Hand the soul of Muḥammad is held, the honour of the believer is more splendid in the sight of Allāh. Unlawful to you are his wealth and his blood, and thinking of him anything but good.'"[1178]

Suspicion is the underlying cause on which abominations are built, and from which the hate-filled enemy emerges. If the intelligent person bases his affairs on certainty, he will seldom be convinced that someone is at fault, and so speak ill of him. In outward appearance, an action may sometimes seem bad, when it is not so in actual fact, since it is possible that the perpetrator is acting absent-mindedly, or that the observer is mistaken.

[Since the Arabic word *ẓann* (pl. *ẓunūn)* sometimes means "thought; idea," rather than "suspicion"] the purpose of His saying (Exalted is He):

> a great deal....
> *kathīran....*

—is to exclude those *ẓunūn* [thoughts] on which good things are based. The Prophet (Allāh bless him and give him peace) [used the corresponding verb *ẓunnū* when he] said:

> Think well of the believer!

His saying (Exalted is He):

> Some suspicion is a sin.
> *inna baʿḍa 'ẓ-ẓanni ithmun.*

—is an admonition to take the utmost precaution. You may not encounter a highwayman every time on the perilous road, but you will not travel that way, because of what has happened on it once or twice, unless you have no choice, in which case you will travel with a company. Suspicion is likewise appropriate only after complete exercise of judgement and serious conviction.[1179]

"Avoid a great deal of suspicion [*ẓann*]" means: "Keep well away from it." The indefinite form of the adjective *kathīran* [much; a great deal] is used to stress the need to be wary of every kind of *ẓann*, and to consider which of the following categories it belongs to:

1. Some *ẓann* is permissible, like the kind of *ẓann* [guesswork] that is involved in dealing with the affairs of everyday life.
2. Some *ẓann* is necessary, like *ẓann* [making assumptions] about religious practices on which there is no unequivocal ruling, such as duties that are established without definitive proof. It is also necessary in the sense of thinking well [*ḥusn aẓ-ẓann*] of Allāh.
3. Some *ẓann* is unlawful, like *ẓann* [suspicion; harbouring doubt] about the attributes of Divinity [*Ilāhiyyāt*] and the attributes of Prophethood [*Nubuwwāt*]. It is also unlawful in the sense of thinking ill [*sū' aẓ-ẓann*] of the believers. According to a traditional report, transmitted by a complete chain of authorities, 'Ā'isha once said: "If someone thinks ill of his brother, he has thought ill of his Lord." Allāh (Exalted is He) says:

> avoid a great deal of suspicion.
> *[-u] 'jtanibū kathīran mina 'ẓ-ẓann:*[1180]

According to the Sacred Law [*Sharī'a*], there are two kinds of *ẓann*: the praiseworthy and the blameworthy.

As for the praiseworthy kind, it includes that which has the effect of preserving the religion of both the *ẓānn* [the one who thinks well of someone] and the *maẓnūn* [the one who is well thought of].

The blameworthy kind is the very opposite if this, as indicated by His saying (Glory be to Him and Exalted is He):

> Some suspicion is a sin.
> *inna ba'ḍa 'ẓ-ẓanni ithmun.*

—and by His saying (Glory be to Him and Exalted is He):

> If only, when you heard it,
> *law lā idh sami'tumū-hu*
> the believing men and women had thought
> *ẓanna 'l-mu'minūna wa 'l-mu'minātu*
> well of themselves!
> *bi-anfusi-him khairan.* (24:12)

—and also by His saying (Glory be to Him and Exalted is He):

> And you thought an evil thought,
> *wa ẓanantum ẓanna 's-saw'i*

> and you were worthless folk.
> *wa kuntum qawman būrā.* (48:12)

—as well as by the saying of the Prophet (Allāh bless him and give him peace):

> If one of you is commending his brother, let him say: 'I have a good opinion of so-and-so, but I esteem no one above Allāh.'[1181]

As for His saying (Exalted is He):

> And do not spy
> *wa lā tajassasū*

—that is to say: "Do not investigate the weak spots of the Muslims, and do not examine their shortcomings." In the words of the Prophetic tradition [*ḥadīth*]:

> O you who believe with your tongues, but whose hearts have not been touched by faith, do not backbite the Muslims and do not probe into their weaknesses. If someone investigates his brother's weak spot, Allāh will investigate his weak spot, and if Allāh investigates a person's weak spot, He will put him to shame, even within the confines of his own home.[1182]

You must not spy on one another, for *tajassus* [spying] usually refers to something bad, whereas *taḥassus* [investigation] refers to something good.[1183] His saying (Exalted is He):

> And do not spy
> *wa lā tajassasū*

—completes what has gone before, because it is thus understood that when He said (Exalted is He):

> avoid a great deal of suspicion.
> *[-u] 'jtanibū kathīran mina 'ẓ-ẓann:*

—the reference was to seeking certainty, for, when someone says: "I shall examine so-and-so," he means: "I shall get to know him for certain. I shall inspect his fault with my own eyes, then express criticism. I shall thus have avoided suspicion." It is as if Allāh (Exalted is He) is saying: "Do not pursue suspicion, and do not endeavour to seek certain knowledge of people's shortcomings."[1184]

To this I would add: It is understood from the obvious meaning of this verse:

> avoid a great deal of suspicion.
> *[-u] 'jtanibū kathīran mina 'ẓ-ẓann:*

—that it signifies the opposite of: "Seek certainty," for this is also forbidden, because it is not permissible for the believer to go on seeking until he uncovers the fault of his fellow believer, and it becomes known to him for certain.

ʿUmar ibn al-Khaṭṭāb (may Allāh be well pleased with him) was out on patrol one night, when he noticed a lamp shining through a door. He went to investigate, and discovered a group of people drinking intoxicating liquor. He was not sure how to act, so he entered the mosque and brought out ʿAbd ar-Raḥmān ibn ʿAwf (may Allāh be well pleased with him). According to one version, ʿUmar said: "This is the house of Rabīʿa ibn Umayya ibn Khalaf, and they are now a party of drunkards, so what do you think?" ʿAbd ar-Raḥmān replied: "I think, by Allāh, that we have done what Allāh has forbidden us to do. Allāh (Exalted is He) has said:

> And do not spy
> *wa lā tajassasū*

—and we have spied. We have invaded the privacy of a group of people. They were concealed from us, and it was not for us to remove the veil of Allāh." ʿUmar then said: "I think you have spoken nothing but the truth," so the pair of them departed from the scene.[1185]

> and do not backbite one another.
> *wa lā taghtab baʿḍu-kum baʿḍā:*

In other words: "Do not speak ill of one of you in his absence, in a way that you know to be disgusting."

> Would one of you love to eat the flesh of his dead brother?
> *a-yuḥibbu aḥadun min-kum an yaʾkula laḥma akhī-hi maitan*

This comparison matches the hideousness and repulsiveness of backbiting with the most disgusting thing imaginable. In other words: "Would one of you love to eat the flesh of his Muslim brother, when he is a corpse?"

> You would consider that disgusting!
> *fa-karihtumū-h:*

That is to say: "Just as you would naturally be disgusted by this, you must regard backbiting with equal disgust, for its penalty is even more severe."

Allāh (Exalted is He) has likened backbiting to eating one's brother's flesh, when his state is that of a corpse. Since a human being loathes the flesh of any human being, let alone a brother, and let alone a dead person, he must loathe backbiting with a loathing that is similar to this, or even more intense.[1186]

The Qur'ānic verse indicates the necessity of preserving the believer's honour in his absence, and it contains several points worth noting:

1. His saying (Exalted is He)

> one another.
> *baʿḍu-kum baʿḍā:*

—is significant, for it really applies to everyone in general.

2. What is forbidden is backbiting the believer, for He has said:

> one another.
> *baʿḍu-kum baʿḍā:*

As for the unbeliever, one may expose him and speak about his condition—and why not? It is also permissible to discuss the state of the flagrant sinner, when the need arises.

3. His saying (Exalted is He):

> Would one of you love to eat the flesh of his dead brother?
> *a-yuḥibbu aḥadun min-kum an ya'kula laḥma akhī-hi maitan*

—is proof that the forbidden backbiting is backbiting the believer, not talking about the unbeliever. That is because He has likened it to eating one's brother's flesh, and He has previously said :

> The believers are nothing but brothers.
> *inna-ma 'l-mu'minūna ikhwatun.* (49:10)

—so there is no brotherhood except between believers.

4. This comparison invites the conclusion that a person's honour is like his blood and his flesh, but this is merely an example of superficial reasoning by analogy. That is because the believer's honour is actually more noble than his flesh. If eating people's flesh is not good for the intelligent person, it cannot be good for him to gnaw on their honour, *a fortiori*, because that is even more painful. His expression (Exalted is He):

> the flesh of his dead brother
> *laḥma akhī-hi maitan*

—adds emphasis to the prohibition, because the enemy is motivated by hatred to chew the flesh of his enemy. Allāh (Exalted is He) has therefore said, in effect: "Your closest friend is the one to whom your own mother gave birth, so eating his flesh is the most disgusting thing there could be."

By using the word "dead," Allāh (Exalted is He) has dispelled a possible misunderstanding, for it might otherwise be said: "Speaking badly in someone's face is a cause of pain, so it is unlawful. As for backbiting, it is unobserved by the victim, so it does no harm." He has therefore answered this by saying (Exalted is He): "It is also true that eating the flesh of one's brother, when he is dead, does not cause pain. This [backbiting] is extremely disgusting, nevertheless, because the victim would suffer pain if he became aware of it, just as it would surely hurt the corpse if it could feel its flesh being eaten."

The following meaning is also implied: "Backbiting is like eating human flesh, the eating of which is unlawful, except for someone compelled by desperate need. If a person in desperate need can choose between the flesh of a sheep and the flesh of a human being, he must not eat the flesh of the human being. Likewise in the case of the backbiter, if he can find an alternative to meet his urgent need, instead of backbiting, it is not permissible for him to resort to backbiting."[1187]

> You would consider that disgusting!
> *fa-karihtumū-h:*

Backbiting him when he is alive is like eating his flesh after his death. The second prospect has been presented to you, for you would consider it disgusting, so you must regard the first with equal disgust.[1188]

As reported by Anas (may Allāh be well pleased with him), Allāh's Messenger (Allāh bless him and give him peace) once said:

> When I was taken on my Heavenly Journey, I passed by a group of people who had fingernails of copper. They were scratching their faces and their flesh (in one copy: and their breasts), so I said: 'Who are these, O Gabriel?' He replied: 'These are the ones who eat people's flesh and attack their good reputations.'[1189]

> And practise true devotion to Allāh.
> *wa 'ttaqu 'llāh:*

In other words: "You must be afraid of offending Allāh, and be on your guard against His punishment, through compliance with His commandments and avoidance of His prohibitions."

> Allāh is Ever-Relenting, All-Compassionate.
> *inna 'llāha Tawwābun Raḥīm.*

That is to say: "He (Glory be to Him and Exalted is He) is very Willing to relent, Tremendous in mercy, for those who practise true devotion to Allāh, and who repent and demonstrate contrition." This contains an incentive to repentance, and an exhortation to make haste in showing remorse and acknowledging sinful error, so that the human being will not despair of Allāh's mercy.[1190]

According to the majority of the religious scholars, the backbiter must take the following steps in his repentance:

1. He must desist from that [backbiting], and make a resolution never to repeat it.

2. He must meet the condition of remorse for what has happened in the past.

3. He must obtain pardon from the victim of his backbiting. According to some, however, the backbiter is not required to obtain his victim's pardon, for, if he lets him know what happened, he may suffer more harm than if he never got to know about it. His procedure must therefore be to extol his merits, when he attends the meetings at which he used to find fault with him, thereby clearing him of the slander, to the best of his ability.[1191] Some maintain that the backbiter must seek his victim's pardon, except when accusations of adultery or fornication are involved, by saying: "I beg you to acquit me of everything that you could rightly hold against me."

The Qur'ānic verse contains several subtle points, for instance:

• Allāh (Exalted is He) has mentioned three things, linked together in sequence, within His saying (Glory be to Him and Exalted is He):

> avoid a great deal....
> *[-u] 'jtanibū kathīran....*

In other words: (1) "Do not say about the believers what you do not know to be true of them, based only on suspicion." (2) "When you ask them about things that are suspected, do not say: 'We are investigating their affairs, in order to be certain about them before discussing them.'" (3) "If you learn something about them without spying, do not talk about it, do not broadcast it, and do not indulge in backbiting."

First of all, He has forbidden that which is not known, then He has forbidden the pursuit of that knowledge, and then He has forbidden the mention of what has become known.

• Allāh (Glory be to Him and Exalted is He) has not said: "Avoid saying something contrary to what you know to be true." Nor has He said: "Avoid doubt." The first thing He has forbidden is talk based on suspicion. That is because saying what is known to be untrue amounts to lying and fabrication, while it amounts to stupidity and folly to say things that are doubtful, thereby indulging in speculation. These vices are both at the extreme of point of infamy, so He has not explicitly forbidden them, contenting Himself with His saying:

> O you who truly believe
> *yā ayyuha 'lladhīna āmanū*

—because, by describing them in terms of belief, He automatically bars them from the falsehood and scepticism that are typical of the unbeliever. He has only barred them explicitly from doing certain things that are common among the Muslims, as when He said (Exalted is He):

> O you who truly believe, one group of people should not scoff
> *yā ayyuha 'lladhīna āmanū lā yaskhar qawmun*
> at another group people.
> *min qawmin.* (49:11)

• Allāh (Glory be to Him and Exalted is He) has concluded the two Qur'ānic verses [49:11 and 49:12] with the mention of *tawba* [repentance; relenting]. In the first, He has said:

> And those who do not repent, such are the wrongdoers.
> *wa man lam yatub fa-ulā'ika humu 'ẓ-ẓālimūn.* (49:11)

—and in the other He has said:

> Allāh is Ever-Relenting, All-Compassionate.
> *inna 'llāha Tawwābun Raḥīm.*

The first verse begins with the prohibition:

> One group of people should not scoff at another group people.
> *lā yaskhar qawmun min qawmin.* (49:11)

—so the verb is in the negative optative form, whereas the second verse begins with the commandment:

> avoid....
> [-*u*] *'jtanibū*....

—so the verb is in the positive imperative form.[1192]

An important point: When you speak to the judge, in the effort to support your claim against someone who has wronged you, it does not constitute backbiting if you say: "So-and-so has wronged me, or robbed me, or struck me, or slandered me, or done me harm." The scholars of the Community are unanimously agreed on that, and the Prophet (Allāh bless him and give him peace) once said:

> The owner of a rightful claim is entitled to speak out.[1193]

A good example is the case of Hind, who said to the Prophet (Allāh bless him and give him peace): "Abū Sufyān is a tight-fisted man. He does not give me enough to provide for myself and my children. Should I take [what we need] without his knowledge?" The Prophet (Allāh bless him and give him peace) said: "Yes, take!"[1194]

Finally, this subtle point should also be noted: The lower self does not tell the truth, and the heart does not tell lies, but the distinction between the lower self and the heart is difficult to make. If someone still retains a trace of his selfish interests, however slight, he is not entitled to claim that he speaks from the heart. He is influenced by his lower self, so long as any part of it continues to affect him. Whenever he is inclined to find fault with someone else, he must be suspicious of his own lower self. The Commander of the Believers, ʿUmar ibn al-Khaṭṭāb (may Allāh be well pleased with him), once said, while delivering a sermon: "All of the people are wiser than ʿUmar. A woman is wiser than ʿUmar."

> And do not spy
> *wa lā tajassasū*

The insightful person does not shift his attention from witnessing the Lord of Truth to witnessing mere creatures, so how could he devote himself to spying on their situations? He does not focus his attention on himself, so how could he focus it on someone else?

> and do not backbite one another.
> *wa lā taghtab baʿḍu-kum baʿḍā:*

Backbiting [*ghība*] creatures comes about only through absence [*ghaiba*] from the Lord of Truth.

> Would one of you love to eat the flesh of his dead brother?
> *a-yuḥibbu aḥadun min-kum an ya'kula laḥma akhī-hi maitan*

According to the traditional commentary, this is intended as a reference to backbiting, and that is consistent with the obvious meaning of the Qur'ānic verse. The most vile and worthless unbelievers are those who eat carrion. Honourable indeed is he who backbites no one in your presence![1195]

These are my own remarks:

You must read the record of your deeds in this world, before you read it in the Hereafter, because the reading of this record is inevitable in the Hereafter. Allāh (Exalted is He) has said:

> And We shall bring forth for him, on the Day of Resurrection,
> *wa nukhriju la-hu yawma 'l-qiyāmati*
> a book which he will find wide open.
> *kitāban yalqā-hu manshūrā.*
>
> [And he will be told:] "Read your record!
> *iqra' kitāba-k:*
> Your own self suffices you this day as a reckoner against you."
> *kafā bi-nafsi-ka 'l-yawma 'alai-ka ḥasībā.* (17:13,14)

This reading on the Day of Resurrection will do nothing but increase your sorrow and regret, and remorse will not help you at all. If you read your record in this world, on the other hand, and turn to Allāh in repentance of all infringements of the Sacred Law, you will be transported from the life of hardship to the good life in this world.

What concern of yours are the faults of other people? Why should you indulge in mockery, defamation and taunting? Why should you indulge in suspicion, spying and backbiting, especially when the believer's reputation is at stake? You will be questioned about it on the Day of Resurrection, especially if it involves your believing brother. Allāh will not pardon that, unless your brother has already pardoned you, because that is his right in relation to you, and this pardon of his cannot simply be taken for granted.

You must therefore exercise restraint, so that you do not speak in any way that casts doubt and suspicion on your believing brother, and do not accept what other people say about him. Such doubt, suspicion and hearsay will cause you to suffer distress and tightness of the breast. Your lower self will gain the upper hand over you, so you will treat your brother abusively. You will violate the good conduct demanded of you by the Sacred Law, and your adherence to the Book and the Sunna. As a consequence, you will fall into a dire predicament. So long as you are faced with this predicament, you must guard your tongue, and think nothing but good of the believers.

If you hear something from them, you must respond by saying: "Allāh hears what they say!" Then, if you are convinced that what they say is true, rejoice, accept their sound advice, and put it into practice. If this is not the case, then pardon and forgive them, for Allāh pardons His servants. We must focus our attention on our Lord, not on ourselves, let alone on other people.

We beg Allāh to show us our own faults, and enable us to struggle with them, so that we may correct them and set them straight, for the sake of the Chosen Prophet, our master Muḥammad (Allāh bless him and give him peace). Peace be upon the Messengers, and praise be to Allāh, the Lord of All the Worlds. There is no might nor any power, except with Allāh, the All-High, the Almighty. May Allāh bless our master Muḥammad, his family and his Companions, and may He grant them peace.

The Seventy-fourth Call

In the Name of Allāh, the All-Merciful, the All-Compassionate.
Bismi'llāhi 'r-Raḥmāni 'r-Raḥīm.

O you who truly believe,
practise true devotion to Allāh,
yā ayyuha 'lladhīna āmanu 'ttaqu 'llāha
and believe in His Messenger.
He will give you twofold
wa āminū bi-Rasūli-hi yu'ti-kum kiflaini
of His mercy, and He will provide for you
a light by which to walk,
min Raḥmati-hi wa yaj'al la-kum nūran tamshūna bi-hi
and He will forgive you.
Allāh is All-Forgiving, All-Compassionate.
wa yaghfir la-kum wa 'llāhu Ghafūrun Raḥīm:

So that the People of the Book may know
that they control nothing
li-allā ya'lama Ahlu 'l-Kitābi allā yaqdirūna 'alā shai'in
of Allāh's bounty,
but the bounty is in Allāh's hand
min faḍli 'llāhi wa anna l-faḍla bi-yadi 'llāhi
to give to whom He will.
Allāh is the Owner of infinite bounty.
yu'tī-hi man yashā': wa 'llāhu Dhu 'l-faḍli 'l-'aẓim.
(57:28,29)

O you who truly believe, practise true devotion to Allāh,
yā ayyuha 'lladhīna āmanu 'ttaqu 'llāha
and believe in His Messenger.
wa āminū bi-Rasūli-hi.

That is to say: "O you who sincerely believe in Allāh, you must practise true devotion to Allāh, through compliance with His commandments and avoidance of His prohibitions, and you must be constant and steadfast in faith."

> He will give you twofold of His mercy
> *yu'ti-kum kiflaini min Raḥmati-hi*

In other words: "He will grant you two portions of His mercy."

> and He will provide for you a light by which to walk
> *wa yaj'al la-kum nūran tamshūna bi-hi*

That is to say: "He will also provide for you, in the Hereafter, a light by which to walk across the Narrow Bridge [*Ṣirāṭ*].[1196] According to Ibn 'Abbās (may Allāh be well pleased with him and his father): "That light is the Qur'ān." Some maintain that it represents right guidance and clarification, in the sense that He will provide for you a clear path in the religion, by which you will be rightly guided.[1197]

> and He will forgive you.
> *wa yaghfir la-kum:*

In other words: "He will also forgive you for your previous acts of sinful disobedience."

> Allāh is All-Forgiving, All-Compassionate.
> *wa 'llāhu Ghafūrun Raḥīm:*

That is to say: "He is Sublime in forgiveness, Bountiful in compassion."[1198]

Concerning the occasion for the revelation of this Qur'ānic verse, Sa'īd ibn Jubair is reported as having said: "The Prophet (Allāh bless him and give him peace) sent Ja'far, in a caravan of seventy riders, to the Negus [Emperor of Ethiopia], in order to invite him [to accept Islām]. He duly invited him, and he responded by believing. Then, at the time of Ja'far's departure, up spoke some of the Emperor's subjects, forty men who had also believed. They said [to the Negus]: "Grant us permission to go to this Prophet, so that we may acknowledge him (in other words: so that we may believe in him, behold him, and enjoy the privilege of seeing him). We can also assist these visitors in sailing the sea, since we are more familiar with the sea than they are."

They then accompanied Ja'far (may Allāh be well pleased with him) to the Prophet (blessing and peace be upon him), who was barely equipped to entertain a single guest. When they saw what privation and hardship the Muslims were suffering, they sought leave of the Prophet (blessing and peace be upon him), saying: "O Prophet of Allāh, we own properties, and we see what privation, what poverty, the Muslims are enduring. If you will permit us, we shall leave at once, then return with our possessions and share them with the Muslims." He gave them permission, so they left at once, then brought their goods and shared them with the Muslims. Allāh (Glory be to Him and Exalted is He) thereupon sent down these revelations about them:

> Those to whom We gave the Book before it, they believe in it.
> *alladhīna ātainā-humu 'l-Kitāba min qabli-hi hum bi-hi yu'minūn.*
>
> And when it is recited to them, they say:
> *wa idhā yutlā 'alai-him qālū*
> "We believe in it. It is the Truth from our Lord.
> *āmannā bi-hi inna-hu 'l-Ḥaqqu*
> Even before it we were among those who surrender."
> *min Rabbi-nā innā kunnā min qabli-hi muslimīn.*
>
> These will be given their reward twice over,
> *ulā'ika yu'tawna ajra-hum marrataini*
> because they are steadfast and repel evil with good,
> *bi-mā ṣabarū wa yadra'ūna bi'l-ḥasanati 's-sayyi'ata*
> and spend of that wherewith We have provided them.
> *wa mimmā razaqnā-hum yunfiqūn.* (28:52–54)

It was this provision that they shared with the Muslims. As for those People of the Book who did not believe, when they heard His words (Exalted is He):

> These will be given their reward twice over.
> *ulā'ika yu'tawna ajra-hum marrataini*

—they spoke boastfully to the Muslims, saying: "O company of the Muslims, as for someone who believes in your Book, as well as in our Book, he will have his reward twice over. As for someone who [believes in our Book but] does not believe in your Book, he will still have a reward equivalent to your rewards, so where is your advantage over us?" It was then that Allāh (Exalted is He) sent down the revelation:

> O you who truly believe, practise true devotion to Allāh,
> *yā ayyuha 'lladhīna āmanu 'ttaqu 'llāha*
> and believe in His Messenger.
> *wa āminū bi-Rasūli-hi.*
> He will give you twofold of His mercy....
> *yu'ti-kum kiflaini min Raḥmati-hi....*

He thereby assigned them their reward, and granted them light and forgiveness in addition.[1199] Then He went on to say (Exalted is He):

> So that the People of the Book may know
> *li-allā yaʿlama Ahlu 'l-Kitābi*
> that they control nothing of Allāh's bounty,
> *allā yaqdirūna ʿalā shaiʾin min faḍli 'llāhi*
> but the bounty is in Allāh's hand, to give to whom He will.
> *wa anna l-faḍla bi-yadi 'llāhi yuʾtī-hi man yashāʾ:*
> Allāh is the Owner of infinite bounty.
> *wa 'llāhu Dhu 'l-faḍli 'l-ʿaẓim.*

In other words: "If We have couched this explanation in seemingly exaggerated terms, We have done so for good reason. The People of the Book must be made to understand that they cannot monopolize the bounty of Allāh, and that they cannot treat Messengership and Prophethood as prerogatives exclusive to them."

In His expression *li-allā* [so that], the word *lā* [which commonly means "not"] is an [emphatic, not negative] addition, and the meaning is: "so that they may know."

According to the Qurʾānic commentators, the People of the Book used to say: "Inspired revelation [*waḥy*] and Messengership [*Risāla*] are peculiar to us, and the Book and the Sacred Law [*Sharʿ*] belong to us alone. Allāh has singled us out, by this momentous favour, from among all the creatures in the universe." Allāh therefore refuted them with this noble Qurʾānic verse:

> but the bounty is in Allāh's hand, to give to whom He will.
> *wa anna l-faḍla bi-yadi 'llāhi yuʾtī-hi man yashāʾ:*

That is to say: "The control of Prophethood, right guidance and faith, is in the Hand of the All-Merciful, to give to whomever He will among His creatures."

> Allāh is the Owner of infinite bounty.
> *wa 'llāhu Dhu 'l-faḍli 'l-ʿaẓim.*

In other words: "Allāh is Bountiful in gracious favour and beneficence."[1200]

The overall meaning is therefore: "You must practise true devotion to Allāh, and be steadfast in your belief in Allāh's Messenger (Allāh bless him and give him peace), for then He will give you what He promised to those who believed, among the People of the Book: namely, the twofold reward that is mentioned in His saying (Exalted is He):

> These will be given their reward twice over.
> *ulāʾika yuʾtawna ajra-hum marrataini.*

—and He will give you nothing less than the equivalent of their reward, because you are like them in belief, and you make no distinction between any of His Messengers."[1201]

According to Ibn Zaid: "The term 'twofold [*kiflain*]' refers to the reward of this world and that of the Hereafter."[1202] It is an allusion to the two benefits requested in the Qurʾānic verse:

> "Our Lord, give us in this world that which is good,
> *Rabba-nā āti-nā fi 'd-dunyā ḥasanatan*
> and in the Hereafter that which is good,
> *wa fi 'l-ākhirati ḥasanatan*
> and guard us against the torment of the Fire [of Hell]."
> *wa qi-nā ʿadhāba 'n-nār.* (2:201)

As related by al-Bukhārī (may Allāh the Exalted bestow His mercy upon him) in his *Ṣaḥīḥ*, on the authority of Sālim ibn ʿAbdi'llāh, the latter reported that his father told him that he once heard Allāh's Messenger (Allāh bless him and give him peace) say:

> Your superior merit, in relation to the religious communities that preceded you, is like the space between the afternoon prayer [*ṣalāt al-ʿaṣr*] and the setting of the sun. The People of the Torah received the Torah, and they put it into practice until, when the day was halfway through, they could do no more, so they were given a single measure [of reward], then another single measure. Then the People of the Gospel received the Gospel, and they put it into practice until the afternoon prayer, at which point they could do no more, so they were given a single measure, then another single measure. Then we received the Qurʾān, and we put it into practice until the setting of the sun, so we were given a double measure, then another double measure.
> The People of the Book objected, saying: 'Our Lord, why have You given these folk a double measure, then another double measure, when you gave us only a single measure, then another single measure, though we were more actively engaged in our religious practice?' Allāh (Almighty and Glorious is He) replied: 'Have I wrongfully deprived you of any part of your reward?' When they said no, He said: 'Such is My gracious favour. I give it to whom I will.'"[1203]

According to another report, likewise related by al-Bukhārī (may Allāh the Exalted bestow His mercy upon him), Abū Burda stated that his father told him: "Allāh's Messenger (Allāh bless him and give him peace) once said:

Three people are entitled two rewards apiece: (1) A man from among the People of the Book, who believes in his [earlier] Prophet and also believes in Muḥammad (Allāh bless him and give him peace). (2) The enslaved servant, provided he fulfils his duty to Allāh and his duty to his masters. (3) A man who once had a female slave, with whom he used to have nothing but sexual intercourse, but then he trained her and trained her well, taught her and taught her well, then emancipated her and married her, and thus became entitled to two rewards."[1204]

O you who truly believe
yā ayyuha 'lladhīna āmanu

—in Jesus. According to one of the two interpretations offered by the traditional commentators, it is to them that this call is specifically addressed. According to the other, it applies in general to everyone who believes in the Messengers before Muḥammad (Allāh bless him and give him peace). As explained by al-Baiḍāwī, the meaning is: "O you who believe in the previous Messengers, practise true devotion to Allāh, by observing what He has forbidden you to do, and believe in Muḥammad (Allāh bless him and give him peace).

He will give you twofold of His mercy.
yu'ti-kum kiflaini min Raḥmati-hi.

"That is to say: '[He will give you] two portions of His mercy, one for your belief in Muḥammad (Allāh bless him and give him peace), and one for your belief in those before him.' It is not far-fetched, that they should be rewarded for their previous religion, even though it has been superseded by the blessed grace of Islām.

"The call may be addressed, as some maintain, to those Christians who lived in the time of the Prophet (Allāh bless him and give him peace). This view is based on a traditional report, which states that the 'twofold giving' obviously refers to someone who believed in Jesus (peace be upon him) and faithfully followed his religion, until our Prophet Muḥammad (Allāh bless him and give him peace) was sent on his mission. That person had remained loyal to the true religion, until it was superseded, and the true nature of the superseding religion became clear to him. Once that had become clear to him, he faithfully followed the second truth, and thereby earned the right to be given twofold. The case of the Jews is different, because Judaism had already been abrogated by the mission of Jesus (peace be upon him), so the Jews were not following the true religion, at the time when they came to believe in our Prophet (peace be upon him)."

Well then, considering all these points, why should they be rewarded for their previous religion? According to al-Baiḍāwī, there are two possible answers to this question:

1. It is not far-fetched, that they should be rewarded for their previous religion.
2. The call is addressed to the Christians, since their religion was not abrogated before the appearance of the Muḥammadan religion, and their becoming familiar with it.

The weakness of this second interpretation, it has been noted, is that the Qur᾿ānic verse was probably revealed in connection with those Jews who accepted Islām, as reported in authentic traditions, on the authority of ʿAbdu'llāh ibn as-Salām and others like him. That is why al-Baiḍāwī preferred the first interpretation, and his preference is supported by the lack of any contextual evidence of specification.[1205]

As for His expression (Exalted is He):

> He will give you....
> *yu᾿ti-kum....*

—it signifies: "He will reward you, for following him [the Messenger (Allāh bless him and give him peace)], with *kiflain*, meaning two copious portions of His mercy, which will protect you from the torment, just as the *kifl* protects the rider from falling off his camel. (The term *kifl* is applied to a kind of blanket, which is strapped over the camel's back, with the front end attached to the withers, and the rear end to the buttocks.) This protection is granted on account of your belief in Muḥammad (Allāh bless him and give him peace), and your belief in those who preceded him. It is granted along with the lightening of work and the removal of burdens."[1206]

These are my own comments:

If someone really understands the worth and value of true belief, he will maintain it steadfastly, and he will spare no effort in climbing towards the highest peak of this faith. It is indeed the faith of the champions of truth [*ṣiddīqīn*], who have entered the sphere of experiential belief [*īmān shuhūdī*] in the wake of doctrinal belief [*īmān iʿtiqādī*]. As for you, O believer, you are a believer in Allāh and His Messenger, in terms of doctrinal belief, but heedlessness may still afflict you, causing you to fall into infringements of the Sacred Law. You must reinforce this doctrinal belief, so that you may enter into experiential belief. In the words of the Prophet (Allāh bless him and give him peace):

> You must worship Allāh as if you could see Him, for even if you do not see Him, He surely sees you!

This can only come about through your frequent remembrance of Allāh (Exalted is He), in a state of awareness that is constant and complete. The believer must not stop there, however, for he must not become attached to witnessing alone. While lovers [of the Lord] do savour the taste of witnessing, they find even greater delight in servanthood, and in intimate friendship with Him. The enjoyment of servanthood is above and beyond the enjoyment of witnessing, because they have transcended not only their selfish and worldly interests, but also their Otherworldly desires. They still seek the Garden of Paradise, but only because the good pleasure of Allāh (Almighty and Glorious is He) resides therein.

O Allāh, grant us the real experience of absolutely certain faith, because the station of servitude is above all other spiritual stations. It is indeed the station of the champions of truth, above whose station there is only station of Prophethood. That is why Allāh (Almighty and Glorious is He) referred specifically to His Prophet (Allāh bless him and give him peace) when He said:

> Praise be to Allāh, who has revealed the Book to His servant,
> *al-ḥamdu li'llāhi 'lladhī anzala ʿalā ʿabdi-hi 'l-Kitāba*
> and has not placed therein any crookedness.
> *wa lam yajʿal la-hu ʿiwajā.* (18:1)

We beg Allāh (Exalted is He) to strengthen our faith, and to transport us to the faith of the champions of truth, in honour of the dignity of our master Muḥammad (Allāh bless him and give him peace), his family and his Companions, and through the blessed grace of our spiritual leaders (may Allāh be well pleased with them all). Peace be upon the Messengers, and praise be to Allāh, the Lord of All the Worlds. There is no might nor any power, except with Allāh, the All-High, the Almighty. May Allāh bless our master Muḥammad, his family and his Companions, and may He grant them peace.

The Seventy-fifth Call

In the Name of Allāh, the All-Merciful, the All-Compassionate.
Bismi'llāhi 'r-Raḥmāni 'r-Raḥīm.

O you who believe, when you conspire together,
yā ayyuha 'lladhīna āmanū idhā tanājaitum
do not conspire for the sake of sinful misconduct
fa-lā tatanājaw bi'l-ithmi
and hostility and disobedience
towards the Messenger,
wa 'l-ʿudwāni wa maʿṣiyati 'r-Rasūli
but conspire for the sake of righteousness
and true devotion,
wa tanājaw bi'l-birri wa 't-taqwā
and practise true devotion to Allāh,
wa 'ttaqu 'llāha 'lladhī
to Whom you will be gathered.
ilai-hi tuḥsharūn.

Conspiracy is only of the devil,
that he may sadden those who believe,
inna-ma 'n-najwā mina 'sh-shaiṭāni
li-yaḥzuna 'lladhīna āmanū
but this cannot harm them at all,
unless by Allāh's leave.
wa laisa bi-ḍārri-him shaiʾan illā bi-idhni 'llāh:
In Allāh let the believers put their trust.
wa ʿala 'llāhi fa-l'-yatawakkali 'l-muʾminūn. (58:9,10)

There are two opinions concerning the identity, in this instance, of those who are addressed by His saying (Exalted is He):

O you who believe!
yā ayyuha 'lladhīna āmanū.

1. If we take His previous saying (Exalted is He):

> Have you not noticed those who were forbidden to conspire?
> *a-lam tara ila 'lladhīna nuhū ʿani 'n-najwā.* (58:8)

—as a reference to the Jews, we should take His saying in this Qurʾānic verse:

> O you who believe!
> *yā ayyuha 'lladhīna āmanū.*

—as a reference to the hypocrites, meaning: "O you who believe with your tongues!"

2. If we take that [previous saying] as a reference to all the unbelievers, including both the Jews and the hypocrites, we should take this as a reference to the believers. That is because, when Allāh (Exalted is He) blamed the Jews and the hypocrites for conspiring to engage in sinful misconduct, and in hostility and disobedience towards the Messenger (Allāh bless him and give him peace), He went on to forbid his believing Companions to follow a path like theirs, for He said:

> Do not conspire for the sake of sinful misconduct
> *fa-lā tatanājaw bi'l-ithmi*

—that being the disgusting behaviour that is typical of them:

> and hostility
> *wa 'l-ʿudwāni*

—that being what results in the wrongful treatment of others:

> and disobedience towards the Messenger.
> *wa maʿṣiyati 'r-Rasūli*

—that being opposition to him. He also commanded them to:

> conspire for the sake of righteousness
> *wa tanājaw bi'l-birri*

—which is the opposite of hostility:

> and true devotion.
> *wa 't-taqwā.*

—which is the means of salvation from the Fire of Hell, for someone who performs the duties of worshipful obedience, and who refrains from sinful acts of disobedience.[1207]

O you who believe, when you conspire together,
yā ayyuha 'lladhīna āmanū idhā tanājaitum
do not conspire for the sake of sinful misconduct
fa-lā tatanājaw bi'l-ithmi
and hostility and disobedience towards the Messenger.
wa 'l-ʿudwāni wa maʿṣiyati 'r-Rasūli

That is to say: "When you discuss your mutual concerns in secret, do not let your discussions involve sinful misconduct, like abusive speech, or hostility towards others, or opposition and disobedience to the commandment of the Messenger (Allāh bless him and give him peace)." Allāh has forbidden the believers to conspire among themselves in the manner practised by the Jews. His saying (Exalted is He):

And they conspire together for the sake of sinful misconduct
wa yatanājawna bi'l-ithmi
and hostility and disobedience towards the Messenger.
wa 'l-ʿudwāni wa maʿṣiyati 'r-Rasūl. (58:8)

—may thus be interpreted to mean: "They hold discussions among themselves about matters involving sinful misconduct, hostility and opposition to the commandment of the Messenger (Allāh bless him and give him peace)." That is because their discussion revolves around plots to deceive and outwit the Muslims.

It was Abū Ḥayyān who said: "He began by mentioning sinful misconduct, because of its generality. Then He mentioned hostility, because of its great importance to the lower selves, which are the tyrannical oppressors of the servants [of the Lord]. Then He went on to mention the most serious offence of all, which is disobedience towards the Messenger (Allāh bless him and give him peace). This also contains a stab at the hypocrites, since their conspiracy was for that very purpose."[1208]

Conspire for the sake of righteousness and true devotion.
wa tanājaw bi'l-birri wa 't-taqwā.

That is to say: "Let your discussions be about matters involving goodness, obedience and beneficence."[1209] Allāh has forbidden the believers to conspire among themselves in the manner practised by the hypocrites and the Jews. He has commanded them to conspire for the sake of obedience, true devotion, and the avoidance of that which Allāh has forbidden.[1210]

As you should also be aware, when people conspire in this fashion, they do very little conspiring, because the subject of this discussion calls for its open declaration. That corresponds closely to His saying:

> There is no good in much of their conspiring,
> *lā khaira fī kathīrin min najwā-hum*
> except him who enjoins almsgiving,
> *illā man amara bi-ṣadaqatin*
> and fairness and peace-making
> *aw maʿrūfin aw iṣlāḥin baina 'n-nās.* (4:114)

Furthermore, when a man is known to practise this kind of conspiracy, no one is offended by his doing so.[1211]

> And practise true devotion to Allāh,
> *wa 'ttaqu 'llāha 'lladhī*
> to Whom you will be gathered.
> *ilai-hi tuḥsharūn.*

In other words: "You must demonstrate your fear of offending Allāh, through your compliance with His commandments and your avoidance of His prohibitions, for He is the One who will assemble you for the Reckoning, and He will recompense each and every one of you for his conduct."[1212]

As the Qurʾānic verse indicates, conspiracy is not forbidden absolutely. It is actually enjoined in certain cases, either as strictly necessary or as strongly recommended, in keeping with the particular situation.

The question may be raised: "How can Allāh command the fear of Him [that is implicit in true devotion], when He is the All-Compassionate Patron, and nearness to Him is the most delightful of all objectives, and when intimate friendship with Him is the ultimate goal? Surely the sense of fear necessitates avoidance, whereas gathering to Him requires making an approach towards Him?"

The answer to this will be: "The sentence does accommodate such a juxtaposition, since the implied meaning is: 'Be devoutly aware of Allāh's punishment, or Allāh's coercion, or something else of the kind."

Suppose someone said: "If the servant could ensure his own deliverance from punishment and coercion, he would make haste to do so, but he is not capable of that. As Allāh (Glory be to Him and Exalted is He) has said:

If Allāh afflicts you with some injury,
wa in yamsas-ka 'llāhu bi-ḍurrin
there is no one who can remove it but He;
fa-lā kāshifa la-hu illā Hū:
and if He desires any good for you,
wa in yurid-ka bi-khairin
there is no one who can drive away His bounty.
fa-lā rādda li-faḍli-h. (10:107)

"The command can only apply to what is practically possible, since:

No one should be charged beyond his capacity.
lā tukallafu nafsun illā wusʿa-hā. (2:233)"

To this I would reply: "The point is this: One must be devoutly on guard against the cause of sins and acts of disobedience, which emanate from the rebellious servant, so the meaning is: 'And be devoutly on guard against that which results in Allāh's punishment, and which makes His coercion inevitable, in the two abodes [this world and the Hereafter]. Beware of sinful misconduct, and hostility and disobedience towards the Messenger (Allāh bless him and give him peace), for these are the causes thereof.' The intention is thus to prohibit involvement with the causes, and to command the avoidance of them."

Someone may say: "That kind of devout awareness is possible only through Allāh's enabling grace. If He enables the servant to achieve it, there is no need for it to be commanded. If He does not enable him, he has no capacity for it, and commandment is only appropriate to what is practically possible."

My response to this will be: "First of all, Allāh (Exalted is He) has taught His servant the Truth. Secondly, He has endowed him with a partial will, by which he can make choices. Thirdly, the existence of the power of choice, within someone who acts of his own volition, is a fact that is recognized by everyone, even by the very young."[1213] (This is a very important matter, where religious doctrine is concerned.)

Allāh (Exalted is He) has then gone on to say:

Conspiracy is only of the devil,
inna-ma 'n-najwā mina 'sh-shaiṭāni
that he may sadden those who believe;
li-yaḥzuna 'lladhīna āmanū
but this cannot harm them at all, unless by Allāh's leave.
wa laisa bi-ḍārri-him shaiʾan illā bi-idhni 'llāh:
In Allāh let the believers put their trust.
wa ʿala 'llāhi fa-l'-yatawakkali 'l-muʾminūn.

As for His saying:

> Conspiracy is only of the devil,
> *inna-ma 'n-najwā mina 'sh-shaiṭāni*
> that he may sadden those who believe.
> *li-yaḥzuna 'lladhīna āmanū*

—this means: "Conspiracy for the sake of sinful misconduct and hostility is nothing but the devil's make-believe, intended to instil sadness in the believers." This emanates only from those whose conspiracy is motivated by the devil's seduction and temptation.[1214]

In the word *al-najwā* [pronounced *(a)n-najwā*], the letters *alif* and *lām* [of the definite article] cannot convey the comprehensive meaning ["all conspiracy"], because some forms of conspiracy are from Allāh and for Allāh's sake. The word must refer to the type of conspiracy described in the preceding verse: namely, conspiracy for the sake of sinful misconduct and hostility. The meaning is that the devil prompts them to engage in the kind of conspiracy that causes the believers to suffer grief. That is because, when the believers see them conspiring, they say: "Whenever we see them [conspiring like that], they have just received news that our close relatives and our brethren, who went forth on the military expeditions, have been killed and routed." That affects their hearts, and they are saddened by it.[1215]

As for His saying:

> but this cannot harm them at all, unless by Allāh's leave.
> *wa laisa bi-ḍārri-him shai'an illā bi-idhni 'llāh:*

—it signifies: "This conspiracy cannot harm the believers in the least, except by the wish of Allāh and His will."[1216]

There are actually two possible interpretations: (1) "This conspiracy cannot cause any harm to the believers." (2) "The devil cannot harm the believers at all, unless by Allāh's leave."

As for His saying:

> unless by Allāh's leave.
> *illā bi-idhni 'llāh:*

—the following interpretations have been suggested:

- "with His knowledge."
- "by His act of creation and His predetermination of sicknesses and the states of the heart, in sorrow and in joy."

• "by His demonstrating the nature of the conspiracy of the unbelievers, so that grief will pass away."

> In Allāh let the believers put their trust.
> *wa ʿala 'llāhi fa-l'-yatawakkali 'l-muʾminūn.*

—for, if someone puts his trust in Him, his hope will not be disappointed, and his earnest endeavour will not be in vain.[1217] The believers must therefore rely and depend on Allāh, and on Him Alone. They must not worry about the conspiracy of the hypocrites, for Allāh will protect them from their wickedness and their deception. In the words of the Prophetic tradition [*ḥadīth*]:

> If there are three of you, two must not conspire without including their companion, for that would make him feel sad.[1218]

An example of such conspiracy is the case where two people speak, in the presence of a third, in a language that is unintelligible to the third, if that makes him feel sad.[1219]

These are my own remarks:

From all of the above, we must understand that all disobedience stems from the lower self, because it is tyrannical by nature, and from the devil, because he is an enemy. The intelligent person must therefore not be one of those who sell their good fortune in the Hereafter, for the pleasure of the moment in this world. He must combat his lower self with scarcity of food, talk and sleep, and not give it anything at all, except by the command of the noble Sacred Law. He must also combat his devil, by refusing to lend him an ear. He must frequently practise the remembrance of Allāh (Glory be to Him and (Exalted is He). He must also be a source of safety and security for all his fellow creatures. The believer's conspiracy is with the élite of those drawn near to Him by righteousness and true devotion.

In his private retreat, the believer must say:

> Our Lord, forgive us and our brothers
> *Rabba-na 'ghfir la-nā wa li-ikhwāni-na 'lladhīna*
> who were before us in the faith, and do not lodge in our hearts
> *sabaqū-nā bi'l-īmāni wa lā tajʿal fī qulūbi-nā*
> any rancour toward those who believe.
> *ghilla 'lladhīna āmanū:*
> Our Lord, You are All-Gentle, All-Compassionate.
> *Rabba-nā inna-ka Raʾūfun Raḥīm.* (59:10)

In his public life, the believer must keep company with people from whose tongue and hand the Muslim is safe. The state of the believer must be entirely good, in his private and his public life, and in his conspiratorial mode.

We beg Allāh (Exalted is He) to grant us protection and safekeeping, and to guide us and direct us. Excellent is He, in responding to requests! Peace be upon the Messengers, and praise be to Allāh, the Lord of All the Worlds. There is no might nor any power, except with Allāh, the All-High, the Almighty. May Allāh bless our master Muḥammad, his family and his Companions, and may He grant them peace.

The Seventy-sixth Call

In the Name of Allāh, the All-Merciful, the All-Compassionate.
Bismi'llāhi 'r-Raḥmāni 'r-Raḥīm.

O you who truly believe, when it is said to you:
yā ayyuha 'lladhīna āmanū idhā qīla la-kum
"Make room in the public sessions," make room;
tafassaḥū fi 'l-majālisi fa-'fsaḥū
Allāh will make space for you.
yafsaḥi 'llāhu la-kum
And when you are told: "Rise up," rise up;
wa idhā qīla 'nshuzū fa 'nshuzū
Allāh will exalt those of you who believe,
yarfa'i 'llāhu 'lladhīna āmanū
and who have been given knowledge,
to high degrees.
min-kum wa 'lladhīna ūtu 'l-'ilma darajāt:
Allāh is Aware of what you do.
wa 'llāhu bi-mā ta'malūna Khabīr. (58:11)

O you who truly believe, when it is said to you:
yā ayyuha 'lladhīna āmanū idhā qīla la-kum
"Make room in the public sessions," make room;
tafassaḥū fi 'l-majālisi fa-'fsaḥū
Allāh will make space for you.
yafsaḥi 'llāhu la-kum

You should know that Allāh (Exalted is He), having already forbidden His believing servants to behave in ways that result in mutual hatred and aversion, has now commanded them to practise a mode of behaviour that is conducive to an increase in love and affection. He has said (Exalted is He):

Make room in the public sessions
tafassaḥū fi 'l-majālisi

In other words: "Spread out in them, and make room for one another." The expression:

> in the public sessions
> *fi 'l-majālisi*

—is grammatically plural. According to al-Wāḥidī, however: "It should be understood in the singular, because it refers to the public session [*majlis*] held by the Prophet (Allāh bless him and give him peace). The use of the plural form alludes to the fact that each participant [*jālis*] has his own place to sit [*mawḍi' julūs*]."

The experts have provided several interpretations of the Qur'ānic verse:

1. It refers to the public session held by Allāh's Messenger (Allāh bless him and give him peace). Those in attendance used to jostle one another, competing for nearness to him in their eager desire to listen to his speech. On the basis of this interpretation, the experts have given various accounts of the reason for the revelation:

• According to Muqātil ibn Ḥayyān: "One Friday, the day of congregation, the Prophet (Allāh bless him and give him peace) was in the porch, in a narrow place. He was honouring the people of Badr, the Emigrants [*Muhājirīn*] and the Helpers [*Anṣār*]. By the time some of the people of Badr arrived, others had reached the meeting before them, so they stood facing the Prophet (Allāh bless him and give him peace), waiting for space to be made available to them.

"Allāh's Messenger (Allāh bless him and give him peace) realized why they were having to stand, and that was distressing to the Messenger (Allāh bless him and give him peace). He said to those around him, who were not people of Badr: 'Stand up, O so-and-so, and you too, O so-and-so!' One by one, he kept telling those in front of him to stand up. That was a nuisance for those who had to get up from their seats, and their displeasure was apparent in their faces. The hypocrites grumbled, saying: 'By Allāh, these people have been treated unfairly. Others have taken their seats. They dearly wished to be close to him, but he has made them get up, and he has seated those who came later.' This Qur'ānic verse was thereupon revealed, on that Friday, the day of congregation."

• Ibn ʿAbbās (may Allāh be well pleased with him and his father) is reported as having said: "This Qurʾānic verse was revealed in connection with Thābit ibn Qais ibn ash-Shammās. He entered the mosque when the people had already taken their seats, and he wanted to be near to Allāh's Messenger (Allāh bless him and give him peace), because of the cavities in his ears. They made space to let him through, but then one of them gave him trouble, and words were exchanged between the two. He explained to the Messenger (Allāh bless him and give him peace) that he would like to be close to him, in order to hear what he had to say, but so-and-so would not make room for him. This Qurʾānic verse was thereupon revealed, and the people were commanded to spread out, and not to obstruct one another."

• They used to be very fond of closeness to Allāh's Messenger (Allāh bless him and give him peace). A man would be annoyed if his own space was cramped, yet he might refuse to make room for his brother, when the latter asked him to do so. That is why Allāh (Exalted is He) commanded them to treat one another kindly, and to be tolerant of what they disliked. There were some among them who disliked being touched by the poor, such as the People of the Bench [*Ahl aṣ-Ṣuffa*], who used to wear wool [*ṣūf*] and who carried strong odours.

2. The meaning is: "Make room in the assemblies of battle," as in His saying:

> positions for the battle.
> *maqāʿida li'l-qitāl.* (3:121)

When a man arrived to join the front rank, he would say: "Make room," but they would refuse, because of their eagerness for martyrdom [*shahāda*].

3. The meaning is: "[Make room in] sessions and gatherings of all kinds." According to al-Qāḍī: "The most probable reference is to the public session held by Allāh's Messenger (Allāh bless him and give him peace), because Allāh (Glory be to Him and Exalted is He) mentioned the session in a context where it must have been a well-known occasion. At the time of the revelation of the Qurʾānic verse, the only such well-known occasion was the public meeting held by the Messenger (Allāh bless him and give him peace), which excited considerable competition among those who wished to attend. Nearness to him was

regarded as a tremendous privilege, because it included the opportunity to hear him speak, and also because it conferred high status. That explains why he said (Allāh bless him and give him peace):

> Let those of you draw close to me who are endowed with faculties of understanding and intelligence.[1220]

That is why the most outstanding among his Companions used to come to the fore. Due to their great number, however, they used to cramp one another's space, so they were commanded to make room, whenever possible. That was more in keeping with endearment, and with shared participation in hearing essential information about the religion. If that behaviour was appropriate at his public meeting, the nature of the sacred struggle is such that it must require the same. Indeed, it may well be more important there, to ensure that the most formidable warrior is not left behind the front rank. The need for his advancement is urgent, so making room for him is vital. This standard can then be applied, by analogy, to sessions of learning and remembrance [*dhikr*].

As for His saying (Exalted is He):

> Allāh will make space for you.
> *yafsaḥi 'llāhu la-kum*

—this is an absolutely general statement, applying to every situation in which people need adequate space, whether in a physical location, in the provision of sustenance, in the feelings within the breast, in the grave, or in the Garden of Paradise. As you should understand, this Qur'ānic verse indicates that, whenever someone makes it easy for Allāh's servants to enter the gates of goodness and comfort, Allāh will supply him in abundance with the good things of this world and the Hereafter. The intelligent person should not restrict the import of the verse to making room in the meeting-place. It actually refers to providing the Muslim with access to all that is good, and allowing happiness to enter his heart. That is why the Prophet (Allāh bless him and give him peace) once said:

> Allāh will never stop helping the servant, so long as the servant persists in helping his Muslim brother.[1221]

Allāh has commanded the believers to behave with modest humility, and to make room in the meeting-place for anyone who wishes to sit next to the Prophet (Allāh bless him and give him peace), so that people may enjoy an equal opportunity to receive their portion from Allāh's Messenger (Allāh bless him and give him peace).[1222]

The Qur᾽ānic verse gives rise to several points of interest:

1. According to the correct interpretation, the verse applies generally to every session at which the Muslims gather for good purpose and spiritual reward. Each individual is fully entitled to his place, when he has been the first to occupy it, for the Prophet (Allāh bless him and give him peace) said:

> When someone reaches a spot where no one has arrived ahead of him, he is better entitled to it [than anyone else].

He should nevertheless make room for his brother, unless he would be gravely inconvenienced thereby, to the point of being crowded out of his spot. As reported by al-Bukhārī and Muslim, on the authority of Ibn ῾Umar (may Allāh be well pleased with him and his father), the Prophet (Allāh bless him and give him peace) also said:

> A man should not make another man get up from his seat, and then sit there himself.

According to the same authority, when the Prophet (Allāh bless him and give him peace) said that a man should not be made to give up his seat for another to occupy, he added:

> You must spread yourselves out and make room.

According to al-Bukhārī, Ibn ῾Umar did not like to have a man get up from his seat, and then sit in that man's place.

On the basis of this, the case can be stated as follows: Before a person gets up from his seat, to let someone else occupy it instead, the situation must be examined. If the spot to which he is about to move is like the first, for the purpose of hearing the speech of the Imām, there is no objection to his making the move. If it is more remote from the Imām, on the other hand, the move is to his detriment, because it entails the loss of a benefit that his rightfully his.

2. If one person orders another to set out early for the congregational mosque [*jāmi*῾], to hold a place for him to sit [when he arrives later],

there is no objection to this. When the person who gave the order arrives, the other must vacate the spot [that he has been holding for him]. This is based on the following report: Ibn Sīrīn used to send his young manservant to hold a seat for him on Friday, the day of congregation, so he would sit there until his master arrived, then he would get up and let him take his place. The same principle applies in the case of someone who sends a rug or prayer-mat, to be spread for him in a place on the floor of the mosque.

3. As related Muslim, on the authority of Abū Huraira (may Allāh be well pleased with him), the Prophet (Allāh bless him and give him peace) once said:

> If one of you gets up, then returns to his seat, he is more entitled to it [than anyone else].[1223]

As for His saying (Exalted is He):

> And when you are told: "Rise up," rise up.
> *wa idhā qīla 'nshuzū fa 'nshuzū*

—that is to say: "And when you are told: 'O believers, arise from the sitting position, and stand up to make room for others,' you must arise and stand." According to Ibn ʿAbbās (may Allāh be well pleased with him and his father), the meaning is: "When you are told: 'Arise [*irtafiʿū*],' you must arise [*fa 'rtafiʿū*]." According to the author of *al-Baḥr* [The Ocean]: "They have been commanded, first of all, to make room in the meeting-place, then, secondly, to comply with the commandment they have received there, and not to regard that as a nuisance."[1224] The expression lends itself to various interpretations:

1. "When you are told: 'Stand up to make space for the newcomer,' stand up."

2. "When you are told: 'Stand up and move away from the presence of Allāh's Messenger (Allāh bless him and give him peace), and do not spend a long time talking,' you must stand up, and not plant yourselves beside him." Allāh (Exalted is He) has said:

> Do not linger for conversation.
> *wa lā mustaʾnisīna li-ḥadīth:*
> That would cause annoyance to the Prophet.
> *inna dhālikum kāna yuʾdhi 'n-Nabiyya.* (33:53)

3. "When you are told: 'Stand up in readiness for the ritual prayer, the sacred struggle, and the performance of good deeds, and prepare yourselves for that,' you must preoccupy yourselves therewith and prepare yourselves for the task, and you must not be sluggish about it." According to aḍ-Ḍaḥḥāk and Ibn Zaid: "A certain group of people were hanging back from the ritual prayer, so they were commanded to stand up for it when it was announced." As you should also know, when Allāh (Exalted is He) forbade them to do certain things, first of all, then commanded them, secondly, to do certain things, He promised to reward them for acts of worshipful obedience, for He said (Exalted is He):

> Allāh will exalt those of you who believe,
> *yarfaʿi 'llāhu 'lladhīna āmanū*
> and who have been given knowledge, to high degrees.
> *min-kum wa 'lladhīna ūtu 'l-ʿilma darajāt:*

In other words: "Allāh will exalt the believers for compliance with the commandments of Allāh's Messenger (Allāh bless him and give him peace), and the learned amongst them in particular, to high degrees." As for what is meant by this exaltation, there are two opinions:

1. According to the first opinion, which is rarely maintained, it means elevated status in the public session held by the Messenger (Allāh bless him and give him peace).
2. According to the second, which is the well-known opinion, it means exaltation in the degrees of spiritual reward and the stages of approval.

You should know that, in commenting on His saying (Exalted is He):

> And He taught Adam all the names.
> *wa ʿallama Ādama 'l-asmāʾa kulla-hā.* (2:31)

—we have discussed the excellent virtue of knowledge at very great length. It was al-Qāḍī who said: "There is no doubt that the knowledge of the religious scholar sets his worshipful obedience on a plane transcending that of the ordinary believer. The latter should therefore be guided by the scholar in all his actions. He should not follow anyone but the scholar, because, when it comes to the nature of precaution against what is strictly unlawful and matters of dubious legality, and to the examination of the lower self, the scholar knows things of which others are quite unaware. When it comes to the nature of repentance, its timing and its attributes, he also knows things of which others are quite unaware. He is careful to observe his obligations, far more careful than others are in observing theirs. He is superior in many respects, but, just as his acts of worshipful obedience rank highly in the degree of spiritual reward, he likewise incurs immense punishment for any sins he may commit, on account of the importance of his knowledge. It is even possible that many sins that are minor, when committed by others, will count as major offences when committed by him."[1225]

It is clearly explained, in this Qur'ānic verse, that exaltation in the sight of Allāh is attained through knowledge and faith, not by winning the race for the front seats at the public sessions. In the words of the Prophetic tradition [*ḥadīth*]:

> The excellence of the religious scholar, over the ordinary worshipper, is like the excellence of the moon on the night when it is full, over all the stars and planets.[1226]

The Prophet (Allāh bless him and give him peace) is also reported as having said:

> Three groups will act as intercessors on the Day of Resurrection: the Prophets, then the religious scholars, and then the martyrs.[1227]

Exalted indeed is a station that is the mid-point between Prophethood and martyrdom, according to the testimony of Allāh's Messenger (Allāh bless him and give him peace)![1228]

> Allāh is Aware of what you do.
> *wa 'llāhu bi-mā ta'malūna Khabīr.*

That is to say: "He is Aware of those who are worthy of gracious favour and spiritual reward, as distinct from those who do not deserve them."[1229]

These are my own remarks:

The true scholar [*'ālim*] is someone who teaches you the principles of your religion, as a system of belief and as a system of legislation, including the rules concerning what is lawful [*ḥalāl*] and what is unlawful [*ḥarām*], and the real meanings of the rules. He also makes you aware of Allāh (Glory be to Him and Exalted is He), and directs your attention towards Allāh (Glory be to Him and Exalted is He), not towards himself. Whenever the scholar acquires an increase in knowledge, he experiences an increase in fear of offending Allāh. Allāh has said (Glory be to Him and Exalted is He):

> Only those of His servants fear Allāh who have knowledge.
> *inna-mā yakhsha 'llāha min ʿibādi-hi 'l-ʿulamāʾ.* (35:28)

> Or is he who is obedient in the watches of the night,
> *am-man huwa qānitun ānāʾa 'l-laili*
> bowing and standing erect, being wary of the Hereafter
> *sājidan wa qāʾiman yaḥdharu 'l-ākhirata*
> and hoping for the mercy of his Lord...?
> *wa yarjū raḥmata Rabbi-h:*
> Say: "Are they equal, those who know
> *qul hal yastawi 'lladhīna yaʿlamūna*
> and those who do not know?"
> *wa 'lladhīna lā yaʿlamūn:*
> Only those with powers of understanding
> will remember and take heed.
> *inna-mā yatadhdhakaru ulu 'l-albāb.* (39:9)

We are held responsible for putting that into practice. It is strictly incumbent upon us to shape our characters in accordance with the standards of the religion and the Qurʾān, because the Qurʾān commands us to follow the true and tolerant religion. It also commands us to make a serious effort to rid ourselves of egoism, so we must prefer our brothers to ourselves, not only in the assembly and by making room, but by doing the best we can for each and every one of them. We shall then be worthy of praise and commendation, like those referred to in His saying (Exalted is He):

> but they prefer them above themselves,
> *wa yuʾthirūna ʿalā anfusi-him*
> even if poverty becomes their lot.
> *wa law kāna bi-him khaṣāṣa.* (59:9)

If someone claims that he is fully in compliance with the Sacred Law and the pure Sunna, it is incumbent upon him to cling tight to one of the radiant branches of the Qurʾān, so that he may be one of those to whom Allāh, in His Book, has ascribed these praiseworthy characteristics. If someone makes such a claim, but without obedience and practical application, his claim goes no further than his statement, for he is obliged to carry out in practice what he has been commanded to do. The ship does not float on dry land!

O Allāh, grant us Your enabling grace, so that we may adhere to the knowledge that will increase us in active commitment, in fear and dread, and in awareness of Allāh. Praise be to Allāh, the Lord of All the Worlds! There is no power nor any strength except with Allāh, the All-High, the Almighty. May Allāh bless our master Muḥammad, and his family and his Companions, and may He grant them peace.

A rule of the Sacred Law: Concerning His saying:

> And when you are told: "Rise up," rise up.
> *wa idhā qīla 'nshuzū fa 'nshuzū*

—the erudite scholar, Ibn Kathīr, has referred to this Qur'ānic verse as: "The rule of standing up [to make room] for the newcomer." He said (may Allāh bestow His mercy upon him): "The jurists have expressed various opinions regarding the permissibility of standing for the new arrival. Some of them allow it, arguing on the strength of the Prophetic tradition [*ḥadīth*]:

> 'Stand up [to make room] for your master!'[1230]

(As I see it, this [Qur'ānic injunction] applies only to the newcomer, not to someone who stands up to make room for him. If someone's heart is infected with the desire to have people stand up for him, let him occupy his seat in the Fire of Hell! As for those who stand up for someone out of respect, whether for his knowledge, or his righteousness, or his age, this is not blameworthy as far as the person who stands up is concerned.)

"Some of them disallow it, arguing on the strength of the Prophetic tradition [*ḥadīth*]:

> 'If someone loves to have people flatter him by standing up, let him occupy his seat in the Fire of Hell![1231]

"Some of them make distinctions, saying: 'It is permissible at the time of arrival from a journey, and for the governor when he is on duty, because of the story of Sa'd ibn Mu'ādh. The Prophet (Allāh bless him and give him peace) sent him to govern the Banī Quraiẓa tribe, and when he approached them he said: "Stand and make room for your master!"'[1232] That was only for the purpose of asserting his authority."

Ibn Kathīr went on to say: "As for its adoption as a regular custom, that is one of the habits peculiar to the Persians. Among his exemplary practices [*sunan*], Allāh's Messenger (Allāh bless him and give him peace) used to sit down at the far end of the assembly, but the place where he was sitting would turn into the front of the assembly (Allāh bless him and give him peace)."[1233]

The Seventy-seventh Call

In the Name of Allāh, the All-Merciful, the All-Compassionate.
Bismi'llāhi 'r-Raḥmāni 'r-Raḥīm.

O you who truly believe,
yā ayyuha 'lladhīna āmanū
when you confer with the Messenger,
idhā nājaitumu 'r-Rasūla
offer a charitable gift before your conference.
fa-qaddimū baina yadai najwā-kum ṣadaqa:
That is better and purer for you.
dhālika khairun la-kum wa aṭhar:
But if you cannot find the means,
fa-in lam tajidū
Allāh is All-Forgiving, All-Compassionate.
fa-inna 'llāha Ghafūrun Raḥīm.

Are you afraid to offer charitable gifts
before your conference?
a-ashfaqtum an tuqaddimū
baina yadai najwā-kum ṣadaqāt:
Then, when you do not,
and Allāh has relented towards you,
fa-idh lam taf'alū wa tāba 'llāhu 'alai-kum
perform the ritual prayer and pay the alms-due
fa-aqīmu 'ṣ-ṣalāta wa ātu 'z-zakāta
and obey Allāh and His Messenger.
wa aṭī'u 'llāha wa Rasūla-h:
Allāh is Aware of what you do.
wa 'llāhu Khabīrun bi-mā ta'malūn. (58:12,13)

O you who truly believe,
yā ayyuha 'lladhīna āmanū
when you confer with the Messenger
idhā nājaitumu 'r-Rasūla

That is to say: "When you wish to converse with him (Allāh bless him and give him peace) in private."

offer a charitable gift before your conference.
fa-qaddimū baina yadai najwā-kum ṣadaqa:

In other words: "You must offer a charitable gift beforehand, in the form of a donation to the poor."[1234] This obligation contains benefits of several kinds:

1. Reverence for the Messenger (Allāh bless him and give him peace) and reverence for the privilege of conferring with him. When a person finds something difficult to obtain, he attaches great importance to it, but if he finds it easy to acquire, he regards it as insignificant.

2. Many of the poor derived benefit from that charitable donation prior to the conference.

3. It was Ibn ʿAbbās (may Allāh be well pleased with him and his father) who said: "The Muslims brought many problems to Allāh's Messenger (Allāh bless him and give him peace), to the point where they caused him a great deal of trouble, and Allāh wished to lighten the load for His Prophet (Allāh bless him and give him peace). When this Qurʾānic verse was revealed, many people became more reserved and refrained from asking questions."

4. It was Muqātil ibn Ḥayyān who said: "The rich folk outnumbered the poor at the public meeting held by the Prophet (Allāh bless him and give him peace), and they frequently engaged him in private conference. The Prophet (Allāh bless him and give him peace) eventually became displeased with the length of their sessions, so Allāh (Glory be to Him and Exalted is He) commanded the giving of a charitable donation at the time of the conference. As for the rich, they were unwilling, and as for the poor folk, they could not find anything [to give], though they yearned to sit in the company of the Messenger (Allāh bless him and give him peace). When this obligation was imposed, therefore, the status of the poor was increased in the sight of Allāh, while the status of the rich was diminished."

5. The intention is probably to lighten his load, because people with problems used to importune the Messenger (Allāh bless him and give

him peace), keeping him preoccupied during the times allotted for delivering the message to the Community, and for the performance of worship.

6. It serves to distinguish the lover of the Hereafter from the lover of this world, since money is the touchstone of motives.

As indicated by the literal meaning of the Qur'ānic verse, the offering of a charitable gift is a necessary duty, because the command is imperative. That is confirmed by His saying at the end of the verse:

> But if you cannot find the means,
> *fa-in lam tajidū*
> Allāh is All-Forgiving, All-Compassionate.
> *fa-inna 'llāha Ghafūrun Raḥīm.*

—since that would not be said of something unless its necessity ceased to exist in its absence.

According to one of the experts, however, that [charitable donation] is not strictly required, but simply recommended. He based his argument on two points:

1. Allāh's saying (Glory be to Him and Exalted is He):

> That is better and purer for you.
> *dhālika khairun la-kum wa aṭhar:*

—is applicable only to voluntary observance [*taṭawwuʿ*], not to obligatory duty [*farḍ*].

2. If it had been a strict requirement, its strict necessity would not have been removed by a sentence connected with it, that being His saying [in the follwoing verse]:

> Are you afraid to offer...?
> *a-ashfaqtum an tuqaddimū....*

The response to this argument is as follows:

1. While it is true that what is merely recommended [*mandūb*] is properly described as "better and purer," that which is strictly required [*wājib*] may also be described in those terms.

2. From the fact that the two Qur'ānic verses are linked in recitation, it does not necessarily follow that they are linked together in terms of revelation.

ʿAlī ibn Abī Ṭālib (may Allāh be well pleased with him) is reported as having said: "When the verse was sent down, Allāh's Messenger (Allāh bless him and give him peace) sent for me and said: "'What do you say about a dīnār [gold coin]?' I replied: 'They will not be able to afford it,' so he said: 'How much?' When I suggested: 'A seed or a barleycorn,' he said: 'You are very frugal [*zahīd*] indeed!'"[1235] (By this he meant: "You have very little property, so you have based your estimate on your own material situation.")

> That is better and purer for you.
> *dhālika khairun la-kum wa aṭhar:*

In other words: "That offering is better for you in your religion, and purer because charitable giving is a form of purity."[1236] That is to say: "Offering that amount to charity is better for you, O believers, than clinging on to it, and purer for yourselves than the squalor of misgiving and the filth of stinginess, arising from the love of wealth, which is a major part of the love of this world, and which is the source of every sinful error."[1237]

> But if you cannot find the means,
> *fa-in lam tajidū*
> Allāh is All-Forgiving, All-Compassionate.
> *fa-inna 'llāha Ghafūrun Raḥīm.*

This is addressed to the poor. It signifies that, if someone cannot find the means to offer a charitable gift, he will be excused, because the obligation is incumbent only on those of you who are capable of discharging it.[1238]

> Are you afraid to offer charitable gifts before your conference?
> *a-ashfaqtum an tuqaddimū baina yadai najwā-kum ṣadaqāt:*

This is a reprimand to the believers, but a gentle one, oh so gentle! It is a way of saying: "Are you afraid of poverty, O believers, if you make charitable gifts before your conference with the Messenger (Allāh bless him and give him peace)? The purpose is to convey: "Do not be afraid, for Allāh will provide for you, because He is Rich, with the treasures of the heavens and the earth at His disposal." This is a gentle reprimand, as we have explained. Then Allāh (Exalted is He) has abrogated the ruling, as a facilitation for the believers.[1239] The interrogative expression is used for the sake of emphasis. It seems that some of them abandoned the conference because of anxiety, not in opposition to the commandment.[1240]

> Then, when you do not,
> *fa-idh lam taf ʿalū*
> and Allāh has relented towards you....
> *wa tāba 'llāhu ʿalai-kum....*

That is to say: "If you do not do what you have been commanded to do, and if that is very difficult for you, and Allāh has exempted you, by allowing you to confer with him without offering a charitable gift...."[1241] There is no reason to take it as referring literally to the acceptance of repentance, since they have not been guilty of shortcoming in respect of this rule, due to the conference having taken place without the charitable donation.

It implies that their fearful apprehension is a sin that Allāh has disregarded, having viewed their ordeal as equivalent to their repentance.[1242] Allāh recognized the distress that many of them would feel, about giving the charitable offering in the future, if the obligation remained intact.

As for His saying (Exalted is He):

> and Allāh has relented towards you
> *wa tāba 'llāhu ʿalai-kum*

—it may be understood to mean: "Provided you are repentant, returning to Allāh, and perform the ritual prayer [*ṣalāt*] and pay the alms-due [*zakāt*], this imposition will be sufficient for you."[1243]

> perform the ritual prayer and pay the alms-due
> *fa-aqīmu 'ṣ-ṣalāta wa ātu 'z-zakāta*

That is to say: "Be content with dutiful observance of the ritual prayer, and payment of the obligatory alms-due."

> perform the ritual prayer
> *fa-aqīmu 'ṣ-ṣalāta*

The ritual prayer [*ṣalāt*] is a lofty connection, a valuable link and a virtuous service between the servant and the Ruler of Sempiternity [*Sulṭān al-Azal*]. Part of the value of that connection is that every spirit loves it dearly, and its modes of remembrance [*adhkār*] embrace the secrets explained in such works as *al-Futūḥāt al-Makkiyya* [The Meccan

Revelatory Disclosures]. Part of the value of those secrets is that every ecstatic rapture [*wijdān*] loves them, and that they are the invitation of the Maker of Sempiternity [*Ṣāni' al-Azal*] to the pavilion of His presence—five invitations in the day and the night to His conference, which is accessible by virtue of the heavenly ascension [*mi'rāj*]. Part of its value is that every heart yearns ardently for it, and that it entails the perpetuation of the concept of the splendour of the Maker in the heart, and the direction of the mind towards it, in order to establish obedience to the rule of Divine justice, and compliance with the Lordly statute [*an-niẓām ar-Rabbānī*].

The human being needs that perpetuation, since he is a human being because he is civilized by nature. Woe, therefore, to anyone who neglects it! Alas for anyone who is lazy about it! How ignorant is anyone who does not recognize its worth! Begone! and away with you! and ugh! and faugh! to the soul of anyone who fails to appreciate it!

As for His saying (Exalted is He):

> and pay the alms-due
> *wa ātu 'z-zakāta*

—it follows in sequence because, just as the ritual prayer [*ṣalāt*] is the pillar of the religion and its means of support, the alms-due [*zakāt*] is likewise the bridge of Islām and the means of mutual assistance between its people. Furthermore, the following preconditions must be satisfied:

- The charitable gift must be allocated to a suitable cause.
- The charitable donor must not be extravagant, so that he becomes the object of blame.
- He must not take from this person and give to that person; he must draw on his own wealth.
- He must not bestow in the expectation of gaining more in return.
- He must not be be afraid of poverty.
- He must not limit his concern to the material aspect, but should also contribute knowledge, consideration and intelligence.
- He must not enable the recipient to squander foolishly, but to spend wisely and meet essential needs.

To secure the benefit of these fine points, and sensitive awareness of these prerequisites, the Qur'ān has conferred a charitable favour on our faculties of understanding.[1244]

and obey Allāh and His Messenger.
wa aṭīʿu 'llāha wa Rasūla-h:

That is to say: "You must obey the commandment of Allāh and the commandment of His Messenger (Allāh bless him and give him peace) in all your situations."[1245]

According to the traditional commentators: "Allāh abrogated that [requirement of a charitable gift], as a relief for His servants. Ibn ʿAbbās (may Allāh be well pleased with him and his father) even said: 'That was only [in force] for an hour of the day.' It seems probable, however, that it remained in force for ten days, then it was abrogated."[1246] Since this charitable donation [*ṣadaqa*] was abrogated by the obligatory prescription of the alms-due [*zakāt*], this proves the possibility of abrogation [of a rule] before [its being applied in] practice. ʿAlī (may Allāh be well pleased with him) is reported as having said:

"There is a verse [*āya*] in Allāh's Book that no one else ever acted upon, neither before me nor after me. I had a dīnār [gold coin] with me, so I gave it to charity, then I conferred with the Messenger (Allāh bless him and give him peace)."[1247]

Let no one suppose that the absence of such action, on the part of any of the other Companions (may Allāh be well pleased with them all), was due to their general non-participation in charitable giving. Certainly not! How could it be so, when it is well known that Abū Bakr and ʿUthmān (may Allāh be well pleased with them) made charitable donations amounting to thousands of gold and silver coins at a time? How could they, or anyone of that calibre, refrain from giving a gold coin to charity? Perhaps no situation arose, that would have made conference necessary at that particular time.

In any case, this does not preclude attendance at his blessed public meeting, and conversing with him for some beneficial purpose, whether religious or worldly, without private conference, since that is a special form of conversation, and the absence of that which is special does not entail the absence of that which is general.[1248]

Allāh is Aware of what you do.
wa 'llāhu Khabīrun bi-mā taʿmalūn.

That is to say: "He is fully Acquainted with your deeds and your intentions."[1249] In other words: "He is One who knows what actions you perform, both outwardly and inwardly." No secret is kept hidden from Him, so He will recompense you for it. You must therefore do what He has commanded you to do, seeking only to obtain His good pleasure, not to make a display and gain a reputation. You must be humbly submissive towards Him, for fear of His chastisements, especially in the congregation on [Friday] the day of congregational prayer. Here is one of the Prophetic supplications [for you to repeat]:

> O Allāh, purify my heart by ridding it of hypocrisy, and my work by ridding it of ostentation, and my tongue by ridding it of lying, and my eye by ridding it of treachery. You surely know the treachery of the eyes, and what the breasts conceal!

Among all the forms of worshipful service, covered by the commandment to practise obedience in general, the ritual prayer [*ṣalāt*] and the alms-due [*zakāt*] have been singled out for specific mention. This is an indication of the height of their importance, for the ritual prayer is the chief of the physical practices, combining all the various acts of worship, such as standing, bowing, prostration and sitting, as well as the plea for refuge [*taʿawwudh*], the invocation of Allāh's Name [*basmala*], the Qurʾānic recitation, the glorification [*tasbīḥ*], the offering of praise [*taḥmīd*], the affirmation that there is no god but Allāh [*tahlīl*], the declaration of Allāh's Supreme Greatness [*takbīr*], and the invocation of blessing on the Prophet (Allāh bless him and give him peace). It also includes the supplication [*duʿāʾ*], which is the marrow of worship, and which is therefore called a *ṣalāt* [prayer; invocation of blessing], though it is referred to as the *duʿāʾ* [supplication; entreaty] in ordinary language.

The ritual prayer is an act of worshipful service [*ʿibāda*]. When someone worships Allāh by performing it, he is protected by the worshipful service of the worshipful servants [*ʿābidīn*] among the people of the heavens and the earths. If someone abandons it, on the other hand, he is deprived. Congratulations, then, to those who observe the ritual prayer, and woe to those who neglect it!

As for the alms-due [*zakāt*], it is the mother of all religious deeds involving material wealth. By it the heart is purified of the filth of stinginess, and material wealth of the rottenness of illegality. This is why the term *zakāt* can also mean "purity." Through payment of the alms-due, wealth in this world actually increases, because He has said (Exalted is He):

> Allāh has blighted usury and made charitable gifts bear fruit.
> *yamḥaqu 'llāhu 'r-ribā wa yurbi 'ṣ-ṣadaqāt.* (2:276)

It also increases in the Hereafter, because of His reward, for He has said (Exalted is He):

> He gives increase manifold to whom He will.
> *yuḍā'ifu li-man yashā'.* (2:261)

As reported on the authority of Abū Huraira (may Allāh be well pleased with him), Allāh's Messenger (Allāh bless him and give him peace) once said:

> If someone makes a charitable gift of a sack of dates, from a good crop, for Allāh accepts only what is good, Allāh will accept them on his oath—an allusion to the virtue of accepting and doing so with alacrity—then He will make them grow, just as one of you rears his colt [*fuluww*], until they are like a mountain.[1250]

(The term *fuluww* is synonymous with *muhr*, meaning a young horse.)[1251]

These are my own comments:

Reverence for the dignity of the Prophet (Allāh bless him and give him peace) is reverence for the shrines of Allāh (Exalted is He), and reverence for the shrines of Allāh (Exalted is He) is an element in the true devotion of the hearts. Reverence for the dignity of the Prophet (Allāh bless him and give him peace) must include following his immaculate Sunna, because reverence and respect are insufficient without loyalty. We entreat Allāh (Exalted is He) to grant those who revere the shrines of Allāh—and Allāh's Messenger (Allāh bless him and give him peace) is the most splendid of those shrines—the honour of following his presence (Allāh bless him and give him peace) in word and deed and state of being. That is not difficult for Allāh!

O Allāh, graciously bestow that upon us, through Your mercy, O Most Merciful of the merciful. Peace be upon the Messengers, and praise be to Allāh, the Lord of All the Worlds. There is no might nor any power, except with Allāh, the All-High, the Almighty. May Allāh bless our master Muḥammad, his family and his Companions, and may He grant them peace.

The Seventy-eighth Call

In the Name of Allāh, the All-Merciful, the All-Compassionate.
Bismi'llāhi 'r-Raḥmāni 'r-Raḥīm.

O you who truly believe,
you must practise true devotion to Allāh.
yā ayyuha 'lladhīna āmanu 'ttaqu 'llāha
And let a soul consider
wa l'-tanẓur nafsun
what it has forwarded for a day ahead.
mā qaddamat li-ghad:
And practise true devotion to Allāh.
wa 'ttaqu 'llāh:
Allāh is indeed Aware of what you do.
inna 'llāha Khabīrun bi-mā taʿmalūn.

And do not be like those who forgot Allāh,
wa lā takūnū ka-'lladhīna nasu 'llāha
so He made them forget themselves.
fa-ansā-hum anfusa-hum:
Such are the profligates.
ulāʾika humu 'l-fāsiqūn.

Not equal are the inhabitants of the Fire of Hell
lā yastawī aṣḥābu 'n-nāri
and the inhabitants of the Garden of Paradise.
wa aṣḥābu 'l-janna:
The inhabitants of the Garden of Paradise—
aṣḥābu 'l-jannati
they are the triumphantly successful ones!
humu 'l-fāʾizūn. (59:18–20)

O you who truly believe,
you must practise true devotion to Allāh.
yā ayyuha 'lladhīna āmanu 'ttaqu 'llāha
And let a soul consider what it has forwarded for a day ahead.
wa l'-tanẓur nafsun mā qaddamat li-ghad:

Allāh (Glory be to Him and Exalted is He) has already described the attributes of the hypocrites and the Jews, and what lies in store for them, in His saying (Exalted is He):

> Their adversity among themselves is very great.
> *ba'su-hum baina-hum shadīd:*
> You think of them as a whole whereas their hearts are diverse.
> *taḥsabu-hum jamī'an wa qulūbu-hum shattā:*
> That is because they are a folk who have no sense.
> *dhālika bi-anna-hum qawmun lā ya'qilūn.*
>
> In the same way as those a short time before them,
> *ka-mathali 'lladīna min qabli-him qarīban*
> they taste the terrible effects of their conduct,
> *dhāqū wabāla amri-him*
> and theirs is a painful torment.
> *wa la-hum 'ādhābun alīm.* (59:14,15)

—so He has now admonished the believers with good counsel, warning them not to be like those He has previously mentioned, and that is addressed to every soul.[1252]

> You must practise true devotion to Allāh.
> [*-u*] *'ttaqu 'llāha*

That is to say: "O you who believe with a faith that is sincere, you must practise true devotion to Allāh in everything you do, and you must not neglect your duty. You must therefore guard against sinful disobedience by means of worshipful obedience, and avoid ingratitude by means of thankfulness. You must guard against forgetfulness by means of remembrance. You must beware of being screened from Him by your actions and your attributes, by means of witnessing His actions and His attributes."[1253]

> And let a soul consider what it has forwarded for a day ahead.
> *wa l'-tanẓur nafsun mā qaddamat li-ghad:*

In other words: "Let every soul consider what righteous deeds it has sent forward to the Day of Resurrection."[1254] The letter *lām* [in *wa l'-tanẓur*] is the *lām* of the imperative mood. As for the indefinite form of the noun *nafsun* [a soul; a self], it indicates that, compared with other souls, those souls that consider their ultimate destination are very few indeed, quite without equal.

As for His saying (Exalted is He):

> what it has forwarded for a day ahead.
> *mā qaddamat li-ghad:*

—this signifies: "Let a soul examine and get to know the work it has forwarded for a day ahead." That is because, whatever you do in this world, you will see its recompense at the Resurrection. The intelligent person must therefore choose between the two rewards, for, as we are told in the Prophetic tradition [*ḥadīth*]:

> The clever person is someone who subdues his lower self, and works for what comes after death. The stupid fool is someone who lets his lower self follow its passionate desire, while expecting Allāh to meet his wishes.[1255]

> for a day ahead.
> *li-ghad:*

The day ahead is the Day of Resurrection. It is called a *ghad* [morrow; day ahead] because of the nearness of its advent. Allāh (Exalted is He) has said:

> And the matter of the Hour is but a twinkling of the eye.
> *wa mā amru 's-Sā'ati illā ka-lamḥi 'l-baṣari.* (16:77)

It seems that its nearness invites comparison with something that is only a single night away, since everything that is coming is close. The indefinite form of the word *ghadin* is intended to inspire awe and uncertainty, as if to say: "for a day ahead, of which the soul does not realize the extent of its awesomeness and terror."[1256] According to al-Ḥasan (may Allāh bestow His mercy upon him): "Allāh does not cease to bring it near, until He has made it like tomorrow." This is reminiscent of His saying (Exalted is He):

> As if it had not flourished yesterday.
> *ka-an lam taghna bi'l-ams.* (10:24)

—in which the past time is brought near. He may also have used the expression because this world, meaning our own time, is like a day, and the Hereafter is like its tomorrow, since similar conditions and rules are assigned to them both.

The Hereafter is like tomorrow because people in this world are asleep, and there is no wakefulness except at the point of death, which is the prelude to the Resurrection, as related in the traditional report [*khabar*]. Death and the Resurrection are both like the morning, where the heedless person is concerned, just as tomorrow is a morning in relation to the sleeper in the night. This indicates that this world is dark and gloomy, whereas the Hereafter is radiant with light.[1257] You must therefore call yourselves to account, before you are called to account. You must consider what you have laid in store for yourselves, in the form of righteous deeds, for the day of your return and your presentation to your Lord.

According to Imām Aḥmad, Jarīr reported that his father told him: "We were in the presence of Allāh's Messenger (Allāh bless him and give him peace) at the beginning of the day, when a group of people came to him, barefooted, wearing nothing but woollen cloaks or wraps, and girded with swords. They were all from the tribe of Muḍar. A change came over the face of Allāh's Messenger (Allāh bless him and give him peace), when he saw their state of poverty. He went indoors, then came out and gave the order to Bilāl, who duly proclaimed the call to prayer. He performed the ritual prayer [*ṣalāt*], then delivered a sermon, in which he recited:

> O humankind, practise true devotion to your Lord,
> *yā ayyuha 'n-nāsu 'ttaqū Rabba-kumu 'lladhī*
> who created you from a single soul.
> *khalaqa-kum min nafsin wāḥidatin* (4:1)

"He also recited this verse from the Sūra of Exile [*al-Ḥashr*]:

> And let a soul consider what it has forwarded for a day ahead.
> *wa l'-tanẓur nafsun mā qaddamat li-ghad:*

"Then he said:

> "Let a man make a charitable donation, whether it be a dīnār [gold coin] or a dirham [silver coin] of his, an article of his clothing, a measure of his wheat, a measure of his dried dates..., or even just a piece of a dried date.

"A man from among the Helpers [*Anṣār*] brought a bag that he could hardly carry—indeed, he could not carry it. Then other people followed, until you saw piles of food and clothing, and you saw the face of Allāh's Messenger (Allāh bless him and give him peace) aglow with joy, as if it had been gilded. He exclaimed (Allāh bless him and give him peace):

"If someone sets a good example in Islām, he will have its reward, and the reward of those who practise it after him, without their losing any part of their rewards. If someone sets a bad example in Islām, he will bear its burden, and the burden of those who practise it, without their burdens being reduced in any way."[1258]

The Qur'ānic verse contains a commandment to practise true devotion, which includes doing what He has commanded and refraining from what He has forbidden.[1259] In His saying (Exalted is He):

And practise true devotion to Allāh.
wa 'ttaqu 'llāh:
Allāh is indeed Aware of what you do.
inna 'llāha Khabīrun bi-mā ta'malūn.

—He has repeated the commandment:

And practise true devotion to Allāh.
wa 'ttaqu 'llāh:

—for the sake of emphasis, or it may be that the first instance applies to the fulfilment of duties, while the second applies to refraining from sinful acts of disobedience.[1260] It may also indicate that it is proper for everything the servant undertakes to be both preceded and concluded with true devotion.[1261] It stresses the importance of true devotion, which is Allāh's directive (Glory be to Him and Exalted is He) to the first and the last:

And We charged those who received the Book before you:
wa la-qad waṣṣaina 'lladhīna ūtu 'l-Kitāba min qabli-kum
"Be sure to practise true devotion to Allāh!"
wa iyyā-kum ani 'ttaqu 'llāh. (4:131)[1262]

Allāh is indeed Aware of what you do.
inna 'llāha Khabīrun bi-mā ta'malūn.

He is fully Aware of the hidden aspects of things, Capable of making known what creatures are incapable of telling, concerning the good and bad things they do,[1263] so He will recompense them accordingly on the Day of Recompense.

True devotion means the avoidance of everything sinful, in action or in abstinence. According to one of the elders: "True devotion means guarding oneself in this world from harmful consequences in the

Hereafter. Where the common folk are concerned, it means guarding against the harmfulness of actions. In the case of the élite, it means guarding against the harmfulness of traits of character. As for the élite of the élite, for them it means guarding against everything apart from Allāh (Exalted is He)."

As the verse also implies, when the human being dies, people say: "What has he left behind?" while the angels say: "What has he sent on ahead?"

Mālik ibn Dīnār (may Allāh the Exalted bestow His mercy upon him) is reported as having said: "I entered the cemetery of Baṣra, and there I encountered the madman Saʿdūn, so I said to him: 'How is your condition, and how are you?' 'O Mālik,' he replied, 'how is the condition of someone who wishes, every morning and night, to go on a distant journey, without any equipment, without any preparation, and without any provision, heading towards an equitable Lord, who judges between His servants?'

"Then he burst into tears, weeping intensely, so I asked him: 'What is making you weep?' He said: 'By Allāh, I have not wept out of greed for this world, nor from fear of death and tribulation. I have wept for the day that has passed from my life, without my having done good work in it. What has made me weep, by Allāh, is the shortage of provision, the distance of the journey, and the insurmountable obstacle. After that, I do not know whether I shall reach the Garden of Paradise or the Fire of Hell.'

"I said: 'People insist that you are a lunatic.' He said: 'Are you affected by the same delusion as the sons of this world?' People claim that I am a lunatic, but I have no insanity. The love of my Master has mingled with my heart, and flowed between my flesh and my blood, so I am enraptured and infatuated with His love.' 'O Saʿdūn,' said I, 'why do you not keep company with people, and relate to them socially?' To this he replied: 'Stay aloof from people, and be content with Allāh as a companion! However you choose to deal with people, you will find them to be scorpions.'"

> And do not be like those who forgot Allāh,
> *wa lā takūnū ka-'lladhīna nasu 'llāha*
> so He made them forget themselves.
> *fa-ansā-hum anfusa-hum:*

That is to say:

> And do not be
> *wa lā takūnū*

—O believers,

> like those
> *ka-'lladhīna*

—like the Jews and the hypocrites

> who forgot Allāh
> *nasu 'llāha*

—for they forgot His rights and did not accord Him His true worth. They did not observe the requirements of His commandments and His prohibitions, as they ought to be properly observed.

> so He made them forget themselves.
> *fa-ansā-hum anfusa-hum:*

In other words: "He made them forgetful of their own selves, so they did not hear what would have been useful to them, and they did not do what would have saved them."[1264]

The meaning may also be: "O company of the believers, do not be like those who abandoned the remembrance of Allāh, forsaking vigilant awareness of Him and worshipful obedience to Him, so He made them forget their own rights and attention to their own best interests."

According to Abū Ḥayyān: "This is a case of recompensing sin with sin. They abandoned the worshipful service of Allāh and compliance with His commandments, so they were punished for that by His making them forget their own interest, so they did not forward to Him anything good for their own benefit."[1265]

In His saying (Exalted is He):

> so He made them forget themselves.
> *fa-ansā-hum anfusa-hum:*

—the particle *fa-* [so] indicates causality. He has mentioned two aspects of causing to forget:

1. Because they forgot the right of Allāh, He caused them to suffer disappointment in this world, and He made them forgetful of their own

selves, so they did not perform any righteous work that could save them, nor did they refrain from any wicked work that could destroy them, and they experienced no incentive to concentrate on perfecting them.

2. Because they forgot the right of Allāh, He has shown them terrors on the Day of Resurrection, in which they will forget themselves, as when He said (Exalted is He):

> Their gaze does not return to them,
> *lā yartaddu ilai-him ṭarfu-hum*
> and their hearts are as air.
> *wa af᾽idatu-hum hawā᾽*. (14:43)

> And you will see human beings as drunkards,
> *wa tara 'n-nāsa sukārā*
> though they will not be drunkards,
> *wa mā hum bi-sukārā*
> but Allāh's torment will be very severe.
> *wa lākinna ʿadhāba 'llāhi shadīd*. (22:2)[1266]

> Such are the profligates.
> *ulā᾽ika humu 'l-fāsiqūn*.

In other words, according to Ibn Jarīr: "the disobedient sinners," or, according to Ibn Zaid: "the liars." The basic idea conveyed by *fisq* is departure, so the meaning is: "those who have departed from obedience to Allāh."[1267] They are those doomed to perish on the Day of Resurrection, and to be the losers on the Day of their ultimate return, as Allāh (Exalted is He) has said:

> O you who truly believe, let neither your possessions
> *yā ayyuha 'lladhīna āmanū lā tulhi-kum amwālu-kum*
> nor your children distract you from the remembrance of Allāh.
> *wa lā awlādu-kum ʿan dhikri 'llāh*:
> Anyone who does that, well, such are the losers.
> *wa man yafʿal dhālika fa-ulā᾽ika humu 'l-khāsirūn*. (63:9)

According to al-Ḥāfiẓ: "As Jarīr ibn ʿUthmān has informed us, Nuʿaim ibn Namḥa once said: 'This was in the sermon of Abū Bakr aṣ-Ṣiddīq [the Champion of Truth] (may Allāh be well pleased with him):

""Are you not aware that you get up in the morning, and take rest in the evening, for a term that is fixed? If someone is able to complete the term, while he is engaged in the work of Allāh (Almighty and Glorious is He), then let him do so. You will never achieve that, however, except with the help of Allāh (Almighty and Glorious is He). Some people have assigned their appointed times to other creatures, so Allāh (Almighty and Glorious is He) has forbidden you to be like them:

> And do not be like those who forgot Allāh,
> *wa lā takūnū ka-'lladhīna nasu 'llāha*
> so He made them forget themselves.
> *fa-ansā-hum anfusa-hum:*

""""Where are those brethren of yours who really understand? They have followed the course that was followed in the days of their righteous predecessors, and they have experienced misery and happiness. Where are the ancient tyrants, who built the cities and fortified them with walls? They have come to be under the rocks and the wells. This is the Book of Allāh; its miracles never cease, so take light from it for a day of darkness, and take light from its splendour and its clarity. Allāh commended our master Zakariyā (peace be upon him) and the people of his household, when He said:

> They used to vie one with the other in good deeds,
> *inna-hum kānū yusāri'ūna fi 'l-khairāti*
> and they cried to Us in longing and in fear,
> *wa yad'ūna-nā raghaban wa rahabā:*
> and were submissive unto Us.
> *wa kānū la-nā khāshi'īn.* (21:90)

""""There is no good in speech that is not for the sake of Allāh's countenance. There is no good in wealth that is not spent in support of Allāh's cause. There is no good in someone whose ignorance overwhelms his tolerance. There is no good in someone who fears, in the presence of Allāh, the blame of a critic.""""

This report has been transmitted by an excellent chain of authorities, all of them trustworthy men. As for the Shaikh of Jarīr ibn 'Uthmān, he being Nu'aim ibn Namḥa, I know of nothing to deny or confirm his reliability, except that Abū Dāwūd as-Sijistānī has declared all the Shaikhs of Jarīr to be trustworthy.[1268]

Next, after urging the believers to forward what will benefit them in the Hereafter, and condemning those who forgot the right of Allāh and obedience to Him, He has described the distance that separates the two parties, for He has said (Exalted is He):

Not equal are the inhabitants of the Fire of Hell
lā yastawī aṣḥābu 'n-nāri
and the inhabitants of the Garden of Paradise.
wa aṣḥābu 'l-janna:
The inhabitants of the Garden of Paradise—
aṣḥābu 'l-jannati
they are the triumphantly successful ones!
humu 'l-fā'izūn.

As al-Baiḍāwī has pointed out, those referred to as the inhabitants of the Garden of Paradise are those who deserve the Garden, because of their constant obedience to Allāh (Exalted is He) and their avoidance of sinful disobedence to Him. As for those referred to as the inhabitants of the Fire of Hell, they are those who deserve the Fire, because they forgot to practise true devotion and obedience to Allāh (Exalted is He), so He made them forget themselves, by causing them to suffer disappointment and withholding from them His enabling grace and His assistance.

By referring to the two parties as the inhabitants of the Garden of Paradise and the inhabitants of the Fire of Hell, He has vividly emphasized the lack of equivalence between them, in respect of Otherworldly values. The vast difference between the Garden and the Fire, and their lack of equivalence, is no mystery to anyone. Nevertheless, despite the fact that their lack of equivalence is certainly well known, Allāh (Exalted is He) has seen fit to explain the difference between them. He has done so for the purpose of drawing attention to the enormity of that difference, and in order to encourage the believers to perfect themselves by the constant practice of true devotion and obedience. He has put them in the position of someone who does not know the difference between the Garden and the Fire, and the vast gulf that separates the inhabitants of the two. He has done so because, by preferring this world and following lustful desires, they are failing to act as knowledge demands.

If someone has knowledge of something, but fails to act in accordance with his knowledge, he sinks to the level of an ignorant person, so he must be addressed in an informative manner, just as you would tell someone who disobeys his father: "He is your father!"—putting him in the position of someone who did not know him to be his father, and urging him to treat him as he ought to be treated.[1269]

The inhabitants of the Garden of Paradise—
aṣḥābu 'l-jannati
they are the triumphantly successful ones!
humu 'l-fā'izūn.

The inhabitants of the Garden of Paradise are those who will enjoy eternal happiness in the Abode of Bliss, and that is the mighty triumph.[1270]

Some useful lessons, derived from His saying (Exalted is He):

O you who truly believe,
you must practise true devotion to Allāh.
yā ayyuha 'lladhīna āmanu 'ttaqu 'llāha
And let a soul consider what it has forwarded for a day ahead.
wa l'-tanẓur nafsun mā qaddamat li-ghad:

• The first requirement of true devotion is to remember the punishment here and now, and to reflect on the good and the bad in one's conduct.

• The second requirement of true devotion is to practise vigilant awareness, and to call oneself to account. If someone fails to take account of his actions, and does not pay careful attention to his spiritual states, he will surely soon be put to shame.

• The mark of someone who considers his tomorrow is that he makes the most of his present day, and he cannot be like that, unless he reflects on the work he did yesterday. In this respect, people are of various types:

1. The type who wonders, while reflecting on his yesterday, what has been allotted to him in sempiternity.
2. The type who wonders, while reflecting on his tomorrow, what he is about to encounter.
3. The type who concentrates on his present moment, and on what is required of him at this very moment. He is completely detached from any spectator, in contact with his Lord, absorbed in the One he remembers. At the ultimate stage of remembrance [*dhikr*], the one who remembers [*dhākir*] becomes completely absorbed in the One who is remembered [*Madhkūr*]. He pays no attention to his past or his future, for the immediacy of his present moment is his sole preoccupation, to the exclusion of the rest of his time.

This explains why they say: "The Ṣūfī is the son of his moment [*ibn waqti-h*]." It means that he is preoccupied with what is most appropriate for him here and now, busy with what is required of him at this instant, submissive to what appears to him from the Unseen, without any choice of his own. If each moment makes a person happy, time for him is but a moment [*waqt*]. If each moment makes a person miserable, time for him is a protracted agony [*maqt*]. The people of heedlessness [*ghafla*] are not equivalent to the people of connectedness [*wuṣla*].

The root of every disaster is forgetting the Lord. But for forgetfulness [*nisyān*], there would be no sinful disobedience [*ʿiṣyān*]. If someone forgets to command his lower self, he will not endeavour to obtain His pardon, and he will postpone the obedience to Him that the moment demands.[1271]

These are my own remarks:

You must recite the noble Qur'ān with the strength of faith, recognizing that this speech is the speech of your Lord (Glorious is His Majesty), and that it ranks above all other speech, even above the speech of Allāh's Messenger (Allāh bless him and give him peace). You must recite with contemplation, because recitation is one thing, and contemplation is something else. Presence of heart is a third matter, for it signifies your conscious acknowledgement to Allāh (Almighty and Glorious is He) that you are reciting His splendid Book.

If you wish to derive real benefit from this recitation, you must practise frequent remembrance of Allāh. That is because, through frequent remembrance of Allāh (Exalted is He), your remembrance will become a true remembrance, your recitation of the noble Qur'ān will become a true recitation, your hearing of it will become a true hearing, and your ritual prayer will become a true ritual prayer.

You must not waste your moments in futility, for the breaths of life are jewels that can never be replaced. You must be keen to seize the moment. Do not postpone the opportunity it represents, for postponement is from the devil.

We beg Allāh (Exalted is He) to grant us the blessing of remembrance [*dhikr*], and its frequent practice with complete and constant awareness, for the sake of His Chosen Prophet (Allāh bless him and give him peace) and in honour of our noble spiritual leaders (may Allāh be well pleased with them all). Peace be upon the Messengers, and praise be to Allāh, the Lord of All the Worlds. There is no might nor any power, except with Allāh, the All-High, the Almighty. May Allāh bless our master Muḥammad, his family and his Companions, and may He grant them peace.

The Seventy-ninth Call

In the Name of Allāh, the All-Merciful, the All-Compassionate.
Bismi'llāhi 'r-Raḥmāni 'r-Raḥīm.

O you who truly believe,
yā ayyuha 'lladhīna āmanū
do not choose My enemy
and your enemy for friends,
lā tattadhidhū ʿaduwwī wa ʿaduwwa-kum awliyāʾa
treating them with affection
tulqūna ilai-him bi'l-mawaddati
when they disbelieve in that Truth
that has come to you,
wa qad kafarū bi-mā jāʾa-kum mina 'l-Ḥaqqi
driving out the Messenger and you
yukhrijūna 'r-Rasūla wa iyyā-kum
because you believe in Allāh, your Lord.
an tuʾminū bi'llāhi Rabbi-kum.

If you have come forth to strive in My cause
in kuntum kharajtum jihādan fī sabīlī
and seeking My good pleasure;
wa 'btighāʾa marḍātī
do you show them affection in secret,
tusirrūna ilai-him bi'l-mawaddati
when I am Best Aware
wa ana Aʿlamu
of what you hide and what you proclaim?
bi-mā akhfaitum wa mā aʿlantum:
Whoever does it among you,
wa man yafʿal-hu min-kum
he has surely strayed from the right path.
fa-qad ḍalla sawāʾa 's-sabīl. (60:1)

O you who truly believe,
yā ayyuha 'lladhīna āmanū
do not choose My enemy and your enemy for friends,
lā tattadhidhū ʿaduwwī wa ʿaduwwa-kum awliyāʾa
treating them with affection....
tulqūna ilai-him bi'l-mawaddati....

As you should know, there is a definite continuity between this and the preceding Sūra, in that both are concerned with explaining the situation of the Messenger (Allāh bless him and give him peace) in relation to his contemporaries among the Jews, the Christians and others. Some of them engaged in peacemaking, and acknowledged his truthfulness, including the tribe of Banu 'n-Naḍīr, who said: "By Allāh, he is the Prophet whose description we find in the Torah." Some of them denied that, however, and engaged in conflict, either explicitly or in secret, so they were with the people of Islām in outward appearance, but inwardly with the people of unbelief.

As for the continuity between the beginning [of this Sūra] and the end [of the preceding Sūra], it is clearly apparent, because the end of that [preceding] Sūra contains the praiseworthy attributes of Allāh (Exalted is He)—the Most Beautiful Names of Allāh [*Asmāʾu'llāh al-Ḥusnā*]—including Singularity [*Waḥdāniyya*] and others, while the beginning of this Sūra contains the prohibition of social intercourse with those who do not acknowledge those attributes.[1272]

This Qurʾānic verse was revealed in connection with Ḥāṭib ibn Abī Baltaʿa al-ʿAbasī. According to the author of *Kashf al-Asrār* [The Disclosure of Secrets]: "He was born in the time of Allāh's Messenger (Allāh bless him and give him peace). He was descended from al-Azd, a tribe in Yemen. He was emancipated by ʿUbaidu'llāh ibn Ḥamīd ibn Zuhair, who was killed by ʿAlī (may Allāh be well pleased with him) on the Day of Badr, as an unbeliever. Ḥāṭib used to sell food. He died in Medina, and ʿUthmān ibn ʿAffān (may Allāh be well pleased with him) conducted his funeral prayer. He was one of the Emigrants [*Muhājirīn*], and he was present at Badr and the Oath of Allegiance [*Baiʿat ar-Riḍwān*]."

([In the Qurʾānic verse] the term *ʿaduww* [enemy] refers to the unbelievers of Quraish.)

"When Allāh's Messenger (Allāh bless him and give him peace) was preparing to launch the campaign of victory [*ghazwat al-fatḥ*], in the eighth year of the Hijra, Ḥāṭib wrote to the people of Mecca: 'Allāh's Messenger (Allāh bless him and give him peace) intends to attack you, so take your precautions, for he has set out towards you with an army like the night.' He sent the letter with Sāra, the freed woman of the Banī ʿAbd al-Muṭṭalib, and he gave her ten dīnārs [gold coins] and a cloak."[1273]

According to one report, she came to the Prophet (Allāh bless him and give him peace), from Mecca to Medina, so he said (Allāh bless him and give him peace): "Have you come as a Muslim woman?" When she said no, he said: "Have you come as an Emigrant [*Muhājira*]?" When she said no, he said: "So what has brought you?" To this she replied: "The patrons departed on the Day of Badr," that is to say, they were killed on that day, "so I was faced with an urgent need." The Banī Muṭṭalib took an interest in her, clothed her, provided her with transport, and supplied her with provisions for the journey,[1274] so she returned to Mecca with Ḥāṭib's letter.

Gabriel (peace be upon him) then came down with the news, so Allāh's Messenger (Allāh bless him and give him peace) dispatched ʿAlī, ʿAmmār, Ṭalḥa, az-Zubair, Miqdād and Abū Marthad, saying: "Travel until you come to Rawḍa Khākh, a place between the two Sanctuaries. There you will find a woman in a camel-borne chair, carrying Ḥāṭib's letter to the people of Mecca, so take it from her and then leave her alone. If she refuses to hand it over, chop off her head!" She denied [having the letter on her], so ʿAlī (may Allāh be well pleased with him) drew his sword, and she promptly produced it from her headband.

It is also related that Allāh's Messenger (Allāh bless him and give him peace) granted immunity, on the day of the conquest of Mecca, to all but four of the people. She was one of the four, so he gave the order for her to be killed. Allāh's Messenger (Allāh bless him and give him peace) summoned Ḥāṭib to his presence, and said: "What motivated you to do this?" "O Messenger of Allāh," he replied, "I have never disbelieved since I accepted Islām, and I have never deceived you since I committed myself to you." (He thereby affirmed his belief in his Prophethood and his Messengership, and his compliance with his commandments and his prohibitions.) "But I was a man attached to Quraish" (an ally, in other words), "though I was not one of themselves. Some of the Emigrants with you had close relatives among them, protecting their families and their properties, but there was no one among them who would protect my family, so I wished to do them a favour. I did not act out of unbelief and apostasy from my religion, and I knew that my letter would not be of any real value to them."

Allāh's Messenger (Allāh bless him and give him peace) believed him and accepted his excuse. ʿUmar (may Allāh be well pleased with him) said: "O Messenger of Allāh, let me chop off the head of this hypocrite," but he said: "O ʿUmar, he was present at Badr, and, for all you know, Allāh may have looked upon those who were present at Badr, and said: 'Do whatever you wish, for I have forgiven you!'" When ʿUmar (may Allāh be well pleased with him) heard this, tears streamed from his eyes.[1275]

Implicit in this story is the permissibility of exposing the cover of spies, and stripping the veils from trouble-makers, if there is genuine benefit in doing so, or if their cover conceals some serious mischief.

If someone engages in illegitimate activity, but then offers a plausible pretext, it should be accepted from him, for excuses are accepted by noble people.

It is also related that, when Ḥāṭib (may Allāh be well pleased with him) heard the call:

> O you who truly believe!
> *yā ayyuha 'lladhīna āmanū*

—he swooned with joy at the address of faith, for he realized that his letter had not expelled him from faith, due to the soundness of his belief. His expression (Exalted is He):

> and your enemy
> *wa ʿaduwwa-kum*

—was proof of his sincerity, since the unbeliever is not an enemy to the hypocrite, but only to him who is sincere.[1276]

The meaning is: "O company of the believers, O you who believe in Allāh and His Messenger, do not choose the unbelievers, who are your enemies and My enemies, for friends and dear ones." The mark of faith includes hatred of Allāh's enemies, not affection and friendship for them.

treating them with affection
tulqūna ilai-him bi'l-mawaddati

That is to say: "loving them, regarding them with affection, and being friendly with them, despite the fact that they are your mortal foes."[1277] In other words: "letting them know the secrets of the Muslims, and being frank with them."[1278]

Suppose you ask: "How could He say:

Do not choose My enemy and your enemy for friends.
lā tattadhidhū ʿaduwwī wa ʿaduwwa-kum awliyāʾa

—when enmity and affection cannot be combined in one place, due to their being mutually incompatible?"

My answer will be: "The unbelievers were enemies to the believers only with regard to their hostility towards Allāh and His Messenger. That being the case, it is permissible to conceive of friendship between them in connection with worldly matters and self-centred concerns, so Allāh has forbidden that too."[1279]

Suppose you say: "Allāh (Exalted is He) has said:

My enemy
ʿaduwwī

—so why was that not sufficient for Him, without adding:

and your enemy
wa ʿaduwwa-kum

—since the enemy of Allāh is none other than the enemy of the believers?"

To this we shall reply: "The commandment is imperative because of this interconnection. The fact that someone is an enemy to the believers does not necessarily mean that he is an enemy to Allāh. As He has said Allāh (Exalted is He):

Among your wives and your children
inna min azwāji-kum wa awlādi-kum
there are enemies for you, so beware of them.
ʿaduwwan la-kum fa-'ḥdharū-hum. (64:14)"

Enmity is the opposite of friendship, and the two of them cannot coexist in one place at one time.[1280]

when they disbelieve in that Truth that has come to you
wa qad kafarū bi-mā jāʾa-kum mina 'l-Ḥaqqi

That is to say: "When the fact is that they are disbelievers in your religion and your Qur᾿ān, which Allāh has sent down to you with the clear Truth."

> driving out the Messenger and you
> *yukhrijūna 'r-Rasūla wa iyyā-kum*

In other words: "expelling Muḥammad (Allāh bless him and give him peace) from Mecca, wrongfully and because of enmity, as they also expel the believers from it." As we read in *al-Baḥr* [The Ocean]: "He mentioned the Messenger (Allāh bless him and give him peace) first, as a mark of honour for him, and because he is the root of the believers. They drove them out in the sense that they harassed them and caused them harm, until they left Mecca and moved to Medina as Emigrants [*Muhājirīn*]."

> because you believe in Allāh, your Lord.
> *an tu᾿minū bi'llāhi Rabbi-kum.*

That is to say: "on account of the fact that you believe in Allāh, the Single, the One." As He has said Allāh (Exalted is He):

> They took revenge on them
> *wa mā naqamū min-hum*
> only because they believed in Allāh,
> *illā an yu᾿minū*
> the Almighty, the Praiseworthy.
> *bi'llāhi 'l-῾Azīzi 'l-Ḥamīd.* (85:8)

> If you have come forth to strive in My cause
> *in kuntum kharajtum jihādan fī sabīlī*
> and seeking My good pleasure....
> *wa 'btighā᾿a marḍātī....*

The condition is expressed elliptically. In other words: "If you have come forth as warriors in Allāh's cause, seeking His good pleasure, do not choose my enemy and your enemy for friends." According to al-Ulūsī: "The fact that the condition is expressed elliptically indicates that its apodosis precedes it. It has been said, in effect: 'Do not choose my enemies, if you are My friends.'"[1281]

The term *jihād* means engaging in combat with the enemy, as does *mujāhada*. As stated in *at-Ta'rīfāt* [Definitions]: "It is the summons to the true religion." In *al-Mufradāt* [Technical Terms] we are told: "The definition of *jihād* and *mujāhada* is 'sparing no effort in opposing the enemy.' This applies to the struggle against the external enemy, and also to the struggle against the devil and the lower self."

In the conjunction linking:

> and seeking My good pleasure
> *wa 'btighā'a marḍātī....*

—with:

> to strive in My cause
> *jihādan fī sabīlī*

—there is an explicit statement of what would necessarily be inferred, since striving in Allāh's cause can only be for the exaltation of the religion of Allāh, not for any other purpose.[1282]

> do you show them affection in secret,
> *tusirrūna ilai-him bi'l-mawaddati*
> when I am Best Aware
> *wa ana A'lamu*
> of what you hide and what you proclaim?

That is to say: "Do you deal with them in terms of confidentiality, when I am Aware of what you do in private and in public? Nothing about you is hidden from Me, in any of your states of being." This is intended as a stern rebuke and reprimand.[1283] In other words: "What can you gain from secrecy, when there is actually no difference between secrecy and publicity, since both are alike in My knowledge, and I keep My Messenger informed of what you try to conceal?"[1284]

> Whoever does it among you,
> *wa man yaf'al-hu min-kum*
> he has surely strayed from the right path.
> *fa-qad ḍalla sawā'a 's-sabīl.*

That is to say: "If anyone befriends the enemies of Allāh, and broadcasts the secrets of the Messenger (Allāh bless him and give him peace), he has turned aside from the path of truth and rectitude."[1285]

All of this, it has been said, is a scolding aimed at Ḥāṭib, which goes to prove his excellent merit, his genuine commitment to the Messenger (Allāh bless him and give him peace), and his sincerity in his faith, because scolding is administered only by the lover to his beloved. As the saying goes: "If scolding departs, it is not true love, for love survives as long as scolding survives."[1286]

The Qur'ānic verse contains an allusion to the enmity of the lower self, passionate desire and the devil, for they hate the worshipful service of Allāh. They also hate the servants of Allāh, if they are not obedient to them in the fulfilment of their lustful appetites and the acquisition of their wishes. Enmity towards the lower self is basically implemented by weaning it of its habits, and trapping it in the prison of the sacred struggle.

The emblem of love for Allāh is hatred for Allāh's enemy. The Prophet (Allāh bless him and give him peace) once said:

> The finest of faith is love for the sake of Allāh, and hatred for the sake of Allāh.[1287]

According to Abū Ḥafṣ (may Allāh bestow His mercy upon him): "If someone loves his own self, he has chosen Allāh's enemy and his own enemy for a friend. The lower self refuses to comply with what it has been commanded to do, turns aside from the path of right guidance, and leads its lover and its follower to destruction."[1288]

The Prophet (Allāh bless him and give him peace) also said:

> Your worst enemy is your own lower self, which is there between your two sides.[1289]

Allāh conveyed to David (peace be upon him) by way of inspiration:

> You must be hostile to your lower self, for I have no other opponent in the kingdom [of the universe].

If someone is hostile to his lower self, he is upholding the Truth of Allāh, but if someone is not hostile to his lower self, he must bear this stain of disgrace. The basis of faith is friendship and enmity for the sake of Allāh. If anyone is inclined towards the unbelievers, or towards those who depart from the domain of Islām, he will be joined to their side.[1290]

These are my own comments:

We have learned that this Qur'ānic verse was revealed in connection with Ḥāṭib ibn Balta'a (may Allāh be well pleased with him), so His saying (Exalted is He):

O you who truly believe,
yā ayyuha 'lladhīna āmanū
do not choose My enemy and your enemy for friends,
lā tattadhidhū ʿaduwwī wa ʿaduwwa-kum awliyāʾa
treating them with affection
tulqūna ilai-him bi'l-mawaddati
when they disbelieve in that Truth that has come to you....
wa qad kafarū bi-mā jāʾa-kum mina 'l-Ḥaqqi....

—means: "[Do not befriend] the polytheists and the unbelievers, who are waging war on Allāh, His Messenger and the believers. Allāh has prescribed hostility and antagonism towards them. and He has forbidden the believers to choose them for friends and comrades and intimate acquaintances." He has also said (Exalted is He):

O you who truly believe,
yā ayyuha 'lladhīna āmanū
do not take the Jews and Christians for friends.
lā tattakhidhu 'l-Yahūda wa 'n-Naṣārā awliyāʾ:
They are friends one to another.
baʿḍu-hum awliyāʾu baʿḍ:
If anyone among you takes them for friends,
wa man yatawalla-hum min-kum
he is one of them.
fa-inna-hu min-hum. (5:51)

This is a stern warning and a telling threat. He has also said (Exalted is He):

O you who truly believe,
yā ayyuha 'lladhīna āmanū
do not choose unbelievers for friends, instead of the believers.
lā tattakhidhu 'l-kāfirīna awliyāʾa min dūni 'l-muʾminīn:
Would you give Allāh a clear warrant against you?
a-turīdūna an tajʿalū li'llāhi ʿalai-kum sulṭānan mubīnā. (4:144)

O you who truly believe, do not choose those who adopt
yā ayyuha 'lladhīna āmanū lā tattakhidhu 'lladhīna 'ttakhadhū
your religion as a joke and for fun.
dīna-kum huzuwan wa laʿiban. (5:57)

O you who truly believe,
yā ayyuha 'lladhīna āmanū
do not choose your fathers nor your brothers for friends,
lā tattakhidhū ābāʾa-kum wa ikhwāna-kum awliyāʾa
if they take pleasure in unbelief rather than faith.
ini 'staḥabbu 'l-kufra ʿala 'l-īmān. (9:23)

You must therefore be on your guard, O my brother, against choosing a friend and a dear one from among the unbelievers, feeling love and affection for him on account of your worldly interest. If there is no bond of faith between you and him, this friendship and affection is at odds with faith, for it is like poison to the body, killing it without its being aware of what is happening. We beseech Allāh (Exalted is He and Glorious is His Majesty) to keep the believers far removed from this condition, except when the relationship is not detrimental to the religion, and does not involve faith and religious love, the location of which is the heart. In this case it is permissible, and likewise when you deal with them from fear of their wickedness and their cunning guile. Allāh (Exalted is He) has said:

> Unless you are guarding yourselves against them,
> *illā an tattaqū min-hum*
> taking precaution.
> *tuqāh*. (3:28)

That is to say: "while your heart is secure in faith." This explains why Allāh's Messenger (Allāh bless him and give him peace) accepted the excuse of Ḥāṭib, because his dealing [with the unbelievers] was a contrivance, which did not affect his faith and his belief. It is thus incumbent on the intelligent believer, who loves Allāh and His Messenger, to withhold affection from someone who opposes the commandments of Allāh and refuses to follow His Messenger (Allāh bless him and give him peace), unless he considers it worth trying to reform that transgressor, by offering him sincere advice and directing him towards Allāh and His Messenger. If he becomes convinced, however, that his effort will not be accepted, he is obliged to abandon the person concerned, out of love for the sake of Allāh and hatred for the sake of Allāh.

We beg Allāh (Exalted is He) to grant us the support of the religion and the blessing of enabling grace. *Āmīn*. Peace be upon the Messengers, and praise be to Allāh, the Lord of All the Worlds. There is no might nor any power, except with Allāh, the All-High, the Almighty. May Allāh bless our master Muḥammad, his family and his Companions, and may He grant them peace.

The Eightieth Call

In the Name of Allāh, the All-Merciful, the All-Compassionate.
Bismi'llāhi 'r-Raḥmāni 'r-Raḥīm.

O you who truly believe,
yā ayyuha 'lladhīna āmanū
when believing women come to you as emigrants, examine them.
idhā jā'a-kumu 'l-mu'minātu muhājirātin fa-'mtaḥinū-hunn:
Allāh is Best Aware of their faith.
Allāhu a'lamu bi-īmāni-hinn
Then, if you recognize them as believers,
fa-in 'alimtumū-hunna mu'minātin
do not send them back to the unbelievers.
fa-lā tarji'ū-hunna ila 'l-kuffār:
They are not lawful for them [the unbelievers],
lā hunna ḥillun la-hum
nor are they [the unbelievers] lawful for them.
wa lā hum yaḥillūna la-hunn:
And give them [the unbelievers] what they have spent.
wa ātū-hum mā anfaqū:
And it is no sin for you to marry such women
wa lā junāḥa 'alai-kum an yankiḥū-hunna
when you have given them their dues.
idhā ātaitumū-hunna ujūra-hunn:
And do not hold to the ties of unbelieving women;
wa lā tumsikū bi-'iṣami 'l-kawāfir
and ask for what you have spent;
wa 's'alū mā anfaqtum
and let them [the unbelievers] ask for what they have spent.
wa 'l-yas'alū mā anfaqū:
That is Allāh's verdict. He judges between you.
dhālikum ḥukmu 'llāh: yaḥkumu baina-kum

Allāh is All-Knowing, All-Wise.
wa 'llāhu ʿAlīmun Ḥakīm. (60:10)

In the arrangement of the Qurʾānic verses in this Sūra, there is a clearly intelligible theme, relating to the cynic and his future prospects. There are three possibilities: (1) that he will continue in his cynicism; (2) that he is not a hopeless case, and may come to abandon his cynicism; (3) that he will indeed abandon his cynicism and surrender [to the Truth].

In these verses, Allāh (Exalted is He) has described the various situations of the cynics, and He has commanded the Muslims to deal with them, in each case, according to the demands of the particular situation.

1. The first situation is indicated by His saying (Exalted is He):

> There is a good example for you in Abraham and those with him,
> *qad kānat la-kum uswatun ḥasanatun fī Ibrāhīma wa 'lladhīna maʿa-hu*
> when they told their people: "We are guiltless of you."
> *idh qālū li-qawmi-him innā buraʾāʾu min-kum.* (60:4)

2. The second situation is indicated by His saying (Exalted is He):

> It may be that Allāh will ordain love between you
> *ʿasa 'llāhu an yajʿala baina-kum*
> and those of them with whom you are at enmity.
> *wa baina 'lladhīna ʿādaitum min-hum mawadda.* (60:7)

3. The third situation is indicated by His saying (Exalted is He):

> O you who truly believe,
> *yā ayyuha 'lladhīna āmanū*
> when believing women come to you as emigrants....
> *idhā jāʾa-kumu 'l-muʾminātu muhājirātin....*

This also conveys a subtle message, a notification, and an incitement to observe the most noble moral standards, because Allāh (Exalted is He) has commanded the believers, in dealing with those three situations, to adopt none but the best course of action, and none but the most proper way of speaking.

You must also understand that He (Exalted is He) has called them "believing women [*muʾmināt*]" for one of the following reasons: (1) They have professed the essential requirement of faith, which is the *shahāda* [testimony that there is no god but Allāh, and that Muḥammad is Allāh's Messenger], and there is no evidence of their having contradicted it. (2) They demonstrate the steadfastness of their faith under examination, when put to the test of swearing a solemn oath. The purpose of the oath is to establish their faith beyond reasonable doubt. Allāh's Messenger (Allāh bless him and give him peace) used to ask the woman under examination to say:

> By Allāh (there is no god but He), [I swear that] I have not left home because of loathing a husband. By Allāh, I have not left home because of a mere desire to move from one country to another. By Allāh (there is no god but He), I have not left home in search of worldly satisfaction. By Allāh, I have not left home for any reason except love of Allāh and His Messenger.[1291]

As for His saying (Exalted is He):

> examine them.
> *fa-'mtaḥinū-hunn.*

—this means: "Put them to the test, with something that will leave you feeling convinced." If a woman among them wished to upset her husband, it has been said, she would tell him: "I am going to emigrate to Muḥammad (Allāh bless him and give him peace)." The Prophet (Allāh bless him and give him peace) was therefore commanded to examine any woman who emigrated to him, apparently because of her faith.

The experts give differing accounts of the method by which he (Allāh bless him and give him peace) used to examine them. According to Ibn ʿAbbās (may Allāh be well pleased with him and his father): "He used to examine them by having them swear by Allāh. That is to say, provided these conditions were accepted, he would call them believing women before the examination, because of their willingness to have their faith examined. When the emigrant women arrived, they would sit in his presence (Allāh bless him and give him peace), and he would say to them (Allāh bless him and give him peace):

> "I call upon you to swear that you do not associate anything with Allāh.

"He would then recite the Qur'ānic verse to them. If they made the necessary affirmation, he would go on to say:

> I have accepted your solemn oath, so you may now get up from your seats."

ʿĀʾisha (may Allāh be well pleased with her) once said: "By Allāh, the hand of a woman never touched his hand (Allāh bless him and give him peace) during the oath-taking ceremony, except with his spoken permission."[1292]

Three aspects of faith [*īmān*] are mentioned in these Qurʾānic verses, namely:

1. The faith that is evidenced merely by affirmation with the tongue, and by the fact of emigration to us. This is referred to in His saying (Exalted is He):

> when believing women come to you as emigrants....
> *idhā jāʾa-kumu 'l-muʾminātu muhājirātin....*

In this case, faith is ascribed to them on the basis of their outward manifestation thereof.

2. The faith that is evidenced by distinctive indications, which point convincingly to full accord between their hearts and their tongues. This is referred to in His saying (Exalted is He):

> Then, if you recognize them as believers....
> *fa-in ʿalimtumū-hunna muʾminātin....*

In other words: "Then, if you are reasonably convinced of their sincerity in faith...." Reasonable conviction is sufficient proof, where the Sacred Law is concerned, and it is considered tantamount to certain knowledge.

3. The real faith that constitutes tranquillity of the heart in true and firm belief. This is referred to in His saying (Exalted is He):

> Allāh is Best Aware of their faith.
> *Allāhu aʿlamu bi-īmāni-hinn*

A valuable purpose is served by the interposition of this sentence, even though its content is a well-known and indubitable fact, because it plainly states that we have no way of comprehending the full reality of the situation. That is not within our capacity, so we must settle for the reasonable conviction obtained through examination.[1293]

> Allāh is Best Aware of their faith.
> *Allāhu aʿlamu bi-īmāni-hinn*

That is to say: "Allāh is Best Aware of their truthfulness in laying claim to faith, because He (Exalted is He) is the Supervisor of their hearts." The sentence is interposed to explain that this examination is for the benefit of the believers, not of Allāh, for He is Aware of the inner consciences, and no secret is hidden from Him.[1294]

Then, if you recognize them as believers,
fa-in ʿalimtumū-hunna muʾminātin
do not send them back to the unbelievers.
fa-lā tarjiʿū-hunna ila ʾl-kuffār:

Such recognition depends on the kind of knowledge that amounts to reasonable conviction, resulting from the solemn oath and other factors.[1295] The overall meaning is: "If you are certain of their faith, after their examination, you must not return them to their unbelieving husbands."[1296]

They are not lawful for them [the unbelievers],
lā hunna ḥillun la-hum
nor are they [the unbelievers] lawful for them.
wa lā hum yaḥillūna la-hunn:
And give them [the unbelievers] what they have spent.
wa ātū-hum mā anfaqū:

That is to say: "You must give their husbands the equivalent of what they have spent on them in the form of marriage dowers." The point is that it was stipulated, in the peace treaty of the year of al-Ḥudaibiyya, that: "If anyone comes to you [Muslims] from the people of Mecca, he must be returned to them, whereas, if anyone of you goes to Mecca, he may not return to you." They inscribed that agreement in a written document, and set their seal upon it. Then Sabīʿa bint al-Ḥārith al-Aslamiyya, a Muslim women, came along while the Prophet (Allāh bless him and give him peace) was still at al-Ḥudaibiyya. Her husband, Musāfir al-Makhrūmī (some say his name was Ṣaifī ibn ar-Rāhib), soon appeared on the scene, and he said: "O Muḥammad, you must return my wife to me, for you have just made a commitment to return to us anyone who comes to you, and this sheet of the document is not yet dry." The Qurʾānic verse was thereupon revealed, to explain that the stipulation applied to men, but not to women.

According to a report from az-Zuhrī: "A woman called Umm Kulthūm bint ʿUqba ibn Abī Muʿīṭ, an emancipated slave, came [to join the Muslims], so her people came to ask Allāh's Messenger (Allāh bless him and give him peace) to return her to them. She had fled from her husband, ʿAmr ibn al-ʿĀṣ, accompanied by her brothers, ʿAmmāra and Walīd, so the Messenger (Allāh bless him and give him peace) returned her two brothers, but kept her from them. They said: "Return her to us," but he replied (Allāh bless him and give him peace): "The stipulation was meant to apply to men, not to women."

The Messenger (Allāh bless him and give him peace) then called on her to swear a solemn oath, and she duly swore. He gave her husband what he had spent [on her marriage dower], then married her to ʿUmar (may Allāh be well pleased with him).[1297]

> They are not lawful for them [the unbelievers],
> *lā hunna ḥillun la-hum*
> nor are they [the unbelievers] lawful for them.
> *wa lā hum yaḥillūna la-hunn:*

That is to say: "The believing woman is not lawful for the polytheist [*mushrik*], nor is it lawful for the believing man to marry the polytheistic woman [*mushrika*]." According to al-Ulūsī: "The repetition is intended to reinforce and emphasize the unlawfulness involved, and to sever the connection between the believing woman and the polytheist."

> And give them [the unbelievers] what they have spent.
> *wa ātū-hum mā anfaqū:*

In other words: "You must reimburse their unbelieving husbands for what they have spent on their marriage dowers." According to the author of *al-Baḥr* [The Ocean]: "Allāh has commanded the reimbursement of the unbelieving husband for what he has spent on his wife, [but only what he has spent on her] since she accepted Islām, so that he does not suffer financial loss, as well as the loss of a wife."

> And it is no sin for you to marry such women
> *wa lā junāḥa ʿalai-kum an yankiḥū-hunna*
> when you have given them their dues.
> *idhā ātaitumū-hunna ujūra-hunn:*

That is to say: "There is no objection to your marrying these emigrant women, nor is there any sin involved, provided you have presented them with their marriage dowers."[1298] Allāh has permitted the Muslims to marry women who have emigrated from the domain of war to the domain of Islām, even if they have unbelieving husbands. That is because [their acceptance of] Islām causes divorce between them and their unbelieving husbands, and the divorce takes effect at the conclusion of their *ʿidda* [legally prescribed waiting period].[1299] Their marriage dowers are [returned to their former husbands in] compensation for the divorce.

> And do not hold to the ties of unbelieving women.
> *wa lā tumsikū bi-ʿiṣami 'l-kawāfir.*

The term *ʿiṣma* [of which *ʿiṣam* is the plural form] is applied to something that is clung to, such as a knot, for instance. The prohibition signifies: "There is no tie between you and those women, and likewise no marriage bond." According to Ibn ʿAbbās (may Allāh be well pleased with him and his father): "The tie is severed by the disparity between the two domains." It has also been said to mean: "Do not make binding contracts with unbelieving women."[1300] According to one interpretation, the meaning is: "Do not adhere to the marriage contracts of your unbelieving wives, for there is no tie between you and them, and no spousal connection. In this context, the 'tie' refers to marriage. If someone has an unbelieving wife in Mecca, he should attach no importance to her, for she is not his wife, since her 'tie' has been severed by the disparity between the two domains."

> and ask for what you have spent;
> *wa 's'alū mā anfaqtum*
> and let them [the unbelievers] ask for what they have spent.
> *wa 'l-yas'alū mā anfaqū:*

That is to say: "You must demand, O believers, what you have spent in the form of the marriage dower, if your wives join the unbelievers, and let them (meaning the polytheists) demand what they have spent on their wives who have emigrated."[1301]

According to Ibn al-ʿArabī: "What it amounts to is this: If one of the apostate Muslim women goes to the unbelievers, the unbelievers must be told: 'Hand over her marriage dower!' As for the Muslims, when one of the [formerly] unbelieving women comes to them as an emigrant Muslim woman, they must be told: 'Return her marriage dower to the unbelievers!' That strikes a fair and equitable balance between the two situations."[1302]

> That is Allāh's verdict. He judges between you.
> *dhālikum ḥukmu 'llāh: yaḥkumu baina-kum*

In other words: "That is the Law of Allāh and His fair judgment between you and your enemies;[1303] that is to say, between the Muslims and the unbelievers."[1304]

> Allāh is All-Knowing, All-Wise.
> *wa 'llāhu ʿAlīmun Ḥakīm.*

That is to say: "Where the best interests of His servants are concerned, He is All-Knowing. He is All-Wise in His legislation for them, prescribing what the utmost wisdom requires."[1305]

According to Ibn al-ʿArabī: "This verdict of Allāh was delivered specifically for that time, and with exclusive reference to that peculiar situation." According to az-Zuhrī: "Had it not been for this truce and the contract between Allāh's Messenger (Allāh bless him and give him peace) and Quraish, on the day of al-Ḥudaibiyya, the women would have been retained, but the marriage dower would not have been returned. That was how he treated those Muslims who came to him before the agreement was contracted."[1306]

In short: Examination is a path to knowledge and understanding, and the essential characters of human beings become apparent through the test of experience. You must not agree with anyone who contradicts the Truth, however little or much.[1307]

These are my own observations:

Your hereditary connection with faith and the people of faith is a tremendous honour. This is one of the greatest blessings bestowed upon you by Allāh, but this splendid honour must be crowned by your obedience to the Prophet (Allāh bless him and give him peace), because that obedience is a genuine proof of the genuineness of faith. Obedience is the test that distinguishes the truthful person from the liar. According to the noble Prophetic tradition [*ḥadīth*], recorded by Imām Muslim in his *Ṣaḥīḥ*, on the authority of our master Abū Huraira (may Allāh be well pleased with him), the Prophet (Allāh bless him and give him peace) once said:

> If someone is retarded by his conduct, his progress will not be accelerated by his family tree.

This indicates that noble lineage alone is not sufficient, and that good conduct is essential. If noble lineage is combined with active obedience, you will attain to goodness in all its many forms.

We beseech Allāh (Exalted is He) to grant us the blessing of obedience to the Prophet (Allāh bless him and give him peace) in all our states and circumstances, for He is Capable of all things, and He is Competent to grant such requests. Peace be upon the Messengers, and praise be to Allāh, the Lord of All the Worlds. There is no might nor any power, except with Allāh, the All-High, the Almighty. May Allāh bless our master Muḥammad, his family and his Companions, and may He grant them peace.

The Eighty-first Call

In the Name of Allāh, the All-Merciful, the All-Compassionate.
Bismi'llāhi 'r-Raḥmāni 'r-Raḥīm.

O you who truly believe,
do not be friendly with a folk
yā ayyuha 'lladhīna āmanū lā tatawallaw qawman
with whom Allāh is angry,
who have despaired of the Hereafter
ghaḍiba 'llāhu ʿalai-him qad yaʾisū mina 'l-ākhirati
as the unbelievers despair of those in the graves.
ka-mā yaʾisa 'l-kuffāru min aṣḥābi 'l-qubūr. (60:13)

O you who truly believe, do not be friendly with a folk
yā ayyuha 'lladhīna āmanū lā tatawallaw qawman
with whom Allāh is angry.
ghaḍiba 'llāhu ʿalai-him.

O company of the believers, do not befriend the unbelievers, the enemies of the religion! Do not choose them as dear ones and friends, whom you follow and whose opinions you accept, for they are a folk with whom Allāh is angry, and whom He has cursed.

According to al-Ḥasan al-Baṣrī (may Allāh be well pleased with him), they must be the Jews, since He [was referring to them when He] said (Exalted is He):

not [the path] of those who haved earned Your wrath.
ghairi 'l-maghḍūbi ʿalai-him. (1:7)

It was Ibn ʿAbbās (may Allāh be well pleased with him and his father) who said: "They must be the unbelievers of Quraish, because every one of them is an unbeliever with whom Allāh is angry."[1308] The obvious interpretation, however, is that this Qurʾānic verse is of general application, referring to the Jews, the Christians, and all the other unbelievers with whom Allāh is angry, and whom He has cursed, and who deserve to be banished and driven into distant exile.[1309]

The expression:

> with whom Allāh is angry
> *ghaḍiba 'llāhu ʿalai-him*

—is a relative clause that qualifies:

> a folk
> *qawman*

—and the same is true of:

> who have despaired of the Hereafter
> *qad ya'isū mina 'l-ākhirati*

They are the species of the unbelievers, because they have all earned the wrath of Allāh, and they will have no share in the mercy of the Hereafter.[1310]

As for the cause of the revelation of this Qur'ānic verse, it was that certain impoverished Muslims were supplying the Jews with information about the Muslims, in order to obtain some of their property.[1311] The despair referred to in:

> who have despaired of the Hereafter
> *qad ya'isū mina 'l-ākhirati*

—is the cessation of ambitious desire. Their hope of the Hereafter has been cut off completely, on account of their disbelief in the Afterlife, and their total lack of conviction.

The People of the Scripture do believe in the Resurrection, but they have persisted in denial, out of envy and obstinacy, because they know that they can have no share in it. This is due to their stubborn rejection of the Messenger (Allāh bless him and give him peace), even though he is described in the Torah and supported by signs. He said (Allāh bless him and give him peace):

> O company of the Jews, woe unto you! You must practise true devotion to Allāh. By Allāh—there is no god but He!—you surely know that I am Allāh's Messenger in truth, and that I have come to you with Truth. You must therefore surrender [to His Will].[1312]

By one account, the meaning is: "They have despaired—they being those Jews with whom Allāh is angry—of Allāh's reward for them in the

Hereafter, and of His gracious favour, because of their unbelief and their denial of His Messenger (Allāh bless him and give him peace), despite their knowledge that he is a Prophet [*Nabī*] for Allāh."[1313] They are well aware that he is Allāh's Messenger, and that they have spoiled their Afterlife by calling him a liar.[1314]

There are two well-known interpretations of:

> as the unbelievers despair of those in the graves.
> *ka-mā ya'isa 'l-kuffāru min aṣḥābi 'l-qubūr.*

1. That is to say: "as the living unbelievers despair of rejoining their close relatives who are in their graves, because they do not believe in a resurrection or a bringing back to life." Their conviction leaves them deprived of hope,[1315] since they do not expect to return to life again, after they die. They have been in the habit of saying, when a close relative or friend of theirs died: "This is the end of time for him, and he will never be resurrected."[1316] This interpretation has the support of Ibn ʿAbbās and al-Ḥasan al-Baṣrī (may Allāh be well pleased with them).

2. The meaning is: "as the unbeliever despairs when he dies, and beholds and contemplates his recompense." This is the interpretation of Mujāhid, ʿIkrima, Muqātil, Ibn Zaid al-Kalbī and Manṣūr, and it is the one preferred by Ibn Jarīr (may Allāh bestow His mercy upon them all).[1317]

The meaning may also be: "as those of them who have died have despaired, because they have discovered the reality of the situation." They have witnessed their exclusion from the everlasting bliss of the Hereafter, and their exposure to its painful torment. In other words, they are characterized by complete and utter despair.

It was Muqātil who said: "As soon as the unbeliever is laid in his grave, an extremely threatening angel will come to him, then ask him: 'Who is your Lord? What is your religion? Who is your Prophet?' His reply will be: 'I do not know,' so the angel will say: 'May Allāh banish you! Look and see your lodging in the Fire of Hell.'" When the unbeliever wails in loud lamentation, the angel will say: 'This is for you.' Then he will open the gate of the Garden of Paradise, and say: 'This is for those who believe in Allāh. If you had believed in your Lord, you would have settled in the Garden.' The unbeliever will suffer a painful shock. He will lose all hope, as he recognizes that he has no share in it, and despairs of the blessing of the Garden."

The Qur'ānic verse also contains an allusion to bodies that are sick, diseased and injured, since the unbelievers have despaired of escaping from the narrowness of the graves of their bad characters, and emerging into the wide space of their good attributes. While this applies to all those who erect thick barriers, there are some occupants of the graves whose condition is the reverse. The Prophet (Allāh bless him and give him peace) alluded to this distinction, when he said:

> Be in this world as if you were a stranger, or someone crossing the road, and count yourself among the occupants of the graves [*aṣḥāb al-qubūr*].[1318]

They are those who die by choice, before they experience death under compulsion, that being through complete waste-disposal [*nafā'*].* Their bodies are for their spirits like graves for the dead. We beseech Allāh to grant a fortunate conclusion, for the sake of him who is endowed with perfect leadership. May Allāh bless our master Muḥammad, his family and his Companions, and may He grant them peace.[1319]

These are my own observations:

The following nine calls [*nidā'āt*] have come from Allāh (Exalted is He) to forbid the believer to cultivate certain kinds of friendship:

> O you who truly believe, if you obey a party of those who have received
> *yā ayyuha 'lladhīna āmanū in tuṭī'ū farīqan mina 'lladhīna*
> the Book, they will make you unbelievers after your belief.
> *ūtu 'l-Kitāba yuruddū-kum ba'da īmāni-kum kāfirīn.*
> How can you disbelieve, when Allāh's signs are recited to you,
> *wa kaifa takfurūna wa antum tutlā 'alai-kum*
> and His Messenger is in your midst?
> *āyātu 'llāhi wa fī-kum Rasūlu-h:*
> And whoever holds fast to Allāh, he is indeed guided to a straight path.
> *wa man ya'taṣim bi'llāhi fa-qad hudiya ilā ṣirāṭin mustaqīm.* (3:100,101)

> O you who truly believe, do not take for intimates
> *yā ayyuha 'lladhīna āmanū lā tattakhidhū*
> others than your own folk, who would spare no pains to ruin you;
> *biṭānatan min dūni-kum lā ya'lūna-kum khabalā : waddū mā 'anittum:*
> they love to hamper you. Hatred is revealed by their mouths,
> *qad badati 'l-baghḍā'u min afwāhi-him*
> but what their breasts hide is greater.
> *wa mā tukhfī ṣudūru-hum akbar:*

* Such is the spelling in the source text. The correct rendering may be "complete annihilation [*fanā'*]," though Allāh knows best.

We have made plain for you the signs if you will understand.
qad bayyannā la-kumu 'l-āyāti in kuntum ta'qilūn. (3:118)

O you who truly believe, if you obey those who disbelieve,
yā ayyuha 'lladhīna āmanū in tuṭī'u 'lladhīna kafarū
they will make you turn back on your heels,
yaruddū-kum 'alā a'qābi-kum
and you will turn back as losers.
fa-tanqalibū khāsirīn.
But Allāh is your Protector, and He is the Best of helpers.
bali 'llāhu Mawlā-kum wa Huwa Khairu 'n-nāṣirīn. (3:149,150)

O you who truly believe, do not choose unbelievers for friends
yā ayyuha 'lladhīna āmanū lā tattakhidhu 'l-kāfirīna awliyā'a
instead of believers.
min dūni 'l-mu'minīn:
Would you give Allāh a clear warrant against you?
a-turīdūna an taj'alū li'llāhi 'alai-kum sulṭānan mubīnā. (4:144)

O you who truly believe, do not take the Jews and Christians for friends.
yā ayyuha 'lladhīna āmanū lā tattakhidhu 'l-Yahūda wa 'n-Naṣārā awliyā':
They are friends one to another.
ba'ḍu-hum awliyā'u ba'ḍ:
He among you who takes them for friends is of them.
wa man yatawalla-hum min-kum fa-inna-hu min-hum:
Allāh does not guide the wrongdoing folk.
inna 'llāha lā yahdi 'l-qawma 'ẓ-ẓālimīn. (5:51)

O you who truly believe, do not choose for friends such of those
yā ayyuha 'lladhīna āmanū lā tattakhidhu 'lladhīna 'ttakhadhū
who received the Book before you, and of the unbelievers
dīna-kum huzuwan wa la'iban mina 'lladhīna ūtu 'l-Kitāba
as make a jest and sport of your religion.
min qabli-lum wa 'l-kuffāra awliyā':
But keep your duty to Allāh if you are true believers.
wa 'ttaqu 'llāha in kuntum mu'minīn. (5:57)

O you who truly believe, do not choose your fathers nor your brothers
yā ayyuha 'lladhīna āmanū lā tattakhidhū ābā'a-kum wa ikhwāna-kum
for friends if they take pleasure in unbelief rather than faith.
awliyā'a ini 'staḥabbu 'l-kufra 'ala 'l-īmān:
Whoever of you takes them for friends, such are wrongdoers.
wa man yatawalla-hum min-kum fa-ulā'ika humu 'ẓ-ẓālimūn. (9:23)

O you who truly believe, do not choose My enemy and your enemy
yā ayyuha 'lladhīna āmanū lā tattadhidhū 'aduwwī wa 'aduwwa-kum
for friends. Do you give them friendship when they disbelieve
awliyā'a tulqūna ilai-him bi'l-mawaddati
in that Truth that has come to you, driving out the Messenger
wa qad kafarū b-mā jā'a-kum mina 'l-Ḥaqqi yukhrijūna 'r-Rasūla

and you because you believe in Allāh, your Lord?
wa iyyā-kum an tuʾminū bi'llāhi Rabbi-kum.
If you have come forth to strive in My cause and seeking My good pleasure;
in kuntum kharajtum jihādan fī sabīlī wa 'btighāʾa marḍātī
do you show them friendship in secret,
tusirrūna ilai-him bi'l-mawaddati
when I am Best Aware of what you hide and what you proclaim?
wa ana Aʿlamu bi-mā akhfaitum wa mā aʿlantum:
Whoever does it among you, he has surely strayed from the right path.
wa man yafʿal-hu min-kum fa-qad ḍalla sawāʾa 's-sabīl. (60:1)

O you who truly believe, do not be friendly with a folk
yā ayyuha 'lladhīna āmanū lā tatawallaw qawman
with whom Allāh is angry, who have despaired of the Hereafter
ghaḍiba 'llāhu ʿalai-him qad yaʾisū mina 'l-ākhirati
as the disbelievers despair of those in the tombs.
ka-mā yaʾisa 'l-kuffāru min aṣḥābi 'l-qubūr. (60:13)

This prohibition is absolute, when it applies to the unbelievers and the hypocrites. As for those whose hypocrisy is expressed in their actions, despite the existence of belief, they are likewise disobeying the commandment of Allāh and His Messenger. It is therefore incumbent upon us to refrain from befriending them, so that we do not provide them with assistance, and do not encourage Satan to tempt them. They are otherwise liable to cause the believers to deviate from the straight path.

According to a traditional account, related by Imām Aḥmad with a continuous chain of transmission, it was Abū Dharr who said: "I once came to the Prophet (Allāh bless him and give him peace) while he was in the mosque, so I sat down, and he said:

'O Abū Dharr, have you performed the ritual prayer?' When I said no, he said: 'Get up and perform the prayer.' I promptly got up and prayed, then I sat down again, and he said: 'O Abū Dharr, take refuge with Allāh from the evil of the devils of humankind and the jinn.' I said: 'O Messenger of Allāh, does the human race have devils, too?' 'Yes,' said he, 'that is why we must choose the fellowship of the righteous, because the human being must seek what is conducive to his righteousness. If a person wishes to engage in trade, he must follow the expert, in order to profit by his expertise in trading. Certain experts in religion are likewise endowed with special skill, like the seller of musk (meaning one of them who is among the people of righteousness): Either you buy from him, or he gives you a free sample, or at least you detect a fragrant scent from him.'"

We beg Allāh to enable us to follow in the footsteps of Allāh's Messenger (Allāh bless him and give him peace). Peace be upon the Messengers, and praise be to Allāh, the Lord of All the Worlds. There is no might nor any power, except with Allāh, the All-High, the Almighty. May Allāh bless our master Muḥammad, his family and his Companions, and may He grant them peace.

The Eighty-second Call

In the Name of Allāh, the All-Merciful, the All-Compassionate.
Bismi'llāhi 'r-Raḥmāni 'r-Raḥīm.

O you who truly believe,
why do you say what you do not do?
yā ayyuha 'lladhīna āmanū li-ma
taqūlūna mā lā taf'alūn:
It is most hateful in the sight of Allāh
kabura maqtan 'inda 'llāhi
that you say what you do not do.
an taqūlū mā lā taf'alūn. (61:2)

Concerning the occasion on which this Qur'ānic verse was revealed, 'Abdu'llāh ibn Salām (may Allāh be well pleased with him) is reported as having said: "Some of us, Companions of Allāh's Messenger (Allāh bless him and give him peace), were sitting together in a group. In the course of our conversation, we said: 'If we knew which deeds are dearest to Allāh, we would surely perform them!' It was then that Allāh (Exalted is He) sent down:

> All that is in the heavens glorifies Allāh,
> *sabbaḥa li'llāhi mā fi 's-samāwāti*
> and [so does] all that is in the earth,
> *wa mā fi 'l-arḍ:*
> and He is the Almighty, the All-Wise.
> *wa Huwa 'l-'Azīzu 'l-Ḥakīm.*
>
> O you who truly believe,
> *yā ayyuha 'lladhīna āmanū*
> why do you say what you do not do?
> *li-ma taqūlūna mā lā taf'alūn.* (61:1,2)"

'Abdu'llāh ibn Salām went on to say: "So Allāh's Messenger (Allāh bless him and give him peace) recited it to us."[1320]

According to the traditional commentators, the believers said: "If we knew which deeds are dearest to Allāh, we would surely perform them, and we would dedicate our possessions and ourselves to them." It was then that Allāh (Magnificent is His Majesty) sent down:

> Allāh loves those who battle for His cause in ranks,
> *inna 'llāha yuḥibbu 'lladhīna yuqātilūna fī sabīli-hi ṣaffan*
> as if they were a solid structure.
> *ka-anna-hum bunyānun marṣūṣ.* (61:4)

Allāh (Exalted is He) also sent down:

> O you who truly believe, shall I show you a commerce
> *yā ayyuha 'lladhīna āmanū hal adullu-kum ʿalā tijāratin*
> that will save you from a painful doom?
> *tunjī-kum min ʿadhābin alīm.* (61:10)

—and the succeeding verses. They were put to that test on the day of [the Battle of] Uḥud, but they turned their backs, despising death and loving worldly life, so Allāh (Glory be to Him and Exalted is He) sent down:

> Why do you say what you do not do?
> *li-ma taqūlūna mā lā tafʿalūn:*

It is said that, when Allāh (Exalted is He) informed His Messenger (Allāh bless him and give him peace) of the spiritual reward of the People of Badr, the Companions said: "If we engage in a battle, we shall surely devote all our energy to it." But they fled on the day of Uḥud, so Allāh rebuked them with this Qurʾānic verse. It was sent down in the context of fighting, by one account, because a man used to say: "I have fought," when he had not fought, and "I have provided food," when he had not provided food, and "I have struck a blow," when he had not struck a blow.[1321]

According to Qatāda and aḍ-Ḍaḥḥāk: "It was revealed in connection with some people who used to say: 'We have engaged in the sacred struggle, and we have stood the test,' when they had done nothing of the kind."

Ṣuhaib said: "A certain man had harmed the Muslims on the day of Badr, and he had killed and wounded some of them, so I killed him." A man said: "O Prophet of Allāh, I have killed so-and-so," and the Prophet (Allāh bless him and give him peace) was pleased to hear it.

Then ʿUmar ibn al-Khaṭṭāb and ʿAbd ar-Raḥmān ibn ʿAwf said: "O Ṣuhaib, why have you not told Allāh's Messenger (Allāh bless him and give him peace) that you killed so-and-so? You should tell him, because so-and-so has claimed that it was he who killed him." Ṣuhaib took this advice, and the Prophet (Allāh bless him and give him peace) said: "Is that the truth of the matter, O Abū Yaḥyā?" He said: "Yes, by Allāh, O Messenger of Allāh!" This Qurʾānic verse was thereupon revealed, concerning the pretender.[1322]

> O you who truly believe,
> *yā ayyuha 'lladhīna āmanū*
> why do you say that which you do not do?
> *li-ma taqūlūna mā lā tafʿalūn.* (61:1,2)

That is to say: "O you who have accepted Allāh and His Messenger as true, why do you say something with your tongues, when you do not act accordingly?" Or: "For what reason do you say, 'We do,' about something good and proper that you never actually do?" The interrogative expression is meant to convey disapproval and reproach.[1323]

The need to inquire is inconceivable, where Allāh is concerned, since He is Aware of all things. (This observation of ours is relevant when inquiry [*istifhām*] means the search for understanding [*fahm*]. It does not apply, however, when the purpose is to exert pressure on someone who has failed to keep his promise, or has denied the truth and persisted in falsehood.)[1324]

The target of the expression and the rebuke is, in fact, their failure to act. In aiming at their speech, He is warning against the doubling of their disobedience, by explaining that what is reprehensible is not only the failure to do the promised good, but also the making of rash promises, which they used to consider right and proper. Had it been said: "Why do you not do what you say?" this would have been taken to mean that what is reprehensible is the failure to do what was promised. The intention, however, is to declare it reprehensible for a person to attribute something good to himself, when he does not actually do it. If he states that he has done something in the past or the present, when he has not done it, he is telling a lie. If he promises to do something in the future, but he does not do it, he is committing a breach of promise. In either case, he is guilty of a blameworthy offence.

According to the author of *al-Kashshāf*: "This expression covers both lying and breach of promise. It does not apply, however, to the case where someone makes a promise, but fails to keep it because of some valid excuse, for he is not guilty of any sin."[1325]

This Qur'ānic verse makes it strictly incumbent, upon anyone who commits himself to an action involving worshipful obedience, to fulfil that commitment. When a promise is made, its fulfilment is obligatory in every case, except on account of a valid excuse.[1326] According to an authentic Prophetic tradition *ḥadīth*, recorded in the two *Ṣaḥīḥ*'s:

> The mark of the hypocrite is threefold: (1) when he makes a promise, he breaks it; (2) when he tells a tale, he is lying; and (3) when he is given a trust, he betrays it....[1327]

Mālik said: "As for what counts as a promise, let us suppose, for instance, that one man asks another man to give him a present, and he says yes to this request, but then it occurs to him that he may not do it. I wonder if that puts him under a binding obligation." I (the commentator) would say: "Yes, in the context of moral excellence and chivalrous refinement." As a general principle, breach of promise with anyone is abhorrent, and with Allāh it is even more abhorrent.

Allāh (Exalted is He) has commended those who keep their promise and fulfil their vow, for He has said [when describing the truly devout]:

> Those who fulfil their covenant
> *wa 'l-mūfūna bi-ʿahdi-him*
> when they have committed themselves to a covenant.
> *idhā ʿāhadū.* (2:177)

He has also said (Exalted is He):

> And make mention in the Book of Ishmael.
> *wa 'dhkur fi 'l-Kitābi Ismāʿīl:*
> He was a keeper of his promise,
> *inna-hu kāna ṣādiqa 'l-waʿdi*
> and he was a Messenger, a Prophet.
> *wa kāna Rasūlan Nabiyyā.* (19:54)

It was an-Nakhaʿī who said: "Three Qur'ānic verses have prevented me from telling people idle tales: (1) Allāh (Exalted is He) has said:

> Do you enjoin righteousness on other people,
> *a-ta'murūna 'n-nāsa*
> while you forget [to practise it] yourselves?
> *bi'l-birri wa tansawna anfusa-kum.* (2:44)

(2) He has said (Exalted is He):

> I do not wish to do behind your backs
> *wa mā urīdu an ukhālifa-kum*
> what I tell you not to do.
> *ilā mā anhā-kum ʿan-h.* (11:88)

—quoting the words of our master Shuʿaib (peace be upon him).

(3) He has also said (Exalted is He):

> O you who truly believe,
> *yā ayyuha 'lladhīna āmanū*
> why do you say what you do not do?
> *li-ma taqūlūna mā lā tafʿalūn.* (61:2)"

As reported by Abū Naʿīm al-Ḥāfiẓ, from the account transmitted by Mālik ibn Dīnār, on the authority of Thumāma, it was Anas ibn Mālik who said: "Allāh's Messenger (Allāh bless him and give him peace) once said:

> During a night when I was transported on a heavenly journey, I came upon some people whose lips were being clipped with scissors of fire. Whenever they were clipped, they grew back. I said: 'Who are these people, O Gabriel?' He said: 'These are the preachers of your Community, who say but do not do, and who recite the Book of Allāh, but do not act.'

It is said that one of the righteous predecessors [*salaf*] was told: "Talk to us!" but he remained silent. When he was again told: "Talk to us!" he replied: "Do you consider it proper for me to say what I do not do, and thereby precipitate the hatred of Allāh?"[1328]

> It is most hateful in the sight of Allāh
> *kabura maqtan ʿinda 'llāhi*
> that you say what you do not do.
> *an taqūlū mā lā tafʿalūn.*

The Arabic word *maqt* is synonymous with *bughḍ* [hate; hatred]. If someone deserves the hatred of Allāh, he is bound to suffer torment. According to the author of *al-Kashshāf*: "[The loathing signified by] *maqt* is the most intense kind of *bughḍ*, the most extreme and most horrible form of it. The meaning is: 'Your saying what you do not do is extremely hateful in the sight of Allāh,' and this is reminiscent of His saying (Exalted is He):

> Utterly disgusting is the word.
> *kaburat kalimatan.* (18:5)"[1329]

In other words: "Your doing this is monstruously hateful in the sight of your Lord."[1330] The expression: "It is most... [*kabura*...]" conveys the sense of great astonishment, and astonishment means that something has a tremendous impact on the hearts of the listeners. The subject of the verb *kabura* is the phrase: "that you say... [*an taqūlū*...]." The noun *maqtan*, in the accusative case, is supplied as an explanatory complement, and as an indication that saying:

> what you do not do.
> *mā lā taf'alūn.*

—is a sheer and unmitigated abhorrence, since it is utterly permeated by loathsomeness. The word *maqt* was chosen because it is more intense and more extreme than *bughḍ*. The expression *nikāḥ al-maqt* [marriage of abhorrence] is used to describe a marriage between a man and his father's ex-wife.

> in the sight of Allāh
> *'inda 'llāhi*

He did not confine Himself to describing the hatefulness as great, but referred to it in its most intense and horrible form. "In the sight of Allāh" makes it even more extreme. That is because, if the enormity of its hatefulness is established in the sight of Allāh, the One in Whose presence (Glory be to Him) everything tremendous becomes insignificant, its enormity and its intensity must be complete, beyond any doubt whatsoever. According to Ibn 'Aṭiyya: "The term *maqt* is applied to hatred [*bughḍ*] on account of sin, or suspicion [*rība*], or something vile committed by the person who is abhorred [*mamqūt*]." According to al-Mubarrad: "A man is abhorred [*mamqūt*] when everybody hates him."[1331]

The Qur'ānic verse contains several implicit indications, including the following:

• Allāh has warned the believers to beware of laying claim to spiritual stations, to which they have not attained, in case they fall into the hatred of Allāh, and deviate from the path of the Truth by making false claims.

• If someone does not fulfil his commitments, and does not pay his dues, he will not attain to Truth [*Ḥaqq*] and Reality [*Ḥaqīqa*].

• The servant [of the Lord] has no [independent power of] action, and no control, because he is a prisoner in the grip of Omnipotence, subject to the rules of the Divine Power and the dispositions of the Divine Will. If someone says: "I have done," or, "I have come," or, "I have witnessed," he has forgotten his Master and laid claim to something that is not his own. If someone attributes to himself an act of worshipful obedience, he is closer to sinful disobedience, because forgetfulness is a form of blindness.

According to the author of *at-Ta'wīlāt an-Najmiyya* [The Starry Interpretations], the meaning is:

"O counterfeit believers, why do you find fault with this world with the tongue of the outer self, and praise it with the tongue of the inner being, as evidenced by your indulgence in all kinds of animal lusts, and all sorts of physical pleasures? Why do you praise the sacred struggle with your tongues, and find fault with it in your hearts? That proves your deviation from the Truth, and your attachment to the lower self and this world, and this is most hateful in the sight of Allāh, as He has said (Exalted is He):

> It is most hateful in the sight of Allāh
> *kabura maqtan ʿinda 'llāhi*
> that you say what you do not do."[1332]
> *an taqūlū mā lā tafʿalūn.*

That is why it is said: "A display of brash self-confidence, without acknowledgment of the need for the Truth with every breath, is a sure sign of pretension, meaning the pretension of the lower self. It signifies that a person has been seduced by his lower self, into imagining that he has some say in the matter, and that his own skill is what makes things possible for him, whereas Allāh loves the renunciation of personal power and strength."

It is also said: "Allāh (Glory be to Him) has issued no sterner threat against any lapse, than when He said:

> It is most hateful in the sight of Allāh
> *kabura maqtan ʿinda 'llāhi*
> that you say what you do not do."[1333]
> *an taqūlū mā lā tafʿalūn.*

These are my own remarks:

As for those who say what they do not do, all of them have followed passionate desire. By following passionate desire, they have fallen into heedlessness, so they have stained their spirits by committing sinful acts of disobedience, and infringements and violations of the Sacred Law. Futhermore, their errant behaviour was conscious and deliberate. From error after right guidance, the only refuge is with Allāh (Exalted is He)!

My believing brother, our spirits have entered our bodies in a state of purity, while intimately acquainted with Allāh, so there are now two possibilities:

1. This spirit will grow strong, through strict adherence to the Book and the Sunna, and frequent remembrance of Allāh (Exalted is He), together with recitation of the Qur᾿ān, and rejection of the vanities of worldly life, until it seems, to the person concerned, as if he is looking at the Throne of his Lord.
2. It will flirt with passionate desire, which will prompt it to acts of disbodience and sins, committed both outwardly and inwardly, and to following the footsteps of the devil. The person concerned will thus become detached—Allāh (Exalted is He) forbid!—from the Sacred Law of Allāh, so his likeness will be the likeness of the animals.

We beg Allāh (Exalted is He) to endow us with safekeeping, steadfastness, and strict adherence to the rules of the noble Sacred Law, both outwardly and inwardly.

O Allāh, help us to remember You, to give thanks to You, and to serve You well. Do not include us among those who are heedless of Your remembrance, through Your mercy, O Most Merciful of the merciful. Peace be upon the Messengers, and praise be to Allāh, the Lord of All the Worlds. There is no might nor any power, except with Allāh, the All-High, the Almighty. May Allāh bless our master Muḥammad, his family and his Companions, and may He grant them peace.

The Eighty-third Call

In the Name of Allāh, the All-Merciful, the All-Compassionate.
Bismi'llāhi 'r-Raḥmāni 'r-Raḥīm.

O you who truly believe,
shall I show you a commerce
yā ayyuha 'lladhīna āmanū hal adullu-kum ʿalā tijāratin
that will save you from a painful torment?
tunjī-kum min ʿadhābin alīm.

You must believe in Allāh and His Messenger,
tuʾminūna bi'llāhi wa Rasūli-hi
and strive for Allāh's cause with your wealth
and your own selves.
wa tujāhidūna fī sabīli 'llāhi bi-amwāli-kum
wa anfusi-kum:
That is better for you, if you did but know.
dhālikum khairun la-kum in kuntum taʿlāmūn.

He then will forgive you your sins
and cause you to enter
yaghfir la-kum dhunūba-kum wa yudkhil-kum
Gardens beneath which rivers flow,
and pleasant dwellings
jannātin tajrī min taḥti-ha 'l-anhāru
wa masākina ṭayyibātan
in Gardens of Eden. That is the mighty triumph.
fī Jannāti ʿAdn: dhālika 'l-fawzu 'l-ʿaẓīm.

And another [blessing] that you love:
wa ukhrā tuḥibbūna-hā:
help from Allāh and a victory near at hand.
naṣrun mina 'llāhi wa fatḥun qarīb:
And give good tidings to the believers.
wa bashshiri 'l-muʾminīn. (61:10–13)

After having explained that the polytheists [*mushrikīn*] are intent on extinguishing the Light of Allāh (Exalted is He), He has commanded the believers to struggle against the enemies of the religion. He has called upon them to make material and personal sacrifice, and to wage the sacred struggle for Allāh's cause. He has also explained to them that this is the truly profitable commerce, for someone who seeks good fortune in the Two Abodes [this world and the Hereafter].[1334]

As for the occasion on which this noble Qur'ānic verse was revealed, al-Muqātil said: "It was sent down concerning ʿUthmān ibn Maẓʿūn, because he said to the Messenger (Allāh bless him and give him peace): 'If you would permit me, I would divorce Khawla and adopt the monastic way of life. I would undergo castration. I would regard meat as unlawful. I would never sleep at night, and I would never break fast in the daytime.' Allāh's Messenger (Allāh bless him and give him peace) responded by saying:

> "Marriage is part of my Sunna, and there is no monasticism in Islām. The monasticism of my Community is the sacred struggle in Allāh's cause. The castration of my Community is fasting, and you must not treat as unlawful the good things that Allāh has made lawful for you. As part of my Sunna [exemplary practice], I sleep and I keep vigil, I break fast and I fast. If anyone dislikes my Sunna, he is not one of mine.

ʿUthmān said: "By Allāh, O Prophet of Allāh, I love whatever types of commerce are dearest to Allāh, so I shall deal in them."[1335] It was then that He sent down His saying (Exalted is He):

> O you who truly believe, shall I show you a commerce
> *yā ayyuha 'lladhīna āmanū hal adullu-kum ʿalā tijāratin*
> that will save you from a painful torment?
> *tunjī-kum min ʿadhābin alīm.*

In other words: "O you who have accepted Allāh and His Messenger as true, and have believed in your Lord with real faith, shall I show you a profitable commerce, that is of splendid worth?"[1336] You should also understand that His expression:

> shall I show you...?
> *hal adullu-kum...*

—conveys an imperative meaning ["let Me show you!"], just as the question: "Will you be quiet?" is a way of saying: "Be quiet!" The

Arabic word *hal* is basically a question mark, but then its emphasis gradually shifts towards incentive and stimulus, and it becomes the mark of a command.[1337] This accounts for the apocopate form [*majzūm*] of the verb *yaghfir* in:

He will then forgive you
yaghfir la-kum

—since the optative mood is used in the apodosis to an imperative protasis.[1338]

a commerce
ʿalā tijāratin

That is the commerce between the people of faith and the presence of Allāh (Exalted is He), as He has said (Exalted is He):

Allāh has bought from the believers
inna 'llāha 'shtarā mina 'l-muʾminīna
their persons and their goods,
anfusa-hum wa amwāla-hum
the Garden [of Paradise] being theirs for the price.
bi-anna la-humu 'l-Janna. (9:111)

—and as indicated by:

You must believe in Allāh and His Messenger
tuʾminūna bi'llāhi wa Rasūli-hi

Commerce [*tijāra*] is a term for the exchange of one thing for another. Just as ordinary commerce rescues the trader from the trial of poverty, and spares him from having to endure its exigencies, the same is true of this commerce. It requires verification with the heart and confirmation with the tongue, as stated in the definition of faith, so this is why He has used the term "commerce."

Just as ordinary commerce involves profit and loss, the same applies here. If someone believes, and does righteous work, he will enjoy the reward of abundant profit and obvious prosperity. If someone shuns righteous work, on the other hand, he will suffer distress and loss that is plain to see.[1339]

a commerce that will save you
tijāratin tunjī-kum

That is to say: "It will be a cause of Allāh's salvation and deliverance for you." The qualifying phrase implies that commerce can also have the opposite result, as indicated by His saying (Exalted is He):

> They look forward to a commerce that will never be unprofitable.
> *yarjūna tijāratan lan tabūr*. (35:29)

—because unprofitability and stagnation in commerce are a painful torment for the trader. Like the accumulation of unsalable goods and having to store them, and the withholding of the payments due to him, it is a disaster in the Hereafter, for it is a losing trade. The same applies to all actions that are not in accordance with the Sacred Law and the Sunna, and which are performed for the sake of someone other than Allāh.

> from a painful torment
> *min ʿadhābin alīm*.

In other words: "from an agonizing physical torment, that being the outer aspect, and an agonizing spiritual torment, that being the experience of regret and discontent."[1340]

> You must believe in Allāh and His Messenger
> *tuʾminūna bi'llāhi wa Rasūli-hi*

It is as if they had said: "O our Lord, show it (profitable trade) to us, so that we may practise it, and so that You may save us, because of it, from the painful torment," and they were answered, by being told:

> You must believe in Allāh....
> *tuʾminūna bi'llāhi wa Rasūli-hi*....

For the sake of simplicity, when His saying (Exalted is He):

> O you who truly believe, shall I show you a commerce
> *yā ayyuha 'lladhīna āmanū hal adullu-kum ʿalā tijāratin*
> that will save you from a painful torment?
> *tunjī-kum min ʿadhābin alīm*.

—was sent down, it was not immediately accompanied by what was sent down after it. They were left with an eager longing to know and understand the nature of it, and they remained in that state for sixteen months. Then down came His saying (Exalted is He):

> You must believe in Allāh and His Messenger,
> *tuʾminūna bi'llāhi wa Rasūli-hi*
> and strive for Allāh's cause....
> *wa tujāhidūna fī sabīli 'llāhi*....

—as an explanation of the commerce [that He had offered to show them].[1341]

> and strive for Allāh's cause....
> *wa tujāhidūna fī sabīli 'llāhi....*

That is to say: "Struggle against the enemies of the religion, materially and personally, in order to exalt the Word of Allāh." According to the traditional commentators: "He has represented faith and the struggle for His cause as 'a commerce [*tijāra*].'"[1342]

In addition to these two aspects of the sacred struggle [*jihād*] (meaning faith and striving for Allāh's cause), there are three other aspects to be considered:

1. The struggle waged between the individual and his own lower self [*nafs*]. This involves the subjugation of the lower self, and preventing it from indulgence in carnal pleasures and lustful desires.
2. The struggle waged in the sphere of relations between the individual and his fellow creatures. This requires him to abandon greediness towards them, and to treat them with kindness and compassion.
3. The struggle waged in the sphere of relations between the individual and this world. This requires him to gather provision for a lengthy process, meaning his cultivation of righteousness throughout his life.

This adds up to a total of five aspects.[1343]

> with your wealth and your own selves.
> *bi-amwāli-kum wa anfusi-kum:*

If someone believes, and strives with his wealth and his own person, he is expending what he has at his disposal, and what is within his capacity.

> That is better for you, if you did but know.
> *dhālikum khairun la-kum in kuntum taʿlāmūn.*

In other words: "That which I have commanded you, in respect of belief and striving for Allāh's cause, is better for you than everything in this life, if you have any understanding and knowledge."[1344] That is to say: "If you are among the people of knowledge, for the ignorant are not accountable for their actions." Or: "If you did but know that it is better for you, belief and the sacred struggle would be dearer to you than yourselves and your possessions, so you would enjoy salvation and triumphant success." It is therefore incumbent on the intelligent person to replace what is transitory with that which is permanent, since that is better for him.[1345]

He then will forgive you your sins
and cause you to enter
yaghfir la-kum dhunūba-kum wa yudkhil-kum
Gardens beneath which rivers flow,
and pleasant dwellings
jannātin tajrī min taḥti-ha 'l-anhāru
wa masākina ṭayyibātan
in Gardens of Eden. That is the mighty triumph.
fī Jannāti ʿAdn: dhālika 'l-fawzu 'l-ʿaẓīm.

He then will forgive you your sins
yaghfir la-kum dhunūba-kum

—is a grammatical apodosis to His saying:

You must believe in Allāh and His Messenger,
tuʾminūna bi'llāhi wa Rasūli-hi
and strive for Allāh's cause....
wa tujāhidūna fī sabīli 'llāhi....

—because this amounts to an imperative command, as previously explained. It is as if He had said [using the imperative forms of the Arabic verbs]: "Believe [*āminū*] in Allāh and strive [*jāhidū*] for Allāh's cause, for then He will forgive you."[1346] The meaning is thus: "If you do that, He will forgive you your sins." In other words: "He will pardon you for them, and erase them from you by His grace."

and cause you to enter Gardens beneath which rivers flow
wa yudkhil-kum jannātin tajrī min taḥti-ha 'l-anhāru

That is to say: "He will cause you to enter parks and orchards, beneath the palaces of which flow the rivers of the Garden of Paradise."

and pleasant dwellings in Gardens of Eden.
wa masākina ṭayyibātan fī Jannāti ʿAdn:

In other words: "He will cause you to dwell in lofty palaces, in the Gardens of permanent abode."

That is the mighty triumph.
dhālika 'l-fawzu 'l-ʿaẓīm.

That is the reward that has been mentioned. It is the mighty triumph, beyond which there is no triumph, and the great and lasting happiness, after which there is no other happiness.[1347]

And another that you love:
wa ukhrā tuḥibbūna-hā:
help from Allāh and a victory near at hand.
naṣrun mina 'llāhi wa fatḥun qarīb:
And give good tidings to the believers.
wa bashshiri 'l-muʾminīn.

And another that you love
wa ukhrā tuḥibbūna-hā:

That is to say: "And another commerce in the present life, with the reward of the Hereafter." According to al-Farrāʾ, it means: "And another feature that you love in this world, together with the reward of Hereafter." The expression:

that you love
tuḥibbūna-hā:

—is something of a rebuke against the love of this present world.[1348]

help from Allāh and a victory near at hand.
naṣrun mina 'llāhi wa fatḥun qarīb:

That is to say: "He will help you against your enemies, and He will enable you to conquer Mecca." According to Ibn ʿAbbās (may Allāh be well pleased with him and his father): "It means victory over the Persians and the Byzantines."[1349]

And give good tidings to the believers.
wa bashshiri 'l-muʾminīn.

It is as if it had been said: "Believe and strive, for then Allāh will help you. And give good tidings, O Messenger of Allāh, to the believers,[1350] and give the good news, O Muḥammad, of this clear and gracious favour." According to the author of *al-Baḥr* [The Ocean]: "Having described the reward that He will bestow upon them in the Hereafter,

Allāh (Exalted is He) has also mentioned something that will delight them in the present life: namely, the fact that Allāh will enable them to conquer certain towns and countries. The best of this world is thus combined with the bliss of the Hereafter."[1351] They will receive grace and beneficence from Allāh in both domains.

This also served as a proof of the truthfulness of the Prophet (Allāh bless him and give him peace), because He foretold what would happen in the days that lay in the future, just as His Messenger (Allāh bless him and give him peace) had foretold it.[1352]

A subtle point: Allāh (Exalted is He) has explained the nature of the profit from that commerce, for He has said:

> He then will forgive you your sins
> *yaghfir la-kum dhunūba-kum*
> and cause you to enter Gardens
> *wa yudkhil-kum jannātin*

He has first mentioned the most important of all things, that being forgiveness, then, when the hearts have been freed from the dread of punishment, He has added:

> and [He will] cause you to enter Gardens
> *wa yudkhil-kum jannātin*

Then, after mentioning the Garden of Paradise and its bliss, He has gone on to say:

> and pleasant dwellings
> *wa masākina ṭayyibātan*

What will make those dwellings pleasant? Nothing less than the vision of the Lord of Truth (Glory be to Him)!

> And another that you love
> *wa ukhrā tuḥibbūna-hā:*

That is to say: "You will also have another blessing that you love."

> help from Allāh
> *naṣrun mina 'llāhi*

—on the day when faith is secure and feet are firmly established on the path of righteousness, and tomorrow on the Narrow Bridge of the Resurrection.

and a victory near at hand.
wa fatḥun qarīb:

—meaning the vision [of the Lord] and the station of nearness, or direct witnessing, or everlasting existence, as indicated by His saying:

dwelling therein forever.
khālidīna fī-hā abadā. (4:57)

And give good tidings to the believers.[1353]
wa bashshiri 'l-mu'minīn.

These are my own observations:

You must be truthful with Allāh (Exalted is He). Let your inner conscience be better than your outward appearance. Do not pay special attention to any of your fellow creatures, nor to any of your worldly and Otherworldly fortunes. You need not worry about what people say, no matter what they may say about you, so long as you are truthfully committed to the Sacred Law of Allāh (Exalted is He), in your outer conduct and your inner being. Then, even if everybody said about you—Allāh forbid!—that you were a liar in your worshipful service, their words would not subtract a single atom from your truthfulness. By the same token, even if they said about someone that he was truthful, when he was a liar in the sight of Allāh, they would not implant a single atom of truthfulness in him. The truthful person is one who is truthful in the sight of Allāh, and the liar is someone who is a liar in Allāh's sight.

We beg Allāh to gather us at the Resurrection in the company of the honest champions of truth. He is Capable of whatever He wills. Peace be upon the Messengers, and praise be to Allāh, the Lord of All the Worlds. There is no might nor any power, except with Allāh, the All-High, the Almighty. May Allāh bless our master Muḥammad, his family and his Companions, and may He grant them peace.

The Eighty-fourth Call

In the Name of Allāh, the All-Merciful, the All-Compassionate.
Bismi'llāhi 'r-Raḥmāni 'r-Raḥīm.

O you who truly believe, be Allāh's helpers,
yā ayyuha 'lladhīna āmanū kūnū anṣāra 'llāhi
even as Jesus son of Mary said to the disciples:
ka-mā qāla ʿĪsa 'bnu Maryama li'l-Ḥawāriyyīna
"Who are my helpers for Allāh's sake?"
man anṣārī ila 'llāh:
The disciples said: "We are Allāh's helpers."
qāla 'l-Ḥawāriyyūna naḥnu anṣāru 'llāhi

And a party of the Children of Israel believed,
fa-āmanat ṭāʾifatun min Banī Isrāʾīla
while a party disbelieved.
wa kafarat ṭāʾifa:
Then We supported those who believed against their enemy,
fa-ayyadna 'lladhīna āmanū ʿalā ʿaduwwi-him
and they became prevailing.
fa-aṣbaḥū ẓāhirīn. (61:14)

Allāh (Exalted is He) is here commanding His believing servants to be Allāh's helpers, in all their situations, in all their words and deeds, and with themselves and their possessions. He is also commanding them to respond to Allāh and His Messenger, just as the disciples responded to Jesus (peace be upon him), when he said:

> "Who are my helpers for Allāh's sake?"[1354]
> *man anṣārī ila 'llāh.*

—for He has said (Exalted is He):

> O you who truly believe, be Allāh's helpers
> *yā ayyuha 'lladhīna āmanū kūnū anṣāra 'llāhi*

In other words: "You must support the religion of Allāh, raise its minaret aloft,[1355] and persevere in the support you are now providing."[1356]

> even as Jesus son of Mary said to the disciples:
> *ka-mā qāla ʿĪsa 'bnu Maryama li'l-Ḥawāriyyīna*

That is to say: "Just as the disciples supported the religion of Allāh, when Jesus (peace be upon him) said to them:

> 'Who are my helpers for Allāh's sake?'
> *man anṣārī ila 'llāh.*

"In other words: 'Who will help me and be my assistant, in order to convey the summons of Allāh and support His religion?'"[1357]

Muqātil said: "This means: 'Who will keep me safe from Allāh?'" ʿAṭāʾ said: "Who will support Allāh's religion?" One of the commentators said: "Allāh has commanded the believers to help our master Muḥammad (Allāh bless him and give him peace), just as the disciples helped Jesus (peace be upon him), and it is implied that victory in the sacred struggle [*jihād*] does not belong exclusively to this Community."[1358]

> The disciples said: "We are Allāh's helpers."
> *qāla 'l-Ḥawāriyyūna naḥnu anṣāru 'llāhi*

In other words: "The followers of Jesus (peace be upon him), meaning his special band of sincere believers, who were always responsive to his call, said: 'We are the helpers of Allāh's religion.'"[1359]

The disciples [*ḥawāriyyūn*], his intimate friends and the first to believe in him, were twelve men. A man's *ḥawārī* [disciple] is his intimate friend and loyal follower. The term is derived from *ḥawar*, which signifies pure whiteness. They are said to have been fullers, meaning tradesmen who bleach [*yuḥawwirūn*] clothes, and bleaching is a whitening process.

As for those helpers [*anṣār*] who were all from the tribe of Quraish, they were our masters Abū Bakr, ʿUmar, ʿUthmān, ʿAlī, Ḥamza, Jaʿfar, Abū ʿUbaida ibn al-Jarrāḥ, ʿUthman ibn Maẓʿūn, ʿAbd ar-Raḥmān ibn ʿAwf, Saʿd ibn Abī Waqqāṣ, ʿUthman ibn ʿAwf, Ṭalḥa ibn ʿUbaidi'llāh, and az-Zubair ibn al-ʿAwwām. May Allāh be well pleased with them, one and all.

In simple terms, the [Qurʾānic] comparison signifies: "Be Allāh's helpers, as were the disciples."[1360]

In similar vein, Allāh's Messenger (Allāh bless him and give him peace) used to say, in the days of the Pilgrimage [*Ḥajj*]:

> Is there any man who will shelter me, so that I may deliver the Message of my Lord, for Quraish have prevented me from delivering the Message of my Lord?[1361]

—until Allāh (Almighty and Glorious is He) decreed that the tribe of al-Aws should leave their homes in Medina, and come to his aid. They duly paid homage to him, offered him their support, and vowed to protect him from "the black and the red,"[1362] if he would emigrate to join them [in Medina]. Once he had emigrated, along with some of his Companions, they protected him as Allāh had made them promise, and that is why Allāh and His Messenger (Allāh bless him and give him peace) called them the Helpers [*Anṣār*]. That term has thus become a proper name for them (may Allāh be well pleased with them, and may He grant them contentment).[1363]

> And a party of the Children of Israel believed,
> *fa-āmanat ṭā'ifatun min Banī Isrā'īla*
> while a party disbelieved.
> *wa kafarat ṭā'ifa:*

It was Ibn ʿAbbās (may Allāh be well pleased with him and his father) who said: "This means those who believed in the time of Jesus (peace be upon him), and those who disbelieved at that time." That is because, when Jesus (peace be upon him) was raised up to heaven, they split into three groups. One group said: "He was God, and now he has ascended." A second group said: "He was the son of God, and now He has raised him unto Himself." Another group said: "He was the servant of Allāh and His Messenger, and now He has raised him unto Himself." The latter were the Muslims.

Each of these groups acquired a party of followers, and the two unbelieving parties joined forces against the Muslim party, killing them and driving them into exile. This state of affairs continued, until Allāh dispatched Muḥammad (Allāh bless him and give him peace), and the believing party then prevailed over the unbelieving one.[1364] That is referred to in His saying (Exalted is He):

> Then We supported those who believed against their enemy
> *fa-ayyadna 'lladhīna āmanū ʿalā ʿaduwwi-him*

In other words: "We strengthened the believers against the unbelievers." It has also been said to mean: "Now We have supported the Muslims against the two groups that have gone astray," because Jesus (peace be upon him) did not fight anyone, and there was no fighting in the religion of his companions after him."[1365]

> and they became prevailing.
> *fa-aṣbaḥū ẓāhirīn.*

Mujāhid said: "This refers to those who followed Jesus." If this interpretation is correct, the meaning of the Qur'ānic verse must be: "Those who believed in Jesus (peace be upon him) prevailed over those who disbelieved in him, so they became predominant over the people of other religions."[1366]

Ibrāhīm said: "The evidence of those who believed in Jesus (peace be upon him) became prevailing through the verification of Muḥammad (Allāh bless him and give him peace), who confirmed that Jesus was the Word [*Kalima*] of Allāh and His Spirit [*Rūḥ*]."

It was al-Kalbī who said: "[They became] prevailing because of the evidence [*ḥujja*]." This coincides with the interpretation of Zaid ibn ʿAlī (may Allāh be well pleased with him),[1367] and likewise that of Qatāda, because they all quoted the traditional saying:

> You must surely know that Jesus (peace be upon him) used to sleep, whereas Allāh never sleeps, and that Jesus (peace be upon him) used to eat, whereas Allāh does not eat.[1368]

In one commentary on the Qur'ānic verse:

> Then We supported those who believed against their enemy
> *fa-ayyadna 'lladhīna āmanū ʿalā ʿaduwwi-him*
> and they became prevailing.
> *fa-aṣbaḥū ẓāhirīn.*

—we are told: "[They became prevailing] when our master Muḥammad (Allāh bless him and give him peace) caused their religion to prevail over the religion of the unbelievers." This is likewise reported by an-Nasā'ī, who notes, by way of commentary on this Qur'ānic verse. "The Community of our master Muḥammad (Allāh bless him and give him peace) will not cease to prevail, in the battle for the Truth, until the commandment of Allāh is fulfilled, while they are in that state, and until others join the fight against the False Messiah [*Dajjāl*], on the side of the True Messiah [*Masīḥ*], Mary's son Jesus (peace be upon him)."[1369]

These are my own comments:

Each and every one of the servants of Allāh (Glorious and Exalted is He) stands in need of help. Our Lord has urged us to to provide it, for He has said:

And help one another to practise piety and true devotion.
wa ta'āwanū 'ala 'l-birri wa 't-taqwā. (5:2)

As for Allāh Himself (Glorious and Exalted is He), He is Independent of the universe in its entirety, because He is the Lord of All the Worlds. His Prophet (Allāh bless him and give him peace) is supported solely by Him, for our Lord (Almighty and Glorious is He) has told him:

So if they turn their backs, say: "Allāh is enough for me.
fa-in tawallaw fa-qul ḥasbiya 'llāhu
There is no god but He. In Him I have put my trust,
lā ilāha illā Hū: 'alai-hi tawakkaltu
and He is the Lord of the Mighty Throne."
wa Huwa Rabbu 'l-'arshi 'l-'aẓīm. (9:129)

Nevertheless, Allāh (Exalted is He) has addressed the believers, requesting them to support Allāh's religion, and to be the helpers of Allāh's Messenger (Allāh bless him and give him peace), for He has said:

O you who truly believe, be Allāh's helpers.
yā ayyuha 'lladhīna āmanū kūnū anṣāra 'llāhi.

What can be the purpose of this support and assistance, except to be of benefit to us? Allāh surely loves those who direct Allāh's servants towards Allāh. When we have directed Allāh's servants, and the Community of the Chosen One [*al-Muṣṭafā*] (Allāh bless him and give him peace), towards Allāh and His Messenger, we shall have fulfilled our duty, and proved the reality of our worshipful servitude. The benefit will surely accrue to us, so we must be helpful and mutually helpful in that endeavour. For those believers who direct Allāh's servants towards Allāh, it is not appropriate to grant ingratiating favours to others. One of the blessings of communal effort is that it strengthens the weak, while the strong make progress, and but for them they would not develop.

Do not grant favours, seeking to gain more [in return].
wa lā tamnun tastakthir. (74:6)

For those who help one another, in support of the religion, it is not appropriate to grant ingratiating favours to those whom they are directing. In the words of the Prophetic saying [*ḥadīth*]:

> The Hand of Allāh is with the congregation.[1370]

We shall thus be among those described by Allāh (Glorious and Exalted is He), when He said:

> You are the best community that has ever been brought into being
> *kuntum khaira ummatin ukhrijat*
> for the sake of mankind. You enjoin what is right and fair
> *li-'n-nāsi ta'murūna bi'l-ma'rūfi*
> and you forbid what is wrong and unfair.
> *wa tanhawna 'ani 'l-munkari.* (3:110)

Such is His reward for us. Support for the religion of Allāh (Glorious and Exalted is He) is not restricted to us, however. As our Lord has said:

> Allāh will surely bring forth a people whom He loves,
> *fa-sawfa ya'ti 'llāhu bi-qawmin yuḥibbu-hum*
> and who love Him.
> *wa yuḥibbūna-hu.* (5:54)

To quote the relevant Prophetic saying [*ḥadīth*]:

> If someone sets a good example in Islām, he will be rewarded for it. He will also receive the reward of those who put his example into practice after him, without their own rewards being reduced in the slightest.

We beg Allāh to grant us enabling grace, and to keep us in compliance with Allāh's commandments and in avoidance of His prohibitions, as long as the spirit remains within the body. Peace be upon the Messengers, and praise be to Allāh, the Lord of All the Worlds. There is no might nor any power, except with Allāh, the All-High, the Almighty. May Allāh bless our master Muḥammad, his family and his Companions, and may He grant them peace.

The Eighty-fifth Call

In the Name of Allāh, the All-Merciful, the All-Compassionate.
Bismi'llāhi 'r-Raḥmāni 'r-Raḥīm.

O you who truly believe!
When the call is proclaimed
yā ayyuha 'lladhīna āmanū idhā nūdiya
for the prayer on the Day of Congregation,
li'ṣ-ṣalāti min yawmi 'l-jumuʿati
hasten to the remembrance of Allāh
fa-'sʿaw ilā dhikri 'llāhi
and leave trading aside.
wa dharu 'l-baiʿ:
That is better for you, if you did but know.
dhālikum khairun la-kum in kuntum taʿlamūn.

And when the prayer is finished,
scatter in the land,
fa-idhā quḍiyati 'ṣ-ṣalātu fa-'ntashirū fi 'l-arḍi
and seek the bounty of Allāh
wa 'btaghū min faḍli 'llāhi
and remember Allāh frequently,
wa 'dhkuru 'llāha kathīran
for then you may prosper.
laʿalla-kum tufliḥūn:

But when they spy some commerce or sport,
wa idhā raʾaw tijāratan aw lahwani 'nfaḍḍū
they break away to it and leave you standing.
ilai-hā wa tarakū-ka qā'imā:
Say: "What is with Allāh is better
qul mā ʿinda 'llāhi khairun
than sport and commerce."
mina 'l-lahwi wa mina 't-tijāra:
And Allāh is the Best of providers.
wa 'llāhu Khairu 'r-rāziqīn. (62:9–11)

As for the connection with what has gone before, it is that those who follow Judaism flee from death to the enjoyment of this world and its delights, and those who believe engage in buying and selling for the enjoyment of this world and its delights, in similar fashion. Allāh (Exalted is He) has therefore admonished them by saying:

> hasten to the remembrance of Allāh
> *fa-'s'aw ilā dhikri 'llāhi*

In other words: "to what will benefit you in the Hereafter, that being attendance at the congregational prayer, because this world and its enjoyment are fleeting, while the Hereafter and its contents are everlasting." Allāh (Exalted is He) has said:

> And the Hereafter is better and more lasting.
> *wa 'l-ākhiratu khairun wa abqā.* (87:17)

There is another aspect to the connection, for, according to one of the experts: "Allāh has declared what the Jews say false on three counts:

1. They boasted that they were Allāh's friends and His loved ones, so He declared them false by His saying:

> If you claim that you are friends of Allāh,
> *in za'amtum anna-kum*
> apart from the rest of mankind,
> *awliyā'u li'llāhi min dūni 'n-nāsi*
> then long for death, if you are truthful folk!
> *fa-tamannawu 'l-mawta in kuntum ṣādiqīn.* (62:6)

2. They boasted that they were the people of the Book, while the Arabs had no Book, so He likened them to the donkey that carries a load of tomes.

3. They boasted that they observed the Sabbath, while the Muslims had nothing like it, so Allāh (Exalted is He) ordained the Day of Congregation.

In His saying (Exalted is He):

> When [the call] is proclaimed
> *idhā nūdiya*

—the verb *nūdiya* refers to the call [*nidā'*]. (The Sacred Law assigns particular, well-known words to the call to the ritual prayer [*ṣalāt*].) In this context, it refers to the call proclaimed while the prayer leader [*imām*] is seated on the pulpit on the Day of Congregation. That is the opinion of Muqātil, and it is surely correct, because, in the time of Allāh's Messenger (Allāh bless him and give him peace), the call to prayer was invariably delivered by Bilāl at the door of the mosque, while the Prophet (blessing and peace be upon him) was seated on the pulpit. The procedure was the same during the Caliphates of Abū Bakr and ʿUmar (may Allāh be well pleased with them both).[1371] It continued until the Caliphate of our master ʿUthmān, who added another muezzin [*muʾadhdhin*] because the people had multiplied and their dwellings were far apart.[1372]

> for the prayer
> *li'ṣ-ṣalāti*

That is to say: "for the time of the ritual prayer [*waqt aṣ-ṣalāt*]," as implied by His saying (Exalted is He):

> on the Day of Congregation
> *min yawmi 'l-jumuʿati*

—since the prayer is not performed all day long, but only at the particular time of day prescribed for it.

According to al-Laith: "[Friday, the Day of] Congregation is a day singled out for the people to gather for that purpose [of praying together]." As reported by Salmān al-Fārisī (may Allāh be well pleased with him), Allāh's Messenger (Allāh bless him and give him peace) once said:

> The Day of Congregation is so called because it was on that day that Adam assembled [*jamaʿa*] his people.

Some say it is because Allāh (Exalted is He) completed the creation of things [on that day], so that all created entities were then gathered together [*ijtamʿat*].

> hasten to the remembrance of Allāh
> *fa-'sʿaw ilā dhikri 'llāhi*

That is to say: "move along," or, "walk [to it]." On the basis of this interpretation, *saʿy* [the verbal noun corresponding to the imperative verb *fa-'sʿaw*] means *mashy* [walking], not *ʿadw* [running]. The term *saʿy* signifies *taṣarruf* [engaging freely and vigorously] in any activity.

An example occurs in His saying (Exalted is He):

> Then, when he had reached the age of walking briskly with him.
> *fa-lammā balagha maʿa-hu 's-saʿya.* (37:102)

It was al-Ḥasan who said: "By Allāh, it is not about hastening on the feet, but striving with the heart, the intention, the aspiration and the like." In this context, according to some, *saʿy* means *ʿamal* [work; effort; exertion; striving], and such is the doctrine of Mālik and ash-Shāfiʿī, since that is what it signifies in the Book of Allāh. He has said (Exalted is He):

> And when he turns away, he strives in the land.
> *wa idhā tawallā saʿā fi 'l-arḍi* (2:205)

—[using the related verb *saʿā*] and He has said (Exalted is He) [using the verbal noun *saʿy*]:

> Surely your effort is dispersed.
> *inna saʿya-kum la-shattā.* (92:4)

The Prophet (Allāh bless him and give him peace) is reported as having said:

> When you approach the ritual prayer, do not approach it while you are in a hurry [*wa antum tasʿūna*], but approach it while you are in a state of calm tranquillity.[1373]

The Islāmic jurists are generally agreed that when the Prophet (Allāh bless him and give him peace) attended the congregational prayer, he always approached it in a leisurely fashion.

> to the remembrance of Allāh
> *ilā dhikri 'llāhi*

In this context, according to most of the traditional commentators, the remembrance [*dhikr*] means the sermon [*khuṭba*], though some say it means the ritual prayer [*ṣalāt*]. As for the legal rules connected with this Qurʾānic verse, they can be ascertained from the books of Islāmic jurisprudence [*fiqh*].

> and leave trading aside.
> *wa dharu 'l-baiʿ*:

According to al-Ḥasan: "When the muezzin gives the call to prayer on the Day of Congregation, it is not permissible to engage in buying and selling." According to ʿAṭāʾ: "When the sun sets [at the end of the previous day], buying and selling become unlawful." According to al-Farrāʾ: "Buying and selling become unlawful only when the call is proclaimed for prayer at the place of congregation."[1374]

The believers have been told: "Move promptly to the trading of the Hereafter, leave the trading of this world aside, and hasten to the remembrance of Allāh, for there is nothing more beneficial and more valuable."[1375]

> That is better for you
> *dhālikum khairun la-kum*

That is to say: "in the Hereafter."

> if you did but know
> *in kuntum taʿlamūn.*

—what is better for you and more righteous."[1376]

According to Jābir ibn ʿAbdi'llāh (may Allāh be well pleased with him and his father): "Allāh's Messenger (Allāh bless him and give him peace) once delivered a sermon to us, in which he said:

> O people, repent to Allāh before you die. Press ahead with righteous works, before you are distracted. Close the gap between you and your Lord, by your frequent remembrance of Him, and by much charitable giving, in private and in public. You will then be sustained, helped and restored. You must also know that Allāh has prescribed the congregational prayer for you, in this place of mine, on this day of mine, in this month of mine, in this year of mine, until the Day of Resurrection. If anyone forsakes it in my lifetime, or after me, when he has a prayer leader [*imām*] who may be just or unjust, treating it as insignificant and dismissing it, Allāh will not bring things together for him, nor will He bless him in his business. Surely he will have no ritual prayer to his credit. Surely he will have no alms-due to his credit. Surely he will have no pilgrimage to his credit. Surely he will have no fast to his credit. Surely he will have no piety to his credit. Not unless he repents, for if someone repents, Allāh will relent towards him."[1377]

As for the first Friday congregation, it was convened by Allāh's Messenger (Allāh bless him and give him peace). When he moved to Medina as an emigrant, he broke his journey at Qubāʾ, home to the clan of ʿAmr ibn ʿAwf, on Monday the 12th of Rabīʿ al-Awwal, well into the forenoon. The Islāmic calendar is reckoned from the date of that *sunna* [action of the Prophet (Allāh bless him and give him peace)]. He stayed there on the Monday, Tuesday, Wednesday and Thursday, and founded their mosque [*masjid*]. Then he left on the Friday, heading for Medina, and the time for the congregational prayer overtook him in the territory of the Banī Sālim ibn ʿAwf, inside a valley of theirs. The clan had prepared a place there as a mosque, so he delivered a sermon and led the congregational prayer. That was the first sermon he delivered in Medina the Illumined, and in the course of it he said:[1378]

> Praise be to Allāh! Of Him I seek help and of Him I seek guidance. In Him I believe. I do not disbelieve in Him, and I am hostile to anyone who disbelieves in Him. I bear witness that there is no god but Allāh, Alone without partner. I also bear witness that Muḥammad is His servant and His Messenger, whom He has sent with right guidance, the religion of Truth, light, counsel and wisdom, in an era of separation from the Messengers, paucity of knowledge, and error on the people's part, when time is short, the Hour is near, and the final term is close. If someone obeys Allāh and His Messenger, he is guided aright, but if someone disobeys Allāh and His Messenger, he is lost and wandering far astray.
>
> I advise you to practise dutiful devotion to Allāh, for a Muslim can best advise a Muslim by urging him to prepare for the Hereafter, and bidding him to practise dutiful devotion to Allāh. Be on your guard against that which Allāh has warned you to guard against, namely Himself. Dutiful devotion to Allāh, if practised in fear and dread of offending your Lord, is a real help to the attainment of what you long for in the Hereafter. If someone works to improve his relationship with his Lord, in private and in public, intending to gain nothing but Allāh's countenance thereby, that will earn him recognition in his present situation, and a treasure in his situation after death, when a man will need what he has sent on ahead, and he will wish for anything other than that to be far removed from him.
>
> And Allāh warns you to beware of Himself,
> *wa yuḥadhdhiru-kumu 'llāhu Nafsah:*
> and Allāh is Kind and Gentle with His servants.
> *wa 'llāhu Raʾūfun bi-'l-ʿibād.* (3:30)
>
> He is the One who has spoken the truth, and has fulfilled His promise. There is no going back on that, for He says (Exalted is He):
>
> The Word is not changed with Me;
> *mā yubaddalu 'l-qawlu ladayya*
> I am no tyrant to the servants.
> *wa mā Ana bi-ẓallāmin li'l-ʿabīd.* (50:29)
>
> You must therefore practise dutiful devotion to Allāh, in private and in public, for:
>
> If someone keeps his duty to Allāh,
> *wa man yattaqi 'llāha*
> He will acquit him of his evil deeds,
> *yukaffir ʿan-hu sayyiʾāti-hi*

and He will grant him a mighty reward.
wa yu'ẓim la-hu ajrā. (65:5)

If someone keeps his duty to Allāh, he has gained a mighty triumph. If he keeps his duty to Allāh, he is guarding against His disgust, guarding against His punishment, and guarding against His displeasure. Dutiful devotion to Allāh makes faces clear and bright, pleases the Lord, and results in promotion to high degree. You must therefore accept your allotted portion, and do not exceed the proper bounds in relation to Allāh, for He has made His Book known to you, and made His path clear to you, in order to teach those who are truthful, and to teach those who are liars. Conduct yourselves well, as Allāh has treated you well. Be hostile towards His enemies, and strive for the sake of Allāh with all the effort He deserves. He has chosen you, and He has called you Muslims:

so that he who perished might perish by a clear proof
li-yahlika man halaka 'an bayyinatin
and he who survived might survive by a clear proof.
wa yaḥyā man ḥayya 'an bayyina. (8:42)

There is no might nor any power, except with Allāh, so make the remembrance of Allāh your frequent practice, and work for what comes after death. If someone works to improve his relationship with his Lord, Allāh will protect his relationship with people. That is because Allāh judges people, but they do not judge Him, and He rules over people, but they do not rule over Him. Allāh is Supremely Great, and there is no might nor any power, except with Allāh, the All-High, the Almighty.[1379]

And when the prayer is finished
fa-idhā quḍiyati 'ṣ-ṣalātu

That is to say: "When you have performed the obligatory prayer on the Day of Congregation."

scatter in the land
fa-'ntashirū fi 'l-arḍi

This is expressed in the form of a command, but with the sense of granting permission. The permissibility of scattering is cancelled by the obligation to perform the prayer, but then, as soon as that obligation has been discharged, permissibility is restored, so they are allowed to disperse in the land and seek the bounty of Allāh, meaning sustenance and the like.

It is no sin for you
laisa 'alai-kum junāḥun
that you seek bounty from your Lord.
an tabtaghū faḍlan min Rabbi-kum. (2:198)

According to Ibn ʿAbbās (may Allāh be well pleased with him and his father): "When you have finished performing the ritual prayer, you may depart if you wish. If you wish, you may move away until the afternoon prayer [*ʿaṣr*], or, if you wish, you may stay where you are."

His saying (Exalted is He):

> and seek the bounty of Allāh
> *wa 'btaghū min faḍli 'llāhi*

—is also expressed in the form of a command, but with the sense of granting permission to procure sustenance by means of commerce, after the prohibition issued in His saying (Exalted is He):

> and leave trading aside.
> *wa dharu 'l-baiʿ*:

According to Muqātil: "He has declared it lawful for them to seek sustenance after the ritual prayer, so whoever wishes may leave, and whoever wishes may stay." According to Mujāhid: "If he wishes he may do it, and if he wishes he may not do it." According to aḍ-Ḍaḥḥāk: "This is permission from Allāh (Exalted is He), granted when one has finished [the prayer]. As for seeking the bounty of Allāh, that is best done by seeking sustenance, or a righteous son, or useful knowledge, or some equally good thing, but the obvious meaning is the first of these."

When ʿArrāk ibn Mālik had performed the congregational prayer, it is reported that he would go and stand by the door of the mosque, then say: "O Allāh, I have answered Your call and performed Your obligatory prayer. I have now scattered, as you commanded me, so provide me with sustenance from Your bounty, for You are the Best of providers!"

> and remember Allāh frequently
> *wa 'dhkuru 'llāha kathīran*

According to Muqātil: "with the tongue." According to Saʿīd ibn Jubair: "through worshipful obedience." According to Mujāhid: "Remembrance is not frequent unless it is practised while standing, while sitting, and while reclining." The meaning may also be: "When you return to commerce, and go off to engage once again in buying and selling, you must remember Allāh frequently." He has said (Exalted is He):

> Men whom neither commerce nor trading diverts
> *rijālun lā tulhī-him tijāratunwa lā baiʿun*

from the remembrance of Allāh
ʿan dhikri 'llāhi
and the performance of the prayer.
wa iqāmi 'ṣ-ṣalāti. (24:37)

As reported by ʿUmar (may Allāh be well pleased with him), the Prophet (Allāh bless him and give him peace) once said:

> When you come to the market, you must say: 'There is no god but Allāh, Alone [*lā ilāha illa 'llāhu Waḥda-h*]. No partner has He [*lā sharīka la-h*]. To Him belongs the sovereignty and to Him belongs the praise [*la-hu 'l-mulku wa la-hu 'l-ḥamd*]. He brings to life and He causes death [*yuḥyī wa yumīt*], and He is Capable of all things [*wa Huwa ʿalā kulli shaiʾin Qadīr*].' If someone says that, Allāh will record a million good deeds to his credit, acquit him of a million sinful errors, and promote him by a million degrees.[1380]

for then you may prosper.
laʿalla-kum tufliḥūn:

That is to say: "so that you may succeed in obtaining the best of the two abodes [this world and the Hereafter]."[1381]

The Qurʾānic verse raises several points for consideration:

1. What is the wisdom in Allāh's having imposed this obligation on the Day of Congregation?

We shall answer this by quoting al-Qaffāl: "It is that Allāh (Almighty and Glorious is He) has created creatures, for He has brought them out of non-existence into existence, and He has made some of them minerals, some of them plants, and some of them animate beings. Of those that are other than minerals, there are various kinds, including animals, angels, jinn and human beings. Then they have various dwelling places, from the high to the low. Of those in the lowest world, the most noble are the human beings, because of their marvellous formation, and because Allāh (Exalted is He) has honoured them with the gift of speech, and endowed them with minds and faculties capable of dedication to the Sacred Laws. He has not concealed the glory of the gracious favour, and the splendid worth of the gift bestowed upon them. He has commanded gratitude for this generosity on one day of the week, the day on which creatures were brought into being, and their existence was perfected, so that their gathering together on that day may be an acknowledgement of the splendour of that which Allāh (Exalted is He) has graciously bestowed upon them. From the time they first began, their condition has never been devoid of blessing, and Allāh's grace was conferred upon them before they deserved it. Each of the well-known religious communities has a day that is venerated: for the Jews it is the Sabbath, for the Christians it is Sunday, and for the Muslims it is [Friday] the Day of Congregation. Allāh's Messenger (Allāh bless him and give him peace) is reported as having said:

> "This Day of Congregation is the day about which they disagreed, so Allāh has guided us to it. For the Jews it is tomorrow, and for the Christians the day after tomorrow.[1382]

"Since the Day of Congregation has been designated as a day of thankfulness, expression of joy and magnification of blessing, it needs to be celebrated collectively, so gatherings are held for it, as for the customary celebration of the festivals [*aʿyād*]. It also needs to include a sermon, as a reminder of the blessing, and as an exhortation to seek its continuance by grateful acknowledgement of the favours received. Since the ritual prayer is the focal point of the celebration, the special prayer for this day has been assigned to the middle of the day, so that the gathering will be complete. This prayer should be held in only one mosque [in the same locality], to facilitate the summoning of the congregation. Allāh knows best, of course."

2. In His saying (Exalted is He):

> and leave trading aside.
> *wa dharu 'l-baiʿ*:

—why, among all activities, has He mentioned trading in particular?

Our answer to this will be: "Because it is one of the most important of a man's daily occupations, for the purpose of gaining the means of livelihood. It also implies refraining from commerce [*tijāra*], because buying and selling are commonly conducted in the markets, and heedlessness is most likely to affect the people of the markets. His saying:

> and leave trading aside.
> *wa dharu 'l-baiʿ*:

—is a wake-up call to the heedless, so trading is most worthy of mention, not because it is unlawful *per se*, but because it is conducive to neglect of duty. The situation therefore resembles the performance of prayer in enemy-occupied territory.

3. What is the difference between remembering Allāh in the first instance, and remembering Allāh in the second instance?

Our answer is as follows: The first has no connection with commerce in any way at all, since it refers to the sermon and the ritual prayer, as mentioned above. The second does have a connection with it, as in His saying (Exalted is He):

> Men whom neither commerce nor trading diverts
> *rijālun lā tulhī-him tijāratunwa lā baiʿun*
> from the remembrance of Allāh....
> *ʿan dhikri 'llāhi....* (24:37)

❧ ❧

> But when they spy some commerce or sport,
> *wa idhā raʾaw tijāratan aw lahwani 'nfaḍḍū*
> they break away to it and leave you standing.
> *ilai-hā wa tarakū-ka qā'imā:*
> Say: "What is with Allāh is better
> *qul mā ʿinda 'llāhi khairun*
> than sport and commerce."
> *mina 'l-lahwi wa mina 't-tijāra:*
> And Allāh is the Best of providers.
> *wa 'llāhu Khairu 'r-rāziqīn.*

According to Muqātil: "Diḥyat al-Kalbī came back from a commercial expedition to Syria, before he accepted Islām, bringing many kinds of merchandise with him. The people of Medina greeted him with drumbeats and handclapping. That was on the Day of Congregation, while the Prophet (Allāh bless him and give him peace) was standing on the pulpit, delivering the sermon, so the people went out and left the Prophet (Allāh bless him and give him peace). No one remained except twelve men, or maybe fewer, like eight, or even fewer, or maybe more, like forty, so the Prophet (Allāh bless him and give him peace) said:

> Were it not for these, they would have been pelted with stones!

"This Qurʾānic verse was then revealed. Among those who stayed with him were Abū Bakr aṣ-Ṣiddīq [the Champion of Truth] and ʿUmar (may Allāh be well pleased with them)."

According to al-Ḥasan: "Hunger afflicted the people of Medina, and prices became inflated. Then a caravan arrived, while the Prophet

(Allāh bless him and give him peace) was delivering a sermon on the Day of Congregation. The people heard the sound of the caravan, and they went out to greet it, so the Prophet (Allāh bless him and give him peace) said:

> "If the last of them had followed the first of them, the valley would have burst into flames, exposing them to fire."

Qatāda said: "They did that on three occasions."

His expression (Exalted is He):

> or sport
> *aw lahwan*

—is a reference to the beating of drums. When they gave maidens in marriage, they used to play musical instruments, and they would go off making music, leaving the Prophet (blessing and peace be upon him) behind.

> they break away to it
> *[-i] 'nfaḍḍū ilai-hā*

In other words: "they disperse." According to al-Mubarrad: "They incline towards it, and turn away towards it. The pronoun *-hā* [it] refers to commerce." According to az-Zajjāj: "The meaning would be the same if the [masculine] pronoun *-hu* had been used instead of *-hā*. The reference here is to returning to commerce, because it is more important to them."

> and leave you standing.
> *wa tarakū-ka qā'imā:*

The commentators agree that this standing occurred during the sermon to the congregation. It was Jābir (may Allāh be well pleased with him) who said: "I never saw Allāh's Messenger (Allāh bless him and give him peace) delivering the sermon unless he was standing."

ʿAbdu'llāh was asked: "Did the Prophet (Allāh bless him and give him peace) deliver his sermons while standing, or while sitting down?" He responded by reciting:

> and leave you standing.
> *wa tarakū-ka qā'imā:*

Say: "What is with Allāh is better
qul mā ʿinda 'llāhi khairun
than sport and commerce."
mina 'l-lahwi wa mina 't-tijāra:

That is to say: "The reward for performing the prayer and remaining loyal to the Prophet (Allāh bless him and give him peace) is better than sport and commerce."[1383] In other words: "The benefit of that is everlastingly confirmed, in contrast with the dubious benefit of those two, for the benefit of sport is not confirmed, and the benefit of commerce is not everlasting."[1384]

And Allāh is the Best of providers.
wa 'llāhu Khairu 'r-rāziqīn.

He is likewise the Fairest of judges and the Best of creators. The meaning is that He has enabled the existence of providers, so He is the Best of providers. Some say that the term *rāziq* [provider] is not applicable to anyone but Him, except by way of metaphor.[1385]

If someone is captivated by the attractions of material things, he will respond to every instinct that invites him to indulge in sport, or that prompts him to absent-minded action. On the other hand, if someone is governed by the power of Reality, he will not deviate from present awareness, and he will not be distracted from the state of witnessing:

Say: "What is with Allāh is better
qul mā ʿinda 'llāhi khairun
than sport and commerce."
mina 'l-lahwi wa mina 't-tijāra.[1386]

These are my own comments:

We must adhere to the Divine commandments, and avoid infringement of the prohibitions, because His commandments and prohibitions are attached to His good pleasure (Glorious and Exalted is He), so they are a test from Him for His servant. If the servant is enabled to pass this test, through His grace and favour, he will obtain approval from his Lord. Allāh has given him intelligence, and He has given him knowledge, and He has taught him the truth, so that he can comprehend this Divine commandment. Then He has given him the element of voluntary discrimination, so that he can distinguish between truth and falsehood.

The scope of this test is a benefit conferred upon the servant. Allāh (Glorious and Exalted is He) has not created His creatures in order to profit from them, but rather so that they may profit from Him (Glory be to Him and Exalted is He). The servant is obliged to obey his Master, whether or not obedience suits his natural constitution and his lower self. That is better for him than following the desire of his lower self, and forsaking the good pleasure of his Lord. That is why our Lord (Glorious and Exalted is He) has told us:

> Surely We have guided him upon the way,
> *innā hadainā-hu 's-sabīla*
> whether he be thankful or unthankful.
> *immā shākiran wa immā kafūrā.* (76:3)

—because the servant is free to choose between doing what he is commanded and abstaining therefrom, since all the obligations imposed by the Sacred Law are subject to this element of voluntary discrimination.

It is incumbent upon us, O companies of the believers, to direct our preparation and our aspiration towards the Hereafter, and to remember our reckoning and our interrogation, as Allāh (Exalted is He) has said:

> And stop them, for they must be questioned.
> *wa qifū-hum inna-hum mas'ūlūn.* (37:24)

They must be questioned about the Muḥammadan Sacred Law, concerning the ritual prayer [*ṣalāt*], attendance at the Friday congregation [*jum'a*] and the pilgrimage [*ḥajj*], payment of the alms-due [*zakāt*], fasting [*ṣawm*], remembrance [*dhikr*], and other such acts of worshipful service.

We beseech Allāh to enable us, and all the Muslims, to accomplish what He loves and finds pleasing, through His gracious favour and His noble generosity. Peace be upon the Messengers, and praise be to Allāh, the Lord of All the Worlds. There is no might nor any power, except with Allāh, the All-High, the Almighty. May Allāh bless our master Muḥammad, his family and his Companions, and may He grant them peace.

The Eighty-sixth Call

In the Name of Allāh, the All-Merciful, the All-Compassionate.
Bismi'llāhi 'r-Raḥmāni 'r-Raḥīm.

O you who truly believe,
let neither your possessions
yā ayyuha 'lladhīna āmanū lā tulhi-kum amwālu-kum
nor your children distract you
from the remembrance of Allāh.
wa lā awlādu-kum ʿan dhikri 'llāh:
Anyone who does that, well, such are the losers.
wa man yafʿal dhālika fa-ulāʾika humu 'l-khāsirūn:

Expend from what We have provided for you,
wa anfiqū mim-mā razaqnā-kum
before death comes to one of you, and he says:
min qabli an yaʾtiya aḥada-kumu 'l-mawtu fa-yaqūla
"My Lord, if only You would reprieve me
for a little while,
Rabbi law lā akhkharta-nī ilā ajalin qarībin
then I would give alms
and I would be among the righteous!"
fa-aṣṣadaqa wa akun mina 'ṣ-ṣāliḥīn:

But Allāh will never reprieve any soul
when its term comes,
wa lan yuʾakhkhira 'llāhu nafsan idhā jāʾa ajalu-hā:
and Allāh is Aware of what you do.
wa 'llāhu Khabīrun bi-mā taʿlamūn. (63:9–11)

O you who truly believe,
yā ayyuha 'lladhīna āmanū
let neither your possessions nor your children
lā tulhi-kum amwālu-kum wa lā awlādu-kum
distract you from the remembrance of Allāh.
ʿan dhikri 'llāh:

Having described the vices of the hypocrites, Allāh (Exalted is He) has forbidden the believers to imitate them in the delusion of possessions and children. The meaning is: "Do not become so preoccupied, O believers, with possessions and children, that you neglect obedience and worshipful service to Allāh, and fail to perform your obligatory religious duties, such as the ritual prayer [*ṣalāt*] and the pilgrimage [*ḥajj*], just as the hypocrites are preoccupied with those distractions."

According to Ibn Ḥayyān: "That is to say: 'Do let your possessions make you so preoccupied with the effort to increase them, and with the pleasure of accumulating them, and do not let your children make you so preoccupied with their enjoyment, and with concern for their interests, that you neglect the remembrance of Allāh.' This applies to all forms of remembrance, including the ritual prayer, glorification [*tasbīḥ*], the offering of praise, and other acts of worshipful obedience."[1387]

You must not become so preoccupied with attending to the management of your affairs, and with concern for their interests and the enjoyment of them, that you pay no attention to His remembrance (Exalted is He), in the ritual prayer and other acts of worship, by which the Master should be remembered.

According to one of the commentators: "Remembrance with the heart is the fear of offending Allāh (Blessed and Exalted is He). Remembrance with the tongue is the recitation of the Qur'ān, and other such recitations. Remembrance with the physical body is fasting and the ritual prayer."

What is forbidden to the believers is letting themselves be distracted by them [their possessions and children]. In other words, they are forbidden to neglect the remembrance of Allāh because of their preoccupation with them. The hypocrites used to be miserly with their possessions, and that is why they said: "You must not spend anything on those who are close to Allāh's Messenger." They used to take tremendous pride in their children and their tribal relatives, and they were preoccupied with them, and with their possessions, to the exclusion of Allāh, obedience to Him, and rendering assistance to His Messenger. That is why He forbade the believers to be like them in that respect.[1388]

> Anyone who does that, well, such are the losers.
> *wa man yafʿal dhālika fa-ulāʾika humu ʾl-khāsirūn:*

If someone is distracted by this world from obedience to Allāh and His service, and by preoccupation with anything apart from Him, for even the shortest time, well, people like that are bound to experience the most total loss. They have chosen what is insignificant and fleeting, instead of that which is important and enduring, and they have preferred immediate worldly profit to investment in the Hereafter.[1389]

According to the Prophetic tradition [*ḥadīth*]:

> Whenever the sun rises, there are two angels at its sides, calling and making themselves heard by all creatures, except the two heavyweights [humans and jinn]: "O people, come to your Lord! That which is little, but sufficient, is better than what is abundant, but distracting."

It was Sahl who said: "You must not be so preoccupied with your possessions or your children, that you fail to perform the obligatory prayers at the beginning of their prescribed times. If someone is distracted from the remembrance of Allāh and His service, by any of the trivia of this world, he is one of the losers. The only refuge is with Allāh!"[1390]

As one interpreter put it: "If someone is preoccupied with the cultivation of his properties [*amwāl*], instead of the development of his spiritual states [*aḥwāl*], and with the enjoyment of his children [*awlād*], instead of the improvement of his prospects in the afterlife [*maʿād*], well, such people are the losers in their trade."[1391]

> Expend from what We have provided for you,
> *wa anfiqū mim-mā razaqnā-kum*
> before death comes to one of you.
> *min qabli an yaʾtiya aḥada-kumu ʾl-mawtu.*

That is to say: "Spend, for the sake of Allāh's good pleasure, some of the things We have given you, and some of the possessions We have graciously bestowed upon you, before death alights on the human being, and he enters the state of demise."[1392]

> Expend from what We have provided for you.
> *wa anfiqū mim-mā razaqnā-kum*

According to Ibn ʿAbbās (may Allāh be well pleased with him and his father): "This is a reference to the alms-due [*zakāt*] assessed on property, and the word *min* [from] indicates subdivision." It has also been said to mean: "the expenditure that is strictly required."

> before death comes to one of you.
> *min qabli an ya᾽tiya aḥada-kumu 'l-mawtu.*

That is to say: "the signs and symptoms of death." These prompt him to beg to be returned to this world:

> and he says: "My Lord,
> *fa-yaqūla Rabbi*
> if only You would reprieve me for a little while."
> *law lā akhkharta-nī ilā ajalin qarībin*

According to one interpretation: "Allāh has urged them to practise constant remembrance, and not to be stingy with their possessions. [When death comes to one of them, and he says]: 'If only You would grant me some delay, and postpone my term for a little while,' he is asking for an extension to his span of life, so that he can make charitable donations and be purified." This is a reference to the words attributed to him in the Qur᾽ānic verse:

> "then I would give alms and I would be among the righteous!"
> *fa-aṣṣadaqa wa akun mina 'ṣ-ṣāliḥīn:*

It was Ibn ʿAbbās (may Allāh be well pleased with him and his father) who said: "This goes to prove that the people concerned were not believers, since believers do not ask to be returned [to this world]."

After saying: "Death does not alight on anyone who has not performed the Pilgrimage, and who has not paid the alms-due, without that person begging to be returned," aḍ-Ḍaḥḥāk went on to recite this Qur᾽ānic verse.

According to the author of *al-Kashshāf*, "before death comes..." means: "before he witnesses that which makes him despair of any respite, and choking suffocates him, and expenditure becomes impossible for him, and the time of acceptance slips away, so that he suffers the distress of deprivation, and bites his nails over the loss of what could have been possible for him."

It was Ibn ʿAbbās (may Allāh be well pleased with him and his father) who said: "You must give alms before the power of death descends upon you, for no repentance will then be accepted, and no deed will be of any use."[1393] Ibn ʿAbbās (may Allāh bestow His mercy upon him) also said: "It is very hard to apply this verse to those who affirm the Divine Oneness [*Tawḥīd*], because none of them wishes to return to this world, or to have his time in it prolonged. For him there is goodness in the Hereafter, in the presence of Allāh." The only exception is the martyr, for he would like to return to the fray, as a matter of honour.[1394]

Every prodigal spendthrift will feel remorse at the point of death, and he will beg for extra time, to make up for what he has missed, but that, alas, is out of the question.[1395]

As reported by at-Tirmidhī, on the authority of aḍ-Ḍaḥḥāk ibn Muzāḥim, Ibn ʿAbbās (may Allāh be well pleased with him and his father) once said: "If someone has enough wealth to take him on the Pilgrimage to the House of his Lord, or he owes the alms-due on it, but does not act accordingly, he will beg to be returned at the point of death." A man who heard this said: "O Ibn ʿAbbās, beware of offending Allāh! Only the unbelievers would beg to be returned." To this he replied: "I shall read you a Qurʾānic verse, to prove my point:

> O you who truly believe,
> *yā ayyuha 'lladhīna āmanū*
> let neither your possessions nor your children
> *lā tulhi-kum amwālu-kum wa lā awlādu-kum*
> distract you from the remembrance of Allāh."
> *ʿan dhikri 'llāh.*

This Qurʾānic verse contains proof of the fact that prompt payment of the alms-due is a strict obligation, and that its postponement is absolutely impermissible. The same is true of other acts of worshipful service, whenever a specific time has been prescribed for their performance.[1396] It also proves that almsgiving is one of the causes of righteous success and worshipful obedience, just as the withholding of alms is one of the causes of corruption and immorality. That is why He has said (Exalted is He):

> [and he says...] "and I would be among the righteous!"
> [*fa-yaqūla...*] *wa akun mina 'ṣ-ṣāliḥīn:*

There is a significant difference between a present [*hadiyya*] and a charitable donation [*ṣadaqa*]. A charitable donation is a gift to someone in need, by way of compassion, whereas a present is a gift to a loved one, for the sake of affection. That is why the Prophet (Allāh bless him and give him peace) used to accept a present, though he would not accept a charitable donation, whether it was an obligatory due [*farḍ*] or a supererogatory offering [*nafl*].

> But Allāh will never reprieve any soul when its term comes.
> *wa lan yu'akhkhira 'llāhu nafsan idhā jā'a ajalu-hā:*

That is to say: "He will not grant it any respite, whether it is obedient or rebellious, great or small, at the end of its life."[1397] In this Qur'ānic verse, Allāh (Exalted is He) has informed us that He will not grant postponement to anyone whose span has expired, and whose final moment is at hand. According to the author of *al-Kashshāf*: "This negation of postponement is expressed in uncompromisingly definitive terms."

In short, His saying:

> let neither your possessions nor your children distract you....
> *lā tulhi-kum amwālu-kum wa lā awlādu-kum....*

—is an exhortation to remember before death, and His saying:

> Expend from what We have provided for you.
> *wa anfiqū mim-mā razaqnā-kum*

—is an exhortation to give thanks for that provision.

> and Allāh is Aware of what you do.
> *wa 'llāhu Khabīrun bi-mā ta'lamūn.*

In other words: "[He is Aware] that, even if he was sent back to this world, he would neither pay the alms-due nor perform the Pilgrimage." This is reminiscent of His saying:

> And if they were sent back, they would return
> *wa law ruddū la-'ādū*
> to that which they have been forbidden.
> *li-ma nuhū 'an-hu.* (6:28)

The traditional commentators maintain that this statement [that He is Aware of what you do] applies to every action, good or bad.[1398]

Note: According to one of the commentators, death is of two kinds:

1. The compulsory kind. That is the kind that is commonly known

and generally recognized. It is the "fixed term [*al-ajal al-musammā*]," about which it has been said:

> When their term comes,
> *fa-idhā jā'a ajalu-hum*
> they shall neither tarry for a moment nor go ahead.
> *lā yasta'khirūna sā'atan wa lā yastaqdimūn.* (7:34)

2. The voluntary kind. That is dying while still in the life of this world. It is the "decreed term [*al-ajal al-maqḍī*]," referred to in His saying:

> Then He decreed a term.
> *thumma qaḍā ajalā.* (6:2)

The human being cannot genuinely experience this kind of death, unless he has realized the Oneness of Allāh (Exalted is He) with the realization of the dead, from whom the veils have been removed.[1399]

Some fine points: You must not be deluded by the apparent security of your lifetimes. You must be vigilantly aware of the suddenness with which your terms may expire. You must prepare for the journey that lies before you. You must not follow a zigzag course through the lands of procrastination.

It is said that Allāh is entitled to what He has obliged you to fulfil, while He has guaranteed the fulfilment of your rightful due, so concentrate on the duty with which you have been charged, and not on your personal satisfaction.

You must not squander the opportunities of your worldly life, on account of your possessions and your children. You must rather give priority to Allāh's rightful due, and make it your preoccupation, for He will then take care of your worldly affairs and your children. If you are for Allāh, Allāh will be for you.[1400]

These are my own remarks:

There is no harm in working in this world, but the heart becomes attached to this world, and that is harmful. Do not invoke your children's needs, to justify your total absorption in this world, because, if your children are righteous, Allāh will befriend and protect them:

> And He befriends and protects the righteous.
> *wa Huwa yatawalla 'ṣ-ṣāliḥīn.* (7:196)

How does your custodianship compare with His custodianship? If they are immature, you must be devoutly cautious:

> And let those fear, who, if they left behind them
> *wa l'-yakhsha 'lladhīna law tarakū min khalfi-him*
> weak offspring, would be afraid for them.
> *dhurriyyatan ḍi'āfan khāfū 'alai-him:*
> So let them practise true devotion to Allāh,
> *fa-'l-yattaqu 'llāha*
> and let them speak words that get straight to the point.*
> *wa yaqūlū qawlan sadīdā.* (4:9)

If your children are badly behaved—Allāh (Exalted is He) forbid!—you must not assist them in their misconduct. If you do so, they will be punished because of their sinful disobedience, and you will also be punished, for letting the accumulation of wealth distract you from the remembrance of Allāh. Your sustenance is the responsibility of Allāh (Exalted is He), as is their sustenance, so take advantage of the material means, but not at the expense of your religion. You must realize that the Provider is Allāh, not the material means. The best form of wealth is what you use for lawful purposes.

You belong to material wealth, so long as you hold on to it, but once you have spent it to good purpose, it belongs to you. Congratulations, then, to a servant who belongs to Allāh (Exalted is He)!

We beseech Allāh (Exalted is He) to keep us, and all of you, safe from the wickedness of our lower selves, and from the vanity of the life of this world, for its poison is deadly. Peace be upon the Messengers, and praise be to Allāh, the Lord of All the Worlds. There is no might nor any power, except with Allāh, the All-High, the Almighty. May Allāh bless our master Muḥammad, his family and his Companions, and may He grant them peace.

* This admonition applies to speech in general, not only to what needs to be said in this particular context.

The Eighty-seventh Call

In the Name of Allāh, the All-Merciful, the All-Compassionate.
Bismi'llāhi 'r-Raḥmāni 'r-Raḥīm.

O you who truly believe,
yā ayyuha 'lladhīna āmanū
among your wives and your children
inna min azwāji-kum wa awlādi-kum
there are enemies for you, so beware of them.
ʿaduwwan la-kum fa-'ḥdharū-hum
And if you pardon and overlook and forgive,
wa in taʿfū wa taṣfaḥū wa taghfirū
Allāh is All-Forgiving, All-Compassionate.
fa-inna 'llāha Ghafūrun Raḥīm.

Your wealth and your children
are merely a temptation,
innamā amwālu-kum wa awlādu-kum fitna:
and with Allāh there is an immense reward.
wa 'llāhu ʿinda-hu ajrun ʿaẓīm.

So practise true devotion to Allāh,
fa-'ttaqu 'llāha
as far as you are able, and listen, and obey,
ma 'staṭaʿtum wa 'smaʿū wa aṭīʿū
and spend on what is best for yourselves.
wa anfiqū khairan li-anfusi-kum:
And whoever is guarded against
his own selfish greed,
wa man yūqa shuḥḥa nafsi-hi
such are those who will prosper.
fa-ulāʾika humu 'l-mufliḥūn.

If you lend Allāh a fine loan,
in tuqriḍu 'llāha qarḍan ḥasanan
He will multiply it for you and forgive you,
yuḍāʿif-hu la-kum wa yaghfir la-kum.
for Allāh is Appreciative, Forbearing,
wa 'llāhu Shakūrun Ḥalīm.

Knower of the invisible
ʿĀlimu ʾl-ghaibi
and the visible, the Almighty, the All-Wise.
wa ʾsh-shahādati ʾl-ʿAzīzu ʾl-Ḥakīm. (64:14–18)

The Sūra of Mutual Cheating [*at-Taghābun*] is one of the Medinan Sūras, which are concerned with legislation, but its tone is that of the Meccan Sūras, which deal with the principles of Islāmic belief. It has commanded obedience to Allāh and obedience to His Messenger, and it has warned against rejecting the summons of Allāh. It has also warned against the hostility of some wives and children, for they often prevent an individual from engaging in the sacred struggle [*jihād*] and the Migration [*Hijra*]. The Sūra concludes with the commandment to spend in support of Allāh's cause, seeking His good pleasure, that being half of the sacred struggle in the cause of Allāh.[1401]

O you who truly believe,
yā ayyuha ʾlladhīna āmanū
among your wives and your children
inna min azwāji-kum wa awlādi-kum
there are enemies for you, so beware of them.
ʿaduwwan la-kum fa-ʾḥdharū-hum

According to al-Kalbī: "When a man proposed to embark on the Migration [*Hijra*], his sons and his wife would cling to him, saying: 'You are going away and leaving us in the lurch!' One man would obey his family, and stay at home, so Allāh warned them against obeying their wives and their children. Another would not obey them, and he would say: 'By Allāh, if we had not migrated, and if Allāh had not brought us together with them in the abode of the Migration, we would not be of any use to you at all.' When Allāh brought them together, He therefore commanded them to spend, to be active in goodness, and to be graciously kind."

According to Abū Mulsim al-Khurāsānī: "It was revealed in connection with ʿAwf ibn Mālik al-Ashjaʿī, whose wife and son used to hold him back from the Migration and the sacred struggle."[1402]

Allāh (Exalted is He) therefore addressed them by saying, in effect: "O company of the believers, some of your wives and children are enemies for you. They divert you from Allāh's cause and deter you from obedience to Allāh, so beware of responding to them and obeying them."

According to the commentators: "A group of people accepted Islām, and they proposed to embark on the Migration, but their wives and children deterred them, so they did not emigrate until some time later. When they eventually came to Allāh's Messenger (Allāh bless him and give him peace), they saw that the people with him had acquired understanding of the religion, so they were filled with remorse and regret, and considered punishing their wives and children. The Qur᾽ānic verse was thereupon revealed. The verse applies to everyone who is distracted from obedience to Allāh by his wives and children."[1403]

there are enemies for you
ʿaduwwan la-kum

They distract you from obedience to Allāh. They may not bear any obvious enmity, but an enemy is identified as such by his conduct, not by his nature, and there is no conduct more vile than intervention between the servant and his Lord.

He has mentioned wives first, because they are the sources of children, and because, since they are the focus of carnal desires, they are more closely attached to people's hearts, and more influential in distracting them from servitude. That explains why He has mentioned them first, in His saying (Exalted is He):

Decked out fair for mankind is the love of the pleasures
zuyyina li'n-nāsi ḥubbu 'sh-shahawāti
derived from women and children.
mina 'n-nisā᾽i wa 'l-banīna. (3:14)

As stated in *al-Lubāb* [The Core]: "His saying:

among your wives
inna min azwāji-kum

—is also applicable to the male, for, just as the man's wife and children may be enemies for him, the woman's husband may be an enemy for her."

so beware of them.
fa-'ḥdharū-hum

That is to say: "Keep yourselves from loving them too much, from extreme attachment to them, and from collusion with them. You must not give their rights precedence over the rights of Allāh (Exalted is He)."

As reported by at-Tirmidhī, on the authority of Abū Huraira (may Allāh be well pleased with him), Allāh's Messenger (Allāh bless him and give him peace) once said:

> If your leaders are the best of you, and your rich folk are the most generous of you, and your affairs are a matter of consultation among you, the surface of the earth will be better for you than its guts. If your leaders are the worst of you, however, and your rich folk are the stingiest of you, and your affairs are assigned to your women, the guts of the earth will be better for you than its surface.

The Prophet (blessing and peace be upon him) had consulted [his wife] Umm Salama (may Allāh be well pleased with her), as reported in the story of al-Ḥudaibiyya, so that became evidence in favour of consulting a virtuous woman. Umm Salama was noted for her virtue and the amplitude of her intelligence, to the point where Imām al-Ḥaramain said: "We know of no woman who aimed an opinion and hit the mark, except Umm Salama."[1404]

> And if you pardon and overlook and forgive,
> *wa in ta'fū wa taṣfaḥū wa taghfirū*
> Allāh is All-Forgiving, All-Compassionate.
> *fa-inna 'llāha Ghafūrun Raḥīm.*

This relates to the situation where one of these men, when he had eventually emigrated, and had seen how people had acquired understanding of the religion, would decide to punish his wife and children. Even if they joined him in the Abode of Migration [*Dār al-Hijra*], he would not spend on them or accord them any good treatment, so down came the revelation:

> And if you pardon and overlook and forgive....
> *wa in ta'fū wa taṣfaḥū wa taghfirū....*

It has thus been made clear that such enmity is relevant only to unbelief and negation of faith, not among the believers, so their believing wives and children are not enemies for them.[1405]

> And if you pardon
> *wa in ta'fū*

—their sins, which are susceptible to pardon because they are connected with the affairs of this world, or with the affairs of the religion, but accompanied by repentance:

> and overlook
> *wa taṣfaḥū*

—by refraining from reproof and censure:

and forgive
wa taghfirū

—by concealing their sins and setting forth their apology:

Allāh is All-Forgiving, All-Compassionate.
fa-inna 'llāha Ghafūrun Raḥīm.

—He will treat you as your behaviour deserves, and He will bestow His grace upon you. This is reminiscent of His saying (Exalted is He):

But if [your parents] strive with you
wa in jāhadā-ka
to make you ascribe to Me as partner
ʿalā an tushrika bī
that of which you have no knowledge,
mā laisa la-ka bi-hi ʿilmun
then do not obey them.
fa-lā tuṭiʿ-humā
Consort with them in this world kindly.
wa ṣāḥib-humā fi 'd-dunyā maʿrūfan. (31:15)

According to al-Qāshānī: "If you pardon them with affability, overlook their transgressions with forbearance, and forgive their offences with compassion, that will incur no sin and no objection. Sin resides only in collusion with them, excessive affection and extreme attachment, not in the cultivation of fairness and good grace."

There is no objection to consorting with them on the basis of moral excellence, for that is strongly recommended. Indeed, it is consistent with the attributes of Allāh, for Allāh is All-Forgiving, All-Compassionate, so you must model your character on His standards.[1406]

Your wealth and your children are merely a temptation.
innamā amwālu-kum wa awlādu-kum fitna:

According to Ibn ʿAbbās (may Allāh be well pleased with him and his father): "[This means that] you must not obey them in disobedience to Allāh (Exalted is He)."

a temptation.
fitna:

In other words: "a trial and a distraction from the Hereafter." Someone said: "Allāh (Exalted is He) has made it known that material possessions and children are included among everything that afflicts them in the form of temptation." This is a general statement, referring to all children, for the human being is tempted by his child, since he will sometimes disobey Allāh (Exalted is He) because of him, and commit an unlawful deed for his sake, such as the misappropriation of someone else's property, for instance.

> and with Allāh there is an immense reward.
> *wa 'llāhu ʿinda-hu ajrun ʿaẓīm.*

In other words: "an abundant reward, that being the Garden of Paradise." He has declared that with Him there is an immense reward, so that they will endure the enormous inconvenience. The meaning is: "Do not commit sinful acts of disbodedience because of your children, and do not prefer them to the immense reward that Allāh has in store."[1407] The Qurʾānic verse contains an inducement to long for the Hereafter, and to abstain from this world and from material possessions and children, by which people are tempted.[1408]

Ibn Masʿūd used to say: "None of you should ever say: 'O Allāh, I take refuge with You from temptation,' for none of you can relate to a wife and property and children, without being subject to temptation. You should rather say: 'O Allāh, I take refuge with You from the misleading effects of temptations.'"

Buraida (may Allāh be well pleased with him) is reported as having said: "Allāh's Messenger (Allāh bless him and give him peace) was delivering a sermon to us, when along came [his grandsons] al-Ḥasan and al-Ḥusain. They were dressed in red shirts, as they walked and stumbled. Allāh's Messenger (Allāh bless him and give him peace) stepped down from the pulpit, picked them up and set them in front of him, then said:

"Allāh spoke the truth when He said:

> Your wealth and your children are merely a temptation.
> *innamā amwālu-kum wa awlādu-kum fitna:*

"I caught sight of these two boys walking and stumbling, so I became impatient to break off my speech and pick them up."[1409]

> So practise true devotion to Allāh, as far as you are able
> *fa-'ttaqu 'llāha ma 'staṭaʿtum*

That is to say: "Devote your effort and your ability, O believers, to obedience to Allāh, and do not burden yourselves with what you cannot do." According to the commentators: "This applies to things that are commanded and to virtuous deeds. Each person must perform them to the extent of his ability. As for things that are forbidden, their total avoidance is strictly required." This is indicated by the saying attributed to the Prophet (Allāh bless him and give him peace):

> When you are given a commandment, you must carry it out as far as you are able. When you are forbidden to do something, you must avoid it.[1410]

> and listen, and obey
> *wa 'sma'ū wa aṭī'ū*

In other words: "and listen to the advice you are being given, and respond obediently to what you are commanded and forbidden to do."

> and spend on what is best for yourselves.
> *wa anfiqū khairan li-anfusi-kum:*

That is to say: "and spend from your wealth in support of Allāh's cause, for that will be best for yourselves."

> And whoever is guarded against his own selfish greed,
> *wa man yūqa shuḥḥa nafsi-hi*
> such are those who will prosper.
> *fa-ulā'ika humu 'l-mufliḥūn.*

In other words: "And if someone is immune to the stinginess and greedy desire to which the lower self incites, he will surely succeed in achieving every goal."[1411]

As for the term *shuḥḥ*, it is synonymous with *bukhl* [greed, avarice; stinginess, miserliness]. It relates to money and other things, and the corresponding adjective *shaḥīḥ* [greedy; stingy, miserly] occurs in expressions like: "So-and-so is stingy with money, greedy for social status, miserly when it comes to being fair." If someone is detached from *shuḥḥ*, that person is one of those who enjoy prosperity.[1412] That is to say: "If Allāh guards and protects someone against the greed of his lower self, that greed being the vice that is kneaded into the clay of the lower self, such are the triumphantly successful in every aspiration." In the words of the Prophetic tradition [*ḥadīth*]:

> It is greed [*shuḥḥ*] enough for a man to say: 'I am taking what rightfully belongs to me. I am not letting go of any part of it.'[1413]

> And whoever is guarded against his own selfish greed....
> *wa man yūqa shuḥḥa nafsi-hi....*

That is to say: "Allāh protects him against the greed of his own lower self, so he does with his wealth whatever Allāh has commanded him to do, with a feeling of conviction and contentment, so that all anxieties are removed from his heart."

The term *shuḥḥ* applies to an internal condition, which is a chronic disease, while *bukhl* is a form of external behaviour, arising from *shuḥḥ*. The lower self is sometimes stingy with abstinence from acts of disobedience, by committing them. It is sometimes stingy with acts of obedience, so it refrains from performing them. It is sometimes stingy with giving money. If someone does what Allāh has assigned to him as an obligatory duty, he says goodbye to *shuḥḥ*.

> If you lend Allāh a fine loan....
> *in tuqriḍu 'llāha qarḍan ḥasanan....*

He has called it a loan in the sense that the duty imposed by Allāh entails a recompense (from His gracious favour). In calling it a loan, there is also an extra incentive to charitable donation, since He has declared it a loan to Allāh, although the servant is actually lending to himself, because the benefit is accruing to him.[1414]

This exhortation is addressed to the rich, urging them to spend their wealth for the sake of the poor, in order to clear their days and moments of their own purposes, and prefer the purpose of the Lord of Truth to the purpose of their lower selves.[1415] That is to say: "If you make charitable donations in support of Allāh's cause, in a cheerful spirit, Allāh will multiply the recompense and the reward." In the depiction of charitable donation as a loan, there is an eloquently subtle allusion to beneficent treatment of the poor.[1416]

> He will multiply it for you
> *yuḍā'if-hu la-kum*

In other words: "He will grant you His reward increased many times. He will record one as ten, seventy, seven hundred and more, according to His will, taking account of the intentions, the times and the situation."

and forgive you
wa yaghfir la-kum.

—through the blessed grace of spending, for some of the sins that have slipped from you.[1417]

for Allāh is Appreciative
wa 'llāhu Shakūrun

He gives abundantly in exchange for very little.

Forbearing
Ḥalīm.

He does not accelerate the punishment,[1418] but delays it for a very long time, so that the servant may consider good behaviour as an option, instead of disobedience, and so repent and not be negligent. One must not be misled by His forbearance, for the anger of the Forbearing is unbearable.

Knower of the invisible
ʿĀlimu 'l-ghaibi
and the visible, the Almighty, the All-Wise.
wa 'sh-shahādati 'l-ʿAzīzu 'l-Ḥakīm.

[He is] the Knower of the secret, Aware of nature's influence on the heart, although the owner of the heart knows nothing of it, let alone anyone else.[1419] In other words: "Allāh (Exalted is He) is the Knower of whatever is absent or present. No secret is hidden from Him, the All-Prevailing in His sovereignty, the All-Wise in His workmanship."[1420]

The Appreciative [*Shakūr*] rewards His servant for thankfulness [*shukr*], which means the acknowledgement of gracious favour with an attitude of humility. He has called the reward for *shukr* [thankfulness] a form of *shukr* [appreciation]. He confers much praise upon His servant, by mentioning his good deeds and his worshipful obedience, for *shukr* means extolling the benefactor by mentioning his beneficence. According to al-Qushairī (may Allāh bestow His mercy upon him): "*Shakūr* is the intensive form of [the participial adjective] *shākir*, which applies to someone who possesses thankfulness [*shukr*]."

One of the righteous experts was asked: "Who is the most thankful of the thankful [*ashkar ash-shākirīn*]?" He replied: "He who is pure and free from sins, yet counts himself among the sinners. He who strives to perform the supererogatory acts of worship [*nawāfil*], after discharging the obligatory religious duties [*farā'iḍ*], yet counts himself among those who fall short. He who is content with little of this world, yet counts himself one of the desirous. He who devotes his entire life to the remembrance of Allāh, yet counts himself among the negligent. He who is diligently committed to good work, yet counts himself among the bankrupt. Such is the most thankful of the thankful."[1421]

These are my own comments:

As for the temptation posed by wives, we are well aware of that. It means that a man obeys his wife in opposition to the rules of the religion. In relating to your wives, however, it is incumbent upon you to observe the duties of the Sacred Law. You must not treat them with indulgence, by complying with their passions and their lustful desires for the love of this world, superficial adornment, clothing, and impressing strangers with their finery. Their intelligence is too easily submerged beneath their carnal appetites and their pleasures, especially when they enjoy an affluent situation, because affluence diverts women from righteousness, due to the predominance of their passion over their intellects.

As far as temperaments are concerned, the intelligent believer is obliged to be tolerant and patient with the temperamental natures of women. Patience with the temperaments of women is one of the distinctive features of the perfect human being. He must therefore treat them gently, with wisdom and counsel, while carefully preserving love and mercy:

> And one of His signs is this:
> *wa min āyāti-hi*
> He created for you wives from among yourselves,
> *an khalaqa la-kum min anfusi-kum azwājan*
> so that you might find rest in them,
> *li-taskunū ilai-hā*
> and He ordained between you love and mercy.
> *wa ja'ala baina-kum mawaddatan wa raḥmā.* (30:21)

—on condition that you must not treat them too indulgently in all circumstances.

Consultation with them is praiseworthy, on the subject of temperaments, provided these matters are not at variance with the Sacred Law, just like consultation over domestic problems, and other such necessities of life. That is because they will be consorts for you in the Hereafter, as in this world, provided they are compliant with the Sacred Law and the Sunna. To treat them unfairly is not consistent with faith. In the words of the Prophetic tradition [*ḥadīth*]:

> The best of you is the one of you who is best for his family, and I am the best of you for my family.[1422]

In the case of children, you must not let them become a barrier between you and Allāh (Exalted is He), through excessive emotional attachment to them. They have rights over the father, as the Prophet (Allāh bless him and give him peace) once said:

> The son is entitled to expect from the father that he will give him a good name, teach him to write, and give him in marriage when he reaches adulthood.

The father must be wary, however, in his attention to livelihood, to ensure that he does not lapse into that which is unlawful, on account of his children. Allāh (Exalted is He) has said:

> We provide for you and for them.
> *naḥnu narzuqu-kum wa iyyā-hum.* (6:151)

If the children are among the people of righteousness, and the father makes every effort to obtain his livelihood in compliance with the Sacred Law, while placing his trust in Allāh and being content with the portion allotted by destiny, he is the recipient of enabling grace. If the child is at odds with Allāh's good pleasure, why should the father accumulate wealth for the child to squander and waste, when the burden of sin will rest upon the father?

We beg Allāh to inspire us with a sense of our right direction, and to improve our children and our future offspring. Peace be upon the Messengers, and praise be to Allāh, the Lord of All the Worlds. There is no might nor any power, except with Allāh, the All-High, the Almighty. May Allāh bless our master Muḥammad, his family and his Companions, and may He grant them peace.

The Eighty-eighth Call

In the Name of Allāh, the All-Merciful, the All-Compassionate.
Bismi'llāhi 'r-Raḥmāni 'r-Raḥīm.

O you who truly believe,
guard yourselves and your families
yā ayyuha 'lladhīna āmanū qū anfusa-kum wa ahlī-kum
against a Fire of which the fuel
is human beings and stones.
nāran waqūdu-ha 'n-nāsu wa 'l-ḥijāratu

In charge of it are angels, tough, severe,
ʿalai-hā malāʾikatun ghilāẓun shidādun
who do not disobey Allāh
in what He commands them,
lā yuʿṣūna 'llāha mā amara-hum
but do what they are commanded.
wa yafʿalūna mā yuʾmarūn. (66:6)

O you who truly believe,
yā ayyuha 'lladhīna āmanū
guard yourselves and your families against a Fire....
qū anfusa-kum wa ahlī-kum nāran....

That is to say: "O you who sincerely believe in Allāh and His Messenger and surrender your faces to Allāh, you must keep yourselves safe, and protect your wives and your children, from a fiercely blazing Fire. That you must do by refraining from sinful acts of disobedience and performing acts of worshipful obedience, and by training and teaching them."

Mujāhid said: "This means: 'You must practise true devotion to Allāh, and instruct your families to practise true devotion to Allāh.'" It was al-Khāzin who said: "It means: '"You must command them to do what is good, and forbid them to do what is bad. You must educate them and train them, in order to guard them from the Fire.' In this context, the family means the women and children, and everything connected with them."[1423] Muqātil said: "It means that the Muslim must train himself and his family in good behaviour."[1424]

You must therefore provide them with the kind of protection exemplified by the Prophet (Allāh bless him and give him peace), through abstinence from all forms of sinful disobedience, and the performance of all forms of worshipful obedience. You must provide your families, meaning the women and children, and anyone else to whom the term "family" applies, with sound advice and proper training.[1425]

According to aḍ-Ḍaḥḥāk and Muqātil: "The duty of the Muslim is to teach his family, meaning his close relatives and his maidservants, that which Allāh has made obligatory for them, and that which Allāh has forbidden them to do." In the words of the Prophetic tradition [*ḥadīth*]:

> You must instruct the young boy to perform the ritual prayer [*ṣalāt*] when he reaches the age of seven. Then, when he reaches the age of seventeen, you must compel him to perform it.[1426]

According to the legal experts [*fuqahā'*]: "This also applies to fasting. This is an effective way of drilling him in worshipful service, so that, by the time he reaches maturity, he will be thoroughly accustomed to worship, obedience, the avoidance of sinful acts, and abstinence from reprehensible conduct. Allāh is the One who enables us to succeed!"[1427]

According to ʿAlī (may Allāh be well pleased with him), Qatāda and Mujāhid, the meaning of the Qurānic verse is: "Guard yourselves with your actions, and guard your families with your sound advice."

The man is obliged to improve himself through worshipful obedience, and to improve his family as a shepherd improves his flock. This saying of the Prophet (Allāh bless him and give him peace) is recorded in the *Ṣaḥīḥ*:

> Each one of you is a shepherd, and each one of you is responsible for his flock.... The man is a shepherd in charge of the people of his household, and he is responsible for them.[1428]

He must therefore teach them what is lawful [*ḥalāl*] and what is unlawful [*ḥarām*], and keep them from committing acts of disobedience and sins, while instructing them in other rules of conduct. The Prophet (Allāh bless him and give him peace) also said:

The father owes it to his son to give him a good name, to teach him to write, and to marry him off when he reaches adulthood.

He must also inform his family of the time prescribed for the ritual prayer [*waqt aṣ-ṣalāt*], and of when it is necessary to keep and break the fast, depending on the sighting of the new moon. As reported by [Imām] Muslim, the Prophet (Allāh bless him and give him peace) used to say [to his wife], whenever he performed the nightly prayer called *witr*:

Get up, O ʿĀʾisha, for you must perform the *witr* prayer![1429]

To quote another Prophetic tradition [*ḥadīth*]:

May Allāh bestow His mercy on the man who says: 'O members of my family, attend to your ritual prayer, your fasting and your alms-due [*zakāt*], and to your needy, your orphan and your neighbours!' Perhaps Allāh will gather them together with him in the Garden of Paradise.[1430]

a Fire of which the fuel is human beings and stones.
nāran waqūdu-ha 'n-nāsu wa 'l-ḥijāratu

This is a special kind of fire, which is kindled only with human beings and stones. According to Ibn ʿAbbās (may Allāh be well pleased with him and his father): "These stones are lumps of sulphur [*kibrīt*], because they are the hottest of all things, when they are ignited."[1431] They are also the most speedily combustible. In other words, this fire is exceptionally hot, because of its peculiar fuel, unlike the fire of this world, which is kindled with wood and similar materials. According to Ibn Masʿūd: "The firewood that is cast into it is the son of Adam [the human being], and its stones are lumps of sulphur, more evil-smelling than the rotting corpse."

In charge of it are angels, tough, severe....
ʿalai-hā malāʾikatun ghilāẓun shidādun....

That is to say: "In charge of this Fire are tough-hearted stokers of Hell [*zabāniyya*], who never show any mercy. They are charged with the task of tormenting the unbelievers."[1432] The angels [mentioned in the Qurʾānic verse] must be the stokers of Hell [*zabāniyya*], since they are tough-hearted and show no mercy when they are begged to be merciful. This is because they were created from anger, and the torment of creatures has been made dear to them, just as the consumption of food and drink has been made dear to human beings. As for their "toughness," it has been said to mean the tremendous force and strength of their colossal bodies.

Ibn ʿAbbās (may Allāh be well pleased with him and his father) once said: "The space between the shoulders of any one of them is the distance of a year's journey. The strength of any one of them is so great, that if he strikes a blow with the goading iron, that blow will knock seventy thousand people into the pit of Hell." As Ibn Wahb has mentioned: "Allāh's Messenger (Allāh bless him and give him peace) once said, concerning the guardians of Hell:

> The space between the shoulders of one of them is like the distance between the east and the west.'[1433]

❧ ❧

> [Angels] who do not disobey Allāh in what He commands them,
> *lā yuʿṣūna 'llāha mā amara-hum*
> but do what they are commanded.
> *wa yafʿalūna mā yuʾmarūn.*

That is to say: "They do not disobey the commandment of Allāh, in any situation whatsoever, and they carry out their orders without delay or postponement."

Then the unbelievers will be told, as they are about to enter the Fire:

> O you who disbelieve, make no excuses for yourselves this day.
> *yā ayyuha 'lladhīna kafarū lā taʿtadhiru 'l-yawm:* (66:7)

In other words: "Make no excuses for your sins and your criminal behaviour. You will gain nothing by making excuses today, because the warning went out to you long ago, along with the opportunity to apologize."

> You are only being paid for what you used to do.
> *inna-mā tujzawna mā kuntum taʿmalūn.* (66:7)

That is to say: "You are simply receiving the recompense for your foul deeds, and you are not being wronged in the slightest." As Allāh (Exalted is He) has said:

> This day each soul is requited according to what it has earned.
> *al-yawma tujzā kullu nafsin bi-mā kasabat*
> There is no wrong this day.
> *lā ẓulma 'l-yawm:*
> Allāh is Swift at reckoning.
> *inna 'llāha Sarīʿu 'l-ḥisāb.* (40:17)[1434]

As for those who:

> do not disobey Allāh in what He commands them
> *lā yuʿṣūna 'llāha mā amara-hum*

—they readily accept His commandments and dutifully carry them out. The expression:

> but they do what they are commanded.
> *wa yafʿalūna mā yuʾmarūn.*

—signifies that they duly perform what they are commanded to do, neither finding it too burdensome nor wavering in its performance.[1435] This implies that the angels are charged, in the Hereafter, with the duty to observe whatever Allāh (Exalted is He) commands them to do, and whatever He forbids them to do. Disobedience on their part would therefore mean noncompliance with the command and the prohibition.[1436] This also goes to prove the impeccable virtue [*ʿiṣma*] of the angels, because they are pure intellects, devoid of desires and lustful appetites, obedient to the Essence [*Dhāt*], in stark contrast to the human being.[1437]

These are my own comments:

For the believer who seeks to point other people in the direction of Allāh (Exalted is He), it is appropriate that he should first consider directing his fellow believers towards Allāh (Magnificent is His Majesty). He should consider being one of those who sacrifice themselves, and who prefer the believers to themselves, by forgetting himself and entrusting his business to his Lord, after fulfilling the Divine religious duties [*farāʾiḍ Ilāhiyya*]. He should dearly wish to see the Community of our master Muḥammad (Allāh bless him and give him peace) entering Allāh's good pleasure, and following His Messenger. This should be dearer to him than protecting himself, through worshipful service intended exclusively for his own benefit. Serving the believers should be dearer to him than securing his own salvation from the torment [of the Hereafter], even if it means neglecting himself and his family, since everyone must do his duty.

This is the aim of those who know Allāh through direct experience [*al-ʿārifīn bi'llāh*]. Abū Bakr aṣ-Ṣiddīq [the Champion of Truth] once said: "I would love to see my body grow big enough to fill Hell completely, so that no room would be left for the Community of my master Muḥammad (Allāh bless him and give him peace)." This is love for the sake of Allāh and His Messenger, not a way of seeking spiritual reward, or anything at all.

Yes indeed, the self is given priority over everything, but this does not apply to everyone.

> Guard yourselves and your families against a Fire....
> *qū anfusa-kum wa ahlī-kum nāran....*

—does not apply to everyone. We beseech Allāh (Exalted is He) to grant us, and all the believers, His good pleasure and His love. The style of the Noble Qur᾽ān is sometimes frightening to His servants, as in this verse, for instance:

> Guard yourselves and your families....
> *qū anfusa-kum wa ahlī-kum....*

At other times, it fills them with ardent yearning for His good pleasure, and with eager longing to follow His Messenger (Allāh bless him and give him peace) in the Garden of Paradise, and to enjoy the lovely maidens, the palaces, and all the other delights of the Gardens of Bliss.

Since this draws attention to our weakness, by inspiring either longing or fear, it is part of His grace and generous favour (Glorious and Exalted is He), because He knows the reality of our origin—nonexistence!

We beg Allāh to enable us to be of service to the true believers, and we beg Him to forgive the Community of our master Muḥammad (Allāh bless him and give him peace). Peace be upon the Messengers, and praise be to Allāh, the Lord of All the Worlds. There is no might nor any power, except with Allāh, the All-High, the Almighty. May Allāh bless our master Muḥammad, his family and his Companions, and may He grant them peace.

The Eighty-ninth Call

In the Name of Allāh, the All-Merciful, the All-Compassionate.
Bismi'llāhi 'r-Raḥmāni 'r-Raḥīm.

O you who truly believe,
yā ayyuha 'lladhīna āmanū
turn to Allāh in repentance—
in sincere repentance!
tūbū ila 'llāhi tawbatan naṣūḥā:
It may be that your Lord will acquit you
ʿasā Rabbu-kum an yukaffira ʿan-kum
of your evil deeds,
and will admit you into Gardens
sayyiʾāti-kum wa yudkhila-kum jannātin
underneath which rivers flow,
tajrī min taḥti-ha 'l-anhāru
on the day when Allāh will not abase the Prophet
yawma lā yukhzi 'llāhu 'n-Nabiyya
and those who believe with him.
wa 'lladhīna āmanū maʿa-h:
Their light will run before them
nūru-hum yasʿā baina aidī-him
and on their right hands.
wa bi-aimāni-him
They will say: "Our Lord,
yaqūlūna Rabba-nā
perfect our light for us, and forgive us!
atmim lā-nā nūra-nā wa 'ghfir la-nā
You are surely Capable of all things."
inna-ka ʿalā kulli shaiʾin Qadīr. (66:8)

O you who truly believe,
yā ayyuha 'lladhīna āmanū
turn to Allāh in repentance—in sincere repentance!
tūbū ila 'llāhi tawbatan naṣūḥā:

When repentance is *naṣūḥ*, it advises [*tanṣaḥu*] the penitent to refrain from reverting to what he has repented, for it is genuine and truthful. According to the author of *al-Kashshāf*: "Repentance is described metaphorically in terms of *naṣḥ* [good advice], since it counsels them to be extremely contrite in repenting their misdeeds, and not to repeat them." The related term *naṣāḥa* is applied to the tailoring of clothes.[1438]

According to ʿUmar ibn al-Khaṭṭāb, Ubayy ibn Kaʿb and Muʿādh (may Allāh be well pleased with them): "When repentance is *naṣūḥ*, it means that one repents and then does not return to the sin, just as milk does not return to the udder." According to al-Kalbī: "It means that the penitent seeks forgiveness with his tongue, feels remorse in his heart, and keeps his physical body under control." According to Muḥammad ibn al-Qurṭubī: "Sincere repentance [*tawba naṣūḥ*] consists of four ingredients: (1) seeking forgiveness with the tongue, (2) physical abstinence, (3) inner commitment to refraining from repetition, and (4) avoiding the misconduct of one's brethren."

According to the religious scholars, it is strictly necessary to repent every sin immediately. It is not permissible to delay repentance, whether the offence be minor or major. If the offence is a matter between the servant and Allāh (Exalted is He), and does not involve any human right, three conditions must be fulfilled by the penitent:

1. He must refrain from the sinful act of disobedience.
2. He must feel remorse for what he has committed.
3. He must be determined never to repeat it.

If all these conditions are fulfilled, his repentance is sincere [*naṣūḥ*], but if any one of them is omitted, his repentance is invalid. If the offence involves a human right, the conditions of repentance are four in number, these same three plus a fourth:

4. He must acquit himself of what he owes to the victim. If the offence involves money and the like, he must return it to the owner. If it incurs a legal penalty, for *qadhf* [false accusation of sexual misconduct] or the like, he must submit himself to retribution by the victim, or else seek his pardon. If it is a case of backbiting, he must ask him to overlook it.

It is necessary for the servant to repent all the sins he has committed. If he repents one of them, his repentance of that particular sin is valid, and he remains responsible for those he has not repented. This is the doctrine of the people of the Sunna.

The necessity of repentance is demonstrated by evidence from the Book, the Sunna and the consensus of the Community.

As reported by Muslim, on the authority of al-Agharr ibn Yasār al-Mazanī, Allāh's Messenger (Allāh bless him and give him peace) once said:

> O people, repent to Allāh, for I repent a hundred times each day.

As reported by al-Bukhārī, it was Abū Huraira (may Allāh be well pleased with him) who said: "I once heard Allāh's Messenger (Allāh bless him and give him peace) say:

> By Allāh, I seek Allāh's forgiveness and I repent to Him more than seventy times each day."

According to a generally accepted report from Anas ibn Mālik (may Allāh be well pleased with him), Allāh's Messenger (Allāh bless him and give him peace) also said:

> For Allāh, delight in the repentance of His servant is greater than the joy experienced by one of you, when he comes across his camel after losing it in a desert land.

As reported by Abū Mūsā al-Ash'arī, the Prophet (Allāh bless him and give him peace) once said:

> Allāh extends His hand by night, to invite the evildoer of the day to repent, and He extends His hand by day, to invite the evildoer of the night to repent, until the sun rises from its setting.[1439]

(That is to say: "He extends His power and His mercy," because He is totally exempt from physical limbs and organs.)

As reported by 'Abdu'llāh ibn 'Umar (may Allāh be well pleased with him and his father), the Prophet (Allāh bless him and give him peace) once said:

> Allāh accepts the servant's repentance, provided he is not gargling his last breath.[1440]

Much more has been said on the subject of repentance [*tawba*]. It is the most important of the Islāmic commandments, the first of the stations of faith, the beginning of the path of the spiritual travellers, and the key to the door of those who reach their destination, so there is no harm in discussing some of the things connected with it.

In everyday language, *tawba* means *rujūʿ* [returning]. As a term of the Sacred Law, it means remorse [*nadam*] for the commission of a sinful act of disobedience, because it is a sinful act of disobedience. Remorse does not constitute repentance [*tawba*] if it is remorse for physical harm, or damage to reputation or property, for example.

As for remorse inspired by fear of the Fire of Hell, or desire for the Garden of Paradise, there is some uncertainty as to whether it constitutes repentance [*tawba*]. It depends on whether or not that remorse is an acknowledgement of the wickedness of the deed committed, and of the fact that it is a sinful act of disobedience. It also depends on whether some other motive is involved.

The truth of the matter is that, if the acknowledgement of wickedness is sufficient to prove that the remorse is genuine, it counts as repentance [*tawba*], but not otherwise. In the case of repentance during an alarming illness, for example, it all depends on whether or not that remorse is an acknowledgement of the wickedness of the act of disobedience, or simply due to fear.

On the basis of traditional reports [*akhbār*], the obvious conclusion is that repentance should be readily accepted, unless the symptoms of death are apparent, and that the penitent's veracity is usually confirmed.

The term *nadam* [remorse] signifies: "experiencing sadness and grief because of what has been done, and wishing that it had not been done." This is essential to the establishment of true repentance, because mere abstinence is typical of the clown [*mājin*], the sinner who plays games, like the drinker of alcoholic liquor. When he gets bored with his clowning, and tries some permissible activities for a change, that does not count as repentance. The Prophet (Allāh bless him and give him peace) said:

> Remorse is an act of repentance [*an-nadam tawba*].[1441]

An additional element is firm resolve to refrain from repetition of the offence, but suppose someone raises this objection: "When it comes to committing the sinful offence in the future, the penitent may not realize what he is doing, because of mental confusion or insanity, or something of the kind. He may actually be incapable of committing it again, due to some affliction he has suffered, like dumbness, for instance, in the case of slanderous accusation [*qadhf*], or the amputation of his testicles, in the case of sexual misconduct [*zinā*]. It is therefore pointless to resolve to abstain, because it presupposes the ability and freedom to act."

The answer to this will be: The resolution to abstain is based on the assumption of sanity and capability. If the penitent has been deprived of the ability to do something, the resolution to abstain from it will not be required of him. Consider what Imām al-Ḥaramain had to say on the subject: "As for the resolution to abstain from repeating an offence, it must accompany repentance in certain cases only. It is not relevant in every case, since the resolution is appropriate only when the penitent is still capable of doing what he committed previously. It is not appropriate for the eunuch to resolve to abstain from adultery and fornication, nor for the dumb mute to resolve to abstain from slanderous accusation."

According to one of the most outstanding experts: "As a matter of fact, the resolution [to remain abstinent] is only for the purpose of clear and emphatic affirmation, not binding restraint and precaution. Since the penitent feels remorse for his sin because of its wickedness, he will never be devoid of that resolution, so long as he retains his sanity and capability."

The symptom of remorse is the prolongation of grief, fear, and the shedding of tears. To quote one of the more unusual sayings on the subject: "The sign that remorse is genuine, in the case of a sin like adultery or fornication, is that the penitent does not dream of committing it voluntarily, since that would indicate his continued liking for it, and the lack of its total eradication from his heart, which would be incompatible with genuine remorse."

According to the authors of *Sharḥ al-Maqāṣid*: "If the offence was a violation of the right of Allāh (Exalted is He), and His alone, remorse is sufficient, as in cases like fleeing from the military advance, and failing to enjoin what is right and proper [*ma'rūf*]. In certain instances, there may be an additional requirement, like submitting oneself to the legal penalty [*ḥadd*] for drinking alcoholic liquor, paying what is outstanding from the alms-due [*zakāt*], and making up for missed performance of the ritual prayer [*ṣalāt*].

"Where the rights of His servants are involved, remorse and the resolution [to abstain] must be accompanied by delivering what is due to the servant concerned, or providing him with compensation, if the offence was an act of cruel injustice, like robbery and deliberate murder. If the offence involved leading the victim astray, the penitent must guide him aright [by informing him of the true facts]. Apology is required in a case of slanderous abuse, like backbiting, if the victim has come to know about it. It is not necessary to provide specific details of the backbiting, unless the victim has already heard an exaggerated version of it."

According to Imām al-Ḥaramain: "This additional element is actually a different obligation, separate from the act of repentance. If the murderer expresses remorse, without submitting himself to retaliation, his repentance is valid with regard to the right of Allāh (Exalted is He). By withholding retaliation from the person entitled to exact it, he is committing a fresh offence, which calls for repentance in turn, but which does not detract from repenting the murder." He then went on to say: "In certain cases, like robbery, repentance cannot be valid unless the right of the servant has been discharged. There is a significant difference between robbery and murder, and the distinction is not hidden from the thoughtful person."

There is no disagreement, among the people of the Sunna and others, concerning the strict necessity of repentance by those who are guilty of major sins [*kabā'ir*].

According to *Sharḥ al-Jawhara*: "Persistence in a sin, by delaying its repentance, counts as a single offence, so long as the perpetrator has not resolved to abstain from repeating it."

The scholars hold various opinions about someone who remembers the sinful offence, after repentance thereof: Is he obliged to renew his remorse? According to al-Qāḍī: "If he does not renew his remorse, that counts as a new offence, for which remorse is strictly required. The first repentance retains its validity, since nothing invalidates a previous act of worship, after it has been established."

Imām al-Ḥaramain has stated explicitly: "[Renewal is not required] provided the penitent does not rejoice and take pleasure and delight in his recollection of the sin, or in hearing about it. Otherwise, renewal is obligatory by general agreement."

There are several degrees of repentance, and one of the best accounts of them occurs in the report from [ʿAlī] the Prince of the Believers (may Allāh ennoble his countenance), who heard an Arab nomad say: "O Allāh, I beg Your forgiveness and I repent to You." ʿAlī said: "O you there, slickness of the tongue in repentance is the repentance of the liars!" The Arab nomad then asked: "And what is repentance?" ʿAlī (may Allāh ennoble his countenance) replied: "It includes six things:

1. Remorse for sins committed in the past.
2. Renewed performance of obligatory religious duties [*farāʾiḍ*].
3. Providing compensation for acts of criminal injustice.
4. Seeking pardon from adversaries.
5. Resolving never to repeat the offence.
6. Dissolving your lower self in worshipful obedience to Allāh, just as you caused it to grow in sinful disobedience, and making it taste the bitterness of obedience, just as you let it taste the sweetness of sinful acts of disobedience, until it comes to enjoy the sweetness and flavours of worshipful obedience."

Allāh (Exalted is He) has then gone on to explain the value of repentance, in His saying (Glory be to Him and Exalted is He):

> It may be that your Lord will acquit you of your evil deeds,
> *ʿasā Rabbu-kum an yukaffira ʿan-kum sayyiʾāti-kum*
> and will admit you into Gardens underneath which rivers flow
> *wa yudkhila-kum jannātin tajrī min taḥti-ha 'l-anhāru*

This means, it has been said, that Allāh (Almighty and Glorious is He) will indeed do that, but the promise is expressed in the form of encouraging expectation, in the sytle of the kings, for they used to say, when they intended to do something: "Perhaps we shall do such-and-such." The implication is that it is a gracious favour from Him (Glory be to Him and Exalted is He), that repentance is not necessarily accepted by Him, and that the servant must be poised between fear and hope, even if he goes to extreme lengths in performing the obligations of worshipful service. The Qurʾānic verse indicates that acceptance of repentance cannot be taken for granted, because expiation comes after acceptance.

Imām an-Nawawī said: "According to the people of the Sunna, Allāh (Glory be to Him and Exalted is He) is not obliged to accept repentance, even if its preconditions are met, but He does accept it (Glory be to Him) as a mark of noble generosity from Him, and as a gracious favour. Our knowledge of its acceptance is based on the Sacred Law and the consensus, so it is not in doubt, as it is clearly stated in the Book, in His saying (Exalted is He):

> And He it is who accepts repentance from His servants,
> *wa Huwa 'lladhī yaqbalu 't-tawbata ʿan ʿibādi-hi*
> and pardons evil deeds,
> *wa yaʿfū ʿani 's-sayyiʾāti*
> and He knows what you are doing.
> *wa yaʿlamu mā tafʿalūn.* (42:25)"[1442]

It may be, O believers, that your Lord will erase your bad deeds that you have previously committed, and that He will admit you to orchards, where rivers flow beneath their trees.[1443]

> on the day when Allāh will not abase the Prophet
> *yawma lā yukhzi 'llāhu 'n-Nabiyya*
> and those who believe with him.
> *wa 'lladhīna āmanū maʿa-h:*

That is to say: "He will not abase him by rejecting his intercession." Abasement means humiliation. In other words: "He will not humiliate them in the presence of the unbelievers, though it is permissible for Him to torment them in a manner that is not perceptible to the unbelievers." His saying (Exalted is He):

> will not abase
> *lā yukhzi*

—is an allusion to those whom Allāh has abased, such as the people guilty of unbelief and immorality. It is also intended to elicit praise from the believers, because He has preserved them from a similar condition.[1444]

> and those who believe with him.
> *wa 'lladhīna āmanū maʿa-h:*

In other words: "those who have accompanied him in the sphere of belief."

> Their light will run before them and on their right hands.
> *nūru-hum yasʿā baina aidī-him wa bi-aimāni-him*

It will run before them on the Bridge over Hell. What is meant by "their right hands" is "every direction they take." According to al-Khaṭīb: "The specific reference to 'before' and 'right hands' does not preclude their having a light on their left hands. They do have such a light, but they pay no attention to it, because they are either among the front-runners, in which case they are moving towards what lies before them, or among the people of the right hand, in which case they are moving towards that which is on their right."

As reported by Ibn Jarīr, concerning His saying (Exalted is He):

> Their light will run before them
> *nūru-hum yasʿā baina aidī-him*

—Ibn Masʿūd said: "In accordance with the scope of their deeds, they will cross the Bridge over Hell. Some among them will have a light like a mountain, and some will have a light like a palm tree. The least of them will have his light in his big toe...."[1445]

As we are informed by Ibn al-Mubārak, on the authority of Abū Dharr and Abu'd-Dardāʾ, Allāh's Messenger (Allāh bless him and give him peace) once said:

> I shall be the first of those summoned to make prostration on the Day of Resurrection, and the first of those summoned to raise his head. I shall then look in front of me, and I shall recognize my Community among the communities. I shall look to my right, and I shall recognize my Community among the communities. I shall look to my left, and I shall recognize my Community among the communities.

A man asked: "O Messenger of Allāh, and how will you recognize your Community among the communities?" To this he replied:

> They will be distinguished by a whiteness on the forehead and on the wrists and ankles, from the effects of ritual purification, and none of the other communities will be like them in that respect. I shall recognize them by the fact that they are receiving their records with their right hands. I shall recognize them by the mark on their faces, from the effect of prostration, and I shall recognize them by their light, which will be running before them.[1446]

> They will say: "Our Lord,
> *yaqūlūna Rabba-nā*
> perfect our light for us, and forgive us!
> *atmim lā-nā nūra-nā wa 'ghfir la-nā*
> You are surely Capable of all things."
> *inna-ka ʿalā kulli shaiʾin Qadīr.*

According to Ibn ʿAbbās (may Allāh be well pleased with him and his father): "They will say that when the light of the hypocrites is extinguished, out of pity." According to al-Ḥasan: "Allāh (Exalted is He) will be perfecting their light for them, but they will appeal for closeness to the presence of Allāh (Exalted is He)." Someone said: "The lowest of them in rank will be he whose light is just sufficient for him to see where his feet are treading. The light is in keeping with the scope of their deeds, so they will be asking for its perfection." Someone said: "The front-runners into the Garden of Paradise will pass like lightning across the Bridge over Hell. Some of them will move like the wind, and some of them at a slow and creeping pace, the latter being those who will say:

> Our Lord, perfect our light for us."[1447]
> *Rabba-nā atmim lā-nā nūra-nā*

It has also been said to mean: "They will plead with constant entreaty and humble supplication."[1448]

These are my own observations:

If the servant never lapsed into error, he would become deluded into thinking himself perfect. The natural constitution of the servant [of the Lord] includes shortcoming, shamefulness and inadequacy.

If Allāh did not afflict us with contradictions, who would prevent us from deluding ourselves? By His grace and noble generosity, He has granted us scope [for personal choice], because the servant must repent, for repentance is Allāh's custom [*sunna*] in relation to His creatures, and so is seeking forgiveness. He has opened this window of opportunity for us till the end of our lives (so long as we are not gargling our last breath), so we must not fail to take advantage of it, and we must make a firm commitment to genuine repentance.

As we can see for ourselves, when we experience a worldly need, we twist and turn from one person to another, so that the doorway of assistance may be opened for us, yet our Lord has already opened it for us. We must not overlook this doorway, for we need our Lord at all times, to block the contradictions, the slips and the mistakes that issue from us. We must not bolt this doorway against us, because the doorway of Allāh's mercy for His servants is open at every moment, including the here and now, so long as the servant does not shut it against himself, by failing to repent and apologize to Him.

We beg You to grant us perfect pardon and complete forgiveness. Peace be upon the Messengers, and praise be to Allāh, the Lord of All the Worlds. There is no might nor any power, except with Allāh, the All-High, the Almighty. May Allāh bless our master Muḥammad, his family and his Companions, and may He grant them peace.

Bibliography

Sources relied upon in the commentary

1 The Commentary *[Tafsīr]* of al-Fakhr ar-Rāzī, commonly known as *at-Tafsīr al-Kabīr wa Mafātīḥ al-Ghaib* [The Great Commentary and the Keys of the Unseen], by Imām Muḥammad ar-Rāzī Fakhr ad-Dīn.

2 *Rūḥ al-Bayān* by Ismā'īl Ḥaqqī al-Burūsawī.

3 *Rūḥ al-Ma'ānī* by al-Ulūsī al-'Allāma Abu'l-Faḍl Shihāb ad-Dīn Maḥmūd al-Ulūsī al-Baghdādī.

4 *al-Jāmi' li-Aḥkām al-Qur'ān* by Abū 'Abdi'llāh Muḥammad ibn Aḥmad al-Anṣārī al-Qurṭubī.

5 *Jāmi' al-Bayān fī Tafsīr al-Qur'ān* by Abū Ja'far Muḥammad ibn Jarīr aṭ-Ṭabarī.

6 *Tafsīr al-Qur'ān al-'Aẓīm* by al-Ḥāfiẓ 'Imād ad-Dīn Abu'l-Fidā' Ismā'īl ibn Kathīr ad-Dimashqī.

7 *Madārik an-Nasafī* by Imām Abu'l-Barakāt 'Abdu'llāh ibn Aḥmad ibn Maḥmūd an-Nasafī.

8 *Mawāhib al-Jalīl min Tafsīr al-Baiḍāwī: Anwār at-Tanzīl wa Asrār at-Ta'wīl* by al-Qāḍī Shaikh Muḥammad Aḥmad Kan'ān.

9 *Laṭā'if al-Ishārāt* by al-Qushairī.

10 *Ḥāshiyat al-Jumal 'ala 'l-Jalālain* by Shaikh Sulaimān ibn 'Umar al-'Ujailī ash-Shāfi'ī. Commonly known as *al-Jumal*.

11 *Ḥāshiyat aṣ-Ṣāwī 'ala 'l-Jalālain* by al-'Ālim al-'Allāma al-'Ārif-bi'llāh Shaikh Aḥmad aṣ-Ṣāwī al-Mālikī.

12 *Ḥāshiya* by Shaikh Zāda, on the *Tafsīr* of al-Baiḍāwī.

13 *Ṣafwat at Tafāsīr* by aṣ-Ṣābūnī.

14 *Ishārāt al-I'jāz fī Bayān al-Ījāz* by Imām al-Mujaddid Badī' az-Zamān Sa'īd an-Nūrsī.

15 *Tafsīr Gharā'ib al-Qur'ān wa Raghā'ib al-Furqān* by al-'Allāma Niẓām ad-Dīn al-Ḥasan ibn Muḥammad ibn Ḥusain al-Qummī an-Nīsābūrī.

16 *Tafsīr al-Khāzin*, entitled *Lubāb at-Ta'wīl fī Ma'āni 't-Tanzīl*, by Imām 'Alā' ad-Dīn 'Alī ibn Muḥammad al-Baghdādī, generally known as al-Khāzin.

17 *Ḥāshiya* by al-'Allāma Abu'l-Faḍl al-Qurashī aṣ-Ṣiddīqī al-Khaṭīb, commonly known as al-Kāzarūnī, on [the *Tafsīr* of] al-Baiḍāwī.

Notes: The First Call

[1] Ibn Kathīr

[2] *Ṣafwat at-tafāsīr*

[3] Shaikh Zāda ʿAlī al-Qāḍī

[4] ar-Rāzī

[5] Ibn Kathīr

[6] At this point in the original text, the author explains that *unẓur-nā* is derived from the Arabic expression *naẓara-hu idha 'ntaẓara-hu* [to watch over someone while waiting for him].

[7] al-Ulūsī

[8] *Ṣafwat at-tafāsīr*

[9] Literally, "the stopping of the means."

[10] The form *dharīʿa* is the singular of *dharāʾiʿ*.

[11] al-Qurṭubī

Notes: The Second Call

[12] *Ṣafwat at-tafāsīr*
[13] aṭ-Ṭabarī
[14] al-Qurṭubī
[15] ar-Rāzī
[16] al-Ulūsī
[17] al-Qurṭubī
[18] *Rūḥ al-Bayān*
[19] Ibn Kathīr
[20] aṭ-Ṭabarī
[21] *Ṣafwat at-tafāsīr*
[22] ar-Rāzī
[23] aṭ-Ṭabarī
[24] *al-Jumal*
[25] al-Ulūsī
[26] *Laṭā'if al-ishārāt*

Notes: The Third Call

[27] ar-Rāzī
[28] aṣ-Ṣāwī
[29] al-Ulūsī
[30] *Ṣafwat at-tafāsīr*
[31] ar-Rāzī
[32] aṭ-Ṭabarī
[33] *Rūḥ al-bayān*
[34] Ibn Kathīr
[35] *Ṣafwat at-tafāsīr*
[36] *Rūḥ al-bayān*
[37] aṣ-Ṣāwī
[38] *Laṭā᾿if al-ishārāt*
[39] al-Ulūsī
[40] al-Khāzin
[41] al-Ulūsī
[42] al-Kāzirūnī's commentary on al-Baiḍāwī

Notes: The Fourth Call

[43] ar-Rāzī
[44] *Ṣafwat at-tafāsīr*
[45] ar-Rāzī
[46] *Ṣafwat at-tafāsīr*
[47] Ibn Māja
[48] *Madārik*
[49] al-Khāzin
[50] *Ṣafwat at-tafāsīr*
[51] al-Khāzin
[52] *Ṣafwat at-tafāsīr*
[53] ar-Rāzī
[54] *Ṣafwat at-tafāsīr*
[55] al-Ulūsī
[56] ar-Rāzī
[57] *Ṣafwat at-tafāsīr*
[58] al-Ulūsī
[59] *Ṣafwat at-tafāsīr*
[60] ar-Rāzī
[61] *Rūḥ al-bayān*
[62] *Laṭā᾽if al-ishārāt*

Notes: The Fifth Call

[63] *Rūḥ al-bayān*

[64] *Ṣafwat at-tafāsīr*

[65] ar-Rāzī

[66] al-Qurṭubī (This saying is reported by al-Bukhārī).

[67] *Ṣafwat at-tafāsīr*

[68] ar-Rāzī

[69] al-Bukhārī

[70] *Rūḥ al-bayān*

[71] *Ṣafwat at-tafāsīr*

[72] ar-Rāzī

[73] *Ṣafwat at-tafāsīr*

[74] al-Qurṭubī

[75] *Rūḥ al-bayān*

[76] al-Baiḍāwī

[77] *Rūḥ al-bayān*

[78] *Laṭā'if al-ishārāt* (This saying is reported by al-Bukhārī and other traditional experts).

Notes: The Sixth Call

[79] ar-Rāzī
[80] *Ṣafwat at-tafāsīr*
[81] ar-Rāzī
[82] al-Ulūsī
[83] *Ṣafwat at-tafāsīr*
[84] ar-Rāzī
[85] al-Baiḍāwī
[86] *Ṣafwat at-tafāsīr*
[87] ar-Rāzī
[88] ar-Rāzī
[89] al-Qurṭubī
[90] *Ṣafwat at-tafāsīr*
[91] ar-Rāzī
[92] *Laṭā'if al-ishārāt*
[93] Reported by Muslim.

Notes: The Seventh Call

[94] *Ṣafwat at-tafāsīr*

[95] al-Qurṭubī

[96] ar-Rāzī

[97] *Ṣafwat at-tafāsīr*

[98] ar-Rāzī

[99] al-Qurṭubī

[100] aṭ-Ṭabarī

[101] al-Ulūsī

[102] *Ṣafwat at-tafāsīr*

[103] *Rūḥ al-bayān*

[104] *Laṭāʾif al-ishārāt*

Notes: The Eighth Call

[105] *Ṣafwat at-tafāsīr*

[106] *Rūḥ al-bayān*

[107] *Ṣafwat at-tafāsīr*

[108] *Rūḥ al-bayān*

[109] *Ṣafwat at-tafāsīr*

[110] *Rūḥ al-bayān*

[111] al-Qurṭubī

[112] *Ṣafwat at-tafāsīr*

[113] al-Qurṭubī

[114] *Ṣafwat at-tafāsīr*

[115] Aḥmad (with very similar wording).

[116] This Prophetic tradition [*ḥadīth*] is reported by at-Tirmidhī, in the chapters on pious abstinence [*zuhd*] (see the section on hypocritical ostentation [*riyā'*] and the effort to gain a good reputation [*sum'a*]). The original version can be found in the *Ṣaḥīḥ* of Muslim, in the Book of the Sacred Struggle [*Kitāb al-Jihād*] (see the section on those who fight for the sake of hypocritical ostentation [*riyā'*] and to gain a good reputation [*sum'a*]).

[117] *Rūḥ al-bayān*

[118] *Ṣafwat at-tafāsīr*

[119] *Rūḥ al-bayān*

[120] *Ṣafwat at-tafāsīr*

[121] al-Khāzin

[122] *Ṣafwat at-tafāsīr*

[123] al-Khāzin

[124] *Ṣafwat at-tafāsīr*

[125] *al-Madārik*

[126] ar-Rāzī

[127] *Ṣafwat at-tafāsīr*

[128] *Rūḥ al-bayān*

[129] *Ṣafwat at-tafāsīr*

[130] *Rūḥ al-bayān*

[131] Ibn Kathīr

[132] *Laṭā'if al-ishārāt*

Notes: The Ninth Call

133 *Rūḥ al-bayān*

134 *Ṣafwat at-tafāsīr*

135 *Rūḥ al-bayān*

136 *Ṣafwat at-tafāsīr*

137 al-Qurṭubī

138 al-Qurṭubī

139 *Ṣafwat at-tafāsīr*

140 al-Qurṭubī

141 aṭ-Ṭabarī

142 *Ṣafwat at-tafāsīr*

143 al-Qurṭubī

144 al-Bukhārī, Muslim and Aḥmad

145 ar-Rāzī

146 *Ṣafwat at-tafāsīr*

147 ar-Rāzī

148 *Ṣafwat at-tafāsīr*

149 ar-Rāzī

150 *Ṣafwat at-tafāsīr*

151 al-Bukhārī and Muslim.

152 Ibn Kathīr (Reported by Aḥmad, but with the wording "his oppression [*ghashmu-hu*]" instead of "his deception [*ghashshu-hu*]").

153 *Iḥyā' 'Ulūm ad-Dīn*

Notes: The Tenth Call

[154] ar-Rāzī

[155] Muslim

[156] *Ṣafwat at-tafāsīr*

[157] *Rūḥ al-bayān*

[158] *Ṣafwat at-tafāsīr*

[159] al-Khāzin

[160] *Ṣafwat at-tafāsīr*

[161] al-Khāzin

[162] *Ṣafwat at-tafāsīr*

[163] *al-Madārik*

[164] al-Khāzin (Reported by Muslim).

[165] *Ṣafwat at-tafāsīr*

[166] *Rūḥ al-bayān*

[167] *Ṣafwat at-tafāsīr*

[168] al-Qurṭubī

[169] ar-Rāzī

[170] al-Qurṭubī

[171] aṭ-Ṭabarī

[172] al-Ḥākim

[173] Aḥmad

[174] *Ṣafwat at-tafāsīr*

[175] al-Khāzin

[176] Reported by al-Bukhārī, with the wording: "If someone is hostile to me as a guardian, I have declared war on him."

[177] Abū Dāwūd

[178] ar-Rāzī

[179] *Ṣafwat at-tafāsīr*

[180] Ibn Kathīr (Reported by Ibn Abī Ḥātim, and also by at-Tirmidhī, but with the wording: "[All of it will] soon [be cancelled]").

[181] al-Qurṭubī

[182] *Ṣafwat at-tafāsīr*

[183] Reported by Aḥmad in his *Musnad* .

[184] Ibn Kathīr (Reported by al-Bukhārī and Muslim).

[185] *Ṣafwat at-tafāsīr*

[186] ar-Rāzī

[187] *Rūḥ al-bayān*

Notes: The Eleventh Call

188 *Ṣafwat at-tafāsīr*

189 *Rūḥ al-bayān*

190 *Ṣafwat at-tafāsīr*

191 *Rūḥ al-bayān*

192 al-Khāzin

193 *Ṣafwat at-tafāsīr*

194 al-Khāzin

195 *Ṣafwat at-tafāsīr*

196 al-Khāzin

197 *Ṣafwat at-tafāsīr*

198 *Rūḥ al-bayān*

199 *Ṣafwat at-tafāsīr*

200 al-Khāzin

201 *Ṣafwat at-tafāsīr*

202 al-Khāzin

203 ar-Rāzī

204 *Ṣafwat at-tafāsīr*

205 ar-Rāzī

206 *Ṣafwat at-tafāsīr*

207 *Rūḥ al-bayān*

208 ar-Rāzī

209 *Ṣafwat at-tafāsīr*

210 ar-Rāzī

211 Ibn Kathīr

212 *Ṣafwat at-tafāsīr*

213 Ibn Kathīr

214 al-Qurṭubī

215 ar-Rāzī

216 *Ṣafwat at-tafāsīr*

217 ar-Rāzī

[218] *Ṣafwat at-tafāsīr*

[219] ar-Rāzī

[220] *Rūḥ al-bayān*

[221] *Ṣafwat at-tafāsīr*

[222] al-Baiḍāwī

[223] al-Qurṭubī (Reported by an-Nasāʾī and others).

[224] *Ṣafwat at-tafāsīr*

[225] ar-Rāzī

[226] *Ṣafwat at-tafāsīr*

[227] al-Baiḍāwī

[228] *Ṣafwat at-tafāsīr*

[229] ar-Rāzī

[230] al-Baiḍāwī

[231] *Ṣafwat at-tafāsīr*

[232] al-Khāzin (Reported by Muslim)

[233] *Ṣafwat at-tafāsīr*

[234] ar-Rāzī

[235] *Ṣafwat at-tafāsīr*

[236] Ibn Kathīr (This report has a sound chain of transmission [*isnād*], and al-Bukhārī has related it in seven places).

[237] *Laṭāʾif al-ishārāt*

Notes: The Twelfth Call

238 *Ṣafwat at-tafāsīr*

239 ar-Rāzī

240 *Ṣafwat at-tafāsīr*

241 al-Baiḍāwī

242 ar-Rāzī

243 al-Qurṭubī

244 al-Khāzin (Reported by Muslim).

245 *Ṣafwat at-tafāsīr*

246 ar-Rāzī

247 *Rūḥ al-bayān*

248 *Laṭāʾif al-ishārāt*

Notes: The Thirteenth Call

249 ar-Rāzī
250 *Ṣafwat at-tafāsīr*
251 al-Qāḍī
252 Shaikh Zāda
253 al-Khāzin
254 *Laṭā'if al-ishārāt*
255 al-Ulūsī
256 al-Bukhārī
257 ar-Rāzī
258 al-Bukhārī and Muslim
259 Ibn Māja, at-Tirmidhī, al-Ḥākim and adh-Dhahabī.
260 *Minhāj al-ʿābidīn*
261 *Ṣafwat at-tafāsīr*
262 ar-Rāzī
263 al-Ulūsī
264 al-Khāzin (Reported by at-Tirmidhī, who calls it "a good, authentic tradition [*ḥadīth*]").
265 *Ṣafwat at-tafāsīr*
266 at-Tirmidhī (with very similar wording).
267 Aḥmad (with very similar wording).
268 ar-Rāzī
269 al-Khāzin
270 Ibn Kathīr
271 *Ṣafwat at-tafāsīr*
272 ar-Rāzī
273 ar-Rāzī
274 *Ṣafwat at-tafāsīr*
275 ar-Rāzī
276 *Ṣafwat at-tafāsīr*
277 *al-Madārik*
278 *Rūḥ al-bayān*

Notes: The Fourteenth Call

279 *Ṣafwat at-tafāsīr*
280 *Rūḥ al-bayān*
281 ar-Rāzī
282 al-Qurṭubī
283 *Ṣafwat at-tafāsīr*
284 ar-Rāzī
285 *Ṣafwat at-tafāsīr*
286 ar-Rāzī
287 *Ṣafwat at-tafāsīr*
288 ar-Rāzī
289 *Ṣafwat at-tafāsīr*
290 Ibn Kathīr
291 *Rūḥ al-bayān*
292 Abū Dāwūd

Notes: The Fifteenth Call

[293] *Ṣafwat at-tafāsīr*

[294] ar-Rāzī

[295] *Ṣafwat at-tafāsīr*

[296] ar-Rāzī

[297] ar-Rāzī

[298] *Rūḥ al-bayān*

[299] *Rūḥ al-maʿānī*

[300] *Ṣafwat at-tafāsīr*

[301] *Rūḥ al-bayān*

[302] Aḥmad

[303] *Rūḥ al-bayān*

[304] *Laṭāʾif al-ishārāt*

Notes: The Sixeenth Call

305 *Ṣafwat at-tafāsīr*

306 *Rūḥ al-maʿānī*

307 ar-Rāzī

308 ar-Rāzī

309 *Ṣafwat at-tafāsīr*

310 ar-Rāzī

311 *Ṣafwat at-tafāsīr*

312 ar-Rāzī

313 *Ṣafwat at-tafāsīr*

314 Reported by Aḥmad, with the wording: "The hearts of the servants are between the fingers of the All-Merciful. O Allāh, transform our hearts into that which You love and approve!"

315 *Rūḥ al-bayān*

316 *Ṣafwat at-tafāsīr*

317 al-Ulūsī

318 al-Bukhārī and an-Nasāʾī

319 *Ṣafwat at-tafāsīr*

320 ar-Rāzī

321 *Ṣafwat at-tafāsīr*

322 ar-Rāzī

323 *Ṣafwat at-tafāsīr*

324 al-Khāzin

325 *Ṣafwat at-tafāsīr*

326 ar-Rāzī

327 Shaikh Zāda

328 *Rūḥ al-bayān*

329 *Rūḥ al-bayān*

330 *Laṭāʾif al-ishārāt*

331 al-Bukhārī and Muslim.

Notes: The Seventeenth Call

[332] ar-Rāzī
[333] *Ṣafwat at-tafāsīr*
[334] al-Khāzin
[335] ar-Rāzī
[336] *Ṣafwat at-tafāsīr*
[337] arl-Qurṭubī
[338] *Ṣafwat at-tafāsīr*
[339] *al-Jumal*
[340] *Rūḥ al-bayān*
[341] *Ṣafwat at-tafāsīr*
[342] *Rūḥ al-bayān*
[343] *Ṣafwat at-tafāsīr*
[344] al-Qurṭubī
[345] ar-Rāzī
[346] ar-Rāzī

Notes: The Eighteenth Call

347 ***Translator's note***: In Islāmic jurisprudence [*fiqh*], a distinction is drawn between *farḍ ʿain*, i.e., a religious duty that is incumbent on every individual Muslim, and *farḍ-kifāya*, meaning a collective duty, incumbent on the Islāmic community as a whole, though not on every individual Muslim.

348 ar-Rāzī

349 al-Qurṭubī

350 ar-Rāzī

351 *Rūḥ al-bayān* (Reported by Ibn Mardawaih and al-Ḥākim).

352 al-Qurṭubī (Reported by Aḥmad and Ibn Māja).

353 *Rūḥ al-bayān*

354 ***Translator's note:*** The count of ten, rather than nine, may suggest that the initial invocation of Allāh's Name [*Bismi'llāhi 'r-Raḥmāni 'r-Raḥīm*] is treated as the first verse [*āya*] of the Sūra. Allāh knows best!

355 Aḥmad, at-Tirmidhī and an-Nasāʾī.

Notes: The Nineteenth Call

356 *Ṣafwat at-tafāsīr*

357 al-Qurṭubī

358 al-Qurṭubī

359 ar-Rāzī

360 ar-Rāzī

361 *Ṣafwat at-tafāsīr*

362 *Rūḥ al-bayān*

363 *Ṣafwat at-tafāsīr* (Reported by Muslim and Aḥmad).

364 al-Bukhārī

365 *Rūḥ al-bayān*

Notes: The Twentieth Call

366 *Ṣafwat at-tafāsīr*

367 ar-Rāzī

368 *Ṣafwat at-tafāsīr*

369 *Rūḥ al-bayān*

370 *Ṣafwat at-tafāsīr*

371 Muslim

372 ar-Rāzī

373 *Ṣafwat at-tafāsīr*

374 *Rūḥ al-bayān*

375 ar-Rāzī

376 *Ṣafwat at-tafāsīr*

377 *Rūḥ al-bayān*

378 *Ṣafwat at-tafāsīr*

379 *Rūḥ al-bayān*

380 al-Baiḍāwī, in the context of His saying (Exalted is He):

> And He thereby leads none astray except the profligate.
> *wa mā yuḍillu bi-hi ila 'l-fāsiqīn*. (2:26)

381 at-Tirmidhī and an-Nasāʾī.

382 Shaikh Zāda, in his commentary on al-Baiḍāwī.

383 *Laṭāʾif al-ishārāt*

384 al-Bukhārī

385 al-Khāzin (Reported by Muslim, with the wording: "and the consumption of usury [*ribā*]," instead of: "and adultery and fornication [*zinā*]").

386 *Ṣafwat at-tafāsīr*

387 *Ṣafwat at-tafāsīr*

388 *Rūḥ al-bayān*

Notes: The Twenty-first Call

389 *Ṣafwat at-tafāsīr* (According to at-Tirmidhī, this is a good authentic tradition).

390 Muslim (with a slight difference in the wording).

391 ar-Rāzī

392 *Ṣafwat at-tafāsīr*

393 ar-Rāzī

394 *Ṣafwat at-tafāsīr*

395 ar-Rāzī

396 ar-Rāzī (Related by al-Bukhārī, without the words "and its soil").

397 *Ṣafwat at-tafāsīr*

398 *Rūḥ al-bayān*

Notes: The Twenty-second Call

399 *Ṣafwat at-tafāsīr*

400 ar-Rāzī

401 al-Bukhārī and Muslim

402 Ibn Kathīr (Reported by al-Bukhārī and Muslim).

403 ar-Rāzī

404 Ibn Kathīr (Reported in the two *Ṣaḥīḥ*'s).

405 al-Qurṭubī

406 *Ṣafwat at-tafāsīr*

407 al-Qurṭubī

408 Ibn Kathīr

409 *Ṣafwat at-tafāsīr*

410 Ibn Kathīr

411 ar-Rāzī

412 *Rūḥ al-bayān*

Notes: The Twenty-third Call

413 *Ṣafwat at-tafāsīr*
414 ar-Rāzī
415 at-Tirmidhī
416 al-Qurṭubī
417 Shaikh Zāda
418 *Ṣafwat at-tafāsīr*
419 *Rūḥ al-bayān* (Reported by Muslim and Aḥmad).
420 *Laṭā᾿if al-ishārāt*

Notes: The Twenty-fourth Call

421 *Rūḥ al-bayān*
422 ar-Rāzī
423 *Ṣafwat at-tafāsīr*
424 *Ṣafwat at-tafāsīr*
425 *Rūḥ al-bayān*
426 *Ṣafwat at-tafāsīr*
427 *Rūḥ al-bayān*
428 ar-Rāzī
429 *Ṣafwat at-tafāsīr*
430 *Rūḥ al-bayān*
431 ar-Rāzī
432 *Rūḥ al-bayān*
433 Ibn Kathīr
434 *Rūḥ al-bayān*
435 aṣ-Ṣāwī
436 *Rūḥ al-bayān*
437 Muslim
438 al-Qurṭubī
439 *Laṭāʾif al-ishārāt*

Notes: The Twenty-fifth Call

440 *Ṣafwat at-tafāsīr*
441 ar-Rāzī
442 *Ṣafwat at-tafāsīr*
443 ar-Rāzī
444 *Ṣafwat at-tafāsīr*
445 al-Bukhārī (with slightly different wording).
446 *Rūḥ al-bayān*
447 *Ṣafwat at-tafāsīr*
448 ar-Rāzī
449 *Ṣafwat at-tafāsīr*
450 Ibn Kathīr
451 ar-Rāzī
452 ar-Rāzī
453 at-Tirmidhī
454 Abū Dāwūd
455 Abū Dāwūd (with slightly different wording).
456 *Rūḥ al-bayān* (Reported by at-Tirmidhī).
457 Ibn ʿĀbidīn
458 Ibn Kathīr
459 *Laṭāʾif al-ishārāt*

Notes: The Twenty-sixth Call

[460] Ibn Kathīr
[461] ar-Rāzī
[462] Ibn Kathīr
[463] ar-Rāzī
[464] Aḥmad
[465] *Rūḥ al-bayān*
[466] *Rūḥ al-bayān*
[467] *Laṭā'if al-ishārāt*
[468] al-Bukhārī and Muslim.

Notes: The Twenty-seventh Call

[469] ar-Rāzī
[470] Ibn Kathīr
[471] ar-Rāzī
[472] Ibn Kathīr
[473] Ibn Kathīr
[474] al-Qurṭubī
[475] ar-Rāzī
[476] Aḥmad
[477] al-Khāzin
[478] Ibn Kathīr
[479] ar-Rāzī
[480] Ibn Kathīr
[481] al-Qurṭubī
[482] ar-Rāzī
[483] Ibn Kathīr
[484] *Ṣafwat at-tafāsīr*
[485] al-Qurṭubī
[486] ar-Rāzī
[487] Ibn Kathīr
[488] ar-Rāzī
[489] *Rūḥ al-bayān*

Notes: The Twenty-eighth Call

490 *Ṣafwat at-tafāsīr*
491 ar-Rāzī
492 al-Khāzin
493 *Ṣafwat at-tafāsīr*
494 al-Khāzin
495 al-Ulūsī in *Rūḥ al-maʿānī* [The Spirit of the Inner Contents].
496 *Rūḥ al-maʿānī*, p. 50.
497 *ash-Shifā' ash-sharīf*, pt. 1, p 440.
498 al-Khāzin
499 *Ṣafwat at-tafāsīr*
500 al-Khāzin
501 ar-Rāzī
502 aṣ-Ṣāwī (in his note on the margin of *al-Jalālān*).
503 al-Qurṭubī (Reported by Aḥmad, with a slight difference in the wording).
504 *Ṣafwat at-tafāsīr*

Notes: The Twenty-ninth Call

505 *Ṣafwat at-tafāsīr*
506 al-Qurṭubī
507 *Ṣafwat at-tafāsīr*
508 ar-Rāzī
509 al-Qurṭubī
510 *Ṣafwat at-tafāsīr*
511 al-Qurṭubī
512 ar-Rāzī
513 al-Ulūsī
514 ar-Rāzī
515 *Ṣafwat at-tafāsīr*
516 al-Ulūsī
517 *Ṣafwat at-tafāsīr*
518 ar-Rāzī
519 *Ṣafwat at-tafāsīr*
520 Ibn Kathīr (Reported by al-Bukhārī).
521 al-Ulūsī
522 *Ṣafwat at-tafāsīr*
523 al-Ulūsī
524 *Rūḥ al-bayān*
525 *Laṭā'if al-ishārāt*

Notes: The Thirtieth Call

526 ar-Rāzī

527 *Ṣafwat at-tafāsīr*

528 al-Bukhārī and Muslim

529 at-Tirmidhī

530 al-Bukhārī

531 al-Khāzin

532 al-Khāzin (The report is generally accepted).

533 al-Khāzin

534 al-Bukhārī and Muslim

535 *Ṣafwat at-tafāsīr*

536 al-Khāzin

537 *Ṣafwat at-tafāsīr*

538 al-Khāzin

539 *Ṣafwat at-tafāsīr*

540 Ibn Māja, Aḥmad and Mālik (without "in Islām").

541 ar-Rāzī

542 *Ṣafwat at-tafāsīr*

543 ar-Rāzī

544 ar-Rāzī

545 al-Khāzin

Notes: The Thirty-first Call

546 *Ṣafwat at-tafāsīr*
547 ar-Rāzī
548 *Ṣafwat at-tafāsīr*
549 al-Khāzin
550 al-Baiḍāwī
551 Shaikh Zāda
552 *Ṣafwat at-tafāsīr*
553 ar-Rāzī
554 *Ṣafwat at-tafāsīr*
555 ar-Rāzī
556 *Ṣafwat at-tafāsīr*
557 al-Khāzin
558 ar-Rāzī
559 *Rūḥ al-bayān*

Notes: The Thirty-second Call

560 ar-Rāzī

561 Reported by al-Bukhārī, in wording very close to this.

562 ar-Rāzī

563 *Ṣafwat at-tafāsīr*

564 *Rūḥ al-bayān*

Notes: The Thirty-third Call

565 ar-Rāzī
566 *Ṣafwat at-tafāsīr*
567 aṭ-Ṭabarī
568 Ibn Kathīr
569 *Rūḥ al-bayān*
570 al-Ulūsī
571 al-Bukhārī
572 Muslim
573 aṣ-Ṣāwī
574 ar-Rāzī
575 *Ṣafwat at-tafāsīr*
576 aṣ-Ṣāwī
577 ar-Rāzī
578 *Rūḥ al-bayān*

Notes: The Thirty-fourth Call

[579] *Ṣafwat at-tafāsīr*

[580] al-Khāzin

[581] *Ṣafwat at-tafāsīr*

[582] al-Baiḍāwī

[583] al-Khāzin

[584] *Ṣafwat at-tafāsīr* (Reported by an-Nisā'ī and Abū Dāwūd).

[585] Shaikh Zāda

[586] al-Qurṭubī

[587] *Rūḥ al-bayān*

[588] ar-Rāzī

[589] al-Khāzin

[590] ar-Rāzī

[591] al-Qurṭubī

[592] ar-Rāzī

[593] *Ṣafwat at-tafāsīr*

[594] ar-Rāzī

[595] Abū Dāwūd

Notes: The Thirty-fifth Call

596 *Ṣafwat at-tafāsīr*
597 ar-Rāzī
598 *Rūḥ al-bayān*
599 *Ṣafwat at-tafāsīr*
600 ar-Rāzī
601 al-Khāzin
602 ar-Rāzī
603 *Ṣafwat at-tafāsīr*
604 al-Khāzin
605 al-Khāzin
606 *Ṣafwat at-tafāsīr*
607 Shaikh Zāda
608 ar-Rāzī
609 *Ṣafwat at-tafāsīr*
610 ar-Rāzī
611 *Ṣafwat at-tafāsīr*
612 ar-Rāzī
613 *Ṣafwat at-tafāsīr*
614 ar-Rāzī
615 *Ṣafwat at-tafāsīr*
616 ar-Rāzī
617 *Ṣafwat at-tafāsīr*
618 ar-Rāzī
619 an-Nawawī
620 Reported by al-Bukhārī, with the wording: "until I am dearer to him than his father, his children and all other people."
621 al-Bukhārī
622 *Rūḥ al-bayān*
623 *Laṭā'if al-minan* (p 22)

Notes: The Thirty-sixth Call

624 ar-Rāzī
625 Ibn Kathīr
626 *Rūḥ al-bayān*
627 ar-Rāzī
628 Ibn Kathīr
629 *Rūḥ al-bayān*
630 ar-Rāzī
631 Ibn Kathīr
632 aṭ-Ṭabarī
633 Ibn Kathīr
634 *Ṣafwat at-tafāsīr*
635 Ibn Kathīr (Reported by Ibn Jarīr and Ibn Abī Ḥātim).
636 ar-Rāzī
637 Ibn Kathīr
638 *Rūḥ al-bayān*

Notes: The Thirty-seventh Call

639 ar-Rāzī

640 al-Khāzin

641 *Ṣafwat at-tafāsīr*

642 ar-Rāzī

643 al-Khāzin

644 *Ṣafwat at-tafāsīr*

645 Ibn Kathīr

646 ar-Rāzī

647 *Ṣafwat at-tafāsīr*

648 al-Khāzin (Reported by Ibn Māja).

649 *Laṭāʾif al-ishārāt*

Notes: The Thirty-eighth Call

650 ar-Rāzī

651 *Ṣafwat at-tafāsīr*

652 ar-Rāzī

653 *Ṣafwat at-tafāsīr*

654 ar-Rāzī

655 *Ṣafwat at-tafāsīr*

656 ar-Rāzī

657 *Ṣafwat at-tafāsīr*

658 aṭ-Ṭabarī

659 *Ṣafwat at-tafāsīr*

660 ar-Rāzī

661 *al-Muʿjam al-wasīṭ*

662 In the version reported by Aḥmad, the wording is: "The servant of strong drink is like the worshipper of idols."

663 Abū Dāwūd

664 *Kashf al-khafāʾ* (Reported by al-Qaḍāʾī on the authority of Ibn ʿUmar, with a good chain of transmission. Also reported by an-Nasāʾī, with the wording: "Leave strong drink aside, for it is the mother of all forms of wickedness.").

665 *Rūḥ al-bayān*

Notes: The Thirty-ninth Call

666 *Ṣafwat at-tafāsīr*
667 al-Baiḍāwī
668 aṣ-Ṣāwī
669 *Ṣafwat at-tafāsīr*
670 ar-Rāzī
671 al-Qurṭubī
672 *Ṣafwat at-tafāsīr*
673 ar-Rāzī
674 *Ṣafwat at-tafāsīr*
675 ar-Rāzī
676 *Rūḥ al-bayān*

Notes: The Fortieth Call

677 *Ṣafwat at-tafāsīr*

678 *Rūḥ al-bayān*

679 al-Khāzin

680 *al-Madārik*

681 *Rūḥ al-bayān*

682 *Ṣafwat at-tafāsīr*

683 *Rūḥ al-bayān*

684 *Ṣafwat at-tafāsīr*

685 *Rūḥ al-bayān*

686 ar-Rāzī

687 *Ṣafwat at-tafāsīr*

688 *al-Madārik*

689 *Ṣafwat at-tafāsīr*

690 al-Khāzin

691 *Ṣafwat at-tafāsīr*

692 *Rūḥ al-bayān*

693 *Ṣafwat at-tafāsīr*

694 *Rūḥ al-bayān*

695 *Ṣafwat at-tafāsīr*

696 aṣ-Ṣāwī

697 *Rūḥ al-bayān*

698 Related by Ibn Ḥabbān, from the traditional report of Anas (may Allāh be well pleased with him).

Notes: The Forty-first Call

699 ar-Rāzī
700 *Ṣafwat at-tafāsīr*
701 Abū Dāwūd
702 Ibn Kathīr
703 *Ṣafwat at-tafāsīr*
704 ar-Rāzī
705 *Ṣafwat at-tafāsīr*
706 ar-Rāzī
707 *Ṣafwat at-tafāsīr*
708 al-Khāzin
709 *Ṣafwat at-tafāsīr*
710 ar-Rāzī
711 *Rūḥ al-bayān*

Notes: The Forty-second Call

[712] Ibn Kathīr

[713] aṣ-Ṣāwī

[714] Ibn Māja

[715] at-Tirmidhī

[716] aṭ-Ṭabarī, citing al-Khāzin

[717] ar-Rāzī

[718] ar-Rāzī

[719] al-Ulūsī

[720] ar-Rāzī

[721] *Ṣafwat at-tafāsīr*

[722] al-Baiḍāwī

[723] *Rūḥ al-bayān*

[724] ar-Rāzī

Notes: The Forty-third Call

[725] *Ṣafwat at-tafāsīr*
[726] al-Khāzin
[727] Shaikh Zāda
[728] *Ṣafwat at-tafāsīr*
[729] *Rūḥ al-bayān*
[730] *Ṣafwat at-tafāsīr*
[731] *Rūḥ al-bayān*
[732] al-Baihaqī and ad-Dailamī (with a slight difference in wording).
[733] al-Qurṭubī
[734] *Ṣafwat at-tafāsīr*
[735] al-Baiḍāwī
[736] *Rūḥ al-bayān*
[737] *Ṣafwat at-tafāsīr*
[738] al-Khāzin
[739] *Ṣafwat at-tafāsīr*
[740] *Rūḥ al-bayān*
[741] *Ṣafwat at-tafāsīr*
[742] al-Khāzin
[743] *Ṣafwat at-tafāsīr*
[744] ar-Rāzī
[745] *Ṣafwat at-tafāsīr*
[746] al-Baiḍāwī
[747] *Ṣafwat at-tafāsīr*
[748] *Rūḥ al-bayān*
[749] *Ṣafwat at-tafāsīr*

Notes: The Forty-fourth Call

[750] Abū Dāwūd

[751] *Ṣafwat at-tafāsīr*

[752] al-Ulūsī

[753] *Ṣafwat at-tafāsīr*

[754] al-Ulūsī

[755] ar-Rāzī

[756] *Ṣafwat at-tafāsīr*

[757] al-Ulūsī

[758] Reported by at-Tirmidhī, with the wording: "No, you are the cunning strategists [*makkārūn*]."

[759] al-Khāzin

[760] *Ṣafwat at-tafāsīr*

[761] ar-Rāzī

[762] *Ṣafwat at-tafāsīr*

[763] *Rūḥ al-bayān*

[764] al-Baihaqī

Notes: The Forty-fifth Call

765 *Ṣafwat at-tafāsīr*
766 *Rūḥ al-bayān*
767 *Ṣafwat at-tafāsīr*
768 ar-Rāzī
769 *Rūḥ al-bayān*
770 *Ṣafwat at-tafāsīr*
771 ar-Rāzī
772 *Rūḥ al-bayān*
773 *Ṣafwat at-tafāsīr*
774 *Rūḥ al-bayān*
775 Ibn Kathīr
776 ar-Rāzī
777 *Rūḥ al-bayān*
778 *Rūḥ al-bayān*
779 *Ṣafwat at-tafāsīr*
780 *Rūḥ al-bayān*
781 *Laṭā᾽if al-ishārāt*
782 *Rūḥ al-bayān*

Notes: The Forty-sixth Call

[783] *Ṣafwat at-tafāsīr*
[784] *Ṣafwat at-tafāsīr*
[785] *Ṣafwat at-tafāsīr*
[786] al-Ulūsī
[787] Aḥmad
[788] ar-Rāzī
[789] *Rūḥ al-bayān*
[790] at-Tirmidhī
[791] *Ṣafwat at-tafāsīr*
[792] Shaikh Zāda
[793] *Ṣafwat at-tafāsīr*
[794] al-Baiḍāwī
[795] *Ṣafwat at-tafāsīr*
[796] *al-Madārik*
[797] *Ṣafwat at-tafāsīr* (Reported by al-Bukhārī).
[798] aṣ-Ṣāwī
[799] al-Khāzin
[800] Imām Aḥmad
[801] Ibn Jarīr
[802] Ibn Kathīr
[803] *Ṣafwat at-tafāsīr*
[804] ar-Rāzī
[805] al-Ulūsī
[806] *Laṭā'if al-ishārāt*
[807] *Rūḥ al-bayān*

Notes: The Forty-seventh Call

808 *Ṣafwat at-tafāsīr*
809 al-Khāzin
810 aṣ-Ṣāwī
811 *Ṣafwat at-tafāsīr*
812 al-Khāzin
813 aṣ-Ṣāwī
814 al-Khāzin
815 *Ṣafwat at-tafāsīr*
816 *Rūḥ al-bayān*
817 ar-Rāzī
818 al-Ulūsī
819 aṭ-Ṭabarī
820 al-Khāzin
821 *Ṣafwat at-tafāsīr*
822 *Rūḥ al-bayān*
823 *Ṣafwat at-tafāsīr*
824 ar-Rāzī
825 *Rūḥ al-bayān*
826 an-Nīsābūrī
827 ar-Rāzī
828 *Ṣafwat at-tafāsīr*
829 *Rūḥ al-bayān*
830 The two Shaikhs [al-Bukhārī and Muslim].
831 Ibn Kathīr
832 *Rūḥ al-bayān*

Notes: The Forty-eighth Call

833 *Ṣafwat at-tafāsīr*
834 Shaikh Zāda
835 al-Qurṭubī
836 *Ṣafwat at-tafāsīr*
837 al-Khāzin
838 *Ṣafwat at-tafāsīr*
839 *Rūḥ al-bayān*
840 ar-Rāzī
841 *Rūḥ al-bayān*

Notes: The Forty-ninth Call

842 *Ṣafwat at-tafāsīr*

843 *Rūḥ al-bayān*

844 Ibn Kathīr

845 *Rūḥ al-bayān*

846 *Ṣafwat at-tafāsīr*

847 ar-Rāzī

848 *Rūḥ al-bayān*

849 al-Khāzin

850 Reported by Muslim in his *Ṣaḥīḥ*, and also by at-Tirmidhī Another version, only slightly different, is reported by Aḥmad in his *Musnad*.

851 Reported with approval by at-Tirmidhī, in the Book of Supplications [*Kitāb ad-Daʿawāt*]; also reported by Ibn Ḥabbān in his *Ṣaḥīḥ*.

852 *Rūḥ al-bayān*

853 ar-Rāzī

854 *Ḥaqāʾiq ʿani ʾt-taṣawwuf*

855 *Nūr at-taḥqīq*, p 173

856 *Rūḥ al-bayān*

857 Ibn Kathīr

858 ar-Rāzī

859 al-Bukhārī

860 Abū Dāwūd

861 al-Khāzin

862 *Rūḥ al-bayān*

863 Muslim

864 Ibn Māja

865 *Laṭāʾif al-ishārāt*

866 *Laṭāʾif al-ishārāt*

Notes: The Fiftieth Call

[867] *Ṣafwat at-tafāsīr*

[868] *Rūḥ al-bayān* (Loosely quoted from ar-Rāzī).

[869] *Ṣafwat at-tafāsīr*

[870] al-Qurṭubī (Reported by al-Bukhārīī).

[871] ar-Rāzī

[872] Margin of *al-Jumal*

[873] *Ṣafwat at-tafāsīr*

[874] *Rūḥ al-bayān*

[875] ar-Rāzī

[876] *Rūḥ al-bayān*

[877] ar-Rāzī

[878] Reported by al-Bukhārī, Muslim, an-Nasāʾī, Ibn Māja, and Aḥmad in the *Musnad*.

[879] *Rūḥ al-bayān*

[880] Ibn Kathīr

[881] *Rūḥ al-bayān*

Notes: The Fifty-first Call

[882] ar-Rāzī

[883] *Ṣafwat at-tafāsīr*

[884] ar-Rāzī

[885] al-Bukhārī

[886] *Ṣafwat at-tafāsīr*

[887] ar-Rāzī

[888] Muslim

[889] Muslim

[890] al-Khāzin (Reported by at-Tirmidhī and Aḥmad).

[891] Mālik

[892] aṣ-Ṣāwī

[893] *Ṣafwat at-tafāsīr*

[894] al-Bukhārī

[895] at-Tirmidhī (who considers it a sound report).

[896] al-Bukhārī

[897] al-Qurṭubī. Reported by al-Bukhārī on the authority of Abū Huraira (may Allāh be well pleased with him).

[898] *Rūḥ al-bayān*

Notes: The Fifty-second Call

899 *Ṣafwat at-tafāsīr*

900 ar-Rāzī

901 *Ṣafwat at-tafāsīr*

902 ar-Rāzī

903 *Rūḥ al-bayān*

904 ar-Rāzī

905 *Ṣafwat at-tafāsīr* (Reported by Ibn Māja).

906 Ibn Kathīr

907 *Ṣafwat at-tafāsīr*

908 aṭ-Ṭabarī

909 al-Qurṭubī

910 *Ṣafwat at-tafāsīr*

911 al-Bukhārī and Muslim.

912 ar-Rāzī

Notes: The Fifty-third Call

913 ar-Rāzī

914 *Ṣafwat at-tafāsīr*

915 ar-Rāzī

916 *Ṣafwat at-tafāsīr*

917 ar-Rāzī

918 Ibn Kathīr

919 al-Qurṭubī (Reported by all-Bukhārī).

920 *Ṣafwat at-tafāsīr*

921 ar-Rāzī

922 *Ṣafwat at-tafāsīr*

923 al-Khāzin

924 al-Bukhārī and Muslim.

925 *Rūḥ al-bayān*

Notes: The Fifty-fourth Call

[926] *Ṣafwat at-tafāsīr*

[927] ar-Rāzī

[928] al-Qurṭubī

[929] al-Khāzin

[930] al-Ulūsī

[931] al-Qurṭubī

[932] *Rūḥ al-bayān*

[933] Shaikh Zāda

[934] *Rūḥ al-bayān*

Notes: The Fifty-fifth Call

935 *Ṣafwat at-tafāsīr*

936 ar-Rāzī

937 *Ṣafwat at-tafāsīr*

938 ar-Rāzī

939 *Rūḥ al-bayān*

Notes: The Fifty-Sixth Call

[940] ar-Rāzī

[941] *Ṣafwat at-tafāsīr*

[942] ar-Rāzī (Reported by aṭ-Ṭabarānī, with the wording: "Set to work, for everyone....")

[943] *Rūḥ al-bayān*

[944] ar-Rāzī

[945] Reported by al-Baghawī without a chain of transmitting authorities.

[946] aṣ-Ṣāwī

[947] ar-Rāzī

[948] *Ṣafwat at-tafāsīr*

[949] ar-Rāzī

[950] *Ṣafwat at-tafāsīr*

[951] aṣ-Ṣāwī

[952] *Ṣafwat at-tafāsīr*

[953] ar-Rāzī

[954] al-Ulūsī

[955] Ibn Kathīr

[956] al-Ulūsī

[957] *Rūḥ al-bayān*

[958] *Laṭā'if al-ishārāt*

Notes: The Fifty-seventh Call

959 ar-Rāzī
960 *Ṣafwat at-tafāsīr*
961 Ibn Kathīr
962 al-Khāzin
963 *Rūḥ al-bayān*
964 *al-Jumal*
965 *Ṣafwat at-tafāsīr*
966 al-Qurṭubī
967 ar-Rāzī
968 al-Khāzin
969 aṣ-Ṣāwī
970 ar-Rāzī
971 ad-Dailamī
972 Abū Dāwūd
973 al-Bukhārī and Muslim.
974 Muslim
975 *Laṭā'if al-ishārāt*

Notes: The Fifty-eighth Call

[976] ar-Rāzī
[977] *Ṣafwat at-tafāsīr*
[978] ar-Rāzī (Reported by Aḥmad with a slight difference in the wording).
[979] al-Qurṭubī (Reported by Mālik)
[980] al-Bukhārī and Muslim
[981] Abū Dāwūd (with a slight difference in the wording).
[982] Abū Dāwūd
[983] ar-Rāzī
[984] al-Qurṭubī
[985] *Ṣafwat at-tafāsīr*
[986] *Ṣafwat at-tafāsīr*
[987] *Rūḥ al-bayān*
[988] *Laṭāʾif al-ishārāt*

Notes: The Fifty-ninth Call

989 Ibn Kathīr

990 ar-Rāzī

991 *Ṣafwat at-tafāsīr*

992 ar-Rāzī

993 *Ṣafwat at-tafāsīr*

994 ar-Rāzī (Reported by Abū Dāwūd)

995 al-Khāzin

996 Abū Dāwūd (with the wording: "You must instruct **your children**...")

997 ar-Rāzī

998 *Ṣafwat at-tafāsīr*

999 *Rūḥ al-bayān*

1000 *Ṣafwat at-tafāsīr*

1001 *Rūḥ al-bayān*

1002 *Laṭā'if al-ishārāt*

1003 at-Tirmidhī

1004 *Rūḥ al-bayān*

1005 al-Khāzin

1006 *Ṣafwat at-tafāsīr*

1007 *al-Madārik*

1008 al-Baiḍāwī

Notes: The Sixtieth Call

1009 *Ṣafwat at-tafāsīr* (p. 509)
1010 *Ṣafwat at-tafāsīr*
1011 ar-Rāzī
1012 *Ṣafwat at-tafāsīr*
1013 ar-Rāzī
1014 *Laṭāʾif al-ishārāt*
1015 *Ṣafwat at-tafāsīr*
1016 al-Qurṭubī
1017 ar-Rāzī
1018 *Ṣafwat at-tafāsīr*
1019 al-Qurṭubī
1020 *Ṣafwat at-tafāsīr*

Notes: The Sixty-first Call

[1021] Aḥmad and al-Baihaqī.
[1022] al-Qurṭubī
[1023] *Rūḥ al-bayān*
[1024] ar-Rāzī
[1025] *Rūḥ al-bayān*
[1026] *al-Jumal*
[1027] ar-Rāzī
[1028] al-Qurṭubī
[1029] *Ṣafwat at-tafāsīr*
[1030] ar-Rāzī
[1031] *Rūḥ al-bayān*
[1032] *Ṣafwat at-tafāsīr*
[1033] *Rūḥ al-bayān*
[1034] al-Bukhārī and Muslim.
[1035] al-Bukhārī and Muslim.

Notes: The Sixty-second Call

1036 ar-Rāzī
1037 *Ṣafwat at-tafāsīr*
1038 *Ṣafwat at-tafāsīr*
1039 Shaikh Zāda
1040 al-Baiḍāwī
1041 *Ṣafwat at-tafāsīr*
1042 al-Baiḍāwī
1043 Shaikh Zāda
1044 al-Baiḍāwī
1045 Shaikh Zāda
1046 al-Baiḍāwī
1047 Muslim
1048 al-Bukhārī

Notes: The Sixty-third Call

[1049] ar-Rāzī

[1050] *Ṣafwat at-tafāsīr*

[1051] ar-Rāzī

[1052] *Ṣafwat at-tafāsīr*

[1053] ar-Rāzī

[1054] al-Khāzin

[1055] *Ṣafwat at-tafāsīr*

[1056] al-Qurṭubī

[1057] al-Khāzin

[1058] ar-Rāzī

[1059] al-Qurṭubī aṣ-Ṣāwī

[1060] al-Bukhārī

[1061] *Ṣafwat at-tafāsīr*

[1062] al-Ulūsī

[1063] al-Qurṭubī

[1064] al-Baiḍāwī

Notes: The Sixty-fourth Call

[1065] ar-Rāzī

[1066] *Ṣafwat at-tafāsīr*

[1067] al-Qurṭubī

[1068] aṣ-Ṣāwī

[1069] *Ṣafwat at-tafāsīr* (Reported by al-Bukhārī and Muslim).

[1070] aṣ-Ṣāwī

[1071] Muslim and at-Tirmidhī.

[1072] al-Qurṭubī

Notes: The Sixty-fifth Call

1073 ar-Rāzī
1074 Reported by al-Bukhārī.
1075 al-Qurṭubī
1076 ar-Rāzī
1077 *Ṣafwat at-tafāsīr*
1078 al-Ulūsī

Notes: The Sixty-sixth Call

1079 al-Ulūsī
1080 ar-Rāzī
1081 *Ṣafwat at-tafāsīr/*
1082 aṭ-Ṭabarī
1083 al-Qurṭubī
1084 *Rūḥ al-bayān*
1085 Aḥmad [ibn Ḥanbal]
1086 Ibn Kathīr
1087 ar-Rāzī
1088 aṭ-Ṭabarī
1089 Ibn Kathīr
1090 ar-Rāzī
1091 aṭ-Ṭabarī
1092 *Rūḥ al-bayān*

Notes: The Sixty-seventh Call

[1093] Ibn Kathīr

[1094] *Rūḥ al-bayān*

[1095] In literal translation, the words *wa yuthabbit aqdāma-kum* mean: "and He will firmly establish your feet." The reader should bear this in mind, in order to grasp the point of certain commentaries and interpretations, cited by the author in the following text.

[1096] *Ṣafwat at-tafāsīr*

[1097] ar-Rāzī

[1098] *Rūḥ al-bayān*

[1099] al-Qurṭubī

[1100] Ibn Kathīr (Reported by aṭ-Ṭabarī, with very similar wording).

[1101] *al-Jumal*

[1102] *Rūḥ al-bayān*

[1103] *Laṭā'if al-ishārāt*

Notes: The Sixty-eighth Call

1104 *Ṣafwat at-tafāsīr*
1105 *Rūḥ al-bayān*
1106 ar-Rāzī
1107 aṣ-Ṣāwī
1108 al-Baiḍāwī
1109 Shaikh Zāda
1110 *Laṭāʾif al-ishārāt*
1111 *Rūḥ al-bayān*

Notes: The Sixty-ninth Call

1112 *Ṣafwat at-tafāsīr*
1113 aṣ-Ṣāwī
1114 *Rūḥ al-bayān*
1115 *Ṣafwat at-tafāsīr*
1116 Ibn Kathīr
1117 al-Qurṭubī
1118 Shaikh Zāda
1119 ar-Rāzī
1120 *Rūḥ al-bayān*
1121 ar-Rāzī
1122 al-Ulūsī

Notes: The Seventieth Call

[1123] ar-Rāzī
[1124] *Rūḥ al-bayān*
[1125] *Ṣafwat at-tafāsīr*
[1126] al-Bukhārī
[1127] ar-Rāzī
[1128] al-Baiḍāwī
[1129] Shaikh Zāda
[1130] *Ṣafwat at-tafāsīr*
[1131] *Rūḥ al-bayān*
[1132] ar-Rāzī
[1133] al-Bukhārī
[1134] al-Qurṭubī
[1135] al-Ulūsī
[1136] *Rūḥ al-bayān*
[1137] ar-Rāzī
[1138] Muslim
[1139] al-Ulūsī
[1140] *Ṣafwat at-tafāsīr*
[1141] ar-Rāzī
[1142] *Ṣafwat at-tafāsīr*
[1143] ar-Rāzī
[1144] *Ṣafwat at-tafāsīr*
[1145] ar-Rāzī
[1146] *Ṣafwat at-tafāsīr*
[1147] al-Baiḍāwī
[1148] *Ṣafwat at-tafāsīr*
[1149] ar-Rāzī

Notes: The Seventy-first Call

[1150] *Ṣafwat at-tafāsīr*

[1151] ar-Rāzī

[1152] al-Ulūsī

[1153] Ibn Kathīr (Reported by at-Tirmidhī).

[1154] al-Khāzin

[1155] al-Baiḍāwī

[1156] Shaikh Zāda

[1157] *Rūḥ al-bayān*

[1158] *Ṣafwat at-tafāsīr*

[1159] ar-Rāzī

[1160] *Rūḥ al-bayān*

Notes: The Seventy-second Call

1161 *Ṣafwat at-tafāsīr*

1162 ar-Rāzī

1163 Shaikh Zāda

1164 al-Qurṭubī

1165 Shaikh Zāda

1166 *Ṣafwat at-tafāsīr* (Reported by Muslim, with the wording: "There is many a person with dishevelled hair, driven away from the doors....")

1167 al-Bukhārī

1168 al-Qurṭubī

1169 *Ṣafwat at-tafāsīr*

1170 aṭ-Ṭabarī

1171 al-Baiḍāwī

1172 al-Khāzin

1173 *Rūḥ al-bayān*

1174 *Laṭā'if al-ishārāt* (Reported by Muslim, with the wording: "There is many a person with dishevelled hair, driven away from the doors....")

Notes: The Seventy-third Call

1175 Ibn Kathīr

1176 *al-Jumal* (mentioned by ath-Thaʿlabī).

1177 al-Qurṭubī

1178 Ibn Kathīr (Reported by Ibn Māja).

1179 ar-Rāzī

1180 al-Ulūsī

1181 al-Bukhārī

1182 *Ṣafwat at-tafāsīr* (Reported by al-Ḥāfiẓ Abū Yaʿlā).

1183 Ibn Kathīr

1184 ar-Rāzī

1185 *Rūḥ al-bayān*

1186 *Ṣafwat at-tafāsīr*

1187 ar-Rāzī

1188 *al-Jumal*

1189 al-Khāzin (Reported by Abū Dāwūd).

1190 *Ṣafwat at-tafāsīr*

1191 Ibn Kathīr

1192 ar-Rāzī

1193 al-Bukhārī

1194 al-Qurṭubī (In the version reported by al-Bukhārī, the wording is: "Take enough to meet the needs of yourself and your children, in fairness.")

1195 *Laṭāʾif al-ishārāt*

Notes: The Seventy-fourth Call

1196 *Ṣafwat at-tafāsīr*
1197 al-Khāzin
1198 al-Khāzin
1199 aṭ-Ṭabarī
1200 *Ṣafwat at-tafāsīr*
1201 *Rūḥ al-bayān*
1202 al-Qurṭubī
1203 *Rūḥ al-bayān*
1204 Ibn Kathīr (Recorded in the two *Ṣaḥīḥ*'s).
1205 Zāda and Shihāb
1206 *al-Jumal*

Notes: The Seventy-fifth Call

1207 ar-Rāzī
1208 *Ṣafwat at-tafāsīr*
1209 *Ṣafwat at-tafāsīr*
1210 al-Qurṭubī
1211 ar-Rāzī
1212 *Ṣafwat at-tafāsīr*
1213 *Rūḥ al-bayān*
1214 *Ṣafwat at-tafāsīr*
1215 ar-Rāzī
1216 *Ṣafwat at-tafāsīr*
1217 ar-Rāzī
1218 *Ṣafwat at-tafāsīr* (Reported by al-Bukhārī and Muslim).
1219 al-Ulūsī

Notes: The Seventy-sixth Call

[1220] at-Tirmidhī and an-Nasāʾī.

[1221] ar-Rāzī (Reported by Muslim and at-Tirmidhī).

[1222] al-Khāzin

[1223] al-Qurṭubī (In the version of Abū ʿUwāna, the wording of this Prophetic tradition [*ḥadīth*] is slightly different).

[1224] *Ṣafwat at-tafāsīr*

[1225] ar-Rāzī

[1226] Abū Dāwūd

[1227] Ibn Māja

[1228] al-Qurṭubī

[1229] *Ṣafwat at-tafāsīr*

[1230] al-Bukhārī and Muslim.

[1231] at-Tirmidhī and Aḥmad (with slightly different wording).

[1232] al-Bukhārī and Muslim.

[1233] *Ṣafwat at-tafāsīr*

Notes: The Seventy-seventh Call

1234 *Ṣafwat at-tafāsīr*

1235 at-Tirmidhī

1236 ar-Rāzī

1237 *Rūḥ al-bayān*

1238 ar-Rāzī

1239 *Ṣafwat at-tafāsīr*

1240 *Rūḥ al-bayān*

1241 *Ṣafwat at-tafāsīr*

1242 *Rūḥ al-bayān*

1243 ar-Rāzī

1244 *Ishārāt al-iʿjāz fī mabāni 'l-ījāz*

1245 *Ṣafwat at-tafāsīr*

1246 *Ṣafwat at-tafāsīr*

1247 al-Qurṭubī

1248 *Rūḥ al-bayān*

1249 ar-Rāzī

1250 al-Bukhārī

1251 *Rūḥ al-bayān*

Notes: The Seventy-eighth Call

1252 aṣ-Ṣāwī

1253 *Rūḥ al-bayān*

1254 *Ṣafwat at-tafāsīr*

1255 Reported by Aḥmad, with the wording: "The incompetent person is someone who lets his lower self follow its passionate desire."

1256 aṣ-Ṣāwī

1257 *Rūḥ al-bayān*

1258 Reported by Aḥmad in his *Musnad*.

1259 Ibn Kathīr

1260 ar-Rāzī

1261 *Rūḥ al-bayān*

1262 *Ṣafwat at-tafāsīr*

1263 aṣ-Ṣāwī

1264 *Rūḥ al-bayān*

1265 *Ṣafwat at-tafāsīr*

1266 Shaikh Zāda

1267 al-Qurṭubī

1268 Ibn Kathīr

1269 Shaikh Zāda

1270 *Ṣafwat at-tafāsīr*

1271 *Laṭā'if al-ishārāt*

Notes: The Seventy-ninth Call

1272 ar-Rāzī
1273 *Rūḥ al-bayān*
1274 ar-Rāzī
1275 al-Bukhārī and Muslim.
1276 *Rūḥ al-bayān*
1277 *Ṣafwat at-tafāsīr*
1278 al-Qurṭubī
1279 *Rūḥ al-bayān*
1280 ar-Rāzī
1281 *Ṣafwat at-tafāsīr*
1282 *Rūḥ al-bayān*
1283 *Ṣafwat at-tafāsīr*
1284 Shaikh Zāda
1285 *Ṣafwat at-tafāsīr*
1286 Shaikh Zāda
1287 Abū Dāwūd (with the wording: "The finest of deeds....")
1288 *Rūḥ al-bayān*
1289 al-Baihaqī
1290 *Laṭā'if al-ishārāt*

Notes: The Eightieth Call

[1291] ar-Rāzī (Reported by at-Tirmidhī).
[1292] al-Bukhārī (with almost identical wording).
[1293] Shaikh Zāda
[1294] *Ṣafwat at-tafāsīr*
[1295] ar-Rāzī
[1296] *Ṣafwat at-tafāsīr*
[1297] ar-Rāzī
[1298] *Ṣafwat at-tafāsīr*
[1299] al-Khāzin
[1300] ar-Rāzī
[1301] *Ṣafwat at-tafāsīr*
[1302] al-Qurṭubī
[1303] *Ṣafwat at-tafāsīr*
[1304] ar-Rāzī
[1305] *Ṣafwat at-tafāsīr*
[1306] *Rūḥ al-bayān*
[1307] *Laṭā'if al-ishārāt*

Notes: The Eighty-first Call

[1308] *Ṣafwat at-tafāsīr*
[1309] Ibn Kathīr
[1310] *Rūḥ al-bayān*
[1311] *al-Jumal*
[1312] *Rūḥ al-bayān*
[1313] aṭ-Ṭabarī
[1314] ar-Rāzī
[1315] Ibn Kathīr
[1316] *Ṣafwat at-tafāsīr*
[1317] Ibn Kathīr
[1318] In the version reported by al-Baihaqī, the wording is *ahl al-qubūr* [the people of the graves].
[1319] *Rūḥ al-bayān*

Notes: The Eighty-second Call

[1320] at-Tirmidhī
[1321] al-Khāzin
[1322] al-Qurṭubī
[1323] *Ṣafwat at-tafāsīr*
[1324] ar-Rāzī
[1325] *Rūḥ al-bayān*
[1326] al-Qurṭubī
[1327] Ibn Kathīr
[1328] al-Qurṭubī
[1329] ar-Rāzī
[1330] *Ṣafwat at-tafāsīr*
[1331] al-Ulūsī
[1332] *Rūḥ al-bayān*
[1333] *Laṭā᾿if al-ishārāt*

Notes: The Eighty-third Call

[1334] *Ṣafwat at-tafāsīr*
[1335] al-Qurṭubī
[1336] *Ṣafwat at-tafāsīr*
[1337] ar-Rāzī
[1338] Shaikh Zāda
[1339] ar-Rāzī
[1340] *Rūḥ al-bayān*
[1341] Shaikh Zāda
[1342] *Ṣafwat at-tafāsīr*
[1343] ar-Rāzī
[1344] *Ṣafwat at-tafāsīr*
[1345] *Rūḥ al-bayān*
[1346] ar-Rāzī
[1347] *Ṣafwat at-tafāsīr*
[1348] ar-Rāzī
[1349] *Ṣafwat at-tafāsīr*
[1350] ar-Rāzī
[1351] *Ṣafwat at-tafāsīr*
[1352] *Rūḥ al-bayān*
[1353] *Laṭā'if al-ishārāt*

Notes: The Eighty-fourth Call

1354 Ibn Kathīr

1355 *Ṣafwat at-tafāsīr*

1356 ar-Rāzī

1357 *Ṣafwat at-tafāsīr*

1358 ar-Rāzī

1359 *Ṣafwat at-tafāsīr*

1360 ar-Rāzī

1361 Aḥmad

1362 ***Translator's note:*** According to the classical Arabic lexicographers, *al-aswad wa 'l-aḥmar* [the black and the red] means "people of any complexion, dark or fair."

1363 Ibn Kathīr

1364 ar-Rāzī

1365 *Ṣafwat at-tafāsīr*

1366 al-Qurṭubī

1367 ar-Rāzī

1368 al-Qurṭubī

1369 Ibn Kathīr

1370 aṭ-Ṭabarānī and at-Tirmidhī.

Notes: The Eighty-fifth Call

[1371] ar-Rāzī

[1372] *Rūḥ al-bayān*

[1373] al-Bukhārī

[1374] ar-Rāzī

[1375] *Rūḥ al-bayān*

[1376] ar-Rāzī

[1377] Ibn Māja and aṭ-Ṭabarānī.

[1378] *Rūḥ al-bayān*

[1379] al-Qurṭubī (Reported by Ibn Jarīr, on the authority of Saʿīd ibn ʿAbd ar-Raḥmān al-Jamḥī [may Allāh be well pleased with them]).

[1380] ar-Rāzī (Reported by at-Tirmidhī).

[1381] *Ṣafwat at-tafāsīr*

[1382] al-Bukhārī

[1383] ar-Rāzī

[1384] *Rūḥ al-bayān*

[1385] ar-Rāzī

[1386] *Laṭāʾif al-ishārāt*

Notes: The Eighty-sixth Call

[1387] *Ṣafwat at-tafāsīr*
[1388] *Rūḥ al-bayān*
[1389] *Ṣafwat at-tafāsīr*
[1390] *Rūḥ al-bayān*
[1391] *al-Madārik*
[1392] *Ṣafwat at-tafāsīr*
[1393] ar-Rāzī
[1394] al-Qurṭubī
[1395] Ibn Kathīr
[1396] al-Qurṭubī
[1397] *Rūḥ al-bayān*
[1398] ar-Rāzī
[1399] *Rūḥ al-bayān*
[1400] *Rūḥ al-bayān*

Notes: The Eighty-seventh Call

[1401] *Ṣafwat at-tafāsīr*

[1402] ar-Rāzī

[1403] *Ṣafwat at-tafāsīr*

[1404] *Rūḥ al-bayān*

[1405] ar-Rāzī

[1406] *Rūḥ al-bayān*

[1407] ar-Rāzī

[1408] *Ṣafwat at-tafāsīr*

[1409] al-Khāzin (Reported by at-Tirmidhī).

[1410] al-Bukhārī and Muslim.

[1411] *Ṣafwat at-tafāsīr*

[1412] ar-Rāzī

[1413] *Rūḥ al-bayān*

[1414] *al-Jumal*

[1415] *Laṭā'if al-ishārāt*

[1416] *Ṣafwat at-tafāsīr*

[1417] *Rūḥ al-bayān*

[1418] al-Baiḍāwī

[1419] *al-Jumal*

[1420] *Ṣafwat at-tafāsīr*

[1421] *Rūḥ al-bayān*

[1422] aṭ-Ṭabarī, at-Tirmidhī and Ibn Māja.

Notes: The Eighty-eighth Call

1423 *Ṣafwat at-tafāsīr*

1424 ar-Rāzī

1425 *al-Jumal*

1426 This is the wording recorded by Abū Dāwūd, and at-Tirmidhī calls it a good tradition [*ḥadīth ḥasan*].

1427 Ibn Kathīr

1428 al-Bukhārī

1429 al-Qurṭubī

1430 an-Nīsābūrī

1431 ar-Rāzī

1432 ar-Rāzī

1433 al-Qurṭubī

1434 *Ṣafwat at-tafāsīr*

1435 *al-Madārik*

1436 ar-Rāzī

1437 *Rūḥ al-bayān*

Notes: The Eighty-ninth Call

1438 ar-Rāzī

1439 Muslim

1440 al-Khāzin (Reported by at-Tirmidhī).

1441 Ibn Māja

1442 al-Ulūsī

1443 aṭ-Ṭabarī

1444 ar-Rāzī

1445 *al-Jumal* (Recorded in as-Suyūṭī's *al-Budūr*).

1446 Ibn Kathīr (Reported by Aḥmad, with very similar wording).

1447 ar-Rāzī (in *al-Kashshāf*)

1448 *Laṭā'if al-ishārāt*

About the Translator

Muhtar Holland was born in 1935, in the ancient city of Durham in the North East of England. This statement may be considered anachronistic, however, since he did not bear the name Muhtar until 1969, when he was moved—by powerful experiences in the *latihan kejiwaan* of Subud—to embrace the religion of Islām.*

At the age of four, according to an entry in his father's diary, he said to a man who asked his name: "I'm a stranger to myself." During his years at school, he was drawn most strongly to the study of languages, which seemed to offer signposts to guide the stranger on his "Journey Home," apart from their practical usefulness to one who loved to spend his vacations traveling—at first on a bicycle—through foreign lands. Serious courses in Latin, Greek, French, Spanish and Danish, with additional smatterings of Anglo-Saxon, Italian, German and Dutch. Travels in France, Germany, Belgium, Holland and Denmark. Then a State Scholarship and up to Balliol College, Oxford, for a degree course centered on the study of Arabic and Turkish. Travels in Turkey and Syria. Then National Service in the Royal Navy, with most of the two years spent on an intensive course in the Russian language.

In the years since graduation from Oxford and Her Majesty's Senior Service, Mr. Holland has held academic posts at the University of Toronto, Canada; at the School of Oriental and African Studies in the University of London, England (with a five-month leave to study Islamic Law in Cairo, Egypt); and at the Universiti Kebangsaan in Kuala Lumpur, Malaysia (followed by a six-month sojourn in Indonesia). He also worked as Senior Research Fellow at the Islamic Foundation in Leicester, England, and as Director of the Nūr al-Islām Translation Center in Valley Cottage, New York.

* The name Muhtar was received at that time from Bapak Muhammad Subuh Sumohadiwidjojo, of Wisma Subud, Jakarta, in response to a request for a suitable Muslim name. In strict academic transliteration from the Arabic, the spelling would be *Mukhtār*. The form *Muchtar* is probably more common in Indonesia than *Muhtar*, which happens to coincide with the modern Turkish spelling of the name.

His freelance activities have mostly been devoted to writing and translating in various parts of the world, including Scotland and California. He made his Pilgrimage *[Ḥajj]* to Mecca in 1980.

Published works include the following:

Al-Ghazālī. *On the Duties of Brotherhood*. Translated from the Classical Arabic by Muhtar Holland. London: Latimer New Dimensions, 1975. New York: Overlook Press, 1977. Repr. 1980 and 1993.

Sheikh Muzaffer Ozak al-Jerrahi. *The Unveiling of Love*. Translated from the Turkish by Muhtar Holland. New York: Inner Traditions, 1981. Westport, Ct.: Pir Publications, 1990.

Ibn Taymīya. *Public Duties in Islām*. Translated from the Arabic by Muhtar Holland. Leicester, England: Islamic Foundation, 1982.

Hasan Shushud. *Masters of Wisdom of Central Asia*. Translated from the Turkish by Muhtar Holland. Ellingstring, England: Coombe Springs Press, 1983.

Al-Ghazālī. *Inner Dimensions of Islamic Worship*. Translated from the Arabic by Muhtar Holland. Leicester, England: Islamic Foundation, 1983.

Sheikh Muzaffer Ozak al-Jerrahi. *Irshād*. Translated [from the Turkish] with an Introduction by Muhtar Holland. Warwick, New York: Amity House, 1988. Westport, Ct.: Pir Publications, 1990.

Sheikh Muzaffer Ozak al-Jerrahi. *Blessed Virgin Mary*. Translation from the original Turkish by Muhtar Holland. Westport, Ct.: Pir Publications, 1991.

Sheikh Muzaffer Ozak al-Jerrahi. *The Garden of Dervishes*. Translation from the original Turkish by Muhtar Holland. Westport, Ct.: Pir Publications, 1991.

Sheikh Muzaffer Ozak al-Jerrahi. *Adornment of Hearts*. Translation from the original Turkish by Muhtar Holland and Sixtina Friedrich. Westport, Ct.: Pir Publications, 1991.

Sheikh Muzaffer Ozak al-Jerrahi. *Ashki's Divan*. Translation from the Original Turkish by Muhtar Holland and Sixtina Friedrich. Westport, Ct.: Pir Publications, 1991.

Shaikh ʿAbd al-Qādir al-Jīlānī. *Revelations of the Unseen (Futūḥ al-Ghaib)*. Translated from the Arabic by Muhtar Holland. Houston, Texas: Al-Baz Publishing, Inc., 1992. Second edition, Fort Lauderdale, Florida: Al-Baz Publishing, Inc., 1998.

Shaikh ʿAbd al-Qādir al-Jīlānī. *The Sublime Revelation (al-Fatḥ ar-Rabbānī)*. Translated from the Arabic by Muhtar Holland. Houston, Texas: Al-Baz Publishing, Inc., 1992. Second edition, Fort Lauderdale, Florida: Al-Baz Publishing, Inc., 1998.

Shaikh ʿAbd al-Qādir al-Jīlānī. *Utterances (Malfūẓāt)*. Translated from the Arabic by Muhtar Holland. Houston, Texas: Al-Baz Publishing, Inc., 1992. Second edition, Fort Lauderdale, Florida: Al-Baz Publishing, Inc., 1998.

Shaikh ʿAbd al-Qādir al-Jīlānī. *The Removal of Cares (Jalāʾ al-Khawāṭir)*. Translated from the Arabic by Muhtar Holland. Ft. Lauderdale, Florida: Al-Baz Publishing, Inc., 1997.

Shaikh ʿAbd al-Qādir al-Jīlānī. *Sufficient Provision for Seekers of the Path of Truth (Al-Ghunya li-Ṭālibī Ṭarīq al-Ḥaqq)*. Translated from the Arabic (in 5 vols.) by Muhtar Holland. Hollywood, Florida: Al-Baz Publishing, Inc., 1997.

Shaikh ʿAbd al-Qādir al-Jīlānī. *Fifteen Letters* (*Khamsata ʿAshara Maktūban*). Translated from the Arabic by Muhtar Holland. Hollywood, Florida: Al-Baz Publishing, Inc., 1997.

Shaikh Walī Raslān ad-Dimashqī. *Concerning the Affirmation of Divine Oneness (Risāla fi't-Tawḥīd)*. Translated from the Arabic by Muhtar Holland. Hollywood, Florida: Al-Baz Publishing, Inc., 1997.

Al-Ghazālī. *The Proper Conduct of Marriage in Islām* (*Ādāb an-Nikāḥ*). (Book twelve of *Iḥyāʾ ʿUlūm ad-Dīn*). Translated from the Arabic by Muhtar Holland. Hollywood, Florida: Al-Baz Publishing, Inc., 1998.

Shaikh Muḥammad ibn Yaḥyā at-Tādifī. *Necklaces of Gems (Qalāʾid al-Jawāhir)*. Translated from the Arabic by Muhtar Holland. Fort Lauderdale, Florida: Al-Baz Publishing, Inc., 1998.

Shaikh Aḥmad Fatḥu'llāh Jāmī. *The Call to the Believers in the Clear Qurʾān (Nidāʾ al-Muʾminīn fi 'l-Qurʾān al-Mubīn)*. Translated from the Arabic by Muhtar Holland. Fort Lauderdale, Florida: Al-Baz Publishing, Inc., 1999.

BOOKS PUBLISHED BY AL-BAZ PUBLISHING INCLUDE:

1. **Revelations of the Unseen** (*Futūḥ al-Ghaib*) $18.00
   78 Discourses by Shaikh ʿAbd al-Qādir al-Jīlānī
2. **The Sublime Revelation** (*Al-Fatḥ ar-Rabbānī*) $29.00
   62 Discourses by Shaikh ʿAbd al-Qādir al-Jīlānī
3. **Utterances of Shaikh ʿAbd al-Qādir** (*Malfūẓāt*) $16.00
4. **The Removal of Cares** (*Jalāʾ al-Khawāṭir*) $24.95
   45 Discourses by Shaikh ʿAbd al-Qādir al-Jīlānī
5. **Sufficient Provision for Seekers of the Path of Truth**
   (*Al-Ghunya li-Ṭālibī Ṭarīq al-Ḥaqq*) $110.00 Set
   by Shaikh ʿAbd al-Qādir al-Jīlānī (may Allāh be well pleased with him)
   This encyclopedic work is a complete resource on the inner and outer aspects of Islām. The translation has been published in 5 volumes. Translated by Muhtar Holland and over five and a half years in the translating, this work is undoubtedly the publishing event of this century and a treasure of unimaginable value to the believers. 1738 pages.
6. **Fifteen Letters** $10.00
   (*Khamsata ʿAshara Maktūban* otherwise known as *Maktūbāt*)
   Fifteen letters by Shaikh ʿAbd al-Qādir al-Jīlānī to one of his disciples. Originally written in Persian, they were translated into Arabic by ʿAlī Ḥusāmu'd-dīn al-Muttaqī (the Devout), who said of them, "... these letters comprise nuggets of wisdom and spiritual counsel, couched in various forms of allegory, metaphor, paraphrase and quotation, including approximately two hundred and seventy-five Qurʾānic verses. They also contain allusions to the experiences *[adhwāq]* and spiritual states *[ḥālāt]* of the Ṣūfis (may Allāh's good pleasure be conferred upon them all). Translated by Muhtar Holland.
7. **Concerning the Affirmation of Divine Oneness** $15.00
   (*Risāla fi't-Tawḥīd*)
   by Shaikh Walī Raslān ad-Dimashqī (d. A.H. 540)
   This is a Risāla on *shirk khafī* (hidden *shirk*). *Shirk* is associating partners with Allāh. Also in the book is a commentary by Shaikh Zakariyyāʾ al-Anṣārī (d. A.H. 926) called *Kitāb Fatḥ ar-Raḥmān*. Also in the book is a commentary by Shaikh ʿAlī ibn ʿAṭiyya ʿAlawān al-Ḥamawī (d. A.H. 936) called *Sharḥ Fatḥ ar-Raḥmān*. This is a very important book. Translated by Muhtar Holland.

8. **The Proper Conduct of Marriage in Islām** $16.00
(*Ādāb an-Nikāḥ*)
by Imām al-Ghazālī
This is Book 12 of *Iḥyā' 'Ulūm ad-Dīn*. Translated by Muhtar Holland.

9. **The Most Beautiful Names of God** $11.00/12.50
(*Al-Asmā' al-Ḥusnā*)
by Jamā'a Majhūla
A chanted recital of the 99 Names of Allāh. Vocals only; men and boys
Track 2: The Boundless Grace of al-Qur'ān
Audio tape and CD.

10. **Necklaces of Gems** (*Qalā'id al-Jawāhir*) $29.95
by Shaikh Muḥammad ibn Yaḥyā at-Tādifī (d. A.H. 963)
A Biography of Shaikh 'Abd al-Qādir al-Jīlānī (may Allāh be well pleased with him), on the Marvelous Exploits of the Crown of the Saints, the Treasure-trove of the Pure, the Sulṭān of the *Awliyā'*, the Sublime *Quṭb*, Shaikh Muḥyi'd-dīn 'Abd al-Qādir al-Jīlānī. Translated by Muhtar Holland.

Books scheduled for publication in 2000 include:

1. **Emanations of Lordly Grace** (*al-Fuyūḍāt ar-Rabbāniyya*)
by Ismā'īl Muḥammad Sa'īd al-Qādirī
A collection of the work and explanations of Shaikh 'Abd al-Qādir al-Jīlānī (may Allāh be well pleased with him), that includes definition and attributes of the seven selves *[nafs]*, an explanation of the names of the seven stations *[maqāmāt]*, the creed *['aqīda]* of the Supreme Helper (may Allāh be well pleased with him), the meaning of the names of the Qādiriyya order, the remarkable virtues of al-Jīlānī the *Quṭb*, the names of our master, 'Abd al-Qādir, litanies *[awrād]* for the taming of hearts and for emergency situations; how to offer the greeting of peace *[salām]*to the men of the unseen *[Ghaib]* and much much more. Translated by Muhtar Holland.

2. **The Path of the Worshipful Servants to the Garden of the Lord of All the Worlds**
(*Minhāj al-'Ābidīn ilā Jannati Rabbi 'l-'Ālamīn*)
by Imām Ḥujjat al-Islām Abū Ḥāmid Muḥammad al-Ghazālī.
The author tells us how he implored Allāh "to make it possible for me to compose a book—one that would meet with unanimous approval, and the reading of which would result in positive benefit—and He inspired me with a marvelous arrangement, the like of which I did not recall in any of the previous compositions dealing with the secrets of religious practices."

He also said, "Worshipful service is the fruit of knowledge, the benefit of life, the income of strong servants, the stock-in-trade of the saints [*awliya'*], the path of the truly devout, the allotted portion of the mighty, the goal of those endowed with aspiration, the emblem of the noble, the vocation of real men, and the choice of those with faculties of vision. It is the way of good fortune and the path [*minhāj*] of the Garden of Paradise."

He went on to say, "We therefore looked into the subject of worshipful service, and made a study of its path, from its beginnings to its destinations, which are the goals of its travelers. It is indeed a rugged path and a hard road, fraught with many obstacles, serious hardships, remote distances, enormous difficulties, frequent hindrances and impediments. It is beset with deadly perils and interruptions, abounding in enemies and highway robbers, and offering very few companions and followers. That is exactly how it needs to be, since it is the path of the Garden of Paradise."

As the very last book composed by Imām Ghazālī, it undoubtedly contains the essence of his profound and remarkable experience, and conveys that essence in a remarkably edifying manner. Near the beginning of the book he tells us, "When the servant of the Lord is first awakened to worshipful service, and devotes himself exclusively to traveling its path, he is motivated by a heavenly vibration from Allāh, and a special enabling grace of Divine origin."

Orders or enquiries, or to be placed on our mailing list, contact:

Al-Baz Publishing, Inc.
P.O. Box 348
Ft. Lauderdale, Florida 33303-0348

Phone: (954) 567-4072
Fax: (954) 563-1311
E-mail: albaz@bellsouth.net *or*
ruslan@herald.infi.net